Greek Islands

David Willett, Carolyn Bain, Michael Clark, Des Hannigan,
Paul Hellander, Jeanne Oliver

Contents

Ionian Islands pp405–47

Athens & Mainland Ports pp65–100

Northeastern Aegean Islands pp323–78

Evia & The Sporades pp379–404

Saronic Gulf Islands pp101–17

Dodecanese pp254–322

Cyclades pp118–201

Crete pp202–53

Destination: Greek Islands

The Greek islands have long been one of Europe's favourite holiday destinations. It's hardly surprising: with more than 1400 islands scattered around the blue waters of the Aegean and Ionian Seas, there's something for everyone. For some it's the opportunity to escape to the far-flung island paradise of their dreams, for others it's the opportunity to explore the remains of some of Europe's oldest civilisations. For most people though, the greatest attraction is the lure of sand, sea – and more than 300 days of guaranteed sunshine a year.

Every island is different. The scenery can vary dramatically, from the semitropical lushness of the Ionian and Northeastern Aegean Islands, to the bare, sunbaked rocks of the Cyclades. There are party islands, quiet romantic islands, islands for walkers, islands for windsurfers, islands for history buffs, islands for gays and islands for lesbians. There's an island for everyone – the challenge is to find it, and that means island-hopping, using Europe's largest ferry network.

The islanders have retained a strong sense of tradition: tradition and religion were the factors that kept the notion of Greek nationhood alive during hundreds of years of foreign occupation, and Greeks have clung to their traditions more tenaciously than most. The traditions manifest themselves in a variety of ways, including ornate regional costumes and energetic festivals, where people express their *joie de vivre* through dancing, singing and feasting.

Festival time or not, the Greek capacity for enjoyment of life is immediately evident. Food and wine are plentiful, and Greeks love to eat out with family and friends. All this adds up to the islands being one of Europe's most friendly and relaxed destinations.

JOHN ELK III

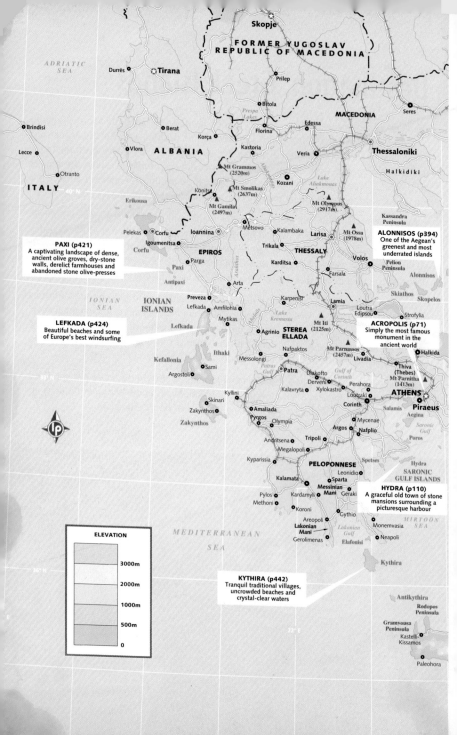

ADRIATIC
SEA

Skopje

FORMER YUGOSLAV
REPUBLIC OF MACEDONIA

Durrës
Tirana
Prilep

Brindisi
Berat
Bitola
Prespa
Lakes

Lecce
Vlora
Korça
Florina
Edessa
MACEDONIA
Seres

Otranto
Mt Grammos
(2520m)
Kozani
Lake
Aliakmonas
Veria
Thessaloniki

ITALY 40° N
Erikousa
Konitsa
Mt Smolikas
(2637m)
Halkidiki

Mt Gamila
(2497m)
Mt Olympus
(2917m)
Kassandra
Peninsula

Pelekas
Corfu
Ioannina
Metsovo
Kalambaka
Larisa
Mt Ossa
(1978m)

ALONNISOS (p394)
One of the Aegean's
greenest and most
underrated islands

Igoumenitsa
Corfu
EPIROS
Trikala
THESSALY
Pelion
Peninsula

Paxi
Parga
Karditsa
Farsala
Volos
Alonnisos

Antipaxi
Arta
Skiathos
Skopelos

IONIAN
SEA
Preveza
Karpenisi
Lamia
Skiros

IONIAN
ISLANDS
Lefkada
Amfilohia
Loutra
Edipsou
Strofylia

LEFKADA (p424)
Beautiful beaches and some
of Europe's best windsurfing

Lefkada
Mytikas
Agrinio
STEREA
ELLADA
Mt Iti
(2125m)

ACROPOLIS (p71)
Simply the most famous
monument in the
ancient world

Ithaki
Nafpaktos
Mt Parnassos
(2457m)
Livadia
Halkida

Kefallonia
Messolongi
Patra
Diakofto
Perahora
Thiva
(Thebes)
Mt Parnitha
(1413m)

Sami
Derveni
Gulf of
Corinth
Xylokastro
ATHENS

Argostoli
Patras
Gulf
Kalavryta
Loutraki
Piraeus

Kyllini
Corinth
Salamis

Skinari
Amaliada
Mycenae
Aegina
Saronic
Gulf

Zakynthos
Pyrgos
Olympia
Argos
Nafplio
Poros

Zakynthos
Andritsena
Tripoli
Spetses
Hydra

Megalopoli
PELOPONNESE
SARONIC
GULF ISLANDS

Kyparissia
Leonidio
Hydra

Kalamata
Sparta
HYDRA (p110)
A graceful old town of stone
mansions surrounding a
picturesque harbour

Pylos
Messinian
Mani
Geraki

Methoni
Kardamyli
MIRTOÖN
SEA

Koroni
Areopoli
Gythio
Monemvasia

Lakonian
Mani
Lakonian
Gulf
Neapoli

MEDITERRANEAN
Gerolimenas
Elafonisi

SEA
Kythira

KYTHIRA (p442)
Tranquil traditional villages,
uncrowded beaches and
crystal-clear waters

Antikythira

Rodopos
Peninsula

22° E
Gramvousa
Peninsula
Kastelli-
Kissamos

Paleohora

ELEVATION

3000m

2000m

1000m

500m

0

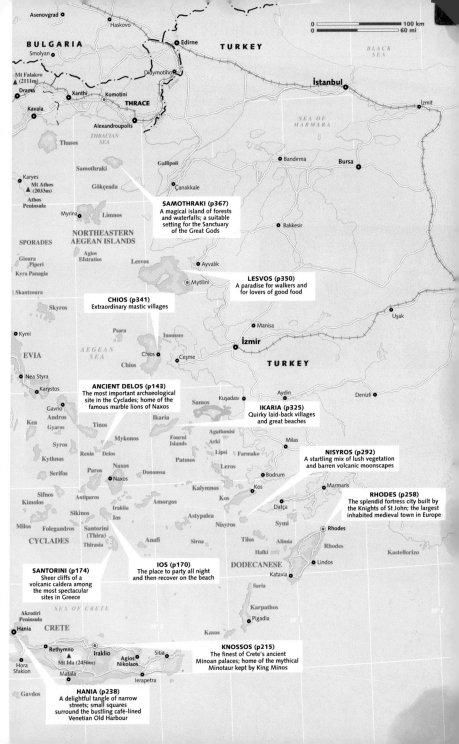

SAMOTHRAKI (p367)
A magical island of forests and waterfalls; a suitable setting for the Sanctuary of the Great Gods

LESVOS (p350)
A paradise for walkers and for lovers of good food

CHIOS (p341)
Extraordinary mastic villages

ANCIENT DELOS (p143)
The most important archaeological site in the Cyclades; home of the famous marble lions of Naxos

IKARIA (p325)
Quirky laid-back villages and great beaches

NISYROS (p292)
A startling mix of lush vegetation and barren volcanic moonscapes

RHODES (p258)
The splendid fortress city built by the Knights of St John; the largest inhabited medieval town in Europe

SANTORINI (p174)
Sheer cliffs of a volcanic caldera among the most spectacular sites in Greece

IOS (p170)
The place to party all night and then recover on the beach

KNOSSOS (p215)
The finest of Crete's ancient Minoan palaces; home of the mythical Minotaur kept by King Minos

HANIA (p238)
A delightful tangle of narrow streets; small squares surround the bustling café-lined Venetian Old Harbour

The Saronic Gulf Islands are the perfect destination for weary souls looking to escape the traffic and pollution of Athens for a few days – or even a few hours. **Aegina Town** (p105), just 35 minutes by hydrofoil from Piraeus, is home to the stunning **Temple of Aphaia** (p106), built at the same time as the Parthenon. **Hydra** (p110) is the Saronic Gulf Island with the most style. Its perfect horseshoe harbour is one of the prettiest, surrounded by hillsides of graceful stone mansions, built at the beginning of the 19th century by the island's wealthy shipowners. Unpretentious **Spetses** (p113) is another island with a proud naval tradition.

Soak up some ancient history at the stunning Temple of Aphaia (p106)

CHRIS CHRISTO

CHRIS CHRISTO

Cool off in the shade of an elegant mansion on the island of Spetses (p113)

Wander up the winding lanes to the hilltop houses of Hydra (p110)

RODNEY HYETT

IZZET KERIBAR

Get lost in the whitewashed streetscape of Santorini (p174)

CHRIS CHRISTO

Explore the ruins of a Roman theatre at Plaka (p67)

Play in the lovely waters around Ios (p170)

CHRIS CHRISTO

HIGHLIGHTS Cyclades

The Cyclades are the archetypal Greek islands: dazzling, whitewashed villages clinging to barren hillsides, geraniums in brightly painted pots, golden beaches and azure seas. Spectacular **Santorini** (p174) is not to be missed – its sheer cliffs are shaped by one of the largest volcanic eruptions in history, while **Folegrandos** (p187) is full of classic Cycladic architecture. Don't miss the temples of **Ancient Delos** (p143), which are guarded by the celebrated marble Lions of Naxos. The smaller islands of the **Little Cyclades** (p162) are full of uncrowded beaches, while **Ios** (p170), **Mykonos** (p134) and **Paros** (p145) are great for party people.

Crete is Greece's largest and most southerly island. It's a favourite with history buffs, who come to visit the celebrated Minoan palaces at **Knossos** (p215) and **Zakros** (p227), built 3500 years ago by one of the Mediterranean's earliest civilisations. The cities of **Iraklio** (p207), **Hania** (p238) and **Rethymno** (p231) are filled with reminders of the island's long Turkish and Venetian past. Crete is also a favourite with walkers, who flock here to trek the famous **Samaria Gorge** (p244), just one of many excellent walks in the rugged southwest. **Ha Gorge** (p229) is perhaps the most challenging gorge to traverse in all of Europe.

JOHN ELK III

Discover the famous Minoan palace complex of Phaestos (p217)

Marvel at the 16th-century monastery of Moni Arkadiou (p235)

NEIL SETCHFIELD

STELLA HELLANDER

Trek across the length of Crete's spectacular Samaria Gorge (p244)

GEORGE TSAFOS

Clamber around the traditional old village of Olymbos (p280)

GEORGE TSAFOS

Climb the stairs leading to a white-washed chapel in Mandraki (p293)

Be amazed at the spectacular location of the ancient Acropolis of Lindos (p269)

PAUL HELLANDER

HIGHLIGHTS **Dodecanese**

It's not for nothing that **Rhodes** (p258) is one of Greece's most popular tourist destinations. The mighty fortress city built by the Knights of St John is the oldest inhabited medieval town in Europe. Other highlights include the dramatic volcanic landscape of **Nisyros** (p292); the traditional villages of northern **Karpathos** (p275) and the **Potami Gorge, Tilos** (p291). **Kalymnos** (p305) is great for rock-climbing junkies, while low-key and remote **Kastellorizo** (p283) is a good place to lie low for a while.

The Northeastern Aegean Islands are perfect for people who want to escape and unwind. There could be no better place to start than the beautiful beaches of laidback **Ikaria** (p325), a place where time seems to stand still, and **Alyki Beach** (p376) on Thasos. **Lesvos** (p350) is a favourite with walkers and nature lovers, while the amazing medieval villages of the Mastihohoria district of southern **Chios** (p346) should be on every visitor's itinerary. Remote **Samothraki** (p367) is a lush paradise of forests and waterfalls, and home to the mystical **Sanctuary of the Great Gods** (p369).

Enjoy a coffee in a quiet square of Pythagorio (p337)

CHRIS CHRISTO

STELLA HELLANDER

Stroll through Mytilini's charming waterfront and visit the domed Church of Agios Therapon (p353)

Chill out on Ikaria's beautiful pale-golden sand of Mesahti beach (p325)

PAUL HELLANDER

GEORGE TSAFOS

Explore some of the unique architecture and old windmills of Skyros (p399)

Get away from the summer crowds
in the old town of Halkida (p383)

GEORGE TSAFOS

GEORGE TSAFOS

Watch out for the horns of Skyros' annual
pre-Lenten goat carnival (p399)

HIGHLIGHTS Evia & The Sporades

Evia and the Sporades is a region of stunning natural contrasts, from the mountain villages of sparsely populated **Evia** (p328) to the bars and beaches of fast-living **Skiathos** (p386), where holiday-makers will find every form of water sport. Unsung **Alonnisos** (p394) boasts the cleanest waters in the Aegean. Tiny **Skyros** (p399), famous for its strange goat carnival and its quirky architecture, is a perfect spot in which to escape the crowds for a few days.

Corfu (p409), blessed with ample rain and fertile soil, is rated by many as Greece's most beautiful island. **Paxi** (p421) and **Antipaxi** (p424) offer a captivating landscape of ancient olive groves; in **Kythira** (p442) villages are linked by narrow, winding lanes flanked by ancient dry-stone walls; **Zakynthos** (p437) is an island of exceptional natural beauty and a tourist mecca; **Kefallonia** (p429) has rugged towering mountains with many species of heavily scented herbs and wildflowers; and **Assos** (p433) is a gem of whitewashed and pastel houses.

Sail into the sunset off the coast of Lefkada's Nydri (p427)

CHRISTINE OSBORNE

GEORGE TSAFOS

See the fishing boats moored along the waterfront in Vathy harbour (p435)

Check out the beguiling blend of British, Greek and Venetian architectural influences of Corfu Town (p413)

JOHN ELK III

Getting Started

The Greek islands are easy to hop around, with good public transport and a range of accommodation to suit every budget, from the backpacker to the five-star traveller. For some, planning involves no more than heading out and buying a ticket; for others, planning the trip is half the fun – and there is certainly no shortage of information to help them on their way.

WHEN TO GO

Spring and autumn are the best times to visit Greece and its islands. Most of the country's tourist infrastructure goes into hibernation during winter, particularly on the islands. Some of the smaller islands close completely, and islanders head off to alternative homes in Athens for a few months. Many hotels, along with seasonal cafés and restaurants, close their doors from the end of November until the beginning of April; bus and ferry services are either drastically reduced or plain cancelled.

See Climate (p452) for more information.

The cobwebs are dusted off in time for Easter, when the first tourists start to arrive. Conditions are perfect between Easter and mid-June, when the weather is pleasantly warm in most places; beaches and ancient sites are relatively uncrowded; public transport operates at close to full schedules; and accommodation is cheaper and easy to find.

Mid-June until the end of August is the high season. It's party time on the islands and everything is in full swing. It's also very hot – in July and August the mercury can soar to 40°C (over 100°F) in the shade just about anywhere in the country; the beaches are crowded, the ancient sites are swarming with tour groups and in many places accommodation is booked solid.

The season starts to wind down in September, and conditions are ideal once more until the end of October.

By November, the endless blue skies of summer have disappeared. November to February are the wettest months. It can get surprisingly cold. Snow is common on the mainland and in the mountains of Evia and Crete; it occasionally snows in Athens. There are also plenty of sunny days, and some visitors prefer the tranquillity that reigns.

DON'T LEAVE HOME WITHOUT...

Most travellers carry far too much gear, filling bags and backpacks with things that will never see the light of day. It's best to bring only the following essentials (you can buy anything else you might need in Greece):

- A sturdy pair of shoes for clambering around ancient sites and historic towns and villages, which tend to have lots of steps and cobbled streets. Footwear with ankle support is preferable, especially for trekking.
- Good sunglasses – essential in summer.
- High UV-protection sunscreen, which can be hard to find and expensive when you do.
- A universal plug – bathrooms rarely have one.
- A few photos of your family, your home and your region: they are great for answering the questions of curious locals.
- A few disposable paperbacks to read and swap.

TOP 10s
BEST BEACHES

The Greek islands are justly famous for their beaches, so don't forget to pack your beach towel, hat and sunscreen. The following is a list of some of the finest beaches as selected by Lonely Planet's researchers:

- Pori beach, Koufonisia, Cyclades (p165)
- Milopotas beach and Manganari beach, Ios, Cyclades (p174)
- Ladiko beach and Glystra beach, Rhodes, Dodecanese (p269, p271)
- Ammoöpi beach, Karpathos, Dodecanese (p278)
- Preveli beach and Elafonisi beach, Crete (p235, p250)
- Alyki beach, Thassos, Northeastern Aegean (p376)
- Psili Ammos, Samos, Northeastern Aegean (p340)
- Banana beach, Skiathos, Sporades (p389)
- Mylos beach, Lefkada, Ionians (p428)
- Myrtos beach, Kefallonia, Ionians (p434)

MUST-SEE MOVIES

Pre-departure planning is best done in a comfy lounge chair with a bowl of popcorn in one hand and a remote in the other. Head down to your local video store to pick up these flicks, from the best-known Greek films to the very cheesiest. For more information on Greek cinema, see p40.

- *Zorba the Greek* (1964)
  Director: Mihalis Cacoyannis
- *My Big Fat Greek Wedding* (2002)
  Director: Joel Zwick
- *Eleni* (1985)
  Director: Peter Yates
- *For Your Eyes Only* (1981)
  Director: John Glen
- *Shirley Valentine* (1989)
  Director: Lewis Gilbert
- *Mediterraneo* (1991)
  Director: Gabriel Salvatores
- *Never on Sunday* (1960)
  Director: Jules Dassin
- *Z* (1969)
  Director: Costa Gavras
- *Alexander the Great* (1980)
  Director: Theo Angelopoulos
- *Eternity & a Day* (1998)
  Director: Theo Angelopoulos

FESTIVALS & EVENTS

Greeks love to celebrate, and there's almost always something, somewhere, that's worth celebrating. The following list is our top 10, but for a comprehensive list of all the main festivals and events throughout the year, go to p455.

- Skyros Carnival (Sporades)
  February to March (p399)
- Easter (everywhere!)
  March to April (p455)
- Miaoulia Festival on Hydra (Saronic Gulf)
  June (p112)
- Summer on Lykavittos Hill (Athens)
  June to August (p73)
- Hellenic Festival, Theatre of Herodes Atticus (Athens)
  June to September (p73)
- Folegandros Festival (Cyclades)
  July (p189)
- Santorini Jazz Festival (Cyclades)
  July (p182)
- Milos Festival (Cyclades)
  July (p192)
- Panagia tou Harou, Lipsi (Dodecanese)
  24 August (p319)
- Samothraki Dance Festival (Northeastern Aegean)
  August (p368)

COSTS & MONEY

Greece is no longer a cheap country. Prices have rocketed since the adoption of the euro at the beginning of 2002. It is hard to believe that inflation is less than 4%, as claimed by the government, when prices for many services have risen by more than 50% in two years. Lonely Planet's researchers have recorded some dramatic price rises, particularly for accommodation options around the country and for restaurant meals.

A rock-bottom daily budget for a solo traveller would be €40. This would mean hitching, staying in youth hostels or camping, staying away from bars, and only occasionally eating out in restaurants or taking ferries. Allow at least €80 per day if you want your own room and plan to eat out regularly as well as travel about and see the sights. You will still need to do a fair bit of self-catering. If you really want a holiday and want comfortable rooms and restaurants all the way, you will need closer to €120 per day per individual. These budgets are for individuals travelling in high season (July/August). Couples sharing a double room can get by on less.

Your money will go a lot further if you travel in the quieter months, outside the high season – there are fewer tourists around and you're able to negotiate better deals. Accommodation, which often eats up a large part of the daily budget, is a lot cheaper outside the high season – particularly on the islands. You will also be able to negotiate much better deals if you stay a few days. Families can achieve big savings by looking for rooms with kitchen facilities.

All prices quoted in this guidebook are for the high season (during July and August).

TRAVEL LITERATURE

Travel writers can be a great source of inspiration for those planning to follow in their footsteps.

The Colossus of Marousi (Henry Miller) Few writers have been able to match the feverish enthusiasm expressed by Henry Miller in this classic tale. Miller's fervour never flags as he leaps from one adventure to the next. Some travellers get upset about being ripped off by a taxi driver on arrival; to Miller, it's another experience to be savoured.

Attic in Greece (Austen Kark) This tale revolves around the author's experience of buying a house in the old town of Nafplio with his wife Nina. It's full of interesting insights gleaned through the author's time in Greece working for the BBC.

Prospero's Cell (Lawrence Durrell) This classic collection of tales record Durrell's experience on Corfu in the 1920s. Worth reading for the fire-engine story alone!

The Greek Islands (Lawrence Durrell) This coffee-table collection of stunning photos is one of the most popular books of its kind.

Hellas: A Portrait of Greece (Nicholas Gage) Another book that's sure to whet the travel appetite.

A Cretan Diary (Edward Lear) The English painter and writer Edward Lear, of *The Owl & the Pussy-Cat* fame, spent some time in Greece in the mid-19th century.

Journeys of a Landscape Painter in Greece & Albania (Edward Lear) More evocative travel tales from Lear.

My Family & Other Animals (Gerald Durrell) Brother Gerald offers an hilarious account of the Durrell family's chaotic and wonderful life on Corfu.

The Mani (Patrick Leigh Fermor) Another ardent philhellene, Patrick Leigh Fermor is well known for his exploits in rallying the Cretan resistance in WWII. He now lives in Kardamyli in the Peloponnese.

Travels in the Morea (Nikos Kazantzakis) Greece's greatest modern writer records his thoughts during a journey around the Peloponnese in the 1930s.

HOW MUCH?

Local telephone call
€0.20 per min

Minimum taxi fare
€2

Milk (1L)
€1.50

Herald Tribune
€1.80

Coffee
€2-3

Soft drink (can)
€0.80

Cinema ticket
€7

LONELY PLANET INDEX

Litre of petrol
€0.70-0.85

Litre of water
€1

Bottle of beer
€2

Souvenir T-shirt
€12

Souvlaki
€1.50

INTERNET RESOURCES

Predictably enough, there has recently been a huge increase in the number of websites providing information about Greece.

Culture Guide (www.cultureguide.gr) Lots of information about contemporary culture and the performing arts.

Greek Ferries (www.greekferries.gr) One-stop site with access to all the latest international and domestic ferry information.

Greek National Tourist Organisation (www.gnto.gr) For more tourist information see p461.

Greek Search Engine (www.in.gr) The best starting point for web browsers.

Lonely Planet (www.lonelyplanet.com) Has postcards from other travellers and the Thorn Tree bulletin board, where you can ask questions before you go or dispense advice when you get back.

Ministry of Culture (www.culture.gr) Information about ancient sites, art galleries, museums and lots more.

Itineraries

ISLAND HOPPING

ONE WEEK TO SPARE

One week / 400km

The first port of call is super chic **Mykonos** (p134). It's also the stepping-off point for the sacred island of **Delos** (p142), where the much-photographed Terrace of Lions from Naxos stand guard over the most important archaeological site in the Greek islands.

The next stop is **Naxos** (p153), famous for its wine, cheese and fresh produce. Hora, the capital, is a maze of alleys surrounding an ancient Venetian *kastro (castle)*. The mountainous interior is ideal for trekking, while Agios Georgios Beach is perfect for windsurfing or sailing.

Onwards to **Santorini** (p174), surely the most spectacular of all the islands. The sheer cliffs of its volcanic caldera, created by one of the largest eruptions ever recorded, are a sight not to be missed.

If ferry schedules permit, try to stop at either **Folegandros** (p187) or **Serifos** (p196) on the journey back to the mainland. Both boast superb examples of Cycladic architecture, and the opportunity to relax away from the crowds.

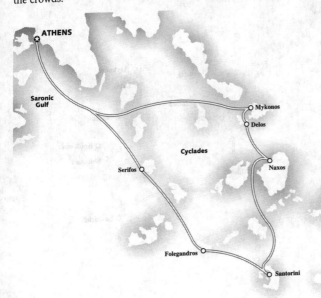

This tour is designed for people without much time who want to get a taste of what the islands have to offer. The island-hop starts and finishes in Athens.

THE CYCLADES

Two weeks / 230km

Head first to **Syros** (p128) and spend a couple of days exploring its graceful capital of **Ermoupolis** (p131), once the busiest and largest port in the Aegean. The next port of call is **Mykonos** (p134), and a stepping-off point for the sacred island of **Delos** (p142). You can recover on **Naxos** (p153), the greenest amd most fertile of the Cyclades and a great place for walkers.

If time permits, take a detour for a couple of days to either **Koufonisia** (p165) or **Shinousa** (p164), otherwise head straight on to spectacular **Santorini** (p174). The sheer cliffs of its volcanic caldera, created by one of largest eruptions ever recorded, are a sight not to be missed, and divers can check out the activities of the new volcano that is developing underwater. The journey back north starts with friendly **Folegandros** (p187), followed by **Milos** (p190), an underrated island that is often overlooked despite a wealth of attractions. The final port of call is **Serifos** (p196), home to arguably the finest of all the Cycladic capitals.

The Cyclades are the quintessential Greek islands. Two weeks should be long enough to complete the circuit, but a month is even better.

EVIA & THE SPORADES

Two weeks / 360km

Start by catching a ferry from **Rafina** (p85) on the mainland to the port of Karystos in southern Evia, and work up the island via **Eretria** (p384) to its capital of **Halkida** (p383), where you can observe the extraordinary tide patterns of the **Evripous Channel** (p382) that once so puzzled Aristotle. The mountain village of **Steni** (p383), in central Evia, is a delightful stop en route to the eastern port of **Kymi** (p383), the departure point for ferries to remote **Skyros** (p399). This quaint island is best known for its strange pre-Lenten goat carnival, and for its pretty Cycladic-style capital.

You'll need to double back to Halkida to continue to Skiathos, reached from the mainland ports of **Agios Konstantinos** (p95) or **Volos** (p85). **Skiathos** (p386) is one of Greece's premier resort areas, with dozens of beaches to choose from as well as all manner of water sports. Next stop is **Skopelos** (p390), where the pace is decidedly slower. **Skopelos Town** (p391) is a delightful place to explore, and there are some good walks. The final stop is **Alonnisos** (p394). It's no longer the Aegean's best-kept secret, but it still boasts the cleanest water in the Aegean and wonderful opportunities for walkers.

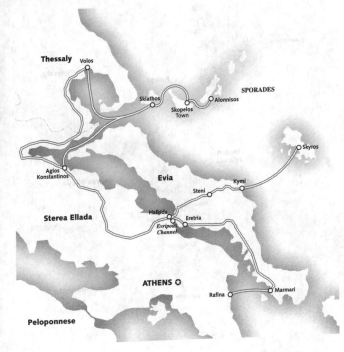

The Sporades represent something of a challenge for the island hopper, thanks to the absence of easy connections between Evia and Skyros and the main islands of the Sporades further north.

IONIAN EXPERIENCE

Two weeks / 500km

Start with a few days on **Corfu** (p409), exploring the sights of the old town and savouring the island's distinctive cuisine. Include a day trip over to the west-coast resort of **Paleokastritsa** (p420), lingering long enough to enjoy the sunset. Next up is tiny **Paxi** (p421), where visitors can explore a lost world of gnarled, ancient olive groves and derelict farmhouses. In the absence of ferry connections, you'll need to return to Corfu to move on to the next island south, **Lefkada** (p424).

The beaches of the west coast are the finest beaches in the Ionians, while **Vassiliki Bay** (p428), in the south, is renowned as a prime windsurfing spot. It's also the departure point for ferries to **Kefallonia** (p429), which arrive at the charming port of **Fiskardo** (p434), the only Kefallonian town not devastated by the great earthquake of 1953. Hop across from Fiskardo to **Ithaki** (p435) and spend a couple of days exploring the homeland of Homer's Odysseus, and then return to Kefallonia. Call in at the stunning west-coast village of **Assos** (p433) and magic **Myrtos beach** (p434) on the journey south to Kefallonia's lively capital of **Argostoli** (p431) for connections to the final island in the group, **Zakynthos** (p437). Known to the Venetians as the 'Flower of the Orient', the island's capital, **Zakynthos Town** (p439), boasts some fine examples of Venetian and neoclassical architecture.

The Ionians are Greece's green islands, blessed with ample winter rains. Visit outside of peak summer season (September to June) and have the islands to yourself.

THE EASTERN ISLAND RUN

Three weeks / 680km

You'll need to spend a few days on **Rhodes** (p258), exploring the old city and visiting the **Acropolis of Lindos** (p269), before setting sail for **Tilos** (p289). Laid-back Tilos is a great place for walkers, and one of the few islands in the Dodecanese to have escaped the ravages of development. The next stop is **Nisyros** (p292), where the eruptions of Mt Polyvotis have created a bizarre volcanic landscape. You'll need to call briefly at **Kos** (p295) to pick up a ferry onward to **Patmos** (p313), an island that St John found sufficiently inspiring to pen his *Book of Revelations*. Patmos has good connections to ultra–laid-back **Ikaria** (p325), where you can laze on some of the Aegean's best beaches before continuing to **Chios** (p341) and the fabulous villages of the south.

The next stop is **Lesvos** (p350), birthplace of the poet Sappho, and which produces Greece's finest olive oil and ouzo. **Limnos** (p362) is little more than a transit point on the journey north to **Samothraki** (p367) and the superbly named **Sanctuary of the Great Gods** (p369). The final leg is to the Thracian port of **Alexandroupolis** (p98), where travellers will find good transport connections to Athens and Thessaloniki.

This route takes travellers island hopping north from Rhodes through the islands of the Dodecanese and the Northeastern Aegean, finishing at the northern city of Alexandroupolis.

THE GRAND TOUR

One month / 1400km

From **Athens** (p67), head first to spectacular **Santorini** (p174), its capital of Fira perched precariously atop the sheer walls of a volcanic caldera, created by one of the greatest eruptions ever recorded. Next up is **Naxos** (p153), followed by **Mykonos** (p134). Be sure to take a day trip to visit the temples and sanctuaries of sacred **Delos** (p142) before moving on to laid-back **Ikaria** (p325) – where Icarus crash-landed after he flew too close to the sun. Next up is **Samos** (p333), where the unspoiled villages of the interior offer lots of opportunities for walkers. **Kos** (p295) need be no more than a stopover en route to **Rhodes** (p258), the amazing fortress city built by the Knights of St John.

The journey west from Rhodes offers the possibilities of stops at either **Karpathos** (p275) or **Kasos** (p280) on the way to the Cretan port of **Sitia** (p225). Travel along Crete's northern coast to **Iraklio** (p207) and **Knossos** (p215), before moving west to **Rethymno** (p231) or **Hania** (p238). The exit point from Crete is the northwestern port of **Kissamos** (p251) to **Kythira** (p442). From Kythira, there's a choice of catching a ferry or flight back to Athens, or travelling back through the Peloponnese.

A month is long enough to have a really good look around the islands, and to experience the huge variety of attractions they have to offer.

TAILORED TRIPS

ANCIENT WONDERS

Two weeks / 1100km

The ancient sites are one of the main reasons why travellers come to Greece, and this itinerary takes in all the biggest names as well as a couple of lesser sites.

Start with a couple of days exploring **Athens** (p67), the **Acropolis** (p71), and a day trip to Aegina to see the **Temple of Aphaia** (p106). Then head to **Mykonos** (p134), the depature point for trips to the sacred island of **Delos** (p142) – guarded by the much photographed **Terrace of Lions** (p145). From Mykonos, go to **Samos** (p333) to view the **Ireon** (p339), a massive temple to Hera that ranked as one of the wonders of the ancient world. Next is **Kos** (p295) and the ancient **Asklipieion** (p300) where the great Hippocrates once taught his approach to medicine. Then continue to **Rhodes** (p258) – the mighty fortress city built by the Knights of St John is Europe's oldest inhabited medieval town, and it's a great base for visiting the spectacular **Acropolis of Lindos** (p269). Continue from Rhodes to **Iraklio** (p207) on Crete for a visit to the Minoan palace of **Knossos** (p215). If time permits, try to include the palaces at **Phaestos** (p217) and **Zakros** (p228) before heading back to Athens.

WALK ON THE WILD SIDE

Three weeks / 1200km

The islands offer wonderful opportunities for walkers. The best time to go is in spring (especially April/May), when the weather is pleasantly warm and wildflowers transform the countryside into a riot of colour.

Start in **Athens** (p67) and use the second port of **Rafina** (p85) as the departure point for **Andros** (p122). **Batsi** (p123), on Andros, is an ideal base for exploring the countryside along ancient cobbled paths. Next is **Naxos** (p153), the largest of the Cyclades. The mountainous interior, especially the **Tragaea** (p160) region, is a favourite walking destination.

From Naxos, go northeast to **Samos** (p333). The coastal resorts may be a tour group fave, but the interior villages remain unspoiled. This journey heads south through the Dodecanese to volcanic **Nisyros** (p292), where you can marvel at the landscape created by the eruptions of **Mt Polyvotis** (p294). Stop in **Tilos** (p289) for its picturesque **Potami Gorge** (p291) or **Symi** (p285) before going to **Rhodes** (p258). Allow a day to explore the **Old Town** (p262) then head to **Crete** (p202). Greece's most southerly island has many possibilities, starting with **Samaria Gorge** (p244), one of many excellent treks.

The Authors

DAVID WILLETT
Coordinating Author plus Athens & the Mainland Ports and Saronic Gulf Islands

David is a freelance journalist based near Bellingen in northern NSW, Australia, where he lives with his partner, Rowan, and their 13-year-old son, Tom. Born in Hampshire, UK, he moved to Australia in 1980 following stints working on newspapers in Iran and Bahrain. David first travelled to Greece in 1978, and has been a regular visitor ever since. He has been coordinating Lonely Planet's coverage of Greece since 1995, specialising in Athens, the Peloponnese. and the Greek islands. He is also the author of LP's guide to The Peloponnese, an area that allows him to pursue his interest in ancient history and mythology.

The Coordinating Author's Favourite Trip

I like to stay in Athens (p67) only long enough to enjoy dinner at a restaurant with a view of the floodlit Acropolis. That done, I'll be off to Piraeus (p82) to catch the first available boat to beautiful Naxos (p153) to relax for a few days. From there, I'll head south to spectacular Santorini (p174) and then onward to Crete (p202), departing from the eastern port of Sitia (p225) for quirky Karpathos (p275). Next up is Rhodes (p258) and its magnificent fortified old town built by the Knights of St John. On the way back to Piraeus, I'll call at Nisyros (p292) for another glimpse of its bizarre volcanic landscape, and finally call at laidback Ikaria (p325) to laze on some of the best beaches in the Mediterranean.

CAROLYN BAIN
Ionian Islands

Carolyn was born in Melbourne, Australia (the third-largest Greek city in the world) and first visited the Greek islands as a teenager. For the last few years Lonely Planet has allowed her to trade a Melbourne winter for a European summer, and she jumped at the chance to return to the Ionian islands in pursuit of more great beaches, unspoilt villages and perfectly char-grilled octopus (another tough day at the office). The search for an unattached shipping magnate continues, but in the meantime Carolyn hopes Lonely Planet will continue to subsidise her quest to find the perfect Mediterranean island.

MICHAEL CLARK
Evia & The Sporades

Born into a Greek-American community in Cambridge, Ohio, Michael's Greek roots go back to the village of Karavostamo on the Aegean island of Ikaria, home of his maternal grandparents. He first worked his way to Greece aboard a Greek freighter, trading English lessons for Greek over wine and backgammon.

When not travelling to Greece, Michael teaches English to international students in San Francisco and Berkeley, California, and continues to study Greek on the side, listen to *rembetika* music after midnight and search out the best sources of olives, feta and retsina.

DES HANNIGAN
Cyclades

Des is a writer and photographer who has written over 20 books, most of them travel and tourism related. He was born on a very cold part of Scotland's east coast and from an early age was fired by dreams of sun-blasted islands and blue seas. He has lived in sunny Cornwall, England, for many years, but has travelled extensively throughout the Greek mainland and islands and has written guidebooks to Corfu and Rhodes. There's hardly a Greek island that he would not hop to, but the Cyclades hold for him an enduring fascination.

PAUL HELLANDER
Crete & Dodecanese

For author Paul Hellander Greece is not merely a destination, it is a lifestyle and a 30-year love affair that sees no end. Fluent in the language after taking a hard-earned degree in Ancient, Byzantine & Modern Greek from his native UK, he has been in and out of Greece more times than he cares to remember. Imbued with a love of rocky, sun-bleached islands in the Aegean, Paul brings to this edition of *Greek Islands* his vast experience of the Dodecanese Islands and Crete. His additional LP regional titles, *Crete* and *Rhodes & the Dodecanese*, bear witness to his enduring passion bordering on obsession with all things Greek. Paul usually lives in Adelaide, South Australia.

JEANNE OLIVER
Northeastern Aegean Islands

Jeanne has been dreaming of Greece and the blue waters of the Mediterranean since her childhood in New Jersey. Her first trip to the country was in 1980 when she fell in love with the island of Crete. Many journeys later, Lonely Planet assigned her to write the first edition of *Crete* as well as *Crete Condensed*. After returning again and again to dig deeper into Greek culture (and not just the sun and raki), she was pleased to discover the boundless pleasures of the Northern Aegean gems. When not dashing around Greek islands, she can be found whipping up *soupa avgolemono* in the south of France.

CONTRIBUTING AUTHORS

Dr Caroline Evans wrote the Health chapter. Caroline studied medicine at University of London, and completed General Practice training in Cambridge. She is the medical adviser to Nomad Travel clinic, a private travel health clinic in London, and also a GP specialising in travel medicine. She has been an expedition doctor for Raleigh International and Coral Cay expeditions.

Snapshot

Not surprisingly, the 2004 Olympic Games are dominating Greek conversation. After a slow start, Athens has become a giant construction site, its streets reverberating to the sound of jackhammers and concrete mixers. Amid all the chaos and dust, it's hard not to wonder how they are going to put it all back together again before August 2004.

The other main topic of conversation has been disclosures emerging from the trial of 18 members of Greece's November 17 terror gang. The shadowy left-wing group's 27-year campaign of assassination and bombing came to an end in July 2002, when a bomb went off prematurely, seriously injuring alleged hitman Savvas Xeros. Far from ending the affair, the arrests have raised as many questions as they have answered. Many people are still asking how the gang managed to evade detection for so long. Greek gossip is full of conspiracy theories involving political patronage and police pay-offs, while some of the biggest names in Greek business and banking have been accused of paying huge sums to have their names removed from November 17 hit lists. Many members of the gang are believed to be still at large, particularly members who were active in the early years.

On the political front, the Greek electorate appears ready to ditch Prime Minister Costas Simitis at the next general election, due before April 2004. Despite an impressive seven-year stint at the helm that has seen Greece become part of Europe's elite Euro Club, his PASOK party has been dogged by a succession of corruption scandals. Their conservative New Democracy rivals are way ahead in opinion polls, although the same polls show little enthusiasm for ND leader Costas Karamanlis.

On the economic front, the euro is being blamed for a host of problems – particularly price rises. Many people are baffled by the official inflation figure, which hovers around 4%, when prices of some services have risen by closer to 30%.

The Greek Orthodox Church continues to play an influential and very visible role in society. The church's patriarch, the ultra-conservative Archbishop Hristodoulos, is frequently in the news. Despite his oft-controversial utterings, Hristodoulos draws crowds that many rock stars would envy. For more information on religion in Greece, see p47.

The campaign to remove Saddam Hussein from Iraq was greeted with predictable outrage. Greeks seldom agree with US foreign policy, and demonstrations continued throughout the war. Greece also finds itself at odds with the US over Israel. It has long supported Palestinian statehood, and Palestinian officials are frequent visitors to Athens.

FAST FACTS

Population: 10,964,020 (2001 census)

Percentage of women: 50.51%

Tourists: 13.5 million annually

Cars: 3.6 million

GDP: US$160 billion

GDP growth: 3.7%

Per capita income: €12,380

Inflation: 4%

Unemployment: 9.6%

History

The Greek islands were the birthplace of two of Europe's earliest civilisations, the Cycladic and the Minoan.

Both can be traced to the introduction of Bronze Age smelting techniques in about 3000 BC by settlers from Phoenicia (on the coast of modern Lebanon). The Cyclades were the first to blossom. The most impressive legacy of this civilisation is the statuettes carved from Parian marble – the famous Cycladic figurines, which depicted images of the Great Mother (the earth goddess). The finest examples were produced during the Early Cycladic period, which lasted from 3000 to 2100 BC.

The people of the Cycladic civilisation were also accomplished sailors who developed prosperous maritime trade links. They exported their wares to Asia Minor (west of present-day Turkey), Europe and north Africa, as well as to Crete and continental Greece. The Cycladic civilisation lasted until about 1100 BC, but its later stages were increasingly dominated by the Minoan civilisation that evolved on nearby Crete.

The Minoans, named after the mythical King Minos, drew their inspiration from two great Middle Eastern civilisations: the Mesopotamian and the Egyptian. The civilisation reached its peak in the period between 2100 and 1500 BC, producing pottery and metalwork of remarkable beauty and a high degree of imagination and skill.

The famous palaces at Knossos, Phaestos, Malia and Zakros were built at this time. They were destroyed by a violent earthquake in about 1700 BC, but were rebuilt to a more complex, almost labyrinthine design with multiple storeys, sumptuous royal apartments, reception halls, storerooms, workshops, living quarters for staff and an advanced drainage system. The interiors were decorated with the celebrated Minoan frescoes, now on display in the archaeological museum at Iraklio (p207).

After 1500 BC, the civilisation began to decline, both commercially and militarily, against Mycenaean competition from the mainland. The Minoan civilisation came to an abrupt end around 1100 BC during a period of major upheaval throughout the eastern Mediterranean that is normally referred to as the Age of Migrations, and which also swept away the Mycenaeans.

Some historians have suggested that the Minoans' demise was accelerated by the effects of the massive volcanic explosion on the Cycladic island of Santorini (Thira) in 1450 BC, an eruption vulcanologists believe was more cataclysmic than any on record. They theorise that the fallout of volcanic ash from the blast caused a succession of crop failures – with resulting social upheaval.

DORIAN GREECE

By time life had settled down, it was the Dorians who had emerged as the new power on the Greek mainland, replacing the old order with new city-states such as Sparta and Corinth. Thought to have arrived from northern Greece, the warrior-like Dorians brought a traumatic break with the past, and the next 400 years are often referred to as Greece's 'dark age'. The Dorians worshipped male gods instead of fertility goddesses and adopted

A Traveller's History of Greece, by Timothy Boatswain and Colin Nicolson, is a good general introduction, covering Greece from Neolithic times to the present day.

Maureen O'Sullivan's *An Iconoclast's Guide to the Greek Gods* presents an entertaining and accessible version of the myths.

3000 BC:	1200–1100 BC:
arrival of the Bronze Age in Greece triggers rise of Cycladic and Minoan civilisations	Age of Migrations ends with the Dorians in control of much of the Greek mainland

the Mycenaean gods of Poseidon, Zeus and Apollo, paving the way for the later Greek religious pantheon. They were also responsible for bringing the Iron Age to Greece, and for the development of a new style of pottery, decorated with striking geometrical designs.

The Dorians also spread their tentacles into the Greek islands, founding the cities of Kamiros, Ialysos and Lindos on the island of Rhodes in about 1000 BC, while Ionians fleeing to the Cyclades from the Peloponnese established a religious sanctuary on Delos.

By the 8th century BC, when Homer's *Odyssey* and *Iliad* were first written down, the Greek city-states were powerful enough to start spreading their wings. Led by Athens and Corinth, which took over Corfu in 734 BC, the city-states created a Magna Graecia (Greater Greece) with southern Italy as an important component. Although the city-states spent much of their time fighting each other, they united behind Athens to repel the Persians twice, at Marathon (490 BC) and Salamis (480 BC).

THE GOLDEN AGE

The period that followed Salamis has become known as the Classical (or Golden) age. For Athens, it was a time of unparalleled growth and prosperity. In 477 BC it founded the Delian League, so called because the treasury was on Delos. Almost every state with a navy, including most of the Aegean islands, was forced to swear allegiance to Athens and to make an annual contribution of ships (and later money).

When Pericles became leader of Athens in 461 BC, he moved the treasury from Delos to the Acropolis and used its contents to build the Parthenon and the other monuments of the Acropolis (p71). The golden age ended with the Peloponnesian War (431–404 BC) in which the militaristic Spartans defeated the Athenians.

So embroiled were they in this war that they failed to notice the expansion of Macedonia to the north under King Philip II, who easily conquered the war-weary city-states.

Philip's ambitions were surpassed by those of his son Alexander the Great, who marched triumphantly into Asia Minor, Egypt, Persia and what are now parts of Afghanistan and India. After Alexander's untimely death in 323 BC at the age of 33, his generals divided his empire between themselves. The Dodecanese became part of the kingdom of Ptolemy I of Egypt, while the remainder of the Aegean islands became part of the League of Islands ruled by the Antagonids of Macedon.

ROMAN RULE & THE BYZANTINE EMPIRE

Roman incursions into Greece began in 205 BC. By 146 BC the mainland had become the Roman provinces of Greece and Macedonia. Crete fell in 67 BC, and the southern city of Gortyn became capital of the Roman province of Cyrenaica, which included a large chunk of North Africa. Rhodes held out until AD 70.

In AD 330 Emperor Constantine chose Byzantium as the new capital of the Roman Empire and renamed the city Constantinople. After the subdivision of the Roman Empire into Eastern and Western empires in AD 395, Greece became part of the Eastern Roman Empire, leading to the illustrious Byzantine age.

DID YOU KNOW?

The first coins produced in Greece were silver turtles minted on the island of Aegina in the last quarter of the 7th century BC.

DID YOU KNOW?

The *Venus de Milo*, now at home in the Louvre in Paris, was carved on the island of Milos in the 4th century BC.

DID YOU KNOW?

The Romans were the first to refer to the Hellenes as Greeks.

480 BC:

the defeat of Persia at the Battle of Salamis heralds the start of Athens' golden age

334 BC:

Alexander the Great invades Persia, greating an empire stretching as far as the River Indus

In the centuries that followed, Venetians, Franks, Normans, Slavs, Persians, Arabs and, finally, Turks all took their turns to chip away at the Byzantine Empire. The Persians captured Rhodes in 620, but were replaced by the Saracens (Arabs) in 653. The Arabs also captured Crete in 824.

Other islands in the Aegean remained under Byzantine control until the sacking of Constantinople in 1204 by renegade Frankish crusaders in cahoots with Venice. The Venetians were rewarded with the Cyclades and they added Crete to their possessions in 1210.

THE OTTOMAN EMPIRE

The Byzantine Empire finally came to an end in 1453 when Constantinople fell to the Turks. Once more Greece became a battleground, this time fought over by the Turks and Venetians. Eventually, with the exception of Corfu, Greece became part of the Ottoman empire.

Much has been made of the horrors of the Turkish occupation in Greece. However, in the early years at any rate, people probably marginally preferred Ottoman to Venetian or Frankish rule. The Venetians in particular treated their subjects little better than slaves. Ottoman power reached its zenith under Sultan Süleyman the Magnificent (ruled 1520–66), who expanded the empire to the gates of Vienna. His successor added Cyprus to their dominions in 1570, but his death in 1574 marked the end of serious territorial expansion.

A History of the Greek City States 700–338 BC, by Ralph Seely, is a good choice for those seeking a clearer understanding of this formative period in Greek history.

Although they captured Crete in 1669 after a 25-year campaign and briefly threatened Vienna once more in 1683, the ineffectual sultans of the late 16th and 17th centuries saw the empire go into steady decline. They suffered a series of reversals on the battlefield, and Venice succeeded in recapturing the Peloponnese (1685–87) in a campaign that saw them advance as far as Athens. The Parthenon was destroyed in the fighting by a shell that struck a store of Turkish gunpowder.

Mistras & Byzantine Style & Civilisation by Sir Steven Runciman, and Fourteen Byzantine Rulers by Michael Psellus are both good introductions to Greece's Byzantine Age.

Chaos and rebellion spread across Greece. Pirates terrorised coastal dwellers and islanders, while gangs of *klephts* (anti-Ottoman fugitives and brigands) roamed the mountains. There was an upsurge of opposition to Turkish rule by freedom fighters – who fought each other when they weren't fighting the Turks.

THE WAR OF INDEPENDENCE

The long-heralded War of Independence finally began on 25 March 1821, when Bishop Germanos of Patras hoisted the Greek flag at the monastery of Agias Lavras, near Patras in the Peloponnese. Fighting broke out almost simultaneously across most of Greece and the occupied islands, with the Greeks making big early gains. The fighting was savage, with atrocities committed on both sides. The islands weren't spared the horrors of war: in 1822, Turkish forces massacred 25,000 people on the island of Chios, while another 7000 died on Kasos in 1824.

Eventually, the Great Powers – Britain, France and Russia – intervened on the side of the Greeks, defeating the Turkish-Egyptian fleet at the Battle of Navarino in October 1827. Although fighting between Russian and Turkish forces continued until 1829, Greece was left free to organise its own affairs. Nafplio, in the Peloponnese, was declared the first capital.

70 BC:	AD 324:
Romans complete the conquest of Greece by destroying Corinth	Emperor Constantine transfers the capital of the Roman Empire to Byzantium; Greece becomes part of Byzantine Empire

It was there that the country's first president, Ioannis Kapodistrias, a Corfiot who had been the foreign minister for Tsar Alexander I, was assassinated in 1831. Amid anarchy, the European powers stepped in again and declared that Greece should become a monarchy. In January 1833, 17-year-old Prince Otto of Bavaria was installed as king of a nation (established by the London Convention of 1832) that consisted of the Peloponnese, Sterea Ellada (Central Greece), the Cyclades and the Sporades.

King Otho (as his name became) displeased the Greek people from the start, arriving with a bunch of upper-class Bavarian cronies to whom he gave the most prestigious official posts. He moved the capital to Athens in 1834.

Patience with his rule ran out in 1843, when demonstrations in the capital, led by the War of Independence leaders, called for a constitution. Otho mustered a National Assembly, which drafted a constitution calling for parliamentary government consisting of a lower house and a senate. Otho's cronies were whisked out of power and replaced by War of Independence freedom fighters, who bullied and bribed the populace into voting for them.

By the end of the 1850s, most of the stalwarts from the War of Independence had been replaced by a new breed of university graduates (Athens University had been founded in 1837). In 1862 they staged a bloodless revolution and deposed the king. But they weren't quite able to set their own agenda because, in 1863, Britain returned the Ionian Islands (a British protectorate since 1815) to Greece. Amid the general euphoria that followed, the British were able to push forward young Prince William of Denmark, who became King George I.

His 50-year reign brought stability to the troubled country, beginning with a new constitution in 1864, which established the power of democratically elected representatives and pushed the king further towards a ceremonial role. An uprising in Crete against Turkish rule (1866–68) was suppressed by the sultan, but in 1881 Greece acquired Thessaly and part of Epiros as the result of another Russo-Turkish war.

In 1897 there was another uprising in Crete, and the hot-headed prime minister Theodoros Deligiannis responded by declaring war on Turkey and sending help to Crete. A Greek attempt to invade Turkey in the north proved disastrous – it was only through the intervention of the Great Powers that the Turkish army was prevented from taking Athens.

Crete was made a British protectorate in 1898, and the day-to-day government of the island was gradually handed over to the Greeks. In 1905 the president of the Cretan assembly, Eleftherios Venizelos, announced Crete's union *(enosis)* with Greece, although this was not recognised by international law until 1913. Venizelos went on to become prime minister of Greece in 1910 and was the country's leading politician until his republican sympathies brought about his downfall in 1935.

Although the Ottoman Empire was in its death throes at the beginning of the 20th century, it was still clinging onto Macedonia. It was a prize sought by the newly formed Balkan countries of Serbia and Bulgaria, as well as by Greece, leading to the Balkan wars. The first, in 1912, pitted

Modern Greece: A Short History, by CM Woodhouse, covers the period from Constantine the Great to 1990, however it has a right-wing bent that not everyone will appreciate.

824:	1204:
Arabs capture Crete	Frankish crusaders carve up Greece after sacking Constantinople (formerly Byzantium)

all three against the Turks; the second, in 1913, pitted Serbia and Greece against Bulgaria. The outcome was the Treaty of Bucharest (August 1913), which greatly expanded Greek territory by adding the southern part of Macedonia, part of Thrace, another chunk of Epiros, and the Northeastern Aegean Islands, as well as recognising the union with Crete.

In March 1913, King George was assassinated by a lunatic and his son Constantine became king.

WWI & SMYRNA

King Constantine, who was married to the sister of the German emperor, insisted that Greece remain neutral when WWI broke out in August 1914. As the war dragged on, the Allies (Britain, France and Russia) put increasing pressure on Greece to join forces with them against Germany and Turkey and they made promises that they couldn't hope to fulfil, including offering land in Asia Minor. Venizelos, the prime minister of Greece, favoured the Allied cause, placing him at loggerheads with the king. Tensions between the two came to a head in 1916, and Venizelos set up a rebel government, first in Crete and then in Thessaloniki, while the pressure from the Allies eventually persuaded Constantine to leave Greece in June 1917. He was replaced by his more amenable second son, Alexander.

Greek troops served with distinction on the Allied side, but when the war ended in 1918 the promised land in Asia Minor was not forthcoming. Venizelos took matters into his own hands and, with Allied acquiescence, landed troops in Smyrna (present-day Izmir) in May 1919 under the guise of protecting the half a million Greeks living in that city (just under half its population). With a firm foothold in Asia Minor, Venizelos now planned to push home his advantage against a war-depleted Ottoman Empire. He ordered his troops to attack in October 1920 (just weeks before he was voted out of office). By September 1921, the Greeks had advanced as far as Ankara.

The Turkish forces were commanded by Mustafa Kemal (later to become Atatürk), a young general who also belonged to the Young Turks, a group of army officers pressing for Western-style political reforms. Kemal first halted the Greek advance outside Ankara in September 1921 and then routed them with a massive offensive the following spring. The Greeks were driven out of Smyrna and many of the Greek inhabitants were massacred. Mustafa Kemal was now a national hero, the sultanate was abolished and Turkey became a republic.

The outcome of the failed Greek invasion and the revolution in Turkey was the Treaty of Lausanne of July 1923. This gave eastern Thrace and the islands of Imvros and Tenedos to Turkey, while the Italians kept the Dodecanese (which they had temporarily acquired in 1912 and would hold until 1947).

The treaty also called for a population exchange between Greece and Turkey to prevent any future disputes. Almost 1.5 million Greeks left Turkey and almost 400,000 Turks left Greece. The exchange put a tremendous strain on the Greek economy and caused great hardship for the individuals concerned. Many Greeks abandoned a privileged life in Asia Minor for one of extreme poverty in shantytowns in Greece.

Farewell Anatolia and *The Dead are Waiting*, by Dido Soteriou, are two powerful novels focusing on the population exchange of 1923. Soteriou was born in Asia Minor in 1909 and was herself a refugee.

1453:	1687:
Turks capture Constantinople; most of Greece becomes part of the Ottoman Empire	Venetians blow up the Parthenon during an artillery assault on the Acropolis of Athens

King Constantine, restored to the throne in 1920, identified himself too closely with the war against Turkey, and abdicated after the fall of Smyrna.

WWII & THE CIVIL WAR

In 1930 George II, Constantine's son, became king and appointed the dictator General Ioannis Metaxas as prime minister. Metaxas' grandiose ambition was to take the best from Greece's ancient and Byzantine past to create a Third Greek Civilisation, though what he actually created was more a Greek version of the Third Reich. His chief claim to fame was his celebrated *ohi* (no) to Mussolini's request to allow Italian troops to traverse Greece in 1940. Despite Allied help, Greece fell to Germany in 1941, after which followed carnage and mass starvation. Resistance movements sprang up, eventually polarising into royalist and communist factions.

Greek Women in Resistance, by Eleni Fountouri, is a compilation of journals, poems and personal accounts of women in the resistance movement from the 1940s to the 1950s. The book also contains poignant photographs and drawings.

A bloody civil war resulted, lasting until 1949 and leaving the country in chaos. More people were killed in the civil war than in WWII and 250,000 people were left homeless. The sense of despair that followed became the trigger for a mass exodus. Almost a million Greeks headed off in search of a better life elsewhere, primarily to Australia, Canada and the USA. Villages – whole islands even – were abandoned as people gambled on a new start in cities like Melbourne, Chicago and New York. While some have drifted back, the majority have stayed away.

THE COLONELS

Continuing political instability led to the colonels' coup d'etat in 1967, led by Georgos Papadopolous and Stylianos Patakos. King Constantine (son of King Paul, who succeeded George II) staged an unsuccessful counter coup, then fled the country. The colonels' junta distinguished itself by inflicting appalling brutality, repression and political incompetence upon the people.

After The War Was Over, edited by Mark Mazower, is a collection of essays dealing with the social history of Greece between 1943 and 1960, with particular emphasis on the lasting divisions created by the Civil War.

In 1974 they attempted to assassinate Cyprus' leader, Archbishop Makarios. When Makarios escaped, the junta replaced him with the extremist Nikos Samson, a convicted murderer. The Turks, who comprised 20% of the population, were alarmed at having Samson as leader. Consequently, mainland Turkey sent in troops and occupied North Cyprus, the continued occupation of which is one of the most contentious issues in Greek politics today. The junta, by now in a shambles, had little choice but to hand power back to the civilians.

In November 1974 a plebiscite voted 69% against restoration of the monarchy, and Greece became a republic. An election brought the right-wing New Democracy (ND) party into power.

THE SOCIALIST 1980S

In 1981 Greece entered the EC (European Community, now the EU). Andreas Papandreou's Panhellenic Socialist Movement (PASOK) won the next election, giving Greece its first socialist government. PASOK promised removal of US air bases and withdrawal from NATO, which Greece had joined in 1951.

Six years into government these promises remained unfulfilled, unemployment was high and reforms in education and welfare had been

1827:	1923:
Ioannis Kapodistrias elected first president of independent Greece	failed military campaign ends with population exchange between Greece and Turkey

limited. Women's issues had fared better however – the dowry system was abolished, abortion legalised, and civil marriage and divorce were implemented. The crunch for the government came in 1988 when Papandreou's affair with air stewardess Dimitra Liana (whom he subsequently married) was widely publicised and PASOK became embroiled in a financial scandal involving the Bank of Crete.

In July 1989, an unprecedented conservative and communist coalition took over to implement a *katharsis* (campaign of purification) to investigate the scandals. It ruled that Papandreou and four ministers should stand trial for embezzlement, telephone tapping and illegal grain sales. It then stepped down in October 1990, stating that the catharsis was complete.

THE 1990S & BEYOND

An election in 1990 brought the ND back to power with a majority of only two seats. The tough economic reforms that Prime Minister Konstantinos Mitsotakis was forced to introduce to counter a spiralling foreign debt soon made his government deeply unpopular. By late 1992, allegations began to emerge about the same sort of government corruption and dirty tricks that had brought Papandreou unstuck. Mitsotakis himself was accused of having a secret hoard of Minoan art. He was forced to call an election in October 1993.

Greeks again turned to PASOK and the ageing, ailing Papandreou, who had been cleared of all the charges levelled in 1990. Papandreou's final spell at the helm was dominated by speculation about his health. He was finally forced to step down in early 1996, and his death on 26 June marked the end of an era in Greek politics.

Papandreou's departure produced a dramatic change of direction for PASOK, with the party abandoning his left-leaning politics and electing experienced economist and lawyer Costas Simitis as the new prime minister. Cashing in on his reputation as the Mr Clean of Greek politics, Simitis romped to a comfortable majority at a snap poll called in October 1996.

His government has focused almost exclusively on the push for further integration with Europe, which has meant more tax reform and more austerity measures. His success in the face of constant protest earned him a mandate in April 2000 for another four years.

The goal of admission to the euro club was achieved at the beginning of 2001, and Greece adopted the euro as its currency in March 2002.

> 'Greece's foreign policy is dominated by its very sensitive relationship with Turkey, its giant Muslim neighbour to the east.'

RECENT FOREIGN POLICY

Greece's foreign policy is dominated by its very sensitive relationship with Turkey, its giant Muslim neighbour to the east.

After decades of constant antagonism, these two uneasy NATO allies have been working hard at being friends in recent years. This about-turn was sparked by the massive earthquake that devastated the Izmit area of western Turkey in August 1999. Greek rescue teams were among the first on the scene, where they were greeted as heroes. The Turks were quick to return the favour when a major earthquake struck Athens a month later. Despite the occasional hiccup, the two sides have been cooperating

1944–49:	1981:
Greek Civil War leaves Greece in tatters, prompting a mass exodus to countries like Australia, Canada and the USA	Greece becomes 10th member of the European Union

ever since – going so far as to mount a failed joint bid to stage the 2008 European soccer championship.

While Turkey remains the top priority, Greece has also had its hands full in recent years coping with events to the north, precipitated by the break-up of former Yugoslavia and the collapse of the communist regimes in Albania and Romania.

The country found itself in an impossible position during the 1999 NATO conflict with Serbia over Kosovo. The Greek public, already strongly sympathetic towards their fellow Orthodox Christian Serbs in the battle against the Muslim Albanian Kosovars, was outraged when the NATO bombing began. The Americans bore the brunt of anti-NATO demonstrations, violent at first, that lasted throughout the war.

Greece was a somewhat reluctant member of the 'coalition of the willing' assembled by the US to attack Iraq in March 2003. Faced with serious domestic opposition to the war, the government kept very quiet about the role played by US forces based at Souda Bay in Crete.

2002:	2004:
Greece drops the drachma and adopts the euro	Athens hosts the 28th Modern Olympic Games

The Culture

THE NATIONAL PSYCHE

Greeks have long enjoyed a reputation as loyal friends and generous hosts, for their pride in the country's rich cultural heritage and for their patriotism. This is certainly how most Greeks would like to see themselves. Scratch the surface a little though, and a slightly different picture starts to emerge.

The Greek psyche is a complex creature, moulded by centuries of foreign occupation.

It's true that Greeks are intensely patriotic. As elsewhere, however, this patriotism often gives way to xenophobia and, on a local level, to general suspicion.

Greek society remains deeply influenced by the Greek Orthodox Church and its surrounding ritual. Many people, even rebellious-looking youths, make the sign of the cross when they pass a church.

The male-female dynamic throws up some interesting paradoxes. Men love to give the impression that they rule the roost. In reality, it's usually the women who run the show, both at home and in business, while men do little more than sit around talking over endless coffees and ouzos. This pattern is developed at home, where boys are waited on hand and foot, while girls are involved in running the household from an early age.

At election time, voting intentions are often determined more by almost feudal local allegiances rather than party loyalty, and it's almost impossible to make any headway with local bureaucracy without the help of a friend or cousin working within the system.

Anti-Americanism is an interesting undercurrent of the Greek psyche. It originates from what many regard as undue US interference in Greek affairs during the Civil War, and was reinforced by suspicions of CIA involvement in the coup that brought the notorious colonels to power in 1967 (p32). It surfaces whenever the opportunity presents itself; the US Embassy seems to be the target of just about every protest staged in Athens. Greeks are also great supporters of the underdog, which is another reason why people took to the streets to protest the invasion of Iraq by the USA and its allies.

LIFESTYLE

The lifestyle of the average Greek has changed beyond all recognition in the last 50 years. Grandparents who recall the devastated country that emerged from the Civil War can hardly believe that Greece now ranks among the members of Europe's economic elite, the Euro Club.

Despite the radical changes, Greek society remains dominated by the family. A survey taken in 2003 showed that more than 90% of young people put family first. It's very rare for Greek children to move out of the family home before they are married – they may leave temporarily for university or work reasons, but invariably return.

Greek women are famously house proud, trained from an early age to maintain the home in spotless condition. Greek women also take great pride in their culinary skills. It's extremely rare for men to be involved in housework, and most confine their cooking activities to turning chops on the barbecue.

Households have been feeling the financial pinch in recent times, with the cost of living rising sharply since the arrival of the euro. Wages, which are tied to the official inflation rate, have failed to keep up. Eating out, a

DID YOU KNOW?

Greece has the highest number of smokers in the EU.

DID YOU KNOW?

In 2003 Greece was found to be serving the most expensive coffee in Europe – a full euro more than Italy, and one drunk in view of the Acropolis costing double that of one by the Eiffel Tower in Paris.

DID YOU KNOW?

Every inhabited island has a ferry service of some sort, even if it is only a weekly supply boat.

favourite activity, has been curtailed radically – and Greeks are masters at making a €2.50 cup of coffee last an hour or more.

Greeks attach great importance to education. The baby boomers of the 1950s, who grew up in a country devastated by war, are determined to provide their children with the educational opportunities they lacked. Given the inadequacies of the public education system, this means spending a fortune at private night schools, known as *frontisteria*.

You'll find the websites of Greece's top football teams, Panathinaikos and Olympiacos, at www.pao.gr and www.olympiacos.org, respectively.

Greeks have what most Westerners regard as a very casual approach to timekeeping. It's almost as if people resent the feeling of obligation created by an appointment; some people speculate that this stems from centuries of answering to foreign masters. After the opening of the new Athens Metro network, it became something of a joke that people were turning up for work on time – because they didn't realise how fast the Metro was.

POPULATION

The 2001 census recorded a population of 10,939,771. Almost a third of the population (3.6 million) live in the Greater Athens area, while more than two-thirds live in cities – confirming that Greece is now largely an urban society. Less than 15% of people live on the islands, the most populous of which are Crete (601,131), Evia (212,534) and Corfu (109,537).

Contemporary Greeks are a mixture of all of the invaders who have occupied the country since ancient times. Additionally, there are a number of distinct ethnic minorities living in the country.

The country's small Roman Catholic population is of Genoese or Frankish origin. They live mostly in the Cyclades (especially on the island of Syros, where they form 40% of the population), which the Franks dominated from 1207 to Ottoman times.

There are a small numbers of Turks on Kos and Rhodes which, along with the rest of the Dodecanese, did not become part of Greece until 1947. There are also small Jewish communities in several towns; in Rhodes they date back to the Roman era, while on the mainland most are descendants of 15th-century exiles from Spain and Portugal.

The collapse of the communist regimes in Albania and Romania produced a wave of economic refugees across Greece's poorly guarded northern borders, with an estimated 1.5 million arriving from Albania alone.

SPORT

Football (soccer) remains the most-popular spectator sport, although it has suffered from a lack of success on the playing field, where the national side has proved a source of much hair-wrenching. The side's only appearance in the World Cup finals, in the USA in 1994, brought a string of heavy defeats. They have continued to disappoint ever since, and the public have responded by staying away in droves.

Check out Greece's demographics at www.statistics.gr

The Greek first division is dominated by the big two: Olympiakos of Piraeus and Panathinaikos of Athens. They are the glamour clubs of Greek soccer, with supporters all around the country. Their rivalry is occasionally interrupted by AEK Athens and POAK from Thessaloniki. These four have put up some top performances in European club competition. The only island team in the top flight is OFI from Iraklio on Crete, a club that has known more of the fervour of its fans than its results.

MULTICULTURALISM

Greece probably qualifies as the least multicultural country in Europe – certainly within the EU. Although the country has a history of continuous migration stretching back over thousands of years, the Greeks have

THE ROCKY ROAD TO 2004

The eyes of the world will be upon Athens for 17 days in August 2004 when athletes from some 200 countries descend on the city for the 28th Olympiad.

It will be the end of a dramatic seven-year emotional roller-coaster ride for the people of Athens. Back in 1997, when the city won the right to host the games, there was jubilation that the games were coming home to Greece after 108 years. Slowly but surely, however, the magnitude of the task ahead began to sink in – and jubilation gave way to anxiety. Anxiety was replaced by alarm after Sydney raised the organisational standard to new heights in 2000. Alarm quickly developed into despondency amid a series of dire warnings from the International Olympic Committee (IOC) about the lack of progress.

Faced with the humiliating prospect of losing the games, the organisers finally got moving – although it wasn't until mid-2002 that the IOC was sufficiently satisfied with progress to issue an assurance that Athens would not be stripped of the games.

Work remains behind schedule at many venues, but at the time of research Athenians were feeling confident that everything would be ready in time – if only just.

Many people have questioned the sanity of staging the games during August in one of Europe's hottest and most-polluted capitals. The environmental watchdog Greenpeace has expressed concerns over the possible effects of traffic fumes on the athletes' health. Organisers argue that August is normally a quiet traffic month, as most Athenians abandon the city for the coast and the islands. It remains to be seen whether this exodus is repeated in an Olympic year.

The Olympics are sure to be a source of constant anxiety right up until the opening ceremony, but Greece is deeply committed – both emotionally and financially – to making them work.

Olympic Venues

The centrepiece is the 80,000-seat Olympic Stadium, in the northern suburb of Maroussi, which will stage the athletic events as well as the opening and closing ceremonies. The stadium has doubled as the city's number one soccer venue since it was completed in 1996.

The stadium is part of the Athens Olympic Sports Complex, next to Irini metro station, which also includes an indoor sports hall for gymnastics and basketball, a swimming complex with a diving pool, velodrome and tennis centre. The rhythmic gymnastics, table tennis and water polo will take place 4km south of the stadium at the Galatsi Olympic Indoor Hall.

The other main area of Olympic activity is in the coastal suburb of Faliro. Karaïskaki Stadium, home ground for the Olympiakos football (soccer) club, will host the soccer finals, while the nearby Peace and Friendship Stadium will hold handball and basketball. Yachting will be held in Faliro Bay, beach volleyball at Faliro Beach, and handball and taekwondo at the Faliro Sports Pavilion.

Naturally enough, the marathon will start from Marathon – the town which gave the race its name – and it will finish at the Panathenaic Stadium – the home of the first modern Olympic Games. The stadium will also host the archery.

Other venues include the Markopoulo Olympic Shooting and Equestrian Centre, 10km south of Peania; the Ano Liossia Olympic Indoor Hall, in northern Athens, which will stage the wrestling; the Nikea Olympic Hall, in western Athens, where the weightlifting will take place; a new Olympic Centre at Ellinikon, the old international airport, which will hold the baseball, softball, hockey and badminton events; as well as the Vouliagmeni Olympic Triathlon Centre, 8km south of Glyfada, and the Goudi Olympic Modern Pentathlon Centre, west of central Athens. The cycling road race will take place through Athens' historical centre and the mountain-biking event will be staged at Mt Parnitha. The rowing and flatwater kayaking events will be held at the controversial new Olympic Rowing Centre at Shinias, near Marathon, built despite protests about the destruction of coastal wetlands. The kayak slalom will be held at Ellinikon.

Soccer is the only event that will be staged outside Attica, with Iraklio, Patras, Thessaloniki and Volos to host group and quarter-final matches.

For updated details on Olympic venues and news, log on to the official Athens 2004 website at www.athens2004.com.

been remarkably successful in persuading newcomers to adopt Greek ways. At the same time, Greek culture has absorbed plenty of influences along the way, particularly during four centuries of Ottoman rule that left an indelible stamp on the nation's music and cuisine. The kebabs and the coffee (called Turkish coffee until the invasion of Cyprus) are two obvious legacies.

Modern immigration has proved more difficult to handle, particularly the enormous influx of refugees from neighbouring Albania. These refugees have proved an invaluable source of cheap labour, but many Greeks resent their presence, holding Albanians responsible for just about every crime committed. Greece has also received a fair number of Kurdish refugees in recent years, and there are small Kurdish communities in most major cities. Athens has a small Asian community, mostly from Bangladesh and Pakistan.

The Cyclades, or Life Among the Insular Greeks, by James Theodore Bent, is still regarded as the greatest book about the people of the Greek Islands.

MEDIA

Greeks are great newspaper buyers and avid television watchers, giving the country's media owners an extremely influential role in shaping public opinion.

Strangely, there is no single company that dominates the media – as in other European nations. Ownership of the key publications is spread around half a dozen major players. The most important of these is the Lampraki Group, which publishes the serious *To Vima* and the populist *Ta Nea*, both of which consistently support the ruling (at the time of research) Panhellenic Socialist Movement (PASOK) party of Costas Simitis. *Eleftherotypa* and *Ethos* are two other important contributors to the cause.

Kathimerini, traditionally a centre-right publication, is the newspaper favoured by the Greek establishment. Its support for New Democracy has been lukewarm of late, leaving publications like *Eleftheros Typos* and *Apogevmatini* to promote the ND line.

Communist-party views are represented by the slickly produced daily *Rizospastis*, while the weeklies *Alfa I* and *Xrisi Efkairia* cater to the far right.

Sport, particularly football and basketball, is deemed sufficiently newsworthy to warrant no less than 10 sports dailies – as well as several more weekly sports publications. Most of these have strong affiliations with one of the major clubs like Olympiakos, Panathinaikos or AEK.

Television ownership is evenly spread among the same main players, all jockeying hard to improve their positions.

RELIGION

About 98% of the Greek population belongs to the Greek Orthodox Church. Most of the remainder are either Roman Catholic, Jewish or Muslim.

The Greek Orthodox Church is closely related to the Russian Orthodox Church; together they form the third-largest branch of Christianity. Orthodox, meaning 'right belief', was founded in the 4th century by Constantine the Great, who was converted to Christianity by a vision of the Cross.

By the 8th century, there were a number of differences of opinion, as well as increasing rivalry, between the pope in Rome and the patriarch of Constantinople, and by the 11th century these differences had become irreconcilable. In 1054 the pope and the patriarch excommunicated one another. Ever since, the two have gone their own ways as the (Greek/Russian) Orthodox Church and the Roman Catholic Church. The brief visit to Athens by Pope John Paul II in May 2001 was the first by a pontiff for more than 1300 years.

Allen Guttman's *The Olympics: A History of the Modern Games* traces the history from 1896 to 2000, contrasting its ideals with political reality.

During Ottoman times, membership of the Orthodox Church was one of the most important criteria in defining a Greek, regardless of where he or she lived. The church was the principal upholder of Greek traditions and culture.

Religion is still an integral part of life in Greece, and the Greek year is centred on the festivals of the church calendar. On the islands you will see hundreds of tiny churches dotted around the countryside. Most have been built by individual families in the name of their selected patron saint as thanksgiving for God's protection.

Regrettably, many churches are kept locked nowadays, but it's usually easy enough to locate caretakers, who will be happy to open them up for you.

ARTS
Architecture

Of all the ancient Greek arts, architecture has perhaps had the greatest influence. Greek temples, seen throughout history as symbols of democracy, have been the inspiration for architectural movements such as the Italian Renaissance and the British Greek Revival.

The islands feature a range of architectural styles. The most striking of these is Cycladic style, characterised by brilliant white cubic houses with bright blue doors and window frames: the quintessential island image as pictured on a thousand postcards. They are designed to provide protection from winter gales, and to stay cool in summer. The labyrinthine layout of island towns was originally intended to disorient pirates, who were a major problem for Mediterranean seafaring communities in the 15th and 16th centuries.

One of the earliest known architectural sites of ancient Greece is the huge palace and residential complex at Knossos on Crete (p215), which was built in the Minoan period. Visitors today can still marvel at the spacious courtyards and grandiose stairways that connect the many living rooms, storerooms and bathrooms, and give us an idea of day-to-day Minoan life.

The Minoan period was followed by the Mycenaean. Instead of open, labyrinthine palaces, the Mycenaeans used their advanced skills in engineering to build citadels on a compact, orderly plan, fortified by strong walls.

The next great advance in ancient Greek architecture came with the construction of the first monumental stone temples during the Archaic and the classical periods. From this time, temples came to be characterised by the famous orders of columns, most notably the Doric, Ionic and Corinthian. These orders were applied to the exteriors of temples, which retained their traditional simple plan of porch and hall but were now regularly surrounded by a colonnade or at least a columnar facade.

Doric columns feature cushion capitals, fluted shafts and no bases; the most famous Doric temple in Greece is, of course, the Parthenon (p71).

Time, Religion & Social Experience in Rural Greece by Laurie Kain Hart is a fascinating account of village traditions – many of which are alive and well buried beneath the tourist veneer.

RA Tomlinson's *Greek Architecture* covers everything from the prehistoric settlements of Troy to the absorption of Hellenic Greece into the Roman Empire.

The shaft of the Ionic column has a base in several tiers and more flutes. Unlike the austere Doric style, its capital has an ornamented neck-ing. In all, the Ionic order is less massive than the Doric, and is generally more graceful. The little temple of Athena Nike, by the entrance to the Athenian Acropolis (p71), and the Erechtheion, opposite the Parthenon, are two famous Ionic temples.

The distinct and ornate Corinthian column features a single or double row of leafy scrolls (usually acanthus). This order was introduced at the end of the classical period and was subsequently used by the Romans in many of their buildings. The Temple of Olympian Zeus in Athens, completed in Hadrian's time, is a good example.

During the Roman period, Athens obtained a new commercial *agora* (now known as the Roman Agora; p71) in the time of Augustus, and a century and a half later Emperor Hadrian endowed the city with a library and built an elegant arch that still stands between the old and new parts of the city.

During the Byzantine period the Parthenon in Athens was converted into a church and other churches were built throughout Greece. These usually featured a central dome supported by four arches on piers and flanked by vaults, with smaller domes at the four corners and three apses to the east. The external brickwork, which alternated with stone, was sometimes set in patterns. On Patmos (p313), where one of the first monasteries was built in the 10th century, the monastic buildings as well as the churches survive, though much has changed through centuries of continuous use.

After the War of Independence, Greece continued the neoclassical style that had been dominant in Western European architecture and sculpture from 1760 to 1820, thus providing a sense of continuity with its ancient past. Architectural sensibilities took a back seat for most of the 20th century, when political necessity and economic constraints determined the shape of events.

Cinema & Television

Greece's best-known film director is Paris-based Costa Gavras. He made his name with *Z* (starring Yves Montand) which won an Oscar for best foreign film back in 1969. Montand played a detective in a story based on the 1967 murder of communist deputy Grigoris Lambrakis in Thessaloniki by right-wing thugs. Gavras collected a second Oscar (best screenplay adaptation) for his 1982 film *Missing*, which cast Jack Lemmon in the role of an American kidnapped in Chile. His more recent works are *Mad City* (1997), which starred Dustin Hoffman, John Travolta and Alan Alda, and *Amen* (2003).

Greece's domestic film industry has long been in the doldrums, largely due to inadequate funding. The problem is compounded by the type of films Greek directors seem to favour, which are famously slow moving and loaded with symbolism.

The leader of this school is Theodoros Angelopoulos, winner of the Golden Palm award at the 1998 Cannes Film Festival for *Eternity and a Day*. It tells the story of a terminally ill writer who spends his last day revisiting his youth in the company of a 10-year-old boy. His best-known work is his epic *Alexander the Great* (1980), while *The Beekeeper* (1986) and *The Suspended Step of the Stork* (1991) have also won critical acclaim.

Although it produces no action films, Greek cinema has shown in recent years that it does have a lighter side. *Safe Sex* (2000), a light-hearted look at sexuality directed by Thanasis Reppas and Mihailis Papathanasiou,

The Greek Film Centre is responsible for the support and development of cinema in Greece. Find out about the latest Greek films in production at www.gfc.gr

was the last Greek film to score at the box office. It was responsible for a large percentage of the 2.3 million ticket sales recorded by Greek films in 2000.

If Greek cinema is in the doldrums, it's hard to come up with words to describe the state of Greek television. Most channels serve up a constant diet of low-budget quiz shows, sport and foreign movies.

Dance

Music and dancing have played an important role in Greek social life since the dawn of Hellenism. Whether it be at a traditional wedding, nightclub, an Athenian *boîte* or a simple village *kafeneio* (coffee house), a song and a dance are not far from people's minds.

The style of dancing often reflects the climate or disposition of the participants. The islands with their bright and cheery atmosphere inspired lilting music and matching dances such as the *ballos* or the *syrtos*, while the graceful *kalamatianos* circle dance, where dancers stand in a row with their hands on one another's shoulders, reflects years of proud Peloponnese tradition. Originally from Kalamata in the Peloponnese, this dance can be seen everywhere, most commonly on festive occasions.

The so-called 'Zorba's dance' or *syrtaki* is a stylised dance for two or three men or women with linked arms on shoulders, while the often spectacular solo male *zeïmbekikos*, with its whirling improvisations, has its roots in the Greek blues of the hashish dens and prisons of prewar times. The women counterpoint this self-indulgent and showy male display with their own sensuous *tsifteteli*, a svelte, sinewy show of femininity evolved from the Middle Eastern belly dance.

There are many translations of the Iliad *and* Odyssey *around, but the versions by EV Rien are worth looking out for.*

The folk dances of today derive from the ritual dances performed in ancient Greek temples. The *syrtos* is one of these dances, and is depicted on ancient Greek vases. There are also references to dances in Homer's works. Many Greek folk dances, including the *syrtos*, are performed in a circular formation; in ancient times, dancers formed a circle in order to seal themselves off from evil influences.

Literature

The first, and greatest, ancient Greek writer was Homer, author of the *Iliad* and *Odyssey*, which tell the story of the Trojan War and the subsequent wanderings of Odysseus. Nothing is known of Homer's life: where or when he lived, or whether, as it is alleged, he was blind. The historian Herodotus thought Homer lived in the 9th century BC, and no scholar has since proved or disproved this.

Herodotus (5th century BC) was the author of the first historical work about Western civilisation. His highly subjective account of the Persian Wars has, however, led him to be regarded as the 'father of lies' as well as the 'father of history'.

Pindar (c 518–438 BC) is regarded as the pre-eminent lyric poet of ancient Greece. He was commissioned to recite his odes at the Olympic Games. The greatest writers of love poetry were Sappho (6th century BC) and Alcaeus (5th century BC), both of whom lived on Lesvos. Sappho's poetic descriptions of her affections for other women gave rise to the term 'lesbian'.

Sappho: A New Translation, by Mary Bernard, is the best translation of this great poet's work.

Dionysios Solomos (1798–1857) and Andreas Kalvos (1796–1869), who were both born on Zakynthos, are regarded as the first modern Greek poets. Solomos' work was heavily nationalistic and his *Hymn to Freedom* became the Greek national anthem.

The best-known 20th-century poets are George Seferis (1900–71), who won the 1963 Nobel Prize for literature, and Odysseus Elytis (1911–96), who won the same prize in 1979. Seferis drew his inspiration from mythology, whereas Elytis' work is surreal.

The most important novelist of the 20th century is the Cretan writer Nikos Kazantzakis (1883–1957), whose unorthodox religious views created such a stir in the 1920s. His works continue to be controversial. Some people regard Kazantzakis as essential reading; others refuse to acknowledge him because of his portrayal of the Greek clergy. Kazantzakis's novels are full of drama and larger-than-life characters, such as the magnificent Alexis Zorba of *Zorba the Greek* and the tortured Michaelis of *Christ Recrucified*, two of his finest works.

Apostolos Doxiadis (born in 1953) achieved international fame in 2000 with his unusual novel *Uncle Petros and Goldbach's Conjecture*. Despite this success, he's better known at home as a film director.

Collected Poems, by George Seferis, and *Selected Poems*, by Odysseus Elytis, are both excellent translations.

Music

Singing and the playing of musical instruments have also been an integral part of life in Greece since ancient times; Cycladic figurines holding musical instruments resembling harps and flutes date back to 2000 BC. Musical instruments of ancient Greece included the lyre, lute, *piktis* (pipes), *kroupeza* (a percussion instrument), *kithara* (a stringed instrument), *aulos* (a wind instrument), *barbitos* (similar to a violoncello) and the *magadio* (similar to a harp).

The ubiquitous stringed bouzouki, closely associated with contemporary music and which you will hear everywhere in Greece, is a relative newcomer to the game. It is a mandolin-like instrument similar to the Turkish *saz* and *baglama*.

The plucked strings of the *bulbous outi* (oud), the strident sound of the Cretan *lyra* (lyre) and the staccato rap of the *toumberlaki* (lap drum) bear witness to a rich range of musical instruments that share many common characteristics with instruments all over the Middle East.

The bouzouki is one of the main instruments of rembetika music – the Greek equivalent of the American Blues. The name rembetika may come from the Turkish word *rembet*, which means outlaw. Opinions differ as to the origins of rembetika, but it is probably a hybrid of several different types of music. One source was the music that emerged in the 1870s in the 'low life' cafés, called *tekedes* (hashish dens), in urban areas and especially around ports. Another source was the Arab-Persian music played in sophisticated Middle Eastern *amanedes* (music cafés) in the 19th century. Rembetika was popularised in Greece by the refugees from Asia Minor.

Road to Rembetika: Music of a Greek Sub-Culture – Songs of Love, Sorrow & Hashish, by Gail Holst-Warhaft, is a passionate account of the development of Greek music.

The songs that emerged from the *tekedes* had themes concerning hashish, prison life, gambling, and knife fights, whereas *café aman* music had themes that centred on erotic love. These all came together in the music of the refugees, from which a subculture of rebels, called *manges*, emerged. The manges wore showy clothes even though they lived in extreme poverty, worked long hours in menial jobs, and spent their evenings in the tekedes, smoking hashish and singing and dancing. Although hashish was illegal, the law was rarely enforced until Metaxas did his clean-up job in 1936. It was in a tekedes in Piraeus that Markos Vamvakaris, now acknowledged as the greatest rembetis, was discovered by a recording company in the 1930s.

The 1950s and '60s saw rembetika become increasingly glitzy and commercialised, although the period also produced two outstanding composers of popular music (including rembetika) in Mikis Theodorakis and Manos Hatzidakis. The best of Theodorakis' work is the music that he composed for the poetry of Seferis, Elytis and Ritsos.

During the junta years, many rembetika clubs were closed down, but interest in genuine rembetika revived in the 1980s – particularly among students and intellectuals. There are now a number of rembetika clubs in Athens.

Other musical forms in Greece include *dimotika* – poetry sung and more often than not accompanied by the *klarino* (clarinet) and *defi* (tambourine) – and the widely popular middle-of-the-road *elafrolaïka*, best exemplified by the songs of Giannis Parios.

Since independence, Greece has followed mainstream developments in classical music. Internationally renowned soprano Elena Kelessidi is the latest to follow in the footsteps of the country's original opera superstar Maria Callas. Conductor Loukas Karytinos and composer Nikos Xydakis are others who have won international acclaim.

Comparatively few Greek popular performers have made it big on the international scene – the best known is Nana Mouskouri. Others include Demis Roussos, the larger-than-life singer who spent the 1980s strutting the world stage clad in his caftan, and the US-based techno wizard Yanni.

You'll also find all the main forms of Western popular music. Rock, particularly heavy metal, seems to have struck a chord with young urban Greeks, and Athens has a lively local scene as well as playing host to big international names. Although two of the most popular local rock bands – Xylina Spathia (Wooden Swords) and Tripes (Holes) – perform in Greek, most local bands prefer English. Septic Flesh are the biggest of many heavy-metal outfits.

Painting

The lack of any comprehensive archaeological record of ancient Greek painting has forced art historians to largely rely on the painted decoration of terracotta pots as evidence of the development of this art.

There are a few exceptions, such as the famous frescoes unearthed on Santorini and now housed in the National Archaeological Museum in Athens (p72). Stylistically the frescoes are similar to the paintings of Minoan Crete, which are less well preserved.

Greek painting came into its own during the Byzantine period. Churches during this era were usually decorated with frescoes on a dark-blue background, with a bust of Christ in the dome, the four Gospel writers in the pendentives supporting the dome and the Virgin and Child in the apse. They also featured scenes from the life of Christ and figures of the saints.

Painting after the Byzantine period became more secular in nature, with 19th-century Greek painters specialising in portraits, nautical themes and pictorial representation of the War of Independence. Major 19th-century painters included Dionysios Tsokos, Andreas Kriezis, Theodoros Vryzakis, Nikiphoros Lytras, Konstantinos Volanakis and Nicholas Gyzis. Gyzis' historical paintings, which were painted at the time of the fascination with the 'Great Idea' of a new Greek empire, feature particularly interesting subject matter.

From the first decades of the 20th century, artists such as Konstantinos Parthenis, Konstantinos Kaleas and, later, George Bouzianis were able to use the heritage of the past and at the same time assimilate various developments in modern art. These paintings are best studied in the National Art Gallery in Athens (p72).

'Greek painting came into its own during the Byzantine period'

Pottery

Say the words 'Greek art' and most people will immediately visualise a painted terracotta pot. Represented in museums and art galleries throughout the world, the pots of ancient Greece have such a high profile for a number of reasons, chief among these being that there are lots of them around! The excavation of these pots, buried throughout Greece over millennia, has enabled us to appreciate in small measure the tradition of ancient pictorial art.

Practised from the Stone Age on, pottery is one of the most ancient arts. At first, vases were built with coils and wads of clay but the art of throwing on the wheel was introduced in about 2000 BC and was then practised with great skill by Minoan and Mycenaean artists.

Minoan pottery is often characterised by a high centre of gravity and beak-like spouts. Painted decoration was applied as a white clay slip (a thin paste of clay and water) or one that fired to a greyish black or dull red. Flowing designs with spiral or marine and plant motifs were used. The Archaeological Museum in Iraklio (p207) has a wealth of Minoan pots.

The 10th century BC saw the introduction of the Protogeometric style, with its substantial pots decorated with blackish-brown horizontal lines around the circumference, hatched triangles, and compass-drawn concentric circles. This was followed by the new vase shape and more-crowded decoration of the pots of the Geometric period. The decorations on these pots are painted in a lustrous brown glaze on the light surface of the clay, and the same dark glaze is used as a wash to cover the undecorated areas; occasionally a touch of white is added. By the early 8th century figures were introduced, marking the introduction of the most fundamental element in the later tradition of classical art – the representation of gods, men and animals.

Reproductions of all the various styles constitute a sizeable proportion of Greece's pottery production, and they are available at souvenir shops throughout the country.

> *Greek Art & Archaeology,* by John Griffiths Pedley, is a super introduction to the development of Greek art and civilisation.

Sculpture

The sculptures of ancient Greece are works of extraordinary visual power and beauty that hold pride of place in the collections of the great museums of the world.

The prehistoric art of Greece has been discovered only recently, most notably the remarkable figurines produced in the Cyclades from the high-quality marble of Paros and Naxos in the middle of the 3rd millennium BC. Their primitive and powerful forms have inspired many artists since.

Displaying an obvious debt to Egyptian sculpture, the marble sculptures of the Archaic period are true precursors of the famed Greek sculpture of the classical period. Seeking to master the depiction of both the naked body and of drapery, sculptors of the period focused on figures of *kouroi* (naked youths), with their set symmetrical stance and enigmatic smiles. Many great *kouros* sculptures and draped female *kore* can be admired at the National Archaeological Museum in Athens (p72).

The sculpture of the classical period shows an obsession with the human figure and with drapery but, unfortunately, little original work of the classical period survives. Most freestanding classical sculpture described by ancient writers was made of bronze and survives only as marble copies made by the Romans.

The quest to attain total naturalism continued in the Hellenistic period; works of this period were animated, almost theatrical, in contrast to their serene Archaic and classical predecessors. The end of the Hellenistic age signalled the decline of Greek sculpture's pre-eminent position in the history of the artform.

Theatre

Drama in Greece dates back to the contests staged at the Ancient Theatre of Dionysos in Athens during the 6th century BC for the annual Dionysia festival. During one of these competitions, Thespis left the ensemble and took centre stage for a solo performance regarded as the first true dramatic performance. The term 'thespian', for actor, derives from this event.

Aeschylus (c 525–456 BC) is the so-called 'father of tragedy'; his best-known work is the Oresteia trilogy. Sophocles (c 496–406 BC) is regarded as the greatest tragedian. He is thought to have written over 100 plays, of which only seven survive. These include *Ajax*, *Antigone*, *Electra*, *Trachiniae* and his most-famous play, *Oedipus Rex*. His plays dealt mainly with tales from mythology and had complex plots. Sophocles won first prize at the Dionysia festival 18 times, beating Aeschylus in 468 BC, whereupon Aeschylus went to Sicily in a huff.

Euripides (c 485–406 BC) was another famous tragedian, more popular than either Aeschylus or Sophocles because his plots were considered to be more exciting. He wrote 80 plays, of which 19 are extant (although one, *Rhesus*, is disputed). His most-famous works are *Medea*, *Andromache*, *Orestes* and *Bacchae*. Aristophanes (c 427–387 BC) wrote comedies – often ribald – which dealt with topical issues. His play *The Wasp* ridicules Athenians, who resorted to litigation over trivialities, *The Birds* pokes fun at Athenian gullibility and *Plutus* deals with the unfair distribution of wealth.

Drama continues to feature prominently in domestic arts, although activity is largely confined to Athens and Thessaloniki. The first couple of the modern Greek theatre are playwrights Thanasis Reppas and Mihailis Papathanasiou, also noted writers of screenplays and movie directors. Unfortunately, performances of their work are only in Greek.

John Boardman's *Greek Sculpture: The Classical Period* is an excellent handbook assessing the development of sculpture in the 5th century BC.

Environment

THE LAND
Geography

Greece lies at the southern tip of the rugged Balkan Peninsula. Most of the mainland is mountainous, and dominated by the Pindos Ranges. The country has land borders to the north with Albania, the Former Republic of Macedonia, and Bulgaria; and to the east with Turkey.

The mainland, however, is but a small part of Greece. It also has some 1400 islands, of which 169 are inhabited. They contribute only a small percentage of the nation's total land mass of 131,900 sq km, but are responsible for extending Greek territorial waters over more than 400,000 sq km.

The majority of islands are spread across the shallow waters of the Aegean Sea between Greece and Turkey. These are divided into four main groups: the Cyclades, the Dodecanese, the islands of the northeastern Aegean and the Sporades. The two largest Aegean islands, Crete and Evia, do not belong to any group.

The other island groups are the Saronic Gulf islands, which lie between Athens and the Peloponnese, and the Ionians, in the Ionian Sea between Greece and southern Italy, while Kythira stands alone below the southeastern tip of the Peloponnese.

Like the mainland, most of the terrain is extremely rugged. Crete has half a dozen peaks over 2000m, the highest of which is Mt Ida at 2456m. Evia, Karpathos, Kefallonia and Samothraki all boast peaks of more than 1500m.

Like the mainland, most of the ground is either too arid, too poor or too steep for intensive agriculture. There are several exceptions, like Naxos and Crete, both of which are famous for the quality of their produce, and verdant Samothraki.

Geology

The earthquake that struck Athens on 7 September 1999, leaving 139 dead and 100,000 homeless, served as a savage reminder of the fact that Greece lies in one of most seismically active regions in the world.

That earthquake was just one of more than 20,000 earthquakes that have been recorded in Greece in the last 40 years. Fortunately, most of them are very minor – detectable only by sensitive seismic monitoring equipment. The reason for all this activity is that the Eastern Mediterranean lies at the meeting point (the North Aegean Fault) of three continental plates: the Eurasian, African and Arabian. The three constantly grind away at each other, generating countless earthquakes as the land surface reacts to the intense activity beneath the earth's crust.

The North Aegean Fault was responsible for the massive eruption (one of the largest ever) that created the spectacular cliffs of Santorini, while the strange moonscape of Nisyros is further evidence of the region's volcanic past.

WILDLIFE
Animals

You're unlikely to encounter much in the way of wildlife on most of the islands. The exception is on larger islands like Crete and Evia, where squirrels, rabbits, hares, foxes and weasels are all fairly common. Reptiles are well

Try Paul Sterry's *Complete Mediterranean Wildlife* for a general guide to the plants and animals of the region.

represented too: snakes include several viper species, which are poisonous; you're more likely to see lizards though, all of which are harmless.

One of the pleasures of island-hopping in Greece is watching the dolphins as they follow the boats. Although there are many dolphins in the Aegean, the striped dolphin has recently been the victim of murbilivirus – a sickness that affects the immune system. Research into the virus is being carried out in the Netherlands.

Bird-watchers, however, have more chance of coming across something unusual in the Greek islands.

Not surprisingly, seabirds are a major feature. Assorted gulls, petrels, shearwaters and shags are common throughout the Aegean. The islands are also home to a rich variety of birds of prey, particularly the mountains of larger islands like Crete and Evia. They include the spectacular griffon vulture and several species of eagle as well as Peregrine falcons, harriers and hawks.

About 350 pairs (60% of the world's population) of the rare Eleonora falcon nest on the island of Piperi, northeast of Alonissos in the Sporades. The Eleonora falcon can also be spotted on a number of other islands, including Naxos and Syros.

There are also a large number of migratory birds, most of which are merely passing by on their way from winter feeding sites in North Africa to summer nesting grounds in Eastern Europe.

The larger islands boast all the usual Mediterranean small birds – tits, wagtails, warblers, bee-eaters, larks, swallows, flycatchers, thrushes and chats – as well as some more distinctive species such as the hoopoe.

The Northeastern Aegean Islands are very popular with bird-watchers, particularly Lesvos where birding has become big business. Other rewarding destinations for birders are the islands of Naxos, Sifnos and Syros in the Cyclades, and Kos and Tilos in the Dodecanese.

> You can get more information about dolphins from the Greek Society for the Protection & Study of Dolphins & Cetaceans at www.delphis.gr (in Greek only).

> The website of the Hellenic Ornithological Society, www.ornithologiki.gr, has loads of information about what to see and where, as well as information about the society's outings and activities.

ENDANGERED SPECIES

Europe's rarest mammal, the monk seal (Monachus monachus), was once very common in the Mediterranean, but is now on the brink of extinction in Europe – it survives in slightly larger numbers in the Hawaiian islands. There are only about 400 left in Europe, 250 of which live in Greece. There

THE EVIL OLIVE

It is a sad irony that the tree most revered by the Greeks is responsible for the country's worst ecological disaster. The tree is the olive. It was the money tree of the early Mediterranean civilisations, providing an abundance of oil that not only tasted great but could also be used for everything from lighting to lubrication. The ancient Greeks thought it was too good to be true and concluded it must be a gift from the gods.

In their eagerness to make the most of this gift, native forest was cleared on a massive scale to make way for the olive. Landowners were urged on by decrees such as those issued in the 6th century BC by the arhon (chief magistrate) of Athens, Solon, who banned the export of all agricultural produce other than olive oil and made cutting down an olive tree punishable by death.

Much of the land planted with olives was unsuitable hill country. Without the surface roots of the native forest to bind it, the topsoil of the hills was rapidly washed away. The olive tree could do nothing to help. It has no surface root system, depending entirely on its impressive tap root.

Thus, the lush countryside so cherished by the ancient Greeks was transformed into the harsh, rocky landscape that greets the modern visitor.

are about 40 in the Ionian Sea and the rest are found in the Aegean. These sensitive creatures are particularly susceptible to human disturbance and now live only in isolated coastal caves. The majority of reported seal deaths are the result of accidental trapping, but the main threat to their survival is the continuing destruction of habitat. Tourist boats are major culprits.

The waters around Zakynthos are also home to the last large sea- turtle colony in Europe, that of the loggerhead turtle *(Careta careta)*. The loggerhead also nests in smaller numbers on the Peloponnese and on Crete.

The golden jackal *(Canis aureus)* is a strong candidate for Greece's most misunderstood mammal. Although its diet is 50% vegetarian, in the past it has shouldered much of the blame for attacks on stock carried out by wild dogs. It was hunted to the brink of extinction until it was declared a protected species in 1990, and it survives only in central Greece and on the island of Samos. It's strictly nocturnal. The other 50% of its diet is made up of carrion, reptiles and small mammals.

The Cretan wild goat, the kri-kri, survives in the wild only in the Samaria Gorge area and on the tiny islet of Kri Kri, off Agios Nikolaos in Crete.

Plants

Greece is endowed with a variety of flora unrivalled in Europe. There are over 6000 species (some of which occur nowhere else) and more than 100 varieties of orchid, which flower from late February to early June. They continue to thrive on the islands because most of the land is too poor for intensive agriculture and has escaped the ravages of chemical fertilisers.

The mountains of Crete boast some of the finest displays. Common species include anemones, white cyclamens, irises, lilies, poppies, gladioli, tulips, and countless varieties of daisy. Look out for the blue and orange Cretan Iris *(Iris cretica)*, one of 120 wildflowers unique to Crete. Others are the pink Cretan ebony, the white-flowered symphyandra and the white-flowered *Cyclamen cretica*.

Other rare species found on the islands include the *Rhododendron luteum*, a yellow azalea, that grows only on Mytilini.

Spectacular plants include the coastal giant reed – you may get lost among its high, dense groves on your way to a beach – as well as the giant fennel, which grows to 3m, and the tall yellow-horned poppy, both of which also grow by the sea. The white-flowered sea squill grows on hills above the coast. The beautifully perfumed sea daffodil grows along southern coasts, particularly on Crete and Corfu. The conspicuous snake's-head fritillary *(Fritillaria graeca)* has pink flowers shaped like snakes' heads, and the markings on the petals resemble a chequerboard – the Latin word *fritillu* means dice box. Autumn brings flowers too, especially crocuses.

Another common species is the Cyprus plane *(Platanus orientalis insularis)*, which thrives wherever there is ample water. It seems as if every village on the mainland has a plane tree shading its central square – and a Taverna Platanos.

Australian eucalypts were widely used in tree-planting programmes from the 1920s onwards, particularly on Crete.

NATIONAL PARKS

Visitors who expect Greek national parks to provide facilities on a par with those in countries such as Australia and the USA will be disappointed. Although all have refuges and some have marked hiking trails, Greek national parks provide little else in the way of facilities. The only national park on the islands is Samaria Gorge (p244) on Crete. There are marine

Visit the Hellenic Society for the Study & Protection of the Monk Seal at www.mom.gr

The Sea Turtle Protection Society of Greece, Archelon, runs monitoring programmes and is always looking for volunteers. For details visit www.archelon.gr

The Flowers of Greece & The Aegean, by William Taylor and Anthony Huxley, is the most comprehensive guide for the serious botanist.

parks off the coast of Alonnisos (p398) in the Sporades, and at the Bay of Laganas (p441) on Zakynthos in the Ionians.

ENVIRONMENTAL ISSUES

Greece is belatedly becoming environmentally conscious; regrettably, it can be a case of closing the gate long after the horse has bolted. Deforestation and soil erosion are problems that date back thousands of years. Olive cultivation (see The Evil Olive, p47) and goats have been the main culprits, but firewood gathering, shipbuilding, housing and industry have all taken their toll.

Forest fires are also a major problem, with an estimated 25,000 hectares destroyed every year. The 2000 summer season was one of the worst on record, particularly on the northeastern Aegean island of Samos.

Water shortages are a major problem on many islands, particularly smaller islands without a permanent water supply. These islands import their water by tanker, and visitors are urged to economise on water use wherever possible: small things, like turning the tap off while you brush your teeth, can make a big difference.

General environmental awareness remains at a depressingly low level, especially where litter is concerned. The problem is particularly bad in rural areas, where roadsides are strewn with soft-drink cans and plastic packaging hurled from passing cars. Environmental education has begun in schools, but it will be a long time before community attitudes change. Sadly, many tourists seem to follow the local lead instead of setting a good example.

Not surprisingly, Greece has been slow to embrace the organic movement. Less than 1% of available agricultural land is farmed organically – the lowest percentage in Europe.

For more details on contemporary environmental issues check out www.greece.gr/environment.

Wildflowers of Greece, by George Sfikas, is one of an excellent series of field guides by this well-known Greek mountaineer and naturalist. His guides are readily available at bookshops throughout the country.

Greek Islands Outdoors

The Greek islands offer a plethora of possibilities for travellers who want to do more with their time than laze around on the beach waiting for the evening's partying to begin. Naturally enough, water sports of all descriptions are a speciality throughout the islands, but nowhere more so than in the Cyclades.

DIVING & SNORKELLING

There are some excellent dive sites around the Greek islands, however, diving is subject to strict regulations in order to protect the many antiquities in the depths of the Aegean.

Any kind of underwater activity using breathing apparatus is strictly forbidden unless under the supervision of a diving school. Diving is only permitted between sunrise and sunset, and only in specified locations. There are also strict controls on diving activities: underwater photography of archaeological finds is prohibited, as is spear fishing with diving equipment.

Don't be put off by all the red tape. Diving is rapidly growing in popularity, and there are diving schools on the islands of Corfu (p417), Crete (at Rethymno; p233), Evia (p383), Hydra (p112), Leros (p312), Milos (p192), Mykonos (p142), Paros (p150) and Antiparos (p152), Rhodes (p225), Santorini (p182) and Skiathos (p389). Most charge around €50 for a dive, and from €250 for courses; prices include all equipment.

Check out the **Internet Scuba Diving Club** (www.isdc.gr) website for more information about diving. You'll also get useful information from the **Professional Association of Diving Instructors** (PADI; www.padi.com); its website has a list of all PADI-approved dive centres in Greece.

Snorkelling is enjoyable just about anywhere in the islands, and has the great advantage of being totally unencumbered by regulations. All the equipment you need – mask, fins and snorkel – are cheaply available everywhere.

Especially good places are Monastiri (p150) on Paros; Paleokastritsa (p442) on Corfu; Telendos Islet (p309; near Kalymnos); Ammoöpi (p278) in southern Karpathos; Xirokambos Bay (p312) on Leros; and anywhere off the coast of Kastellorizo (p283). Many dive schools also use their boats to take groups of snorkellers to prime spots.

Organised Tours

Trekking Hellas (☎ 210 323 4548; www.trekking.gr; Filellinon 7, Athens 105 57) offers four-day diving holidays on Paros (p145) that include dives off the islands of Iraklia (p163), Shinousa (p164), Koufonisia (p165) and Naxos (p153). It also offers dives off Corfu (p409) and Lesvos (p350).

GOLFING

Golf has yet to take off in Greece, and the country's few courses are located with expatriates and tourists in mind rather than locals.

Afandou Golf Club (☎ 2241 051 771; www.oasis-hotel.gr; Paralia Afandou, Rhodes; green fees weekdays/weekends €30/35) Afandou's 18-hole course is right next to Afandou Beach, 18km from Rhodes Town on the road to Lindos.

Corfu Golf Glub (☎ 2661 094 220; www.corfugolfclub.com; near Paleokastritsa, Corfu; green fees for 18 holes/1 week €60/258) The Corfu Golf Club's testing 18-hole, par-72 championship layout is spread around a series of man-made lakes in the Rapa Valley near Paleokastritsa (p420) on the island's west coast.

Elounda Golf Club (☎ 2841 041 903; www.ellada.net/elounda-mare/pem.htm; near Agios Nikolaos, Crete) This small pitch-and-putt course is attached to the deluxe Porto Elounda resort.

Glyfada Golf Club (☎ 2108 946 459; www.athensgolfclub.com; off Konstantinos Karamanli; 18 holes €60) Golfers travelling via Athens can get a game at Greece's oldest course, by the coast 10km southeast of the city centre. Clubs and buggies are available for hire.

SAILING

Sailing facilities are harder to find, although the same locations recommended for windsurfing (see p54) are all also ideal for sailing.

Hrysi Akti (p152) on Paros and Mylopotas Beach (p171) on Ios are two of the best locations. Hire charges for Hobie cats (catamarans) range from €20 to €25 per hour, depending on the gear and the location.

The best season (for experienced sailors) is during July and August, when the *meltemi* (northeasterly wind) blows, guaranteeing a solid northerly wind up to 30 knots. Beginners will prefer the lighter winds found in June and September.

The country's main racing club is the **Hellenic Offshore Racing Club** (☎ 2104 122 357; www.horc.gr; Akti Dilaveri 3, Mikrolimano, Piraeus 185 33). Most events are contested in the waters of the surrounding Saronic Gulf, but the club also organises the annual Aegean Rally in mid-July. The 2003 event visited the islands of Amorgos, Patmos and Syros; check the club's website for details and links to other sailing sites.

Organised Tours

Trekking Hellas (☎ 2103 234 548; www.trekking.gr; Filellinon 7, Athens 105 57) runs seven-day catamaran sailing schools at Almirada, between Hania (p238) and Rethymno (p231) in northern Crete, for €430, which includes half-board.

Sea Kayaking Trekking Hellas has eight-day sailing trips around the Ionians for €1995, and eight-day sea-kayaking trips around Lefkada (p424), Ithaki (p435) and some of the smaller Ionian islands. Prices depend on numbers.

TREKKING

The Greek islands are a veritable paradise for trekkers, offering an extraordinary variety of landscapes ranging from remote coastal paths to dramatic mountain gorges.

Spring (April to May) is the best time. Walkers will find the countryside green and fresh from the winter rains, and carpeted with the spectacular array of wildflowers for which the islands are justly famous. Autumn (September to October) is another good time, but July and August, when the temperatures are constantly up around 40°C, are not much fun at all. Whatever time of year you opt to set out, you will need to come equipped with a good pair of walking boots to handle the rough, rocky terrain, a wide-brimmed hat and a high UV-factor sunscreen.

Some of the most-popular treks, such as the Samaria Gorge (p244) on Crete, are detailed in this book, but there are possibilities just about everywhere. On small islands it's fun to discover pathways for yourself, and you are unlikely to get into danger as settlements or roads are never far away. You will encounter a variety of paths – *kalderimi* are cobbled or flagstone paths that link settlements and date back to Byzantine times – sadly, many have been bulldozed to make way for roads.

If you're going to be venturing off the beaten track, a good map is essential. Unfortunately, most of the tourist maps sold around the islands are pitifully inadequate. The best maps are produced by Athens company Road Editions (see Maps, p458, for details).

The following is brief description of the best trekking possibilities around the islands.

Hiking in a narrow part of Samaria Gorge (p244), Crete.

JOHN ELK III

Crete

The spectacular Samaria Gorge (p244) needs little introduction as it is one of Europe's most-popular treks, as well as being one of the island's main tourist attractions, drawing thousands of walkers every year.

The gorge begins at Xyloskalo high on the southern slopes of the lofty Lefki Ori (White Mountains), and finishes at the coastal settlement of Agia Roumeli (p245). Its width varies from 150m to 3.5m (the famous Iron Gates), and its vertical walls reach 500m at their highest points. The gorge has an incredible number of wildflowers, which are at their best in April and May. It is also home to a large number of endangered species, including the Cretan wild goat, the kri-kri. You are unlikely to see too many of these shy animals, which show a marked aversion to trekkers!

Winter rains render the gorge impassable from mid-October until mid-April.

People who prefer to walk without the company of a cast of thousands will enjoy the coastal path that links the southwest coastal villages of Agia Roumeli and Hora Sfakion (p246). Another favourite is the two-hour stroll from Zakros to the remote Minoan palace site of Kato Zakros (p227) in eastern Crete. The walk passes through the mysterious sounding Valley of the Dead, so named because of the cave tombs dotted along the rugged cliffs that line the valley.

Cyclades

Naxos (p153) has long been a favourite destination for walkers, particularly the beautiful Tragaea region (p160) – a broad central plain of olive groves dotted with unspoiled villages and ancient Byzantine churches. The more energetic will enjoy the short but strenuous climb from the village of Filoti to the Cave of Zeus. Andros (p122) is another good choice, particularly the hills around the small west-coast resort of Batsi.

Dodecanese

Tranquil Tilos (p289) is one of the few islands in this group that has escaped the ravages of mass tourism. It's a terrific place for walkers, with dramatic cliff-top paths that lead to uncrowded beaches. For something completely different, there's nothing to rival the bizarre landscape of volcanic Nisyros (p292), where walkers can check the hissing craters that dot Mt Polyvotis for signs of activity.

Evia & the Sporades

Alonnisos (p394) enjoys a glowing reputation as the Aegean's cleanest and greenest islands. In recent years it's been attracting growing numbers of walkers, who come to trek a network of established trails and swim at remote pristine beaches.

Ionian Islands

Nice things come in small packages, or so the saying goes. It's certainly the case on tiny Paxi (p421), the smallest of the main Ionian islands. Its landscape of gnarled, ancient olive groves and snaking dry-stone walls is a great choice for walkers who really want to escape the crowds.

On Ithaki (p435), the long-lost island homeland of Trojan War–hero Odysseus, mythology fans will enjoy seeking out the handful of sites associated with the Homeric legend.

Northeastern Aegean Islands

The Northeastern Aegean Islands are a long-time favourite with walkers. Samos (p333) is one of the most-visited islands in Greece, but most visitors stick to the busy resorts of the south coast – leaving the interior almost unscathed. The best walking area is around the delightful mountain villages of Manolates and Vourliotes (p340), set on the densely forested northern slopes of Mt Ampelos. Walkers who are still out and about around dusk may be lucky enough to spot one of the country's most-endangered species, the golden jackal (p48), which survives only on Samos and in parts of Central Greece. Lesvos (p350) is another good choice, especially for those who enjoy bird-watching.

Saronic Gulf Islands

Walking has always been the main form of transport on traffic-free Hydra (p110), where a well-maintained network of paths links the island's various beaches and monasteries.

WINDSURFING

Windsurfing is the most popular water sport in Greece. Many people reckon that Vasiliki Bay (p428), on the south coast of the Ionian island of Lefkada, is one of the best places in the world to learn the sport. Hrysi Akti (p152) on Paros is another favourite.

There are numerous other prime locations around the islands, including Ormos Korthiou (p125) on Andros; Kalafatis Beach (p141) on Mykonos; Agios Giorgios Beach (p157) on Naxos; Mylopotas Beach (p171) on Ios; Prasonisi (p271) in southern Rhodes; around Tingaki (p301) on Kos; Kokkari (p340) on Samos; around Skala Sotira (p377) on Thasos; Koukounaries Beach (p389) on Skiathos; and Skyros (p399).

You'll find sailboards for hire almost everywhere. Hire charges range from €10 to €25, depending on the gear and the location. If you are a novice, most places that rent equipment also give lessons; reckon on about €200 to €250 for a 10-hour beginners' course.

Sailboards can be imported freely from other EU countries, but importing boards from other destinations, such as Australia and the USA, is subject to some quaint regulations. Theoretically, importers need a Greek national residing in Greece to guarantee that the board will be taken out again. Contact the **Hellenic Windsurfing Association** (☎ 2103 230 330; www.ghiolman.com; Filellinon 7, Athens) for more information.

YACHTING

Despite some disparaging remarks among backpackers, yachting is *the* way to see the Greek islands. Nothing beats the peace and serenity of sailing the open sea, and the freedom of being able to visit remote and uninhabited islands.

The free EOT booklet, *Sailing the Greek Seas*, although long overdue for an update, contains lots of information about weather conditions, weather bulletins, entry and exit regulations, entry and exit ports and guidebooks for yachties. You can pick up the booklet at GNTO/EOT offices either abroad or in Greece. The Internet is the place to look for the latest information – **Hellenic Yachting Server** (www.yachting.gr) has general information on sailing around the islands and lots of links.

The sailing season lasts from April until October, although the best time to go depends on where you are going. The most popular time is between July and September, which ties in with the high season for tourism in general. Unfortunately, it also happens to be the time of year when the *meltemi* is at its strongest (see Climate on p452 for details). The *meltemi* is not an issue in the Ionian Sea, where the main summer wind is the *maistros*, a light to moderate northwesterly that rises in the afternoon and usually dies away at sunset.

Organised Tours

Individuals can consider joining a yachting cruise. Ghiolman Yachts & Travel has a range of seven-day island cruises, including an Ionian cruise leaving Corfu every Saturday, a Dodecanese cruise leaving Rhodes every Thursday and a Cycladic cruise leaving Piraeus every Friday. Berths on board these boats are priced from €670, and include half-board and the services of an English-speaking guide. All three cruises operate weekly from early May to the end of September.

Trekking Hellas also offers a range of yachting and sailing holidays around the Cyclades and the Ionians by caïque or by yacht.

Yachting off Fourni Beach (p271), southwest of Rhodes Town, Rhodes, Dodecanese.

JUDI WILLOUGHBY

Yacht Hire

You can hire a bare boat (a yacht without a crew) if two crew members have a sailing certificate. Prices start at about €1000 per week for a 28-footer that will sleep six and it will cost an extra €840 per week to hire a skipper.

Most of big hire companies are based in and around Athens. They include:

Aegean Cruises (☎ 2109 649 967; www.aegean-cruises.gr; cnr Poseidonos & Davaki, Alimos 174 55)
Alpha Yachting (☎ 2109 680 486; www.alphayachting.com; Poseidonos 67, Glyfada 166 75)
Ghiolman Yachts & Travel (☎ 2103 233 696; www.ghiolman.com; Filellinon 7, Athens)
Hellenic Charters (☎ 2109 607 174; www.hellenic-charters.gr; Arsitotelous 19-21, Glyfada 166 74)
Vernicos Yachts (☎ 2109 896 000; www.vernicos.gr; Poseidonos 11, Alimos 174 55)

You'll find details about yacht-charter companies on the islands of Milos (p128), Paros (p145) and Syros (p190) in the Cyclades chapter.

Food & Drink

Greek cuisine will give you sensory memories to savour forever. You'll marvel at the bread and wonder why they don't make it like that at home. You'll quaff wine straight from the barrel, eat cheese that was milk only that morning and enjoy sweets made from recipes that are over a thousand years old. In fact, Greek cuisine is Western history right in your mouth.

STAPLES & SPECIALITIES

The true taste of Greek cuisine depends on fresh, unadulterated staples. Masking or complicating original flavours is not the done thing, especially when you're dealing with oven-fresh bread, rosy tomatoes and fish fresh from the Mediterranean.

Bread

The most common type of bread is *psomi horiatiko*, country bread, which is made with whatever is available. It is usually wheat bread, and may incorporate cornmeal, sprinkled with sesame seeds or enlivened with aniseed or herbs. Perhaps the best-known Greek bread is *pita:* unlike what you're probably able to buy at home, Greek pita is thick, often whole grain and absorbent.

Paksimadya (rusks) have been a staple of Greece since ancient days. Made from barley flour or whole wheat, after baking it is allowed to cool but then returned to a very slow oven and dried for several hours to produce a hard loaf that can keep, literally, for years.

Lonely Planet's *World Food Greece* takes an in-depth look at the culture of eating and drinking in Greece.

Cheese

Cheese is the original meze. But how many different kinds of cheese does Greece produce? The most accurate answer would be the same number as there are villages in Greece. Cheese, like wine, is greatly influenced by climate and soil, and the innumerable microclimates of Greece produce an infinite variety of organoleptic (taste and smell) qualities in the flora. Those qualities affect the milk of any mammal that eats them.

FETA

Feta is the national cheese of Greece. It's made from sheep's milk, though it may contain up to 30% goat's milk. Most feta comes from mountainous areas, where pesticides and other agricultural chemicals are rare. In this high-altitude environment, grazing is limited so the flocks have to cover great distances in order to feed adequately. This has a double advantage: because of the wide grazing pattern the sheep feed on a greater variety of plants and transmit their characteristics to the milk; secondly, because the sheep are constantly in motion they don't get fat, their milk has less fat, and the resulting cheese has less fat and its characteristic dazzling white colour.

In 2002 the European Commission ruled that, by 2007, only feta produced in Greece can be called feta. At the moment three-quarters of the world's 'feta' is produced outside the country. While renaming the cheese may not cause too much consternation for producers in France and Germany, Cyprus has been producing the cheese for over a hundred years and feels it had as much right to claim the name. They hope to get around the ruling by calling it 'feta'.

Fish & Seafood

In a land with countless miles of coastline, it's not surprising that fish *(psari)* has long been a staple. Some of the more common items on the fish menu include *barbunya* (red mullet) – delicious grilled or fried – and *melanuri* (sea bream). *Kalamari* (squid) is simply cut into rings and deep fried. Grilled *ohtapodi* (octopus) is so common it's taken for granted. You'll often see it whole, precooked, and hanging from a nail on a wall or a post.

Greek Cuisine by Vefa Alexiadrou is packed with authentic recipes and easy-to-follow instructions.

Fruit & Vegetables

Tomatoes *(domates)*, aubergines *(melidzanes)*, onions *(kremidia)* and garlic *(skordo)* are indispensable in the Greek kitchen, making special appearances in the classic dishes *gemistes domates* (stuffed tomatoes) and mousaka.

Wild greens *(horta)* are extremely popular. It's useless to try to distinguish this leaf from that blade or another shoot: what you get depends on where you are and in what season. Vine leaves *(klimato-filo)* are most commonly used to hold packets of aromatic rice in dolmades.

Horiatiki salata, variously translated as 'country salad' or 'village salad', is what we have come to know as Greek salad. Like so much of Greek gastronomy, what goes into it is widely open to interpretation. The original was nothing more than a slab of feta and some sliced onions dressed with oil.

Fruit *(fruta)* is an important part of the Greek diet. Dried figs have been popular since antiquity, and citrus fruits are especially abundant.

The Illustrated Greek Wine Book by Nicos Manessis is the definitive book for the connoisseur, tracing the history of the Greek wine industry and providing hundreds of reviews of wineries and their wines.

Legumes & Pulses

Many islanders and country folk rely on beans and pulses as the foundation of their winter diet. Legumes are also popular as snacks. At the markets you'll see roasted and salted green peas as well as chickpeas. At harvest time they are eaten fresh. Raw fava beans are often removed from the pod, peeled and eaten as a meze with ouzo. Fresh chickpeas are eaten in the pod.

Yigandes look like giant white lima beans. Their most common preparation is in a light tomato sauce seasoned with sweet dill.

Meat & Poultry

In the home, meat plays a small but important part in the family's diet. In poorer times it was likely to be offal: popular dishes included *patsas* (offal soup) and *kokoretsi* (offal wrapped in lamb intestines). The home kitchen remains largely vegetarian.

Beef is relatively rare since there is very little grazing space for cattle. The most common meats you'll see on the menu are pork and lamb. Italian-style salami can be found here and there, but cured meats are not all that common as the climate is not suitable.

There's very little game remaining in Greece. Where it's available, hare and quail are the usual choices. *Stifado* – a stew made from hare or rabbit and onions – is almost the Greek national dish.

Perhaps the most famous of the grilled meat pantheon is *gyros*, from the Greek verb 'to spin'. At first glance it appears to be a great haunch of beef turning on a vertical spit. But look closer and you'll see that the haunch is actually hundreds of thin slices of meat tightly stacked in a tower about 1m high and skewered with the spit.

From the acclaimed New York restaurant, Molyvos, *The Foods of the Greek Islands* by Aglaia Kremezi and Jim Botsacos captures the essence of the islands through their cuisine.

Another grilled meat favourite is souvlaki: basically cubes of meat on a skewer.

Now that prosperity has brought many other animal foods to the table, chicken seems to have taken a back seat, at least in the taverna. Most country folk keep hens, not so much for the meat as for the *avga* (eggs).

Olives & Olive Oil

There could be no Greek cuisine as we know it without olive oil *(eleoladho)*. The Greeks consume more oil per capita than any other people: 20L annually. There are hundreds of olive varieties, but most Greek olive oil is pressed from the smaller variety of *kalamata*, which is unique to Greece. The larger kalamata olives are used as table olives *(elyes)*.

Pasta

It will come as a surprise to many that Greeks are great eaters of pasta *(zimarika)*. It is believed they acquired the taste from their former Venetian overlords. Most frequently you'll see spaghetti with tomato or meat sauce, but there's also *pastitsio*, a sort of Greek lasagne. Another standard taverna item is *yuvetsi*, a hearty dish of roasted meat or poultry in a fresh tomato sauce with *kritharaki* (rice-shaped pasta).

Pies

Pies *(pites)* are among the most common daily fare in Greece. Most are made with filo dough and can be filled with anything and everything. Favourites include *tyropita* (cheese pie) and *spanakopita* (spinach pie).

Rice

Rice *(rizi)* has been known to the Greeks since Alexander's expedition to India in the 3rd century but became a real staple during Ottoman rule. Perhaps the most visible use of rice is as a stuffing, as found with the dish gemista (stuffed vegetables).

TRAVEL YOUR TASTE BUDS

While mezedes are a relatively new feature of the Greek table, in their present form at any rate, the concept is as old as Socrates. What is a meze? Theoretically anything, as long as it's small and goes well with ouzo! We recommend the following:

Bekri meze – meat pieces cooked in tomato and red wine.

Dolmades – vine leaves stuffed with rice, tomato, onion and herbs.

Keftedes – small rissoles or fritters, often made with minced lamb or pork; *psarokeftedes* are made with fish and *tirokeftedes* are made with cheese.

Melidzanosalata – a purée of grilled, mashed aubergine, onion, garlic, oil and lemon juice.

Saganaki – most commonly a sharp, hard cheese cut into flat squares and fried until crispy on the outside and soft in the centre; you'll also see prawn, crab and lobster saganaki.

Taramasalata – a thick pink purée of fish roe, bread crumbs, oil and lemon juice.

Tirokafteri – a cheese spread, usually made from feta.

Tsiros – small dried mackerel, generally served char-grilled with oil and vinegar.

Tzatziki – cucumber, yogurt and garlic purée.

Yogurt

Yogurt *(yaurti)* in Greece is something about which to swoon. Normally made from sheep's milk, Greek yogurt is thick, rich, fat and flavourful. Have it for breakfast with Greek honey.

DRINKS

Retsina and ouzo may be Greece's most famous (or infamous) tipples, but there are plenty of other options. Wine has been produced here since ancient times, and innumerable springs provide natural refreshment. Then there's the coffee...

Wine

Wine *(krasi)* in Greece predates the written record. The wine god Dionysus was tramping the vintage even before the Bronze Age. By the time of Greek independence in 1829, there was little of what could be called a wine industry. Farmers grew small vineyards alongside their crops and made wine for their own consumption. It wasn't until about 1970 that a new thinking began to emerge in the Greek wine mind, and soon wine was also being produced for commercial reasons. The reasons are many, not the least of which are the migrations to the cities (especially Athens) and growing prosperity. Over the last 30 years or so, the industry has been transformed, making Greece an exciting source of modern wines.

> For comprehensive details of the country's wine regions and producers, visit www.greekwine.gr.

Retsina

As the name implies, retsina is wine that has been flavoured with the resin of pine trees. It goes very well with Greek food (especially seafood) and it makes a fine apéritif.

Tsipuro

Tsipuro is produced from the grape skins left over from winemaking. They are fermented and distilled to produce a highly potent, though largely unremarkable, spirit. The same drink is also known as *raki*, and as *tsikouda* on the island of Crete.

Ouzo

Ouzo is also made from distilled grapes, but it may have many flavourings (including mint, fennel, and even hazelnut), the chief among them being aniseed. And no matter what the distiller may add, there is always a touchstone to let you know that it's the real thing: when you add water to ouzo (the proper way to drink it) it turns a milky white.

Ouzo is a superb appetiser. In a taverna many Greeks have ouzo as an apéritif, then have wine with the main meal. Afterwards they may enjoy brandy or more wine, but not more ouzo.

Brandy

Greece produces a number of brandies. The dominant brand is Metaxa (no relationship to the dictator). Greek brandies tend to be sweet and flowery in the nose, with some deliberately sweetened by the addition of Monemvasya or other sweet grapes.

Beer

For the most part your choice will be between Amstel and Heineken imports. However, there are a few small independent breweries in Greece, the most common being Mythos – a Pilsner-type brew in a distinctive green bottle.

Coffee

Greek coffee used to be known by the universal term Turkish coffee. But in 1974 Turkey invaded Cyprus and thereafter it was called Greek coffee. Some say it tastes, smells and has the texture of mud. Nevertheless, thanks to its rich aroma and distinctive taste, the Greeks gulp it with gusto. Who are we to argue?

The singlemost common beverage throughout the land of Homer is the frappé – a mix of instant coffee, sugar and condensed milk whipped into a frothy mess and garnished with two (always two) plastic straws.

Tea

For a social history of the country's cuisine, try Andrew Dalby's *Siren Feasts: A History of Food & Gastronomy in Greece*.

While caffeinated tea *(tsai)* is a sorry story in Greece (ask for a cuppa and you'll get some indifferently heated water and a teabag full of suspect leaves), the chamomile and mountain teas are excellent. Both grow wild all over Greece, although chamomile tea from the Peloponnese is the best. Just be sure to drink it hot and with a generous dollop of Greek honey.

Water

Greece's diverse topography ensures a huge variety of underground springs. Every region has its own unique, refreshing bottled spring water *(nero)* on the market. Tap water is a drink of a different order. We can assure you that tap water in Greece will not kill you – it meets European sanitation standards and in the major cities is quite drinkable – in small coastal towns and on many islands, however, it tastes like harbour water. The water tables here are close to the surface and the sea leaches in. You can survive a shower in this stuff, but you don't want to drink it.

CELEBRATING WITH FOOD

In Greece, history, religion and identity are intrinsically entwined, and this is no more evident than in the nation's celebratory foods. Every morsel is laced with symbolism, from Christmas biscuits to the spit-roast lamb of Easter. Even the fasting days of Lent have culinary attraction.

Carnival

Award-winning *The Glorious Foods of Greece* by Diane Kochilas is a must-have tome on any self-respecting cook's shelf.

In Greek, carnival is called *apokries* (abstinence from meat) and refers to the three weeks before lent. This is a time for indulgence. In the first week, families will slaughter a pig if they have one. In the second, all are free to eat as much meat as they like. Week three is *tirofagos* (cheese week).

Lent

The 40 days of Lent are days of prayer and reflection. This is the best time of the year to eat vegetarian fare. Of course there are exceptions allowed, such as on the Feast of the Annunciation (March 25; also Greek Independence Day) when folk may gorge themselves on platters of fish and tankards of wine.

Easter

Easter is the most important time of the Greek calendar, and Easter Sunday is the main event. The table is set with traditional Easter dishes such as cheese pies and salads, but lamb, after so many meatless days, is the centrepiece.

Christmas & New Year

The end of the year brings on another 40 days of fasting prior to Christmas. On Christmas day those who have one slaughter and roast a piglet. New Year celebrations are much like Christmas. A golden-glazed bread called *vasilopita* is baked with a coin inside. At midnight the family tears into it, and whoever finds the coin can expect good fortune for the ensuing year.

WHERE TO EAT & DRINK

Perhaps the question should be 'where not?'. The traditional public eating house of Greece is the taverna. It amounts to an extension of the Greek home table. Nowadays almost any food service operation may call itself a taverna. And that is what most Greeks are comfortable with. A couple of variations include the *hasapotaverna*, a basic restaurant attached to a butcher in a market. Then there's the *biraria*, a taverna specialising in dishes that, hopefully, go particularly well with beer. Another variant is the *psistaria*, which specialises in char-grilled meat, or meat roasted on a spit, while a *psarotaverna* specialises in fish.

Estiatorio is the Greek word for restaurant. The chief difference between a taverna and an *estiatorio* is that you will pay more for the same dish in an *estiatorio*.

The obvious purpose of an ouzeri is to sell ouzo but, naturally, food is served here too. The traditional order is for a plate of mezedes and a quarter litre of ouzo (the alcoholic equivalent of a bottle of wine).

The *kafeneio* is one of the oldest gastronomic institutions in Greece. A product of the Ottoman occupation, it is the original coffee shop. Traditionally, *kafeneia* serve Greek coffee and little else. And traditionally only men above a certain age patronise them. Nowadays you may have beer or ouzo, as well as gritty Greek coffee, and women may also stop by.

Quick Eats

Souvlaki used to be the fast food of Greece. But now fast food is the fast food of Greece and it has its own slavish imitators of the standard burgers-and-fries joint – Goody's and Everest.

VEGETARIANS & VEGANS

Wherever you call home, no matter how tofu-friendly it is, it's easier and tastier to go vegetarian in Greece. This is ironic since no Greek would claim to be a vegetarian, at least none of our acquaintance. It would be almost unthinkable to observe the Greek Orthodox faith without the paschal lamb at Easter. But the same Orthodox faith that calls for flesh also calls for fasting, which regularly makes the Greeks accidental vegans. Wednesday and Friday are traditional fast days, and some village tavernas serve only vegetarian fare on these days.

WHINING & DINING

Greeks love children, and if you bring yours you'll probably end up having to share them. All tavernas are child-friendly. There is no such thing as a children's menu. Kids eat what their parents eat, often just sharing what's on their plates.

In *Prospero's Kitchen*, Diana Farr Louis and June Marinos present both rare and traditional recipes from the Ionian Islands.

With as many anecdotes as recipes, Emma Tennant's *Corfu Banquet: A Seasonal Memoir with Recipes* is a delightfully evocative book.

> **SMOKED OUT**
>
> Greece is home to the greatest number of smokers in the EU; they smoke all the time, everywhere, through all occasions. They will not only smoke right up to and immediately after a meal, they'll smoke *during* the meal and not only between courses, but during courses!
>
> Restrictions were introduced in 2003, however, banning smoking in public areas (bars and clubs are exempt). All restaurants are now required to have nonsmoking areas – let us know if you find any!

HABITS & CUSTOMS
How Greeks Eat

Matt Barrett's website is an excellent introduction to Greece's food culture: www.greecefoods.com.

Most Greeks think of breakfast as a cigarette and a cup of coffee. If you want something more substantial, your best recourse is to take to the streets. The pie shops are open early, and street vendors all over the country sell *kuluri,* a bagel-like ring of baked dough studded with sesame seeds. The midday meal is the big one and does not start until about 2pm. There will be mezedes including olives, octopus drizzled with oil and vinegar, stuffed vine leaves, dips, spreads and innumerable other culinary bits and bobs. There is no succession of courses: food is brought to the table as it is ready. Then there may be more substantial fare such as fish or a meat dish. In the evening around 10pm the ritual is repeated, though somewhat reduced in calories.

Etiquette

Greek table manners and settings are simple. Take a seat in the taverna. The waiter will arrive with bread (it'll show up on your bill as a small amount). Unless you are in a very smart place, you will keep the same knife and fork throughout the meal. You will have one wine glass and one water glass. Drink as much wine as you like but do not appear greedy for it: never drink your glass dry and never refill it more than two thirds. It is customary for tablemates to pour for each other. A service charge is levied but tipping is not customary: if you want to show your appreciation just round up the bill.

EAT YOUR WORDS

Get behind the cuisine scene by getting to know the language. For pronunciation guidelines, see p481.

Useful Phrases

I want to make a reservation for this evening.   Θέλω να κλείσω ένα τραπέζι για απόψε.
*the·*lo na *kli·*so e·na tra·*pe·*zi ya a·*po·*pse

Rustle up your favourite dishes with the recipes at www.eatgreektonight.com.

A table for ... please.   Ένα τραπέζι για ... παρακαλώ.
e·na tra·*pe·*zi ya ..., pa·ra·ka·*lo*

I'd like the menu, please.   Το μενού, παρακαλώ.
to me·*nu,* pa·ra·ka·*lo*

Do you have a menu in English?   Έχετε το μενού στα αγγλικά;
e·hye·te to me·*nu* stah·gli·*ka?*

I'd like ...   Θα ήθελα ...
tha *i·*the·la ...

Please bring the bill.   Το λογαριασμό, παρακαλώ.
to lo·ghar·ya·*zmo,* pa·ra·ka·*lo*

I'm a vegetarian.
i·me hor·to·*fa*·ghos

Είμαι χορτοφάγος.

I don't eat meat or dairy products.
dhen *tro*·o *kre*·as i gha·la·kto·ko·mi·*ka* pro·i·*on*·da

Δε τρώω κρέας ή γαλακτοκομικά προϊόντα.

Glossary

STAPLES

bread	to pso·*mi*	το ψωμί
butter	to *vu*·ti·ro	το βούτυρο
cheese	to ti·*ri*	το τυρί
eggs	ta a·*vgha*	τα αυγά
honey	to *me*·li	το μέλι
milk	to *gha*·la	το γάλα
olive oil	to e·le·o·la·dho	το ελαιόλαδο
olives	i e·*lyes*	οι ελιές
pepper	to pi·*pe*·ri	το πιπέρι
salt	to a·*la*·ti	το αλάτι
sugar	i *za*·ha·ri	η ζάχαρη
vinegar	to *ksi*·dhi	το ξύδι

MEAT, FISH & SEAFOOD

beef	to vo·dhi·*no*	το βοδινό
chicken	to ko·*to*·pu·lo	το κοτόπουλο
grey mullet	o *ke*·fa·los	ο κέφαλος
hare	o la·*ghos*	ο λαγός
kid (goat)	to ka·tsi·*ka*·ki	το κατσικάκι
lamb	to ar·*ni*	το αρνί
lobster	o a·sta·*kos*	ο αστακός
mackerel	o ko·li·*os*	ο κολιός
mussels	ta *mi*·di·a	τα μύδια
octopus	to hta·*po*·dhi	το χταπόδι
pork	to hyi·ri·*no*	το χοιρινό
prawns	i gha·*ri*·dhes	οι γαρίδες
rabbit	to ku·*ne*·li	το κουνέλι
red mullet	ta bar·*bu*·nya	τα μπαρμπούνια
sardines	i sar·*dhe*·les	οι σαρδέλες
sea bream	to fa·*ghri*/li·*thri*·ni/me·la·*nu*·ri	το φαγρί/λιθρίνι/μελανούρι
squid	to ka·la·*ma*·ri	το καλαμάρι
veal	to mo·*sha*·ri	το μοσχάρι
whitebait	i ma·*ri*·dhes	οι μαρίδες

FRUIT & VEGETABLES

apple	to *mi*·lo	το μήλο
artichoke	i ang·gi·*na*·ra	η αγγινάρα
asparagus	ta spa·*rang*·gi·a	τα σπαράγγια
aubergine (eggplant)	i me·li·*dza*·nes	οι μελιτζάνες
carrot	to ka·*ro*·to	το καρότο
cherry	to ke·*ra*·si	το κεράσι
garlic	to *skor*·dho	το σκόρδο
grapes	ta sta·*fi*·li·a	τα σταφύλια
greens, seasonal wild	(*a*·ghri·a) *hor*·ta	(άγρια) χόρτα
lemon	to le·*mo*·ni	το λεμόνι
onions	ta kre·*mi*·dhi·a	τα κρεμμύδια
orange	to por·to·*ka*·li	το πορτοκάλι

Glossary (Continued)

peach	to ro·*dha*·ki·no	το ροδάκινο
peas	o a·ra·*kas*	ο αρακάς
peppers	i pi·per·*yez*	η πιπεριές
potatoes	i pa·*ta*·tes	οι πατάτες
spinach	to spa·*na*·ki	το σπανάκι
strawberry	i *fru*·u·la	η φράουλα
tomato	i do·*ma*·ta	η ντομάτα

DRINKS

beer	i *bi*·ra	η μπύρα
coffee	o ka·*fes*	ο καφές
tea	to *tsa*·i	το τσάι
water	to *ne*·ro	το νερό
wine (red/white)	to kra·*si* (*ko*·ki·no/*a*·spro)	το κρασί (κόκκινο/άσπρο)

Athens & the Mainland Ports

CONTENTS

Named in honour of Athina, the goddess of wisdom, the Greek capital was always going to have a difficult time living up to expectations. The sprawling, polluted city that awaits the modern visitor is a far cry from the romantic vision of Athens as the home of democracy and great patron of the arts. Despite its glorious past and its enduring influence on Western civilisation, it is a city that few fall in love with.

To appreciate Athens (Athina in Greek), it's important to be aware of the city's traumatic history. Unlike most national capitals, Athens does not have a history of continuous expansion; it is one characterised by glory, followed by decline and near annihilation, and then resurgence in the 19th century – when it became the capital of independent Greece.

Athens has spent the best part of the past decade dragging itself into the new millennium as a modern, efficient European capital and sprucing itself up for the 2004 Olympics. The games proved a catalyst for fast-tracking solutions to serious transport, infrastructure and environmental challenges and addressing the city's image as the continent's ugly duckling. Whatever happens in the sporting arena, the city that emerges from the Olympics will be a better place than the city that won the right to host the Games in 1996.

Perhaps most significant of all is the fact that wherever you are in the centre of the city, the Acropolis, with its transcendent and compelling aura, stands proudly on the skyline. It serves as a constant reminder that whatever trials and tribulations might have befallen the city, its status as the birthplace of Western civilisation is beyond doubt.

HIGHLIGHTS

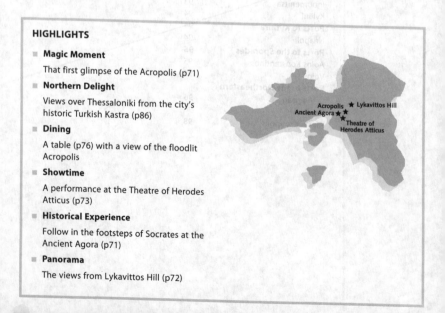

- **Magic Moment**

  That first glimpse of the Acropolis (p71)

- **Northern Delight**

  Views over Thessaloniki from the city's historic Turkish Kastra (p86)

- **Dining**

  A table (p76) with a view of the floodlit Acropolis

- **Showtime**

  A performance at the Theatre of Herodes Atticus (p73)

- **Historical Experience**

  Follow in the footsteps of Socrates at the Ancient Agora (p71)

- **Panorama**

  The views from Lykavittos Hill (p72)

ATHENS AΘHNA

pop 3.7 million

HISTORY

The early history of Athens is so interwoven with mythology that it's hard to disentangle fact from fiction.

The Acropolis has been occupied since Neolithic times. It was an excellent vantage point, and the steep slopes formed natural defences on three sides. By 1400 BC the Acropolis was a powerful Mycenaean city.

Its power peaked during the so-called golden age of Athens in the 5th century BC, following the defeat of the Persians at the Battle of Salamis. The city fell into decline after its defeat by Sparta in the long-running Peloponnesian War, but rallied again in Roman times when it became a seat of learning. The Roman emperors, particularly Hadrian, graced Athens with many grand buildings.

After the Roman Empire split into east and west, power shifted to Byzantium (modern day Istanbul) and Athens fell into obscurity. By the end of Ottoman rule, Athens was little more than a dilapidated village (the area now known as Plaka).

Then, in 1834, the newly-crowned King Otho transferred his court from Nafplio in the Peloponnese and made Athens the capital of independent Greece. The city was rebuilt along neoclassical lines, featuring large squares and tree-lined boulevards with imposing public buildings. The city grew steadily and enjoyed a brief heyday as the 'Paris of the Mediterranean' in the late 19th and early 20th centuries.

This came to an abrupt end with the forced population exchange between Greece and Turkey, which followed the Treaty of Lausanne in 1923. The huge influx of refugees from Asia Minor virtually doubled the population overnight, forcing the hasty erection of the first of the concrete apartment blocks that dominate the city today. The belated advent of Greece's industrial age in the 1950s brought another wave of migration, this time of rural folk looking for work.

The city's infrastructure, particularly road and transport, could not keep pace with such rapid and unplanned growth, and by the end of the '80s the city had developed a sorry reputation as one of the most traffic-clogged and polluted in Europe.

The 1990s appear to have been a turning point in the city's development. Jolted into action by the failed bid to stage the 1996 Olympics, authorities embarked on an ambitious programme to prepare the city for the 21st century. Two key elements have been an extension of the metro network, and the construction of a new international airport.

These projects played an important role in the city's successful bid to stage the 2004 Olympics.

ORIENTATION

Although Athens is a huge, sprawling city, nearly everything of interest to short-term visitors is located within a small area bounded by Omonia Square (Plateia Omonias) to the north, Monastiraki Square (Plateia Monastirakiou) to the west, Syntagma Square (Plateia Syntagmatos) to the east and the Plaka district to the south. The city's two major landmarks, the Acropolis and Lykavittos Hill, can be seen from just about everywhere in this area.

Plaka, the delightful old Turkish quarter that was virtually all that existed when Athens was declared the capital of independent Greece, lies nestled on the northeastern slope of the Acropolis. It may be touristy, but it's the most attractive and interesting part of Athens and the majority of visitors make it their base.

INFORMATION
Bookshops

Booknest (Map pp74-5; ☎ 2103 231 703; mezzanine level, Panepistimiou 25-29, Syntagma) Stocks books in French, German, Italian, Spanish, Russian and English.

Compendium (Map pp74-5; ☎ 2103 221 248; Nikis 28, Plaka) Specialises in books in English, and has a popular second-hand section.

Eleftheroudakis Books Syntagma (Map pp74-5; ☎ 2103 314 180; Panepistimiou 17); Plaka (Map pp74-5; ☎ 2103 229 388; Nikis 20) The Panepistimiou store is the biggest bookshop in Athens, with a floor dedicated to books in English.

Road Editions (Map pp68-9; ☎ 2103 613 242; Ippokratous 39, Exarhia) You'll find a wide range of travel literature as well as the complete selection of Road Editions maps. International newspapers reach the *periptera* (kiosks) in Syntagma on the same day they are published at 3pm on weekdays and 7pm on weekends.

ATHENS

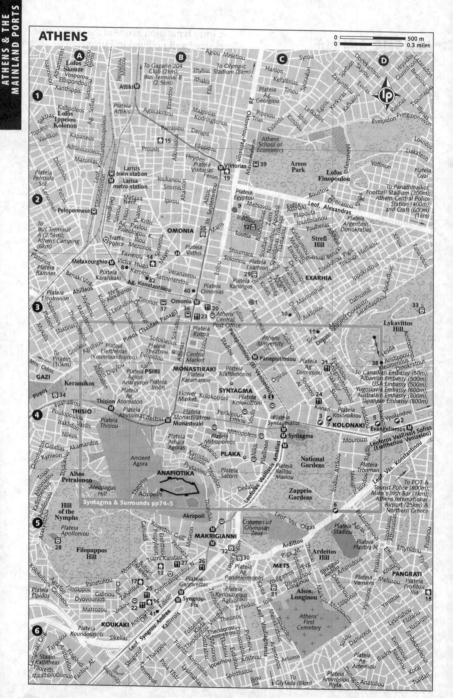

Emergency

Athens Central Police Station (Map pp68–9; ☎ 2107 705 711/5717; Leof Alexandras 173)

Duty Doctor (☎ 105; ☾ 2pm–7am)

Duty Hospital (☎ 106)

Duty Pharmacy (☎ 107)

First-aid advice (☎ 166) US citizens can ring ☎ 2107 212 951 for emergency medical aid.

SOS Doctors (☎ 2103 220 046/0015) This 24-hour call-out service employs doctors who speak English and a range of other languages.

Tourist Police (Map pp68–9; ☎ 2108 707 000; Tsoha 7, Ambelokipi; ☾ 24hr)

Tourist Police 24-hour Information Service (☎ 171) General tourist information and emergency help. In theory, someone who speaks English is always available.

Traffic Police (Map pp68–9; ☎ 2105 284 000; Deligianni 24-26, Omonia)

Internet Access

The following is a list of Internet cafés around the city centre. Most charge from €3 to €4 per hour of computer time, whether you're online or not.

Arcade Internet Café (Map pp74–5; ☎ 2103 210 701; Stadiou 5, Syntagma, behind Flocafé; ☾ 10am–10pm Mon-Sat, 1-9pm Sun)

Bits & Bytes Internet Café (Map pp68–9; ☎ 2103 306 590; Akadimias 78, Exarhia; ☾ 24hr)

easyInternetaccess (Map pp74–5; Plateia Syntagmatos, above Everest; ☾ 24hr)

Museum Internet Café (Map pp68–9; ☎ 2108 833 418; Oktovriou-Patission 46, Omonia, next to National Archaeological Museum; ☾ 9-3am)

Plaka Internet World (Map pp74–5; Pandrosou 29, Monastiraki; ☾ 11am–11pm)

Skynet Internet Centre (Map pp74–5; cnr Voulis & Apollonos, Plaka; ☾ 9am–11pm Mon-Sat)

Laundry

Laundry Self Service (Map pp68–9; Psaron 9, cnr Plateia Karaïskaki; ☾ 8am–8pm Mon-Fri, 8am–2pm Sat & Sun) Charges €8.50.

Plaka Laundrette (Map pp74–5; Angelou Geronta 10, Plaka; ☾ 10am–6pm Mon-Sat, 10am–2pm Sun) Charges €8 to wash and dry 5kg.

Left Luggage

Many of Athens' hotels are happy to store luggage free for guests, although a lot of them will do little more than pile the bags up in a hallway. You'll find left-luggage facilities at the airport and at the train station.

Money

Most of the major banks have branches around Plateia Syntagmatos. The banks at the airport open 7am to 9pm daily. The following may be useful:

Acropole Foreign Exchange (Map pp74–5; ☎ 2103 312 765; Kydathineon 23, Syntagma; ☾ 9am–midnight)

American Express (Map pp74–5; ☎ 2103 223 380, 2103 244 979; Ermou 7, Syntagma; ☾ 8.30am–4pm Mon-Fri, 8.30am–1.30pm Sat)

Eurochange (Map pp74–5; ☎ 2103 220 155; Karageorgi Servias 4, Syntagma; ☾ 8am–8pm Mon-Fri, 10am–6pm Sat & Sun) Changes Thomas Cook travellers cheques without commission.

National Bank of Greece (Map pp74–5; cnr Karageorgi Servias & Stadiou, Syntagma; foreign exchange only 🕓 3.30-6.30pm Mon-Thu, 3-6.30pm Fri, 9am-3pm Sat, 9am-1pm Sun) It also has a 24-hour automatic exchange machine outside on Stadiou.

Post

Athens Central Post Office (Map pp68-9; Eolou 100, Omonia; 🕓 7.30am-8pm Mon-Fri, 7.30am-2pm Sat) Unless specified otherwise, poste restante will be sent here.

Parcel Post Office (Map pp74-5; Stadiou 4, Syntagma; 🕓 7.30am-2pm Mon-Fri) Parcels that weigh over 2kg must be taken here and unwrapped for inspection. The office is in the arcade between Amerikis and Voukourestiou.

Syntagma Post Office (Map pp74-5; cnr Mitropoleos & Plateia Syntagmatos, Syntagma; 🕓 7.30am-8pm Mon-Fri, 7.30am-2pm Sat) If you're staying in Plaka, it's far more convenient to get your mail sent here.

Telephone

Greek Travel Phones (Map pp74-5; ☎ 2103 224 932; blakjohn@athena.compulink.gr; Voulis 38, Plaka) Specialises in providing mobile phones for English-speaking visitors. It charges €135 for up to 45 days' rental, and provides a phone that is fully charged, programmed in English and ready to use.

Toilets

Public toilets are a rarity in Athens – and those that do exist are best avoided except in an absolute emergency. Fortunately there are fast-food outlets with toilet facilities everywhere in central Athens. Failing that, head to a café, although you'll usually be expected to buy something.

Tourist Information

EOT (Map pp68-9; ☎ 2108 707 000; www.gnto.gr; Tsoha 7, Ambelokipi; 🕓 9am-4pm Mon-Fri) EOT was in turmoil at the time of research, following the relocation of its administrative headquarters from Amerikis 2, near Syntagma, to Ambelokipi. The move has also meant the closure of the ground-floor information office at Amerikis 2, leaving the city temporarily without a city centre tourist office. Until a new location is found, EOT will be dispensing its usual range of information sheets from Tsoha 7. These information sheets include a useful timetable of the week's ferry departures from Piraeus, and details about public-transport prices and schedules from Athens. Its free map of Athens is in need of an update, although most places of interest to travellers are clearly marked. The office is situated about 500m from Ambelokipi metro station.

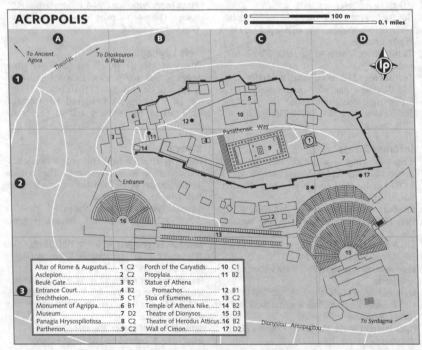

ACROPOLIS

Altar of Rome & Augustus	1	C2
Asclepion	2	C2
Beulé Gate	3	B2
Entrance Court	4	B2
Erechtheion	5	C1
Monument of Agrippa	6	B1
Museum	7	D2
Panagia Hrysospiliotissa	8	C2
Parthenon	9	C2
Porch of the Caryatids	10	C1
Propylaia	11	B2
Statue of Athena Promachos	12	B1
Stoa of Eumenes	13	C2
Temple of Athena Nike	14	B2
Theatre of Dionysos	15	D3
Theatre of Herodus Atticus	16	B2
Wall of Cimon	17	D2

EOT Airport Office (☎ 2103 530 445, 2103 545 101; arrivals hall; ⏰ 9am-7pm Mon-Fri, 10am-3pm Sat & Sun) EOT's airport office has the same information sheets and maps.

DANGERS & ANNOYANCES

Lonely Planet continues to hear from readers who have been taken in by one of the various bar scams that operate around central Athens, particularly around Syntagma.

The basic scam runs something like this: friendly Greek approaches solo male traveller and discovers that the traveller knows little about Athens; friendly Greek then reveals that he, too, is from out of town. Why don't they go to this great little bar that he's just discovered and have a beer? They order a drink, and the equally friendly owner then offers another drink. Women appear, more drinks are provided and the visitor relaxes as he realises that the women are not prostitutes, just friendly Greeks. The crunch comes at the end of the evening when the traveller is presented with an exorbitant bill and the smiles disappear. The con men who cruise the streets playing the role of the friendly Greek can be very convincing: some people have been taken in more than once.

Other bars don't bother with the acting. They target intoxicated males with talk of sex and present them with outrageous bills.

SIGHTS
The Acropolis

Most of the buildings that are now gracing the **Acropolis** (Map p70; ☎ 2103 210 291; site & museum adult/concession €12/6; ⏰ site 8am-6.30pm Apr-Oct, museum 8am-6.30pm Tue-Sun & noon-6.30pm Mon Apr-Oct, site & museum 8am-4.30pm Nov-Mar) were commissioned by Pericles during the golden age of Athens in the 5th century BC. The site had been cleared for him by the Persians, who destroyed an earlier temple complex on the eve of the Battle of Salamis.

The entrance to the Acropolis is through the **Beulé Gate**, a Roman arch that was added in the 3rd century AD. Beyond this is the **Propylaia**, the monumental gate that was the entrance in ancient times. It was damaged by Venetian bombing in the 17th century, but has since been restored. To the south of the Propylaia is the small, graceful **Temple of Athena Nike** (not accessible to visitors).

> ### MORE FOR YOUR MONEY
>
> The €12 admission charge to the Acropolis buys a collective ticket that also gives entry to all the other significant ancient sites in Athens: the Ancient Agora, the Roman Agora, the Keramikos, the Temple of Olympian Zeus and the Theatre of Dionysos. The ticket is valid for 48 hours, otherwise individual site fees apply.

Standing supreme over the Acropolis is the monument which, more than any other, epitomises the glory of ancient Greece: the **Parthenon**. Completed in 438 BC, this building is unsurpassed in grace and harmony. To achieve perfect form, its lines were ingeniously curved to counteract optical illusions. The base curves upwards slightly towards the ends, and the columns become slightly narrower towards the top, with the overall effect of making them both look straight.

Above the columns are the remains of a Doric frieze, which was partly destroyed by Venetian shelling in 1687. The best surviving pieces are the controversial Parthenon Marbles, carted off to Britain by Lord Thomas Elgin in 1801. The Parthenon, dedicated to Athena, contained an 11m-tall gold-and-ivory statue of the goddess completed in 438 BC by Phidias of Athens (only the statue's foundations exist today).

To the north is the **Erechtheion** with its much-photographed Caryatids, the six maidens who support its southern portico. These are plaster casts – the originals (except for the one taken by Lord Elgin) are in the site's museum.

Ancient Agora

The **Agora** (Map pp74-5; ☎ 2103 210 185; western end of Adrianou; adult/concession €4/2; ⏰ 8.30am-3pm Tue-Sun) was the marketplace of ancient Athens and the focal point of civic and social life. The main monuments are the well-preserved **Temple of Hephaestus**, the 11th-century **Church of the Holy Apostles** and the reconstructed **Stoa of Attalos**, which houses the site's museum.

Roman Agora

The Romans built their own **Agora** (☎ 2103 245 220; cnr Pelopida Eolou & Markou Aureliou; adult/concession €2/1; ⏰ 8.30am-3pm Tue-Sun) just east of the Ancient Agora. The main attraction is the

Tower of the Winds, built in the 1st century BC by a Syrian astronomer named Andronicus. This ingenious construction functioned as a sundial, weather vane, water clock and compass.

Keramikos

The **Keramikos** (☎ 2103 463 552; entrance at Ermou 148; adult/concession €2/1; ⌚ 8am-3pm Tue-Sun) was the city's cemetery from the 12th century BC to Roman times. It has an astonishing array of funerary monuments. The finest are to be found on the Street of Tombs, which was reserved for Athens' most prominent citizens. What you see are replicas; the originals are in the National Archaeological Museum.

Temple of Olympian Zeus

This **temple** (☎ 2109 226 330; adult/concession €2/1; ⌚ 8.30am-3pm Tue-Sun) is the largest in Greece, and took over 700 years to build. It was begun in the 6th century BC but was abandoned for lack of funds. It was finally completed by Hadrian in AD 131. The temple is impressive for the sheer size of its 104 Corinthian columns (17m high with a base diameter of 1.7m), of which 15 remain.

Changing of the Guard

Every Sunday at 11am a platoon of traditionally costumed *evzones* (guards) marches down Vasilissis Sofias, accompanied by a band, to the Tomb of the Unknown Soldier in front of the **parliament building** (Map pp74-5; Syntagma).

Museums & Galleries

The **National Archaeological Museum** (Map pp68-9; ☎ 2108 217 717; Oktovriou-Patission 44; www.culture.gr; adult/concession €6/3; ⌚ 12.30-7pm Mon & 8am-7pm Tue-Sun Apr-Oct, 10.30am-5pm Mon & 8am-5pm Tue-Sun Nov-Mar) is one of the world's greatest museums, housing the most important finds from archaeological sites around the country. The crowd-pullers are the magnificent, exquisitely detailed gold artefacts from Mycenae and the spectacular Minoan frescoes from Santorini (Thira).

The museum has been closed as part of a major pre-Olympic reorganisation that began in 2002. It is due to open again in early 2004. The museum is a 10-minute walk from Viktorias metro station, or a 30-minute walk from Plaka.

The **Benaki Museum** (Map pp74-5; ☎ 2103 671 000; cnr Vasilissis Sofias & Koumbari 1, Kolonaki; adult/concession €6/3; ⌚ 9am-5pm Mon, Wed, Fri & Sat, 9am-midnight Thu, 9am-3pm Sun) contains the sumptuous collection of Antoine Benaki, accumulated during 35 years of avid collecting throughout Europe and Asia. The collection includes ancient sculpture, Bronze Age finds from Mycenae and Thessaly, two early works by El Greco and a stunning collection of Greek regional costumes.

The **Goulandris Museum of Cycladic & Ancient Greek Art** (Map pp74-5; ☎ 2108 015 870; cnr Vasilissis Sofias & Neofytou Douka, Kolonaki; adult/concession €3.50/2; ⌚ 10am-4pm Mon & Wed-Fri, 10am-3pm Sat) houses a collection of Cycladic art second in importance only to that displayed at the National Archaeological Museum. The museum was custom-built for the collection and the finds are beautifully displayed and labelled.

The emphasis in the **National Art Gallery** (☎ 2107 235 857; Leof Vasileos Konstantinou 50, adult/concession €6.50/3; ⌚ 8.30am-7pm Tue-Sun Jul-Oct, 9am-3pm Mon-Sat, 6-9pm Mon & Wed, 9am-2pm Sun Nov-June), opposite the Hilton Hotel, is on Greek painting and sculpture from the 19th and 20th centuries. There are also 16th-century works, a few works by European masters, including paintings by Picasso, Marquet and Utrillo, and Magritte's sculpture *The Therapist*. Greek sculpture of the 19th and 20th centuries is effectively displayed in the sculpture garden and sculpture hall, reached from the lower floor. There are several works by Giannolis Halepas (1851–1937), one of Greece's foremost sculptors.

Lykavittos Hill

The name Lykavittos means 'hill of wolves' and derives from ancient times when the hill's pine-covered slopes were inhabited by wolves. Today it rises out of a sea of concrete to offer the finest views in Athens. Pollution permitting, there are panoramic views of the city, the Attic basin, the surrounding mountains and the islands of Salamis and Aegina. A path leads to the summit from the top of Loukianou. Alternatively, you can take the funicular railway (Map pp68-9; one way/return €2/4; h9.15am-11.45pm) from the top of Ploutarhou.

The open-air Lykavittos Theatre, northeast of the summit, is used during the Summer on Lykavittos Hill programme (see Festivals & Events following).

FESTIVALS & EVENTS
Hellenic Festival
The annual **Hellenic Festival** is the city's most important cultural event, running from mid-June to late September. It features a line-up of international music, dance and theatre at the **Theatre of Herodes Atticus** (Map pp74-5). The setting is superb, backed by a floodlit Acropolis.

The festival has been going from strength to strength in recent years. The 2003 line-up included Marcel Marceau, the French National Opera Company of Paris and Ian Anderson's Jethro Tull, as well as a mix of opera, modern dance and theatre both ancient and modern.

Tickets can be bought at the **festival box office** (Map pp74-5; ☎ 2103 221 459; fax 2103 235 172; Stadiou 39, Syntagma; ⏱ 8.30am-4pm Mon-Fri, 9am-2.30pm Sat). Tickets go on sale three weeks before a performance. There are student discounts for most performances on production of an International Student Identity Card (ISIC; see Discount Cards p453).

Summer on Lykavittos Hill
The **Lykavittos Theatre** (Map pp68-9; ☎ 2107 227 233) on the Hill of Lykavittos makes a spectacular setting for a series of performances by Greek and international stars from June to the end of August. The line-up for 2003 included the Dandy Warhols, Moby, Massive Attack and flamenco star Joaquin Cortes.

SLEEPING
Camping
Athens Camping (☎ 2105 814 114; fax 2105 820 353; Leof Athinon 198; site per adult/tent €5/3; ⏱ year-round) This place is 7km west of the city centre on the road to Corinth, making it the nearest camping ground to the city centre. It has reasonable facilities but nothing else going for it.

Hostels
Athens International Youth Hostel (Map pp68-9; ☎ 2105 234 170; fax 2105 234 015; Victor Hugo 16, Omonia; members €8.66, nonmembers €8.66 plus daily stamp, joining fee €15, daily stamp €2.50) A large question mark hung over the future of this HI-affiliated hostel at the time of research. It was still open, but its phone had been disconnected and it looked like the cleaners hadn't called for weeks.

Youth Hostel No 5 (Map pp68-9; ☎ 2107 519 530; y-hostel@otenet.gr; Damareos 75; dm €10) The rooms here are very basic, but it's a cheery place in a quiet residential neighbourhood. Owner Yiannis is something of a philosopher and visitors are encouraged to contribute their jokes and words of wisdom to the hostel noticeboard. Hostel facilities include coin-operated hot showers, a communal kitchen, a TV room and a washing machine (€3). You can get there on trolleybus No 2 or 11 from Syntagma to the Filolaou stop on Frinis, or alternatively you can walk from Evangelismos metro station.

Hotels
PLAKA & SYNTAGMA
Student & Travellers' Inn (Map pp74-5; ☎ 2103 244 808; info@studenttravellersinn.com; Kydathineon 16; dm €15-22, s/d €45/50, d/tr with bathroom €60/75; 🖳 🕱) Most travellers make a bee-line for this place. This well-run inn is a veritable maze of rooms large and small – some have lovely old timber floors. The dorms here are good value, especially in the quieter months. All dorms share communal bathrooms and facilities include a courtyard with big-screen TV, Internet access and a travel service. Rooms are heated in winter.

John's Place (Map pp74-5; ☎ 2103 229 719; Patrovu 5; s/d/tr €30/45/60; 🕱) This small, old-fashioned, family-run place is ideally situated just west of Syntagma.

Hotel Adonis (Map pp74-5; ☎ 2103 249 737; fax 2103 231 602; Kodrou 3; s/d/tr €44/59/77; 🕱) This comfortable modern hotel represents one of the best deals around. All the rooms come with TV. There are good views of the Acropolis from the 4th-floor rooms, and from the rooftop bar.

Hotel Nefeli (Map pp74-5; ☎ 2103 228 044; fax 2103 225 800; Iperidou 16; s/d/tr with breakfast €65/75/96; 🕱) The Nefeli is in a quiet location and comfortable rooms with TV.

MONASTIRAKI
Hotel Tempi (Map pp74-5; ☎ 2103 213 175; www .travelling.gr/tempihotel; Eolou 29; s/d €30/42, s/d/tr with bathroom €40/48/60) This friendly, family-run place was named one of the world's top 50 budget hotels by Britain's *Independent* newspaper. Yiannis and Katerina keep the place spotless, and the rooms at the front have balconies overlooking pretty

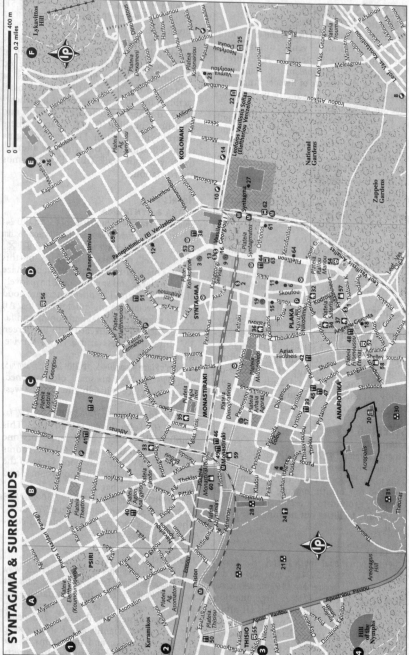

SYNTAGMA & SURROUNDS

Plateia Agia Irini with its flower market and church – not to mention views to the Acropolis. There is also a communal kitchen with a refrigerator and facilities for preparing hot drinks and snacks. Credit cards are accepted – an unusual feature for a Greek budget hotel.

Hotel Attalos (Map pp74-5; ☎ 2103 212 801; www .attaloshotel.com; Athinas 29; s/d/tr with bathroom €53/62/ 80; ✷) This is a comfortable, if characterless, modern hotel. Its best feature is the rooftop bar which offers wonderful views of the Acropolis at night. All rooms have TV and breakfast is offered (€5.90).

MAKRIGIANNI & KOUKAKI

Marble House Pension (Map pp68-9; ☎ 2109 234 058, 2109 228 294; www.marble-house.gr; Zini 35a; d/tr €37/44, s/d/tr with bathroom €35/43/50; ✷) This isn't exactly backpacker territory, but this pension, on a quiet cul-de-sac off Zini, is one of Athens' better budget hotels. All rooms have a bar fridge and ceiling fans, and breakfast is offered (€4.50).

Tony's Hotel (Map pp68-9; ☎ 2109 230 561; www .hoteltony.gr; Zaharitsa 26; s/d/tr €50/55/72, d with bathroom €60) This is a clean, well-maintained pension. There is a small communal kitchen downstairs for tea,coffee and breakfast. Tony also has well-equipped studio apartments nearby for long- or short-term rental. Short-term prices are the same as for rooms at the pension.

Art Gallery Hotel (Map pp68-9; ☎ 2109 238 376; ecotec@otenet.gr; Erehthiou 5; s/d/tr €63/90/109; ✷) This is a small, friendly place that's full of personal touches – like fresh flowers. It's run by brother-and-sister team Ada and Yannis Assimakopoulos, who are full of information about the city. The rooms are heated in winter, when cheaper long-term rates are available. A generous breakfast costs €6.

OMONIA & SURROUNDS

Hostel Aphrodite (Map pp68-9; ☎ 2108 810 589; info@hostelaphrodite.com; Einardou 12; dm €16-18; d/tr €45/60, d with bathroom €50; ▣) This hostel is definitely worth checking out. It's 10 minutes' walk from the train stations, and has very clean, good-sized rooms – many with balconies. It seems to be party time every night at the downstairs bar. In the morning, the bar becomes the breakfast room. Facilities include Internet access. The nearest metro station is Viktorias, five minutes' walk southeast at Plateia Viktorias.

Zorba's Hotel (Map pp68-9; ☎ 2108 234 239; www .zorbashotel.com; Gilfordiou 10; dm €16-18, d/tr with bathroom €50/75; ☐) This hotel occupies a quaint old building 100m east of Plateia Viktorias. Facilities include Internet access and a laundry service. Breakfast is available in the bar.

EATING
Plaka

For most people, Plaka is the place to be. It's hard to beat the atmosphere of an afternoon coffee break in its cobbled streets or dining out beneath the floodlit Acropolis.

Taverna Vizantino (Map pp74-5; ☎ 2103 227 368; Kydathineon 18; mains €4.50-12) This place is the best of the restaurants around Plateia Filomousou Eterias. It prices its menu realistically and is popular with locals year-round. The daily specials are good value, with dishes like stuffed tomatoes (€4.50), *pastitsio* (baked macaroni with cheese and minced lamb; €4.50) and baked fish (€7).

Taverna tou Psara (Map pp74-5; ☎ 2103 218 734; Eretheos 16; mains €5-18, fish from €40/kg) Hidden away from the main hustle and bustle of Plaka, Taverna tou Psara is a cut above the Plaka crowd. The menu includes a fabulous choice of mezedes – the *melizanakeftedes* (aubergine croquettes; €5.30) are particularly good. You'll need to get in early to secure a table on the terrace, which has views out over the city.

Paleo Taverna Stamatopoulos (Map pp74-5; ☎ 2103 228 722; Lyssiou 26; mains €5-8.50; ☺ 7pm-2am Mon-Sat, 11-2am Sun) Stamatopoulos is something of a Plaka institution: reasonable food, very reasonable prices and live music every night. It's very popular with locals and can get very busy later in the evening, so you'll need to get in early to be assured of a table. The waiters are famous for the astonishing number of plates they can handle!

Eden Vegetarian Restaurant (Map pp74-5; ☎ 2103 248 858; www.edenveg.gr; Lyssiou 12; mains €4.70-8.50; ☺ 11am-midnight Wed-Mon) The Eden is unchallenged as the best vegetarian restaurant in Athens. It's been around for years, substituting soya products for meat in tasty vegetarian versions of mousaka (€6.80), and other Greek favourites. You'll also find vegie burgers (€5.30), mushroom *stifado* (stew made with rabbit and onions; €8.80), as well as organic beer and wine.

Syntagma

Neon Café (Map pp74-5; ☎ 2103 246 873; Mitropoleos 3; mains €5.10-7.50) This is a stylish modern caféteria with a good selection of meals, as well as coffee and cakes. You'll find spaghetti or fettuccine napolitana (€3.40) and bolognese or carbonara (€4.40). Main dishes include mousaka (€5.50), roast beef with potatoes (€7) and pork kebab (€7.50). It's located in the southwestern corner of Plateia Syntagmatos.

Monastiraki

There are some excellent cheap eats around Plateia Monastirakiou, particularly for gyros and souvlaki fans. Recommended are **Thanasis** (Map pp74-5; ☎ 2103 244 705; Mitropoleos 69) and **Savas** (Map pp74-5; ☎ 2103 245 048; Mitropoleos 86) at the western end of Mitropoleos.

Thisio

To Steki tou Elia (Map pp74-5; ☎ 2103 458 052; Epahalkou 5; mains €4.40-7; ☺ 8pm-late) This place specialises in lamb chops (€22/kg). Locals swear that they are the best chops in Athens, and the place has achieved some sort of celebrity status. Eat here with Greek friends, and they will constantly be pointing out famous personalities rolling up their sleeves to tuck into great piles of chops and a few jars of retsina. There are pork chops (€6.50) and steaks (€5) for those who don't eat lamb, as well as dips, chips and salads.

Makrigianni & Koukaki

Gardenia Restaurant (Map pp68-9; ☎ 2109 225 831; Zini 31; mains €3-5) The Gardenia is a typical old-fashioned neighbourhood place turning out solid taverna food at old-fashioned prices. Cheerful owners Nikos and Gogo reckon they have the best prices in Athens.

To 24 Hours (Map pp68-9; ☎ 2109 222 749; Syngrou 44; mains €4.50-7; ☺ 24hr) This is something of an institution among Athenian night owls. The place never closes, except on Easter Sunday, and seems to be at its busiest in the wee small hours. The customers are as much of an attraction as the food: you'll be rubbing shoulders with an assortment of hungry cabbies, middle-aged couples dressed for the opera, and leather-clad gays from the area's many bars – all tucking into steaming bowls of the house speciality, *patsas* (tripe soup). It also has a constantly changing choice of other popular taverna dishes.

Stoa of Attalos, Ancient Agora (p71),
Athens

GEORGE TSAFOS

JOHN ELK III

Theatre of Herodes Atticus (p73),
Athens

Restaurant in Plaka (p76), Athens

NEIL SETCHFIELD

ANDERS BLOMQVIST

Detail of the Parthenon
Marbles (p71), Athens

Evzones outside the Greek parliament (p72),
Athens

DIANA MAYFIELD

Parthenon (p71), Acropolis, Athens

ANDERS BLOMQVIST

Kolonaki

The Food Company (Map pp68-9; ☎ 2103 630 373; Anagnostopoulou 47; mains €5-7) The Food Company turns out an interesting range of salads and pasta dishes at prices below the Kolonaki norm.

Self-catering

MARKETS

You'll find the widest range of whatever's in season, and the best prices at the central markets on Athinas, halfway between Plateia Omonias and Plateia Monastirakiou. The **fruit and vegetable market** (Map pp74-5) is on the western side of Athinas, and the **meat market** (Map pp74-5) is opposite on the eastern side. The stretch of Athinas between the meat market and Plateia Monastirakiou is the place to shop for nuts and nibblies.

SUPERMARKETS

You can find the following supermarkets in central Athens:

Bazaar Discount Supermarket (Map pp68-9; Eolou 104, Omonia)

Marinopoulos (Map pp68-9; Kanari 9, Kolonaki)

Marinopoulos (Map pp68-9; Athinas 60, Omonia)

Papageorgiou (Map pp68-9; Dimitrakopoulou 72, Veikou)

Vasilopoulou (Map pp74-5; Stadiou 19, Syntagma)

Veropoulos (Map pp68-9; Parthenos 6, Koukaki)

DRINKING

Cafés

Brazil Coffee Shop (Map pp74-5; ☎ 2103 235 463; Voukourestiou 1, Syntagma) It's very hard to ignore the delicious aromas emanating from the Brazil Coffee Shop. It offers a range of coffees, including Greek coffee (€1.50), cappuccino and filter coffee (both €1.80). Cakes and croissants cost from €1.05.

Kotsolis (Map pp74-5; ☎ 2103 221 164; Adrianou 112, Plaka) This is a smart pastry shop with a mouth-watering array of goodies to accompany an extensive choice of coffees (€1.70-5). It includes such traditional Greek favourites as *galaktoboureko* (custard slice; €3), baklava (€2.70) and *kataifi* ('angel hair' pastry; €2.70).

Embros (Map pp74-5; ☎ 2103 213 285; Plateia Agion Anargyron 4, Psiri) Serves the usual range of coffees, but specialises in tea. There's a long list of exotic brews to choose from, including favourites like Earl Grey and Orange Pekoe. In winter, it becomes a haven for chocoholics with an irresistible array of chocolate fondues from €4.50.

ENTERTAINMENT

The best source of entertainment information is the weekly listings magazine *Athenorama*, but you'll need to be able to read some Greek to make much sense of it. It costs €1.50 and is available from *periptera* all over the city.

English-language listings appear daily in the *Kathimerini* supplement that accompanies the *International Herald Tribune*, while the *Athens News* carries a weekly entertainment guide.

Bars

Brettos (Map pp74-5; ☎ 2103 232 110; Kydathineon 41, Plaka; ☉ 10am-midnight) This is a delightful place right in the heart of Plaka. Very little has changed here in years, except that being old fashioned has become very fashionable. It's a family-run business that acts as a shopfront for the family distillery and winery in Kalithea. Huge barrels line one wall, and the shelves are stocked with a colourful collection of bottles. Shots of Brettos brand spirits (ouzo, brandy and many more) cost €1.50, as does a glass of wine.

Mike's Irish Bar (☎ 2107 776 797; www.mikesirish bar.gr; Sinopsis 6, Ambelokipi; ☉ 8pm-4am) Mike's is a longtime favourite of the city's expat community, which comes here to play darts and sup pints of Guinness or Murphy's stout (both €7). There's live music every night from 11.30pm. Try to catch 1950s and '60s revivalists, Johnny Vavouras and The Cadillacs.

Craft (☎ 2106 462 350; www.craft.gr; Leof Alexandras 205, Ambelokipi; ☉ 10am-1.30am) This is Greece's first (and only) boutique brewery – or microbrewery as Craft likes to call itself. Drinkers can sample the various house brews safe in the knowledge that there's plenty more bubbling away in the giant stainlesss steel vats in the background. It also serves a large range of beer-drinking finger food, like *weisswurst* and mustard (€5.80).

Gay & Lesbian Venues

The greatest concentration of gay bars is to be found around Makrigianni, south of the Temple of Olympian Zeus. Most places open about 11pm, but you won't find much of a crowd until after midnight. Popular spots include the long-running **Granazi Bar** (Map pp68-9; ☎ 2109 244 185; Lembesi 20, Makrigianni; admission €6 with free drink) and the **Lamda Club** (Map pp68-9; ☎ 2109 224 202; Lembesi 15, Makrigianni; admission €6 with free drink).

Greek Folk Dancing

Dora Stratou Dance Company (Map pp68-9; ☎ 2109 214 650; www.grdance.org; Dora Stratou Theatre, Filopappos Hill; adult/concession €13/6.50; performances 9.30pm Tue-Sat, 8.15pm Sun, 23 May–28 Sep) The Dora Stratou company has been around for many years, performing its repertoire of folk dances from all over Greece. Formed originally with the goal of preserving the country's folk culture, it has gained an international reputation for authenticity and professionalism. It performs at its own theatre on the western side of Filopappos Hill, signposted from the western end of Dionysiou Areopagitou.

Live Music

The city's main rock venues are the **Rodon Club** (Map pp68-9; ☎ 2105 247 427; Marni 24, Omonia) and **Gagarin 205 Club** (Liossion 205). Both have gigs most Friday and Saturday nights. Tickets are available from **Ticket House** (Map pp68-9; ☎ 2103 608 366; Panepistimiou 42).

Top-name international acts play at a variety of venues, including the spectacular **Lykavittos Theatre** (p73) on Lykavittos Hill and the **Panathinaïkos Football Stadium** (Leof Alexandras).

Jazz fans should head for the **Half Note Jazz Club** (Map pp68-9; ☎ 2109 213 310; Trivonianou 17, Mets) opposite the Athens Cemetery. It hosts an interesting array of international names.

Nightclubs

Admission to most places ranges from €5, Monday to Thursday, to €10 Friday and Saturday. The price often includes one free drink. Subsequently, expect to pay about €3 for soft drinks, €5 for a beer and €8 for spirits. Clubs don't start to get busy until around midnight.

Lava Bore (Map pp74-5; ☎ 2103 245 335; Filellinon 25; admission €6 with free drink; 10-5pm) The Lava Bore is one city-centre club that stays open year-round, although this is its third address in five years. The formula remains much the same: a mixture of mainstream rock and techno and large beers for €2.95.

Plus Soda (Map pp68-9; ☎ 2103 456 187; Ermou 161, Thisio) A glamorous club with a cast of chic DJs turning out a diet of techno, trance and psychedelia for an energetic crowd of under-25s.

SHOPPING
Flea Market

This market is the first place to spring to most people's minds when they think of shopping in Athens. It's the commercial area that stretches west of Plateia Monastirakiou and consists of shops selling goods running the whole gamut from high quality to trash. These shops are open daily during normal business hours.

However, when most people speak of the Athens flea market, they are referring to the **Sunday market** (Map pp74-5; 7am-2pm), which spills over into Plateia Monastirakiou and onto Ermou.

A visit to Athens isn't complete without a visit to the Sunday market. All manner of things – from new to fourth-hand – are on sale. There's everything from clocks to condoms, binoculars to *bouzouki* (stringed lute-like instrument associated with *rembetika* music), tyres to telephones, giant evil eyes to jelly babies, and wigs to welding kits to be found.

Traditional Handicrafts

Hellenic Folk Art Gallery (Map pp74-5; ☎ 2103 250 524; cnr Apollonos & Ipatias, Plaka; 9am-8pm Tue-Fri, 9am-3pm Mon & Sat) Run by the National Welfare Organisation, this is a good place for purchasing handicrafts. It has top-quality merchandise and your money goes to a good cause – the preservation and promotion of traditional Greek handicrafts. It has a wide range of knotted carpets, kilims, flokatis, needlepoint rugs and embroidered cushion covers, as well as a small selection of pottery, copper and woodwork.

Mado (Map pp74-5; ☎ 2103 223 628; Sellev 6, Plaka; noon-8pm Mon-Sat) Next to the Lysicrates monument, this workshop produces beautiful, hand-woven wall hangings. Many depict island scenes.

Stavros Melissinos (Map pp74-5; ☎ 2103 219 247; Pandrosou 89; 10am-2pm & 4-7pm Mon-Sat, 10am-2pm Sun) Athens' famous sandalmaker/poet is still turning out good-quality leather sandals from only €16 per pair.

GETTING THERE & AWAY
Air

Athens is served by **Eleftherios Venizelos International Airport** (☎ 2103 530 000; www.aia.gr) at Spata, 27km east of Athens.

The airport, named after the country's leading 20th-century politician, opened in 2001. The facilities are immeasurably better than the former airport, Ellinikon. Built by a German consortium, it's state of the art.

See Getting Around (p80) for public transport to/from the airport. For international flights to/from see the Transport chapter (p464).

DOMESTIC FLIGHTS

Most domestic flights are operated by **Olympic Airways** (Map pp68-9; ☎ 2103 569 111, 8011 144 444; www.olympic-airways.gr; Leof Syngrou 96), which also has branch offices at **Syntagma** (Map pp74-5; ☎ 2109 264 444; Filellinon 15) and **Omonia** (Map pp68-9; ☎ 2109 267 218; Kotopouli Merakas 1). For flight information call ☎ 2109 666 666. The following tables give flight details from Athens to the islands and mainland ports.

OLYMPIC AIRWAYS FLIGHTS FROM ATHENS TO THE GREEK ISLANDS (HIGH SEASON)

Destination	Flights/week	Duration	Fare
Astypalea	4	1hr	€74.55
Chios	28	50min	€75
Corfu	20	1hr	€96
Crete (Hania)	28	50min	€89
Crete (Iraklio)	43	50min	€89
Crete (Sitia)	3	80min	€91
Ikaria	4	55min	€65
Karpathos5	1	25min	€106
Kefallonia	12	65min	€81
Kos	19	55min	€89
Kythira	7	45min	€61
Leros	7	1hr	€72
Lesvos	28	50min	€84
Limnos	7	55min	€71
Milos	10	45min	€55
Mykonos	34	40min	€82
Naxos	8	45min	€81
Paros	19	40min	€78
Rhodes	35	1hr	€96
Samos	30	1hr	€79
Santorini	35	50min	€88
Skiathos	7	50min	€71
Skyros	2	35min	€51
Syros	5	35min	€70
Zakynthos	11	1hr	€80

OLYMPIC AIRWAYS FLIGHTS FROM ATHENS TO OTHER MAINLAND PORTS

Destination	Flights/week	Duration	Fare
Alexandroupolis	14	65min	€92
Kavala	14	1hr	€89
Preveza	5	1hr	€68
Thessaloniki	70	55min	€96

Aegean Airlines (reservations ☎ 801 11 20000; www.aegeanair.com) provides welcome competition on some of the most popular routes. It has up to 12 flights per day to Thessaloniki, seven daily to Iraklio, six daily to Rhodes, at least four daily to Mykonos and Santorini, three daily to Hania and Lesvos, two daily to Alexandroupolis and Corfu, and one daily flight to Kavala. Aegean Airlines has a convenient city centre sales office at **Syntagma** (Map pp74-5; ☎ 2103 315 502; Othonos 10).

Bus

There are two main intercity bus stations in Athens.

The first of these stations, Terminal A, is about 7km northwest of Plateia Omonias at Kifissou 100 and has regular departures to the Peloponnese, the Ionian Islands, and western and northern Greece. City bus No 051 runs between the terminal and the junction of Zinonos and Menandrou, near Omonia, every 15 minutes from 5am to midnight.

Terminal B is about 5km north of Plateia Omonias off Liossion and has departures to central Greece and Evia. The EOT information sheet misleadingly lists the address of the terminal as being Liossion 260, which in fact turns out to be a small car-repair workshop. Liossion 260 is where you will need to get off the No 024 bus that travels from outside the main gate of the National Gardens on Amalias. From Liossion 260, you should turn right onto Gousiou and you'll then see the terminal at the end of the road on Agiou Dimitriou Oplon.

Buses for Rafina and Lavrio leave from the **Mavromateon bus terminal** (Map pp68-9; cnr Alexandras & 28 Oktovriou-Patission), which is 250m north of the National Archaeological Museum.

For international bus services see p467 in the Transport chapter.

BUS DEPARTURES FROM ATHENS
BUS TERMINAL A

Destination	Duration	Fare	Frequency
Corfu*	11hr	€29.50	2 daily
Gythio	4½hr	€16.30	5 daily
Igoumenitsa	8½hr	€29.85	4 daily
Kalamata	3½hr	€15	9 daily
Kavala	10hr	€39.40	3 daily
Kefallonia*	8hr	€23.85	4 daily
Lefkada	5½hr	€22.50	4 daily
Nafplio	2½hr	€9	hourly
Patra	3hr	€12.90	half-hourly
Thessaloniki	7½hr	€29.40	8 daily
Zakynthos*	7hr	€22.60	8 daily

*prices inclusive of ferry transfers

BUS TERMINAL B

Destination	Duration	Fare	Frequency
Agios Konstantinos	2½hr	€10.90	hourly
Halkida	1 hr	€4.80	half-hourly
Kymi	3½hr	€10.45	3 daily
Volos	5hr	€18.60	9 daily

MAVROMATEON BUS TERMINAL

Destination	Duration	Fare	Frequency
Lavrio	1½hr	€3.25	half-hourly
Rafina	45min	€2	half-hourly

Car & Motorcycle
National Road 1 is the main route north from Athens. It starts at Nea Kifissia. To get there from central Athens, take Vasilissis Sofias from Syntagma. National Road 8, which begins beyond Dafni, is the road to the Peloponnese. Take Agiou Konstantinou from Omonia.

The northern reaches of Syngrou, situated just south of the Temple of Olympian Zeus, are packed solid with car-rental firms.

Train
All intercity services are due to start operating from the city's new Central Station at Arharnon in May 2004. Despite the name, Central Station is actually a good 20km north of the city centre. The main access will be by suburban train.

Travellers arriving before May 2004 can expect to find the old system still in operation with trains to central and northern Greece leaving from Larisis station, and

trains to the Peloponnese leaving from Peloponnese station. These two stations are located a few hundred metres apart, about 1km northeast of Plateia Omonias. The easiest way to get to the stations is to catch the metro to the Larisa stop on Line 2, which is right outside Larisis station. To get to the Peloponnese station, cross over the metal bridge at the southern end of Larisis train station.

Under the new system, Larisis station will become a stop on the suburban line between Piraeus and Arharnon, while the Peloponnese station will become a museum.

More information on services is available from the **OSE offices** Omonia (Map pp68-9; ☎ 2105 240 647; Karolou 1; ☺ 8am-6pm Mon-Fri, 8am-3pm Sat) Syntagma (Map pp74-5; ☎ 2103 624 402; Sina 6; ☺ 8am-3.30pm Mon-Fri, 8am-3pm Sat). Both offices also handle advance bookings.

See the Transport chapter (p467) for information on international train services.

GETTING AROUND
To/From the Airport
BUS
There are two special express bus services operating between the airport and the city and a service between the airport and Piraeus.

Service E94 operates between the airport and the eastern terminus of Metro Line 3 at Ethniki Amyna. There are departures every 16 minutes, according to the official timetable, between 6am and midnight. The journey takes about 25 minutes. This service is likely to be discontinued when Metro Line 3 is extended to the airport (see Metro, opposite).

Service E95 operates between the airport and Plateia Syntagmatos. This line operates 24 hours with services approximately every 30 minutes. The bus stop is outside the National Gardens on Amalias on the eastern side of Plateia Syntagmatos. The journey takes between an hour and 1½ hours, depending on traffic conditions.

Service E96 operates between the Athens airport and Plateia Karaïskaki in Piraeus. This line also operates 24 hours, with services approximately every 40 minutes.

KTEL Attikis runs buses from the airport to the port of Rafina.

Tickets for all these services cost €2.90. The tickets are valid for 24 hours, and can be used on all forms of public transport in Athens – buses, trolleybuses and the metro.

METRO

Metro Line 3 is scheduled to start operating to Athens airport in May 2004, providing an ultra-convenient express service to the city centre.

TAXI

It seems to be virtually impossible to catch a cab from the airport without getting involved in an argument about the fare.

Whatever happens, make sure that the meter is set to the correct tariff (see the following Taxi section for details). You will also have to pay a €0.90 airport surcharge and a €0.60 toll for using the tollroad connecting the airport to the city. Fares vary according to the time of day and level of traffic, but you should expect to pay €20 from the airport to the city centre, and €25 to Piraeus, depending on traffic conditions. Both trips should take no longer than an hour. If you have problems, don't hesitate to threaten to involve the tourist police.

TRAIN

Trains are also scheduled to start operating to Athens airport in May 2004. If all goes according to plan, there will be regular trains to the new Athens Central Station at Arharnon. The trip should take 25 minutes.

Bus & Trolleybus

Since most of Athens' ancient sites are within easy walking distance of Syntagma, and many of the museums are close by on Vasilissis Sofias near Syntagma, you won't have much need for public transport.

There are 24-hour buses between the city centre and Piraeus (every 20 minutes, 6am to midnight then hourly). Bus No 040 runs from Filellinon to Akti Xaveriou in Piraeus, and No 049 from the northern end of Athinas to Plateia Themistokleous in Piraeus.

There is a flat fare of €0.45 throughout the city on both buses and trolleybuses. Tickets must be purchased before you board, either at a transport kiosk or at most *periptera*, and validated using the red ticket machine as soon as you board. Plain-clothed inspectors make spot checks and the penalty for travelling without a validated ticket is €28.

Metro

The Metro system has transformed travel around central Athens. Coverage is still largely confined to the city centre, but that's good enough for most visitors.

Travel on Lines 2 and 3 costs €0.70, while Line 1 is split into three sections: Piraeus–Monastiraki, Monastiraki–Attiki and Attiki–Kifissia. Travel within one section costs €0.60, and a journey covering two or more sections costs €0.70. The same conditions apply everywhere, though: tickets must be validated at the machines at platform entrances before travelling. The penalty for travelling without a validated ticket is €28.

The trains operate between 5am and midnight. They run every three minutes during peak periods, dropping to every 10 minutes at other times.

The following is a brief outline of the three lines that make up the network.

LINE 1

This is the old Kifissia–Piraeus line. Until the opening of Lines 2 and 3, this was the metro system. It is indicated in green on maps and signs. Useful stops include Piraeus (for the port), Monastiraki and Omonia (city centre), Plateia Viktorias (National Archaeological Museum) and Irini (Olympic Stadium). Omonia and Attiki are transfer stations with connections to Line 2; Monastiraki is the transfer station for Line 3.

LINE 2

This line runs from Sepolia in the northwest to Dafni in the southeast. It is indicated in red on maps and signs. Useful stops include Larisa (for the train stations), Omonia, Panepistimiou and Syntagma (city centre) and Akropoli (Makrigianni). Attiki and Omonia are transfer stations for Line 1, while Syntagma is the transfer station for Line 3.

LINE 3

This runs northeast from Monastiraki to Ethniki Amyna, and is indicated in blue on maps and signs. Useful stops are Syntagma, Evangelismos (for the museums on Vasilissis Sofias) and Megaro Musikis (Athens Concert Hall). Syntagma is the transfer station for Line 2. This line is scheduled to be extended to Athens airport by May 2004.

Taxi

Athens' taxis are yellow. To hail a taxi, stand on a pavement and shout your destination as they pass. If a taxi is going your way the driver may stop even if there are already passengers inside. This does not mean the fare will be shared: each person will be charged the fare shown on the meter. If you get in one that does not have other passengers, make sure the meter is switched on.

The flag fall is €0.75, with a €0.60 surcharge from ports and train and bus stations, and a €0.90 surcharge from the airport. After that, the day rate (tariff 1 on the meter) is €0.23 per km. The rate doubles between midnight and 5am (tariff 2 on the meter). Baggage is charged at the rate of €0.30 per item over 10kg. The minimum fare is €1.50.

Train

A new suburban train network is to begin operation in May 2004, centred on the new Athens Central Station at Arharnon. The line south to Piraeus will stop at Larisis station, giving access to the Metro system. Another line will run southeast to the airport, stopping at the Olympic Stadium on the way.

THE MAINLAND PORTS

This section is designed to provide all the information a traveller needs to get from the mainland to the islands. It begins with the ports that serve more than one island group: Piraeus, Rafina, Thessaloniki and Gythio. The remaining ports are grouped according to the island groups they serve.

WHICH PORT?

The following list details the ports serving each island group:

Crete Piraeus, Thessaloniki, Gythio

Cyclades Piraeus, Rafina, Thessaloniki, Lavrio

Dodecanese Piraeus, Thessaloniki, Alexandroupolis

Evia & the Sporades Rafina (Evia only), Agios Konstantinos, Volos

Ionians Patra, Igoumenitsa, Kyllini, Piraeus (Kythira only), Gythio (Kythira and Antikythira only), Neapoli (Kythira only)

Northeastern Aegean Piraeus, Thessaloniki, Kavala, Alexandroupolis

Saronic Gulf Islands Piraeus, Porto Heli, Ermione, Galatas

PIRAEUS ΠΕΙΡΑΙΑΣ

pop 175,697

Piraeus is the port of Athens, the main port of Greece and one of the Mediterranean's major ports. It's the hub of the Aegean ferry network, centre for Greece's maritime export-import and transit trade and base for its large merchant navy. Nowadays, Athens has expanded sufficiently to meld imperceptibly into Piraeus.

History

The histories of Athens and Piraeus are inextricably linked. Themistocles transferred his Athenian fleet from the exposed port of Phaleron (modern Faliro) to the security of Piraeus at the beginning of the 5th century BC. Piraeus was a flourishing commercial centre during the classical age but, by Roman times, it had been overtaken by Rhodes, Delos and Alexandria. During medieval and Turkish times Piraeus diminished to a tiny fishing village, and by the time Greece became independent, it was home to fewer than 20 people.

Its resurgence began in 1834 when Athens became the capital of independent Greece. By the beginning of the 20th century, Piraeus had superseded the island of Syros as Greece's principal port.

Orientation

Piraeus is 10km southwest of central Athens. The largest of its three harbours is the Great Harbour (Megas Limin), on the western side of the Piraeus peninsula, which is the departure point for all ferry, hydrofoil and catamaran services. Zea Marina (Limin Zeas) and the picturesque Mikrolimano (small harbour), on the eastern side, are for private yachts.

The metro and train lines from Athens terminate at the northeastern corner of the Great Harbour on Akti Kalimassioti. Most ferry departure points are a short walk from here.

Information

Emporiki Bank (cnr Antistaseos & Makras Stoas) Has a 24-hour automatic exchange machine.

Internet Center (☎ 2104 111 261; Akti Poseidonos 24; ❂ 10am-11pm)

National Bank of Greece (cnr Antistaseos & Tsamadou)

Post Office (cnr Tsamadou & Filonos; ⏰ 7.30am-8pm
Mon-Fri, 7.30am-2pm Sat)

Sleeping

There's no reason to stay at any of the
shabby cheap hotels around Great Harbour when Athens is so close. The cheap
hotels are geared more towards accommodating sailors than tourists. Whatever
happens, don't attempt to sleep out –
Piraeus is the most dangerous place in
Greece to do so.

Eating

There are dozens of cafés, restaurants and
fast-food places along the waterfront at
Great Harbour.

Tiny **Restaurant I Folia** (☎ 2104 210 781; Akti
Poseidonos 30; mains €3-5), opposite Plateia Karaïskaki, is perfect for a quick bite before you
board a ferry.

If you would like to stock up on supplies before your ferry trip, you should
head straight for the area just inland from
Poseidonos. You will find fresh fruit and
vegetables at the **markets** on Demosthen-
ous. Opposite the markets is **Pairaikon Supermarket** (☎ 2104 117 177; ⏰ 8am-8pm Mon-Fri,
8am-4pm Sat).

Getting There & Away

AIR

Olympic Airways (☎ 2109 267 560) has an office
at Akti Miaouli 27.

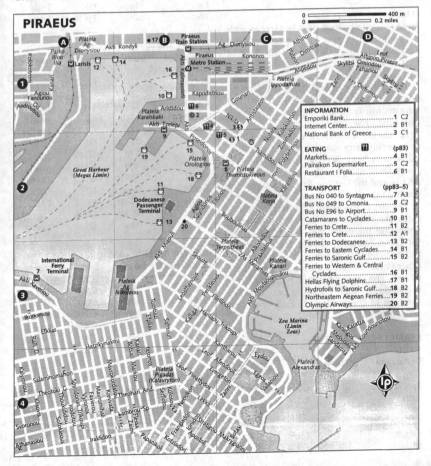

PIRAEUS

0		400 m
0		0.2 miles

INFORMATION	
Emporiki Bank	1 C2
Internet Center	2 B1
National Bank of Greece	3 C1

EATING	(p83)
Markets	4 B1
Pairaikon Supermarket	5 C2
Restaurant I Folia	6 B1

TRANSPORT	(pp83–5)
Bus No 040 to Syntagma	7 A3
Bus No 049 to Omonia	8 C2
Bus No E96 to Airport	9 B1
Catamarans to Cyclades	10 B1
Ferries to Crete	11 B2
Ferries to Crete	12 A1
Ferries to Dodecanese	13 B2
Ferries to Eastern Cyclades	14 B1
Ferries to Saronic Gulf	15 B2
Ferries to Western & Central Cyclades	16 B1
Hellas Flying Dolphins	17 B1
Hydrofoils to Saronic Gulf	18 B2
Northeastern Aegean Ferries	19 B2
Olympic Airways	20 B2

BUS

Special buses (Nos 040 and 049) operate 24 hours a day between Piraeus and central Athens; they run every 20 minutes from 6am until midnight and then hourly.

No 040 runs between Akti Xaveriou in Piraeus and Filellinon in Athens and is the service that passes by closest to Zea Marina; the most convenient stop is outside Hotel Savoy on Iroön Polytehniou. No 049 runs between Plateia Themistokleous in Piraeus and Plateia Omonias in Syntagma, Athens. The fare is €0.45 on each service. E96 buses to the airport leave from the southwestern corner of Plateia Karaïskaki.

There are no intercity buses to or from Piraeus.

FERRY

Piraeus is the busiest port in Greece with a bewildering array of departures and destinations, including daily services to all the island groups except the Ionians and the Sporades.

The following table lists all the destinations that can be reached by ferry. The information is for the high season – from mid-June to September.

For the latest departure information, pick up a weekly ferry schedule from the tourist office in Athens. See the Getting There & Away sections for each island for specific details, and the Getting Around chapter for general information about ferry travel.

The departure points for ferry destinations are shown on the map of Piraeus. Note that there are two departure points for Crete. Ferries for Iraklio leave from the western end of Akti Kondyli, but ferries for other ports in Crete occasionally dock there as well. The other departure point for Crete is on Akti Miaouli it's a long way between the two, so check where to find your boat when you buy your ticket.

FERRIES FROM PIRAEUS
CRETE

Destination	Duration	Fare	Frequency
Agios Nikolaos	12hr	€25.30	3 weekly
Hania	10hr	€23.80	2 daily
Iraklio	10hr	€27.50	2 daily
Kissamou	12hr	€17.10	2 weekly
Rethymno	10-12hr	€23.10	daily
Sitia	14½hr	€25.30	3 weekly

CYCLADES

Destination	Duration	Fare	Frequency
Amorgos	10hr	€17.20	2 daily
Anafi	11hr	€22.80	3 weekly
Folegandros	6-9hr	€17	4 weekly
Ios	7½hr	€18	4 daily
Kimolos	6hr	€15.30	2 weekly
Kythnos	2½hr	€10.50	2 daily
Milos	7hr	€16.90	2 daily
Mykonos	5½hr	€17.50	3 daily
Naxos	6hr	€20	6 daily
Paros	5hr	€17.30	6 daily
Santorini	9hr	€20.24	daily
Serifos	4½hr	€13.20	daily
Sifnos	5½hr	€14.80	daily
Sikinos	8-10hr	€19.90	daily
Syros	4hr	€15	3 daily
Tinos	4½hr	€16.10	2 daily

DODECANESE

Destination	Duration	Fare	Frequency
Astypalea	12hr	€23.20	3 weekly
Halki	22hr	€31.80	2 weekly
Kalymnos	10-13hr	€24	daily
Karpathos	18½hr	€27	4 weekly
Kasos	17hr	€26.70	4 weekly
Kos	12-15hr	€25.80	2 daily
Leros	11hr	€21.80	daily
Lipsi	16hr	€24.90	weekly
Nisyros	13-15hr	€25.60	2 weekly
Patmos	9½hr	€21	daily
Rhodes	15-18hr	€30.70	2 daily
Symi	15-17hr	€30.10	2 weekly
Tilos	15hr	€25.70	2 weekly

NORTHEASTERN AEGEAN ISLANDS

Destination	Duration	Fare	Frequency
Chios	8hr	€19.50	daily
Fourni	10hr	€18	3 weekly
Ikaria	9hr	€17.60	daily
Lesvos	12hr	€24.20	daily
Limnos	13hr	€24	3 weekly
Samos	13hr	€22.80	2 daily

SARONIC GULF ISLANDS

Destination	Duration	Fare	Frequency
Aegina	1¼hr	€5	hourly
Hydra	3½hr	€8.10	2 daily
Poros	2½hr	€7.20	4 daily
Spetses	4½hr	€11.20	daily

HYDROFOIL & CATAMARAN

Hellas Flying Dolphins has hydrofoil and high-speed catamaran services from Piraeus to the Saronic Gulf Islands and the Cyclades.

The information in the hydrofoil and catamarans timetable following is for the high season, from mid-June to September.

For more information about these services, see the Transport chapter and the Getting There & Away sections for each island throughout this book.

HYDROFOILS & CATAMARANS FROM PIRAEUS

CYCLADES

Destination	Duration	Fare	Frequency
Kythnos	1¾hr	€20.40	5 weekly
Milos	3¾hr	€33.20	6 weekly
Mykonos	3½hr	€34.40	3 daily
Naxos	3¼hr	€34.10	2 daily
Paros	3-5hr	€34.10	3 daily
Santorini	5¼hr	€39.70	daily
Serifos	2¼hr	€25.80	daily
Sifnos	2¾hr	€29	daily
Syros	2½hr	€29.40	2 daily
Tinos	3¾hr.	€31.60	daily

PELOPONNESE

Destination	Duration	Fare	Frequency
Ermioni	2hr	€18.40	3 daily
Porto Heli	2hr	€20	4 daily

SARONIC GULF ISLANDS

Destination	Duration	Fare	Frequency
Aegina	35min	€8.40	hourly
Hydra	1¼hr	€16	6 daily
Poros	1hr	€14.20	4 daily
Spetses	2hr	€22.20	4 daily

METRO

The metro is the fastest and easiest way of getting from the Great Harbour to central Athens (see Line 1 p81). The station is at the northern end of Akti Kalimassioti. Travellers should take extra care of valuables on the metro; the section between Piraeus and Monastiraki is notorious for pickpockets.

TRAIN

At the time of research, the former train station for the Peloponnese was undergoing refurbishment to become the Piraeus terminus of the new suburban rail network. Starting in May 2004, there will be regular trains from here to the new Athens Central Station at Arharnon.

RAFINA ΡΑΦΗΝΑ

pop 11,909

Rafina, on Attica's east coast, is Athens' main fishing port and second-most important port for passenger ferries. It is much smaller than Piraeus and less confusing – and fares are about 20% cheaper, but you have to spend an hour on the bus and €2 to get there.

The **port police** (☎ 2294 022 888) occupy a kiosk near the quay, which is lined with fish restaurants and ticket agents. The main square, Plateia Plastira, is at the top of the ramp leading to the port.

BUS

There are frequent buses from the Mavromateon terminal in Athens to Rafina (€2, one hour) between 5.45am and 10.30pm. The first bus leaves Rafina at 5.50am and the last at 10.15pm.

CATAMARAN

Blue Star Ferries and Hellas Flying Dolphins operate high-speed catamarans to the Cyclades.

Blue Star operates a daily 7.40am service to Tinos (€25.90, 1¾ hours), Mykonos (€29.30, 2¼ hours) and Paros (€29.70, three hours), and a 4pm service to Tinos and Mykonos. Hellas Flying Dolphins operates an 8am service to Tinos (€25.90, 1¾ hours) and Mykonos (€29.30, 2¼ hours), and a 4.30pm service to Tinos, Mykonos and Syros (€24.70, 2¾ hours). It then returns to Lavrio via Kythnos.

FERRY

Blue Star Ferries operates a daily service at 8am to Andros (€8.50, two hours), Tinos (€13, 3½ hours) and Mykonos (€14.70, 4½ hours). It also has a 7.15pm daily ferry to Andros. Hellas Ferries sails the same route daily at 7.45am and at 5.30pm every day except Sunday.

There are also five ferries daily to the port of Marmari on the island of Evia (€4.50, one hour).

THESSALONIKI
ΘΕΣΣΑΛΟΝΙΚΗ

pop 363,987

Thessaloniki (thess-ah-lo-*nee*-kih) is Greece's second-largest city. However, being second does not mean Thessaloniki lies in the shadow of, or tries to emulate, the capital. It is a sophisticated city with its own distinct character.

Thessaloniki sits at the top of the wide Thermaic Gulf. The oldest part of the city is the kastro, the old Turkish quarter, whose narrow streets huddle around a Byzantine fortress on the slopes of Mt Hortiatis.

Orientation

Thessaloniki is laid out on a grid system stretching back from Leof Nikis, which runs from the port in the west to the White Tower (Lefkos Pyrgos) in the east. The two main squares, both abutting the waterfront, are Plateia Eleftherias, which doubles as a local bus terminal, and Plateia Aristotelous.

The other principal streets of Mitropoleos, Tsimiski, Ermou and Egnatia run parallel to Leof Nikis. Egnatia is the city's main thoroughfare, running east from Plateia Dimokratias. Kastra, the old Turkish quarter, is north of Plateia Dimokratias.

Information
BOOKSHOPS

Malliaris Kaisia (☎ 2310 277 11; Aristotelous 9) Stocks English-language books, foreign-language newspapers and magazines as well as a reasonable selection of Lonely Planet titles and maps of Greece.

EMERGENCY

First-Aid Centre (☎ 2310 530 530; Navarhou Koundourioti 10)

Ippokration Hospital (☎ 2310 837 921; Papanastasiou 50) Two kilometres east of the city centre.

Tourist Police (☎ 2310 554 871; 5th floor, Dodekanisou 4; ⏰ 7.30am-11pm)

INTERNET ACCESS

Enterprise (☎ 10 211 722; Gounari 52; ⏰ 9am-3am)

MultiPlay (☎ 2310 968 289; Olymbou 124; ⏰ 9.30-3am)

LAUNDRY

Bianca Laundrette (Panagias Dexias 3; ⏰ 8am-8.30pm Tue, Thu & Fri, 8am-3pm Mon, Wed & Sat; €6 for a 6kg load)

MONEY

National Bank of Greece (Tsimiski 11) Opens at the weekend for currency exchange.

POST

Main Post Office (Aristotelous 26; ⏰ 7.30am-8pm Mon-Fri, 7.30am-2.15pm Sat, 9am-1.30pm Sun)

Port Post Office (Koundouriotou 6; ⏰ 7.30am-2pm)

TOURIST INFORMATION

EOT (☎ 2310 500 310; port passenger terminal; ⏰ 7.30am-3pm Mon-Fri, 8am-2pm Sat)

Sights

The **Archaeological Museum** (☎ 2310 830 538; Manoli Andronikou 6; adult/concession €4/2; ⏰ 8.30am-3pm Tue-Sun, 10.30am-5pm Mon) houses finds from prehistoric Thessaloniki, including a well-preserved **Petralona hoard** – a collection of early axes and chisels, and some exquisite filigree gold wreaths and jewellery from burial sites all over Macedonia.

The **Museum of Ancient Greek & Byzantine Instruments** (☎ 2310 555 263; Katouni 12-14; admission €4.40; ⏰ 9am-3pm & 5-10pm Tue-Sun) houses a superb collection of instruments from antiquity to the 19th century.

The imposing **Arch of Galerius**, at the eastern end of Egnatia, is the finest of the city's Roman monuments. It was erected in AD 303 to celebrate the emperor's victories over the Persians in 297. The nearby **Rotonda** was built as a mausoleum for Galerius, but never fulfilled this function; Constantine the Great transformed it into a church.

The 15th-century **white tower** (☎ 2310 267 832; Lefkos Pyrgos; admission free; ⏰ 8am-6pm Tue-Sun) is both the city's symbol and most prominent landmark. During the 18th century the tower was used as a prison for insubordinate janissaries. In 1826 they were massacred there and it became known as the 'bloody tower'. After independence it was whitewashed as a symbolic gesture to expunge its Turkish function. You can climb to the top of the tower via a wide circular stairway – the views from the top are very impressive and there is a small café at the top level.

The Turkish quarter of **Kastra**, with its narrow steep streets flanked by timber-framed houses and tiny, whitewashed dwellings with shutters, is all that is left of 19th-century Thessaloniki. The original ramparts of Kastra were built by Theodosius (379–475), but were rebuilt in the 14th century. From Kastra there are stunning views of modern Thessaloniki and the Thermaic Gulf.

Take bus No 22 or 23 from Plateia Eleftherias, or walk north along Agias Sofias, which becomes Vlatadon then Dimadou Vlatadou after Athinas, and turn right into Eptapyrgiou at the top.

Sleeping

Hotel Acropol (☎ 2310 536 170; fax 2310 528 492; Tandalidou 4; s/d €18/26) The Acropol is the best budget option. It's clean and quiet, and the rooms are basic but comfortable. There is a small courtyard for bicycle storage and luggage can also be stored for free.

Orestias Kastoria (☎ 2310 276 517; fax 2310 276 572; Agnostou Stratioti 14; s/d €35/40; 🏠) The Orestias Kastoria occupies a beautifully renovated neoclassical building a little away from the main hotel strip. While the hotel is nominally D-class, the comfortable rooms are bright and airy and come with TV and phone.

Hotel Alexandria (☎ 2310 536 185; fax 2310 536 154; Egnatia 18; s/d €40/45) This D-class hotel was renovated in 2003 and offers clean, tidy rooms with bathroom and TV. There's a rather impressive modern lift to hoist your heavy backpacks to the rooms.

Hotel Tourist (☎ 2310 270 501; fax 2310 226 865; Mitropoleos 21; s/d €53/67.50) The C-class Hotel Tourist has a spacious lounge with comfortable armchairs and a TV. Rooms are good enough, though the reception area is a little spartan and small.

Eating

Ta Nea Ilysia (☎ 2310 536 996; Leondos Sofou 17; mains €3-60) This is a clean and cheery place equally popular with travellers and locals, conveniently near the west-end budget-hotel strip with moderately priced *mayirefta* (ready-cooked meals) including filling mousakas and a range of olive oil–based dishes (*ladera*).

Ta Spata Psistaria (☎ 2310 277 412; Aristotelous 28; mains €4.50-6) At this no-nonsense old-style restaurant, you choose from the dishes on display – a simple meal of beans, feta cheese and half a litre of retsina is a good choice. Service is smart and business-like.

Myrsini (☎ 2310 228 300; Tsopela 2; mains €5-10) The only dedicated Cretan restaurant in town, patrons graze on dishes such as *dakos* (tomato and cheese on oil-softened rusks), small cabbage pies, or roasted goat, all washed down with Cretan firewater known as *raki* or *tsikoudia*.

Ouzeri Taverna 1901 (☎ 2310 553 141; Katouni 9; mains €4-6) This ever-popular ouzeri is housed in an old pink building in the Ladadika district. A couple of its specialities are prawns and baked pasta (*garidoyiouvetsi*) and the spicy aubergine dip.

Drinking

Kourdisto Gourouni (☎ 2310 274 672; Agias Sofias 310) There's an old-world feel about this neat pub-cum-restaurant with its wood-panelled baroque décor, and prominent bar and seven types of draught beer.

Dore Zythos (☎ 2310 279 010; Tsirogianni 7) Another classic hangout for revellers of all ages. Beers such as Fosters and Schneider Wheat beers and a range of wines are on offer, as well as good Mediterranean food.

Getting There & Away

AIR

Thessaloniki's **airport** (☎ 2310 473 212) is 16km southeast of the city. **Olympic Airways** (☎ 2310 368 666; Navarhou Koundourioti 1-3) and **Aegean Airlines** (☎ 2310 280 050; Venizelou 2) have offices in town.

Olympic Airways has seven flights daily to Athens (€45 to €94, 55 minutes); daily flights to Limnos (€56, 50 minutes); six flights a week to Mytilini (€74, one hour 50 minutes); and between two and four flights weekly to Corfu (€74, 55 minutes), Iraklio (€97, 1½ hours), Mykonos (€92, one hour), Hania (€104, 2½ hours), Chios (€77, 2¾ hours), Skyros (€57, 40 minutes) and Samos (€88, one hour 20 minutes).

Aegean Airlines has similar flights to Athens (€76), and with lesser frequency to Iraklio (€90), Mytilini (€81), Rhodes (€108) and Santorini (€105).

There is no Olympic Airways shuttle, but bus No 78 plies the airport route; it runs between the local bus station on Filippou and the airport – via the train station – every 30 minutes. A taxi to the airport costs around €8.50.

See the Transport chapter (p464) for details on international flights to and from Thessaloniki.

THESSALONIKI

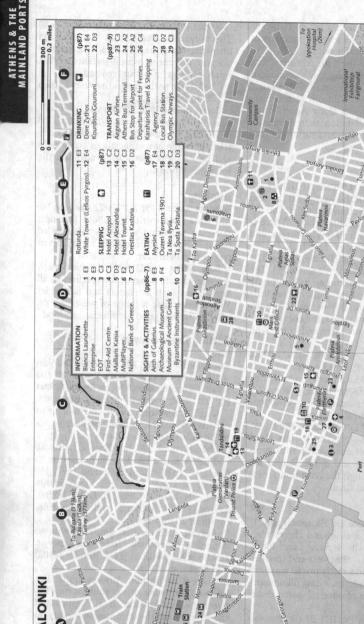

BUS

Thessaloniki's main **KTEL Macedonias bus station** (☎ 2310 595 408; Monastiriou 319), situated 3km west of the city centre, has departures to Athens (€29.40, six hours, 13 daily), Alexandroupolis (€20.70, six hours, eight daily) and Kavala (€9.70, 1½ hours, hourly). Athens buses also depart from a small terminal located opposite the train station. Local bus No 1 travels between the bus station and the train station every 10 minutes.

FERRY

Minoan Lines operates three ferries weekly to Iraklio on Crete (€40, 23 hours), via Mykonos (€33, 13½ hours) and Santorini (€35.50, 19 hours). These boats also call twice weekly at Tinos (€32.50, 12½ hours) and Paros (€33; 15 hours), and once weekly at Skiathos (€15, 5¾ hours) and Syros (€30.50, 12¼ hours).

There are a further three boats (offering weekly services) just to Skiathos in July and August, as well as a Sunday ferry to Chios (€30, 18 hours) via Limnos (€20, eight hours) and Lesvos (€30, 13 hours), and a weekly boat that goes to Rhodes (€48, 21 hours) via Samos and Kos throughout the year.

Ferry tickets are available from **Karaharisis Travel & Shipping Agency** (☎ 2310 524 544; fax 2310 532 289; Navarhou Koundourioti 8).

HYDROFOIL & CATAMARAN

In summer hydrofoils and a catamaran travel more or less daily to the Sporades islands of Skiathos (€29, 3¼ hours), Skopelos (€28, four hours) and Alonnisos (€29, 4½ hours), via Nea Moudania (€15, one hour) in Halkidiki. Tickets for these can also be purchased from **Karaharisis Travel & Shipping Agency** (☎ 2310 524 544; fax 2310 532 289; Navarhou Koundourioti 8).

TRAIN

There are four regular trains daily to Athens (€14, 7½ hours), three daily to Alexandroupolis (€9.70, eight hours) and Larisa with connections to Volos (€6.80, 4½ hours).

There are seven additional express intercity services to Athens (€27.60, six hours) and two to Alexandroupolis (€16.20, 5½ hours).

GYTHIO ΓΥΘΕΙΟ

pop 4489

Gythio (*yee-thih-o*), once the port of ancient Sparta, is an attractive fishing port at the head of the Lakonian Gulf. It is a convenient port of departure for the island of Kythira, and for Kissamos on Crete.

Orientation

Gythio is not too hard to figure out. Most things of importance to travellers are along the seafront on Akti Vasileos Pavlou. The bus station is at the northeastern end, next to the small triangular park known as the Perivolaki.

Vasileos Georgiou runs inland past the main square, Plateia Panagiotou Venetzanaki, and becomes the road to Sparta.

The square at the southwestern end of Akti Vasileos Pavlou is Plateia Mavromihali, the hub of the old quarter of Marathonisi. The ferry quay is situated opposite this square.

Information

BOOKSHOPS

Hassanakos Bookstore (☎ 2733 022 064; Akti Vasileos Pavlou 39).

EMERGENCY

Tourist Police (☎ 2733 022 271; Akti Vasileos Pavlou)

INTERNET ACCESS

Café Mystery (☎ 2733 025 177; cnr Kapsali & Grigoraki; €4/hr; 9am-1pm) Despite being almost opposite the telephone exchange, poor lines are a problem.

POST

Post Office (cnr Ermou & Arhaia Theatrou; ⏰ 7.30am-2pm Mon-Fri)

TOURIST INFORMATION

EOT (☎ /fax 2733 024 484; Vasileos Georgiou 20; ⏰ 11am-3pm Mon-Fri) This is the information equivalent of Monty Python's famous 'cheese shop' sketch: it's remarkably information-free, even by EOT's lamentable standards.

Sights

Tranquil pine-shaded **Marathonisi Island** is linked to the mainland by a causeway at the southern edge of town. According to mythology, it was here that Paris (prince of Troy) and Helen (wife of Menelaus) consummated the affair that sparked the

Trojan Wars. The 18th-century Tzanetakis Grigorakis tower at the centre of the island houses a small **Museum of Mani History** (☎ 2733 024 484; admission €1.50; ⊗ 9am-7pm).

Sleeping

Xenia Karlaftis Rooms to Rent (☎ 2733 022 719; s/d/tr with bathroom €25/35/40) This is the best budget option in town, situated opposite Marathonisi Island on Kranais. There's a communal kitchen area upstairs with a fridge and small stove for making tea and coffee. Manager Voula (daughter of Xenia) is a wonderful host, full of suitably laconic observations about life. Voula also has studios for rent 3km west of town, beyond Mavrovouni.

Saga Pension (☎ 2733 023 220; fax 2733 024 370; s/d with bathroom €28/40; ⊗) Situated only 150m from the port on Kranais, the French-run Saga is good value with its comfortable rooms with TV.

Eating

Taverna Petakou (☎ 2733 022 889; mains €3-6) There are no frills at this taverna, located beside the stadium on Xanthaki. The day's menu is written down in an exercise book in Greek and normally includes a hearty fish soup (€6), which comes with a large chunk of bread on the side.

General Store & Wine Bar (☎ 2733 024 113; Vasileos Georgiou 67; mains €6.50-13; ⊗ 6-11pm Mon-Sat) For something completely different, head inland to this tiny restaurant run by the Greek-Canadian Thomakos family. You'll find an unusually varied and imaginative menu featuring dishes like orange and pumpkin soup (€3.50) and fillet of pork with black pepper and ouzo (€10.50).

Getting There & Away

BUS

The **KTEL Lakonias bus station** (☎ 2733 022 228; cnr Vasileos Georgios & Evrikleos) has buses north to Athens (€16.30, 4¼ hours, five daily) via Sparta (€2.90, one hour).

FERRY

ANEN Lines (www.anen.gr) operates five ferries weekly to Kissamos on Crete (€19.20, 6½ hours), travelling via Kythira (€8.90, 2½ hours) and Antikythira (€13.40, 4½ hours), from July to early September. The frequency drops to two services weekly

in winter. **Rozakis Travel** (☎ 2733 022 207; rosakigy@otenet.gr), on the waterfront near Plateia Mavromihali, sells tickets.

PORTS TO THE SARONIC GULF ISLANDS

There are connections to the Saronic Gulf Islands from several minor ports around the Argolis Peninsula of the eastern Peloponnese.

Porto Heli, at the southwestern tip of the peninsula, has at least four hydrofoils a day to Spetses (€4.50, 10 minutes) and Hydra (€9.80, 45 minutes), while nearby **Ermioni** has four a day to Hydra (€6.20, 20 minutes).

Galatas, on the east coast, is just a stone's throw from Poros. Small boats (€0.50, five minutes) shuttle back and forth constantly across the adjoining Poros Strait from 6am to 10pm.

All three ports can be reached by bus from **Nafplio**, the main town and transport hub of the Argolis. There are two buses daily from Nafplio to Galatas (€5.60, two hours), while travelling to Ermioni and Porto Heli involves changing buses at Kranidi (€5.30, two hours, three daily). There are hourly buses to Nafplio (€9, 2½ hours) from Terminal A in Athens.

PORTS TO THE CYCLADES

LAVRIO Λαύριο
pop 8558

Lavrio, an unattractive industrial town on the east coast of Attica 43km southeast of Athens, is the departure point for ferries to the islands of Kea and Kythnos, and for high-season catamaran services to the western Cyclades.

Getting There & Away
BUS

Buses run every 30 minutes to Lavrio from the Mavromateon terminal in Athens (€3.25, 1½ hours).

CATAMARAN

Hellas Flying Dolphins operates from Lavrio between mid-June to September.

There are departures daily except Wednesday to Kythnos (€14.50, 40 minutes), Syros (€25.50, 1¾ hours) and Mykonos (€30, 2¾ hours).

FERRY

Goutos Lines runs the F/B Myrina Express from Lavrio to Kea (€5.30, 1¼ hours) and Kythnos (€7.20, 3½ hours). From mid-June, there are ferries to Kea every morning and evening Monday to Friday, and up to six daily at weekends. Six ferries weekly continue to Kythnos. In winter there are ferries to Kea every day except Monday, returning every day except Wednesday. One service a week continues to Kythnos. The EOT in Athens gives out a timetable for this route. The ticket office at Lavrio is opposite the quay.

PORTS TO THE IONIANS

PATRA ΠΑΤΡΑ
pop 160,400

Patra (Patras in English), is Greece's third-largest city and the principal port for boats travelling to and from Italy and the Ionian Islands. It is named after King Patreas, who ruled the Peloponnese prefecture of Achaïa in about 1100 BC. Despite a history stretching back 3000 years, Patra is not wildly exciting. Few travellers stay around any longer than it takes to catch the next boat, bus or train.

The city was destroyed during the War of Independence and rebuilt on a modern grid plan of wide, arcaded streets, large squares and ornate neoclassical buildings. Many of these old buildings, such as the Apollon Theatre, were being restored at the time of research in preparation for the city's role as Europe's City of Culture for 2006.

Orientation

Patra's grid system means easy walking. The waterfront is known as Iroön Polytehniou at the northeastern end, Othonos Amalias in the middle and Akti Dimeon to the south. Customs is at the Iroön Polytehniou end, and the main bus and train stations are on Othonos Amalias. Most of the agencies selling ferry tickets are on Iroön Polytehniou and Othonos Amalias.

Information

BOOKSHOPS
News Stand (☎ 2610 273 092; Agios Andreou 77) A small selection of novels, as well as international news papers and magazines.
Road Editions (☎ 2610 279 938; Agiou Andreou 50) Stocks a large range of Lonely Planet guides, as well as maps and travel literature.

EMERGENCY
First-Aid Centre (☎ 2610 277 386; cnr Karolou & Agiou Dionysiou; ✆ 8am-8pm)
Port Police (☎ 2610 341 002)
Tourist Police (☎ 2610 695 191; ✆ 7am-9pm) Upstairs in the embarkation hall at the port;

INTERNET ACCESS
Netp@rk (☎ 2610 279 699; Gerokostopoulou 37; ✆ 10-2am)
Plazanet Internet Café Bar (☎ 2610 222 192; Gerokostopoulou 25; ✆ 10am-midnight)

LAUNDRY
Skafi Laundrette (Zaïmi 49, ✆ 9am-3pm Mon-Sat, 5-8.30pm Tue, Thu & Fri) Charges €7 to wash and dry a load.

LEFT LUGGAGE
Train Station (✆ 6am-11pm) Charges €3.20 per item per day, or €1.60 if you have a train ticket.

MONEY
National Bank of Greece (Plateia Trion Symahon, opp train station)

POST
Main Post Office (cnr Zaïmi & Mezonos; ✆ 7.30am-8pm Mon-Fri, 7.30am-2pm Sat, 9am-1.30pm Sun)

TOURIST OFFICES
EOT (☎ 2610 620 353; international arrivals terminal at port; ✆ 7am-8pm) This place is invariably closed despite the extended hours advertised.
Info Centre (☎ 2610 461 740; infopatras@hol.gr; Othonos Amalias 6; ✆ 8am-10pm) Friendly and well organised, with maps, hotels and brochures about local points of interest. It also has an attractive display of local wine, olive oil and other produce.

Sights

Kastro's wonderful old **fortress** (admission free; ✆ 8am-7pm Tue-Sun Apr-Oct, 8.30am-5pm Tue-Fri, 8.30am-3pm Sat-Sun Nov-Mar) stands on the site of the acropolis of ancient Patrai. The structure is of Frankish origin, remodelled many times over the centuries by the Byzantines,

Venetians and Turks. It was in use as a defensive position until WWII and remains in good condition.

Set in an attractive park, it is reached by climbing the steps at the end of Agiou Nikolaou.

Festivals & Events

Patra is noted for the exuberance with which its citizens celebrate the city's annual **carnival**. The carnival programme begins in mid-January, and features a host of minor events leading up to a wild weekend of costume parades, colourful floats and celebrations at the end of February or early March. The event draws big crowds, so hotel reservations are essential if you want to stay overnight. Contact the Greek National Tourist Organisation (p461) for dates and details.

Sleeping & Eating

Pension Nicos (☎ 2610 623 757; cnr Patreos & Agiou Andreou; d/tr €30/40, s/d/tr with bathroom €20/35/45) Nicos is easily the best budget choice in town. The sheets are clean, the water is hot and it's close to the waterfront.

Hotel Rannia (☎ 2610 220 114; fax 2610 220 537; Riga Fereou 53; s/d/tr with bathroom €40/55/60; 🖭) The Rannia is the best option after Nicos, although it has little to recommend it other than air-con and TV.

Hotel Byzantino (☎ 2610 243 000; info@byzantino -hotel.gr; www.byzantino-hotel.gr; Riga Fereou 106; s with

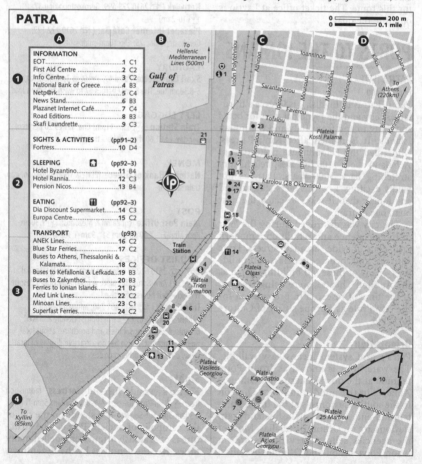

PATRA

bathroom €112, d with bathroom €140-156; 🔀 🖳)
The Byzantino occupies a graceful old neoclassical building that has been tastefully restored. Every room is different, but all offer the same facilities: TV, fax, Internet access, minibar and safety box. Prices include breakfast.

Europa Centre (☎ 2610 437 006; Othonos Amalias 10; mains €5.50-7; ⏰ 7am-midnight) This convenient caféteria-style place is close to the international ferry dock. It has taverna dishes, spaghetti and a good choice of vegetarian meals. It also serves a hearty breakfast (€7), and offers free luggage storage to customers.

Dia Discount Supermarket (Agiou Andreou 29) This supermarket is ideally located for travellers planning to buy a few provisions and keep moving.

Getting There & Away
BUS
The **KTEL Achaias bus station** (☎ 2610 623 888; Othonos Amalias) has buses to Athens (€12.90, three hours, half-hourly) via Corinth (€8.60, 1½ hours). It also has buses to Thessaloniki (€30.60, 9½ hours, three daily) and Kalamata (€14.30, four hours, two daily).

The **KTEL Kefallonia bus station** (☎ 2310 274 938; cnr Othonos Amalias & Gerokostopoulou) has five buses a day to Kyllini (€4.40, 1¼ hours), timed to meet ferries to Argostoli and Poros.

Buses to Zakynthos (€5.20 plus ferry, 3½ hours, five daily) leave from the **KTEL Zakynthos bus station** (☎ 2610 220 219; Othonos Amalias 58). They also travel via Kyllini.

FERRY
There are daily ferries to Kefallonia (€11.50, 2½ hours) and Ithaki (€11.70, 3¾ hours). Fares to Corfu (7 hours) range from €21 with Blue Star Ferries up to €25.50 with ANEK.

See p468 for services to Italy. Ferry offices include the following:

ANEK Lines (☎ 2610 226 053; Othonos Amalias 25) Ancona and Trieste via Corfu and Igoumenitsa.
Blue Star Ferries (☎ 2610 634 000; Othonos Amalias 12-14) Brindisi direct; Ancona and Venice via Igoumenitsa and Corfu.
Hellenic Mediterranean Lines (☎ 2610 452 521; cnr Iroön Polytehniou & Pente Pigadion) Brindisi via Kefallonia and Corfu.

Med Link Lines (☎ 2610 623 011; Giannatos Travel, Othonos Amalias 15) Located 500m north of port; Brindisi direct or via Kefallonia and Igoumenitsa.
Minoan (☎ 2610 455 622; cnr Norman 1 & Athinon) Ancona via Igoumenitsa; Venice via Igoumenitsa and Corfu.
Superfast Ferries (☎ 2610 622 500; Othonos Amalias 12) Ancona direct or via Igoumenitsa; Bari via Igoumenitsa.

TRAIN
If track work goes according to plan, from May 2004 catching a train to Athens will involve changing at Corinth. At the time of research there were at least eight trains daily from Patra to Corinth, five are slow trains (€3.55, 2½ hours) and three are Intercity (€7, two hours). All trains between Patra and Corinth stop at Diakofto.

IGOUMENITSA ΗΓΟΥΜΕΝΙΤΣΑ
pop 9104
Igoumenitsa (ih-goo-meh-*nit*-sah), opposite the island of Corfu, is the main port of northwest Greece. Few travellers hang around any longer than it takes to buy a ticket out. Ferries leave in the morning and evening, so there is little reason to stay overnight.

Orientation
Ferries for Italy and Corfu leave from three separate quays reasonably close to one another on the waterfront of Ethnikis Andistasis. Ferries to Ancona and Venice (in Italy) depart from the new port on the south side of town; those for Brindisi and Bari (in Italy) use the old port in front of the main shipping offices; and ferries for Corfu (Kerkyra) and Paxi depart from slightly north of the new port. A larger quay will be opened in 2004 and will be situated at the southern end of the harbour.

The bus station is situated on Kyprou, two blocks back from the waterfront.

Sleeping & Eating
Hotel Egnatia (☎ 2665 023 648; fax 2665 023 633, Eleftherias 2; s/d with bathroom €32/40; 🔀) The Hotel Egnatia is the place to head to if you need a bed for the night. All the rooms have TV.

Alekos (☎ 2665 023 708; Ethnikis Andistasis 84; mains €3.50-5.50) Popular with locals, Alekos is one of the better eating choices in town. It does an excellent mousaka.

O Salonikios (☎ 2665 026 695; Pargas 5; breakfast €5) For breakfast and excellent Greek coffee try this brilliant little place tucked away in the backstreets near the Corfu ferry terminal.

Getting There & Away

BUS

The **bus station** (☎ 2665 022 309; Kyprou 29) has departures to Athens (€28.45, eight hours, five daily), Preveza (€7.40, 2½ hours, two daily) and Thessaloniki (€27.70, eight hours, one daily).

FERRY

There are ferries heading to Corfu Town hourly between 5am and 10pm (€5.10, 1¾ hours). Ferries also travel to Lefkimmi in southern Corfu (€2.80, one hour, six daily) and to Paxi (€6.10, 1¾ hours, three weekly).

Most of the ferries to/from Italy also stop at Corfu.

HYDROFOIL

There is a weekly hydrofoil service to/from Corfu (€10.20, 35 minutes) and Paxi (€11.70, one hour) in summer. Contact **Milano Travel** (☎ 2665 023 565; milantvl@otenet.gr) for further details.

KYLLINI ΚΥΛΛΗΝΗ

The tiny port of Kyllini (kih-*lee*-nih), which sits about 78km southwest of Patra, warrants a mention only as the jumping-off point for ferries to Kefallonia and Zakynthos. Most people pass through Kyllini on buses from Patra that board the ferries that ply the Ionian.

GETTING THERE & AWAY

BUS

There are 10 buses daily to Kyllini (€4.40, 1¼ hours) from Patra, five from the KTEL Kefallonia bus station and five from the KTEL Zakynthos bus station.

FERRY

There are boats travelling to Zakynthos (€5.10, 1¼ hours, up to six daily), Poros (€6.50, 1½ hours, three daily) and Argostoli on Kefallonia (€10.50, 2½ hours, two daily).

PORTS TO KYTHIRA

Kythira is the odd island out. Dangling from the southeastern tip of the Peloponnese, it belongs to no other island group to the far-off Ionian Islands. The best access is from the ports of Gythio and Neapoli.

NEAPOLI ΝΕΑΠΟΛΗ

pop 2727

Neapoli (neh-*ah*-po-lih) lies close to the tip of the eastern finger of the Peloponnese. It's a fairly uninspiring town, in spite of its location on a huge horseshoe bay. Most travellers come here only to catch a ferry to the island of Kythira, clearly visible across the bay.

Sleeping & Eating

Hotel Aivali (☎ 2734 022 287; Akti Voion 164; s/d with bathroom €37/42; ✿) This small family hotel is ideally located right on the seafront close to the ferry dock for Kythira. All the rooms are equipped with TV and fridge. Like all the hotels in town, it's booked out during August.

Psarotaverna O Bananas (☎ 2734 022 464; Akti Voion 158; mains €4-7.50, fresh fish from €26/kg) This excellent taverna is the perfect place to indulge your seafood cravings. Ask to take a look at the day's catch, or check out the daily specials, such as the seafood risotto (€7), or the fish baked with wine and herbs (€6).

There are numerous ouzeria along the waterfront serving up the local speciality, grilled octopus (€2.70 with ouzo).

Getting There & Away

BUS

There are four buses daily from Neapoli to Sparta (€9.50, three hours), from where there are frequent buses to Athens.

FERRY

There are daily ferries travelling from Neapoli to Agia Pelagia on Kythira (€5.20, one hour). Tickets are sold at **Voiai ANE** (☎ 2734 023 980; fax 2734 023 981), signposted on the seafront 100m west of the Hotel Aivali. The frequency varies from one a day in mid-winter up to four a day in July/August.

PORTS TO THE SPORADES

AGIOS KONSTANTINOS
ΑΓΙΟΣ ΚΩΝΣΤΑΝΤΙΝΟΣ
pop 2574

Agios Konstantinos, 175km northwest of Athens, is the closest port serving the Sporades for travellers setting out from Athens.

SLEEPING & EATING

With judicious use of buses from Athens, you will not need to stay overnight.

Hotel Olga (☎ 2235 031 766; fax 2235 033 266; Eivoilou 6; s/d €22/31.50; 🔀) The Olga is a good option if you get stuck. Like most of the town's hotels, it's right on the seafront.

Taverna O Stephanos (☎ 2235 032 110; mains €3-6.50) Near the central square, Stephanos serves up tasty grills, generous salads and traditional oven-dishes.

Getting There & Away
BUS

There are hourly buses (from 6.15am) between Agios Konstantinos and Athens Terminal B bus station (€10.90, 2½ hours).

FERRY

Two fast ferries make twice-daily runs from Agios Konstantinos to Skiathos (€20.80, 2½ hours), Skopelos (€28.40, 3½ hours) and Alonnisos (€28.40, 4 hours).

HYDROFOIL

There are three hydrofoils daily to Skiathos (€20.80, 1½ hours) and Skopelos Town (€28.40, 2½ hours), and two daily to Glossa (Skopelos; €23.70, two hours) and Alonnisos (€28.40, 2¾ hours). **Bilalis Travel Agency** (☎ 2235 031 614), near the quay, sells tickets.

VOLOS ΒΟΛΟΣ
pop 122,458

Volos is a bustling city on the northern shores of the Pagasitic Gulf, and the main port for ferry and hydrofoil services to the Sporades.

According to mythology, Volos was ancient Iolkos, from where Jason and the Argonauts set sail on their quest for the Golden Fleece.

Orientation

Volos is laid out on an easy grid system stretching inland parallel to the waterfront (called Argonafton), which is where most things of importance to travellers are to be found. The main square, Plateia Riga Fereou, is at the northwestern end of Argonafton.

Information

Magic Net Café (☎ 2421 020 992; Iasonos 41; 🕑 9am-2am) Volos' largest Internet café.
National Bank of Greece (Argonafton)
Post Office (cnr Dimitriados & Agios Nikolaou)
Tourist Police (☎ 2421 039 065; 28 Oktovriou 179)
Volos Association of Hotels (☎ 2421 020 273; www.travel-pelion.gr; Sekeri & Zachou; 🕑 9am-5pm Mon-Fri) Gives out town maps, bus and ferry schedules as well as information about hotels.

Sleeping & Eating

Hotel Jason (☎ 2421 026 075; fax 2421 026 975; Pavlo Mela 1 at Argonafton; s/d €25/35, d with bathroom €40; 🔀) You won't miss the ferry to the Sporades if you stay at this clean and roomy budget option located just opposite the ferry quay.

Hotel Philippos (☎ 2421 037 607; fax 2421 039 550; info@philoppos.gr; Solonos 9; s/d €45/65; 🔀) The well-managed Philippos has bright, modern rooms with satellite TV, along with a spacious bar where breakfast and drinks are served.

O Haliabalias (☎ 2421 020 234; Orpheos 8; mains €6-10) This charming taverna located on a pedestrian street offers well-prepared traditional Greek dishes. Rabbit with fresh tomatoes and carrots, pork with white wine and lemon, and chicken stuffed with cheese and ham are all highly recommended, and the organic red wine is excellent. Note that Orpheos is also called Kontaratou.

Apostolis Restaurant (☎ 2421 026 973; Argonafton 15; mains €3-5) You can grab a quick lunch at this traditional waterfront eatery opposite the ferry quay; they'll pack it for takeaway if you're in a hurry to catch a ferry.

Getting There & Away
BUS

There are 10 buses daily to Athens (€18.60, five hours) and seven to Thessaloniki (€12.50, three hours).

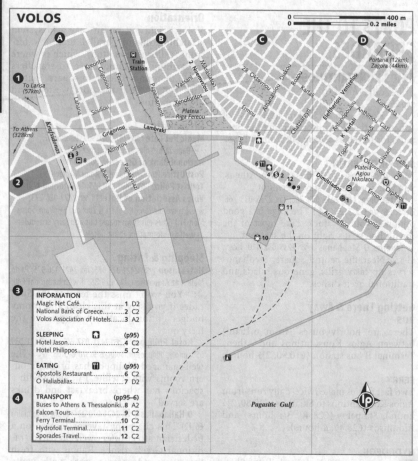

VOLOS

0 — 400 m
0 — 0.2 miles

INFORMATION
Magic Net Café....................... 1 D2
National Bank of Greece............ 2 C2
Volos Association of Hotels........ 3 A2

SLEEPING (p95)
Hotel Jason............................... 4 C2
Hotel Philippos......................... 5 C2

EATING (p95)
Apostolis Restaurant................. 6 C2
O Haliabalias............................ 7 D2

TRANSPORT (pp95–6)
Buses to Athens & Thessaloniki.. 8 A2
Falcon Tours............................. 9 C2
Ferry Terminal.......................... 10 C2
Hydrofoil Terminal.................... 11 C2
Sporades Travel......................... 12 C2

Pagasitic Gulf

FERRY

There are two ferries daily to Skiathos (€11.50, 2½ hours), Glossa (Skopelos; €9.70, 3½ hours), Skopelos Town (€15.10, four hours) and Alonnisos (€15.70, four hours). You can buy tickets from **Sporades Travel** (☎ /fax 2421 035 846; Argonafton 33).

HYDROFOIL

There are four hydrofoils travelling daily to Skiathos (€19.80, 1¼ hours) and to Skopelos Town (€25.20, 2¼ hours), and three travelling to Glossa (Skopelos; €19.10; 1¾ hours) and Alonnisos (€26.60, 2½ hours). Tickets are available from **Falcon Tours** (☎ 2421 021 626, 2421 033 586; ☎ /fax 2421 025 688; Argonafton).

TRAIN

There is one intercity train daily to Athens (€18), and one to Thessaloniki (€14.40).

PORTS TO THE NORTH-EASTERN AEGEAN

KAVALA ΚΑΒΑΛΑ
pop 60,802

Kavala, 163km east of Thessaloniki, is one of the nicest of Greece's large cities, spilling gently down the foothills of Mt Symvolon to a large harbour. The old quarter of Panagia nestles under a big Byzantine fortress.

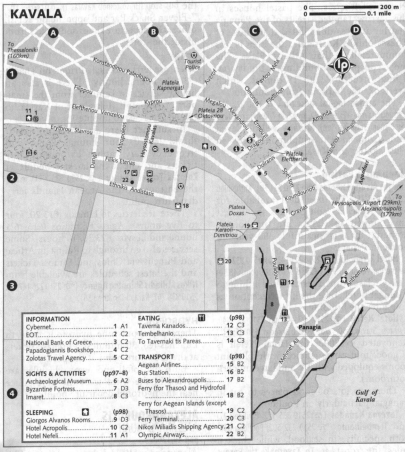

KAVALA

0 — 200 m
0 — 0.1 mile

It is the main port for the island of Thasos, and also has connections to the Northeastern Aegean and the Dodecanese.

Orientation

Kavala's focal point is Plateia Eleftherias. The two main thoroughfares, Eleftheriou Venizelou and Erythrou Stavrou, run west from here parallel with the waterfront Ethnikis Andistasis. The old quarter of Panagia occupies a promontory to the southeast of Plateia Eleftherias reached by a steep signposted access road at the east side of the harbour.

Information

Cybernet (☎ 2510 230 102; Erythrou Stavrou 64; ⏱ 6-4am)

EOT (☎ 2510 222 425; Plateia Eleftherias; ⏱ 8am-2pm Mon-Fri) Staff can provide a map of the town and transport information.

National Bank of Greece (cnr Megalou Alexandrou & Dragoumi) Exchange machine and ATM.

Papadogiannis Bookshop (Omonias 46) Stocks a wide range of international newspapers and magazines.

Post Office (cnr Hrysostomou Kavalas & Erythrou Stavrou)

Tourist Police (☎ 2510 222 905; Omonias 119) In the same building as the regular police.

Sights

If you've got time to spare, spend it exploring the streets of **Panagia**, the old Turkish quarter surrounding the massive Byzantine fortress on the promontory south of

Plateia Eleftherias. The pastel houses in the narrow, tangled streets of the Panagia quarter are less dilapidated than those of Thessaloniki's Kastra and the area is less commercialised than Athens' Plaka. The most conspicuous building is the **Imaret**, a huge structure with 18 domes, which overlooks the harbour from Poulidou.

The **archaeological museum** (☎ 2510 222 335; Erythrou Stavrou 17; adult €2, free Sun & public holidays; ⊗ 8.30am-3pm Tue-Sun) houses well-displayed finds from ancient Amphipolis, between Thessaloniki and Kavala.

Sleeping & Eating

Giorgos Alvanos Rooms (☎ 2510 221 781; Anthemiou 35; s/d €18/25) The best deal available for budget travellers and perhaps the cosiest environment in Kavala are the homely domatia in this beautiful 300-year-old house in Panagia.

Hotel Acropolis (☎ 2510 223 543; fax 2510 832 291; Eleftheriou Venizelou 29; s €29, d with bathroom €48.50) This C-class property is the closest thing to a budget hotel. Take the lift to reception as you enter the building.

Hotel Nefeli (☎ 2510 227 441; fax 2510 227 440; Erythrou Stavrou 50; s/d with bathroom €50/65; ⊠) Renovated in 2002, the Hotel Nefeli is a good mid-range choice with pleasant rooms equipped with TV and large modern bathrooms.

There are lots of good places to eat in Panagia, particularly on Poulidou.

Taverna Kanados (☎ 2510 835 172; Poulidou 27) and **Tembelhanio** (☎ 2510 232 502; Poulidou 33b) both specialise in seafood, while chicken rules the roost at **To Tavernaki tis Pareas** (☎ 2510 226 535; Poulidou 25).

Getting There & Away

AIR

Olympic Airways (☎ 2510 223 622; Ethnikis Andistasis 8) and Aegean Airlines offers three flights a day to Athens from Hrysoupolis airport, 29km east of town. A taxi to the airport will cost around €17.

BUS

The **bus station** (☎ 2510 223 593) has departures to Athens (€37.60, 9½ hours, three daily), Keramoti (€3, one hour, hourly) and Thessaloniki (€9.70, two hours, hourly).

Buses for Alexandroupolis (€10.35, two hours, seven daily) depart from outside the **bus stop** (Hrysostomou Kavalas 1), outside the 7-Eleven Snack Bar and opposite the KTEL office. Get departure times and tickets from inside the store.

FERRY

There are ferries to Skala Prinou on Thasos (€3, 1¼ hours, hourly). There is also an hourly service in summer from the small port of Keramoti, 46km east of Kavala, to Limenas (€1.50, 40 minutes).

In summer there are ferries to Samothraki (€9.70, four hours). Times and frequency vary month by month. Buy tickets and check the latest schedule at **Zolotas Travel Agency** (☎ 2510 835 671) near the entrance to the Aegean Islands ferry departure point.

There are ferries to Limnos (€13.20, four to five hours), Agios Efstratios (€13, 6¾ hours) and Lesvos (€23.30, 10 hours). Some services also go through to Rafina (in Attica) and Piraeus via Chios and Samos. Tickets and the latest schedules are available from **Nikos Miliadis Shipping Agency** (☎ 2510 226 147; fax 2510 838 767; Karaoli-Dimitriou 36).

HYDROFOIL

There are about nine hydrofoils daily to Limenas (€8, 30 minutes). Purchase tickets at the departure point at the port.

Both hydrofoil and ferry schedules are posted in the window of the port police near the hydrofoil departure point.

ALEXANDROUPOLIS

ΑΛΕΞΑΝΔΡΟΥΠΟΛΗ

pop 49,176

Alexandroupolis (ah-lex-an-*droo*-po-lih), the capital of the prefecture of Evros, is a modern and friendly town with a lively student atmosphere supplemented by a considerable population of young soldiers. Most travellers come here simply in transit heading east to Turkey, or to catch ferries to Samothraki or to the Dodecanese Islands. The maritime ambience of this town, and its year-round liveliness, make it a pleasant stopover. The town was named Alexandroupolis (Alexander's City) in honour of Greece's King Alexander and has been part of the Greek state since 1920. Sights as such are fairly minimal, except for its prominent operating 19th-century lighthouse parked conspicuously on the main promenade, along which crowds flock on warm summer evenings, to stroll and relax in the many cafés and restaurants that stretch westwards from the port.

Orientation

The town is laid out roughly on a grid system, with the main streets running east–west, parallel with the waterfront, where the lively evening *volta* (promenade) takes place. Karaoli Dimitriou is at the eastern end of the waterfront, with Megalou Alexandrou at the western end.

The two main squares are Plateia Eleftherias and Plateia Polytehniou, both just one block north of Karaoli Dimitriou.

The train station is on the waterfront just south of Plateia Eleftherias and east of the port where boats leave for Samothraki and other ports south. The bus station is at Eleftheriou Venizelou 36, five blocks inland. The local bus terminal is on Plateia Eleftherias, just outside the train station.

Information

Bank of Piraeus & Eurobank (Leof Dimokratias) Both have ATMs, as do other banks along the same street.

Kendro Typou (Leof Dimokratias) Foreign newspapers and magazines available here.

La Strada (☎ 2551 033 639; Nikiforou Foka 7; ☻ 9-3am) Internet access, €3/hr.

Municipal Tourist Information office (Camping Alexandroupolis; ☎ /fax 2551 028 735; Leof Makris) Handles all official tourist information.

Post Office (cnr Nikiforou Foka & Megalou Alexandrou)

Port Police (☎ 2551 226 468)

Public Toilets (admission €0.50) Near the harbour entrance.

Tourist Police (☎ 2551 037 424; Karaïskaki 6)

Sights

The **Ethnological Museum of Thrace** (☎ 2551 036 663; www.emthrace.com; 14th Maiou 63; adult €3; ☻ 10am-2pm & 6-9pm Tue-Sat) houses a superb collection of traditional artefacts and tools.

The excellent **Ecclesiastical Art Museum of Alexandroupolis** (☎ 2551 026 359; Plateia Agiou Nikolaou; free; ☻ 9am-2pm Tue-Fri, 10am-1pm Sat) is one of the best in the country. It has a priceless collection of icons and ecclesiastical ornaments brought to Greek Thrace by refugees from Asia Minor. The museum is in the grounds of the Agios Nikolaos Cathedral.

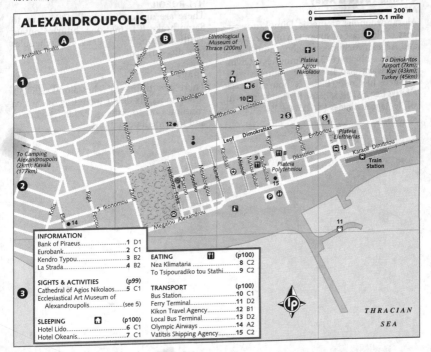

ALEXANDROUPOLIS

INFORMATION	
Bank of Piraeus	1 D1
Eurobank	2 C1
Kendro Typou	3 B2
La Strada	4 B2

SIGHTS & ACTIVITIES	(p99)
Cathedral of Agios Nikolaos	5 C1
Ecclesiastical Art Museum of Alexandroupolis	(see 5)

SLEEPING	(p100)
Hotel Lido	6 C1
Hotel Okeanis	7 C1

EATING	(p100)
Nea Klimataria	8 C2
To Tsipouradiko tou Stathi	9 C2

TRANSPORT	(p100)
Bus Station	10 C2
Ferry Terminal	11 D2
Kikon Travel Agency	12 B1
Local Bus Terminal	13 D2
Olympic Airways	14 A2
Vatitsis Shipping Agency	15 C2

THRACIAN SEA

Sleeping & Eating

Camping Alexandroupolis (☎ /fax 2551 028 735; Leof Makris; site per adult/tent €3.60/2.80) This spacious but rather characterless camping ground is on the beach 2km west of town. It's a clean, well-run site with good facilities. Take local bus No 7 from Plateia Eleftherias to reach the site.

Hotel Lido (☎ 2551 028 808; fax 2551 025 156; Paleologou 15; s/d €27/35, with bathroom €35/43) The Lido is a good budget choice.

Hotel Okeanis (☎ 2551 028 830; okeanis@otenet.gr; Paleologou 20; s/d €40/50; ✖) Almost opposite the Lido, this is a step up in comfort and style. Rooms have TV and telephone.

Nea Klimataria (☎ 2551 026 288; Plateia Polytehniou; mains €3.5-5) This is the place to head for hearty, home-cooked fare. Choose from the dishes on display. Draft wine is available.

To Tsipouradiko tou Stathi (☎ 2551 080 547; Markou Botsari 6; mezedes €3-5) This cozy place is a favourite with locals, serving mainly fish-based mezedes. Fried rice with mussels washed down with draft Cretan retsina makes for a satisfying meal.

Getting There & Away

AIR

Alexandroupolis' domestic Dimokritos airport is 7km east of town. Olympic Airways and Aegean Airlines offer about four flights a day to Athens (€75, 55 minutes). Olympic Airways also has three flights a week to Siteia in Crete (€78, 1¾ hours). **Olympic Airways** (☎ 2551 026 361; Ellis 6 & Koletti) is in town, while **Aegean Airlines** (☎ 2551 089 150) is at the airport.

A **taxi** (☎ 2551 028 358) to the airport costs about €5.

BUS

The **bus station** (☎ 2551 026 479; Eleftheriou Venizelou) has buses to Athens (€43.15, 12 hours, one daily) and Thessaloniki (€19.75, six hours, six daily) via Xanthi and Kavala. Contact **Kikon Travel Agency** (☎ 2551 025 455; Eleftheriou Venizelou) for tickets and reservations.

FERRY

There are up to three boats daily to Samothraki (€7.80, two hours) in summer, dropping back to one daily in winter. Contact **Vatitsis Shipping Agency** (☎ 2551 026 721; saos@orfeasnet.gr; Kyprou 5) for timetables and tickets. Some services continue to Limnos, Agios Evstratios and Psara.

There is also a Sunday G&A ferry to Rhodes (€38.85, 18 hours) via Limnos (€14.10, five hours) and Lesvos (€19.60, 11½ hours). See **Kikon Travel Agency** (☎ 2551 025 455; Eleftheriou Venizelou) for tickets and reservations.

HYDROFOIL

There are up to three hydrofoils daily to Samothraki (€15.60; one hour). Contact Vatitisis Shipping Agency for schedules (see Bus earlier).

TRAIN

There are trains to Thessaloniki (€9.50, seven hours, six daily), including one which continues on to Athens (€23.80, 14 hours) and intermediate stations.

Saronic Gulf Islands
Νησιά του Σαρωνικού

SARONIC GULF ISLANDS

The five Saronic Gulf Islands are the closest group to Athens. The closest, Salamis, is little more than a suburb of the sprawling capital. Aegina is also close enough to Athens for people to commute to work. Along with Poros, the next island south, it is a popular package-holiday destination. Hydra, once famous as the rendezvous of artists, writers and beautiful people, manages to retain an air of superiority and grandeur. Spetses, the most southerly island in the group, is a favourite with British holiday-makers.

Spetses has the best beaches, but these islands are not the place to be if you want long stretches of golden sand. And, with the exception of the Temple of Aphaia on Aegina, the islands have no significant archaeological remains.

Nevertheless, the islands are a popular escape for Athenians. Accommodation can be impossible to find between mid-June and mid-September, and weekends are busy all year round. If you plan to go at these times, it's a good idea to reserve a room in advance.

The islands have a reputation for high prices, which is a bit misleading. What is true is that there are very few places for budget travellers to stay – no camping grounds and only a couple of cheap hotels. There is plenty of good accommodation available if you are happy to pay €60 or more for a double and midweek visitors can get some good deals. Food is no more expensive than anywhere else in Greece.

The Saronic Gulf is named after the mythical King Saron of Argos, a keen hunter who drowned while pursuing a deer that had swum into the gulf to escape.

SARONIC GULF ISLANDS

HIGHLIGHTS

- **Wining & Dining**
  Ouzo and grilled octopus in Aegina Town (p105)

- **Ancient Wonder**
  The magnificent Temple of Aphaia on Aegina (p106)

- **Adrenaline Rush**
  Diving in the waters around Hydra (p112)

- **Living in Style**
  Staying in Hydra (p112) and Spetses' (p116) gracious old stone mansions

- **Naval Tradition**
  Check out the fine collection of ships' figureheads at the museum on Spetses (p115)

SARONIC GULF ISLANDS

(map shows:) Megara, Salamis, Piraeus, Salamis, Diaporioi, Saronic Gulf, Ypsili, Souvala, Agia Marina, Kira, Aegina Town, Aegina, To Corinth (20km), Angistri, Moni, Gulf of Epidavros, To Nafplio (25km), Epidavros, Methana, Poros Town, Poros, Cape Spathi, Argolic Gulf, PELOPONNESE, Ermioni, Gulf of Hydra, Cape Zourvas, To Leonidio (25km), Kranidi, Dokos, Monemvasia (82km), Porto Heli, Hydra Town, Kosta, Hydra, Spetses, Spetses Town, Trikeri, Spetsopoula, MIRTOÖN SEA

`0 —— 10 km`
`0 —— 6 miles`

Getting There & Away

FERRY
See the table for ferries departing Piraeus' Great Harbour.

FERRIES FROM PIRAEUS' GREAT HARBOUR

Destination	Time	€	Frequency
Aegina	1¼hr	€5	hourly
Hydra	3½hr	€8.10	2 daily
Poros	2½hr	€7.20	4 daily
Spetses	4½hr	€11.20	daily

HYDROFOIL & CATAMARAN

Hellas Flying Dolphins (☎ 2104 199 100; www .dolphins.gr) operates a busy schedule to the islands and the nearby Peloponnesian ports with its Flying Dolphin hydrofoils and Flying Cat catamarans; see the destination sections for full details. **Saronic Dolphins** (☎ 2104 224 777) is a company that operates less frequently on the very same routes, but offers good discounts for all advance bookings that are made. All services depart from the Great Harbour at Piraeus in Athens.

ORGANISED TOURS

The cruise ships *Aegean Glory* and *King Saron* offer daily cruises from Piraeus to the islands of Aegina, Poros and Hydra.

The cruises leave Piraeus at 9am, returning at about 7pm. Passengers are given pass-outs and are allowed to spend approximately an hour on shore at each island – long enough to buy a souvenir and take the obligatory 'been there, done that' photo.

The official price is €65, including buffet lunch, but it's possible to pick up a heavily discounted ticket if you book through your hotel.

AEGINA ΑΙΓΙΝΑ

pop 13,552

Once upon a time, unassuming Aegina (*eh-yee-nah*) was a major player in the Hellenic world, thanks largely to its strategic position at the mouth of the Saronic Gulf. In time, it began to emerge as a commercial centre in about 1000 BC. By the 7th century BC, it was the premier maritime power in the region and went about amassing great wealth through its strong trade links with Egypt and Phoenicia. The silver 'turtle' coins minted on the island at this time are widely thought to be the first coins ever produced in Europe. Aegina's fleet made a major contribution to the Greek victory over the Persian fleet at the Battle of Salamis in 480 BC.

Athens, uneasy about Aegina's maritime prowess, attacked the island in 459 BC. Defeated, Aegina was forced to pull down its city walls and surrender its fleet. It did not recover.

The island's only other brief moment in the spotlight came during 1827–29, when it was declared the temporary capital of partly liberated Greece. The first coins of the modern Greek nation were minted here.

Aegina has since slipped into a more humble role as Greece's premier producer of pistachio nuts.

Aegina was named after the daughter of the river god, Asopus. According to ancient Greek mythology, Aegina was abducted by Zeus and taken to the island. Her son by Zeus, Aeacus, was the grandfather of Achilles of Trojan War fame.

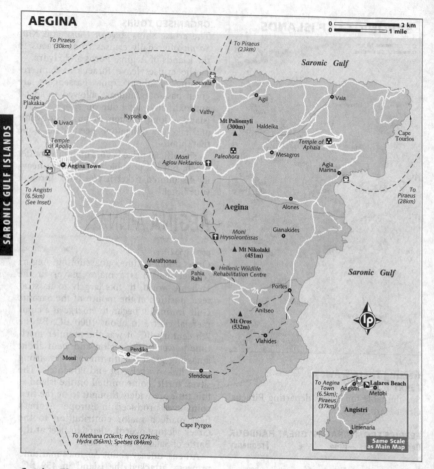

AEGINA

Saronic Gulf

Saronic Gulf

To Piraeus (30km)
To Piraeus (23km)
Souvala
Cape Plakakia
Livadi
Agii
Vala
Temple of Apollo
Kypseli
Vathy
Mt Paliomyli (300m)
Haldeika
Cape Tourlos
Aegina Town
Moni Agiou Nektariou
Paleohora
Mesagros
Temple of Aphaia
Agia Marina
To Angistri (6.5km) (See Inset)
To Piraeus (28km)
Aegina
Alones
Moni Hrysoleontissas
Gianakides
Marathonas
Mt Nikolaki (451m)
Pahia Rahi
Hellenic Wildlife Rehabilitation Centre
Portes
Anitseo
Mt Oros (532m)
Vlahides
Moni
Perdika
Sfendouri
Cape Pyrgos
To Methana (20km); Poros (27km); Hydra (56km); Spetses (84km)

To Aegina Town (6.5km); Piraeus (37km)
Angistri
Lalares Beach
Metobi
Angistri
Limenaria
Same Scale as Main Map

Getting There & Away
FERRY
In summer there are at least 10 ferries daily from Aegina Town to Piraeus (€5, 1½ hours), and at least four boats daily to Poros (€3.85, one hour) via Methana (€3.25, 40 minutes), two daily to Hydra (€4.70, two hours) and one to Spetses (€7.35, three hours).

The ferry companies have ticket offices at the quay, where you'll find a full list of the day's sailings. There are also services to Piraeus from Agia Marina (€4, 1½ hours) and Souvala (€3.60, 1¼ hours).

HYDROFOIL & CATAMARAN
Hellas Flying Dolphins (☎ 2297024456; www.dolphins .gr) operates almost hourly from 7am to

8pm between Aegina Town and the Great Harbour at Piraeus (€8.90, 35 minutes), but there are no services south to Poros, Hydra or Spetses. Tickets are sold at the quay in Aegina Town.

Getting Around
There are frequent buses running from Aegina Town to Agia Marina (€1.40, 30 minutes), via Paleohora and the Temple of Aphaia. Other buses go to Perdika (€0.80, 15 minutes) and Souvala (€1.10, 20 minutes). Departure times are displayed outside the ticket office on Plateia Ethnegersias.

There are numerous places in Aegina to hire motorcycles. Advertised prices start from around €15 per day for a 50cc machine.

AEGINA TOWN

pop 7410

Aegina Town, on the west coast, is the island's capital and main port. The town is a charming and bustling, if slightly ramshackle, place; its harbour is lined with colourful caïques (little boats). Some crumbling neoclassical buildings survive from its glory days as the Greek capital.

Orientation

The ferry dock and small quay used by hydrofoils are on the western edge of town. A left turn at the end of the quay leads to Plateia Ethnegersias, home of the bus terminal and post office. The town beach is 200m further along. A right turn at the end of the quay leads to the main harbour.

Information

Aegina doesn't have an official tourist office. The 'tourist offices' you'll see advertised on the waterfront are booking agencies, which will do no more than add a substantial commission fee to the price of whatever service you care to nominate.

Credit Bank About 150m beyond the National Bank of Greece, around the harbour.

Kalezis Bookshop (☎ 2297 025 956) On the waterfront. Has foreign newspapers and books.

National Bank of Greece On the waterfront just past Aiakou.

Nesant Internet Café (☎ 2297 024 053; Afeas 13; ☯ 10am-2am)

Post office (Plateia Ethnegersias; ☯ 7.30am-2pm Mon-Fri)

Port Police (☎ 2297 022 328) Next to the hydrofoil ticket office at the entrance to the hydrofoil quay.

Tourist Police (Leonardou Lada; ☎ 2297 027 777) Opposite the hydrofoil quay.

Sights & Activities

'Temple' is a bit of a misnomer for the one Doric column standing at the **Temple of Apollo** (☎ 2297 022 637; adult/concession €2/1; ☯ 8.30am-3pm Tue-Sun). The column is all that's left of the 5th-century BC temple, which once stood on the Hill of Koloni. The hill was the site of the ancient acropolis, and there are remains of a Helladic (early) settlement. There is a museum on the far side of the town beach.

Aegina's Water Park (☎ 2297 022 540; adult/child under 10 €3/free; ☯ 10am-8pm May-Oct), on the coast 1.5km south of Aegina Town, is a big hit with kids. The park charges from €4 for five rides on the slides to €10 for all day.

Sleeping

Aegina Town doesn't have a huge choice of accommodation.

Hotel Plaza (☎ 2297 025 600; plazainaegina@yahoo.co.uk; s/d with bathroom €20/25, d with seaview €30) The Plaza, on the waterfront 100m north of Plateia Ethnegersias, is a long-standing favourite with travellers. It has some good rooms overlooking the sea.

Xenon Pavlou Guest House (☎ 2297 022 795; Aiginitou 21; s/d/tr with bathroom €30/47/50) The Xenon Pavlou is a small family-run guesthouse tucked away behind the Church of Panagytsa on the southeastern side of the harbour.

Hotel Brown (☎ 2297 022 271; brownhotel@aig.forth net.gr; s/d/tr with bathroom €55/75/93; ☒) This fine old hotel has finally reopened after closing several years ago for renovations and extensions. It's named after the owner, Giorgos Brown, a local with an English grandfather. It's on the seafront south of the Church of Panagytsa.

Eginitiko Arhontiko (☎ 2297 024 968; fotis voulgarakis@aig.forthnet.gr; cnr Thomaïdou & Agios Nikoloau; s/d/tr with bathroom €50/60/70, ste €120) This 19th-century sandstone *arhontiko* (mansion once belonging to an *arhon*, a leading town citizen) has the most interesting rooms in town, particularly the ornate two-room suite.

There are several **domatia** (s/d €25/35), or cheap rooms, at the top of Leonardou Lada.

Eating

The harbour front is lined with countless cafés and restaurants – good for relaxing and soaking up the atmosphere, but not particularly good value.

Locals prefer to head for the cluster of lively ouzeria and restaurants around the fish markets at the eastern side of the harbour.

Mezedopoleio To Steki (☎ 2297 023 910; Pan Irioti 45; seafood mezedes €4-8) This tiny place, tucked away behind the fish markets, must be the most popular restaurant in town. It's always packed with people tucking into the local specialities, barbecued octopus (€4), grilled sardines (€4) or other mezedes, over a glass or two of ouzo.

Taverna I Synantasis (☎ 2297 024 309; Afeas 40; mains €5-6.50) This place comes to life on Friday and Saturday nights when there's live music from 10pm.

Ouzomezedopoleio Ippokampos (☎ 2297 026 504; Faneromenis 9; mezedes €2.50-10) This tiny, old-fashioned place is around the corner from the Hotel Brown, opposite the primary school on the street leading up to the old jail. It serves only mezedes, brought round on a large tray for the customer to choose.

Kritikos Supermarket (☎ 2297 027 772; Pan Irioti 53) Self-caterers will find most things at this supermarket behind the fish markets.

Delicious local pistachio nuts are on sale everywhere, priced from €3.25 for 500g.

Entertainment

There are dozens of music bars dotted around the maze of small streets behind the waterfront.

One For the Road (☎ 2297 022 340; Afeas 3) This lively bar draws a young crowd with a mixture of modern Greek and rock music.

Avli (☎ 2297 026 438; Pan Irioti 17) Avli attracts an older audience with a mixture of '60s and Latin music.

Mousiki Skini (☎ 2298 022 922; Spirou Rodi 44) Mousikini Skini is for serious night owls, with rembetika music on Wednesday, Friday, Saturday and Sunday nights from midnight until 5am.

AROUND AEGINA
Temple of Aphaia

The splendid, well-preserved Doric **Temple of Aphaia** (☎ 2297 032 398; adult/concession €4/2; ⊙ 8am-7pm), a local deity of pre-Hellenic times, is the major ancient site of the Saronic Gulf Islands. It was built in 480 BC when Aegina was at its most powerful.

The temple's pediments were décorated with outstanding Trojan War sculptures, most of which were spirited away in the 19th century and eventually fell into the hands of Ludwig I (father of King Otho). They now have pride of place in Munich's Glyptothek. The temple is impressive even without these sculptures. It stands on a pine-covered hill and commands imposing views over the Saronic Gulf as far as Cape Sounion.

Aphaia is 10km east of Aegina Town. Buses to Agia Marina (€1.20, 20 minutes) stop at the site. A taxi from Aegina Town costs about €7.50.

Paleohora Παλαιοχώρα

The ruins of Paleohora, on a hillside 6.5km east of Aegina Town, are fascinating to explore. The town was the island's capital from the 9th century to 1826, when pirate attacks forced the islanders to flee the coast and settle inland. It didn't do them much good when the notorious pirate Barbarossa arrived in 1537, laid waste the town and carried the inhabitants off into slavery.

The ruins are far more extensive than they first appear. The only buildings left intact are the churches. There are more than two dozen of them, in various states of disrepair, dotted around the hillside. Remnants of frescoes can be seen in some.

In the valley below Paleohora is **Moni Agiou Nektariou**, an important place of pilgrimage. The monastery contains the relics of a hermit monk, Anastasios Kefalas, who died in 1920. When his body was exhumed in 1940 it was found to have mummified – a sure sign of sainthood in Greek Orthodoxy,especially after a lifetime of performing miracle cures. Kefalas was canonised in 1961 – the first Orthodox saint of the 20th century. The enormous new church that has been built to honour him is a spectacular sight beside the road to Agia Marina. A track leads south from here to the 16th-century **Moni Hrysoleontissas**, in a lovely mountain setting.

The bus from Aegina Town to Agia Marina (€0.90, 10 minutes) stops at the turn-off to Paleohora.

Hellenic Wildlife Rehabilitation Centre

If you want to get an idea of the kind of toll that hunting takes on the nation's wildlife, pay a visit to the **Hellenic Wildlife Rehabilitation Centre** (Elliniko Kentro Perithalifis Agrion Zoon; ☎ 2297 028 367; www.ekpaz.gr in Greek; ⊙ 11am-1pm).

The centre recently moved to new, custom-built premises about 10km southwest of Aegina Town and 1km west of Pahia Rahi on the road to Mt Oros. Admission is free, but donations are appreciated.

It is designed to handle the 4000-odd animals and birds that are brought here every year. They come from all over Greece; the majority have been shot.

Volunteers are welcome: the need is greatest in the winter months. The new centre has accommodation for volunteer workers. There is no public transport – most visitors hire motorbikes or bicycles to get here; a taxi will cost about €10.

Perdika Πέρδικα

The small fishing village of Perdika, 21km south of Aegina Town at the southern tip of the west coast, is popular for its fish tavernas, with half-a-dozen places overlooking the harbour.

Beaches

Beaches are not Aegina's strong point. The east-coast town of **Agia Marina** is the island's premier tourist resort, but the beach is not great – if you can see it for package tourists. There are a couple of sandy patches that almost qualify as beaches between Aegina Town and Perdika.

MONI & ANGISTRI ISLETS
ΜΟΝΗ & ΑΓΚΙΣΤΡΙ

The Moni and Angistri Islets lie off the west coast of Aegina, opposite Perdika. Moni, the smaller of the two, is a 10-minute boat ride from Perdika – frequent boats (€0.80, 10 minutes) make the trip in summer.

Angistri is much bigger with around 500 inhabitants. The island achieved a certain notoriety when alleged November 17 hitman Dimitris Koufonidas was arrested on Lalares Beach, better known as a nudist hangout, in September 2001. There's a decent sandy beach at the port and other smaller beaches around the coast. Both package-holiday tourists and independent travellers find their way to Angistri, which is served by regular boats from Aegina Town and Piraeus.

POROS ΠΟΡΟΣ

pop 4348

The island of Poros is little more than a stone's throw from the mainland. The slender passage of water that separates it from the Peloponnesian town of Galatas is only 360m wide at its narrowest point.

Poros was once two islands, Kalavria and Sferia. These days they are connected by a narrow isthmus, cut by a canal for small boats and rejoined by a road bridge. The vast majority of the population lives on the small volcanic island of Sferia, which is more than half-covered by the town of Poros. Sferia hangs like an appendix from the southern coast of Kalavria, a large, well-forested island that has all the package hotels. Poros Town is not wildly exciting,

but it can be used as a base for exploring the ancient sites of the adjacent Peloponnese (p109).

The island was once a popular spot with British holidaymakers, but they have virtually disappeared from the scene. It's been bad news for the island economy, but good news for travellers in search of accommodation bargains.

Getting There & Away
FERRY

There are at least four ferries daily to Piraeus (€7.50, 2½ hours), via Methana (€2.50, 30 minutes) and Aegina (€4.50, one hour), two daily to Hydra (€3.70, one hour), and one to Spetses (€4.80, two hours). Ticket agencies are opposite the ferry dock.

Small boats shuttle constantly between Poros and Galatas (€0.50, five minutes) on the mainland. They leave from the quay opposite Plateia Iroön in Poros Town. Car ferries to Galatas leave from the dock on the road to Kalavria.

HYDROFOIL & CATAMARAN

Hellas Flying Dolphins (www.dolphins.gr) has four services daily to Piraeus (€14.90, one hour), and four south to Hydra (€7.30, 30 minutes), two of which continue to Spetses (€11.60, one hour). The **Flying Dolphin agency** (☎ 2298 023 423; Plateia Iroön) has a timetable of departures posted outside.

Saronic Dolphins also operate to these destinations. **Hellenic Sun Travel** (☎ 2298 025 901), opposite the ferry dock, is the local agent.

Getting Around

The Poros bus operates almost constantly along a route that starts near the hydrofoil dock on Plateia Iroön in Poros Town. It crosses to Kalavria and goes east along the south coast as far as Moni Zoödohou Pigis (€0.70, 10 minutes), then turns around and heads west as far as Neorion Beach (€0.70, 15 minutes).

Some of the caïques operating between Poros and Galatas switch to ferrying tourists to beaches in summer. Operators stand on the waterfront and call out destinations.

There are several places on the road to Kalavria offering bikes for hire, both motorised and pedal-powered. **Moto Stelios** (☎ 2298 023 026) has bikes for €5 per day, and mopeds and scooters priced from €15.

POROS

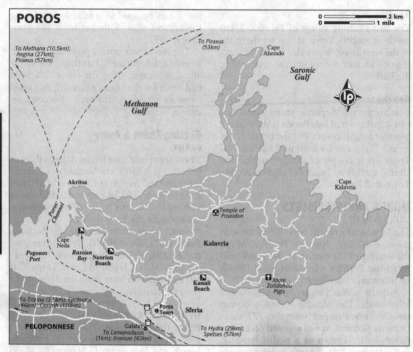

To Methana (10.5km);
Aegina (27km);
Piraeus (57km)

To Piraeus
(53km)

Cape
Aherado

Saronic
Gulf

Methanon
Gulf

Akritsa

Poros
Channel

Cape
Neda

Russian
Bay

Pogonos
Port

Neorion
Beach

Temple of
Poseidon

Kalavria

Cape
Kalavria

Moni
Zoödohou
Pigis

Kanali
Beach

To Trizina (3.5km); Epidavros
(46km); Corinth (110km)

PELOPONNESE

Poros
Town

Sferia

Galatas

To Lemonodasos
(1km); Ermioni (42km)

To Hydra (29km);
Spetses (57km)

POROS TOWN

pop 4102

Poros Town is the island's main settlement. It's a pretty place of white houses
with terracotta-tiled roofs, and there are
wonderful views over to the mountains
of Argolis.

Orientation

The main ferry dock is at the western tip
of Poros Town, overlooked by the striking
blue-domed clock tower.

A right turn from the ferry dock leads
along the waterfront facing Galatas. The
first square (triangle actually) is Plateia
Iroön, where the hydrofoils dock. The
square is lined with cafés and tourist
shops. The island bus leaves from right
next to the kiosk at the very eastern end
of the square. The next square along is
Plateia Karamis.

A left turn from the dock puts you on
the waterfront road leading to Kalavria.
Dimosthenous runs inland from the road
to Kalavria, starting just beyond the small
supermarket.

Information

Poros does not have a tourist office, but
you can find information on the Internet at
www.poros.gr.

Alpha Bank (Plateia Iroön)

Bank Emporiki (Plateia Iroön)

Coconuts Internet Café (☎ 2298 025 407; Plateia
Karamis; ☼ 9am-2am)

National Bank of Greece 100m from the dock.

Post office (Plateia Karamis; ☼ 7.30am-2pm Mon-Fri)

Suzi's Laundrette Service (☼ 8am-2pm & 6-9pm
Mon-Sat) Next to the National Bank of Greece; €10 to wash
and dry a 5kg load.

Tourist Police (☎ 2298 022 462/256; Dimosthenous
10) Behind the Poros high school.

Sleeping

Villa Tryfon (☎ 2298 022 215/025 854; off Plateia Agios
Georgiou; s/d with bathroom €30/50; ☼) This is the
place to head for a room with a view. It's
on top of the hill overlooking the port. All
rooms have bathroom and kitchen facilities
as well as great views over to Kalavria. To
get there, turn left from the ferry dock and
take the first right up the steps 20m past the
Agricultural Bank of Greece. Turn left at the

Windmills of Mykonos (p134),
Cyclades

CHRIS CHRISTO

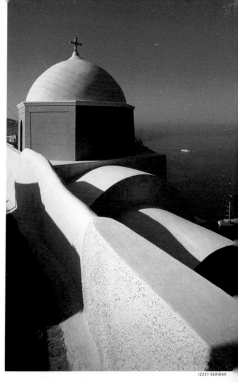

IZZET KERIBAR

View from Santorini (p174), Cyclades

Houses along the waterfront, Mykonos (p134), Cyclades

CHRIS CHRISTO

Octopus on grill, Aegina (p103), Saronic Gulf Islands

ALAN BENSON

ALAN BENSON

Ouzo display, Aegina (p103), Saronic Gulf Islands

Port Hydra, Hydra Town (p111), Saronic Gulf Islands

KIM WILDMAN

top of the steps on Aikaterinis Hatzopoulou Karra, and you will see the place signposted up the steps to the right after 150m.

Seven Brothers Hotel (☎ 2298 023 412; 7brothrs@hol.gr; Plateia Iroön; s/d/tr with bathroom €40/ 50/55; 🖭) Seven Brothers is a smart modern hotel with large, comfortable rooms equipped with fridge and TV. No sign of any brothers, though.

Hotel Dionysos (☎ 2298 023 511/022 530; Papadopoulou 78; s/d with bathroom €40/60) The Dionysos occupies a beautifully restored mansion opposite the car ferry dock from Galatas. The rooms are comfortably furnished with air-con and TV. Breakfast is €4.40.

If things are quiet, you may be offered a room by one of the domatia owners when you get off the ferry. Otherwise, head left along the waterfront and turn right after about 400m, beyond the small supermarket. There are several domatia on the streets around there.

Eating
Poros has some good restaurants.

Taverna Karavolos (☎ 2298 026 158; mains €4.50-7.40; 🕒 7pm-late) Karavolos means 'big snail' in Greek and is the nickname of cheerful owner Theodoros. Sure enough, snails are a speciality of the house – served in a delicious thick tomato sauce (€4). You'll find a range of imaginative mezedes like *taramokeftedes* (fish-roe balls), and a daily selection of main courses like pork stuffed with garlic (€6). The restaurant is signposted behind Cinema Diana on the road to Kalavria.

Taverna Platanos (☎ 2298 024 249; Plateia Agios Georgiou; mains €4.50-10) The Platanos is another popular spot, with seating beneath a large old plane tree in the small square at the top of Dimosthenous. Owner Tassos is a butcher by day and the restaurant specialises in spit-roast meats. You'll find specialities like *kokoretsi* (offal) and *gouronopoula* (suckling pig).

Taverna Apagio (☎ 2298 026 219; off Plateia Karamanos; mains €4-8.50) New owners and a new menu have made the Apagio the place to head for something a bit different. You'll find dishes like chicken with fresh mango (€6) and pork spare ribs with spicy barbecue sauce (€6) as well as taverna standards. The place is about 800m from the ferry dock, signposted off the road to Kalavria.

AROUND POROS
Poros has few places of interest and the beaches there are no great shakes. **Kanali Beach**, on Kalavria 1km east of the bridge, is a mediocre pebble beach. **Neorion Beach**, 3km west of the bridge, is marginally better. The best beach is at **Russian Bay**, 1.5km past Neorion.

The 18th-century **Moni Zoödohou Pigis**, on Kalavria, has a beautiful gilded iconostasis from Asia Minor. The monastery is well signposted, 4km east of Poros Town.

From the road below the monastery you can strike inland to the 6th-century **Temple of Poseidon**. The god of the sea and earthquakes was the principal deity worshipped on Poros. There's very little left of this temple, but the walk is worthwhile for the scenery on the way. From the site there are superb views of the Saronic Gulf and the Peloponnese. The orator Demosthenes, after failing to shake off the Macedonians who were after him for inciting the city-states to rebel, committed suicide here in 322 BC.

From the ruins you can continue along the road, which eventually winds back to the bridge. The road is drivable, but it's also a fine 6km walk that will take around two hours.

See the Getting There & Around section (below) for details on buses to the monastery.

PELOPONNESIAN MAINLAND
The Peloponnesian mainland opposite Poros can easily be explored from the island.

The celebrated citrus groves of **Lemonodassos** (Lemon Forest) begin about 2km southeast of **Galatas**. There's no public transport, but it's an easy walk.

The ruins of ancient **Troizen**, legendary birthplace of Theseus, lie in the hills near the modern village of Trizina, 7.5km west of Galatas. There are buses to Trizina (€0.90, 15 minutes) from Galatas, leaving a walk of about 1.5km to the site.

Getting There & Around
Small boats run constantly between Galatas and Poros (€0.50, five minutes). A couple of buses daily depart Galatas for Nafplio (€5.60, two hours) and can drop you off at the ancient site of Epidavros.

HYDRA ΥΔΡΑ

pop 2719

Hydra (*ee*-drah) is the Saronic Gulf island with the most style. The gracious white and pastel stone mansions of Hydra Town are stacked up the rocky hillsides that surround the fine natural harbour. Film-makers were the first foreigners to be seduced by the beauty of Hydra. They began arriving in the 1950s when the island was used as a location for the film *Boy on a Dolphin*, among others. The artists and writers moved in next, followed by the celebrities, and nowadays it seems the whole world is welcomed ashore.

If you've been in Greece for some time you may fall in love with Hydra for one reason alone – the absence of kamikaze motorcyclists. Hydra has no motorised transport except for sanitation and construction vehicles. Donkeys (hundreds of them) are the only means of transport.

History

Like many of the Greek islands, Hydra was ignored by the Turks, so many Greeks from the Peloponnese settled on the island to escape Ottoman suppression and taxes. The population was further boosted by an influx of Albanians. Agriculture was impossible, so these new settlers began building boats. By the 19th century, the island had become a great maritime power. The canny Hydri-ots made a fortune by running the British blockade of French ports during the Napoleonic Wars. The wealthy shipping merchants built most of the town's grand old arhontika from the considerable profits. It became a fashionable resort for Greek socialites, and lavish balls were a regular feature.

Hydra made a major contribution to the War of Independence. Without the 130 ships supplied by the island, the Greeks wouldn't have had much of a fleet with which to block-ade the Turks. It also supplied leadership in the form of Georgios Koundouriotis, who was president of the emerging Greek na-tion's national assembly from 1822 to 1827, and Admiral Andreas Miaoulis, who com-manded the Greek fleet. Streets and squares all over Greece are named after these two.

Getting There & Away
FERRY

There are two ferries daily to Piraeus (€8.40, 3½ hours), sailing via Poros (€3.70, one hour), Methana (€5.40, 1½ hours) and Ae-gina (€5.60, two hours). There's also a daily boat to Spetses (€4.70, one hour). Departure times are listed on a board at the ferry dock.

You can buy tickets from **Idreoniki Travel** (☎ 2298 054 007), next to the Flying Dolphin office overlooking the port.

HYDROFOIL & CATAMARAN

Hellas Flying Dolphins (☎ 2298 053 814; www.dolphins .gr) have six services daily to Piraeus (€16.70). Direct services take 1¼ hours, but

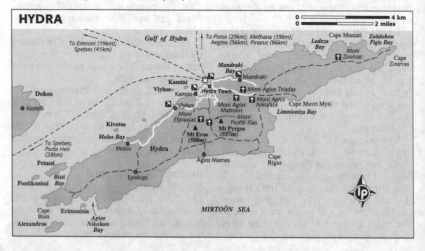

HYDRA

| 0 | 4 km |
| 0 | 2 miles |

Gulf of Hydra

To Poros (29km); Methana (39km); Aegina (56km); Piraeus (86km)

To Ermioni (19km); Spetses (41km)

Cape Maniati
Zoödohou Pigis Bay

Ledeza Bay
Moni Zourvas
Cape Zourvas

Mandraki Bay
Mandraki

Kamini
Vlyhos
Kamini
Hydra Town
Moni Agios Triadas

Dokos
Kastelli

Vlyhos
Moni Agias Matronis
Moni Agios Nikolaos
Cape Mavri Myti
Limnioniza Bay

Kivotos
Moni Efpraxias
Moni Profiti Ilias
Mt Eros (588m)
Mt Pyrgos (557m)

Molos Bay
To Spetses; Porto Heli (28km)
Molos
Hydra

Petassi
Agios Mamas
Cape Rigas

Bisti Bay
Pontikonissi
Episkopi

Cape Bisti
Alexandros
Erimonisia
Agios Nikolaos Bay

MIRTOÖN SEA

most go via Poros (€7.40, 30 minutes) and take 1½ hours. There are also frequent services to Spetses (€8.50, 30 minutes), some of which call at Ermioni, adding 20 minutes to the trip. Many of the services to Spetses continue on to Porto Heli (€9.80, 50 minutes). The Flying Dolphin office is on the waterfront opposite the ferry quay.

Saronic Dolphins also calls a couple of times daily. **Saitis Tours** (☎ 2298 052 184) located on the waterfront sells tickets.

Getting Around
In summer, there are caïques from Hydra Town to the island's beaches. There are also **water taxis** (☎ 2298 053 690) which will take you anywhere you like.

The donkey owners clustered around the port charge around €10 to transport your bags to the hotel of your choice.

HYDRA TOWN
pop 2526
Most of the action in Hydra Town is concentrated around the waterfront cafés and shops, leaving the upper reaches of the narrow, stepped streets virtually deserted – and a joy to explore.

Information
There is no tourist office, but **Saitis Tours** (☎ 2298 052 184; fax 2298 053 469), on the waterfront near Tombazi, puts out a useful free guide called *Holidays in Hydra*. You can find information about the island on the Internet at www.compulink.gr/hydranet.

Most things of importance are close to the waterfront. The **post office** (☼ 7.30am-2pm Mon-Fri) is on a small side street between the **Bank Emporiki** and the **National Bank of Greece**. The **Tourist Police** (☎ 2298 052 205; Votsi; ☼ mid-May–end-Sep) can be found sharing an office with the regular police.

You can check email at the **Flamingo Internet Café** (☎ 2298 053 485; Tombazi; ☼ noon-11pm).

Sights & Activities
The star attraction is the grand **Lazaros Koundouriotis Historical Mansion** (☎ 2298 052 421; nhmuseum@tee.gr; adult/concession €4/2; ☼ 10am-5pm Tue-Sun), former home of one of the major players in the Greek independence struggle. It's a great example of traditional architecture at the end of the 18th century, boasting some superb wood-panelled ceilings. The

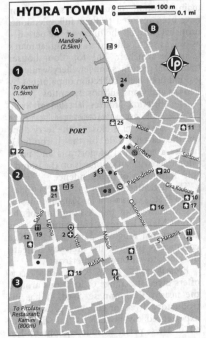

HYDRA TOWN

main reception rooms of the second floor have been restored to their full splendour, furnished with all the finery of the period – as well as such oddments as the great man's favourite armchair. The top floor houses traditional costumes and jewellery, while the ground floor has a collection of paintings by Periklis and Constantinos Byzantios.

The **Historical Archives Museum of Hydra** (☎ 2298 052 355; museumhy@otenet.gr; adult/concession €3/2; 🕑 9am-4.30pm) is close to the ferry dock on the eastern side of the harbour. It houses a collection of portraits and naval oddments, with an emphasis on the island's role in the War of Independence.

The **Byzantine Museum** (☎ 2298 054 071; admission €1.50; 🕑 10am-5pm Tue-Sun), upstairs at the Monastery of the Assumption of the Virgin Mary, houses a collection of icons and assorted religious paraphernalia. The entrance is through the archway beneath the clock tower on the waterfront.

Hydra Divers (☎ 2298 053 900; www.divingteam.gr) offers dives at a range of locations around the nearby Peloponnese coast. It has introductory dives for €60, and packages for experienced divers such as four dives for €170. These prices include equipment. Enthusiastic owner, Alexander, also runs daily boat trips to beautiful Bisti Bay (€10), on the southwestern side of the island, where people can hire snorkelling gear or try their hand at kayaking in the sheltered waters.

Festivals

Hydriots celebrate their contribution to the War of Independence struggle by staging a mock battle in Hydra harbour during the **Miaoulia Festival**, held in honour of Admiral Miaoulis, in late June. It's accompanied by much carousing, feasting and fireworks.

Sleeping

Accommodation in Hydra is of a high standard, and you pay accordingly. These prices are for the high season, which in Hydra means weekends as well as July and August.

BUDGET

Hotel Dina (☎ 2298 052 248; Stavrou Tsipi; s/d with bathroom €40/45) The cheapest rooms are found at this small, old-fashioned place, run by the only hotel owner on the island who speaks no English. The high location means there are great views over the town and harbour.

Pension Erofili (☎/fax 2298 054 049; info@pensionerofili.gr; Tombazi; s/d/tr with bathroom €40/50/60; ❄) This popular place is about 300m from the waterfront, and has clean, comfortable rooms with TV and fridge. It also has a large family room with private kitchen.

Pension Alkionides (☎/fax 2298 054 055; off Oikonomou; s/d/tr with bathroom €45/50/60; ❄) The Alkionides is a good budget choice, tucked away on a quiet side street about 250m from the port. All rooms have a fridge.

Hotel Hydra (☎/fax 2298 052 102; hydrahotel@aig.forthnet.gr; Voulgari; s/d/tr with bathroom €45/63/81; ❄) This hotel has a great setting, overlooking the town from the west, and large, comfortable rooms. It's a fair haul to get there – more than 100 steps up Sahini from Lignou – but the views over the town and harbour are worth it. Prices include breakfast.

MID-RANGE

Hotel Leto (☎ 2298 053 385; soflau@otenet.gr; off Miaouli; s with bathroom €60-79, d with bathroom €77-103.50, tr with bathroom €96-127.50; ❄) This is a stylish place with beautiful timber floors. Prices include buffet breakfast. It's hidden away in the maze of streets behind the port, but signposted to the left off the first square on Miaouli.

Hotel Miranda (☎ 2298 052 230; mirhydra@hol.gr; Miaouli; s/d/tr with bathroom €75/100/150; ❄) Originally the mansion of a wealthy Hydriot sea captain, the Miranda has been beautifully renovated and converted into a very smart hotel. Prices include buffet breakfast.

TOP END

Hotel Orloff (☎ 2298 052 564; orloff@internet.gr; Rafalia; s/d with bathroom from €82/94; ❄) This is a beautiful old stone mansion with a cool, vine-covered courtyard at the back. The furnishings are elegant without being overstated, and each of the 10 rooms has a character of its own. Prices include buffet breakfast, served in the courtyard in summer. The hotel is about 250m from the port; head inland from the port on Miaouli and turn right onto Rafalia after the square.

Hotel Bratsera (☎ 2298 053 971; bratsera@yahoo.com; Tombazi; d with bathroom €116-180, 4-bed ste €220; ❄ 🏊) The Bratsera is another place with loads of character. It occupies a converted sponge factory about 300m from the port. It also has the town's only swimming pool. It's for guests only, but you'll qualify if you eat at its restaurant. Prices include breakfast.

Eating

Hydra has dozens of tavernas and restaurants. Unlike the hotels, there are plenty of cheap places around – especially if you're prepared to head away from the waterfront.

Taverna Gitoniko (☎ 2298 053 615; Spilios Haramis; mains €3.80-10.80) The Gitoniko taverna is better known by the names of its owners, Manolis and Christina. The menu looks nothing special, but they have built up an enthusiastic local following through the simple formula of turning out consistently good traditional taverna food. Try the beetroot salad – a bowl of baby beets and boiled greens served with garlic mashed potato. The flavours complement each other perfectly. Get in early or you'll have a long wait.

Verandah (☎ 2298 052 259; Sahini; mains €4.50-11) Nowhere else comes close to matching the views enjoyed from the terrace at Verandah, where diners can gaze out over the town and harbour while enjoying such treats as spaghetti marina (€9.50) or pork fillet with gorgonzola cheese (€10.50).

Pirofani Restaurant (☎ 2298 052 259; mains €6-11.50; ⏰ 7pm-late Wed-Sun Easter-Oct) For something really special, head out to this excellent restaurant at Kamini. Owner Theo specialises in desserts – so be sure to leave room for a slice of lemon meringue pie or chocolate and pear cake. The restaurant is at the base of the steps on the inland route between Kamini and Hydra Town; to get there, follow Kriezi over the hill from Hydra Town.

Entertainment

Hydra boasts a busy nightlife. The action is centred on the bars on the southwestern side of the harbour where places like **Pirate** (☎ 2298 052 711) and **Saronikos** (☎ 2298 052 589) keep going until almost dawn. Pirate plays Western rock while Saronikos plays Greek. For something more laidback, try **Amalour** (☎ 69-7746 1357; Tombazi), which sells a wide range of fresh juices as well as cocktails.

AROUND HYDRA

It's a strenuous but worthwhile 2km walk up to **Moni Profiti Ilias**, starting from Miaouli. Monks still live in the monastery, which has fantastic views down to the town. It's a short walk from here to the convent of **Moni Efpraxias**.

The beaches on Hydra are a dead loss, but the walks to them are enjoyable. **Kamini**,

about a 1.5km walk along the coastal path from town, has rocks and a very small pebble beach. **Vlyhos**, a 1.5km walk further on, is an attractive village with a slightly larger pebble beach, two tavernas and a ruined 19th-century stone bridge.

From here, walkaholics can continue to the small bay at **Molos**, or take a left fork before the bay to the inland village of **Episkopi**. There are no facilities at Episkopi or Molos.

A path leads east from Hydra Town to the pebble beach at **Mandraki**.

A water taxi from Hydra Town to Kamini costs €7, or €10 to Mandraki and Vlyhos.

SPETSES ΣΠΕΤΣΕΣ

pop 3916

Pine-covered Spetses, the most distant of the group from Piraeus, has long been a favourite with British holiday-makers.

Spetses' history is similar to Hydra's. It became wealthy through shipbuilding, ran the British blockade during the Napoleonic Wars and refitted its ships to join the Greek fleet during the War of Independence. Spetsiot fighters achieved a certain notoriety through their pet tactic of attaching small boats laden with explosives to the enemy's ships, setting them alight and beating a hasty retreat.

The island was known in antiquity as Pityoussa (meaning 'pine-covered'), but the original forest cover disappeared long ago. The pine-covered hills that greet the visitor today are a legacy of the far-sighted and wealthy philanthropist Sotirios Anargyrios.

Anargyrios was born on Spetses in 1848 and emigrated to the USA, returning in 1914 an exceedingly rich man. He bought two-thirds of the then largely barren island and planted the Aleppo pines that stand today. He also financed the island's road system and commissioned many of the town's grand buildings, including the Hotel Possidonion. He was a big fan of the British public (ie private) school system, and established Anargyrios & Korgialenios College, a boarding school for boys from all over Greece. British author John Fowles taught English at the college in 1950–51, and used the island as a setting for his novel The Magus.

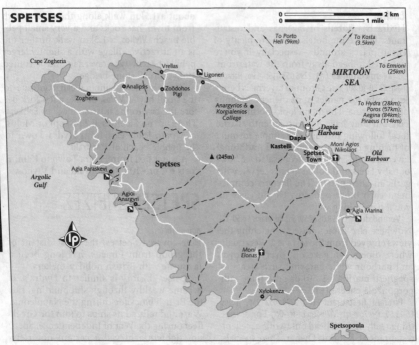

SPETSES

Cape Zogheria

Vrellas

Ligoneri

MIRTOÖN
SEA

To Porto
Heli (9km)

To Kosta
(3.5km)

To Ermioni
(25km)

Analipsis

Zoödohos
Pigi

Zogheria

Anargyrios &
Korgialenios
College

To Hydra (28km);
Poros (57km);
Aegina (84km);
Piraeus (114km)

Dapia
Harbour

Dapia

Kastelli

Moni Agios
Nikolaos

Old
Harbour

Spetses
Town

▲ (245m)

Spetses

Agia Paraskevi

Argolic
Gulf

Agioi
Anargyri

Agia Marina

Moni
Elonas

Xylokenza

Spetsopoula

Getting There & Away

FERRY

There is a daily ferry to Piraeus (€11.70, 4½ hours), via Hydra (€4.20, one hour), Poros (€5.80, two hours) and Aegina (€8.70, three hours). You'll find departure times on the waterfront outside **Alasia Travel** (☎ 2298 074 098), which sells tickets.

There are also water taxis to Kosta (€12, 15 minutes), on the Peloponnese mainland. There are three buses daily from Kosta to Nafplio (€5, 2¼ hours).

HYDROFOIL & CATAMARAN

Hellas Flying Dolphins (www.dolphins.gr) runs at least six services a day to Piraeus (€23.20, 2½ hours). Most services travel via Hydra (€8.50, 30 minutes) and Poros (€11.60, 70 minutes). There are also daily connections to Ermioni (€6.40, one hour) and Porto Heli (€4.50, 20 minutes). Tickets are available from **Bardakos Tours** (☎ 2298 073 141; Dapia Harbour).

Saronic Dolphins operates less frequently on the same route. Tickets are available from **Mimoza Travel** (☎ 2298 0 75 170; Plateia Limenarheiou).

Getting Around

Spetses has two bus routes. There are three or four buses daily from Plateia Agios Mamas in Spetses Town to Agio Anargyri (€2, 40 minutes), travelling via Agia Marina and Xylokeriza. All departure times are displayed on a board by the bus stop. There are also hourly buses to Ligoneri (€0.95) departing from right in front of the Hotel Possidonion.

No cars are permitted on the island. Unfortunately this ban has not been extended to motorbikes, resulting in there being more of the critters here than just about anywhere else. There are motorbike-rental shops everywhere; rental is around €15 per day.

Those who prefer pedal power will find an assortment of bikes (€5 per day) to suit all ages, as well as baby seats, at the **Bike Center** (☎ 2298 074 143) behind the fish markets.

The colourful horse-drawn carriages are a pleasant but expensive way of getting around. Prices are displayed on a board on Plateia Limenarheiou by the port.

BOAT
Water taxis (☎ 2298 072 072; Dapia Harbour) go anywhere you care to nominate from opposite the Flying Dolphin office. Fares are displayed on a board. Sample one-way fares include €18 to Agia Marina and €38 to Agioi Anargyri.

In summer, there are caïques from the harbour to Agioi Anargyri (€6 return) and Zogheria (€4 return).

SPETSES TOWN
pop 3846

Spetses Town sprawls along almost half the northeast coast of the island, reflecting the way in which the focal point of settlement has changed over the years.

There's evidence of an early Helladic settlement near the old harbour, about 1.5km east of the modern commercial centre, and at the port of Dapia. Roman and Byzantine remains have been unearthed in the area behind Moni Agios Nikolaos, halfway between the two.

The island is thought to have been uninhabited for almost 600 years before the arrival of Albanian refugees fleeing fighting between the Turks and the Venetians in the 16th century. They settled on the hillside just inland from Dapia, in the area now known as Kastelli.

The Dapia district has a few impressive arhontika, but the prettiest part of town is around the old harbour.

Orientation
The quay at Dapia Harbour serves both ferries and hydrofoils. A left turn at the end of the quay leads east along the waterfront on Sotirios Anargyris, skirting Plateia Limenarheiou where the horse-drawn carriages wait. The road is flanked by a string of uninspiring, concrete C-class hotels, and emerges after 200m on Plateia Agios Mamas, next to the town beach.

The waterfront to the right of the quay is also called Sotirios Anargyris. It skirts Dapia Harbour, passes the grand old Hotel Possidonion and continues west around the bay to Hotel Spetses and becomes the road to Ligoneri.

The main road inland from Dapia is N Spetson, which runs southwest off the small square where horse-drawn carriages wait. It soon becomes Botassi, which continues

inland to Kastelli. These two streets are among the few on Spetses with street signs.

Information
There is no tourist office on Spetses.

Delfinia Net Café (☎ 2298 075 051; Plateia Agios Mamas; ⏱ 9am-2am)

National Bank of Greece Behind Dapia Harbour; one of three banks in town.

Post Ofice (⏱ 7.30am-2pm Mon-Fri) On the street running behind the hotels on Sotirios Anargyris; coming from the quay, turn right at Hotel Soleil and then left.

Port Police (☎ 2298 072 245) Opposite the quay.

Tourist Police (☎ 2298 073 100; ⏱ mid-May–Sep) Based in the police station – on the well-signposted road to the museum.

Sights
The **old harbour** is a delightful place to explore. It is ringed by old Venetian buildings, and filled with boats of every shape and size – from colourful little fishing boats to sleek luxury cruising yachts. The shipbuilders of Spetses still do things the traditional way and the shore is dotted with the hulls of emerging caïques. The walk from Dapia Harbour is about 1.5km long. **Moni Agios Nikolaos** straddles a headland at the halfway mark.

The **museum** (☎ 2298 072 994; adult/concession €3/2; ⏱ 8.30am-2.30pm Tue-Sun) is housed in the

---

LASCARINA BOUBOULINA

Spetses contributed one of the most colourful figures of the War of Independence, the dashing heroine Lascarina Bouboulina. Her exploits on and off the battlefield were the stuff of legend. She was widowed twice by the time the war began – both her ship-owning husbands had been killed by pirates, leaving her a very wealthy woman – and she used her money to commission her own fighting ship, the *Agamemnon*, which she led into battle during the blockade of Nafplio in April 1921.

Bouboulina was known for her fiery temperament and her countless love affairs, and her death was in keeping with her flamboyant lifestyle – she was shot during a family dispute in her Spetses home. Bouboulina featured on the old 50 drachma note, depicted directing cannon fire from the deck of her ship.

arhontiko of Hadzigiannis Mexis, a ship-owner who became the island's first gover-nor. While most of the collection is devoted to folkloric items and portraits of the island's founding fathers, there is also a fine collec-tion of ships' figureheads. The museum is clearly signposted from Plateia Orologiou.

The mansion of Lascarina Bouboulina (p115), behind the OTE building, has now been converted into a **museum** (☎ 2298 072 416; adult/concession €4/1; 🕑 9am-5pm Tue-Sun). Bill-boards around town advertise the starting times for tours.

Sleeping
BUDGET
The prices listed here are for the high sea-son in July and August. Travellers should be able to negotiate substantial discounts at other times – particularly for longer stays.

Villa Marina (☎ 2298 072 646; off Plateia Agios Mamas; s/d with bathroom €40/56; 🗷) This small, traveller-friendly place is just off the square beyond the row of restaurants. It has good rooms with bathrooms looking out onto a delightful little garden full of fresh flowers. All rooms have refrigerators and there is a well-equipped communal kitchen down-stairs.

Hotel Kamelia (☎ 2298 072 415; d/tr with bathroom €40/45; 🗷) The Kamelia is a small, old-fashioned, family hotel tucked away in the back streets inland from Plateia Agios Mamas, where it lies almost hidden behind a brilliant burgundy bougainvillea. It's sign-posted to the right at the supermarket 150m beyond Plateia Agios Mamas.

For other options, you might be forced to fall back on one of the uninspiring concrete hotels that line the waterfront between the ferry dock and Plateia Agios Mamas, or seek help from one of the travel agents.

MID-RANGE & TOP END
Orloff Apartments (☎ 2298 072 246; info@orloff studios.com; s with bathroom €80-150; 🗷 🗷) Man-ager Christos has 16 well-equipped studio rooms set in the gardens of the family's stone mansion on the road leading out to Agioi Anargyri, above the old harbour about 1.5km from the port. All the rooms come with fridge and facilities for making tea and coffee.

Hotel Possidonion (☎ 2298 072 308/006; fax 2298 072 208; s/d/tr with bathroom €50/60/75) The Hotel

Possidonion, which overlooks the seafront just south of the Dapia harbour, was once one of the grand hotels of the Mediterranean – a wonderful old Edwardian-style hotel where the crowned heads of Europe would meet to dance the night away. The hotel was originally built in Egypt, and was then shipped over to be reassembled in situ. It has seen better days, but it remains an imposing building with wide wrought-iron balconies looking out to sea. Prices include breakfast.

Nisia (☎ 2298 075 000; nissia@otenet.gr; d/tr €200/ 250; 🗷 🗷) Nisia, about 200m west of Hotel Possidonion, represents the luxury end of the market with apartment-style rooms clustered around a large swimming pool.

Eating
Taverna O Lazaros (☎ 2298 072 600; 🕑 7pm-midnight; mains €5-6.50) This taverna is in the district of Kastelli, about 600m inland at the top end of Spetson. Treat yourself to a plate of *tarama-salata* (€2.35); its home-made version of this popular fish-roe dip is utterly different from the mass-produced muck served at many restaurants. The speciality of the house is baby goat in lemon sauce (€5.30).

Restaurant Patralis (☎ 2298 072 134; mains €6-10) Fish fans should head out to the Patralis, about 1.5km west of Dapia on the road to Ligoneri. It has a great setting, good menu and the fish are supplied by the restaurant's own boat. The fish a la Spetses (€8), a large tuna or swordfish steak baked with vegeta-bles and lots of garlic, goes down perfectly with a cold beer. You can also buy fresh fish here from €42 per kilo.

Orloff (☎ 2298 075 255; mezedes €5-14, mains €8-14) If character is what you want, you won't find a better place than this, 600m from Plateia Agios Mamas on the coast road to the old harbour. The early-19th-century port-authority building has been converted into a stylish restaurant special-ising in mezedes.

Self-caterers will find everything they need at **Kritikos Supermarket** (☎ 2298 074 361; Kentriki Agora), next to the fish market on the waterfront near Plateia Agios Mamas.

Entertainment
Bar Spetsa (☎ 2298 074 131; 🕑 8pm-late) Owner Costas likes to joke that he has the best collection of music from the '60s and '70s,

whiskies from the '80s – and the worst views of the Saronic Gulf! The views don't really matter, since he doesn't open until 8pm. The bar is 50m beyond Plateia Agios Mamas on the road to Agioi Anargyri.

Balconi Wine Bar (☎ 2298 72 594; ☉ 10am-3am May-Oct, 6.30pm-3am Nov-Apr) This stylish bar plays mainly classical/orchestral music during the day, and jazz in the evening. The terrace is the perfect spot to unwind with a cocktail or a glass of wine, overlooking the Saronic Gulf. The bar also serves a selection of fine cheeses and salami or hand-cut smoked salmon. Balconi is between the seafront and the post office.

AROUND SPETSES

Spetses' coastline is speckled with numerous coves with small, pine-shaded beaches. A 24km sealed road skirts the entire coastline,

so a motorcycle is the ideal way to explore the island.

The beach at **Ligoneri**, west of town, has the attraction of being easily accessible by bus. **Agia Paraskevi** and **Agioi Anargyri**, on the southwest coast, have good, albeit crowded, beaches; both have water sports of every description. A large mansion between the two beaches was the inspiration for the Villa Bourani in John Fowles' *The Magus*. **Agia Marina**, to the south of the old harbour, is a small resort with a crowded beach.

There's accommodation at Agioi Anargyri at the **Hotel Akrogiali** (☎ 2298 073 695; s/d incl breakfast €70/80) as well as a couple of tavernas.

The small island of **Spetsopoula** to the south of Spetses is owned by the family of the late shipping magnate Stavros Niarchos. (Unfortunately, they don't take visitors).

SARONIC GULF ISLANDS

Cyclades
Κυκλάδες

The Cyclades (kih-*klah*-dez) are what Greek island dreams are made of – rugged, multi-coloured outcrops of rock, anchored in azure seas and strewn with snow-white cubist buildings and blue-domed Byzantine churches. Add in golden beaches, olive groves and the scented wild gardens of mountains and terraced valleys, all under a brilliant Mediterranean sun, and it's easy to believe that the Cyclades were once the closest that humanity ever got to paradise on earth.

The reality is, of course, more prosaic; not least for native islanders who still struggle for a living, raising livestock on the more barren islands, or chasing a diminishing supply of fish from seas that are not always mirror calm. Added to this are winters that are often grey, bleak and unrewarding.

Yet, for many, the Cyclades will always be utterly seductive; not least because of their fascinating variety. They range from big, fertile Naxos and its landlocked valleys, to tiny outliers like Donoussa, Iraklia or Sikinos, where the sea dominates at every turn.

Some islands, such as Mykonos, Santorini (Thira) and Ios, seem to be engulfed by tourism – their beaches are awash with the packaged hedonism of the sun lounger, dance culture and fun water-sports; their main towns seethe with commercialism and exploitation. Yet other islands, such as Andros, Amorgos, Folegandros and Serifos, have kept tourism to a human scale.

The Cyclades are so named because they form a circle *(kyklos)* around the island of Delos, one of Greece's – and the world's – most significant and haunting ancient sites. For the dedicated traveller, closing that circle is still one of the world's most exhilarating and rewarding experiences.

CYCLADES

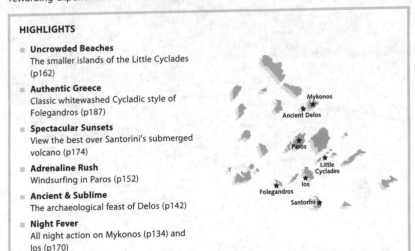

HIGHLIGHTS

- **Uncrowded Beaches**
  The smaller islands of the Little Cyclades (p162)

- **Authentic Greece**
  Classic whitewashed Cycladic style of Folegandros (p187)

- **Spectacular Sunsets**
  View the best over Santorini's submerged volcano (p174)

- **Adrenaline Rush**
  Windsurfing in Paros (p152)

- **Ancient & Sublime**
  The archaeological feast of Delos (p142)

- **Night Fever**
  All night action on Mykonos (p134) and Ios (p170)

Mykonos
Ancient Delos
Paros
Little Cyclades
Ios
Folegandros
Santorini

History

The Cyclades have been inhabited since at least 7000 BC, awesome proof of their antiquity. Around 3000 BC, the Cycladic civilisation, a culture sustained by its sea-farers, first achieved cohesion. During the Early Cycladic period (3000–2000 BC) there were settlements on the islands of Keros, Syros, Naxos, Milos, Sifnos and Amorgos, while colonisation of other islands must have taken place. During this period the tiny, yet compelling, Cycladic marble figurines were sculpted.

In the Middle Cycladic period (2000–1500 BC), many of the islands were occupied by the Minoans – at Akrotiri, on Santorini, a Minoan town has been excavated. At the beginning of the Late Cycladic period (1500–1100 BC), the Cyclades passed to the Mycenaeans. The Dorians followed in the 8th century BC, bringing Archaic culture with them.

By the middle of the 5th century BC the islands were members of a fully fledged Athenian empire. In the Hellenistic era (323–146 BC) they were controlled by Egypt's Ptolemic dynasties and, then, by the Macedonians. In 146 BC, the islands became a Roman province and lucrative trade links were established with many parts of the Mediterranean.

After the division of the Roman Empire into western and eastern entities in AD 395, the Cyclades were ruled from Byzantium

(Constantinople). Following the fall of Byzantium in 1204, the Franks ceded the Cyclades to Venice, which parcelled the islands out to opportunistic aristocrats. The most powerful was Marco Sanudo (self-styled Duke of Naxos), who acquired Naxos, Paros, Ios, Santorini, Anafi, Sifnos, Milos, Amorgos and Folegandros, thus bringing an indelible Venetian gloss that survives to this day in island architecture.

The Cyclades came under Turkish rule in 1537. Neglected by the Ottomans, they became backwaters prone to pirate raids, hence the labyrinthine, hilltop character of their towns – the mazes of narrow lanes were designed to disorientate invaders. Nevertheless, the impact of piracy led to massive depopulation; in 1563 only five out of 16 islands were still inhabited.

The Cyclades' participation in the Greek War of Independence was minimal, but they became havens for people fleeing those islands where insurrections against the Turks had led to massacres. During WWII the islands were occupied by the Italians.

The fortunes of the Cycladics have been revived by the tourism boom that began in the 1970s. Until then, many islanders lived in deep poverty; many more gave up the battle and headed for the mainland, and for America and Australia, in search of work.

Getting There & Away
AIR
Olympic Airways links Athens with Naxos, Syros, Santorini, Mykonos, Paros and Milos. From Santorini there's direct flights to/from Mykonos, Thessaloniki, Iraklio (Crete) and Rhodes, and from Mykonos there's flights to/from Thessaloniki, Santorini and Rhodes (see individual island sections for details).

Aegean Airlines flies to Mykonos and Santorini from Athens and Thessaloniki.

FAST BOAT & CATAMARAN
Large high-speed boats and cats are now significant on Cyclades routes. The travel time is usually half that of regular ferries. Seats fill fast in July and August, especially on weekends, so it's worth booking your ticket a day or so in advance.

FERRY
Ferry routes separate the Cyclades into western, northern, central and eastern subgroups

Most ferries serving the Cyclades connect one of these subgroups with Piraeus, Lavrio or Rafina on the mainland. The central Cyclades (Paros, Naxos, Ios and Santorini) are the most-visited and have the best links with the mainland, usually Piraeus.

The northern Cyclades (Andros, Tinos, Syros and Mykonos) have excellent connections with the mainland. The jumping-off

FERRY CONNECTIONS TO THE CYCLADES

Origin	Destination	Time	€	Frequency
Agios Nikolaos				
(Crete)	Milos	7hr	€16.60	3 weekly
Iraklio (Crete)	Mykonos	9hr	€21.50	3 weekly
	Naxos	7½hr	€18.50	1 weekly
	Paros	7-8hr	€20.50	2 weekly
	Santorini	3¾hr	€14	3 weekly
	Syros	10hr	€20	1 weekly
	Tinos	10¼hr	€22.50	2 weekly
Lavrio	Kea	1¼hr	€5.30	2 daily
	Kythnos	3½hr	€7.20	6 weekly
	Syros	3½hr	€13	2 weekly
Piraeus	Amorgos	10hr	€17.20	10 weekly
	Anafi	11hr	€22.80	3 weekly
	Donousa	7hr	€15.80	3 weekly
Piraeus	Folegandros	6-9hr	€17	4 weekly
	Ios	7hr	€18	4 daily
	Iraklia	6¾hr	€15.40	3 weekly
	Kimolos	6hr	€15.30	2 weekly
	Koufonisia	8hr	€15.20	5 weekly
	Kythnos	2½hr	€10.50	2 daily
	Milos	5-7hr	€16.90	2 daily
	Mykonos	6hr	€17.50	3 daily
	Naxos	6hr	€17.30	6 daily
	Paros	5hr	€17.30	6 daily
	Santorini	9hr	€20.20	4 daily
	Serifos	4½hr	€13.20	1 daily
	Sifnos	5hr	€14.80	1 daily
	Sikinos	10hr	€19.90	7 weekly
	Syros	4hr	€15	3 daily
	Tinos	5hr	€16.10	2 daily
Rafina	Andros	2hr	€8.50	2 daily
	Mykonos	4½hr	€14.70	2 daily
	Paros	7hr	€14.40	6 weekly
	Syros	1¾hr	€25	1 daily
	Tinos	3½hr	€13	2 daily
Sitia (Crete)	Milos	9hr	€20	3 weekly
Thessaloniki	Mykonos	15hr	€33	3 weekly
	Naxos	15hr	€31	1 weekly
	Paros	15-16hr	€33	2 weekly
	Santorini	19hr	€35.50	3 weekly
	Syros	12hr	€30.50	1 weekly
	Tinos	13hr	€32.50	2 weekly

point for Andros is Rafina, but it's possible to also access it from Piraeus by catching a ferry to Syros, Tinos or Mykonos and connecting from there.

The western Cyclades (Kea, Kythnos, Milos, Serifos, Sifnos, Folegandros and Sikinos) have less frequent connections with the mainland. Lavrio is the mainland port for ferries serving Kea from where connections south to the other western Cyclades can be made.

The eastern Cyclades (Anafi, Amorgos, Iraklia, Shinousa, Koufonisia and Donousa) are the least-visited and have the fewest links with the mainland. Amorgos, Iraklia, Shinousa, Koufonisia are best visited from Naxos; Anafi from Santorini.

When you plan your island-hopping, it pays to bear this pattern of ferry routes in mind. However, Paros is the ferry hub of the Cyclades, and connections between different groups are usually possible via Paros.

The following table gives an overview of high-season ferry services to the Cyclades from the mainland and Crete.

Getting Around

For information on travel within the Cyclades, see the individual island entries.

The Cyclades are more exposed to the northwesterly *meltemi* wind than other island groups. This is a fierce wind; it may be warm, but it can blast, and it often plays havoc with ferry schedules (especially on smaller vessels that ply the Little Cyclades routes and on small hydrofoils). Keep this in mind if on a tight schedule.

ANDROS ΑΝΔΡΟΣ

pop 9999

Andros is an escapist's dream. It is the most northerly of the Cyclades, is not overwhelmed by tourism, and has lonely mountains and terraced valleys to wander through. The second-largest island of the group after Naxos, Andros boasts neoclassical mansions and Venetian tower-houses that contrast with the rough unpainted stonework of farm buildings and patterned dovecotes. Elaborate slate walls wriggle everywhere across the landscape, intertwined with old cobbled footpaths. Andros is also

one of the most fertile of the Cyclades; it produces citrus fruit and olives, and supports large swathes of pine, plane and cypress trees. The island has several beaches, many of them isolated. There are three main settlements; the unpretentious port of Gavrio, the cheerful resort of Batsi and the handsome main town, the Hora, known also as Andros.

Getting There & Away

FERRY

At least two ferries daily leave Andros' main port of Gavrio for Rafina (€8.50, two hours). Daily ferries run to Tinos (€6.20, 1½ hours) and Mykonos (€7.80, 2½ hours); conveniently allowing daily connections to Syros and Paros in the high season. Services run direct to Syros twice a week (€6.60, two hours). There is a daily service, except on Sunday, to Paros (€11.10, four hours), a weekly service to Naxos (€12.80, five hours), Kythnos (€10, five hours) and Kea (€7.30, six hours).

Getting Around

Around nine buses daily (fewer on weekends) link Gavrio and Hora (€2.70, 50 minutes) via Batsi (€1, 15 minutes); schedules are posted at the bus stop in Gavrio and Hora and outside Andros Travel in Batsi; otherwise, call ☎ 2282 022 316 for information.

A **taxi** Gavrio (☎ 2282 071 171) Batsi (☎ 2282 041 081) Hora (☎ 2282 022 171) from Gavrio to Batsi costs €5 and to Hora €17. Car hire is about €45 in August.

GAVRIO ΓΑΥΡΙΟ

Gavrio, on the west coast, is the main port of Andros. Apart from the flurry of ferry arrivals, Gavrio is very low key; but there are pleasant beaches nearby.

Orientation & Information

The ferry quay is mid-waterfront and the bus stop is next to it. Turn left from the quay and walk along the waterfront for the post office. There is a small **tourist information kiosk** (☎ 2282 071 770; ⏰ Jul-Aug) to the right of the ferry quay where the road to Batsi bears off. From 2004 Greek Sun Holidays (see Batsi, p124) will have an office at Gavrio. The **port police** (☎ 2282 071 213) are on the waterfront.

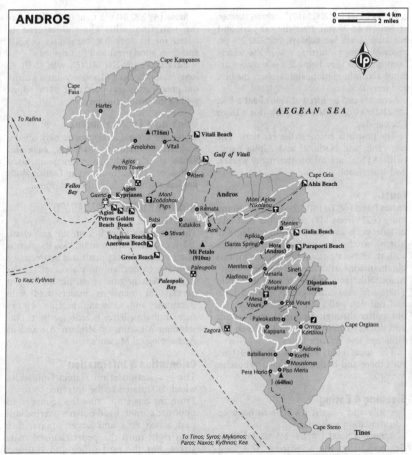

ANDROS

0 ———— 4 km
0 ———— 2 miles

Cape Kampanos

AEGEAN SEA

Cape Fasa

Hartes

To Rafina

▲ (716m)

Vitali Beach

Amolohos   Vitali

Gulf of Vitali

Agios
Petros Tower

Ateni

Cape Gria

Ahla Beach

Fellos
Bay

Gavrio

Agios
Kyprianos

Moni
Zoödohou
Pigis

Andros

Moni Agiou
Nikolaou

Agios
Petros Golden
Beach Beach

Batsi   Remata

Katakilos

Stivari   Arni

Stenies

Gialia Beach

Apikia
(Sariza Spring)

Hora
(Andros)

Paraporti Beach

Delavoia Beach
Anerousa Beach

Mt Petalo
(910m)

Green Beach

Paleopolis

To Kea; Kythnos

Menites

Mesaria

Sineti

*Paleopolis
Bay*

Aladinou

Moni
Panahrandou

Dipotamata
Gorge

Mesa
Vouni

Exo Vouni

Zagora

Paleokastro

Kapparia

Ormos
Korthiou

Cape Orginos

Batsilianos

Korthi

Aidonia

Pera Horio

Mousianos

Piso Meria

(648m)

Cape Steno   *Tinos*

*To Tinos; Syros; Mykonos;
Paros; Naxos; Kythnos; Kea*

Sleeping & Eating

Ostria Studios (☎ 2282 071 551; www.ostria-studios.gr; s/d €55/60, apt €67) These decent apartments in a big and quiet complex are a good choice, especially for reduced prices off season. It is about 300m along the Batsi road.

Andros Holiday Hotel (☎ 2282 071 384; www.andros holiday.com; s/d €74/93; ◷ Easter–mid-Oct; Ⓟ ⊗ ⊛) Breakfast is included in the price at this fairly smart place that has an exclusive air about it. There's direct access to a small beach. The hotel is reached by turning right down a side road just before Ostria Studios.

Veggera (☎ 2282 071 077; mains €2.80-6) Seafood is sold by the kilo, and there's a fine selection of dishes at this pleasant taverna with

its peaceful and tree-shaded plateia. It's along to the right of the ferry quay and is reached up an alleyway, just before the Batsi road bears off left.

To Konaki (☎ 2282 071 733; mains €2.50-8.50) A pleasant little ouzeria, To Konaki is just to the left of the ferry quay and is fronted by trees and shrubs.

BATSI ΜΠΑΤΣΙ

Bright and friendly Batsi, 8km south of Gavrio, is Andros' main resort. The village stands on the curve of a pretty bay and has a tiny fishing harbour at one end and a pleasant, sandy beach at the other. Mulberry trees punctuate the colourful waterfront. A great source of information is **Andros Travel** (☎ 2282 041 252; androstr@otenet.gr; ☺ 9am-2pm & 6-9.30pm), near the car park and bus stop. **Greek Sun Holidays**, (☎ 2282 041 198; greeksun@travelling.gr), further round the waterfront are also very helpful. Both places arrange accommodation, sightseeing, car hire and ferry tickets.

Scooters can be hired at **Dino's Rent-a-Bike** (☎ 2282 041 003) by the car park, for €16 to €22 per day.

The post office is near the car park. The taxi rank, and National and Alpha banks (with ATMs) are all on the main square, mid-waterfront.

Tours

Andros Travel (☎ 2282 041 252) organises island tours (€22) from May to October that take in Paleopolis and the charming villages of Korthi on the Bay of Korthiou; Menites, with its elaborate fountain; Apikia with its old mansions and the 8th-century Moni Agiou Nikolaou and its beautiful murals. There are also small-group, guided half- and full-day walks (€17 to €27) following old paths through beautiful countryside and donkey treks (€30 to €70). Greek Sun Holidays also arrange tours.

The local boat, **Poseidon** (☎ 2282 041 696) runs there-and-back trips to nearby beaches for €10.

Sleeping & Eating

For July and August it's wise to book accommodation well ahead.

Karanasos Hotel (☎ 2282 041 480; s/d €50/65) Set back from the waterfront, this long-established place has rather dark and old-fashioned furnishings and decor, but the style enhances the quiet charm.

Hotel Chryssi Akti (☎ 2282 041 237; s/d €48/66; ✖ ☷) Bright, cool rooms and acres of gleaming marble are the style at this modern hotel that also has a lift. It's right across the road from the beach. Breakfast starts at €3.80.

Likio Studios (☎ 2282 041 050; fax 2282 042 000; d/f €65/100; ✖) Treat yourself to one of these spacious and well-equipped studios in flower-filled surroundings. Open year-round, they are in a quiet location about 250m past Dino's Rent-a-Bike.

Cavo d'Ora (☎ 2282 041 766; mains €5-12) Shaded by trees and big umbrellas, Cavo d'Ora offers good traditional cooking, including tasty moussaka.

Koala (☎ 2282 041 696; mains €4-11) Right on the waterfront, this cheerful taverna is noted for its very big breakfasts (€5.50) and does good meat and fish dishes.

Pizza Litsa's (☎ 2282 041 477; mains €6-12) A long-established popular eatery, Litsa's turns out great pizzas and pastas for €4 to €8, as well as meat and chicken dishes.

Drinking & Entertainment

There are several lively music bars on the waterfront, including **Nameless**, **Aqua** and **Kimbo**, all of which play mainstream disco with some Greek music. The **Capricio Music Bar** has a stronger line in Greek music.

HORA (ANDROS) ΧΟΡΑ (ΑΝΔΡΟΣ)
pop 1508

The intriguing Hora lies on the east coast, 35km east of Gavrio and unfolds its charms along a narrow rocky peninsula between two bays. It's an enchanting place that reflects its Venetian origins in numerous elegant neoclassical mansions underscored with Byzantine and Ottoman accents. Hora's rich cultural pedigree is reflected in its outstanding Museum of Modern Art and its Archaeological Museum.

Orientation & Information

The bus station is on Plateia Goulandri, which is situated at the entrance to town. From the bus stop, cross the square to its opposite corner, head down a narrow lane past a taxi rank and larger square, then turn right onto the pedestrianised main street. For the post office and National Bank of Greece, with ATM, turn left at the main street. There's also an Alpha Bank, with ATM as well, to the right and halfway down the main street, beside the big church and its palm trees. Right opposite the church, steps lead down to the old harbour area of Plakoura and to Nimborio Beach.

Further down the main street is the pretty central square, Plateia Kaïri with its shaded tavernas and cafés, overlooked by the Archaeological Museum. Steps descend from the square, north to Plakoura and Nimborio Beach and south to Paraporti Beach. The street continues along the promontory and ends at Plateia Riva, a big, airy square with crumbling balustrades.

Sights & Activities

Hora has two outstanding museums; both were donated to the state by Vasilis and Elise Goulandris of a wealthy shipowning Andriot family. The **Andros Archaeological Museum** (☎ 2282 023 644; Plateia Kaïri; adult/student €3/free; ☺ 8.30am-3pm Tue-Sun) contains impressive finds from the 9th to 8th centuries BC settlements of Zagora and Paleopolis on Andros' east coast as well as items of the Roman, Byzantine and Early Christian periods. They include a splendid marble copy of the 4th-century bronze **Hermes of Andros** by Praxiteles.

The **Museum of Modern Art** (☎ 2282 022 650; adult/student Jul-Sep €6/3, Oct-Jun €3/1.50; ☺ main gallery 10am-2pm & 6-8pm, sculpture gallery 10am-2pm Wed-Mon Jul-Sep; both galleries 10am-2pm Wed-Mon Oct-Jun) has earned Andros an international reputation in the art world. The main gallery features the work of prominent Greek artists, but each year, from July to September, the gallery stages an exhibition of one of the world's great artists. To date there have been impressive exhibitions featuring the work of Picasso, Matisse, Braque, Toulouse-Lautrec and Miro. To reach the gallery head down the steps from Plateia Kaïri towards the old harbour.

A huge **bronze statue** of a sailor stands in Plateia Riva, more Russian triumphalist than Andriot in its scale and style. The ruins of a **Venetian fortress** stand on an island that is linked to the tip of the headland by the shaky remnants of a steeply arched bridge.

Scooters and motorbikes can be hired at **Riva** (☎ 2282 024 412) down at Nimborio, and through Karaoulanis Rooms for €12 to €15.

Sleeping & Eating

Karaoulanis Rooms (☎ 2282 024 412; www.andros rooms.gr; Plakoura; d/apt €30/75) The rooms in this tall harbourside house are neat and clean and the building has a terrific traditional ambience. Apartments are self-contained. To get there, head down the steps opposite the big church halfway down the main street.

Alcioni Inn (☎ 2282 024 522; Nimborio; s/d €50/90) Development at Nimborio Beach is mixed, but these self-catering rooms are very smart and comfortable and are just across the road from the beach.

Niki (☎ /fax 2282 029 155; s/d €45/56) Right on the main street and handy to just about everything, these lovely rooms are in a handsome old house that has retained its beautiful timber ceilings and galleries. Downstairs is a large veranda where you can get breakfast for €7.50 and where coffee is available.

Nonnas (☎ 2282 023 577; Plakoura; mains €3-9) A small, down-to-earth mezedes place on the old harbour next to Karaoulanis Rooms, Nonnas rattles out standard fare as well as more pricey fish dishes such as red mullet, when available.

Palinorio (☎ 2282 022 881; Nimborio; mains €8-15; ☺ 11am-2am) Of the line-up of restaurants at the town end of Nimborio Beach, this is an excellent choice for well-prepared traditional dishes, good service and great value. Shellfish dishes are more expensive, but are superb.

Red Pepper (☎ 2282 022 778; Plateia Goulandri; mains €6-12) Usefully located next to the bus station this big cheerful place dishes up filling meat and chicken dishes as well as a wide range of tasty pizzas and pastas (€4 to €8). There's a balcony with fine views over the hills.

Ernis (☎ 2282 022 233; Plateia Kaïri), by the square, is a fine little café and pastry shop. **Mickey's Café-Bar** (☎ 2282 023 508; ☺ 10am-4pm & 9pm-2.30am), just up the street from Ernis, is the buzzing music scene for young locals, by day and night.

AROUND ANDROS

About 2.5km from Gavrio, the **Agios Petros tower**, an impressive circular watchtower in rough stone and dating from the 4th century BC, is signposted.

Between Gavrio and Paleopolis Bay are several pleasant beaches, including **Agios Kyprianos**, where there's a little church with a taverna close by; **Delavoia**, one half of which is naturist, **Anerousa** and **Green Beach**.

Paleopolis, 9km south of Batsi on the coast road, is the site of Ancient Andros, where the Hermes of Andros was found. There is little to see, but the mountain setting is compelling.

The blue-green bay and resort at **Ormos Korthiou**, 20km south of Hora, has a lot of faded charm. You'll find several standard hotels and domatia, as well as a handful of reasonably priced restaurants.

CYCLADES

TINOS ΤΗΝΟΣ

pop 8574

On the very picturesque island of Tinos religious pilgrims are regularly brought to their knees by their devotion to the sacred icon of the Megalochari, the Holy Virgin. Yet beyond the religious tourism of the main town of Hora, where the icon resides in the very splendid Church of Panagia Evangelistria, Tinos is an incredibly beautiful island covered with mountains and terraced slopes that are dotted with unspoilt and remote hill villages and elaborately ornate whitewashed dovecotes; arguably reward enough for any kind of pilgrim.

Getting There & Away

EXCURSION BOAT

The excursion boat *Tinos Sky* runs trips to Delos (€20) from the north end of the waterfront, 9.30am Tuesday to Saturday and 9am Sunday, returning about 6pm, July to the first week in September.

FAST BOAT & CATAMARAN

There are at least three services daily to Mykonos (€7.10, 15 minutes) and Rafina (€26, 1¾ hours). Also, daily services to Paros (€16, 1¼ hours), five weekly to Piraeus (€33, three hours) and one daily to Syros (€6.80, two hours).

FERRY

At least six ferries daily go to Mykonos (€3.60, 30 minutes), and one daily to Rafina (€13, 3½ hours) and Andros (€6.20, 1½ hours). There are at least two daily to Syros (€4, 50 minutes) and Piraeus (€16.80, six hours).

Four weekly ferries go to Ikaria via Mykonos (€16, 3½ hours).

Two ferries weekly go to Thessaloniki (€22.50, 12 hours), and there are daily services to Paros (€8, 2½ hours) and Santorini (€15, five hours).

Two weekly services run to Naxos (€8.30, 4¼ hours) and Iraklio on Crete (€22, 10¼ hours).

There are two weekly ferries to Amorgos (€15, 2¼ hours) and one weekly ferry to Skiathos (€19, 7¼ hours).

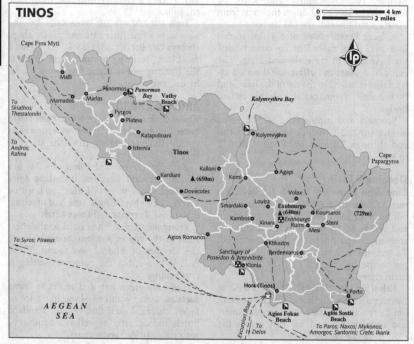

TINOS

0 — 4 km
0 — 2 miles

Cape Fyra Myti

Malli

Panormos · *Panormos Bay* · Vathy Beach

Mamados · Marlas

To Skiathos; Thessaloniki

Pyrgos · Plateia

Katapolioani

Kolymvythra Bay

To Andros; Rafina

Isternia

Tinos

Kolymvythra

Kalloni · Komi

Kardiani · ▲ (650m)

Agapi

Dovecotes

Cape Papargyros

Volax

Smardaki · Loutra · **Exobourgo** ▲ (640m) · Koumaros

Kambos · *Exobourgo Ruins* · Steni

Xinara · Mesi

▲ (729m)

To Syros; Piraeus

Agios Romanos

Sanctuary of Poseidon & Amphitrite · Kionia

Ktikados

Berdemiaros

Hora (Tinos)

Porto

AEGEAN SEA

Excursion Boat To Delos

Agios Fokas Beach

Agios Sostis Beach

To Paros; Naxos; Mykonos; Amorgos; Santorini; Crete; Ikaria

Getting Around

There are frequent buses from Hora (Tinos) to Porto and Kionia (€0.90) and several daily to Panormos (€2.80) via Pyrgos and Kambos. Buses leave from the station on the waterfront, opposite the Blue Star Ferry Office where there's a timetable in the window.

Motorcycles (€20 a day) and cars (€40 a day) can be hired from a number of outfits along the waterfront at Hora.

HORA (TINOS)

Hora, also known as Tinos, is the island's capital and port. It's a busy, everyday sort of place, where the waterfront is lined with cafés and hotels. The narrow streets behind the waterfront are full of restaurants and tavernas and there are numerous shops and stalls crammed with religious ware.

Orientation

The 'new' ferry quay, where large ferries dock, is rather isolated at the northwestern end of the waterfront, about 300m from the main harbour; but there are two more central quays where catamarans and smaller ferries dock. When you buy a ferry ticket, it's essential to check which quay your boat leaves from. Allow at least 20 minutes to walk from the centre to the new quay.

The uphill street of Leof Megaloharis, straight ahead from the main harbour, is the route pilgrims take to the church. The narrower Evangelistria, to the right facing inland, also leads to the church.

Information

Malliaris Travel (☎ 2283 024 241; fax 2283 024 243; malliaris@thn.forthnet.gr; Paralía), on the waterfront near Hotel Posidonion, and **Windmills Travel & Tourism** (☎ 2283 023 398; www.windmills-travel.com; Kionion 2), halfway between the new ferry quay and the central waterfront, are both very helpful.

The post office is at the southeastern end of the waterfront, just past the bus station and the Agricultural Bank of Greece (with ATM), next door to Hotel Tinion – turn right from the quay. The pebbled town beach of Agios Fokas is a 10-minute walk south from the waterfront.

The **port police** (☎ 2283 022 348; Akti Elis) are on the waterfront, near the Oceanis hotel.

Sights

The intriguing neoclassical **Church of the Annunciation** (Church of Panagia Evangelistria; ⊙ 8am-8pm) is built of marble from the island's Panormos quarries. Inside the main building, the acclaimed icon of the Holy Virgin is draped with gold, silver, jewels and pearls, and is surrounded by gifts from suppliants.

Set into the surface of the street on one side of Leoforos Megaloharis, there is a rubberised strip, complete with sidelights, on which no cars ever park. This is used by pilgrims, who may be seen at any time of year crawling on hands and knees to the church, pushing long candles before them. The final approach is up carpeted steps.

There's a lucrative trade in candles, reproduction icons, incense and evil-eye charms (see Beware the Evil Eye, p128) on Evangelistria and Leoforos Megaloharis, where religious shops rub shoulders happily with places selling those competing icons of the 21st century, mobile phones. The largest candles, which are about 2m long, cost €5.

Within the church complex, several **museums** house religious artefacts, icons and secular artworks.

The small **archaeological museum** (☎ 2283 022 670; Leof Megaloharis; admission €2; ⊙ 8am-3pm Tue-Sun) on the right-hand side of the street as you descend from the church, has a small collection that includes impressive clay *pithoi* (storage jars), grave reliefs and sculptures.

Sleeping

Avoid Hora on 25 March (Annunciation), 15 August (Feast of the Assumption) and 15 November (Advent), unless you want to join the roofless masses who sleep on the streets at these times.

Camping Tinos (☎ 2283 022 344; fax 2283 025 55; camp sites per adult/tent €5/3, bungalows €15, with bathroom €20) This is a fine site with good facilities. It's south of the town, near Agios Fokas, about a five-minute walk from the ferry quay, and is clearly signposted from the waterfront. A minibus meets ferries.

Oceanis (☎ 2283 022 452; oceanis@mail.gr; Akti G Drósou; s/d €35/55; ⊠) Although blandly modern in style, the rooms at this big hotel, at the southern end of the waterfront, are smart and adequate. There's a lift to all floors.

BEWARE THE EVIL EYE

You may notice when travelling through Greece that some bus drivers keep a chain bearing one or two blue stones dangling over the dashboard. Or you may spot a small, plastic blue eye attached to a cross hanging around someone's neck. These are powerful tokens against the 'evil eye'.

The evil eye is associated with envy, and can be cast – unintentionally even – upon someone or something that is praised or admired. Those most vulnerable to the evil eye include people, creatures or objects of beauty, rarity and value. Babies are particularly vulnerable, and those who admire them will often effect the sound of spitting gently on them to repel any ill effects. Adults and older children who are worried about being afflicted by the evil eye wear blue.

Hotel Posidonion (☎ 2283 023 121; fax 2283 025 808; 4 Paralía; s/d €50/70) This well-placed and long-established hotel is on the waterfront, opposite the bus station and near the ferry quay. It has fairly well worn, but decent rooms, although high season prices are steep.

Hotel Tinion (☎ 2283 022 261; kchatzi@ath.forth net.gr; 1 Constantinou Alavanou; s/d €35/70) Rooms at this handsome place, near the roundabout at the southern end of the waterfront, are high-roofed, elegant and comfortable. There is some traffic noise at the front.

Eating & Drinking

Waterfront places serve standard fare, but in the narrow streets behind there are some worthwhile restaurants.

Pallada Taverna (☎ 2283 023 516; Plateia Palladas; mains €2.50-11) Seafood is by the kilo at this popular taverna that offers tasty Greek dishes and particularly fine retsina and other local wines from the barrel. It's a block inland from the northern end of the waterfront.

Metaxy Mas (☎ 2283 025 945; mains €4-15) You'll pay a bit more for the privilege of eating in this stylish restaurant, but it has a refreshingly modernist ambience and the mezedes and main dishes are worthwhile.

Koursaros (☎ 2283 023 963; ☻ 8am-3am) Making a healthy bid as the centre of non-religious music on Tinos, this relaxing music bar at the northern end of the main waterfront plays a mix of rock, funk and jazz.

AROUND TINOS

To make the most of Tinos and its 42 villages, its dovecotes and enticing countryside you need to get out of Hora's religious-commercial grip and go exploring.

Kionia, 3km northwest of Hora, has several small beaches. Here too is the 4th-century BC site of the **Sanctuary of Poseidon & Amphitrite**.

At **Porto**, 6km east of Hora, there's a lovely, uncrowded beach facing Mykonos, while about 1km further on from Porto is the even lovelier **Pacheia Ammos** Beach.

The ruins of the Venetian fortress of **Exobourgo**, atop a 640m-high rocky hill, stand sentinel over a cluster of unspoiled villages. The ascent can be made from several villages; the shortest route is from Xinara and, though steep, the great views are reward enough.

Tinos is noted for its basket-making and most weavers are based in the tiny, white-walled village of **Volax**, nestled amid rocky monoliths on a spectacular plain in the centre of the island. Car or bike are the best ways of getting to Volax, where there is a small **folklore museum** (ask at the nearest basket-makers for someone to open it for you) and an attractive Catholic chapel. There are a couple of popular tavernas in Volax.

About 12km north of Hora on the north coast is **Kolymvythra Bay**, where there are two fine sandy beaches.

On the north coast, 28km northwest of Hora there's a small beach at **Panormos** from where the distinctive green marble, quarried in nearby **Marlas** was once exported. **Pyrgos**, on the way to Panormos, is a picturesque village where marble is still carved and where there is a wealth of fine architecture as well as two art museums and a marble sculpture school. The village also has several marble and woodcarving workshops.

SYROS ΣΥΡΟΣ

pop 16,766

Syros is the big boss of the Cyclades, a ferry hub of the northern islands, the legal and administrative centre of the entire group and home to Ermoupolis, the handsomest of all Cycladic towns. If you break the lightest of laws anywhere in the Cyclades, they'll whisk you off immediately to court in Syros. Make your visit voluntary instead. The rewards are substantial; they include authentic Greek culture and society, great eating and sleeping options, and a handful of small, but pleasant beaches. Because Syros' core economy does not depend on tourism, there is none of the overt commercialism of more tourist-bound islands. Local shipbuilding has declined, but Syros still has textile manufacturing, dairy farms and a thriving horticultural industry.

History
Excavations of an Early Cycladic fortified settlement and burial ground at Kastri in the island's northeast, dating from 2800–2300 BC, show that early inhabitants followed the typical Neolithic life of farmers and fishermen and had trading and cultural connections with other communities.

In the Middle Ages, Syros was the only Greek island with an entirely Roman Catholic population, a result of conversion by the Catholic Franks who took over the island in 1207. This ensured that during Turkish rule, Syros enjoyed effective neutrality, and the protection of the French. During the War of Independence thousands of refugees from islands ravaged by the Turks fled to the island. They brought with them an infusion of Greek Orthodoxy and fresh commercial incentives. Through their energies they built a new settlement (now called Vrodado), and made the port town of Ermoupolis the commercial, naval and cultural centre of Greece during the 19th century.

Getting There & Away
AIR
Olympic Airways (☎ 2281 088 018; fax 2281 083 536; Akti Papagou) operates at least one flight daily except Thursday and Saturday to Athens (€63). The Olympic Airways office is on the waterfront in Ermoupolis, near the bus station, around the corner from Naxou street.

FAST BOAT & CATAMARAN
Services depart daily for Piraeus (€31, 2½ hours), Rafina (€25, 1¾ hours), Paros (€12, 45 minutes), Naxos (€13, 1½ hours), Mykonos (€11, 30 minutes) and Tinos (€7, two hours).

FERRY
There are at least four ferries daily from Syros to Piraeus (€19, four hours), two to Tinos, except Tuesday (€4, 50 minutes), and four to Mykonos (€5.10, 1¼ hours).

There are two daily to Paros (€7, 1¾ hours) and Naxos (€8, three hours). There are daily connections to Andros via Tinos (€6, 2¾ hours) and two direct connections weekly (1¾ hours).

At least four ferries weekly go to Amorgos (€11, 4½ hours), Ios (€15, 2¾ hours), Ikaria (€10, 2½ hours), Milos (€14, six hours), Samos (€16, 4½ hours) and Santorini (€18, 5¼ hours); and one weekly serves Crete (€24, 8½ hours).

At least twice weekly there are boats to Andros (€6, 1¾ hours), Kea (€8, three hours), Kythnos (€7, two hours), Sifnos (€10, four hours), Serifos (€8, two to four hours), Kimolos (€11, five hours) and Anafi (€15.20, eight hours).

Five ferries weekly go to Patmos (€21, 4½ hours).

Each week, three ferries head to Sikinos (€9, five hours), Folegandros (€10, six hours), Lavrio (€13, 3½ hours) and Leros (€23, seven hours).

Two ferries a week go to Kos (€26, nine hours) and Rhodes (€31, 15½ hours), and one goes to Thessaloniki (€26, 12 hours).

There are weekly ferries to Iraklio (€24, 7½ hours) and Nisyros (€19, 11 hours).

Getting Around
About nine buses per day run a circular route from Ermoupolis to Galissas (€1.15) and Vari (€1.15) calling at all beaches mentioned in this section. Buses leave Ermoupolis every half hour from June to September and every hour the rest of the year, alternating clockwise and anticlockwise. All of these buses will eventually get you to where you want to go, but its always worth checking which service is quickest.

There is a bus that travels Ano Syros every morning at 10.30am, except Sunday (€0.90). **Taxis** (☎ 2281 086 222) charge €3 to Ano Syros from the port; it's a very pleasant and easy walk of about 1.5km back down.

Cars can be hired from about €40 a day, and mopeds from €10 per day, from numerous hire outlets on the waterfront.

SYROS

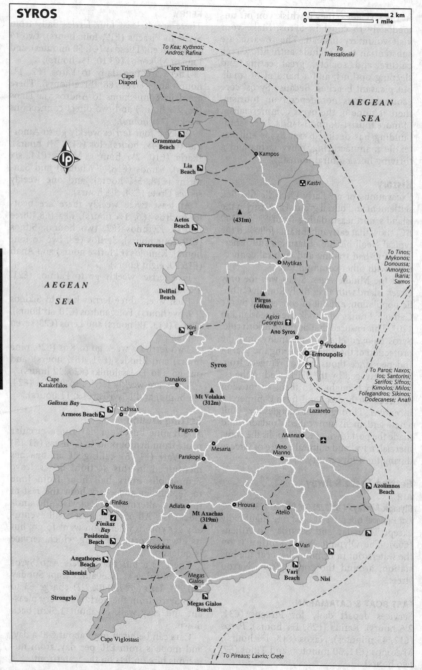

0   2 km
0   1 mile

To Kea; Kythnos;
Andros; Rafina

To
Thessaloniki

Cape
Diapori

Cape Trimeson

AEGEAN
SEA

Grammata
Beach

Kampos

Lia
Beach

Kastri

Aetos
Beach

(431m)

Varvarousa

Mytikas

Delfini
Beach

To Tinos;
Mykonos;
Donoussa;
Amorgos;
Ikaria;
Samos

Pirgos
(440m)

Agios
Georgios

AEGEAN
SEA

Kini

Ano Syros

Vrodado

Ermoupolis

Syros

To Paros; Naxos;
Ios; Santorini;
Serifos; Sifnos;
Kimolos; Milos;
Folegandros; Sikinos;
Dodecanese; Anafi

Cape
Katakefalos

Danakos

Mt Volakas
(312m)

Lazareto

Galissas Bay

Armeos Beach

Galissas

Pagos

Manna

Mesaria

Parakopi

Ano
Manno

Vissa

Azolimnos
Beach

Finikas

Adiata

Mt Axachas
(319m)

Hrousa

Atelio

Finikas
Bay
Posidonia
Beach

Posidonia

Vari

Angathopes
Beach

Vari
Beach

Shinonisi

Megas
Gialos

Nisi

Strongylo

Megas Gialos
Beach

Cape Viglostasi

To Pireaus; Lavrio; Crete

CYCLADES

ERMOUPOLIS ΕΡΜΟΥΠΟΛΗ

pop 11,799

Ermoupolis is named after Hermes, the god of commerce. Its position as the maritime centre of Greece was finally relinquished to Piraeus in the 20th century, but it remains the Cyclades' capital and its largest town. It's a lively and likeable place full of restored neoclassical mansions. There are bustling commercial areas and well-kept central streets, although there is some decline in the outer neighbourhoods, where crumbling ruins and cracked and sagging stairways regularly punctuate the general tidiness.

The Catholic settlement of Ano Syros and the Greek Orthodox settlement of Vrodado lie to the left and right, looking inland, and both spill down from high hilltops, with higher hills rising behind.

Orientation

The main ferry quay is at the southwestern end of the port. The bus station is on the waterfront, just along from the main ferry quay.

To reach the central square, Plateia Miaouli, walk to the right from the ferry quay for about 200m, and then turn left into El Venizelou. There are public toilets at the eastern end of the port, and off Antiparou.

Information

In summer there is an **information booth** (☎ 2281 080 356; ☽ 10am-2pm & 4-8pm Jun-Aug) run by the Syros Hotels' Association on the waterfront, about 100m northeast of the main ferry quay. The travel agencies **Enjoy Your Holidays** (☎ 2281 087 070; 4 Akti Papagou), opposite the bus station on the waterfront, and **Teamwork Holidays** (☎ 2881 083 400; 18 Akti Papagou) just across from the main ferry quay are very helpful with accommodation information, ferry tickets and other details.

There are ATMs at a number of convenient points throughout town.

Internet Café (☎ 0281 085 330; ground fl, town hall, Plateia Miaouli; €2 per 20 min)

Police station (☎ 2281 082 610; Plateia Vardaka) Beside the Apollon Theatre.

Port police (☎ 2281 082 690/088 888; Plateia Lakis Kyriarchias) On the eastern side of the port.

Post office (Protopapadaki)

Sights

This splendid town square of **Plateia Miaouli** is the hub of Ermoupolis. It's flanked by palm trees and is lined along its south–side by cafés and bars, some of them engagingly seedy. The north–side of the plateia is dominated by the magnificent neoclassical **town hall**. The small **archaeological museum** (☎ 2281 088 487; Benaki; admission free; ☽ 8.30am-3pm Tue-Sun) at the rear, founded in 1834 and one of the oldest in Greece, houses a tiny collection of ceramic and marble vases, grave stelae and some very fine Cycladic figurines.

The Vrodado district and Ermoupolis merge fairly seamlessly, but **Ano Syros** – a medieval settlement with narrow alleyways and whitewashed houses has great individuality. It's a fascinating place to wander around and has views of neighbouring islands. Be wise and catch the bus up to Ano Syros. From the bus terminus, head into the steeply rising alleyways and bear up right through peaceful enclaves to reach the finest of the Catholic churches, the 13th-century **Agios Georgios** cathedral, with its star-fretted barrel roof and baroque capitals. Follow your nose down from the church, past stunning viewpoints to reach the main street where you'll find a little **museum** (☽ 10am-1pm Mon-Sat Jul-Aug) celebrating the life of Markos Vamvakaris, the famous rembetika singer, who was born in Ano Syros. It's next to a lovely little balcony with terrific views and a handsome bust of Vamvakaris overseeing it all.

Just down some steps at the midpoint of the main street are, potentially, the best-kept public toilets in Greece.

Activities

Cyclades Sailing (☎ 2281 082 501; csail@otenet.gr) can organise yachting charters, as can **Nomikos Sailing** (☎ 2281 088 527); call direct or book through Teamwork Holidays.

Tours

You can book a day coach trip (adult/child €15/5) round the island on Tuesday, Thursday and Saturday through **Teamwork Holidays** (☎ 2881 083 400).

Sleeping

Ermoupolis has a varied selection of rooms although there are not many budget options. Most places are open all year.

CYCLADES

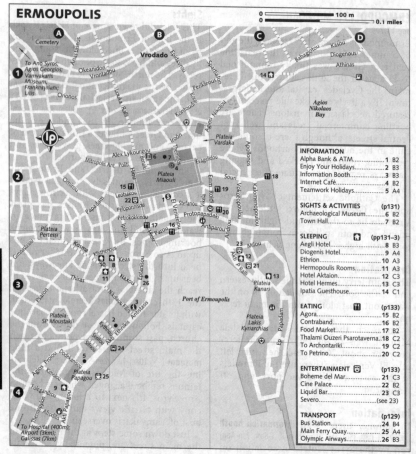

ERMOUPOLIS

0 ———————— 100 m
0 ———————— 0.1 miles

Ipatia Guesthouse (☎ 2281 083 575; ipatiaguest@ yahoo.com; 3 Babagiotou; s/d €30/40, with bathroom €45/ 65) Set in a fine position overlooking Agios Nikolaou Bay, the Ipatia has been lovingly preserved and retains all the finest features of its 19th-century past. Spacious rooms have antique furnishings and remnants of original ceiling frescoes. There's a warm welcome in keeping with the house's family character.

Aegli Hotel (☎ 2281 079 279; www.lux-hotels.com /aegli; 14 Klisthenous; s/d incl breakfast €80/95; ⛄ 🖵) There's an enjoyable sense of exclusivity in this handsome hotel with its elegant and comfortable rooms. Upper balconies at the front have great views over the port and the town centre is just a stroll away.

Hotel Aktaion (☎ 2281 082 675; Akti P Ralli; s/d €45/50; ⛄ 🖵) This award-winning hotel is reached down an alleyway from the busy eastern waterfront and then up several flights of a beautiful staircase. The reception area is a lovely room that was once a dance studio with a minstrels' gallery. Bedrooms have exposed brickwork and canopied beds.

Ethrion (☎ 2281 089 066; www.ethrion.gr; 24 Kosma; d €50; ⛄) These charming apartments are in a modern, but traditionally designed building. Balconies are pleasantly secluded. The building is in a quiet location, just uphill from Hermopoulis Rooms, yet is just a few minutes from the centre.

Hotel Hermes (☎ 2281 083 011; fax 2281 087 412; Plateia Kanari; s/d incl breakfast €52/88) There's a great deal of old-fashioned charm in the air at this long-established hotel that dominates the eastern side of the waterfront. Rooms are smart, with bright interiors.

Hermopoulis Rooms (☎ 2281 087 475; Naxou; d €45) Tucked away in narrow Naxou, a short climb up from the waterfront, these compact self-contained rooms open onto small, bougainvillea-cloaked balconies.

Diogenis Hotel (☎ 2281 086 301; fax 2281 083 334; Plateia Papagou; s/d €55/70) The rooms in this smart hotel are quite swish, although the location, near the shipyard, is a bit dreary. You pay more for sea views, such as they are.

Eating

The waterfront, especially along Akti P Ralli, and the southern edge of Plateia Miaouli is lined with fairly standard restaurants and cafés, but dip into the quieter corners and you'll find some splendid eateries.

To Archontariki (☎ 2281 081 744; 8 Emm Roidi; dishes €3.50-12) This great favourite of locals and visitors alike has an extensive menu of classical Greek dishes with a good selection of regional wines to go with them. Even such simple items as fennel pie and herb pie are delicious. There's a roof garden and there's Greek music at times.

To Petrino (☎ 2281 087 427; 9 Stefanou; dishes €3.50-13.20) Superb traditional dishes and cheerful service are on offer at this excellent restaurant amid swathes of bougainvillea in the pleasant little enclave of Stefanou. There's a delightful sense of being in the heart of some mountain village.

Contraband (☎ 2281 081 028; dishes €3.30-8.80) This is a friendly, unpretentious place in a narrow alleyway off El Venizelou, a block in from the waterfront. It offers delicious seafood and generous helpings.

Agora (☎ 2281 088 329; Plateia Miaouli, Parou; dishes €9-17) Great style and a relaxed atmosphere characterise this wonderful place in a building that predates the town hall. Classical Mediterranean cuisine with modern flair and a selection of fine wines, that are enthusiastically sourced throughout Greece by the owners, go well with the ambience.

Thalami Ouzeri Psarotaverna (☎ 2281 085 331; Souri; dishes €6-20) Seafood is by the kilo at this stylish restaurant that occupies an old waterside mansion on Agios Nikolaos Bay. Fish dishes are well prepared here and reasonably priced treats such as mussels in wine sauce,

or *kakavia*, a local soup comprising fish, onions and tomatoes, are a delight. To get there, follow Souri (which runs off the eastern side of Plateia Miaouli) east to its end.

Frankosyriani (☎ 2282 084 888; Piatsa; dishes €3.50-8) Evening mezedes in this attractive restaurant in Ano Syros, near the Vamvakaris museum, comes with superb views over the port and the dusky sea.

There's a cluster of bars in Ano Syros' main street and **Lilis** (☎ 2282 088 087; dishes €3-8) is another fine evening eatery on the main street with great views. Down at the port, the best place for fresh produce is the small, but well-stocked morning **food market** (Hiou).

Entertainment

The best music bars are clustered along the waterfront on Akti P Ralli. They play mostly lounge music by day and a mix of house, funk and modern Greek music by night, when they draw a great local crowd and are rocking into the early hours.

Boheme del Mar (☎ 2281 083 354) heads up the young scene while the nearby **Liquid Bar** (☎ 2281 082 284) is also lively. Next door, **Severo** (☎ 2281 088 243) has a great racy atmosphere and good DJs.

Cine Palace (☎ 2281 082 313; Plateia Miaouli; admission €6; ☯ 9.30pm Jun-Sep) is an outdoor cinema that screens mainstream new release English- and French-language films subtitled in Greek.

GALISSAS ΓΑΛΗΣΣΑΣ

The west-coast resort of Galissas is a nice relaxed place and has one of the best beaches on Syros, and several cheerful bars and restaurants. There are helpful location maps at bus stops. The beach is a long crescent of sand, shaded by tamarisk trees. The smaller **Armeos**, a scramble round the church-crowned headland on the south–side of the bay, is a nudist beach. The main bus stop is at an intersection behind the beach. The travel agent, **Galissas Tours** (☎ 2281 042 801; galtours@syr.forthnet.gr) is just across from the bus stop. It arranges accommodation and car hire for €40 a day, or scooter hire for €10 to €15 a day.

Sleeping

Two Hearts Camping (☎ 2281 042 052; www.twohearts -camping.com; camp sites per adult/tent €6/4) Set in a pistachio orchard about 4000m from the village and beach, this camping ground has reasonable facilities; from the main bus stop, cross the intersection, keep right of Baroque Café and follow the signs. A minibus meets ferries in high season.

Karmelina Rooms (☎ 2281 042 320; s/d €20/30) There's a charming, old-fashioned welcome at these pleasant little rooms that have a communal kitchen and overlook a garden. Stay on the bus beyond the main bus stop for about 500m until a bus shelter at the junction with the main road.

Oasis (☎ 2281 042 357; s/d €20/35, studio €45) On a delightful and friendly little farm about 400m back from the village, the rooms here are extremely pleasant, while brand new studios are due to open in 2004. Head down the track opposite Karmelina's, or follow the signs from the main bus stop intersection.

Hotel Benois (☎ 2281 042 833; h-benois@otenet.gr; s/d incl breakfast €50/70; ✖) A pleasant hotel close to the beach at the north–entrance to the village, this sizeable place has a friendly family atmosphere.

Dolphin Bay Hotel (☎ 2281 042; dbh@otenet.gr; s/d incl breakfast €95/115; ✖ Easter-Oct; ▢ ✖) Dominating Galissas, this swish hotel, complete with separate units climbing up the hillside, is the place for costly cosseting. The beach is only seconds away.

Eating & Drinking

To Aithrio (☎ 2281 043 950; dishes €4-9) right by the main bus stop does sandwiches (€3 to €4) and pizzas (€7 to €9) as well as standard Greek fare and breakfast (€5). Nearby **Markos** (☎ 2281 043 924; dishes €3.50-9), next to the minimarket, offers similar fare.

For music while you drink try the friendly **Green Dollars Bar** on the beach road, where rock and reggae are favourites from 10am to 4am. Heavier late-night clubbing action drives things along at nearby **Kaldera**.

AROUND SYROS

The beaches south of Galissas all have domatia and some have hotels. Some are narrow roadside strips of dullish sand; but they're not too busy. The first is **Finikas**, with a line of trees serving as a road-break and with potential for fairly brisk windsurfing at times. You'll need your own equipment. **Posidonia**, further south has a sand-and-pebble beach shaded by

tamarisk trees. Further south again, and off the main road, **Angathopes** has a pleasant, south-facing, beach backed by trees. Back on the main road and on the south coast proper, **Megas Gialos** has a couple of roadside beaches.

The pleasant **Vari Bay** further east, has a decent sandy beach with some development including a couple of hotels and a beachfront taverna. **Kini**, out on its own on the west coast, north of Galissas, has a good long beach and is becoming a popular and developing resort.

Sleeping & Eating

Hotel Domenica (☎ 2281 061 216; Vari; s/d €50/65) At Vari, this is a modern seaside place that has bright, clean rooms and friendly service.

Hotel Kamelo (☎ 2281 061 217; Vari; s/d €36/60; ✖) Just down the road from Domenica, but with a frontage right on the sand, this is another friendly place with decent rooms and a reasonable beachside restaurant (dishes €3.80 to €6).

MYKONOS ΜΥΚΟΝΟΣ

pop 9306

Mykonos carries its glamorous and faintly louche reputation with ease, but expensively so. Under the gloss it's a charming and hugely entertaining place, where high camp and celebrity posturing are balanced by the Cubist charms of a traditional Cycladic town and by local people who have had 40 years to get a grip on tourism without losing too much of their Greek identity.

Be prepared for the oiled-up lounger life of the island's packed main beaches, the jostling street scenes and the relentless, and sometimes forlorn, partying. Yet there's still a handful of off-track beaches worth fighting for, while the stylish bars, restaurants and shops have great appeal, and you can still find a quieter pulse amid the labyrinthine old town. Add to all this the nearby sacred island of Delos, and Mykonos really does live up to expectations of marvellous variety.

Mykonos is packed with visitors in July and August and earlier in the season crowds of youngsters arrive in swarms, on school and college trips that are not necessarily educational.

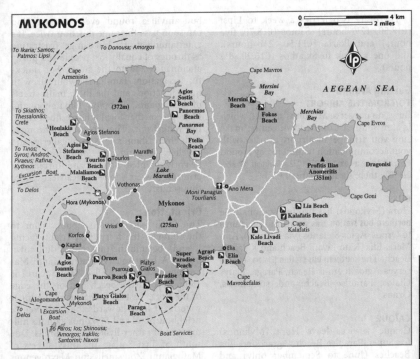

MYKONOS

0 —— 4 km
0 —— 2 miles

To Ikaria; Samos;
Patmos; Lipsi

To Donousa; Amorgos

Cape
Armenistis

Cape Mavros

Mersini
Bay

AEGEAN SEA

Agios
Sostis
Beach
(372m)

Mersini
Beach

Panormos
Beach

Panormos
Bay

Fokos
Beach

Merchias
Bay

Cape Evros

To Skiathos;
Thessaloniki;
Crete

Houlakia
Beach

Agios Stefanos

Ftelia
Beach

To Tinos;
Syros; Andros;
Piraeus; Rafina;
Kythnos

Agios
Stefanos
Beach

Marathi

Profitis Ilias
Anomeritis
(351m)

Dragonisi

Tourlos
Beach

Tourlos

Lake
Marathi

Ano Mera

Excursion Boat

Malaliamos
Beach

To Delos

Vothonas

Moni Panagias
Tourlianis

Lia Beach

Kalafatis Beach

Hora (Mykonos)

Mykonos

Cape
Kalafatis

Cape Goni

Vrissi

(275m)

Kalo Livadi
Beach

Korfos

Kapari

Ornos

Super
Paradise
Beach

Agrari
Beach

Elia

Elia
Beach

Agios
Ioannis
Beach

Psarou

Platys
Gialos

Psarou Beach

Paradise
Beach

Cape
Mavrokefalas

Cape
Alogomandra

Nea
Mykonos

Platys Gialos
Beach

To
Delos

Excursion
Boat

Paraga
Beach

To Paros; Ios; Shinousa;
Amorgos; Iraklio;
Santorini; Naxos

Boat Services

Getting There & Away

AIR
Olympic Airways has five flights daily to Athens (€76), as well as flights to Santorini (€65 one way, daily except Friday) and Rhodes (€90, daily except Sunday). **Aegean Airlines** (☎ 2289 028 720) has daily flights to Athens and Thessaloniki (€99.50).

The **Olympic Airways office** (☎ 2289 022 490, 0109 666 666; Plateia Remezzo; ◷ 8am-3.30pm Mon-Fri) is by the southern bus station in Hora.

FAST BOAT & CATAMARAN
There are at least three daily services connecting Mykonos with Tinos (€7.30, 15 minutes). Four daily services go to Rafina (€29, two hours) and three go to Piraeus (€36, three hours) and Syros (€10.90, 30 minutes). There are three daily services to Paros (€12, 45 minutes), which connect with services to Naxos (€13.80, 1½ hours), Santorini (€24.30, three to four hours) and Ios (€22.80, 2¾ hours). One service daily continues to Iraklio on Crete (€41.30, 4¾ hours).

One service weekly goes directly to Ios (€16, 1¾ hours) and Shinousa (€13, 2½ hours). One weekly service goes to Amorgos (€18.60, 2¼ hours) and Kythnos (€19.90, 1¼ hours).

FERRY
Mykonos has two ferry quays. The town quay where some conventional ferries and smaller fast ferries dock, and the new quay, which is 2.5km north of town and where the bigger fast ferries and some conventional ferries dock. You should always check when buying outgoing tickets which quay your ferry leaves from. Buses connect the new quay with Hora.

Mykonos has daily services to Rafina (€15, 4½ hours) via Tinos (€3.80, 30 minutes) and Andros (€8.60, 2½ hours); to Piraeus (€18.50, six hours) via Tinos and Syros (€5.60, 1½ hours) and to Paros (€7.45, two hours). Connect at Paros for Naxos.

There are three ferries a week to Santorini (€12, six hours) and two weekly to Amorgos (€13.20, 2½ hours).

There are three ferries a week to Thessaloniki (€33, 15 hours), Patmos (€16.50, nine hours) and Crete (€20.50, nine hours).

There are two ferries a week to Lipsi (€18.50, 12½ hours), Samos (€18.70, five hours) and Ikaria (€11.50, 2¾ hours), and one a week to Skiathos (€16.20, 8½ hours).

Getting Around
TO/FROM THE AIRPORT
Buses do not serve Mykonos' airport, which is 3km southeast of the town centre; make sure you arrange an airport transfer with your accommodation (expect to pay around €6); or take a **taxi** (☎ 2289 022 400, airport ☎ 2289 023 700); there's a fixed fare of €5.

BUS
Hora (Mykonos) has two bus stations. The **northern bus station** has frequent departures to Ornos, Agios Stefanos (via Tourlos), Ano Mera, Elia, Kato Livadi Beach and Kalafatis Beach. The **southern bus station** (Plateia Remezzo) serves Agios Ioannis Beach, Paraga, Platys Gialos, Paradise Beach, and, sometimes, Ornos.

CAÏQUE
Caïque services leave Hora (Mykonos) for Super Paradise Beach, Agrari and Elia Beaches (June to September only) and from Platys Gialos to Paradise (€3.70), Super Paradise (€4), Agrari (€3.50) and Elia (€4) Beaches.

CAR & MOTORCYCLE
Most car and motorcycle rental firms are around the southern bus station in Hora. Expect to pay around €40 for car hire.

TAXI
Taxis gather at Hora's Taxi Square and by the bus stations. The minimum fare is €1.50, but there's a charge of €0.30 for each item of luggage. Fares to beaches are: Paradise €6.50, Ornos €3.50, Platys Gialos €4.70 and Elia €9.20.

HORA (MYKONOS)
pop 6467

Mykonos, or Hora, the island's port and capital, is a warren of narrow alleyways that wriggle between white-walled buildings, their stone surfaces webbed with white paint. In the heart of the Little Venice area tiny flower-bedecked churches mix it with trendy boutiques and there's a deluge of bougainvillea round every corner. You can soon pass the same junction twice. It's entertaining at first, but can get frustrating as throngs of equally lost people and pushy aficionados add to the stress. For quick-fix navigation, familiarise yourself with main junctions and the three main streets of Matogianni, Enoplon Dinameon and Mitropoleos that form a horseshoe behind the waterfront. The streets are thronged with chic fashion salons, cool galleries and jewellers, languid and loud music bars, brightly painted houses and torrents of crimson flowers – plus a theatrical cast of thousands.

Orientation
The town waterfront is about 400m to the south of the ferry quay (right, facing inland), beyond the tiny, rather dull, town beach. A busy square, Plateia Manto Mavrogenous (usually called Taxi Square) is 150m beyond the beach and on the edge of the hora. East of Taxi Square, the inner waterfront leads towards the Little Venice neighbourhood and Mykonos' famous hilltop row of rather flyblown windmills. Due south of Taxi Square the busy streets of Matogianni, Zouganelli and Mavrogenous lead into the heart of the hora.

The northern bus station is 250m south of the ferry quay, just beyond where the road bends sharply left. The southern bus station is on Plateia Remezzo, on the southern edge of town. The quay for boats to Delos is at the western end of the waterfront.

Information
Mykonos has no official tourist office. When you get off at the town ferry quay, you will see a low building with four numbered offices. No 1 is the **Hoteliers Association of Mykonos** (☎ 2289 024 540; www.mykonosgreece.com; ☺ 8am-midnight) The Association does not take telephone bookings. No 2 is the **Association of Rooms, Studios & Apartments** (☎ 2289 026 860; ☺ 9am-10pm); No 3 has **camping information** (☎ 2289 022 852), but is rarely open.

BOOKSHOPS
International Press (☎ 2289 023 316; 5 Kambani) Has international newspapers and a good range of magazines and books; it's a block in from the waterfront, just along from Taxi Square.

HORA (MYKONOS)

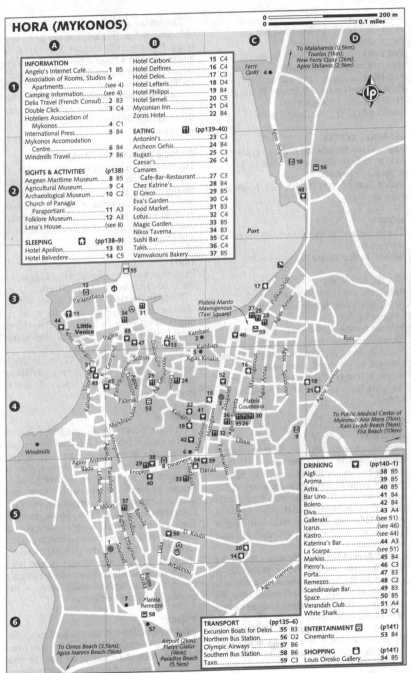

CYCLADES

EMERGENCY

Police (☎ 2289 022 235; Plateia Laka) Next door to the post office.

Port police (☎ 2289 022 716; Akti Kambani) On the waterfront, near the Delos boat quay.

Post office (Laka) In the southern part of town.

Public Medical Center of Mykonos (☎ 2289 023 994/023 996) On the road to Ano Mera.

Tourist police (☎ 2289 022 482; airport)

INTERNET ACCESS

Angelo's Internet Café (☎ 2289 024 106; Xenias; €3.80 per hr) On the road between the southern bus station and the windmills.

Double Click (☎ 2289 027 070; 18 Florou Zouganeli; €6 per hr)

MONEY

There are several banks with ATMs by the ferry quay.

National Bank of Greece (Taxi Sq) Has an ATM.

TRAVEL AGENCIES

Delia Travel (☎ 2289 022 322; travel@delia.gr; Paralia) Halfway along the inner waterfront; this is also the French Consul.

Mykonos Accommodation Center (☎ 2289 023 408; www.mykonos-accommodation.com; 1st fl, 10 Enoplon Dinameon) Very helpful and can find mid-range to top-end, and gay-friendly, accommodation.

Windmills Travel (☎ 2289 023 877; www.windmills -travel.com; Fabrica Sq) By the southern bus station; also helpful.

Sights

MUSEUMS

There are five museums. The **archaeological museum** (☎ 2289 022 325; admission €2; ☉ 8.30am-3pm Tue-Sun) is near the quay. It houses pottery from Delos and some grave stelae and jewellery from the island of Renia (Delos' necropolis). Chief exhibits are a *pithos* (Minoan storage jar), featuring a Trojan War scene in relief, and a statue of Heracles.

The **Aegean Maritime Museum** (☎ 2289 022 700; Tria Pigadia; admission €2; ☉ 10.30am-1pm & 6.30-9pm Apr-Oct) has a fascinating collection of nautical paraphernalia from all over the Aegean, including models of ancient vessels and an old lighthouse.

Next door, **Lena's House** (☎ 2289 022 390; Tria Pigadia; admission free; ☉ 6.30-9.30pm Mon-Sat Apr-Oct) is a 19th-century, middle class Mykonian house with furnishings intact.

The **folklore museum** (☎ 2289 022 591; Paraportianis; admission free; ☉ 4.30-8.30pm Mon-Sat Apr-Oct), housed in an 18th-century sea captain's house, features a large collection of memorabilia and furnishings. The museum is near the Delos quay.

The **agricultural museum** (☎ 2289 022 748; Agiou Ioannou; admission free; ☉ 4-6pm Jun-Sep), near the road to Ano Mera, is housed in a renovated windmill.

CHURCH OF PANAGIA PARAPORTIANI

The Panagia Paraportiani is Mykonos' most famous church. It is five small churches amalgamated, in classical Byzantine style, into one entity, asymmetrical and rock-like in its naturalness. The interplay of light and shade on the multifaceted structure make it a photographer's delight.

Tours

Excursion boats run day trips to Delos. See the Delos section (p143) for details.

Windmills Travel (☎ 2289 023 877; www.windmills -travel.com) is the booking agent for snorkelling (€30 for 30 minutes) and horse-riding tours (from €29; sunset ride €50) and island cruises (€34.90, four weekly).

A Gay Island Cruise (€48) with lunch provided can be booked through **Kyklomar Travel** (☎ 2289 027 091; Plateia Remezzo) or ask at Porta (see Gay Bars, p141).

Sleeping

There are scores of sleeping options in Mykonos, but between July and September if you arrive without a reservation and find reasonably priced accommodation, grab it ('budget' in Mykonos is relative to high prices generally). Otherwise check out local accommodation organisations (see Information, p136). If you choose domatia from owners meeting ferries – they rev up into one of the most raucous scrums in the Cyclades – ask if they charge for transport – some do. If you plan to stay in the hora and want somewhere quiet, think carefully about domatia on the main streets – bar noise till dawn is de rigueur.

BUDGET

Hotel Philippi (☎ 2289 022 294; fax 2289 024 680; 25 Kalogera; s/d €60/75) Although at the heart of Hora, this charming place has the style and atmosphere of a colonial garden house.

Bright, clean rooms open onto a railed veranda overlooking a lush oasis of trees, flowers and shrubs.

Hotel Apollon (☎ 2289 022 223; fax 2289 024 237; Paralia; d €50, s/d with shower €50/€65) Right on the middle of the main waterfront, this is a delightful slice of traditional Mykonos, from the time-lock of the entrance foyer to the satisfyingly old-fashioned and well-kept rooms. Its appealing character is matched by the friendly owner.

Hotel Carboni (☎ 2289 022 217; fax 2289 023 264; Matogianni; s/d €46/100) There's not a lot of character about this functional place, but the rooms are a good size. Those at the back overlook a quiet garden area and manage to retain a nice sense of detachment from crowded Mykonos.

Hotel Delfines (☎ 2289 024 505; Mavrogenous; s/d €38/59) Midway along main drag Mavrogenous, this long-established place was in at the dawn of tourist Mykonos. Don't expect contemporary design features or lavish, spacious rooms, but the welcome is kind.

MID-RANGE

Hotel Lefteris (☎ 2289 027 117; lefterisot@yahoo.com; 9 Apollonos; s/d €79/99) This is a great choice if you want a refuge from the hubbub. It's tucked away above the main streets, just up from Taxi Square. Rooms are comfy and there's a very friendly and sociable welcome. The roof terrace is a great place to relax.

Zorzis Hotel (☎ 2289 022 167; www.zorzishotel.com; 30 Kalogera; s/d €92/115; ❄) There's a stylish ambience at this attractive hotel in the heart of the hora, where good design and distinctive furnishings make the most of occasionally cramped spaces. Rooms at the back overlook a quiet garden.

Hotel Delos (☎ 2289 022 517; fax 2289 022 312; s/d €70/80) In a quiet spot at the town end of Hora's little beach, life at Hotel Delos really does feel peacefully uninterrupted. Rooms are refreshingly bright and large and those at the front have a clear sea view.

TOP END

Hotel Belvedere (☎ 2289 025 122; www.belvedere hotel.com; Rohari; s €145-430, d €150-435; P ❄ ⎚) Wispy Mykonos style enhances the decor and furnishings of this swish hotel where sea and town views are panoramic in all but the cheapest rooms. The reception areas and pool are luxurious and there's even a

sushi bar as well as a mainstream restaurant. Throw in Jacuzzis, massage therapy, a fitness studio and a cinema, and who needs a backpack?

Hotel Semeli (☎ 2289 027 466; semeliht@otenet.gr; Rohari; s/d €240/260, ste €330-400; P ❄ ⎚) Right next door to the Belvedere, the Semeli has the same luxuriousness, but in traditional Cycladic style with a soothing pastel decor. You'll not escape the Jacuzzi or gym, though.

Myconian Inn (☎ 2289 023 420; mycinn@hotmail .com; Agiou Ioannou; s/d/ste incl breakfast €70/130/180) Some of the best views in Mykonos can be enjoyed from the front rooms of this pleasant place; it's high above the hora, yet is only a minute or two from the centre. There's a bit of traffic noise from the road behind.

For more top-end listings, see the Beaches (p141) and Ano Mera (p142) sections.

Eating

High prices don't necessarily reflect high quality in many Mykonos eateries. There are, however, excellent, good value restaurants of all kinds.

BUDGET

Nikos Taverna (☎ 2289 024 320; Porta; dishes €4-13) Seafood is by the kilo at this bustling, busy place just inland from the Delos quay. It usually has a tasty dish of the day, such as rabbit or baked fish, with tomatoes and spinach, for about €8.

Antonini's (☎ 2289 022 319; Taxi Sq; dishes €3.50-12.50) You won't go wrong at this local hang-out with its standard, but reliable, Greek food. It's on the edge of Taxi Square and the world passes by in front of its outside terrace.

Camares Café-Bar-Restaurant (☎ 2289 028 570; Akti Kambani; dishes €3.50-14) This place is on the waterfront just round from Taxi Square. It offers decent helpings of meat dishes, salads and seafood and the surroundings and style suggest that Mykonos might be an everyday Greek harbour town after all.

Vamvakouris Bakery (☎ 2289 027 207; Aghios Efthymios) The engaging medieval ambience of this bakery makes it a tourist attraction in its own right; but you still won't beat the wood-fired bread or the tasty walnut cake for taste.

There's a cluster of cheap fast-food outlets and creperies around town; **Bugazi** (☎ 2289 024

066; snacks €3-6) is off the edge of Taxi Square; **Takis** (☎ 2289 024 848; Agion Saranta) is a good bet for tasty gyros (Greek-style doner kebabs) at €1.50, and souvlaki at €1.20. There are also several supermarkets and excellent fruit stalls, particularly around the southern bus station area, and there's a bit of a food market on the waterfront where Mykonos' famous pelicans hang out.

MID-RANGE

Magic Garden (☎ 2289 026 217; Tourlianis; dishes €6-14) There's a unique atmosphere here, where you are drawn in to a genuine garden environment. The food's interesting too, with treats such as shrimps in ouzo, and baked lamb with yoghurt, garlic and nutmeg.

Sushi Bar (☎ 2289 026 969; Platia Goumenio; dishes €7.70-9.40) Mykonos keeps abreast of things with this fine sushi place that offers a good selection of special *makis* (small sushi roll), combination rolls and assorted courses, including a two-person combo for €46.

Also recommended are **Eva's Garden** (☎ 2289 022 160; Platia Goumenio; dishes €9-18.50) where authentic Greek cooking makes for tasty dishes, from the dolmades and *spanakopitas* (spinach pie) to generous meat treats. Nearby the friendly **Caesar's** (☎ 2289 027 003; Platia Goumenio; dishes €9-16) serves up excellent fish and meat dishes.

TOP END

Chez Katrine's (☎ 2289 022 169; cnr Gerasimou & Nikou; meals €54) This Mykonos' institution deals in full-on meals rather than mere dishes; the traditional Greek cuisine has more than a worthwhile touch of international flair and the service and surroundings are equally classy.

Archeon Gefsis (☎ 2289 079 256; 19 Dilou; dishes €10-22) This fairly pricey place offers interesting dishes cooked in the alleged old ways of classical Greece. There's much use of adventurous sauces, fruit and vegetables to accompany traditional goat, lamb, pork and liver dishes or cuttlefish and shrimps.

El Greco (☎ 2289 022 074; Tria Pigadia; dishes €8-21) Seafood is by the kilo at El Greco. Prices are fairly high and the service is a touch bland at this prime streetside location. But dishes are creative and good use is made of local produce.

Lotus (☎ 2289 022 881; 47 Matogianni; dishes €5-12) A local favourite with great character and

style; you can also enjoy drinks here to the soothing strains of classical greats such as Puccini.

Drinking

Waterside bars in the Little Venice quarter (Venetia) are a major draw, with rosy sunsets, windmill views, glowing candles and lapping water at your feet. The music leans towards smooth soul and easy-listening; but at quieter times bar staff play more esoteric and satisfying sounds. A good spot is the friendly **Galleraki** (☎ 2289 027 188) where they turn out superb cocktails. Nearby is the view-happy **Verandah Café** (☎ 2289 027 400) while **La Scarpa** (☎ 2289 023 294) leans back a touch from the sea on its cosy cushions. Further north **Katerina's Bar** (☎ 2289 023 084; Agion Anargiron) has a cool balcony.

Deeper into town the relentlessly stylish **Aroma** (☎ 2289 027 148; Enoplon Dinameon) maintains a watching brief on the evening cat walk at the strategic corner of Matogianni with Enoplon Dinameon. It's open for breakfast and coffee as well.

Further down Enoplon Dinameon is **Astra** (☎ 2289 024 767), where the decor is modernist Mykonos at its best, and where some of Athens top DJs feed the ambience with rock, funk, house and drum 'n base. Just across from Astra, cocktail-cool **Aigli** (☎ 2289 027 265) has a useful terrace for people-watching. Matogianni has a couple of music bars including **White Shark** (☎ 2289 024 273), the renamed Angyra, that sticks with easy listening and mainstream.

Bar Uno (☎ 2289 026 144; Kalogera) is a lively corner place that rocks happily to just about every playlist. **Bolero** (☎ 2289 024 877; Malamatenias), in a quiet alleyway off Kalogera, has a more restrained diet of jazz, funk and Latin. **Scandinavian Bar** (☎ 2289 022 669; 9 Ioanni Voinovich), just in from the east end of the waterfront, is more down-to-earth, although its cocktail nomenclature is a bit weary.

For dance club action **Space** (☎ 2289 024 100; Laka) is the place. The night builds superbly through a mix of techno, house and progressive and the bar-top dancing really fires up the late-night action. **Remezzo** (☎ 2289 024 100; Polikandrioti) is run by the same team but features lounge and dance for a more relaxing scene. Entry is around €10 to both clubs.

GAY BARS

Mykonos has long been feted as a gay travel destination, combining camp style with sun-seducing indulgence. The blurring of fashion gender and a healthy, and mutual, tolerance of tendencies has made gay life less overt, but the island still maintains many gaycentric clubs and hang-outs.

Kastro (☎ 2289 023 072; Agion Anargiron) in Little Venice is a good place to start the night with cocktails as the sun sets. The exquisitely stylish **Markiss** (☎ 2289 026 696; Mitropoli), for lounge music, is more of a fashion statement than a social hang-out. Just round the corner is relaxing **Diva** (☎ 2289 027 271) where a mixed crowd has a loyal lesbian element. Around 11pm, things get a bit livelier at **Porta** (☎ 2289 027 807; Ioanni Voinovich), a popular, cruisey bar that gets close-quarters crowded late in the evening. The night rounds off – usually with sensation – at **Pierro's** (☎ 2289 022 177; Agia Kyriaki), just in from Taxi Square, a dance club, playing heavy-beat house, that also has superbly extrovert drag action. Adjoining, and under the same management, is Icarus which is just as overt, but less full frontal.

Entertainment

Cinemanto (☎ 2289 027 190; admission €6) Screenings are at 9pm and 11pm in the garden setting of this open-air cinema that runs new films every few days.

Shopping

You could spend out in a mere 10m of Mykonos' packed shopping streets. Everyone's there, from Dolce & Gabbana, and Naf Naf, to Diesel and the Body Shop. There are plenty of art and craft galleries, but try the **Louis Orosko Gallery** (off Enoplon Dinameon) for some individuality, and look out for photographer **Christos Katsios** (☎ 6944 328 607) out on the street with his very Mykonos take on portraiture.

AROUND MYKONOS
Beaches

Mykonos' beaches are plentiful and popular. Don't expect seclusion, but in some places you'll certainly get a sense of exclusivity as various cliques commandeer the sun loungers, while segregation zones for style and sheer snobbery dominate at some locations. Expect to pay a terribly mundane €2 to €3 for lounger and umbrella hire; but be early.

THE PARADISE CLUB SCENE

Paradise wakes up after midday and by 3pm the Beach Bar and the Tropicana Bar, crank out the dance tunes. You can forget about lounging, as the long arc of beach becomes filled with gyrating bodies.

Cavo Paradiso (☎ 2289 027 205), 300m above Paradise Beach, is the mega club of Mykonos. It picks up round about 2am when the rest of the world leaves off, and hosts top international DJs. Admission is from €20 and it's open May to August.

To whet your dancing appetite, check out www.cavoparadiso.gr for a line-up of upcoming acts.

The best beaches really do get packed and you need to be a party person for the likes of Paradise and Super P. One-time escapist beaches on the windier north–side are in turn becoming overcrowded. On some popular beaches, gin-palace cruisers and other boats are allowed to anchor very close to shore. It can all get very claustrophobic, but it's heaven for the gregarious.

The nearest beaches to the hora, and the island's least glamorous, are **Malaliamos** and the tiny, crowded **Tourlos**, 2km to the north and **Agios Stefanos**, 2km beyond. About 3.5km south of the hora is the packed and noisy **Ornos**, from where you can hop on boats for other beaches. Just west again is **Agios Ioannis**, busy and popular with families. **Platys Gialos**, 4km from the hora on the southwest coast is dismissed by aficionados as 'packaged pop' but is a good beach for youngsters and is the caïque jump-off point for the islands best, and busiest, beaches of **Paradise**, **Super Paradise**, **Agrari** and **Elia**. Nudity is commonplace on all these beaches. Gay-friendly **Elia** is the last caïque stop, so, notionally, it should be the least crowded. Caïques from beach to beach cost about €4.50 return.

The next beach along from Elia, and reached by road rather than caïque, is **Kalo Livadi**, 9km from the hora. It has open space to either side of the sun loungers. Nearby **Kalafatis** specialises in watersports.

North-coast beaches can be exposed to the meltemi wind, but **Panormos** and **Agios Sostis** are fairly sheltered. Panormas is now high on the popular list; Agios Sostis less so because of poor road access.

For out-of-the-way beaching you need to head for the likes of **Lia** on the southeast coast, or the smaller **Fokos** and **Mersini** on the east coast; but you'll need tough wheels and undercarriage to get there.

ACTIVITIES
Mykonos Diving Club (☎ 2289 026 539; www.dive adventures.gr; Paradise Beach) offers a full range of diving courses with multilingual instructors. Two introductory dives cost €115, snorkelling costs €30 and an introductory diving course is €410, plus €60 certification fee.

Planet Windsailing (☎ 2289 072 345; www.pezi -huber.com; Kalafatis Beach for) has one hour/day of windsurfing for €19/50, or take a three-hour beginner's course for €60. You can also hire mountain bikes for €18 a day.

SLEEPING
Mykonos has two camping grounds; minibuses from the camping grounds meet ferries.

Paradise Beach Camping (☎ 2289 022 852; fax 2289 024 350; camp sites €25, s/d bungalows €60/75) If you want to be close to the beach action, this site fits the bill, but there's not much else going for it and don't expect peace and quiet.

Mykonos Camping (☎ 2289 024 578; www.mycamp .gr; camp sites per adult/tent €10/4; bungalows per person €25) This is a quieter site on the less full-on Paraga Beach (a 10-minute walk from Platys Gialos) and has reasonable facilities and bungalows that sleep two.

There are many top-end places around the coast.

Villa Katerina (☎ 2289 023 414; fax 2289 022 503; 2-6 person studios €110-234; P ⌨) Classic Cycladian style and blue-and-white colour scheme enhance the quiet charms of this pleasant place. It's 300m uphill from Agios Ioannis' popular family beach.

Princess of Mykonos (☎ 2289 023 806; fax 2289 023 031; s/d €150/176; P ⌨) It costs about 25% more for sea views at this swish hotel that merges traditional island style with Art-Deco touches. You're never short of an interesting conversation piece. It's above the fairly oversubscribed Agios Stefanos beach.

Aphrodite Beach Hotel (☎ 2289 071 367; sales@ aphrodite-mykonos.com; s/d/ste €187/212/312; P ⌨) Tree-sheltered and with a distinctly secluded feel, the Aphrodite has good-sized rooms and bungalow accommodation.

Kalafatis Beach is nearby. The hotel can organise everything from windsurfing to horse riding.

Ornos Beach Hotel (☎ 2289 023 216; fax 2289 022 483; d €150; P ⌨) Overlooking the busy beach, the traditional-style Ornos is right in the midst of the action and is handy for beach-hopping caïques.

Ano Mera Ανω Μέρα
The village of Ano Mera, 7km east of Hora, is the island's only inland settlement, founded in the 16th century by Cretan settlers who had island-hopped from Folegandros. The central square was recently pedestrianised and has brought more visitors, and more development, although it's fairly low-key. You can visit the 6th-century **Moni Panagias Tourlianis** (☎ 2289 071 249) by arrangement. It has a fine carved marble bell tower, an ornate wooden iconostasis carved in Florence in the late 1700s and 16th-century icons painted by members of the Cretan School. Amplifiers blast out beautiful Orthodox hymns.

Ano Mera Hotel (☎ 2289 071 215; fax 2289 071 230; s/d €70/74; ⌨) This pleasant hotel makes a change from town or resort sleeping. It keeps abreast of things and updates steadily. Recent additions include a sauna and gym and there's a restaurant.

The central square is edged with tavernas including the popular **Vangelis** (☎ 2289 071 577; dishes €4-12), which offers tasty spit roasts, and fish dishes including *kakavia* (fish soup).

DELOS ΔΗΛΟΣ

The sacred island of **Delos** (☎ 2289 022 259; sites & museum €3.50; ☉ 9am-3pm Tue-Sun) is a marvellous contrast to the relentless liveliness of modern Mykonos. The island is one of the most important archaeological sites in Greece, and certainly the most important in the Cyclades. It lies a few kilometres off the west coast of Mykonos and is the mythical birthplace of the twins Apollo and Artemis.

History
Delos was first inhabited in the 3rd millennium BC. In the 8th century BC, a festival in honour of Apollo was established; the oldest temples and shrines on the island

(many donated by Naxians) date from this era. Political and economic interests rather than religious fervour led to the island's growing importance. The dominant Athenians coveted Delos, seeing its strategic position as one from where they could control the Aegean. By the 5th century BC, it was under their jurisdiction.

In 478 BC Athens established an alliance known as the Delian League that kept its treasury on Delos. A cynical decree ensured that no-one could be born or die on Delos, thus strengthening Athens control over the island by removing the native population.

Delos reached the height of its power in Hellenistic times, becoming one of the three most important religious centres in Greece and a flourishing centre of commerce. Many of its inhabitants were wealthy merchants, mariners and bankers from as far away as Egypt and Syria. They built temples to their homeland gods, although Apollo remained the principal deity.

The Romans made Delos a free port in 167 BC. This brought even greater prosperity, due largely to a lucrative slave market that sold up to 10,000 people a day. During the following century, as ancient religions lost relevance and trade routes shifted, Delos began its long, painful decline. By the 3rd century AD there was only a small Christian settlement on the island, and in the following centuries the ancient settlement was looted of many of its antiquities; its stonework and fittings were pillaged for buildings elsewhere. The island became a pirate lair during the Ottoman period and it was not until the Renaissance that its antiquarian value was recognised.

Getting There & Away

Excursion boats for Delos (€6 return, 30 minutes) leave Hora (Mykonos) at 9am, 9.30am, 10.15am, 11am, 11.40pm and 12.50pm, from the quay at the western end of the port. The boats return between 12.20pm and 3pm daily except Monday (when the site is closed). Departure and return times are posted on the noticeboard at the quay.

Between May and September, guided tours are conducted in English, French and German; check with travel agents for times. Tickets are available from several travel agencies.

A boat departs for Delos from Platys Gialos (€8) at 10.15am daily. Boats also operate to Delos from Tinos (€20) and Paros (€20).

ANCIENT DELOS

The quay where excursion boats dock is south of the tranquil Sacred Harbour. Many of the most significant finds from Delos are in the National Archaeological Museum in Athens, but the **site museum** still has an absorbing collection, part of which includes the lions from the Terrace of the Lions (those on the terrace itself are plaster-cast replicas).

Overnight stays on Delos are forbidden, and boat schedules allow a maximum of six or seven hours there. Bring water and food, as the cafeteria's offerings are poor value for money. Wear a hat and sensible shoes.

Exploring the Site

Following is an outline of some significant archaeological remains on the site. For further details, buy a guidebook at the ticket office, or take a guided tour if you are happy being shepherded around.

The island is very flat, but the rock-encrusted **Mt Kythnos** (113m) rises elegantly to the southeast of the harbour. From its summit there are terrific views of the surrounding islands on clear days. The path to Mt Kythnos is reached by walking through the **Theatre Quarter**.

It was in this quarter that Delos' wealthiest inhabitants built their houses. These houses surrounded peristyle courtyards, with mosaics (a status symbol) the most striking feature of each house. These colourful mosaics were exquisite art works, mostly representational and offset by intricate geometric borders. The most lavish dwellings were the **House of Dionysos (12)**, named after the mosaic depicting the wine god riding a panther, and the **House of Cleopatra (9)**, where headless statues of the owners were found. The **House of the Trident (17)** was one of the grandest. The **House of the Masks (15)**, probably an actors' hostelry, has another mosaic of Dionysos resplendently astride a panther, and the **House of the Dolphins (14)** has another exceptional mosaic.

The **theatre (42)** dates from 300 BC and had a large cistern **(4)**, the remains of which can be seen. It supplied much of the town

ANCIENT DELOS

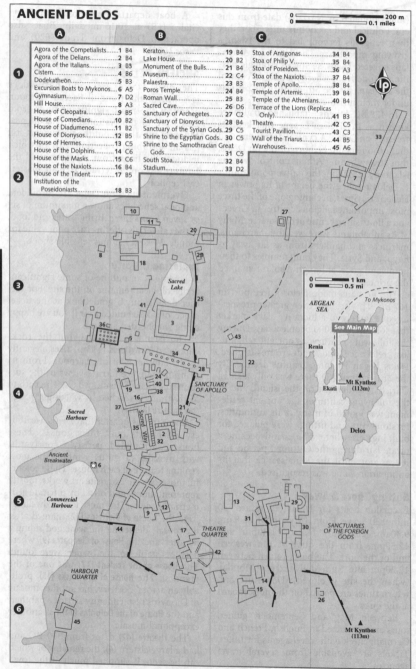

Agora of the Competialists	1 B4	Keraton	19 B4	Stoa of Antigonas	34 B4
Agora of the Delians	2 B4	Lake House	20 B2	Stoa of Philip V	35 B4
Agora of the Italians	3 B3	Monument of the Bulls	21 B4	Stoa of Poseidon	36 A3
Cistern	4 B6	Museum	22 C4	Stoa of the Naxiots	37 B4
Dodekatheon	5 B3	Palaestra	23 B3	Temple of Apollo	38 B4
Excursion Boats to Mykonos	6 A5	Poros Temple	24 B4	Temple of Artemis	39 B4
Gymnasium	7 D2	Roman Wall	25 B3	Temple of the Athenians	40 B4
Hill House	8 A3	Sacred Cave	26 D6	Terrace of the Lions (Replicas
House of Cleopatra	9 B5	Sanctuary of Archegetes	27 C2	Only)	41 B3
House of Comedians	10 B2	Sanctuary of Dionysos	28 B4	Theatre	42 C5
House of Diadumenos	11 B2	Sanctuary of the Syrian Gods	29 C5	Tourist Pavillion	43 C3
House of Dionysos	12 B5	Shrine to the Egyptian Gods	30 C5	Wall of the Triarus	44 B5
House of Hermes	13 C5	Shrine to the Samothracian Great		Warehouses	45 A6
House of the Dolphins	14 C6	Gods	31 C5		
House of the Masks	15 C6	South Stoa	32 B4		
House of the Naxiots	16 B4	Stadium	33 D2		
House of the Trident	17 B5				
Institution of the					
Poseidoniasts	18 B3				

0 — 200 m
0 — 0.1 miles

Sacred Lake

Sacred Harbour

Sacred Way

SANCTUARY OF APOLLO

Ancient Breakwater

Commercial Harbour

THEATRE QUARTER

SANCTUARIES OF THE FOREIGN GODS

HARBOUR QUARTER

Mt Kynthos (113m)

0 — 1 km
0 — 0.5 mi

AEGEAN SEA

To Mykonos

See Main Map

Renia

Ekati

Mt Kynthos (113m)

Delos

CYCLADES

with water. The houses of the wealthy had their own cisterns – essential as Delos was almost as parched and barren then as it is today.

Descending from Mt Kythnos, explore the **Sanctuaries of the Foreign Gods**. Here, at the **Shrine to the Samothracian Great Gods** (31), the Kabeiroi (the twins Dardanos and Aeton) were worshipped. At the **Sanctuary of the Syrian Gods** (29) there are the remains of a theatre where an audience watched ritual orgies. There is also an area (30) where Egyptian deities, including Serapis and Isis, were worshipped.

The **Sanctuary of Apollo**, to the north of the harbour, contains temples dedicated to him. It is the site of the much-photographed **Terrace of the Lions** (41). These proud beasts, carved from marble, were offerings from the people of Naxos, presented to Delos in the 7th century BC to guard the sacred area. To the northeast is the **Sacred Lake** (dry since it was drained in 1925 to prevent malarial mosquitoes breeding) where, according to legend, Leto gave birth to Apollo and Artemis.

PAROS ΠΑΡΟΣ

pop 12,853

Paros draws you in persuasively to its engaging port, its handful of pleasant resorts and its tawny hills with their peaceful mountain villages. The island rises through undulating slopes to Mt Profitis Ilias (770m). The almost-translucent white marble of Paros made the island famous and prosperous from the Early Cycladic period onwards – most famously the Venus de Milo was carved from Parian marble, as was Napoleon's tomb.

Paros is the main ferry hub of the Cyclades and for onward travel to other island chains in the Aegean. The busy port town of Parikia bursts into frantic activity around the ferry quay whenever vessels arrive. The other major settlement, Naoussa, on the north coast, is a delightful resort with a colourful fishing harbour. At the island's heart is the peaceful mountain village of Lefkes.

The smaller island of Antiparos, 1km southwest of Paros, is easily reached by car ferry and excursion boat.

Getting There & Away

AIR

Olympic Airways airport (☎ 2284 091 257) Parikia (☎ 2284 021 900; fax 2284 022 778; Plateia Mavrogenous) has daily flights to Athens (€72).

FAST BOAT & CATAMARAN

There are three services daily to Piraeus (€30.25, 2½ hours) and Rafina (€29.70, 2½ hours), at least two daily to Naxos (€9.90, 30 minutes), Tinos (€16, 1¼ hours), Syros (€12, 45 minutes), Mykonos (€12, one hour), Ios (€16.70, 1½ hours), Santorini (€21.80, 2¼ hours) and Amorgos (€16.90, 1½ to two hours). There is also one service daily to Iraklio on Crete (€41.40, four hours).

FERRY

There are around six boats daily to Piraeus (€18.60, five hours), Naxos (€4.60, one hour), three daily to Ios (€8.30, 2½ hours), Santorini (€10.90, three to four hours) and Mykonos (€7.45, 1¾ hours). There are daily services to Syros (€5.60, 1½ hours), Tinos (€8, 2½ hours) and Amorgos (€9.80, three to 4½ hours).

Six weekly go to Koufonisia (€9.90, 4½ hours) and Sikinos (€6.20, three to four hours), and five to Anafi (€12.20, six hours).

Five weekly go to Andros (€11.10, 4½ hours).

Four weekly go to Astypalea (€19, six hours) and Samos (€15.20, 7½ hours).

There are three ferries weekly to Folegandros (€6.80, 3½ hours), Ikaria (€12.30, four hours), Samos (€15.20, six to seven hours), Thessaloniki (€33, 15 to 16 hours) and Crete (€20.50, seven to eight hours).

There are two ferries weekly to Serifos (€6.90, three hours), Sifnos (€3.70, two hours), Milos (€10.55, 4½ hours), Kimolos (€8.70, 4½ hours), Shinousa (€6.70, four hours) and Donousa (€8.30, two to four hours).

There is one boat weekly that travels to Skiathos (€26, 10 hours), Rhodes (€24.80, 12 to 15 hours), Kos (€16, six to eight hours), Kalymnos (€20.55, seven hours), Patmos (€14.75, four hours), Leros (€16.20, five hours), Kastellorizo (€28.30, 20 hours), Nisyros (€18, 11 hours), Tilos (€22.90, 10½ hours) and Symi (€25.60, 11 hours).

CYCLADES

PAROS & ANTIPAROS

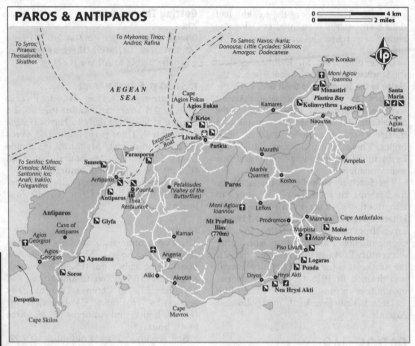

To Syros; Piraeus; Thessaloniki; Skiathos

To Mykonos; Tinos; Andros; Rafina

To Samos; Naxos; Ikaria; Donousa; Little Cyclades; Sikinos; Amorgos; Dodecanese

Cape Korakas

AEGEAN SEA

Moni Agiou Ioannou

Monastiri
Plastira Bay
Kolimvythres Lageri

Santa Maria

Cape Agios Fokas
Agios Fokas

Kamares

Naoussa

Cape Agias Marias

Krios

Livadia

Excursion Boat

Parikia

Marathi

Ampelas

Parasporos

Sunset

Antiparos

Pounta
Antiparos Thea Restaurant

Petaloudes (Valley of the Butterflies)

Paros

Marble Quarries

Kostos

To Serifos; Sifnos; Kimolos; Milos; Santorini; Ios; Anafi; Iraklio; Folegandros

Antiparos

Glyfa

Moni Agiou Ioannou

Mt Profitis Ilias (770m)

Lefkes

Prodromos

Marmara

Cape Antikefalos

Cave of Antiparos

Agios Georgios

Karnari

Marpissa Molos
Moni Agiou Antonios

Agios Georgios

Apandima

Angeria

Piso Livadi

Logaras
Punda

Soros

Aliki

Akrotiri

Dryos Hrysi Akti

Despotiko

Nea Hrysi Akti

Cape Mavros

Cape Skilos

0   4 km
0   2 miles

Getting Around

BUS

There are around seven buses daily from Parikia to Naoussa via Dryos, Hrysi Akti, Marpissa, Marmara, Prodromos, Kostos, Marathi and Lefkes, and frequent buses to Pounta (for Antiparos, €0.90) and Aliki (via Petaloudes and the airport). Around 12 buses daily link Parikia and Naoussa directly.

CAR, MOTORCYCLE & BICYCLE

There are rental outlets along the waterfront in Parikia and all around the island. One of the best in Parikia is **Iria** (☎ 2284 021 232; iriacars@hotmail.com) opposite the marina. Rental is about €40 a day in August.

TAXI

Taxis (☎ 2284 021 500) gather at River Rd opposite the roundabout. Fares include airport €9, Naoussa €8, Pounta €7 and Lefkes €8.

TAXI BOAT

Taxi boats leave from the quay for beaches around Parikia. Tickets ranging from €6 to €10 are available on board.

PARIKIA ΠΑΡΟΙΚΙΑ

pop 4522

Paros' capital and port is Parikia. It's a bright, cheerful town with an often-frantic waterfront that's in remarkable contrast with its Cycladic old quarter, where narrow streets wriggle around the built-over shell of the 13th-century Venetian kastro. The kastro crowns a slight rise above the waterfront, southeast of the ferry quay.

Orientation

The busy hub of Parikia is the windmill roundabout, at the town end of the ferry quay. The main square, Plateia Mavrogenous, is straight ahead from the windmill. The busy road to the left leads along the northern waterfront to the beach at Livadia. The road to the right follows the café-lined southwestern waterfront, a pedestrian precinct in high season.

Market St (Agora in Greek) is the main commercial thoroughfare running southwest from Plateia Mavrogenous through the narrow and pedestrianised streets of the old town.

The bus station is 50m left of the quay (looking inland), and the post office is 300m further along.

Information

Kiosks on the quay give out information on domatia and hotels.

Commercial Bank of Greece (Plateia Mavrogenous)

Memphis.net (9am-midnight; €1 per 15 min) On the waterfront close to the bus station; with an impressive range of services, including hook-ups for notebooks and digital picture transfer.

National Bank of Greece (Plateia Mavrogenous)

Police (2284 023 333; Plateia Mavrogenous)

Port police (2284 021 240) Back from the northern waterfront, near the post office.

Santorineos Travel Services (2284 024 245; bookings@santorineos-travel.gr) On the waterfront, just along to the right of windmill roundabout. Santorineos can help with accommodation, ferry tickets and tours, and is also the representative for American Express and MasterCard.

Wired Café (2284 022 003; Market St; 10.30am-2.30pm & 6-11pm Mon-Sat, 6-11pm Sun; €1.80 per 30 min) Relaxed Internet access.

Sights

The **Panagia Ekatontapyliani** (2284 021 243; 7.30am-9.30pm), which dates from AD 326, is one of the most splendid churches in the Cyclades. The building is three distinct churches: Agios Nikolaos, the largest, with superb columns of Parian marble and a carved iconostasis, is in the east of the compound; the others are the Church of Our Lady and the Baptistery. The name translates as Our Lady of the Hundred Gates, but this is wishful rounding up of a still impressive tally of doorways. The **Byzantine Museum** (admission €1.50; 9.30am-2pm & 6-9pm), within the compound, has a collection of icons and other artefacts.

Next to a school behind the Panagia Ekatontapyliani, the **Archaeological Museum** (2284 021 231; admission €2; 8.30am-3pm Tue-Sun) has some interesting reliefs and statues, including a Gorgon, but the most important exhibit is a fragment of the 4th-century Parian Chronicle, which lists the most outstanding artistic achievements of ancient Greece. It was discovered in the 17th century and most of it ended up in the Ashmolean Museum, Oxford. Typically, some of the most exquisite pieces are only plaster casts – the originals having long since been 'displaced' to museums in New York and Germany.

North along the waterfront there is a fenced **ancient cemetery** dating from the 7th century BC; it was excavated in 1983. Roman graves, burial pots and sarcophagi are floodlit at night.

The **Frankish Kastro** was built on the remains of a temple to Athena by Marco Sanudo, Venetian Duke of Naxos, in AD 1260. Not much remains, save a large wall that is a jigsaw of unpainted column bases and dressed blocks, where pigeons roost in the cracks. To find it, head southwest along Market St and take the first right.

Tours

Santorineos Travel Services (see Information) can book bus tours of Paros (€20), boat trips to Mykonos and Delos (€35), and to Santorini (€50), including a bus tour of Santorini.

Excursion boats also make the trip to Antiparos in summer.

Sleeping
BUDGET

All camping grounds have minibuses that meet ferries.

Camping Koula (2284 022 081; fax 2284 022 740; koula@otenet.gr; camp sites per adult/tent €6/4;) About 1km along the northern waterfront at Livadia, this smallish camping ground is pleasantly shaded by trees and offers good, clean facilities.

Parasporos Camping (2284 022 268; camp sites per adult/tent €6/4) A popular and well-equipped site 2km south of Parikia, Parasporos is 300m from the beach.

Krios Camping (2284 021 705; www.compulink.gr/krios; camp sites per adult/tent €7/2;) This appealing site, on the north shore of Parikia Bay, is about 2.5km from the port. It has a restaurant (dishes €3 to €6) and a minimarket. It runs a taxi boat across the bay to Parikia every 10 minutes for €2 per person (return). The boat pulls in just to the left of the ferry quay, facing inland.

Rooms Association (2284 022 772, after hrs 2284 022 220) This association on the quay has information on domatia; otherwise domatia owners meet ferries. For hotel details, call 2284 024 555 (Parikia) or 2284 041 333 (around the island).

Rooms Rena (2284 022 220; fax 2284 021 427; Epitropakis; s/d €25/35) In a quiet, but handy location back from the waterfront, these

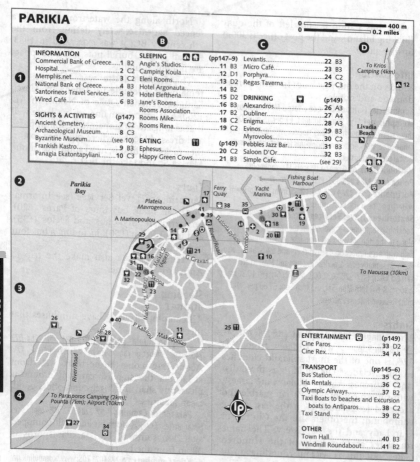

PARIKIA

0 — 400 m
0 — 0.2 miles

INFORMATION	
Commercial Bank of Greece.....1	B2
Hospital......2	C2
Memphis.net.....3	C2
National Bank of Greece.....4	B3
Santorineos Travel Services.....5	B2
Wired Café.....6	B3

SIGHTS & ACTIVITIES	(p147)
Ancient Cemetery.....7	C3
Archaeological Museum.....8	C3
Byzantine Museum.....(see 10)	
Frankish Kastro.....9	B3
Panagia Ekatontapyliani.....10	C3

SLEEPING	(pp147–9)
Angie's Studios.....11	B3
Camping Koula.....12	D1
Eleni Rooms.....13	D2
Hotel Argonauta.....14	B2
Hotel Eleftheria.....15	D2
Jane's Rooms.....16	B3
Rooms Association.....17	B2
Rooms Mike.....18	C2
Rooms Rena.....19	C2

EATING	(p149)
Ephesus.....20	C2
Happy Green Cows.....21	B3

Levantis.....22	B3
Micro Café.....23	B3
Porphyra.....24	C2
Regas Taverna.....25	C3

DRINKING	(p149)
Alexandros.....26	A3
Dubliner.....27	A4
Enigma.....28	A3
Evinos.....29	B3
Myrovolos.....30	C2
Pebbles Jazz Bar.....31	B3
Saloon D'Or.....32	B3
Simple Cafe.....(see 29)	

To Krios
Camping (4km)

12

Livadia
Beach

Parikia
Bay

Fishing Boat
Harbour

Ferry
Quay

Yacht
Marina

17

38

35

24

36   7

Plateia
Mavrogenous

A Marinopoulou

41

5   39

Ektotonpliani

3

30

18

19

River Road

Prombona

14   37

4

1

9

21

G Gravari

2   20

16

31

6

Market St (Agora)

22

32

6

Agora

23

10

8

To Naoussa (10km)

26

40

P Kallirou

11

Makedonias

25

28

D Valleou

River Road

ENTERTAINMENT	(p149)
Cine Paros.....33	D2
Cine Rex.....34	A4

TRANSPORT	(pp145–6)
Bus Station.....35	C2
Iria Rentals.....36	C2
Olympic Airways.....37	B2
Taxi Boats to beaches and Excursion boats to Antiparos.....38	C2
Taxi Stand.....39	B2

OTHER	
Town Hall.....40	B3
Windmill Roundabout.....41	B2

To Parasporos Camping (2km);
Pounta (7km); Airport (10km)

27

34

pleasant and well-kept rooms are excellent value, and there's a charming welcome.

Jane's Rooms (☎ 2284 021 338; Kastro; s/d €35/55; ☒) A great location at the heart of the atmospheric Kastro enhances these pleasant rooms that have fridges, sea views and balconies, and a communal roof terrace. Inquire for details of apartments that are also available on the north side of the bay at Krios.

Rooms Mike (☎ 2284 022 856; roommike@otenet.gr; s/d/tr €22/32/40, studio €25/35/45) You'll never be short of friendly chat and advice at Mike's place, which is very popular, especially with backpackers. There's a shared kitchen and a roof terrace. Some rooms are in another building, a block inland.

Hotel Eleftheria (☎ 2284 022 047; s/d €30/50; ☒) This cheerful and welcoming hotel is near Livadia Beach and has bright, clean rooms and a rooftop terrace; breakfast is available.

MID-RANGE

Hotel Argonauta (☎ 2284 021 440; www.argonauta.gr; d €60; ☒) You simply cannot beat this long-established family-run hotel for its central location, overlooking Plateia Mavrogenous, or for its welcoming atmosphere. There are charming traditional touches to furnishings and rooms are spotless and comfy and have double-glazing.

Eleni Rooms (☎ 2284 022 714; www.eleni-rooms.gr; s/d/tr €55/60/80) Spacious and sparkling rooms surrounding a lovingly tended courtyard that contains brilliant bougainvillea and flowers make Eleni's a worthwhile option. It's about 800m from the ferry quay near Livadia Beach but transfer to/from the port is available.

Angie's Studios (☎ 2284 023 909; www.angies-studios.gr; Makedonias; d €60; P ❀) These fine studios are a short stroll from the centre of town. They're spacious, immaculate and each has its own kitchen area. There's a delightful patio and surrounding garden area, glowing with bougainvillea and flowers. There are generous discounts in the off season.

Eating

Happy Green Cows (☎ 2284 024 691; dishes €5-19; ❂ 7pm-midnight) Fast becoming a Parian institution, this little vegetarian eatery (the name inspired by a dream) has witty kitsch decor that lifts the spirits, as does the cheerful service. Food is ethnic with a creative flair and there's a delicious line in mezedes. You can drink into the early hours after the kitchen closes.

Regas Taverna (☎ 2284 023 532; dishes €3-12) This place is tucked away at the back of town but is great for Greek cuisine in pleasant surroundings. It's accompanied by excellent traditional music live on Tuesday, Thursday, Friday and Saturday nights.

Ephesus (☎ 2284 021 491; dishes €2.50-11) Turkish, Greek and Anatolian specialities are the style at this popular backstreet restaurant that offers delicious, herb-strewn dips and appetisers and a large selection of kebabs and pizzas cooked in a wood-fired oven, or charcoal grilled.

Levantis (☎ 2284 023 613; Kastro; dishes €4-15.50) Stylish and with attentive service, Levantis has a courtyard garden setting and attractive grey and orange decor at the heart of Kastro. There's a subtle international touch to the cuisine with dishes such as lamb smothered in herbs, fava and roasted garlic.

Porphyra (☎ 2284 022 693; dishes €5-12.50) Set back from the busy eastern waterfront Porphyra does a great line in creative seafood, including raw shellfish, as well as traditionally prepared fresh fish, calamari and prawns.

Café Micro (☎ 2284 024 674; Market St) A friendly gathering spot for locals and visitors, this bright place at the heart of the old town does good breakfasts for €4 and offers coffee and snacks, with drinks and music at night.

Drinking

Pebbles Jazz Bar (☎ 2284 022 283) Perched above the waterfront, on the edge of Kastro is this rewardingly cool bar that plays classical music by day and jazz in the evenings, with occasional live performances.

Alexandros (☎ 2284 023 133) Relaxed evening lounging is the style at this restored windmill above the water's edge, on the southwest end of the waterfront.

Saloon D'Or (☎ 2284 022 176) Nights start with warm-up drinks on the waterfront here.

Enigma (☎ 2284 024 664) A stylish place that goes strong into the small hours when there's a touch more Greek to the sounds.

Dubliner (☎ 2284 021 113; admission €6) The Dubliner houses under the same roof the Down Under Bar, the Scandinavian Bar and Paros Rock, all offering a variety of sounds; but loud and large. If you want a dizzy, drink-fuelled night this is the place.

Myrovolos (☎ 2284 021 634; admission €15) Next door to Iria car hire, this authentic Greek music experience, with virtual miniorchestras, is the thing here at Easter and from mid-June to mid-September. It's terrific stuff, but it's not cheap and you'll be expected to drink. The action starts about midnight.

More bars are along the southwestern waterfront and include some busy rooftop places, like Evinos and Simple Café.

Entertainment

Popular open-air cinemas are Cine Paros, in Livadia's backstreets, and Cine Rex near the Dubliner at the southern end of the waterfront. Admission is €6 for both places and screening times are 9pm and 11pm.

NAOUSSA ΝΑΟΥΣΑ

pop 2316

Naoussa, on the north coast of Paros, has transformed itself from a quiet fishing village into a popular tourist resort, and has done so with style and without losing its charm, or its harbourside atmosphere. There are good beaches nearby and the resort is fast becoming a food fanciers' destination with plenty of decent tavernas and restaurants and a couple of exceptional eateries. Behind the waterfront is a maze of narrow, whitewashed streets peppered with fish and flower motifs and with a mix of smart boutiques and souvenir shops.

CYCLADES

Orientation & Information

The bus from Parikia terminates at the main square just in from the waterfront, where a dried-up river bed, whose stream is now channelled, leads inland. The main street of Naoussa lies to the left of the river bed.

Naoussa Information (☎ 2284 052 158; ☺ 10am-midnight Jul-Aug, 11am-1pm & 6-10pm mid-Jun–Jul) can find accommodation and is based in a booth by the main square, where the bus terminates.

The very helpful and efficient **Nissiotissa Tours** (☎ 2284 051 480), left of, and just up from, the main square, can book accommodation and tours to Naxos, Delos, Mykonos, Santorini and Amorgos. It also sells ferry tickets and has a book exchange.

The post office is a tedious uphill walk from the central square. An Alpha Bank (with ATM) is by the bus station and there's an ATM outside Nissiotissa Tours.

Sights

Naoussa's **Byzantine museum** (admission €1.70; ☺ 11am-1.30pm & 7-9pm Tue, Thu, Sat & Sun) is housed in the blue-domed church, about 200m uphill from the central square on the main road to Parikia. A small **folklore museum** (☎ 2284 052 284; admission €1.70; ☺ 7-9pm), which focuses on regional costumes, can be reached by heading inland from the main square to another blue-domed church. Turn right behind the church.

The best beaches in the area are **Kolimvythres**, which has interesting rock formations; and **Monastiri**, which has some good snorkelling and a clubbing venue. Low-key **Lageri** is also worth seeking out. **Santa Maria**, on the other side of the eastern headland, is good for windsurfing. They can all be reached by road, but caïques go from Naoussa to each of them during July and August.

Activities & Tours

X-ta Sea Divers (☎ 0932 417 083; www.isdc.gr/santamaria) offers scuba-diving courses, including introductory dives for €50 and a week-long course for €440.

Naoussa Paros Sailing Center (☎ 2284 052 646; sailing@par.forthnet.gr) offers sailing tours to Naxos, Delos or Iraklia. A full day is €90 per person. Departs 10am. Half-day tours and yacht charters are also available.

Kokou Riding Centre (☎ 2284 051 818; 1/2/3 hr €20/35/45) has morning and evening horse rides and can arrange pick up from Naoussa's main square for €1.50; book through travel agents.

Sleeping

There are two camping grounds. Minibuses from both meet ferries.

Naoussa Camping (☎ 2284 051 595; camp sites per adult/tent €6/4) This shady camping ground is at Kolimvythres. It has a small taverna and lovely bays nearby.

Surfing Beach (☎ 2284 052 491; fax 2284 051 937; info@surfbeach.gr; camp sites per adult/tent €6/4) A fairly large site, but with reasonable facilities and a good location at Santa Maria. The site has a windsurfing and a water-ski school.

Pension Anna (☎ 2284 051 328, 6973 901 135; s/d €35/56) Anna's has immaculate, comfortable rooms in a charming building surrounded by colourful shrubs and flowers. Turn right as you come into town from Parikia, just before the main square.

Hotel Galini (☎ 2284 051 210; fax 2284 051 949; s/d €41/51) Opposite the blue-domed local church (Byzantine museum), on the main road into town from Parikia, this charming and friendly little hotel has unfussy rooms that are being steadily updated.

Hotel Madaky (☎ 2284 051 475; fax 2284 052 968; s/d €41/51; ✷) You pay €10 extra for air-conditioning at this very pleasant family-run hotel where rooms are spacious and comfortable. It's a quiet place, set well back to the right of the main square facing inland.

Hotel Stella (☎ 2284 051 317; www.hotelstella.gr; s/d €45/60) Deep in the heart of the old town and within a leafy, colourful garden, this friendly hotel has excellent rooms and good facilities. It's best reached by heading up the main street, turning left at the National Bank, going beneath an archway, then turning right and up past a small church.

Naoussa has a good range of self-contained accommodation.

Sunset Studios & Apartments (☎ 2284 052 060; sunsetmm@otenet.gr; studios €70-85, apt €90-115; ✷) Charming studio rooms and apartments in traditional surroundings make Sunset a great option. Head inland and uphill from the main square, and turn right at the T-junction.

Hotel Fotilia (☎ 2284 052 581; fax 2284 052 583; d €70; P ⊠ ⚲) Breakfast is €5 at this elegant hotel, 200m uphill from the town centre. Rooms are spacious, furnished tastefully in traditional style, and have good views. There's converted windmill accommodation also.

Eating

Papadakis (☎ 2284 051 047; dishes €6-14) A superb restaurant, in a great harbourside setting, Papadakis is fast putting Paros on the gourmet map with its multitude of tasty Greek dishes, based on strong traditional recipes, but with a distinctive modern slant. Argyro Barbarigou, who runs the restaurant with her husband Manolis, has recently published a celebrated book on Greek cuisine.

Christos (☎ 2284 051 442; dishes €12-22) There's style and quality in abundance at this outstanding restaurant where you eat in a beautiful courtyard sheltered by succulent vines overhead and with fine art work on the walls. The food matches the attentive service and is modern Mediterranean with exquisite touches, all backed by a superb wine list.

Perivolaria (☎ 2284 051 598; dishes €5.60-18) Another of Naoussa's better eateries, Perivolaria has a delightful garden area where you can enjoy first class Greek and international cuisine including delicious pizzas and pastas. It is reached along the river road from the main square.

Moshonas (☎ 2284 051 623; dishes €2.50-8.80) Seafood is by the kilo at this long established and popular ouzeria. It's right on the edge of the harbour where the restaurant's own fishing caïques tie up and deliver the freshest of fish straight to the kitchen.

Entertainment

In July and August, **Naoussa Paros** (parafolk@otenet.gr; admission €8), a nationally known folk-dancing group based in Naoussa, performs every Sunday; book at Naoussa Information (p150).

AROUND PAROS
Marathi Μαράθι

In antiquity Parian marble was considered the world's finest. The **marble quarries** here have been abandoned, but the area is worth exploring and the marble fairly glows with light. Take the Lefkes bus and get off at Marathi village, from where the quarries are signposted.

Lefkes to Moni Agiou Antoniou
Λεύκες προς Μονή Αγίου Αντωνίου

Lefkes, 9km southeast of Parikia, is the island's highest and loveliest village, and was its capital during the Middle Ages. It boasts the magnificent **Agias Trias** cathedral, an impressive building whose entrance is shaded by olive trees. But the village's real charm is the serenity of its pristine alleyways and buildings. Lefkes clings to a natural amphitheatre amid hills whose summits are dotted with old windmills. Siesta is taken seriously here, so tread lightly in the afternoon heat.

From the central square, a signpost points to a well-preserved Byzantine path, which leads in 3km to the village of **Prodromos**. At the edge of the village, keep left at a junction (signposted) with a wider track. Sections of the route retain their original paving.

From Prodromos, it's about 1km by road to **Marmara** or **Marpissa**. From Marmara, it's another 1km to the sandy beach at **Molos**; The 16th-century **Moni Agiou Antoniou** stands atop a 200m-high hill above Marpissa. Down on the coast is the developing resort and harbour of **Piso Livadi**, where there is a pleasant beach.

Candaca Travel (☎ 2284 041 449; fax 041 449; candaca@otenet.gr) can arrange accommodation and car rental, and also has Internet access.

SLEEPING & EATING

There are a few domatia on the road into Lefkes, but the most charming sleeping option in Lefkes is the **Hotel Pantheon** (☎ 2284 041 700; s/d €38/46) a mansion-like building, now the property of the local community. The whole place is bright and airy, and charming paintings and mobiles by the manager enliven the walls. There's a restaurant as well and there are several good tavernas and bars in Lefkes.

Piso Livadi has a number of modern rooms and apartments and a few decent tavernas and there's a camping ground on the outskirts of town.

Petaloudes Πεταλούδες

In July and August, spectacular tiger moths enshroud the copious foliage at **Petaloudes**

(Valley of the Butterflies; admission €2; ⏰ 9am-7pm Mon-Sat, 9am-1pm & 4-8pm Sun Jul & Aug). It's 8km south of Parikia. Travel agents organise tours from both Parikia and Naoussa; or take the Aliki bus and ask to be let off at the Petaloudes turn-off.

Beaches

Apart from the beaches already mentioned, there is a good beach at **Krios**, accessible by taxi boat (€3 return) from Parikia. Paros' top beach, **Hrysi Akti** (Golden Beach), on the southeast coast, is nothing spectacular, but it has good sand, several tavernas and is popular with windsurfers.

The coast between Piso Livadi and Hrysi Akti has some decent, empty beaches, although there are newish beach resorts springing up and swallowing up the coastline all the time, such as those at **Nea Hrysi Akti** (New Golden Beach).

ACTIVITIES

The waters around Paros are ideal for adventure watersports, including diving and windsurfing. The straits between Paros and Antiparos are especially suited to windsurfing and the spectacular new sport of kiteboarding, effectively windsurfing in mid-air.

Eurodivers Club (☎ 2284 092 071; www.euro divers.gr; Pounta), down the coast at Pounta, offers an impressive range of diving courses and dives for all levels and interests. A PADI open-water certification course costs €412. It also runs instruction in windsurfing and kiteboarding.

Aegean Diving College (☎ 2284 041 778, 6974 840 084), based at New Hrysi Akti (Golden Beach), offers an equally impressive range of courses and dives. A PADI open-water certification costs €410.

Fanatic Fun Centre (☎ 6938 307 671; www.fanatic -paros.com) at Hrysi Akti, has equipment for various watersports, including catamaran sailing, water-skiing and windsurfing. Board hire cost from €15 per hour, and one-week courses are €140.

ENTERTAINMENT

Punda Beach Club (☎ 2284 041 717; www.punda beach.gr in Greek) This all-day clubbing venue at Viva Punda is a huge complex with a swimming pool, bars, restaurants, gym, live music shows and a relentlessly crowded beach scene.

ANTIPAROS ΑΝΤΙΠΑΡΟΣ

pop 1037

Antiparos is proud of its distinctiveness as an independent island. Forget this at your peril in front of local people. Although development continues, the island is still a more relaxing and quieter alternative to Paros. The main village and port (also called Antiparos) is a bright and friendly place. There's a touristy gloss round the waterfront and main streets, but the village runs deeply inland to quiet squares and alleyways that give out suddenly onto open fields. Off the waterfront, streets are pedestrianised.

Getting There & Away

In summer, frequent excursion boats depart for Antiparos from Parikia.

There is also a half-hourly car ferry that runs from Pounta on the west coast of Paros to Antiparos (€0.90 one way, €6 car, 10 minutes); the first ferry departs for Antiparos at around 7am, and the last boat returning leaves Antiparos at 1.30am.

Getting Around

The only bus service on Antiparos runs to the cave in the centre of the island (€1). In summer, this bus continues to Soros and Agios Georgios.

Orientation & Information

To reach the village centre from the Pounta ferry quay, head right along the waterfront and turn left into the main street by Anarghyros restaurant. If you've come by excursion boat, walk straight ahead from your arrival quay.

The post office is 200m up the main street. The central square is reached by turning left at the top of the main street and then right, behind Smiles Café.

There are several travel agencies, including **Antiparos Travel Agency** (☎ 2284 061 3000; fax 2284 061 465; ⏰ Jun–mid-Oct) by the waterfront, which can organise accommodation.

To reach the kastro, another Marco Sanudo creation, go under the stone arch that leads north off the central square.

Cave of Antiparos

Despite previous looting of stalactites and stalagmites, the **Cave of Antiparos** (admission €3;

10.15am-3pm summer) is still awe-inspiring. In 1673, the French ambassador, Marquis de Nointel, organised a Christmas Mass (enhanced by a large orchestra) inside the cave for 500 Parians.

There are buses every hour from the village of Antiparos (€1 one way).

Activities & Tours

Blue Island Divers (☎ 2284 061 493; www.blueisland -divers.gr) is based on the main pedestrian thoroughfare. With a gear and clothes shop attached the Blue Island is friendly and helpful and has a wide range of dive options and can organise accommodation. A four-day PADI open-water course is €350 and an advanced course is €285. A snorkelling day trip is €20/10 per adult/child.

The **MS Thiella** tours around the island daily, stopping at several beaches. The tour includes lunch; book at travel agents.

Sleeping & Eating

Camping Antiparos (☎ 2284 061 221; camp sites per adult/tent €4.50/2.20) This well-equipped camping ground is planted with bamboo and is on a pleasant beach 1.5km north of the quay; signs point the way.

Anarghyros (☎ 2284 061 204; mak@par.forthnet.gr; s/d €30/45; 🞬) This is a good-value option; it's right on the waterfront but there's double glazing to counter noise. Rooms are clean and comfortable. There's a **restaurant** (dishes €3.50-8) attached.

Hotel Mantalena (☎ 2284 061 206; mantalenahotel@ par.forthnet.gr; s/d €65/70; 🞬) This hotel is further along from Anarghyros, to the left. It's set back from the main drag and has a fairly peaceful atmosphere. There's a pleasant terrace and rooms are comfortable.

Stillwaters Restaurant (☎ 2284 024 537; stillwaters ap@aol.com; Apandima Beach; dishes €5-12) Located 8km south of the port and only a step away from the water, Stillwaters offers an adventurous menu of modern European and Asian dishes and is also a great place for evening cocktails.

Thea (☎ 2284 091 220; dishes €9-12) Thea is an experience in every sense. It has a marvellous waterside location right by the Antiparos ferry quay on the Paros side of the straits. Delicious traditional food is prepared with the finest ingredients; even the olive oil is carefully sourced. Thea also has one of the finest wine lists anywhere in Greece, and

the background music is from a selection of 2500 CDs of world music.

The main street of Antiparos has many cafés and tavernas serving Greek staples and fish dishes. One of the best is **Maki's** (☎ 2284 061 616; dishes €3.50-10) where the fish and seafood is generally excellent, and includes such treats as prawn souvlaki with calamari.

Entertainment

Signposted left off Market St, Yam Bar Café is a relaxing open-air spot, with views of the sea. It plays a mix of Latin and house and occasional jazz. Soul Sugar is along to the right from the top of the main street and plays funk, disco and house into the small hours.

NAXOS ΝΑΞΟΣ

pop 18,188

Legend has blessed beautiful Naxos with racy romanticism. It was here that Theseus is said to have abandoned Ariadne after she helped him escape the Cretan labyrinth. She didn't pine long, and was soon entwined with Dionysos, the god of wine and ecstasy and the island's favourite deity. Naxian wine has long been considered a fine antidote for a broken heart; but the very air of Naxos is intoxicating enough and you should take time over this delightful island and its captivating mix of superb beaches, lively port, mountainous interior and enchanting villages such as Halki and Apiranthos.

The island is deeply fertile and produces olives, grapes, figs, citrus fruit, corn and potatoes. Mt Zeus (1004m; also known as Mt Zas or Zefs) is the Cyclades' highest peak and is the central focus of inland Naxos.

Naxos is believed to have been inhabited continuously since the Neolithic period and was a cultural centre of classical Greece; its abundant marble facilitated fine sculpture and architecture. It was a flourishing centre of Byzantinium, while Venetian and Frankish influences have also left a powerful mark.

The island is a wonderful place to explore on foot as many old paths between villages, churches and other sights still survive. There are a number of walking guides and maps including the useful *Central Naxos – A Guide with Map* (€8), available from local bookshops.

CYCLADES

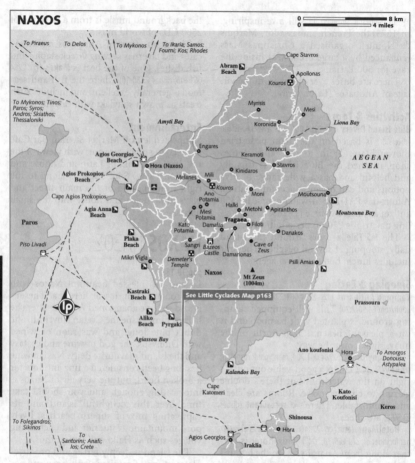

NAXOS

0 — 8 km
0 — 4 miles

To Piraeus To Delos To Mykonos To Ikaria; Samos; Fourni; Kos; Rhodes

Cape Stavros

Abram Beach
Kouros
Apollonas
Myrisis
Mesi
Koronida
Liona Bay

To Mykonos; Tinos; Paros; Syros; Andros; Skiathos; Thessaloniki

Amyti Bay

Engares
Keramoti
Koronos

AEGEAN SEA

Agios Georgios Beach
Hora (Naxos)
Melanes Mili
Kinidaros
Stavros
Kouros
Moni
Moutsouna

Agios Prokopios Beach
Ano Potamia
Halki
Metohi
Apiranthos
Moutsouna Bay

Cape Agios Prokopios
Mesi Potamia
Tragaea
Filoti
Danakos

Agia Anna Beach
Kato Potamia
Damalas

Paros

Piso Livadi

Plaka Beach
Sangri
Bazeos Castle
Damarionas
Cave of Zeus

Mikri Vigla
Demeter's Temple

Naxos

Psili Amas

Mt Zeus (1004m)

Kastraki Beach

See Little Cyclades Map p163

Prassoura

Aliko Beach
Pyrgaki

Ano koufonisi
Hora
To Amorgos; Donousa; Astypalea

Agiassou Bay

Kalandos Bay

Kato Koufonisi

Keros

To Folegandros; Sikinos

Cape Katomeri

Shinousa
Hora

To Santorini; Anafi; Ios; Crete

Agios Georgios
Iraklia

Getting There & Away

AIR

There is at least one flight daily and two on Sunday to Athens (€63). Olympic Airways is represented by **Naxos Tours** (☎ 2285 022 095; naxostours@naxos-island.com; harbour front), which also sells ferry tickets.

FAST BOAT & CATAMARAN

There are at least two catamarans travelling daily to Paros (€9.90, 30 minutes), Mykonos (€13.80, 1½ hours) and Piraeus (€32.30, 3¼ hours). There are also daily services to Ios (€14.80, 50 minutes), Santorini (€20.30, 1½ hours) and Iraklio on Crete (€35.20, 3¼ hours), and four weekly to Syros (€13, 1½ hours).

FERRY

Naxos has around six ferry connections daily with Piraeus (€21.35, six hours), Paros (€6.25, one hour), Ios (€9, 1¼ hours) and Santorini (€12.65, three hours), as well as four daily with Mykonos (€8.70, three hours).

There is one daily boat to Tinos (€8.70, 4¼ hours), Syros (€9.25, three hours), Iraklia (€5.20, 1¼ to 5¼ hours), Shinousa (€5.50, 1¾ to five hours), Koufonisia (€6, 2½ to 4¼ hours), Amorgos (€8.30, two to 5¾ hours), Donousa (€5.60, one to four hours), Samos (€19, 3½ hours) and Ikaria (€10.20, 1½ hours).

There are five ferries weekly to Anafi (€10, seven hours).

There are two boats weekly to Astypalea (€14.60, 5½ hours), Rhodes (€21, 14 hours), Sikinos (€7, three hours) and Folegandros (€8.50, three hours).

One goes weekly to Thessaloniki (€33, 15 hours), Kos (€16, 8¼ hours), Iraklio (€21, seven hours) and Andros (€12.80, five hours).

Getting Around
TO/FROM THE AIRPORT
The airport is 3km south of Hora. There is no shuttle bus, but buses to Agios Prokopios Beach and Agia Anna pass close by. A taxi costs €10.

BUS
Frequent buses run to Agia Anna (€1.20) from Hora. Five buses daily serve Filoti (€1.60) via Halki (€1.20), four serve Apiranthos (€2.30) via Filoti and Halki, at least three serve Apollonas (€4), Pyrgaki (€2) and Melanes (€1.20). There are less frequent departures to other villages.

Buses leave from the end of the wharf in Hora; timetables are posted outside the bus information office and the Naxos Tourist Information Centre in Hora.

CAR, MOTORCYCLE & BICYCLE
You can hire cars from about €40 and motorcycles, as well as 21-speed all-terrain bicycles, from the waterfront outlets in Hora. **Fun Car** (☎ 2285 026 084; Plateia Protodikiou) is a good bet. Bicycle hire starts at €8. You'll need all the gears – the roads are steep and winding and although surfaces are being improved, recent winter storms have caused damage on lesser-used mountain roads.

HORA (NAXOS)
pop 6533
Naxos' bustling and hugely enjoyable Hora, on the west coast, is the island's port and capital. It's a large town, divided into two historic neighbourhoods – Bourgos, where the Greeks lived, and the hilltop kastro, where the Venetian Catholics lived.

Orientation
A causeway to the north of the port leads to the Palatia Islet and the unfinished Temple of Apollo, Naxos' most famous landmark.

There are a few swimming spots along the waterfront promenade below the temple.

The town's northern shore, called Grotta, is too rocky and too exposed to harsh winds for enjoyable swimming. Southwest of the town is the pleasant, but busy, beach of Agios Georgios.

The ferry quay is at the northern end of the waterfront, with the bus terminal at its inland end. The waterfront, Protopapadaki, is lined with cafés and restaurants. Behind the waterfront, narrow alleys scramble up to the kastro.

Information
Booths on the quay have information about hotels and domatia, but a good bet is to head for the privately owned **Naxos Tourist Information Centre** (NTIC; ☎ 2285 025 201, emergency ☎ 2285 024 525; apollon-hotel@naxos-island.com), opposite the quay. It's an excellent source of in-depth advice on accommodation, excursions and rental cars; luggage storage is available (€1.50). The NTIC does not sell ferry tickets.

Zas Travel (☎ 2285 023 330; fax 2285 023 419) and **Naxos Tours** (☎ 2285 022 095; naxostours@naxos-island.com) sell ferry tickets and organise accommodation, tours and rental cars.

There's an ATM outside NTIC and several more scattered along the waterfront. There's half a dozen phone kiosks outside the OTE (telecommunications office), 150m further south along Protopapadaki. For the post office, continue past the OTE, cross Papavasiliou and take the left branch where the road forks. There's Internet access at **Rental Center** (☎ 2285 023 395; Plateia Protodikiou) for €3 an hour.

Zoom (Protopapadaki) newsagent and bookshop has most international newspapers and one of the biggest selection of books, in various languages, in the entire Cyclades.

The **police** (☎ 2285 022 100) are southeast of Plateia Protodikiou. The **port police** (☎ 2285 023 300) are just south of the quay.

Sights
Head inland and up to the right from the main square into the winding backstreets of Bourgos. The most alluring part of Hora is the residential **Kastro**, with its winding alleyways, timber-lined archways and whitewashed houses. Marco Sanudo made the town the capital of his duchy in 1207, and there are some handsome Venetian dwellings, many with well-kept

HORA (NAXOS)

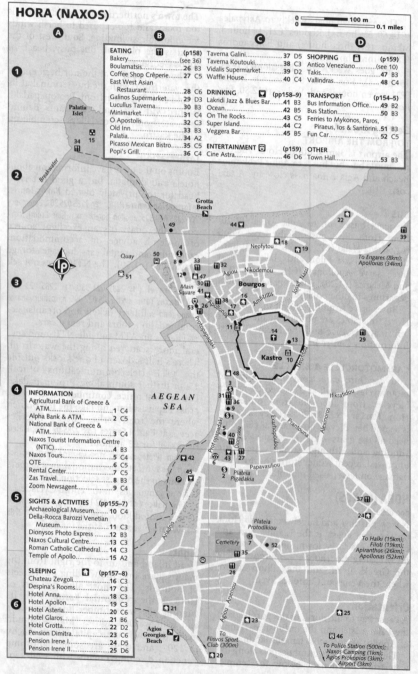

gardens and the insignia of their original residents. Take a stroll around the Kastro during siesta to experience its hushed, medieval atmosphere.

The **archaeological museum** (☎ 2285 022 725; admission €3; 🕒 8.30am-3pm Tue-Sun) is in the Kastro, housed in the former Franciscan school where the novelist Nikos Kazantzakis was briefly a pupil. The contents include Hellenistic and Roman terracotta figurines. There are also, more interestingly, some early Cycladic figurines.

Close by, the crumbling **Della Rocca-Barozzi Venetian Museum** (☎ 2285 022 387; 🕒 10am-3pm & 7-10pm), is within the kastro ramparts by the northwest gate. It was, until recently, still a residence; a visit is a brief, voyeuristic journey back in time. Multilingual guided tours cost €5/2 for adults/students. Kastro tours are €12/6. Sunset concerts are held here several times a week.

The Roman Catholic **cathedral** (🕒 6.30pm), also in the kastro, is worth visiting (tours at 6pm). The **Naxos Cultural Centre** nearby has exhibitions over summer.

Activities & Tours

NTIC (☎ 2285 025 201, emergency ☎ 2285 024 525; apollon-hotel@naxos-island.com) offers day tours of the island by bus (€18) or caïque (€38, including barbecue). One-day walking tours (€44 for two people) are offered three times weekly.

You can windsurf on Naxos and the **Flisvos Sport Club** (☎ 2285 024 308; www.flisvos -sportclub.com) in Agios Georgios offers a range of options starting with a beginner's windsurfing course of three hours for €65 and a four-hour Hobie Cat sailing course for €88 The club also organises walking trips and rents mountain bikes.

Photo-Tours Naxos (☎ 2285 022 367; www.naxos photoworkshop.com) runs one day photo outings for small groups (€35 per person) to great locations with on-the-spot advice on taking better pictures from professional Stuart Thorpe. When on Naxos you can inquire at Dionysos Photo Express on the harbour front.

EXCURSION BOATS
There are daily excursions to Mykonos (€38) and frequent excursions to Delos; book through travel agents.

Sleeping
BUDGET
Naxos has a rapacious mob of domatia hawkers meeting ferries. Be firm but polite, and keep moving, if you're not interested.

Pension Irene I (☎ 2285 023 169; irenepension@ hotmail.com; s/d €25/35) This pension is a little bit out of the town centre but is refreshingly peaceful and well run and has pleasant leafy surroundings. Rooms are comfortable and there are cooking facilities.

Pension Irene II (☎ 2285 023 169; irenepension@ hotmail.com; s/d €30/50; 🏊) Run by the same people, Irene II is an excellent option. Rooms are bright and comfortable with pleasant balconies; the swimming pool is irresistible.

Pension Dimitra (☎ /fax 2285 024 922; s/d/tr €45/53/70) Although some way from the centre and in an anonymous street, this is a charming, very Greek place, with clean and comfy rooms. Agios Georgios Beach is just over 100m away.

Despina's Rooms (☎ 2285 022 356; fax 2285 022 179; s/d €40/45) Tucked away on the edge of the kastro, this cheerful family home has a selection of rooms, some with great sea views. Tiny rooms on the roof terrace are popular despite their small size. There's a communal kitchen.

Hotel Anna (☎ 2285 025 213; hotelannanaxox@ yahoo.gr; s/d/tr €45/50/60) Triples have small kitchens at this family-run place, which is more of a small guest house than hotel. It's in a fairly quiet area.

There are several camping grounds near Hora. All have good facilities. Minibuses meet the ferries. The sites are all handy to good beaches and there's a general price of €5 per person. **Naxos Camping** (☎ 2285 023 500; 🏊) is about 1km south of Agios Georgios Beach; **Camping Maragas** (☎ 2285 024 552) is at Agia Anna Beach and **Plaka Camping** (☎ 2285 042 700; fax 2285 042 701) is 6km from town at Plaka Beach.

MID-RANGE
Hotel Apollon (☎ 2285 022 468, 6976 618 384; www .naxostownhotels.com; Fontana; s/d incl breakfast €65/85; P ⊗ 🖥) The stylish Apollon has thoughtful touches that capture a sense of Naxian good living in spacious, well-equipped rooms. The hotel is in a quiet area only a few minutes from the main waterfront.

Chateau Zevgoli (☎ 2285 026 123; www.naxostown hotels.com; Kastro Bourgo; s/d €70/80; ⊗) situated in a charming garden setting at the heart of Bourgos, Zevgoli's ambience is enhanced even more by the traditional Naxian style of rooms and furnishings.

Hotel Glaros (☎ 2285 023 101; fax 2285 024 877; s/d incl breakfast €62/80; ❄ 🖳) This bright and cheerful hotel has decor that reflects the colours of beach and sea. Agios Georgios beach itself is only a few steps away. Rooms at the front have equally cheerful sea views.

Hotel Grotta (☎ 2285 022 215; www.hotelgrotta.gr; s/d incl breakfast €65/80) Don't be put off by the desolate-looking clifftop that overlooks Grotta Beach below the building. It awaits archaeological decisions. The hotel is comfortably smart, has immaculate rooms and great sea views from its front.

Hotel Asteria (☎ 2285 023 002; www.hotelasteria .com; s/d €50/100; 🅿) A location just a block inland from Agios Georgios makes this fairly smart hotel a good base for beach lovers, and the town centre is only a short stroll away. Rooms are a good size and are well equipped.

Eating

Naxian specialities include *kefalotiri* (hard cheese), honey, *kitron* (a liqueur made from the leaves of the citron tree; see the Glory Days of the Citron p159), raki, ouzo and fine white wine.

Lucullus Taverna (☎ 2285 022 569; Agiou Nikodemou; dishes €2.50-12.50) Lucullus takes the prize for being one of the oldest tavernas in Naxos. It's been operating for over 100 years and still offers great local food. The atmospheric surroundings are liberally hung with all sorts of fascinating artefacts.

O Apostolis (☎ 2285 026 777; dishes €1.50-25) Tucked away behind the main square, in a quiet corner of town with an almost village feel to it, this traditional eatery offers excellent mezedes, fresh fish and grilled octopus.

East West Asian Restaurant (☎ 2285 024 641; off Agiou Arseniou; dishes €5-11.50) There's great ambience and friendly service at this fine restaurant where you can enjoy something different in the form of Thai, Chinese or Indian favourites. Dishes include excellent vegetarian options.

Old Inn (☎ 2285 026 093; dishes €4-12.50) There's a good selection of northern-European food with Mediterranean touches at this popular place that has a lovely tree-shaded garden.

There's also a children's playground, as well as a children's menu, and there's even an in-house flea market full of fascinating odds and ends.

Palatia (☎ 2285 026 588; dishes €3.50-10) At the northern end of the promenade, Palatia is a charming spot for light meals and seafood (by the kilo). Tables are right on the water's edge and there's the cultural bonus of the Temple of Apollo behind.

Picasso Mexican Bistro (☎ 2285 025 408; dishes €3.50-9; ⏰ 7pm) To sample great Tex-Mex tastes, head for this popular place. Tables fill quickly for aficionados of tacos, nachos and burritos. It also does great salads as well as hefty Buffalo steaks.

Plateia Pigadakia, just inland from the OTE, is buzzing place with a couple of tavernas as well as the excellent Coffee Shop Crêperie and the Waffle House, which has a great selection of ice creams among its tasty offerings. Just next to the coffee shop is a splendid fruit and veg shop.

Naxos has numerous good tavernas and popular local favourites include Taverna Koutouki, famous for its outside tables in a narrow alleyway, Boulamatsis, Popi's Grill (the best place for souvlaki) and Taverna Galini, all charging about €3 to €9 for a main dish.

Immediately adjacent to Zoom newsagent and bookshop is the town's best bakery. Next door is a minimarket. The cheapest supermarkets are Galinos and Vidalis, both a little way out of town.

Drinking
BARS

Plateia Pigadakia adds further to its happy buzz with On The Rocks, a place brimming with character, where cocktails are a specialty and you can enjoy Havana cigars with Cuban-style daiquiris. Sounds range from funk, house, electronic to live acts. It's open till the early hours. Just across the way is the long-established Jam, a cosy, atmospheric music bar that plays rock and assorted sounds.

Veggera Bar cranks out '70s and '80s mainstream from the word go and runs 'Disco Fever' nights on Saturday and 'Latin Parties' on Wednesday.

Lakridi Jazz & Blues Bar on the way to the Kastro, is a great place to quietly withdraw from the noisier frontline.

GLORY DAYS OF THE CITRON

The citron *(Citrus medica)* looks like a very large, lumpy lemon. It has a thick rind and yields little juice. It was introduced to the Mediterranean area in about 300 BC. In antiquity the citron was known for its medicinal qualities and was also a symbol of fertility and affluence.

Citron trees need abundant water and are intolerant of wind and cold – but they thrived on Naxos for centuries. Although the fruit is barely edible in its raw state, the Naxians discovered that the rind tastes delicious when preserved in syrup. They also put the aromatic leaves to good use by creating *kitroraki*, a raki distilled from grape skins and citron leaves. By the late-19th century the preserved fruit and a sweet version of kitroraki, known as kitron, had cult followings outside Greece and were popular exports to Russia, Austria, France and the USA. Kitron was so much in demand that it became the mainstay of the island's economy and, by the early 20th century, Naxos was carpeted with citron orchards.

Alas, kitron went out of vogue after WWII; even the islanders abandoned it, seduced by the invasion of exotic drinks from the outside world. In the 1960s most citron trees were uprooted to make way for more useful, profitable crops. However, the citron has enjoyed a happy renaissance in recent years.

On Naxos, Vallindras distillery in Halki still distils kitron the old-fashioned way, using leaves collected from the orchards in the autumn and winter. The leaves are laid out in a dry room, dampened with water and then placed with alcohol and water in a boiler fuelled by olive wood. The distillate is added to water and sugar, and kitron is born.

It is nearly impossible to find kitron outside Greece, so be sure to track some down while visiting its island home. It comes in three strengths and degrees of sweetness: the green is the traditional Naxian liqueur and has the most sugar and least alcohol; the yellow has little sugar, more aroma and more alcohol; the white falls somewhere in between and resembles Cointreau.

NIGHTCLUBS

For clubbing, head to Ocean near Veggera. It's a big space and features house and techno and runs special nights with guest DJs. Super Island right on the waterfront, at Grotta Beach, is even bigger and features similar sounds.

Entertainment

CINEMAS

Cine Astra (☎ 2285 025 381; admission €6) is about a five-minute walk from Plateia Protodikiou. It shows new release mainstream films and has a bar. Sessions are 9pm and 11pm.

SUNSET CONCERTS

Evening concerts, featuring traditional instruments, are held several times weekly in the outdoor grounds of the **Venetian Museum** (☎ 2285 022 387; Kastro) accompanied by wine and food.

Shopping

At **Vallindras** (☎ 2285 022 227; Protopapadaki) on the waterfront, you can find kitron liqueur in beautiful French and Italian bottles, as well as ouzo. **Takis'** (☎ 2285 023 045) is a block behind the waterfront and also sells kitron

and other spirits and liquors as well as interesting jewellery.

In the streets heading up to the kastro there are several shops selling fine embroidery and hand-made silver jewellery.

Antico Veneziano (☎ 2285 026 206; Kastro) an upmarket antique store and gallery, in a restored home in the kastro, makes for a fascinating visit.

AROUND NAXOS

Beaches

Agios Georgios is Naxos' town beach and starts right on the southern edge of the waterfront. It gets crowded, but is safe for youngsters as the water is very shallow.

The next beach south is **Agios Prokopios** in a sheltered bay. This is followed by **Agia Anna**, a stretch of shining white sand, quite narrow but long enough to feel uncrowded. Development is increasing here, but not too heavily.

Cruises run to different destinations daily from Agia Anna. Cruises head either to Irak lia and Koufonisia, Shinousa and Koufo sia, or Antiparos; book at travel agents Sandy beaches continue down as **Pyrgaki** and include **Plaka**, **Aliko**, M

CYCLADES

and **Kastraki**. There are domatia and tavernas aplenty along this stretch, and any of these beaches are good places to stop for a few days. To the north of Hora, **Abram** is also a nice spot.

Tragaea Τραγαία

The lovely Tragaea region is a vast plain of olive groves and unspoilt villages harbouring numerous little Byzantine churches. **Filoti**, on the slopes of Mt Zeus, is the region's largest village. It has an ATM booth, accessed with card, just down from the main bus stop. On the outskirts of the village (coming from Hora), an asphalt road leads off right into the heart of the Tragaea. This road brings you to the isolated hamlets of **Damarionas** and **Damalas**.

From Filoti, you can also reach the **Cave of Zeus**. About 800m south of Filoti there's a junction signposted Aria Spring and Zas Cave. If travelling by bus ask to be dropped here. The side road ends in 1.2km. From the road-end parking, follow a walled path past the **Aria Spring**, a fountain and picnic area, and continue uphill to reach the cave. Continuing to the summit of **Mt Zeus** (1004m) or 'Zas' is a rewarding, if fairly steep slog and some careful route-finding is required. The path zigzags up Zas beyond the cave then bears left and up right. You then have to follow a faint path uphill to reach the summit plateau, bearing right once more for the summit. You can retrace your steps to the Aria Spring or, head west along the summit plateau on a path that descends steadily as it turns north, eventually reaching the main road near the little church of Agia Marina. From here a combination of road walking and excellent old stepped tracks lead down to Filoti. Allow at least five to six hours for the full 8km circuit, carry a map and compass and be prepared for wet, windy and even cold conditions at any time of year.

The delightful village of **Halki** has seen something of a renaissance in recent years, as befits its rich history as the one-time centre of Naxian commerce, and its architectural legacy of handsome villas and tower houses. The latter were built by aristocratic families as refuges and lookouts in the days of pirate raids and feuds between the islanders and the Venetians and Turks.

Vallindras Distillery (☎ 2285 031 220) in a fine old building in the magical centre of Halki, has impromptu tours of its atmospheric rooms with their ancient jars and copper stills. Kitron tastings round off the trip (see Glory Days of the Citron, p159) and a selection of the distillery's products are on sale. Halki's renaissance owes much to the distillery and to the nearby **L'Olivier** (☎ 2285 032 829), a superb ceramics shop full of the enthralling work of Katharina and Alex Bolesch. Katharina Bolesch's exquisite stoneware pottery, the designs of which are inspired by the ancient and sacred themes of the olive and the fish, is fast building her an international reputation, while Alex Bolesch's designs and highly original pendants and jewellery, are irresistible. L'Olivier also has beautiful artefacts in olive wood, and sells olive products, including oil and candles. (Poor quality imitations of Katharina Bolesch's work are sold elsewhere on the island, so be warned.)

PANAGIA DROSIANI
The **Panagia Drosiani** (☒ 10am-7pm May–mid-Oct) just below **Moni**, 2.5km north of Halki, is one of the oldest and most revered churches in the Balkans. It has a warren of cave-like chapels and several of its surviving frescoes date back to the 7th century. Donations are appreciated.

Melanes Μέλανες
Near the hillside villages of Melanes and Mili, there is a 6m, unfinished 7th-century BC **kouros** (male statue), known as 'The Greek', abandoned in a quarry that is now encircled by orchards. A broad sandy track leads on from the end of the surfaced approach road. In about 200m bear up right along a rocky path to reach the kouros. Another kouros lies nearby. To reach it, continue along the broad track and then follow orange paint marks to the right, along a rising, rough path for about 500m to reach the kouros, a strangely haunting figure on a wild hillside.

Sangri Σαγκρί
The handsome tower-like building of **Bazeos Castle** (☎ 2285 031 402; ☒ 10am-5pm & 6-9pm) stands prominently in the landscape about 2km east of the village of Sangri and was built in its original form as the Monastery of Timios Stavros (True Cross) during the 17th century. The monks abandoned the

site in the early 19th century and it was later bought by the Bazeos family whose modern descendants have refurbished the building and its fascinating late-medieval rooms with great skill and imagination. The castle now functions as a cultural centre and stages art exhibitions and the annual **Naxos Festival** during July and August when concerts, plays and literary readings are held.

About 1.5km south of Sangri is the impressive **Temple to Demeter** (Dimitra's Temple; ☎ 2285 022 725; ☒ 8.30am-3pm Tue-Sun). This is fast becoming a popular attraction, and deservedly so. The ruins and reconstructions are not large, but they are historically fascinating and the hilltop location is impressive. There is a site **museum** with some fine reconstructions of temple features. Signs point the way from Sangri.

SLEEPING & EATING
There are no domatia in Halki, or Sangri, but Filoti has serviceable rooms at much lower prices than you'll find anywhere in the Cyclades. Ask at the tavernas by the main bus stop.

Yianni's (☎ 2285 031 214; dishes €3-5.50) At the heart of Halki's main square Yianni's has one of the most romantic settings imaginable. It offers superb salads, including the delicious *dakos*, a Cretan specialty with a rusk base, as well as tasty meat dishes and persuasive local wine. Just across the way is a marvellous bakery.

Taverna Xenakis (☎ 2285 062 374; dishes €2.50-7) in Melanes has excellent and hugely filling dishes that make good use of local produce, including rabbit.

Axiotissa (☎ 2285 075 107; Alyko; dishes €5-12) You'd be wise to book in high season for a table at this hugely popular restaurant near Kastraki, 18km south of Hora and about 3km north of Pyrgaki. The food is superb and there's a commitment to recapturing natural flavours in the use of local produce. The wine list encompasses excellent Cycladean vintages.

Apiranthos Απείρανθος
Apiranthos is an atmospheric village of stone houses and marble-paved streets and alleyways that scramble up the slopes of Fanari mountain. It was once an emery mining centre. Its inhabitants are descendants of refugees who fled Crete to escape

Turkish repression and they have retained an impressive richness in their dialect and a strong individual character. The village was always noted for its spirited politics and its populism. Its most famous son is Manolis Glezos, the resistance fighter who during WWII replaced the Nazi flag with the Greek one atop the Acropolis. He later became the parliamentary representative for the Cyclades. Apiranthos is also known for producing a notable number of academics and has a fascinating tradition of popular versifying as a conversational skill. It also has an impressive trio of museums.

To the right of the beginning of the village's main thoroughfare (coming from the Hora–Apollonas road) is the **museum of natural history** (☒ 8.30am-2pm Tue-Sun). Both the **geology museum** (☒ 8.30am-2pm Tue-Sun) and the **archaeology museum** (☒ 8.30am-2pm Tue-Sun) are along the main street. The latter has a marvellous collection of small artefacts. The museums are sometimes open from 7pm to 10pm in summer, but it should be noted that all the opening times stated here are 'flexible'.

Just before the atmospheric main square, which is dominated by a huge plane tree, is **Stoy Lefteris** (☎ 2285 061 333; dishes €3-8) where you can eat in a peaceful terrace garden overlooking the valley. There are good local meat dishes and there's a selection of delicious home-made sweets and baklava, and a range of local products on sale in the street-front shop.

Moutsouna Μουτσούνα
The road from Apiranthos to Moutsouna descends an exhilarating series of S-bends through spectacular mountain scenery. Formerly a busy port, shipping the emery mined in the region, Moutsouna is a quiet place, although there is some development. Seven kilometres south of the village is the fine beach of **Psili Amas**.

There are a few pensions and tavernas mainly at Moutsouna but some scattered along the coast road.

Apollonas Απόλλωνας
Apollonas, on the north coast, tranquil fishing village, but lar resort. It has a pleasa

Coachloads of day-t the gargantuan 7th-c

lies in an ancient quarry a short walk from the village. The largest of the three on the island, it is signposted to the left as you approach Apollonas on the main inland road from Hora. This 10.5m statue may have been abandoned unfinished because it cracked. Apollonas has several domatia and tavernas.

The inland route from Hora to Apollonas winds through spectacular mountains – a worthwhile trip. With your own transport you can return to Hora via the west-coast road, passing through wild and sparsely populated country with awe-inspiring sea views. Several tracks branch down to secluded beaches.

LITTLE CYCLADES
ΜΙΚΡΕΣ ΚΥΚΛΑΔΕΣ

For the dedicated island lover the chain of small islands between Naxos and Amorgos is paradise regained. Variously called the Little Cyclades, Minor Islands, Back Islands and Lesser Islands, only four – Donousa, Koufonisia (comprising Ano Koufonisia and Kato Koufonisia), Iraklia and Shinousa – have permanent populations. All were densely populated in antiquity, indicated by the large number of ancient graves found here. In the Middle Ages, the islands were inhabited by pirates and goats. After independence, intrepid souls from Naxos and Amorgos began to re-colonise, but until recently, the only visitors were Greeks returning to their roots. These days the islands receive growing numbers of independent-minded tourists. Most are looking for fine beaches and a relaxed lifestyle without overt commercialism, although Koufonisia especially is edging towards becoming a conventional, if still low-key, resort.

Donousa is the northernmost of the group and farthest from Naxos. The others are clustered near the southeast – coast of Naxos. Each has a public telephone and agency. Money can usually be changed neral store or post agency, but rates bring cash with you.

& Away

tle Cyclades are regular affected by bad sea re you have plenty of time before committing yourself – these islands are not meant for last minute flying visits.

For anyone planning to explore the Little Cyclades, the sturdy little ferry **Express Skopelitis** (☎ 2285 071 256/519; Katapola, Amorgos) provides a lifeline daily service in season between Naxos and Amorgos via the islands. It's impressively punctual, but can be curtailed by bad weather. Sailings may be cancelled if wind speeds rise above Force 5 on the Beaufort scale. Most seating is second deck level. When it's windy, work out which is the leeward side of the vessel. Regardless of the weather, locals head straight below for the comfy, air-conditioned cabin.

In high season the Skopelitis starts its weekly schedule from Katapola (Amorgos), at 6am on a Monday morning and calls at Aegiali (Amorgos; €3.50, 50 minutes), Donousa (€4.60, 1 hour 20 minutes), Koufonisia (€5.70, 3½ hours), Shinousa (€5.90, four hours), Iraklia (€7, 4½ hours) and Naxos (€8.30, six hours). It then leaves Naxos at 1pm and reverses the circuit, reaching Katapola at 4.45pm, from where it returns to Naxos direct. This is the schedule on Monday, Wednesday, Friday, Saturday and Sunday (excluding Donousa on Sunday, and Aegiali on Monday, Wednesday and Sunday evenings). On Tuesday and Thursday the Skopelitis does just one complete circuit, leaving Naxos at 3pm and docking overnight at Katapola.

There is also one weekly ferry from Donousa to Syros (€8.20, 3½ hours) and three weekly ferries to Paros (€8.30, two to four hours).

A useful weekly link from Donousa to Astypalea and the Dodecanese is the rather lumbering MV *Dimitrouli*. It calls at Donousa on its outward trip from Piraeus to Rhodes via Paros and Naxos on Tuesday, and calls in again on its return trip on Friday.

Three weekly ferries go from Shinousa to Paros (€6.70, four hours).

Three times a week the fast boat Blue Star Naxos travels from Piraeus to Koufonisia and twice a week to Iraklia and Shinousa via Naxos, continuing on to Amorgos. A few other large ferries stop at the islands during high season, often at the most ungodly of hours.

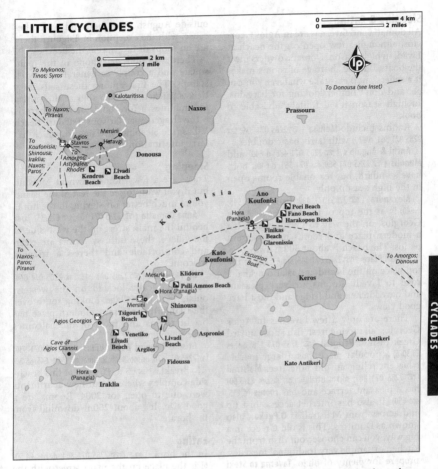

LITTLE CYCLADES

IRAKLIA ΗΡΑΚΛΕΙΑ
pop 151

Iraklia is where you can really switch off. Forget the sightseeing, the nightlife option, the massed ranks of souvenir shops. Instead, bring expectations of a serene and quiet life and Iraklia will never lose its charm. The island is only 19 sq km in area and its only 'sight' is a **cave**, complete with stalactites, where the sacred icon of Agios Giannis, a painting of the saint, was said to have been discovered by a shepherd at the end of the 19th century. The icon is now in the church at the village of Panagia, where a **festival** is held on the last weekend in August.

The port and main village is **Agios Georgios**. It's very quiet and has an attractive cove-like harbour complete with a pleasant little beach. The way into town is to turn right at the end of the ferry quay and go along behind the beach, before turning left uphill. From here the town's two main roads fork around a ravine.

The right fork leads to the right of Perigiali Taverna and passes a supermarket to reach Melissa, the general store that sells ferry tickets. Melissa also has a cardphone, serves as the island's post office and has domatia.

A surfaced road leads off to the left from the end of the ferry quay. This leads, in about 500m, to **Livadi** – the island's best beach. About 1km further on is the village of **Hora**, also known as Panagia. The Cave of Agios Gioannis is 1.25km from Agios Georgos.

Sleeping & Eating

All domatia and tavernas are in Agios Georgios, although a few open on the beach at Livadi in high season. Domatia owners meet the boats, but the shortage of rooms makes it a sellers' market – take whatever you can get and don't bother looking for bargains. In high season it's definitely advisable to book.

Rooms include **Melissa** (☎ 2285 071 539; fax 2285 071 561; d €20) with fairly basic doubles.

Anthi & Angelo's (☎ 2285 071 486; d €40) and **Manolis** (☎ 2285 071 569; fax 071 561; d €40), both have standard, but reasonable rooms open in the high season only.

Alexandra (☎ 2285 071 482; fax 2285 071 545; d €40) is at the top of the hill above Agios Georgios, on the way to Livadi beach. It's a modern place and rooms have pleasant patios. The beach is about 500m away.

Anna's Place (☎ 2285 071 145; s/d €35/65) is the top place on the island and is also near the road to Livadi. Rooms are very pleasant and have kitchen and fridge and most have good views.

There are only a few tavernas in Agios Georgios, all serving fresh fish and standard Greek dishes. **Perigiali** (☎ 2285 071 118; dishes €3.30-6) a popular place, has a large marble table encircling an old pine tree. **Maistrali** (☎ 2285 071 807; nickmaistrali@in.gr; dishes €3-6.80) has a pleasant terrace and has **rooms** (d €35, apt €50). It also has Internet access. Just up and across from Maistrali is **0 Pevkos**, also known as Dimitri's. This is old Greece in a big way; you can choose your dish from the kitchen or sample very traditional mezedes; prepare for plenty of ouzo. **Taverna to Steki** (☎ 2285 071 579; dishes €3-6), in Panagia, does excellent traditional food, with a view and has a good bakery.

SHINOUSA ΣΧΙΝΟΥΣΑ
pop 206

Shinousa (skih-*noo*-sah) is a quietly engaging place with a couple of fine beaches and a thoroughly lived-in **Hora (Panagia)** located on the breezy crest of the island and with sweeping views of the sea.

Ferries dock at the fishing harbour of **Mersini**. The hora is a hot 1km uphill, so try to get a lift with one of the locals offering rooms. Dirt tracks lead from the hora to several beaches around the coast; nearest to the hora are **Tsigouri** and **Livadi**, both uncrowded

outside August. Take food and water, because, with the exception of Tsigouri, there are no shops or tavernas at the beaches.

There's a public telephone in the main square and a couple of general stores sell stamps. The first among these sells ferry tickets. Tickets are also sold at the port a few minutes before boats arrive. There is a travel agency at Grispos Tsigouri Beach Villas (see Sleeping) in Tsigouri, which has ferry information and tickets.

Sleeping

There are a few rooms down at Mersini, but if you want to see the rest of the island you're much better off staying in the hora.

Anna Domatia (☎ 2285 071 161; s/d €20/35) Just behind the main street on the west-side of the village, these unfussy rooms are clean and comfortable and there's a friendly welcome.

Ili Vasilema (☎ 2285 071 948; fax 2285 074 064; s/d €35/45) Ideally located on the western outskirts of the village, looking south over the island, this pleasant modern place has bright rooms and most of the balconies have fine views.

Grispos Tsigouri Beach Villas (☎ 2285 071 930; fax 2285 071 176; grispos@nax.forthnet.gr; s/d/tr €45/65/80; 🖳) Breakfast is €5 to €6 extra at this beach-side complex where brand new apartments were due to open for 2004. Rooms are a good size. It's about 250m downhill from the hora.

Eating

In the hora, **Loza** (☎ 2285 071 864; dishes €4.50-6) is the place on the main street with the very big umbrella shading its terrace. It does breakfasts for €6 as well as salads and pizzas, but it's also a bakery producing delicious pastries, including baklava and walnut pie. To Kentro Kafeneio is a popular local bar. **Grispos** (dishes €3-6) has a restaurant attached to its villa complex and offers good island standards.

Margarita (☎ 2285 074 278; dishes €4-8) is the best place to eat on Shinousa. It's midway along the village street, down an alleyway. The terrace has superb views of the sea and the food is modern Greek and includes pricier seafood options, all creatively prepared and backed by a good wine list.

A couple of standard tavernas at the port serve freshly caught fish and lobster.

KOUFONISIA ΚΟΥΦΟΝΗΣΙΑ

pop 366

Koufonisia is the most visited of the Little Cyclades, yet it retains its small-island charm, while its sizeable fishing fleet imparts a strong down-to-earth element to island life. It's really two islands, Ano Koufonisi and Kato Koufonisi, but it's Kato that's permanently inhabited. Its population is a balanced one, because there has not been too great an exodus of young people to the mainland.

The beaches are picture-perfect swathes of golden sand lapped by crystal-clear turquoise waters; locals are hospitable and friendly; and food and accommodation options are more plentiful and sophisticated than on any of the neighbouring islands.

A caïque ride away, **Kato Koufonisi** has some beautiful beaches and a lovely church. Archaeological digs on **Keros**, the large lump of rock that looms over Koufonisia to the south, have uncovered over 100 Early Cycladic figurines, including the famous harpist and flautist now on display in Athens' archaeological museum. There are no guides at the site.

Orientation & Information

Koufonisia's only settlement spreads out behind the ferry quay and around an attractive harbour filled with moored fishing boats. The large town beach, which is flat and used by traffic, gives a great sense of openness to the waterfront. The older part of town, the hora, is on the low hill behind the quay.

From the quay head right and, where the sand begins, take the first road to the left. Continue to the crossroads, then turn left onto the village's pedestrianised main street.

Along here you'll find a small minimarket and an inconspicuous ticket agency (look for the dolphins painted right above the door). The post office is on the first road to the left as you come from the ferry quay.

Koufonisia Tours (see Tours on this page) organises accommodation on the island.

The flat, hard sand of the town beach draws a few swimmers. Cars drive across it to reach the south-coast road and local youngsters use it as a football pitch.

Beaches

Koufonisia has several outstanding beaches amid its coastal landscape of low sand dunes punctuated by rocky coves and caves.

A walk along the south coast road is the best way to reach the island's beaches. The road runs for a couple of kilometres from the eastern end of the town beach to **Finikas**, **Harakopou** and **Fano** beaches.

However, the best beaches and swimming places are further along the path that follows the coast from Fano to the superb stretch of sand at **Pori**, which can also be reached by an inland road that heads east from the crossroads in the hora.

Tours

Koufonisia Tours (☎ 2285 071 671; www.koufonissia tours.gr) based at Villa Ostria (see Sleeping below) organises caïque trips to Keros, Kato Koufonisi and to other islands of the Little Cyclades. Bike hire is also available.

Sleeping

Wild camping is not permitted on Koufonisia. There is an excellent selection of domatia and hotels.

Koufonisia Camping (☎ 2285 071 683; camp sites per person €5) This site is by the tree-lined beach at Harakopou. Facilities are fairly basic but closeness to the beach is a great bonus.

Akrogyali (☎ 2285 071 685, 6942 448 263; s/d €40/50) This is a very friendly family-run place with clean, comfy rooms, just beyond the eastern end of the town beach.

Lefteris Rooms (☎ 2285 071 458; d €40 3-/4-bed r €45/50) This place is right on the town beach above the restaurant of the same name and the rooms are colourful and pleasant.

Katerina's (☎ 2285 071 670; fax 2285 071 455; d €45) On the road leading from the port to the hora, Katerina's has decent doubles with balcony and shared kitchen.

Ermis (☎ 2285 071 693; fax 2285 074 214; s/d €50/60) Fine spacious rooms with stylish fittings and big generous balconies overlooking the sea makes this quiet and attractive place a good choice. Not all rooms have sea views. It's on the road running parallel to the waterfront and adjoins the post office.

Villa Ostria (☎ 2285 071 671; www.koufonissia tours.gr; s/d incl breakfast €60/70) This excellent hotel is up on the hill, above the beach. Rooms are smart and comfortable and have fridges. There's a charming garden area.

The hotel is reached by going up the road at the eastern end of the beach, then taking the first left.

Eating

Capetan Nikolas (☎ 2285 071 690; dishes €4.50-6) This is a terrific place that overlooks the little harbour on the west–side of the village. It's family-run and bursting with life and good nature. The food is delicious, with lip-smacking grilled fish a specialty.

Karnagio (☎ 2285 071 243; dishes €2.50-7) Treat yourself to this little quayside ouzeria, just below Capetan Nikolas, where tables straggle along the harbour's edge in the rosy-hued evening light. There's excellent mezedes and octopus and squid dishes. The shrimp with tomatoes and feta cheese is a treat.

Fanari (☎ 2285 071 834; dishes €2.50-7) This is a popular place on the road up above the ferry quay near an old windmill. It offers good wood-fired pizzas, *pastitsio* (layers of buttery macaroni and seasoned minced lamb) and gyros, as well as well prepared fish dishes.

Lefteris (☎ 2285 071 458; dishes €3.50-5.50) This is a friendly, down-to-earth restaurant below the rooms of the same name. It does reasonably priced Greek standards and is also open for lunch. There's a huge open area with tables in front of it, overlooking the town beach.

Out of town, there's a taverna by the beach at Finikas and a good fish taverna, **Taverna Venetsanos** (☎ 2285 074 074; Kato Koufonisi).

Drinking

Scholeio (☎ 2285 071 837; ⏲ 6pm-3am) At the west–end of the village's main street, just before it descends to the west–side of the harbour, is this fine little bar and creperie in an atmospheric old schoolhouse. It does great cocktails and plays jazz, blues and rock among other choice sounds.

En Plo (☎ 6972 409 561; ⏲ 9pm-5am) Just next to Fanari is this music bar playing a range of harder sounds and some Greek.

Sorokos (☎ 2285 071 704; ⏲ 4pm-3am) Down at the end of the eastern waterfront beyond the town beach, in a terrific location overlooking the water, this place has a nice Bohemian flavour, great drinks and snacks and good sounds, ranging from early-hours lounge music to hotter notes in the night.

DONOUSA ΔΟΝΟΥΣΑ

pop 110

Stop the world and get off at Donousa, the least accessible of the Little Cyclades, and too far north to be on the schedules of many ferries en route to more popular islands. There's a great castaway atmosphere on Donousa, so have time on your hands.

Agios Stavros is the main settlement and the island's port. It has a pleasant little beach, which also serves as a drive-through for vehicles and foot traffic. Behind the beach there are lush vegetable gardens and vineyards. **Kendros**, 1.25km to the east along a dusty, bulldozed track, is a sandy and secluded beach with a seasonal taverna. **Livadi**, a dusty 1km trek further east, sees even fewer visitors. Both are popular with nudists. Bulldozed roads have marred Donousa in places but there are still delightful paths and tracks that lead into the hills to utterly timeless little hamlets such as Mersini. At a number of points on the island there are taps supplying drinkable water.

There is one public telephone, up a steep hill above the waterfront; look for the skeletal satellite dish. You can get telecards at the souvenir shop just up from the quay-end of the beach.

There is a ticket agency, **Roussos Travel** (☎ 2285 051 648) on the waterfront.

Sleeping & Eating

Wild camping is tolerated at Kendros. Although Donousa is out of the way it's wise to book rooms in advance in high season. Most rooms are fairly basic but are well kept and clean and in good locations.

Spiros Skopelitis Rooms (☎ 2285 051 586; s/d €35/ 38) Just behind the town beach, these pleasant little bungalows have kitchens and are in a garden setting.

Prassinos Studios (☎ 2285 051 579; d €35-41, apt €65) Overlooking the beach is this pleasant complex with a mix of rooms.

To Ilio Vasilema (☎ 2285 051 570; d €35, studio €45) Also overlooking the beach, this place has reasonable rooms, some with kitchens.

Aposperitis (dishes €3.50-6) next to Spiros Skopelitis, serves standard dishes. **To Ilio Vasilema** (dishes €8-20) also has a popular restaurant with a fine terrace and a good selection of food. The hub of village life is **Kafeneio To Kyma** by the quay, where things liven up late into the night.

AMORGOS ΑΜΟΡΓΟΣ

pop 1869

Amorgos (ah-mor-*ghoss*) the most easterly of the Cyclades, is a dramatic and beautiful island, a long, dragon's back of rugged mountains wriggling its way through the vibrant blue sea. The south coast is steep and perpendicular in places and boasts an extraordinary monastery embedded in a huge cliff. The north coast is less forbidding and has a narrow coastal plain on its southern half, where most settlement is concentrated.

Amorgos has two ports, Katapola and Aegiali, where there is a fine beach. The beautiful, unspoilt capital, Hora (also known as Amorgos), nestles high in the mountains above Katapola.

Getting There & Away

See Getting There & Away in the Little Cyclades (p162) for *Express Skopelitis* service details to Naxos and other islands of the Little Cyclades.

Most ferries stop at both Katapola and Aegiali, but check precisely if this is the case with your ferry. There are daily boats to Paros (€9.80, three hours) and Piraeus (€18, 10 hours). There are also services to Astypalea (€9, 2½ hours, three weekly) and Syros (€11, 4½ to 9½ hours, four weekly).

FAST BOAT & CATAMARAN

Weekly services run from Katapola to Paros (€16.90, 1½ to 2½ hours), Mykonos (€18.60, 2¼ to four hours), Ios (€12.80, 1½ hours), Tinos (€26, 2¾ hours) and Andros (€27.50, 3½ to 6¼ hours). Several services will also stop at Aegiali.

Getting Around

Regular buses go from Katapola to Hora (€0.80, 15 minutes), Moni Hozoviotissis (€0.80, 15 minutes), Agia Anna Beach (€1, 20 minutes) and less frequent services go to Aegiali (€1.60, 30 minutes); however there are fewer services on weekends. There are also buses from Aegiali to the picturesque village of Langada. Schedules are posted on bus windscreens.

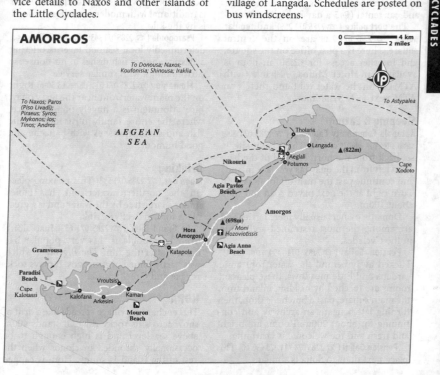

AMORGOS

0 —————— 4 km
0 —————— 2 miles

To Donousa; Naxos; Koufonisia; Shinousa; Iraklia

To Naxos; Paros (Piso Livadi); Piraeus; Syros; Mykonos; Ios; Tinos; Andros

To Astypalea

AEGEAN SEA

Tholaria

Langada

Nikouria

Aegiali
Potamos

▲(822m)

Cape Xodoto

Agia Pavlos Beach

Amorgos

▲(698m)
Moni Hozoviotissis

Hora (Amorgos)

Katapola

Agia Anna Beach

Gramvousa

Paradisi Beach

Cape Kalotassi

Vroutsis

Kalofana   Kamari

Arkesini

Mouron Beach

CYCLADES

Cars and motorcycles are available for rent from the travel agency N Synodinos in Katapola and **Aegialis Tours** (☎ 2285 073 107; fax 2285 073 394; www.amorgos-aegialis.com) in Aegiali.

KATAPOLA ΚΑΤΑΠΟΛΑ

Katapola, the principal port, is a pretty place that straggles along the curving shoreline of a dramatic bay in the most verdant part of the island. A smattering of remains from the ancient Cretan city of Minoa, as well as a Mycenaean cemetery, lie above the port. Amorgos has also yielded many Cycladic finds; the largest figurine in the National Archaeological Museum in Athens was found in the vicinity of Katapola.

Boats dock either in front of the central square or to the right (facing inland). The bus station is to the left along the main waterfront and on the western shore of the bay.

The very helpful travel agency **N Synodinos** (☎ 2285 071 201; synodinos@nax.forthnet.gr; ☼ year-round) offers ferry tickets, money exchange and car rental (€45 a day in high season).

The **port police** (☎ 2285 071 259) and **regular police** (☎ 2285 071 210) are on the central square. There is a post office on the square, and Internet access for €2.50 an hour is available at Hotel Minoa. A bank (with ATM) is on the waterfront and there's an ATM next to N Synodinos.

Sleeping & Eating

Katapola Community Camping (☎ 2285 071 802; camp sites per adult/tent €4/4) This shady site is set back from the northern end of the bay. Turn left from the quay (as you face inland) and continue past the turn-off for the Hora. Turn right at the next paved road and walk about 100m.

Domatia owners usually meet ferries and are among the most restrained and polite in the Cyclades.

Pension Sofia (☎ 2285 071 494; s/d €35/45) Tucked away behind the waterfront amid gardens and little meadows, these pleasant rooms are reached by heading inland from the main square, past a butcher's shop, then turning left beneath an archway and continuing for about 200m. Rooms are bright and fresh and the welcome is charming.

Pension Galini (☎ 2285 071 711; s/d €30/40) This place next door to Sofia is similar.

Pension Amorgos (☎ 2285 071 013, 69 32 24 8 867; s/d €40/45; ☒) This sturdy hotel is mid-waterfront and very handy for the main part of town. Rooms are clean and well kept and some even have canopied beds. Front room balconies have good views over the bay.

Hotel Minoa (☎ 2285 071 480; www.interamorgos .com; s/d incl breakfast €50/60; ☒ ☐) This busy central hotel has comfy rooms. Attached to the hotel and creating a pleasant waterfront scene is taverna **Mythos** (dishes €3-7), serving standard dishes.

Diosmarini (☎ 2285 071 636; diosmarini@yahoo .com; d/tr €46/60, apt €90) On the northern shores of the bay and about 1km from the ferry quay, Disomarini is a delightful option with lovely big rooms in a handsome modern Cycladic-style building. There are airy views from most balconies.

Vitsentzos (☎ 2285 071 518; dishes €2.70-6.50) On the northern side of the bay Vitsentzos is a deservedly popular eatery with a cheerful terrace and a spotless interior of exposed stonework and varnished wood floor. Food is traditional with modern touches. Seafood is by the kilo.

Psaropoula (☎ 2285 071 343; dishes €4-6) This is a determinedly local seafood taverna offering a classic range of fish dishes in no-nonsense surroundings, with similar service.

Mouragio (☎ 2285 071 011; dishes €3.50-6) Right on the main waterfront near the ferry quay, busy Mouragio is a hugely popular place, where the entire family turns out terrific fish and shellfish dishes with panache and good humour.

Drinking

Moon Bar (☎ 2285 071 598) This relaxing place on the northern waterfront, has tables under a large tree by the water and is a great place for a reflective drink.

Le Grand Bleu (☎ 2285 071 633) Just along from Psaropoula is this very popular bar named after the film *The Big Blue*, which was partly filmed in Amorgos. It plays rock, reggae and Greek music.

HORA

This enchanting village spreads like a drift of snow across its rocky ridge. It stands 400m above sea level and is high enough to be occasionally shrouded in clouds when the rest of the island is sunny. Hora is capped with a 13th-century kastro atop a prominent rock pinnacle and old windmills stand like sentinels on surrounding cliffs. Yet in spite of its traditional style the village has several sophisticated shops, bars and cafés that enhance its appeal without eroding its timelessness.

The bus stop is on a small square at the edge of town. The post office is on the main square, reached by a pedestrian laneway from the bus stop.

Hora's **archaeology museum** (☺ 9am-1pm & 6-8.30pm Tue-Sun) is on the main pedestrian thoroughfare, near Café Bar Zygos.

Sleeping & Eating

In Hora there are domatia only.

Rooms to Rent (☎ 2285 071 216; s/d €25/30) This handy little domatia is on the main pedestrian thoroughfare and has decent rooms.

By the main bus square, **Pension Ilias** (☎ 2285 071 277) and **Pension Panorama** (☎ 2285 071 606), both with pleasant doubles for about €35 to €40, have views over the valley.

Café Bar Zygos (☎ 2285 071 350; ☺ 8am-3am) This café lies at the heart of Hora's enchanting main street. It's a charming place inside and out and has a rooftop terrace. You can enjoy coffee, snacks, delicious cakes, candied fruit and ice cream by day to accompanying Greek music, and then relax with drinks to late-night '80s and '90s rock.

Keep heading up the winding main street to reach **Tsagaradiko** (☎ 0977 740 480; dishes €3-7) a great little mezedes place with tables on a lovely little square.

MONI HOZOVIOTISSIS
ΜΟΝΗ ΧΩΖΟΒΙΩΤΙΣΣΑΣ

A visit to the 11th-century **Moni Hozoviotissis** (☺ 8am-1pm & 5-7pm) is unforgettable, as much for the spectacular scenery as for the monastery itself. The dazzling white building clings precariously to a cliff-face above the east coast. A few monks still live there and tours are sporadic, but worthwhile.

The monastery contains a miraculous icon found in the sea below the cliff, having arrived, allegedly unaided, from Asia Minor, Cyprus or Jerusalem, depending on which legend you're told. Modest dress is required (long trousers for men, and a long skirt or dress and covered shoulders for women).

A great round-trip is to catch the bus from Katapola to Hora, stroll the length of

Hora's main street and on to an upper car park below a radio tower. Go down to the right of the car park viewpoint, go through a gate and then follow a zigzag track with exhilarating views, to reach the road. Turn left here to reach a junction; the left branch leads in 500m to the monastery. You can then catch the bus back to Katapola from the junction, or walk down to Agia Anna beach, which is 1.5km downhill, and catch the bus from the car park there.

AEGIALI ΑΙΓΙΑΛΗ

Aegiali is Amorgos' other port and has more of a resort style, not least because of the fine sweep of sand that lines the inner edge of the bay on which it stands. Above the main village lie steep slopes and impressive crags.

Nautilus Travel Agent (☎ 2285 073 032), opposite Aegiali's Tours, sells ferry tickets and provides general tourist information.

Tours

Aegiali's Tours (☎ 2285 073 107; fax 2285 073 394; www.amorgos-aegialis.com) organises a bus outing (€20) around the island that departs at 9.30am and returns at 4.30pm, with stops at Agia Pavlos, Moni Hozoviotissis, Hora and Mouron. Afternoon donkey-riding expeditions cost €17 per hour.

Sleeping

As in Katapola, domatia owners meet the ferries.

Aegiali Camping (☎ 2285 073 333; camp sites per adult/tent €5/3) This is a pleasant and shaded site on the road behind Lakki Village; go left from the port and follow the signs.

Rooms in the Garden (☎ 2285 073 472; s/d €35/45) These small bungalows, with verandas and kitchens, are buried at the heart of a semitropical garden amid an air of pleasant torpor. They're at the far end of the beach; a path leads from the beach to the bungalows.

Lakki Village (☎ 2285 073 253; fax 2285 072 344; s/d/tr incl breakfast €55/65/75, 2-/3-/4-person apt incl breakfast €82/92/109) Right behind the middle of the beach, Lakki has good rooms and apartments within a fairly extensive complex. There's a pleasant garden area between the beach and the buildings, which serves as the terrace of the attached taverna.

CYCLADES

Pension Poseidon (☎ 2285 073 453; fax 2285 073 007; s/d/studio €35/45/55) Behind the waterfront at the base of the hill, Poseidon has decent rooms, some with views. The studios have kitchens.

Grispos Hotel (☎ 2285 073 412; fax 2285 073 557; 2-/4-person studio €70/94; P 🐾) Reached by a bit of an uphill climb, these rooms are well worth the effort. Located in a well maintained, modern building and with very friendly owners, they are big, bright and well equipped.

Eating

To Limani (☎ 2285 073 269; dishes €2.50-6) Excellent traditional fare is prepared with home-grown produce at Limani. It's behind the little church and just up from the waterfront. There's a lovely roof garden, to which food is whisked up in a little lift. The downstairs walls exhibit works by local artists. Seafood is by the kilo.

To Koralli (☎ 2285 073 217; dishes €2.50-6) A great location with extensive views enhances the excellent food at this cheerful restaurant, which offers delicious fish and mezedes platters. It's reached up a flight of steps at the eastern end of the waterfront.

Restaurant Lakki (☎ 2285 073 253; dishes €2.50-9) The popular beachside restaurant of Lakki Village uses home-grown ingredients in its good traditional dishes. They are complemented by a fine wine list.

Disco The Que (☎ 2285 073 212; dishes €3-5) Merging seamlessly with the beach, this relaxing, long-established place keeps going late into the night. Youngsters are cherished. Food is a healthy choice of risotto, rice and chicken dishes, as well as vegetarian, and the music ranges from funk and rock 'n' roll to ambient, trance and jazz.

AROUND AMORGOS

Agia Anna Beach, on the east coast, south of Moni Hozoviotissis, is the nearest beach to both Katapola and Hora. Don't get excited; the car park is bigger than any of the little pebbly beaches strung out along the rocky shoreline and all the beaches fill up quickly. There's a small cantina next to the car park on the cliff-top selling food and drinks.

Langada and **Tholaria** are the most picturesque of the villages inland from Aegiali.

IOS ΙΟΣ

pop 1838

Ios is branded – unfairly at times – as being the party capital of the Cyclades, and not very much else. Commercial interests play up the image and there are certainly wall-to-wall bars and nightclubs in places and a relentless routine of incredibly heavy drinking. It's all fuelled by a sometimes shrill insistence that everyone is having a fantastic time, whether they like it or not. But all of this packaged hedonism is concentrated in corners and Ios rises above the image; not least because of its beautiful beaches, the intrinsic charm of its old hora, its very pleasant port, and the stark beauty of its landscape. The island has formidable recommendations; British poet and novelist Lawrence Durrell thought highly of Ios as a place of poetry and beauty and there's an enduring claim that the island was Homer's burial place, his alleged tomb is on the slopes of Mt Pirgos, in the north.

Getting There & Away
FAST BOAT & CATAMARAN
There are daily catamarans to Santorini (€11.30, 40 minutes), Naxos (€14.90, one hour), Paros (€16.70, 1½ hours) and Iraklio on Crete (€30.90, 2½ hours). Services travel twice a week to Tinos (€25.10, three hours); and once a week to Amorgos (€17.10, two hours) and Mykonos (€22.80, 2¾ hours).

FERRY
There are at least four daily connections with Piraeus (€18.80, seven hours), Paros (€8.40, 2½ hours) and Naxos (€7.40, 1¼ hours). There are daily boats to Santorini (€5.70, 1¼ hours), five weekly to Sikinos (€3.40, 30 minutes), Folegandros (€4.80, 1½ hours) and Anafi (€7.10, three hours) and four weekly to Syros (€15.50, 2¾ hours).

There are two boats weekly to Kimolos (€8, 2½ hours), Sifnos (€10.40, five hours), Serifos (€10.90, six hours) Kythnos (€14, 8½ hours), and three weekly to Milos (€12.50, 3½ hours).

Getting Around
In summer, crowded buses run between Ormos, Hora (€0.90) and Milopotas Beach (€0.90) about every 15 minutes. Private excursion buses go to Manganari Beach (€5, 10.30am and 12.30am) and Agia Theodoti Beach (€0.90).

Caïques travelling from Ormos to Manganari cost €8 per person for a return trip (departing 11am daily). Ormos and Hora both have car and motorcycle rental firms.

HORA, ORMOS & MILOPOTAS
ΗΩΡΑ, ΟΡΜΟΣ & ΜΥΛΟΠΟΤΑΣ
Ios has three population centres, all very close together on the west coast: the port (Ormos); the capital, Hora (also known as the 'village'), 2km inland from the port; and Milopotas, the beach 1km downhill from Hora. Gialos Beach stretches west of the port.

Orientation
The bus terminal in Ormos is straight ahead from the ferry quay on Plateia Emirou. If you don't mind the heat it's possible to walk from the port to Hora, by turning left from Plateia Emirou, then immediately right where a stepped path leads up right after about 100m. It's about 1.2km.

In Hora, the big church opposite the bus stop and on the other side of the dusty car park and play area is the main landmark. To reach the central square of Plateia Valeta head uphill to the right from in front of the church and turn left at the junction. There are public toilets up the hill behind the main square.

The road straight ahead from the bus stop leads to Milopotas Beach.

Information
Plakiotis Travel Agency (☎ 2286 091 221; fax 2286 091 118) on the Ormos waterfront and with an office in Hora, opposite the bus stop, is very helpful; **Acteon Travel** (☎ 2286 091 343; acteon@otenet.gr) on the square near the quay and with branches in Hora and Milopotas needs to shake up its rather unsmiling service at its Ormos office. It has Internet access for €5 an hour. There is a **hospital** (☎ 2286 091 227) 250m northwest of the quay, on the way to Gialos, and there are several doctors in Hora. The **port police** (☎ 2286 091 264) are at the southern end of the waterfront, just before Ios Camping.

There's an ATM right by the information kiosks at the ferry quay. In Hora, the National Bank of Greece, behind the church, and the Commercial Bank, nearby, both have ATMs. The post office is a block behind town hall side of the main road.

Sights
Hora (pop 1632) is a lovely Cycladic village with myriad laneways and attractive houses and shops. It's at its most charming during daylight hours when the bars are shut and it recaptures the atmosphere of other island towns.

The **archaeological museum** (admission free; ◷ 8.30am-3pm Tue-Sun) is in the town hall by the bus stop. It has a selection of historic exhibits.

The views from the top of the hill in Hora are worth the climb, especially at sunset. On the way, pause at **Panagia Gremiotissa**, the large church next to the palm tree.

Activities
Yialos Watersports (☎ 2286 092 463; ralfburgstahler@hotmail.com) is a friendly outfit, right on the beach, and offers banana rides (€10) canoe rental (€12 an hour) and mountain bike rental (€10 a day). It also hires windsurfing

equipment for €12 for one hour and €30 per half day. A lesson is €5.

Snorkel and windsurfing gear, pedal boats and canoes can be hired on Milopotas beach from **Mylopotas Water Sports Center** (☎ 2286 091 622; iossport@otenet.gr). Windsurfing rental is €18/50 per hour/day and waterskiing is €20/30 per 10/15 minutes.

Hotel Ios Plage (☎ 2286 091 301; www.iosplage.com; Milopotas Beach) rents motor boats for €60 per half day, €110 per day.

Sleeping
ORMOS
There are many advantages to staying in Ormos. The port has several good sleeping options, plenty of reasonable eating places, a couple of handy beaches and regular bus connections to the hora.

Ios Camping (☎ 2286 092 035; fax 2286 092 101; camp sites per person €6; 🏊) Tucked away on the west–side of Ormos, this site has good facilities including a restaurant in high season. Sleeping bunks (slabs of concrete) are available for those without a tent. Turn right at Plateia Emirou and walk all the way round the waterfront.

Zorba's Rooms (☎ 2286 091 871; s/d/tr €45/50/70, apt €100) There are good off-season discounts at this fairly well worn but friendly place in a quiet location at Ormos. Go straight ahead from the quay along a lane.

Hotel Poseidon (☎ 2286 091 091; www.poseidon hotelios.gr; s/d/tr €55/75/90; 🍴 🏊) An excellent option, the Poseidon has terrific views over Ormos from its front balconies and a lovely swimming pool. Rooms are spacious and well equipped. Head along the waterfront from the ferry quay and it's to the left of Enigma Bar. A flight of steps leads up to the hotel.

Sun Club (☎ 2286 092 140; fax 2286 092 140; acteon@ otenet.gr; s/d/tr €110/130/160; P 🍴 🏊) Sun Club, on the road to Hora, has immaculate rooms with bathroom, TV, phone and sea view. There's also a pool and bar.

GIALOS BEACH
I Corali (☎ 2286 091 272; www.iosgreece.com; s/d incl breakfast €50/60; P 🍴) These sparkling rooms are attached to the restaurant of the same name and are right on Gialos beach. There's a colourful garden at the rear.

There's a clutch of decent places set back from the mid-point of the beach.

Hotel Glaros (☎ 2286 091 876; www.thegreektravel .com/ios/glaros; s/d incl breakfast €60/70) This is a quiet and relaxed, family-run place with good-sized rooms.

Hotel Helena (☎ 2286 091 276; www.iosgr.com/ helena; s/d €35/55) This is a friendly, well-run place with a cool patio and bright, clean rooms.

HORA
Markos Village (☎ 2286 091 059; dm/s/d €17/32/44; 🍴 🏊) Friendly Markos is popular with young people and has pleasant rooms. There's an easygoing ambience round the pool and bar. To get there, head uphill from the bus stop, turn up right and then left.

Francesco's (☎ 2286 091 223; www.francescos.gr; dm €10, d €30, with bathroom €45) The well-run Francesco's, with good clean rooms, is near the centre of things and is a lively meeting place for backpackers. The party spirit rules supreme. It has a busy bar and terrace with great views of the bay.

MILOPOTAS
Far Out Camping (☎ 2286 091 468; www.faroutclub .com; camp sites per adult/tent €7/1.50, small/large bungalows €9/15; 🖳 🏊) If you want efficient, wall-to-wall facilities this is the place, for everything from bungy jumping to five-a-side football. You'll never walk alone. It has a bar, restaurant and four swimming pools (open to everyone on the beach). The basic 'bungalows' are small tent-sized affairs; the larger ones have double and single beds.

Stars Camping (☎ 2286 091 302; fax 2286 091 612; purplepigios@hotmail.com; camp sites €7, dm €18, bungalows per person €20; 🏊) The smaller Stars is shaded pleasantly by trees and has a more relaxed pace.

Hotel Nissos Ios (☎ 2286 091 610; nisosios@ otenet.gr; dm/s/d €26/45/65; 🍴) Dorms have three beds to a room and all rooms are bright and well kept at this friendly place right across from the beach. Colourful wall murals add a cheerful touch and there's a good restaurant out front.

Hotel Ios Plage (☎ 2286 091 301; www.iosplage .com; d/tr €62/82) With a touch of distinctive Gallic style, this place at the far end of Milopotas Beach has simple rooms with distinctive colour schemes and interesting items, such as mosquito nets draped over the beds. There is a great terrace bar and a restaurant.

There are several domatia on the road to Milopotas Beach. **Hermes Rooms** (☎ 2286 091 471; hermesio@otenet; ✖ ✉), **Pelagos** (☎ 2286 091 112) and **Petradi** (☎ 2286 091 510; fax 2286 091 660) all have good singles/doubles with terrace views for €60/70.

Eating
ORMOS
Susana (☎ 2286 051 108; dishes €2.50-7) A standard taverna that offers efficient service and straightforward food. It's set back from the street in a wide square by Acteon Travel and does pastas and pizzas for €4 to €7.

Ciao Café (☎ 2286 091 940; dishes €1.20) This smart self-service place, right opposite the ferry quay, has snacks such as filled baguettes and ciabatta and tasty cheese pies, but it can be pricey on drinks.

GIALOS BEACH
To Corali (☎ 2286 091 272; dishes €5-9) Right by the beach, this bright and well-run place offers good Italian food with Greek touches. It does terrific wood-fired pizzas as well as pastas and salads and is also great for coffee, drinks and ice cream.

HORA
Pithari Taverna (☎ 2286 091 379; dishes €3-7.50) A friendly, unfussy taverna in the pleasant little square beside the big church, above the car park and play area, Pithari is an excellent option for good Greek food. Its tables, set out in front of the church, make you think that Hora really is a traditional Greek village after all.

Lord Byron (☎ 2286 092 125; dishes €3-15) This is another great traditional place just up the main street from the church square. It has a comfortable, close-knit ambience and offers good mezedes to the accompaniment of rembetika.

Pinocchio Ristorante (☎ 2286 091 470; dishes €5-15) There's good pizza and pasta at this popular place right at the heart of Hora. It has a pleasant garden terrace and there's a takeaway next door. Look for the little figure of a well nailed-down Pinocchio standing outside.

Ali Baba's (☎ 2286 091 558; dishes €6.50-9) Tasty Asian and international dishes, including curry and spare ribs, are on offer at this popular and lively place (see p174 for details). From the main square go past Porky's, take the first right then at junction, go straight ahead, then turn left.

Saini's (☎ 2286 091 106; dishes €4.30-14) Saini's main restaurant is further round from the Ios Club (p174) and does authentic Greek food, as well as steaks and pastas, all backed by good wine by the barrel and bottle. It also stages live Greek music. In Hora, just up and left from Ali Baba's, is Saini's other place, which opens in the early hours and even offers nourishing soup.

There are also numerous gyros stands where you can get a cheap bite. Porky's, just off the main square, is a long time favourite that also does toasties, crepes and hamburgers.

MILOPOTAS
Drakos Taverna (☎ 2286 091 281; dishes €2.20-9) It's seafood by the kilo at this popular taverna at the southern end of the beach where you get the feeling that the fish may well hop straight from the sea.

Hotel Ios Plage (☎ 2286 091 301; meals €12) You can have standard *plat de jour* or a special gourmand's dish (€16) at this entertaining venue, where there's a distinct French flair to the fare and the beach is laid out below.

Harmony (☎ 2286 091 613; dishes €3-12) Just along the northern arm of Milopotas beach, this place has the franchise on relaxation with its hammocks and deckchairs and great music. Children are well catered for. Tex-Mex food is the main attraction, although the pizza, pasta, grills and breakfasts are also worthwhile.

Entertainment
Ios nightlife is relentless in its promise of full-on fun, even for those being sick down the front of the free T-shirts handed out by at least one bar to anyone who sinks seven shots in a row. At night Hora's tiny central square is transformed into a noisy, open-air party and by midnight it's so crowded you won't be able to fall down, even if you need to. Be young and carefree – but women especially should also be careful.

Popular bars and clubs on the square include: **Superfly** (☎ 2286 092 259) for funky house; **Disco 69** (☎ 2286 091 064) which is hard core drinking to a background of disco and current hits; **Slammer Bar** (☎ 2286 092 119) for house, rock and Latin, and **Red Bull** (☎ 2286 091 019), **Flames Bar** (☎ 2286 092 448) and **Blue**

Note (☎ 2286 092 271) – all long-established favourites.

For a taste of mainstream and table-top dancing, you can visit **Sweet Irish Dream** (☎ 2286 091 141) where on-tap Guinness has probably travelled further than you have.

Ios Club (☎ 2286 091 410) is high above the rest with its terrific terrace and sweeping views. Head there for a cocktail to watch the sunset to the tune of classical, Latin and jazz. It also does Greek food with international influences (dishes €3.50 to €7). To find it, walk right along the pathway by Sweet Irish Dream.

Ali Baba's (☎ 2286 091 558) goes the distance for a good mix of entertainment, with the latest Hollywood films most nights at 7pm, mainstream music, open-mike stand-up comedy and live gigging, as well as a restaurant (p173).

Orange Bar (☎ 2286 091814) is about 150m beyond the main square and is an easier paced music bar playing rock, Reggae and fave pop.

Café Astra (☎ 2286 921 830) is a dark little bar that attracts an older, less desperate-to-drink crowd. It's above the Hora branch of Acteon Travel and plays disco, funk and Latin.

For Greek music, head for sea level to **Di Porto** (☎ 2286 091 685; Gialos Beach), near To Corali.

There are a couple of big dance clubs on the Milopotas road, but they don't open until July. **Mojo Club** (☎ 6972 759 318; admission €15) brings in international DJs from the slightly fading North European dance scene for floor-burning progressive, drum 'n' bass and trance. Scorpion's is another late-night dance-to-trance and hip-hop venue with laser shows.

Watch out for bars offering cheap cocktails, they are often made from local *bombes* (moonshine), a disaster for belly and brain.

AROUND IOS

Apart from the nightlife, the beaches are what lure travellers to Ios. From Ormos, it's a 10-minute walk past the little church of Agia Irini for **Valmas Beach**. **Kolitzani Beach**, south of Hora, down the steps by Scorpion's, is also nice. **Koubara**, a 1.3km walk northwest of Ormos, is the official nudist beach. **Tsamaria**, nearby, is nice and sheltered when it's windy elsewhere.

Agia Theodoti, **Psathi** and **Kalamos Beaches**, all on the northeast coast, are more remote. **Moni Kalamou**, on the way to Manganari and Kalamos, stages a huge **religious festival** in late August and a **festival of music and dance** on 7 September.

Manganari Μαγγανάρι

Vying with Milopotas for best beach is Manganari, a long swathe of fine white sand on the south coast, reached by bus or by excursion boat in summer.

Dimitri's (☎ 2286 091 483; d €43.50) Dimitri's, behind Antonio's Restaurant, has lovely rooms.

Hotel Manganari (☎ 2286 091 200; fax 2286 091 204; villas €113) This very private hotel is accessible only by boat and has villas for two people. Breakfast, dinner and port transfer are included.

Antonio's Restaurant (☎ 2286 091 483; dishes €3-7) Noted for its fresh fish, Antonio's also does tasty grilled meat and has a good selection of home-made cheeses and other island specialities.

SANTORINI (THIRA)
ΣΑΝΤΟΡΙΝΗ (ΘΗΡΑ)

pop 13,402

Fabulous Santorini, officially known as Thira, is regarded by many as the most spectacular of all the Greek islands. Vast numbers visit annually to gaze in wonder at the submerged caldera, epicentre of what was probably the biggest volcanic eruption in recorded history. Santorini is unique and should not be missed but you need to brace yourself for relentless crowds and commercialism. The caldera is truly awesome and if you want to experience the full dramatic impact it's worth arriving by a slower ferry with open decks, rather than by catamaran or hydrofoil. The main port is Athinios. Buses (and taxis) meet all ferries and cart passengers to Fira, the capital, which fringes the edge of towering cliffs like a snowy cornice.

History

Greece is an earthquake zone of mostly minor eruptions, but on Santorini these have been so violent through the centuries

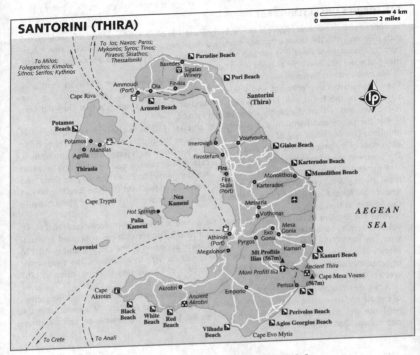

SANTORINI (THIRA)

that they have changed the shape of the island several times.

Dorians, Venetians and Turks occupied Santorini, as they did all other Cycladic islands, but its most influential early inhabitants were the Minoans. They came from Crete some time between 2000 and 1600 BC, and the settlement at Akrotiri dates from the apogee of their great civilisation.

The island was circular then and was called Strongili (the Round One). About 1650 BC, a colossal volcanic eruption caused the centre of Strongili to sink, leaving a caldera with high cliffs – now one of the world's most dramatic sights. Some archaeologists have speculated that this catastrophe destroyed not only Akrotiri but the whole Minoan civilisation. Another theory that has fired the already overheated imaginations of some writers, artists and mystics since ancient times, claims that the island was part of the mythical lost continent of Atlantis. See Santorini's Unsettling Past (p176) for more details on the volcano.

Getting There & Away

AIR

Olympic Airways operates five flights daily to Athens (€82), five weekly to Rhodes (€90) four to Mykonos (€65) and two weekly to Iraklio (€65). The **Olympic Airways** (☎ 2286 022 493; ⊗ 8.30am-8pm Mon-Sat & 8.30am-3pm Sun) is on the road to Kamari in Fira. **Aegean Airlines** (☎ 2286 028 500) has three flights daily to Athens and daily flights to Thessaloniki (€110).

FAST BOAT & CATAMARAN

Daily services go to Ios (€11.30, 30 minutes), Naxos (€20.30, 1½ hours), Paros (€21.80, 2¼ hours), Mykonos (€24.10, three to four hours), Iraklio on Crete (€26, 1¾ hours) and Piraeus (€42, 5¼ hours).

Six boats weekly run to Syros (€25.90, three hours). Twice weekly boats go to Sifnos (€15.40, 2½ hours).

FERRY

Santorini is the southernmost island of the Cyclades, and as a major tourist destination it has good connections with Piraeus

CYCLADES

SANTORINI'S UNSETTLING PAST

Santorini's violent volcanic history is visible everywhere – in black sand beaches, raw lava-layered cliffs plunging into the sea, earthquake-damaged dwellings and in the soil's fertility, which supports coiled-up grape vines. The volcano may be dormant, but it's not dead. Minor tremors – that may just wake you fleetingly at night – are fairly common.

Always unstable, Santorini was once part of a series of volcanoes over a million years ago. The volcanoes became dormant and around 3000 BC the first human settlers arrived to take advantage of the fertile soil. From evidence found at Akrotiri, it appears that they led very idyllic lives and fashioned a highly sophisticated culture.

But the peace and harmony didn't last, and around 1650 BC a chain of earthquakes and eruptions culminated in one of the largest explosions in the history of the planet. Thirty cubic kilometres of magma spewed forth and a column of ash 36km high jetted into the atmosphere. The centre of the island collapsed, producing a caldera that the sea quickly filled. The eruption also generated huge tsunamis that travelled with dangerous force all the way to Crete and Israel. Nearby Anafi was engulfed by a gigantic wave. It's widely held that the catastrophe was responsible for the demise of Crete's Minoan culture, one of the most powerful civilisations in the Aegean at that time.

After the Big One, Santorini settled down for a time and was even recolonised. In 236 BC volcanic activity separated Thirasia from the main island. Further changes continued intermittently. In 197 BC the islet now known as Palia Kameni appeared in the caldera, and in AD 726 there was a major eruption that catapulted pumice all the way to Asia Minor. The south coast of Santorini collapsed in 1570, taking the ancient port of Eleusis with it. An eruption in 1707 created Nea Kameni Islet next to Palia Kameni.

A major earthquake measuring 7.8 on the Richter scale savaged the island in 1956, killing scores of people and destroying most of the houses in Fira and Oia. The renaissance is remarkable; the resilience and insouciance of locals even more so. For lovers of impermanence, precariousness and drama, Santorini is incomparable.

and Thessaloniki on the mainland, as well as with Crete. Santorini also has useful services to Anafi, Folegandros and Sikinos.

There are at least four boats daily to Naxos (€10.40, three hours), Paros (€10.40, three to four hours), Ios (€5.70, 1¼ hours), Piraeus (€21.30, nine hours) and Tinos (€13.50, five hours), and two weekly for Kythnos (€18, eight hours) and Folegandros (€6.50, 1½ to 2½ hours). Change at Naxos for Amorgos.

Seven boats weekly go to Anafi (€6.50, one hour), Sifnos, (€11.20, six hours), Thessaloniki (€36, 18 to 19½ hours), Sikinos (€6.60, 2½ hours), Iraklio on Crete (€12, 3¾ hours) and also Skiathos (€29.30, 13½ hours).

There are two weekly ferries running to Mykonos (€12, six hours), Milos (€14, four hours), Kimolos (€12, 3½ hours) and Syros (€15.60, 5¼ hours) and Serifos (€15, seven hours).

Getting Around
TO/FROM THE AIRPORT
There are frequent bus connections in summer between Fira's bus station and the airport. Enthusiastic hotel and domatia staff meet flights and some also return guests to the airport.

BOAT
From the seafront at Ancient Akrotiri, you can catch a caïque to Red Beach, White Beach and Black Beach for around €5. Caïques also run regularly from Perissa to Red Beach.

BUS
In summer, buses leave Fira hourly for Akrotiri (€1.30) and every half-hour for Oia (€1), Monolithos (€0.90), Kamari (€0.90) and Perissa (€1.50). There are less frequent buses to Exo Gonia (€0.90), Perivolos (€1.50) and Vlihada (€1.60).

Buses leave Fira, Kamari and Perissa for the port of Athinios (€1.30) 1½ hours before most ferry departures. Buses for Fira meet all ferries, even late at night.

CABLE CAR & DONKEY
Cable cars (every 20 minutes, 7am to 10pm daily) shunt cruise-ship and excursion-boat

passengers up to Fira from the small port below, known as Fira Skala. Tickets cost adult/child €3/1.50 one way, luggage €1.50. You can make a more leisured upward trip by donkey for €3.

CAR, MOTORCYCLE & BICYCLE
Fira has many firms that rent cars, motorcycles and bicycles. Car hire is the best way to explore the island as the buses are intolerably overcrowded in summer and you'll usually be lucky to get on one at all; be very patient and cautious when driving – the narrow roads, especially in Fira, can be a nightmare.

TAXI
For **taxis** (☎ 2286 023 951/022 555) there's a stand in the main square. A taxi from Athinios to Fira costs €8 (set fare).

FIRA ΦHΡΑ
pop 2113
The sometimes brash commercialism of Fira has not diminished the town's dramatic aura. Views from the edge of the caldera of the layered, multi-coloured cliffs are breathtaking and at night the caldera's edge is a frozen cascade of lights that eclipses the displays of the jewellery shops in the streets behind.

Orientation
The central square is Plateia Theotokopoulou. The main road, 25 Martiou, runs north–south, intersecting the square and is lined with travel agencies. The **bus station** (25 Martiou) is 50m south of Plateia Theotokopoulou. West of 25 Martiou, towards the edge of the caldera, the streets are pedestrian alleyways; Erythrou Stavrou, one block west of 25 Martiou, is the main commercial thoroughfare.

Another block west, Ypapantis, known also as Gold Street because of its many jewellers, runs along the crest of the caldera and provides some staggering panoramic views. Head north on Nomikou for the cable-car station. If you keep walking along the caldera – the way steepens, but it's well worth it – you'll come to the Nomikos Convention Centre and, eventually, the cliff-top villages of Firostefani and Imerovigli. Keep going and you'll reach Oia, but it's a long, hot 8km.

Information
Fira doesn't have an EOT (national tourist organisation) or tourist police. It's best to seek out the smaller travel agents in Fira, where you'll receive more helpful service.

There are toilets just down from the bus station.

EMERGENCY
Hospital (☎ 2286 022 237) On the road to Kamari and Akrotiri.
Police station (☎ 2286 022 649; Dekigala) South of Plateia Theotokopoulou.
Port police (☎ 2286 022 239; 25 Martiou) North of the square.

INTERNET ACCESS
Lava Internet Café (☎ 2286 025 551; 25 Martiou; €1.50 per 15 min, €4.90 per hr) Up from the main square and set back from the street.

LAUNDRY
Laundrette (Danezi) Next to Pelican Hotel; it charges €9 for washing and drying an average load. Locked luggage storage (€1.50) is also available.

MONEY
There are numerous ATMs scattered around town.
Alpha Bank (Plateia Theotokopoulou) Represents American Express and has an ATM.
National Bank of Greece (Dekigala) Between the bus station and Plateia Theotokopoulou, on the caldera side of the road. With an ATM.

POST
Post office (Dekigala) About 150m south of the bus station.

TRAVEL AGENCIES
Dakoutros Travel (☎ 2286 022 201; Dekigala) Sells ferry tickets and tours.
Pelican Tours & Travel (☎ 2286 022 220; fax 2286 022 570; Plateia Theotokopoulou) A useful agency that books accommodation and ferry tickets.

Museums
A single ticket costing €9 is valid for the Museum of Prehistoric Thera, the Archaeological Museum and the sites at Akrotiri and Ancient Thira.

The **Museum of Prehistoric Thera** (☎ 2286 023 217; Mitropoleos; admission €3; ⊗ 8.30am-3pm Tue-Sun) is near the bus station. It houses extraordinary finds that were excavated from Akrotiri (where, to date, only 5% of the area has been excavated). Most impressive is the glowing gold ibex figurine, measuring around 10cm in length and dating from the 17th century BC. Many of Akrotiri's thrilling wall paintings are on display.

Megaron Gyzi Museum (☎ 2286 022 244; Agiou Ioannou; admission €3; ☺ 10.30am-1pm & 5-8pm Mon-Sat, 10.30am-4.30pm Sun), behind the Catholic cathedral, has local memorabilia, including fascinating photographs of Fira before and immediately after the 1956 earthquake.

The **archaeological museum** (☎ 2286 022 217; adult/student €3/free; ☺ 8.30am-3pm Tue-Sun), opposite the cable-car station, houses finds from Akrotiri and Ancient Thira, some Cycladic figurines, and Hellenistic and Roman sculpture.

For the past few years the **Nomikos Convention Centre** (Thera Foundation; ☎ 2286 023 016; Nomikou; adult/student €3/free; ☺ 10am-8pm Sun-Fri, 10am-2pm Sat) has displayed three-dimensional photographic reproductions of the Akrotiri frescoes. To get there, follow the rising path along the caldera rim beyond the cable-car station.

Tours

Tour agencies operate various trips including a bus-and-boat tour (€30) taking in Akrotiri, Thirasia, the volcanic island of Nea Kameni, Palia Kameni's hot springs and Oia; book at travel agencies.

The *Bella Aurora*, an exact copy of an 18th-century schooner, scoots around the

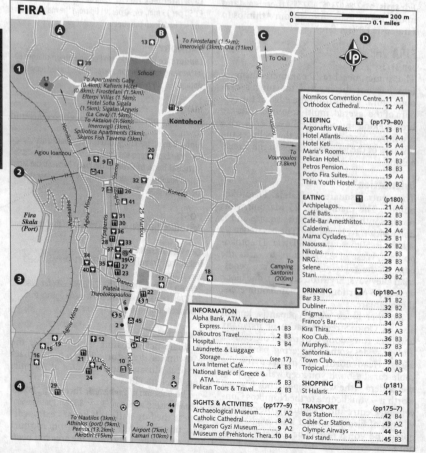

FIRA

0 ─────── 200 m
0 ─────── 0.1 miles

To Firostefani (1.5km);
Imerovigli (3km); Oia (11km)

To Oia

School

To Apartments Gaby
(0.4km); Kafieris Hotel
(0.8km); Firostefani (1.5km);
Efterpi Villas (1.5km);
Hotel Sofia Sigala
(1.5km); Sigalas Argyris
(La Cava) (1.5km);
To Aktaion (1.5km);
Imerovigli (3km);
Spiliotica Apartments (3km);
Skaros Fish Taverna (3km)

Kontohori

Agiou Ioannou

To
Vourvoulos
(3.8km)

Koneou

Fira
Skala
(Port)

To
Camping
Santorini
(200m)

Danezi

Plateia
Theotokopoulou

Mitropoleos

To Nautilos (3km);
Athinios (port) (9km);
Perissa (13.2km);
Akrotiri (15km)

To
Airport (7km);
Kamari (10km)

Nomikos Convention Centre..	11 A1
Orthodox Cathedral	12 A4

SLEEPING	(pp179–80)
Argonaftis Villas	13 B1
Hotel Atlantis	14 A4
Hotel Keti	15 A4
Maria's Rooms	16 A4
Pelican Hotel	17 B3
Petros Pension	18 B3
Porto Fira Suites	19 A4
Thira Youth Hostel	20 B2

EATING	(p180)
Archipelagos	21 B3
Café Batis	22 B3
Café-Bar Amesthistos	23 B3
Calderimi	24 A4
Mama Cyclades	25 B1
Naoussa	26 B2
Nikolas	27 B3
NRG	28 B3
Selene	29 A4
Stani	30 B2

DRINKING	(pp180–1)
Bar 33	31 B2
Dubliner	32 B2
Enigma	33 B3
Franco's Bar	34 A3
Kira Thira	35 A3
Koo Club	36 B3
Murphys	37 B3
Santorinia	38 A1
Town Club	39 B3
Tropical	40 A3

SHOPPING	(p181)
St Halaris	41 B2

INFORMATION	
Alpha Bank, ATM & American Express	1 B3
Dakoutros Travel	2 B3
Hospital	3 B4
Laundrette & Luggage Storage	(see 17)
Lava Internet Café	4 B3
National Bank of Greece & ATM	5 B3
Pelican Tours & Travel	6 B3

SIGHTS & ACTIVITIES	(pp177–9)
Archaeological Museum	7 A2
Catholic Cathedral	8 A2
Megaron Gyzi Museum	9 A2
Museum of Prehistoric Thera	10 B4

TRANSPORT	(pp175–7)
Bus Station	42 B4
Cable Car Station	43 A2
Olympic Airways	44 B4
Taxi stand	45 B3

CYCLADES

caldera every afternoon on a sunset buffet dinner tour (€35), stopping for sight-seeing at Nea Kameni and for ouzo at Thirasia. Most travel agencies sell tickets.

Sleeping

BUDGET

Throughout Fira there are scores of sleeping options, but few budget places; prices soar in high season. Domatia touts at the port reach impressive heights of hysteria in their bid for attention and in their ability to 'escape' the constraints of port police. Some claim their rooms are in town, when such rooms are a long way out; be very tough and ask to see a map showing the exact location. If you're looking for a caldera view, expect to pay at least double the prices elsewhere.

Camping Santorini (☎ 2286 022 944; fax 2286 025 065; www.santorinicamping.gr; camp sites per adult/tent €7/3; Ⓟ 🛋) This camping ground has some shade and modest facilities and is handy for town, but it's a long way from the nearest beach. There may be school groups staying in high season. There's a self-service restaurant and a pool. It's 400m east of Plateia Theotokopoulou.

Thira Youth Hostel (☎ 2286 023 864; 25 Martiou; dm €12, d €40) This massive complex is a dilapidated, shabby old place albeit with some remarkable decor and furnishings from its days as part of a Catholic monastery. Do not have high expectations.

Maria's Rooms (☎ 2286 025 143, 6973 254 461; Agiou Mina; d €45; 🛋) These entertaining rooms just down from Hotel Keti, open onto a shared terrace that offers unbeatable caldera and sunset views. The rooms are small, but are immaculate and blissfully peaceful.

Kafieris Hotel (☎ 2286 022 189; Nomikou; s/d €35/50) This place is a bit of a hike if you're walking from Fira. It's on the caldera rim path to Firostefani. Rooms are a touch small but there's a fine old-fashioned welcome.

MID-RANGE

Apartments Gaby (☎ 2286 022 057; Nomikou; s/d €45/65, 3-/4-bed rooms €78/110) These fine rooms and apartments are just beyond the convention centre on the caldera edge path. They have a wonderful local feeling that transcends Fira's surface gloss. The rooms on the series of roof terraces guarantee fantastic sunset views.

Petros Pension (☎ 2286 022 573; fax 2286 022 615; s/d €55/60) A long-established place run by friendly family owners, Petros is on the east–side of town in a quiet street, but without much outlook. Pick up and drop off to the port and airport is by arrangement.

Hotel Keti (☎ 2286 022 324; www.hotelketi.gr; Agiou Mina; d €70; 🛋) One of the smaller view-to-die-for places, Keti is tucked away at the quieter southern end of town on the edge of the caldera and features attractive traditional rooms dug into the cliffs.

Argonaftis Villas (☎ 2286 022 055; d €65, apt €85) Quirky paintings by the owner adorn the walls of these highly individualistic rooms. One apartment is a traditional cave house; another is a splendid old windmill. They're a bit out from the centre, and fairly viewless, but make up for it with character and a cheerful welcome.

Hotel Sofia Sigala (☎ 2286 022 802; Firostefani; s/d €48/69; 🛋) This place is in the narrow lane leading on to Firostefani's main square next to La Caba. It's a long trek to the centre of town, but rooms are clean and well equipped.

TOP END

Pelican Hotel (☎ 2286 023 113; www.pelican.gr; Danezi; s/d/tr €67.90/80.40/96) This is a fairly sombre place without too many frills, but it has comfy rooms and good facilities. It's well back from the glamorous caldera edge scene, but handy for everywhere.

Porto Fira Suites (☎ 2286 022 849; www.porto fira.gr; Agiou Mina; s/d incl breakfast €150/200; 🛋 🛋) One of Fira's top-rated hotels, this caldera-edge place is an old Venetian mansion that merges traditional style with all the modern conveniences. Rooms are stylishly furnished and have huge stone-based beds and Jacuzzis.

Hotel Atlantis (☎ 2286 022 232; www.atlantishotel.gr; Mitropoleos; s/d incl breakfast €158/225; Ⓟ 🛋 🛋) The Atlantis dominates the southern end of Ypapantis and is a handsome place with cool, relaxing lounges and terraces and bright, airy bedrooms, most of which have great views.

Efterpi Villas (☎ 2286 022 541; www.efterpi.gr; Firostefani; 2-3 person studios €155-186, apt €200-260; 🛋 🛋) Another of those famous caldera-edge hotels, Efterpi has pleasant traditional rooms carved into the cliffside. Furnishings are simple and there's a wonderful sense of detachment from the crush of the main town.

Spiliotica Apartments (☎ 2286 022 637; fax 2286 023 590, spiliot@san.forthnet.gr; Imerovigli; d/tr €117/145; 🛋) In Imerovigli, these are traditional abodes dug into the caldera. Spiliotica has a nice little café-bar and a small swimming pool.

Eating

Fira has many tourist-trap eateries with dismal and overpriced food. In some places, singles, and even families with young children, may find themselves unwelcome in the face of a pushy attitude from owners desperate to keep tables full and turnover brisk. There are excellent exceptions however.

Nikolas (☎ 2286 024 550; Erythrou Stavrou; dishes €5-7) At the heart of Fira, this long-established restaurant has tasty traditional Greek cuisine, ranging from lamb to cuttlefish in wine. Its culture is emphatically traditional and there's scant tolerance of non-traditional manners; or of scant dress for that matter.

Naoussa (☎ 2286 024 869; Erythrou Stavrou; dishes €3-17) Serves excellent, reasonably priced Greek classics, with new specials daily. It's a pleasant upstairs venue and should not be confused with the short-season, average place right by the entrance at ground level.

Stani (☎ 2286 023 078; Erythrou Stavrou; dishes €4.20-12) Just up from Bar 33, Stani's has a terrific range of Greek standards in a rooftop setting.

Calderimi (☎ 2286 023 050; dishes €16-20) Downhill from the cathedral and Hotel Atlantis is this superbly located Italian-style place. It has a lovely terrace with views and does excellent pasta and pizza that's a cut above the ordinary.

Archipelagos (☎ 2286 023 673; Ypapantis; dishes €15-25) Caldera-hugging on several levels this popular restaurant offers classic Mediterranean cuisine in memorable surroundings. It prepares quality fish such as John Dory, monkfish and hake with panache, as well as offering a mix of other dishes including mussels, and octopus – and duck, for high fliers.

Selene (☎ 2286 022 249; Agiou Mina; dishes €18-21) You need deep pockets for the full treatment at classy Selene. It's south of the cathedral in a great setting and also prepares top-quality fish extremely well, including delectable sea bass. Romance blooms unabated, but you may vie with fashionable wedding parties at times.

Nautilos (☎ 2286 027 052; Ayia Irini; dishes €5-10) This rewarding restaurant is about 3km south of Fira on the main road. It's worth the trip for excellent modern Greek cuisine, while a real bonus is the chance of hearing live, superb Greek music, with terrific bouzouki. Nautilos also has very luxurious **apartments** (€170) complete with a swish pool.

Among the best town-centre cafés are **NRG** (Erythrou Stavrou; dishes €3-5) next to Koo Club, for coffee, crepes, tortillas, ice cream, and cool ambience; and **Café-Bar Amesthistos** (Erythrou Stavrou; dishes €2.50-8). Good breakfast places are Mama Cyclades, near Thira Youth Hostel and the friendly **Café Batis** (Plateia Theotokopoulou).

There are several gyros stands up from the main square.

FIROSTEFANI & IMEROVIGLI

To Aktaion (☎ 2286 022 336; dishes €3.50-10) On the edge of the square in Firostefani, this above-the-ordinary taverna has been going for years and offers tasty Greek specialities to go with spectacular views.

Skaros Fish Tavern (☎ 2286 023 616; dishes €3-12) A classic *mezedopoleio* (mezedes restaurant) further along the caldera's edge in Imerovigli, Skaros has a great range of mezedes and fish dishes.

Drinking

Kira Thira (☎ 2286 022 770; Erythrou Stavrou) The oldest bar in Fira has entrances on the streets to either side. Guess which one the locals use and you'll feel even more at home in this candle-lit bar with its smooth jazz and ethnic sounds and occasional live music.

Tropical (☎ 2286 023 089; Marinatou) Tropical has a winning mix of rock, soul and occasional jazz, a cheerful fast-mixing staff, and unbeatable balcony views. There's an international crowd on most nights and a stylish local crew.

Franco's Bar (☎ 2286 024 428; Marinatou) Sheer elegance and impeccable musical taste – wholly classical – makes Franco's famous as the ultimate sunset scene. This is the highest of high life and the ambience alone is sublime.

After midnight Erythrou Stavrou is the clubbing caldera of Fira. The five-bar **Koo Club** (☎ 2286 022 025) fills its spacey levels with mainstream and Greek hits, plus a touch of hip hop and drum 'n' base. **Murphys** (☎ 2286 022 248) is a hot-spot bar that soothes with afternoon lounge sounds, then really rocks from late evening; they're dancing on the bar by the early hours. **Town Club** (☎ 2286 022 820) is delightfully kitsch and fashion conscious and plays a mix of Greek and mainstream, while **Enigma** (☎ 2286 022 466) is all white walls and chrome with muslin drapes; cool, edgy and favouring house and mainstream hits.

For ethnic music including rembetika and *laïko* (popular music) you need to seek out **Santorinia** (☎ 2286 023 777), tucked away in an old wine cellar beyond the north–end of Agiou Ioannou. Back on Erythrou Stavrou **Bar 33** (☎ 2286 023 065) is a lively bouzouki place popular with locals.

Just down from Thira Youth Hostel, the **Dubliner** (☎ 2286 024 888; 25 Martiou) pulls them in with a great raw mix of rock and hits till the early hours.

Shopping
Shopoholics will swoon over Fira's swathe of fashion shops in which you can get anything from Armani and Versace to Timberland and Reef. It will cost you.

Fira's jewellery and gold shops are legion, but browse **St Halaris** (☎ 2286 023 284; Erythrou Stavrou) for a marvellous collection of *komboloï* (worry beads) ranging in price from €15 to €2000.

Grapes thrive in Santorini's volcanic soil, and the island's wines are famous all over Greece and beyond. Local wines are widely available in Fira and elsewhere. Try the pricey 50-50 (so-called because 50% of the grapes are from the mainland and 50% are grown on Santorini) or the wines from Oia.

Sigalas Argyris (La Cava; ☎ 2286 022 802) in Firostefani has a good selection of wines and also caper leaves (a delicacy) and thyme honey.

AROUND SANTORINI
Ancient Akrotiri Παλαιά Ακρωτήρι
Akrotiri (☎ 2286 081 366; adult/student €5/3; ⏲ 8.30am-3pm Tue-Sun) was a Minoan outpost; excavations begun in 1967 have uncovered an ancient city beneath the volcanic ash. Buildings, some three storeys high, date to the late 16th century BC. The absence of skeletons and treasures indicates that inhabitants were forewarned of the eruption and escaped.

SANTORINI WINES

Santorini's two lauded wines are its crisp, clear dry whites, and the amber-coloured, unfortified dessert wine *vinsanto*, both produced from the ancient indigenous cultivar *assyrtiko*. Most vineyards hold tastings and tours, and there are also two fascinating wine museums.

There are several wineries that hold tastings in summer:

Antoniou (☎ 2286 023 557; Megalohori; ⏲ 10am-7pm)
Boutaris (☎ 2286 081 011; www.boutari.gr; Megalohori; ⏲ 10am-7pm)
Canava Roussos (☎ 2286 031 349; ⏲ 10am-10pm) On the way to Kamari.
Hatzidakis (☎ 2286 032 552; hatzidakiswinery@san.forthnet.gr) Call before you visit this small organic winery based in the village of Pyrgos near Moni Profiti Ilia.
Santo Wines (☎ 2286 022 596; santowines@san.forthnet.gr; ⏲ 9am-sunset) Near Pyrgos.
Sigalas (☎ 2286 071 644; ⏲ 11am-1pm & 6-8pm) Off the beach road near Oia.

Antoniou winery was designed early this century by a winemaker with his eye on the export market. Built into the cliffs directly above Athinios port, the *canava* (wine cellar) is a masterpiece of free-form ingenuity: wine was once piped down to waiting boats. Wine is no longer made at this site, but it's a fascinating place to visit.

The winegrowers cooperative, **Santo Wines** (☎ 2286 022 596, santowines@san.forthnet.gr; ⏲ 9am-sunset) in Megalohori has a showcase selection of regional produce taken from all over Greece.

The atmospheric **Volcan Wine Museum** (Lava; ☎ 2286 031 322; www.waterblue.gr; admission €1.70; ⏲ noon-7pm), housed in a traditional *canava* on the way to Kamari, has some interesting displays, including a 17th-century wooden wine press. Admission to the museum includes three tastings.

There's also the Art Space gallery-winery outside Kamari, see p392.

CYCLADES

At the time of writing – and possibly for a long time ahead – the site is visually disappointing, its overall context blurred by the construction of a 'bio-climatic' roof aimed at protecting the ruins from damaging climatic effects. Masses of scaffolding and concrete supports create an impression of a construction zone or, indeed, an earthquake site. Yet the historical drama of Akrotiri is still potent. It's best to go with a guide to get the most from the site.

Outstanding finds are the stunning frescoes and ceramics, many of which are now on display at the Museum of Prehistoric Thera in Fira (there are none on display at the excavation site). Accurate fresco replicas are on display at the Nomikos Convention Centre also.

On the way to Akrotiri, pause at the enchanting traditional settlement of **Megalohori** for some fine wineries – see Santorini Wines on p181.

SLEEPING & EATING

Caldera View Camping (☎ 2286 082 010; fax 2286 081 889; caldera@hol.gr; camp sites per adult/tent €7/4; 2-/4-person bungalows €110/170; P ☒) This pleasant, peaceful camping ground, near Akrotiri, is well out of town but the facilities are very good. Breakfast is included and there's free transfer to/from the port.

On the beach below the archaeological site there are some reasonable fish tavernas, and **Hotel Akrotiri** (☎ 2286 081 375; fax 2286 081 377; hotelakrotiri@yahoo.com; s/d incl breakfast €60/70) offers 10% reduction for web bookings of its pleasant rooms.

Kamari Καμάρι
pop 1351

Kamari is 10km from Fira and is Santorini's best-developed resort. It has a long beach of black sand in a terrific setting with the limestone cliffs of Cape Mesa Vouno at its southern end. The beachfront road is pedestrianised and is thick with eateries and bars. There's an enviable mood of easy living here.

Lisos Tours (☎ 2286 033 765; lisostours@san.forthnet.gr) on the main road into Kamari, is especially helpful and knowledgeable about Santorini generally. They arrange accommodation, sell ferry tickets, organise all kinds of tours including fixed-wing flights over the caldera, and have Internet access.

Volcano Diving Centre (☎ 2286 033 177; www.scubagreece.com) just inland from the beach, offers dives from €55 to €80 for caldera dives. It also has courses for beginners (from €65) and snorkel trips (€30).

Cinema Kamari (☎ 2286 031 974; www.cinekamari.gr; admission €6), on the main road coming into Kamari, is a great open-air theatre set in a thicket of trees and showing recent releases at 9pm and 11.15pm daily. In July it hosts the three-day **Santorini Jazz Festival** (☎ 2286 033 452; www.jazzfestival.gr), featuring lively performances by Greek and foreign musicians.

Just outside Kamari, do not miss **Art Space** (☎ 2286 032 774; Exo Gonia), at one of the oldest wineries on the island. The atmospheric old wine caverns are hung with superb art works while sculptures transform lost corners and niches. The works are all curated by the owner and feature some of Greece's finest modern artists. Wine making is still in the owner's blood, so a tasting of his vinsanto greatly enhances the whole experience.

SLEEPING
Kamari has plenty of domatia and hotels.

Perissa Camping (☎ 2286 081 343; camp@otenet.gr; Perissa Beach; camp sites per adult/tent €7/3; ☒) This fairly shaded site is in a good location just across from the beach at the north–end of the resort.

Anna's Rooms (☎ 2286 022 765; s/d €25/35) Straightforward furnishings without frills, these rooms above Lisos Tours office in Kamari are an ideal budget option. It's a bit of a hike to the beach but the location is quiet.

Hotel Selini (☎ /fax 2286 032 625; s/d incl breakfast €35/45) This is an excellent family-run, mid-range hotel. Rooms are a good size and the hotel is centrally placed just a few blocks in from Kamari beach.

Hotel Santellini (☎ 2286 031 301; santelin@otenet.gr; s/d incl breakfast 70/85; ☒ ☒) Santellini was in its first year at the time of writing and is a sparkling and spacious place with good-sized rooms and friendly staff. It's close to the beach and at the heart of the resort.

Hostel Anna (☎ 2286 082 182; annayh@otenet.gr; dm €8, 4-bed r €40; ☼ Feb-Oct; ☒ ☒) At the entrance to Perissa, this friendly, relaxed hostel is a great place to meet fellow travellers. A minibus picks up guests from the port. To find the hostel contact office at the port, look for the sign on the Blue Star Ferry Office.

Stelio's Place (☎ 2286 081 860; www.steliosplace .com; s/d €50/60; P ⊠ ♨) Just in from the beach at Perissa and down a quiet cul-de-sac, Stelio's is a bright and well-run complex, popular with young travellers. Airport and port transfers are by arrangement.

There are numerous domatia scattered around Perissa and at Perivolos.

EATING
Kamari has numerous eateries along its waterfront and inland streets. Many are fairly standard but there are some choice places.

Eanos (☎ 2286 031 161; dishes €4.20-14.60) Right on the beach, towards the south end of the waterfront, this is a long-established taverna that does excellent Greek food, including terrific moussaka. Food is cooked on a wood-burning stove and pasta is also on offer.

Amalthia (☎ 2286 032 780; dishes €3.50-12) A couple of blocks inland at the southern end of town, Amalthia has a marvellous garden area and terrace, and friendly service. It offers well prepared Greek dishes, the lamb is particularly good as, is the pasta and pizza.

Taverna the Fat Man (☎ 2286 032 932; dishes €3.20-9) This place is right at the back of town on the road into Kamari and is worth visiting for traditional Greek cuisine, including the meat and fish, but also the vegetarian dishes. Arthuro's chicken in tasty 'Zorba Sauce' is a speciality.

There are several good tavernas near Perissa, including **Perivolos** (☎ 2286 082 007; dishes €3.50-8) on Perivolos beach, which does excellent char-grilled fish. On the beachfront in Perissa, **Taverna Lava** (☎ 2286 081 776; dishes €3-6) is a local favourite island-wide. Choose from a mouthwatering selection of dishes on display.

Ancient Thira Αρχαία Φήρα
First settled by the Dorians in the 9th century BC, **Ancient Thira** (admission €2; ☉ 8.30am-2.30pm) consists of Hellenistic, Roman and Byzantine ruins. These include temples, houses with mosaics, an agora, a theatre and a gymnasium. The site has splendid views.

It takes about 45 minutes to walk to the site along the path from Perissa on rocky, difficult ground. If you're driving, take the road from Kamari.

Oia Οία
pop 763
The village of Oia (*ee*-ah), known locally as Ia or Pano Meria, was devastated by the 1956 earthquake, although for the visitor there's little overt evidence as marvellous restoration work has taken place. It's a delightful place, once home to wealthy sea captains. Though much quieter than tourist-frenzied Fira, its streets still have their share of trendy boutiques and expensive jewellery shops. Built on a steep slope of the caldera, many of its dwellings nestle in niches hewn into the volcanic rock. Oia is famous for its dramatic sunsets and its narrow passageways get crowded in the evenings.

ORIENTATION & INFORMATION
From the bus turnaround, head left and uphill to reach the rather empty-looking central square and the main street, Nikolaou Nomikou, which skirts the caldera. There is an Alpha Bank (with ATM) on the main street just past the blue-domed church and another outside Kargounas Tours.

You can get information, book hotels, cars and bikes, and exchange money at **Ecorama** (☎ 2286 071 507; www.santorinitours.com) by the bus turnaround. **Karvounas Tours** (☎ 2286 071 290; Nikolaou Nomikou) is also very helpful.

There are toilets just before the Strogili restaurant.

SIGHTS & ACTIVITIES
The **maritime museum** (☎ 2286 071 156; adult/student €3/1.50; ☉ 10am-2pm & 5-8pm Wed-Sun) is housed in an old mansion and has entertaining displays on Santorini's maritime history. Exhibits include a very arch figurehead.

Ammoudi, the tiny port with good fish tavernas and colourful fishing boats, lies 300 steps below Oia. In summer boats and tours go from Ammoudi to Thirasia daily; check travel agents for departure times.

SLEEPING
Oia Youth Hostel (☎ 2286 071 465; Nikolaou Nomikou; dm incl breakfast €15; ☉ May–mid-Oct) Oia's hostel is well above the ordinary. It has a bright rooftop terrace and bar with great views.

Lauda Traditional Pension (☎ 2286 071 204; fax 2286 071 274; Nikolaou Nomikou; s/d €50/60) Flights of steps lead directly down from the main street to these traditional caldera-cliff rooms.

CYCLADES

Furnishings are fairly basic but the ambience works.

Hotel Museum (☎ 2286 071 515; museumhotel@msn.com; Nikolaou Nomikou; studio/apt €118/135; ☒) Once a consular mansion this lovely building later became a museum and is now restored with great style. The swimming pool is a work of art in itself and decor and furnishings are delightful.

Katikies (☎ 2286 071 401; katikies@otenet.gr; Nikolaou Nomikou; d €234, studio €260; ☒ ☐ ☒) One of Santorini's most beautiful hotels, Katikies is at the east end of the village below the main street. It revels in luxury and its cliff-edge pool is spectacular. Rooms are traditional swish.

Chelidonia (☎ 2286 071 287; www.chelidonia.com; Nikolaou Nomikou; studio €135, 2-/3-/4-person apt €120/149/179) These excellent traditional cave apartments have pleasant wooden furnishings and their verandas have great views. The office is right on the main street.

Zoe-Aegeas (☎ 2286 071 466; www.zoe-aegeas.gr; 2-4 person studios €110-255) These lovely studios are in traditional houses in the quieter western part of town.

EATING & DRINKING

Thomas Grill (☎ 2286 071 769; dishes €3.50-7.40) This grill has a strong local ambience to go with good, inexpensive food – sample such dishes as *kokoretsi* (coarsely chopped lamb offal wrapped in lamb's intestines, flavoured with oregano and lemon juice and grilled). It's just up from the bus stop on the way towards the main street.

Skala (☎ 2286 071 362; Nikolaou Nomikou; dishes €5-14) A terrific caldera-view terrace enhances the good Greek cuisine of Skala. This includes lamb and meat dishes, salads and imaginative starters that make good use of traditional produce, while mixing in international influences.

1800 (☎ 2286 071 485; Nikolaou Nomikou; dishes €16-25; ☺7.30pm) The finest Mediterranean cuisine, with magical use of herbs and subtle sauces, make seafood, such as bass and bream, scallops and cuttlefish, delectable at this one-time sea-captain's mansion. The dining room and terrace-patio are exquisite.

Strogili (☎ 2286 071 415; Nikolaou Nomikou; dishes €4.50-14) There are two levels at this busy place that has the essential terrace-with-view. Its café has tasty beefburgers and the

restaurant offers Greek cuisine with international touches.

GETTING THERE & AWAY

The last bus for Fira leaves Oia at 11.20pm in summer. After that, three to four people can bargain for a shared taxi for about €9. Six buses daily connect Oia with Baxedes beach.

Oia has no petrol station, the nearest being about 10km along the road to Fira.

Other Beaches

Santorini's black-sand beaches become so hot at times that a sun lounger, or mat is essential. The best beaches are on the east coast.

The beach at **Perissa** is very long and can get very busy. **Perivolos** and **Agios Georgios**, further south, are more relaxed. **Red Beach**, near Ancient Akrotiri, is breathtaking – high red cliffs and hand-size pebbles submerged under clear water. **Vlihada**, also on the south coast, is even nicer. On the north coast near Oia, **Paradise** and **Pori** are both worth a stop.

THIRASIA & VOLCANIC ISLETS
ΘΗΡΑΣΙΑ & ΗΦΑΙΣΤΕΙΑΚΕΣ ΝΗΣΙΔΕΣ

Unspoilt Thirasia was separated from Santorini by an eruption in 236 BC. The cliff-top hora, **Manolas**, has tavernas and domatia. It's an attractive place noticeably more relaxed and reflective than Fira ever could be.

The *Nissos Thirasia* leaves Athinios port for Thirasia on Monday and Friday at the inconveniently early hour of 7am, returning at 2pm. On Wednesday it leaves Athinios at 7.45pm but does not return to Santorini. Tickets are available only at the port. There are also morning and afternoon boats to Thirasia from Oia's port of Ammoudi.

The islets of **Palia Kameni** and **Nea Kameni** are still volcanically active and can be visited on half-day excursions from Fira Skala and Athinios. Two-hour trips to Nea Kameni are also possible. A day's excursion taking in Nea Kameni, the **hot springs** at Palia Kameni, Thirasia and Oia is about €28. An underwater tour around Nea Kameni by the 'submarine' vessel **Atlantis Santorini I** (☎ 2286 028 901), which descends to 25m, costs €50. Shop around Fira's travel agencies for the best deals and the nicest boats.

ANAFI ΑΝΑΦΗ

pop 273

Elusive Anafi may sometimes feel hopelessly out of reach, even though it's a mere hour's ferry ride east of Santorini. This is due mainly to often uncertain and unreliable ferry schedules. Persevere; the rewards are uncrowded beaches, a slow-paced, traditional lifestyle and a refreshing lack of commercialism; but pencil in a potential extra day or two.

The island's small port is **Agios Nikolaos**. The main town, **Hora**, is a 10-minute bus ride or steep 1km walk from the port. Hora's main pedestrian thoroughfare leads uphill from the first bus stop and has most of the domatia, restaurants and minimarkets, and a post office that opens occasionally.

There are several lovely beaches near Agios Nikolaos; palm-lined **Klissidi**, a 10-minute walk east of the port, is the closest and most popular.

Anafi's main sight, **Moni Kalamiotissas**, is a 6km walk from the hora in the extreme east of the island, near the meagre remains of a sanctuary to Apollo. **Monastery Rock** (470m) is the highest rock formation in the Mediterranean Sea. There is also a ruined Venetian kastro at **Kastelli**, east of Klissidi.

Jeyzed Travel (☎ 2286 061 253; fax 2286 061 352), down at the port, organises Monastery Rock trips, boat excursions, sells ferry tickets,

exchanges money and can help with accommodation.

Getting There & Away

There are five ferries weekly to Ios (€7.10, three hours), Naxos (€10.30, four hours) and Paros (€12.20, six hours). Seven ferries weekly go to Santorini (€6.50, one hour), four go to Folegandros (€8.60, five hours) and Sikinos (€8, four hours). Three go to Piraeus (€21, 11 hours), and two go to Syros (€15.20, eight hours).

Getting Around

A small bus takes passengers from the port up to the hora. Caïques serve various beaches and nearby islands.

Sleeping & Eating

Camping is tolerated at Klissidi Beach, but the only facilities are at nearby tavernas.

Rooms in the hora are pricey in high season; demand outstrips supply and the standard is generally reasonable, but not luxurious. Shop around if you can, but be careful not to miss out altogether. Domatia owners prefer long stays – if you're only staying one night you should take whatever you can get. In high season, contact Jeyzed Travel in advance to be sure of a room; places at Klissidi fill fast.

Paradisos (☎ 2286 061 243; d €35) Rooms are on the main street, and are bright and clean with good views from the balconies.

Panorama (☎ 2286 061 292; d €35) Next to Paradisos, this place has similar rooms and views from its balconies.

Anafi Rooms (☎ 2286 061 271; d €30) These are clean and simple and have views of the Monastery Rock.

Villa Apollon (☎ 2286 061 348; fax 2286 061 287; vapollon@panafonet.gr; d/studio €120/150) At Klissidi Beach, these pleasant rooms are a good size and have an authentic traditional style.

Rooms to Let Artemis (☎ 2286 061 235; d €40) These are just above the sea at Klissidi and there's a restaurant attached.

Tavernas in the hora are all reasonably priced with dishes from about €3.50 to €8. Most have pleasant terraces and have nice views. These include **Alexandra's** (☎ 2286 061 212), **Astrakan** (☎ 2286 061 249) and **To Steki** (☎ 2286 061 380). Klissidi has a few tavernas, with similar prices.

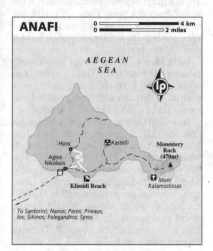

ANAFI

0 — 4 km
0 — 2 miles

AEGEAN SEA

Hora
Kastelli
Agios Nikolaos
Monastery Rock (470m)
Klissidi Beach
Moni Kalamiotissas

To Santorini; Naxos; Paros; Pireaus; Ios; Sikinos; Folegandros; Syros

CYCLADES

SIKINOS ΣΙΚΙΝΟΣ

pop 238

Off-the-beaten-track Sikinos (*see*-kee-noss) is a welcome refuge after the heat and hubbub of Santorini. It has pleasant beaches and a swooping landscape of terraced hills and mountains that plunge down to the sea. The port of **Alopronia**, and the villages of **Hora** and **Kastro** that comprise the hilltop capital, are the only settlements. Hora/Kastro has a post office and there's a futuristic ATM booth, all shiny glass, and with card-slot access in the central square of Kastro. Ferry tickets are sold at **Koundouris Travel** (☎ 2286 051 168) in Kastro and down at the port before departures. There's no petrol station on the island.

Getting There & Away

Seven ferries weekly go to Piraeus (€21, 10 hours) and six weekly go to Santorini (€6.50, 2½ hours). There are five weekly to Ios (€4, 30 minutes), two to Naxos (€7, three hours) and Syros (€12, six hours), six to Paros (€7, four hours), four to Folegandros (€4, 45 minutes), Kimolos (€6, 2½ hours) and Anafi (€8, four hours), three weekly to Milos (€10, three hours), two weekly to Sifnos (€9, five hours), Serifos (€10.40, five hours) and Kythnos (€13.70, seven hours).

Getting Around

The local bus meets all ferries and runs between Alopronia and Hora/Kastro every

half hour in August and less frequently at other times of the year. A timetable is sometimes posted near the minimarket.

Sights

The **Kastro** is a charming place with winding alleyways, brilliant white in the sun, with lovely old houses. At its heart is the main square and the church of Pantanassa. On its northern side, the land falls steeply to the sea. The fortified **Moni Zoödohou Pigis** stands on a hill above the town.

Sikinos' main excursion is a one-hour scenic trek (or five-minute drive along an ugly, bulldozed road) southwest to **Episkopi**. The remains are believed to be those of a 3rd century AD Roman mausoleum that was first transformed, in the 7th century, into a church, and then became **Moni Episkopis** (☼ 6.30-8.30pm) in the 17th century. From here you can climb to a little church and ancient ruins perched on a precipice to the south, from where the views are spectacular.

Caïques run to good beaches at **Agios Georgios**, **Malta** – with ancient ruins on the hill above – and **Karra. Katergo**, a swimming place with interesting rocks, and **Agios Nikolaos Beach** are both within easy walking distance of Alopronia.

Sleeping & Eating

Alopronia has most of the accommodation.

Lucas Rooms (☎ 2286 051 076; fax 2286 051 075; s/d €35/45, studio €60) These very pleasant rooms are in a quiet location on the hillside, 500m uphill from the port. They are bright and clean and have airy views from their balconies. Studios are similar in quality, but are down at the beach.

Porto Sikinos (☎ 2286 051 220; portosikinos@hit 360.com; d incl breakfast €69.60) This attractive hotel is about 100m from the quay. Rooms rise in a series of terraces and have great balcony views. There's also a bar and restaurant.

In Hora/Kastro, there are a few basic domatia that charge about €30 for a double; ask at tavernas and the local shop. **To Steki tou Garbi** (dishes €3-6) is a good grill house just round the corner from the ticket office. There are also good tavernas at Agio Georgios. Down at the port, **Lucas** (dishes €3.50-6) is the local favourite. Up on the cliff directly above the quay is the **Rock Café** (dishes €3.60-7.50); it also rents doubles for €35. There's a supermarket next to Lucas.

SIKINOS

0 — 4 km
0 — 2 miles

AEGEAN SEA

Moni Zoödohou Pigis
Malta Beach
Kastro
Agios Georgios Beach
Hora
▲ (552m)
Agios Nikolaos Beach
Sikinos
Alopronia
Katergo
Moni Episkopis
Kalogeri
▲ (432m)
Kardiotissa
Karra Beach

To Ios; Anafi; Santorini

To Folegandros; Kimolos; Milos; Naxos; Paros; Syros; Sifnos; Serifos; Kythnos; Pireaus

FOLEGANDROS
ΦΟΛΕΓΑΝΔΡΟΣ

pop 667

The charm of Folegandros (fo-*leh*-gandross) lies in its dramatic landscape of cultivated terraces and precipitous sea cliffs and in the friendliness of its residents. Tourism has not overwhelmed it in spite of Folegandros being popular with visitors looking for quieter holidays. The island is a rocky ridge, barely 12km in length and just under 4km at its widest point. Much of the landmass is over 200m in height, the highest point being Agios Eleftherios at 414m. Throughout a long history of human settlement the island's ruggedness led to its use as a place of exile for political prisoners; it was so used by the Romans and by the Greek state during the 20th century and as late as the military dictatorship of 1967–74.

There are several good beaches; but be prepared for strenuous walking to reach some of them.

The capital is the concealed cliff-top Hora, one of the most appealing villages in the Cyclades. Boats dock at the cheerful little harbour of Karavostasis, on the east coast. The only other settlement is Ano Meria, 4km northwest of Hora.

Getting There & Away

There are four services weekly to Piraeus (€18.40, six to nine hours), Santorini (€6, 1½ to 2½ hours), Ios (€4.80, 1½ hours), Paros (€6.80, four hours), Naxos (€7.90, three hours) and Sikinos (€4, 45 minutes).

Three weekly services go to Syros (€10, five hours), Milos (€6, 2½ hours), Sifnos (€7.20, four hours) and Serifos (€9.20, five hours).

Two weekly ferries go to Kimolos (€6, 1½ hours) and Anafi (€8.60, five hours).

Once weekly there's a ferry to Kythnos (€12.90, six hours).

Getting Around

The local bus meets all boats and takes passengers to Hora (€0.90). From Hora there are buses to the port one hour before all

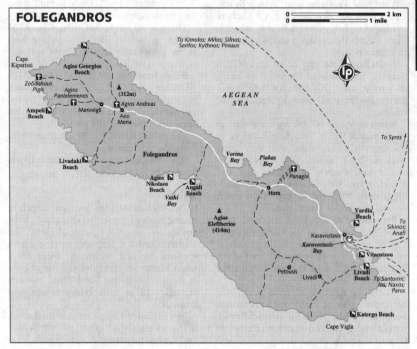

FOLEGANDROS

0 ─────── 2 km
0 ─────── 1 mile

To Kimolos; Milos; Sifnos;
Serifos; Kythnos; Pireaus

Cape Kiparissi

Zoödohous Pigis

Agios Georgios Beach

Agios Pantelemenos

Merovigli

Ampeli Beach

(312m)

Agios Andreas

Ano Meria

AEGEAN SEA

To Syros

Livadaki Beach

Folegandros

Vorina Bay

Piakas Bay

Panagia

Agios Nikolaos Beach

Vathi Bay

Angali Beach

Hora

Agios Eleftherios (414m)

Vardia Beach

To Sikinos; Anafi

Karavostasis

Karavostasis Bay

Vitsentzou

Petousis

Livadi

Livadi Beach

To Santorini; Ios; Naxos; Paros

Katergo Beach

Cape Vigla

ferry departures, even late at night. Buses from Hora run hourly to Ano Meria (€0.20), stopping at the road leading to Angali Beach. The bus stop for Ano Meria is on the western edge of town, next to the Sottovento Tourism Office. There is one **taxi** (☎ 2286 041 048, 6944 693 957) on the island, and you can only hire motorbikes.

KARAVOSTASIS ΚΑΡΑΒΟΣΤΑΣΙΣ
pop 55
Folegandros' port is a sunny little place with a sprinkling of domatia and tavernas and a pleasant little beach called Hochlida. The beach is pebbly but pleasant and there's a line of Tamarisks offering some shade. Within a kilometre to north and south of Karavostasis lie a series of pleasant beaches easily reached by short walks. In season boats leave Karavostasis for beaches further afield.

Karavostasis is also a terrific place to watch the world of boats go by.

Sleeping & Eating
Camping Livadi (☎ 2286 041 204; camp sites per adult/tent €5/3) This site is at Livadi Beach, 1.2km from Karavostasis. It has a kitchen, minimarket, bar, restaurant and laundry. Turn left on the cement road skirting Karavostasis Beach.

Aeolos Beach Hotel (☎ 2286 041 205; s/d €35/60, studio €85) Right behind Karavostasis beach in a quiet area, this friendly hotel has a pretty garden and clean straightforward rooms.

Vrahos (☎ 2286 041 450; www.hotel-vrahos.gr; s/d incl breakfast €75/90) This fine hotel is in traditional Cycladic style, with ever-rising terraces. Room balconies have great views of the bay. There's an outdoor bar and breakfast area with views of the surrounding islands. It's at the far end of the beach beyond the Aeolos Beach Hotel.

Restaurant Kati Allo (☎ 2286 041 272; dishes €4.10-6.20) Seafood is by the kilo at this reliable eatery where food, including salads, is prepared fresh on ordering. It's part of the Poseidon Hotel, and is right behind the Karavostasis beach.

There are a couple of good beach-side bars. Evangelos is right on Karavostasis beach and is the place for relaxed drinks, snacks and great conversation. Its list of famous visitors is impressive.

HORA ΧΟΡΑ
pop 316
The captivating Hora, complete with a dozen pretty little churches and a medieval kastro filled with whitewashed houses draped in bougainvillea, draws you in with unassuming charm to its meandering main street that drifts happily from leafy square to leafy square. On its north-side Hora stands on the edge of a very formidable cliff.

Orientation & Information
The port–Hora bus turnaround is in the square, called Pounta. From here follow a road to the left into Dounavi Square, from where an archway on the right, the Paraporti, leads to the densely-packed kastro, where the walls have been incorporated into dwellings. Heading on from Dounavi Square leads to Kontarini Square and then to Piatsa Square and, finally, to Maraki Square. Keep on through Maraki Square to reach most of the music bars and the bus stop for Ano Meria and most beaches.

The post office is 200m downhill from the bus turnaround, on the port road.

There is no bank, but there's an ATM on the far side of Dounavi Square next to the community offices. Travel agencies exchange travellers cheques.

Maraki Travel (☎ 2286 041 273; fax 2286 041 149; ☼ 10.30am-noon & 5-9pm) in Dounavi Square, has a monopoly on the sale of ferry tickets, and provides limited Internet access; it also has a ticket booth at the port.

The **police** (☎ 2286 041 249) are straight on from Maraki Square.

Scooters can be rented from Spiridoulas Rooms (p189) for €15 a day.

Sights
It is an absolute pleasure just lingering among the well-preserved churches, cubist houses and cheerful squares of Hora. The medieval **Kastro**, a tangle of narrow streets spanned by low archways, dates from when Marco Sanudo ruled the island back in the 13th century. The houses' wooden balconies blaze with bougainvillea and hibiscus.

The extended village, outside the kastro, is just as attractive. From Pounta Square and the bus turnaround, a steep path leads

Sanctuary of Apollo (p145), Delos,
Cyclades

CHRIS CHRISTO

BILL WASSMAN

Potter, Sifnos (p194), Cyclades

View of Nea Kameni (p184) from Imerovigli, Santorini, Cyclades

DIANA MAYFIELD

Fira (p177), Santorini, Cyclades

TAMSIN WILSON

ALAN BENSC

Apiranthos (p161), Naxos, Cyclades

Santorini's caldera (p176), Cyclades

LEE FOSTE

up to the large church of the Virgin, **Panagia** (6-8pm), which sits perched on a dramatic cliff-top above the town.

Tours
Sottovento Tourism Office (2286 041 444; sottove nto94@hotmail.com) runs boat trips (adult/child €25/10) including lunch. Departures are 10am Monday, Wednesday and Friday in summer. The office is by the bus stop at the eastern end of Hora. If you have snorkelling gear, take it along.

Festivals & Events
The annual **Folegandros Festival**, staged in late July, features a series of concerts, exhibitions and special meals at venues around the island.

Sleeping
In July and August most domatia and hotels will be full, so book well in advance. **Diaplous General Tourism Office** (2286 041 158; fax 2286 041 159; diaplous@x-treme.gr), by the port–Hora bus stop books accommodation, as does Sottovento Tourism Office (see above).

Hotel Polikandia (2286 041 322; polikandia@ hotmail.com; s/d €49/65;) Just before the port–Hora bus turnaround, this is a likeable place. It has pleasant, good-sized rooms arranged round a delightful reception and flower-filled garden area, to which a swimming pool was being added for 2004.

Folegandros Apartments (2286 041 239; www.folegandros-apartments.com; studios from €95;) These very fine studios are tastefully decorated and furnished throughout and are arranged round an excellent pool. They're just uphill from the bus turnaround.

Anemomilos Apartments (2286 041 309; d €155-200) Exhilarating views from seaward rooms are among the delights of these superb apartments. Stylish decor and furnishings, including fine antiques, add to the ambience. They are just up from the bus turnaround. One unit is equipped for disabled use.

Kallisti (2286 041 555; www.kallisti.net.gr; s/d €85/90;) The very smart Kallisti merges sparkling modern facilities with charming Cycladic style – beds have the traditional stone, rather than wooden, base of Cycladic custom. The hotel is on an airy hillside at the western edge of Hora, but is just a short walk from the centre.

Also recommended are **Spiridoulas Rooms** (2286 041 078; fax 2286 041 034; s/d €40/50) at the western end of Hora in a bright and pleasant house tucked away in a quiet corner.

Eating
Punta (2286 041 063; dishes €3.50-7.50) Full of character in every sense, Punta is in a walled garden area in Pounta Square, next to the bus turnaround. Bursts of colourful flowers enhance the friendly service and the food is excellent, from tasty breakfasts to evening meals of rabbit stew, lamb and vegetarian dishes. It's all served on delightful crockery made by one of the owners.

Apanemo (2286 041 562; dishes €4-11) Next to the Sottovento Tourism Office, this is a terrific wine bar that serves delicious food, including the Cretan salad *dakos*, served with a rusk base, and herb pie and risotto. It has a great Greek wine list and the service is charming.

Piatsa Restaurant (2286 041 274; dishes €3-8) Piatsa is on Hora's second square and offers excellent Greek cuisine.

Chic (2286 041 515; dishes €3.50-9) Chic is upstairs from Piatsa, with similar classical Greek cuisine as well as tasty vegetarian dishes.

Other eateries are **Pizza Pasta** (2286 041 549; dishes €4-10) above the Greco Café-Bar (see below) and offering delicious pizzas and pastas. **Melissa** (2286 041 067; Kontarini; dishes €1.70-6), under an umbrella of pepper trees, has good home-cooked food, while **Nicolas** (22 86 041 226; Dounavi; dishes €2.50-6) dispenses much advice and entertaining chat with a range of dishes, including grills and pastas.

Entertainment
Kellari (2286 041 515) Opposite Punta, this is a cosy little wine bar that plays Greek music and has a good selection of Greek wines.

Carajo (2286 041 463) This is a good place for a late-night drink to the tones of Latin and jazz. It's on the road that leads west towards the Ano Meria bus stop.

Next door to Sottovento, the vivid and appealing wall murals in **Greco Café-Bar** (2286 041 456) enhance the friendly ambience and great mix of sounds from its stock of over 1000 CDs. Nearby is the stylish **Avli Club** (2286 041 100) where early evening lounge music gives way to rock, disco, Latin and Greek as things liven up into the night. Just along the road to the left is the long established Laoumi, a fine little music bar that plays ethnic, funk, soul and South American and Caribbean sounds, with style.

AROUND FOLEGANDROS
Ano Meria Ανω Μεριά
pop 291

The settlement of Ano Meria is a scattered community of small farms and dwellings that stretches for several kilometres. This is traditional island life where tourism makes no intrusive mark.

The **folklore museum** (admission €1.50; ☯ 5-8pm) is on the eastern outskirts of the village. Ask the bus driver to drop you off nearby.

There are several good traditional tavernas in Ano Meria, including **I Synantisi** (☎ 2286 041 208; dishes €4-7.50) and **Mimi's** (☎ 2286 041 377; dishes €2.50-7), which specialise in *matsada*, a type of handmade pasta served with rabbit or rooster.

Beaches
For **Livadi Beach**, 1.2km south east of Karavostasis, follow the signs for Camping Livadi. Further round the coast on the southeastern tip of the island is **Katergo Beach**, best reached by boat.

The sandy and pebbled **Angali** beach on the coast opposite to Hora, is a popular spot, but you should remember that while it's a 1km downhill walk from where the bus drops you off, it's a steep and sweaty hike back up. There are several domatia here and two reasonable tavernas. About 750m over the hill by footpath, west of Angali is the nudist beach of **Agios Nikolaos**. **Livadaki** beach is over 2km further west again, but is best reached by another 1.5km trek from the bus stop near the church of Agios Andreas at Ano Meria. Boats connect these west coast beaches in high season. **Agios Georgios** is north of Ano Meria and requires another demanding walk. Have tough footwear and sun protection and, because most beaches have no shops or tavernas, make sure you take food and water.

In July and August, weather permitting, excursion boats make separate trips from Karavostasis to Kartergo, Angali and Agios Nikolaos and from Angali to Livadaki beach. Check with Diaplous General Tourism Office for schedules.

MILOS ΜΗΛΟΣ

pop 4771

Milos (*mee*-loss), the most westerly of the Cyclades, is a big, good-natured island. It has dramatic coastal landscapes with colourful and crazy rock formations that reflect its volcanic origin. This is a landscape to rival Santorini's in places, but it is all on a much smaller scale. Milos also has hot springs, marvellous beaches and some absorbing ancient sites. A boat trip around the island allows you to visit most of Milos' beaches (many inaccessible by road), coves and geologically interesting places.

Filakopi, an ancient Minoan city in the island's northeast, was one of the earliest settlements in the Cyclades. During the Peloponnesian Wars, Milos remained neutral, and was the only Cycladic island not to join the Athenian alliance. It paid dearly in 416 BC when avenging Athenians massacred the adult males and enslaved the women and children.

The island's most celebrated export, the beautiful *Venus de Milo* (a 4th-century BC statue of Aphrodite, found in an olive grove in 1820) is far away in the Louvre (allegedly having lost its arms on the way to Paris in the 19th century).

Getting There & Away
AIR
There is a daily flight to/from Athens (€49 one way). The **Olympic Airways office** (☎ 2287 022 380; fax 2287 021 884) is in Adamas, just past the main square, on the road to Plaka (and is worth going in just for the original '70s decor).

FAST BOAT & CATAMARAN
One weekly service goes to Santorini (€27, 1¾ hours), and one daily to Sifnos (€11.50, 1¾ hours) and Serifos (€12.50, 1¼ hours). At least one daily goes to Piraeus (€35, 3¾ hours). Three weekly go to Kythnos (€20, 2½ hours).

FERRY
The *Nissos Kimolos* departs five times daily from Pollonia for Kimolos at 9am, 11am, 2.15pm, 6.30pm and 10.40pm (€1.65/1.30/7 per person/motorbike/car, 20 minutes).

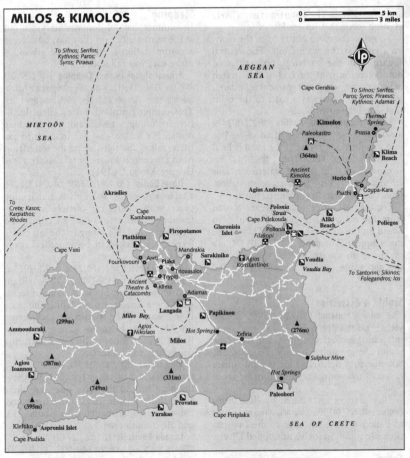

MILOS & KIMOLOS

There are two ferries daily to Piraeus (€18.35, five to seven hours); one daily to Sifnos (€6.50, 1¼ hours), Serifos (€6.50, two hours) and Kythnos (€10, 3½ hours); and six weekly to Kimolos (€5, one hour).

Five times weekly a ferry sails to the Cretan port of Sitia (€20, nine hours), sometimes continuing on to Kasos (€35, 11 hours), Karpathos (€35, 12 hours) and Rhodes (€50, 13 hours).

There are three weekly ferries to Folegandros (€6, 2½ hours) and Sikinos (€10, three hours), and two weekly to Paros (€10.50, 4½ hours).

There is one weekly ferry to Santorini (€14, four hours), Ios (€12.50, 5½ hours) and Syros (€10, six hours).

Getting Around

There are no buses to the airport, so you'll need to take a **taxi** (☎ 2287 022 219) for €6, plus €0.30 per piece of luggage, from Adamas.

Buses leave Adamas for Plaka and Trypiti (both €0.90) every hour or so. Buses run to Pollonia (€0.90, four daily), Paleohori (€1.10, three daily), Provatas (€1.10, three daily) and Arhivadolimni (Milos) Camping, east of Adamas (three daily). Cars, motorcycles and mopeds can be hired along the waterfront.

ADAMAS ΑΔΑΜΑΣ
pop 1391

Although Plaka is the capital, the incredibly pleasant port of Adamas has most of the accommodation. The waterfront has a lively evening scene that proves lots of fun.

To get to the town centre from the quay, turn right at the waterfront. The central square, with the bus stop, taxi rank and outdoor cafés, is at the end of this stretch of waterfront, where the road curves inland. Just past the square is a road to the right that skirts the town beach.

Milos' **municipal tourist office** (☎ 2287 022 445; www.milos-island.gr; ☼ 8am-midnight mid-Jun–mid-Sep), opposite the quay, is one of the most helpful in the Cyclades. **Vichos Tours** (☎ 2287 022 286; vichostours@in.gr) right on the waterfront, sells air and ferry tickets, finds accommodation, rents cars and handles organised tours.

For the post office, follow the main road from the main square and it's about 50m ahead on the right. There are ATMs on the main square. The **police** (☎ 2287 021 378) are on the main square, next to the bus stop; the **port police** (☎ 2287 022 100) are on the waterfront.

Sights & Activities
The **mining museum** (☎ 2287 022 481; admission free; ☼ 9.15am-1.45pm & 6.45-9.15pm) has some interesting geological exhibits and traces the island's long mining history. To get there, take the first right after the central square and continue along the waterfront for about 500m.

Dive courses are offered by **Milos Diving Center** (☎ 2287 041 296; www.milosdiving.gr), based at Pollonia. It's a member of the International Association for Handicapped Divers.

Tours
Milos Round 1 & 2 (☎ 2287 023 411; tours €20) Tour boats depart at 9am and stop at beaches around the island, pausing at Kimolos for lunch; buy tickets on the waterfront.

Andromeda Yachts (☎ 2287 023 680; ☼ May-Sep) Andromeda has sailing trips (€50 per person) to the island's nicest beaches and coves; they feature a seafood lunch, ouzo and sweets. Sailing tours (sailing tours €240 per tour) take place in the southwest Cyclades. Book through travel agencies or visit Andromeda on the waterfront.

Festivals & Events
The **Milos Festival**, a well-orchestrated event, is held in early July and features traditional dancing, cooking and jazz.

Sleeping
In summer, lists of domatia are given out at the tourist office on the quay, but decent accommodation is thin on the ground – make sure you call ahead.

Arhivadolimni (Milos) Camping (☎ 2287 031 410; fax 2287 031 412; www.miloscamping.gr; Arhiva-dolimni; camp sites per adult/tent €5/4, bungalows €65) This camping ground has excellent facilities, including a restaurant, bar and bike rental. It's 4.5km east of Adamas; to get there, follow the signs along the waterfront from the central square or take the bus (see Getting Around, p191).

Hotel Delfini (☎ 2287 022 001; fax 2287 022 294; d incl breakfast €60; P ✿) This is a charming place with charming owners and old-fashioned courtesy. Rooms are comfy and well appointed. It's along to the left of the ferry quay, tucked in behind the Lagada Beach Hotel.

Portiani Hotel (☎ 2287 022 940; fax 2287 022 766; sirmalen@otenet.gr; s/d €90-110; P ✿ ✿) Right next to the square, but with an air of seclusion, these fine rooms are worth the price if you want all the mod-cons, including a lift. The upper balconies have great views. Rates include a buffet breakfast featuring delicious local products.

Villa Helios (☎ 2287 022 258; fax 2287 023 974; heaton.theologitis@utanet.gr; apt €75; ✿) High above the port, behind the ferry quay, are these delightfully stylish, beautifully furnished, two-person apartments with phone, TV and air-conditioning.

Lagada Beach Hotel (☎ 2287 023 411; fax 2287 023 416; s/d/tr incl breakfast €48/60/72; P ✿) To the left of the ferry quay and dominating the fairly scrappy Langada Beach is this big complex of rather barrack-like rooms. They are good and functional, however, and new additions are quite swish.

Hotel Corali (☎ 2287 022 216; fax 2287 022 144; d €69) Standard rooms in this modern, functional place are a good size and have reasonable facilities. The surroundings are uninspiring and they are uphill from the waterfront.

Eating
Flisvos (☎ 2287 022 275; dishes €4.50-7) Fish is by the kilo at this excellent waterfront taverna along to the right of the ferry quay. It serves up good charcoal-grilled Greek specialities without fuss. Just try the delicious cheese pie, or mushroom pie for starters.

Aragosta (☎ 2287 022 292; dishes €12-26) Pricey, but good, food is the rule at this smart Italian restaurant that lies on the first staircase up from the waterfront just past the municipal tourist office. It serves quality items such as duck and lobster as well as tasty pasta.

Navagio (☎ 2287 023 392; dishes €3.50-10) This popular fish taverna is about 300m beyond the Portiani Hotel. It's a favourite with locals and sits right above the waterfront.

There's a terrific bakery and a mouth-watering cake shop just round from the main square on the left-hand side of the road.

Entertainment

Halfway up the first staircase along from the ferry quay there are a couple of popular music bars including Ilori and Vipera Leb-etina, playing disco-pop and Greek music during July and August. Further uphill is **Akri** (☎ 2287 022 064) below and opposite Villa Helios. It's a very stylish place that favours house, funk, and Latin and has an airy ter-race high above the port. Upstairs is a cool gallery selling jewellery, paintings, pottery and sculpture, many by island artists.

PLAKA & TRYPITI ΠΛΑΚΑ & ΤΡΥΠΗΤΗ

Plaka, 5km uphill from Adamas, is a typi-cal Cycladic town with white houses and labyrinthine laneways. It merges with the settlement of Trypiti to the south and rises above a sprawl of converging settlements, yet it retains an endearing character.

Both Plaka and Trypiti have domatia; ask at tavernas.

The **archaeology museum** (☎ 2287 021 629; ad-mission €3; ☺ 8.30am-3pm Tue-Sun) is in Plaka, just downhill from the bus turnaround. It's in a handsome old building and contains some compelling exhibits including a plaster cast of Venus de Milo and a perky little herd of Late Cycladic bull figurines.

The **Milos Folk & Arts Museum** (☎ 2287 021 292) was closed for refurbishment at the time of research but was due to re-open in 2004. It's signposted from the bus turnaround in Plaka.

At the bus turnaround, go right for the path to the **Frankish Kastro** built on the ancient acropolis and offering panoramic views of most of the island. The 13th-century church, **Thalassitras**, is inside the walls.

Plaka is built on the site of Ancient Milos, which was destroyed by the Athen-ians and rebuilt by the Romans. There are some Roman ruins near Trypiti, including Greece's only Christian **catacombs** (☎ 2287 021 625; ☺ 8am-7pm Tue-Sun). Stay on the bus towards Trypiti and get off at a T-junction by a big signpost indicating the way. Follow the road down for about 500m to where a track (signed) goes off to the right. This leads to the rather forlorn, but somehow thrilling spot where a farmer found the Venus de Milo in 1820. You can't miss the huge sign. A short way further along the track is the well-preserved **ancient thea-tre**, which hosts the **Milos Festival** every July. Back on the surfaced road, keep downhill to reach the 1st-century catacombs. A stepped path leads down from the road past a small cave, then on down to the well-lit main chamber with its side galler-ies that contained the tombs. Take plenty of drinking water.

Eating

Arhontoula (☎ 2287 021 384; dishes €2.60-10) Just along the main street from the bus turn-around in Plaka, this happily busy restaur-ant does great mezedes, main dishes of meat and fish, and fresh salads, all served up cheerfully.

Alisahni (☎ 2287 023 485; dishes €6-15) Smart, crisply furnished Alisahni is in the nar-row alleyway just around the corner from Arhontoula and offers modern Greek cuis-ine with international touches and flair.

Utopia Café (☎ 2287 023 678) The sunset views from the cool terrace of Utopia make you wonder why you bothered with Santorini. Head down the narrow alley opposite Arhontoula and prepare to be breathtaken.

Methysmeni Politia (☎ 2287 023 100; dishes €4.50-10) This reliable and popular taverna is halfway down the road to the catacombs. It offers a great selection of Greek dishes, and pasta.

AROUND MILOS

The shoreside village of **Klima** below Trypiti and the catacombs was once the port of an-cient Milos. Whitewashed buildings, with blue, green and red doors and balconies, have boat houses on the ground floor and living quarters on the 1st floor.

Plathiena is a lovely sandy beach below Plaka, to the north. On the way to Plathiena you can detour to the fishing villages of **Areti** and **Fourkovouni**. **Mandrakia** is a lovely fishing hamlet northeast of Plaka. The beaches of **Provatas** and **Paleohori**, on the south coast, are long and sandy, and Paleohori has hot springs, too. **Pollonia**, on the north coast, is a fishing village-cum-resort with a small beach and domatia. It serves as the jumping-off point for the boat to Kimolos.

KIMOLOS ΚΙΜΩΛΟΣ

pop 769

This small island lies just northeast of Milos. It receives a steady trickle of visitors, especially day-trippers arriving on the boat from Pollonia, on the northeastern tip of Milos. There are domatia, tavernas, bars and decent beaches. Domatia owners meet ferries.

The boat docks at the port of **Psathi**, from where it's 3km to the pretty capital of **Horio**. The taverna **To Kyma** (☎ 2287 051 001; dishes €3-6.50) is fine for Greek standards.

There's no petrol station on Kimolos so, if bringing a car or moped from Milos, make sure you've got enough fuel.

There are thermal springs at the settlement of **Prassa** on the northeast coast. **Beaches** can be reached by caïque from Psathi. At the centre of the island is the 364m-high cliff on which sits the fortress of **Paleokastro**.

Getting There & Away

Boats go daily to/from Pollonia on Milos, departing from Kimolos at 8am, 10am, 1.15pm, 5.30pm and 10pm (see the Milos Getting There & Away section on p190 for details on boats to Kimolos).

There are daily boats to Sifnos (€4.40, 1½ hours) and Serifos (€5.90, 3¾ hours). There are six weekly boats to Piraeus (€17.50, eight hours) and Kythnos (€9.10, three hours).

There are three ferries weekly to Adamas (€4.65, one hour) and Syros (€11, five hours) and two weekly to Folegandros (€6, 1½ hours) and Sikinos (€6, 2½ hours).

Two weekly ferries go to Paros (€8.70, 4½ hours) and Santorini (€12, 3½ hours).

SIFNOS ΣΙΦΝΟΣ

pop 2900

Sifnos (see-fnoss) hides its assets from passing ferry passengers behind a curtain of high barren hills. Beyond all this, however, is a fascinating and abundant landscape of terraced olive groves and almond trees, with oleanders in the valleys and hillsides covered in wild juniper. There are numerous dovecotes, whitewashed houses and chapels. Plenty of old paths link the villages and Sifnos is ideal for walking. The Anavasi map series *Topo 25/10.25 Aegean Cyclades/Sifnos* is quite useful for footpath details.

During the Archaic period the island was very wealthy because of its gold and silver resources, but by the 5th century BC the mines were exhausted and Sifnos' fortunes were reversed. The island has a long history of producing superior pottery because of the quality of its clay, and many shops sell local ceramics. Some potters' workshops are open to the public.

Getting There & Away

FAST BOAT & CATAMARAN

There is a daily catamaran to Piraeus (€30.30, 2¾ hours), four weekly to Kythnos (€11.20, 1¼ hours) and one daily to both Serifos (€10.30, 20 minutes) and Milos (€11.50, ¾ hour). There are five weekly catamarans to Santorini (€22.30, 2½ hours).

FERRY

There are daily ferries to Milos (€6, two hours), Piraeus (€16, five hours) via Serifos (€5.20, one hour) and Kythnos (€7.10, 2½ hours). There are three ferries weekly to Kimolos (€5.20, 1½ hours), Folegandros (€7.20, four hours), Sikinos (€9, five hours) and Santorini (€11.20, six hours), and two weekly to Paros (€3.70, two hours) and Syros (€7.20, 5½ hours).

Getting Around

Frequent buses link Apollonia with: Kamares (€0.90), with some services continuing on to Artemonas; Kastro (€0.90), Vathi (€1.80), Faros (€0.90) and Platys Gialos (€1.80).

I Meropi Taverna runs a taxi-boat service to anywhere on the island. **Taxis** (☎ 2284 031 347) hover around the port and Apollonia's

SIFNOS

AEGEAN SEA

Cape Heronisos

Heronisos

To Serifos; Paros; Syros; Kythnos; Piraeus

Agios Dimos

476m

Kamares Bay

Kamares

Sifnos

Ano Petali

Artemonas

Kastro

Seralia

To Kimolos; Milos; Santorini; Sikinos; Folegandros

Apollonia

Kato Petali

Katavati

Exambelas

680m

Moni Profiti Ilia

Platys Gialos

Faros

Fasolou Beach

Vathi

Moni Hrysopigis

Hrysopigis Beach

Vathi Bay

201m

Platys Gialos Bay

Cape Kondou

Kitriani

main square. It's €7 from Kamares to Apollonia. Cars can be hired from **Stavros Hotel** (2284 031 641) in Kamares, and from **Apollo Rent a Car** (2284 032 237) in Apollonia for €35 to €40.

KAMARES ΚΑΜΑΡΕΣ

The port of Kamares (kah-mah-rehs) has a resort atmosphere, not least because of its large beach. There are lots of waterfront cafés and tavernas and a very good mix of shops from food stores to craft shops. The bus stop is the stand of tamarisk trees just past the inland end of the ferry quay.

Opposite the bus stop is the very helpful **municipal tourist office** (2284 031 977; 10am-midnight Sun-Tue & Thu, 11am-5pm Wed, 10am-10pm Fri-Sat). It can find accommodation anywhere on the island. It also offers free luggage storage and sells a useful clutch of information sheets about the island, walking trips, bus schedules and ferry times.

There are toilets near the tourist office and an ATM booth that is accessed by card insert. It has the best air-conditioning in the Cyclades.

Sleeping & Eating

Camping Makis (2284 032 366; www.makiscamping.gr; camp sites per adult/tent €4.20/2.30, r from €40;) This pleasant site is just behind the beach, 600m north of the port. There's a relaxed, friendly atmosphere and there's an outdoor café, a barbecue area, laundry and shaded sites. There's Internet access for €6 per hour.

Hotel Afroditi (2284 031 704; www.hotel-afroditi.gr; d €60;) A gem of a place, with charming family owners, Afroditi is right behind the beach, beyond Hotel Boulis. Rooms are very pleasant; there are sea views to the front and mountain views to the rear. Breakfast (€3 to €4) is available .

Simeon (2284 031 652; fax 2284 031 035; d €50) Try for one of Simeon's front rooms; they're small, but the balconies have exhilarating views down across the port and along the beach to soaring mountains beyond. It's high above the waterfront, up steepish steps. You can't miss the sign.

Stavros Hotel (2284 031 641; www.sifnostravel.com; s/d €44/50) is right on the mid-waterfront and has good clean rooms. **Hotel Kamari** (2284 033 383; www.sifnostravel.com) is owned by the same family and has similar prices and standards. It's 400m up the road to Apollonia. Attached to Stavros Hotel is an information office that can arrange car hire and has a book exchange.

There are several reasonably priced waterfront eateries serving good Greek staples for about €3.50 to €8; they include O-Simos, I Meropi, Ouzeri Kamares and Captain Andreas, which is the best place for fish.

Just up a level from mid-waterfront is **Collage Bar** (2284 032 351), which is good for relaxed drinking to some great blues and rock.

Domatia owners rarely meet boats, and in high season it's best to book ahead.

APOLLONIA ΑΠΟΛΛΩΝΙΑ

The capital is situated on a plateau 5km uphill from the port.

The bus stop for Kamares is on the busy central square where the post office is located. Because of congestion, all other buses pick up passengers about 50m further on, at a junction outside Hotel Anthousa. Initial impressions of Apollonia are of frantic traffic, but step onto the main pedestrian thoroughfare, which is reached from opposite the Kamares

CYCLADES

bus stop and is behind the museum, and things are charmingly transformed. There is an Alpha Bank (with ATM) next to Hotel Sofia and the Piraeus Bank and National Bank of Greece, both with ATMs are just round the corner on the road to Artemonas; the police are another 50m beyond.

The interesting little **Museum of Popular Art** (☎ 2284 033 730; admission €1; ⏰ 10am-2pm & 7.30-11.30pm Tue-Sun), on the central square and just opposite the post office, contains a splendid mass of old costumes, pots, textiles and photographs.

Sleeping & Eating

Hotel Sifnos (☎ 2284 031 624; s/d/tr €49/59/69) Right at the heart of the pretty street is this family-run hotel with adjoining taverna. It has well-kept rooms and its taverna offers tasty Greek dishes for €3.50 to €8.50.

Also recommended are **Peristeronas Apartments** (☎ 2284 071 288; d €85) in a traditional Sifnos-style house that overlooks terraced fields. For basic accommodation try **Hotel Sofia** (☎ 2284 031 238; s/d €30/45). It has fairly functional, but very conveniently located rooms.

Apostoli tou Koutouki (☎ 2284 031 186; dishes €3-8.50) Fish is by the kilo at this excellent place on the main street. It also serves meat and chicken specialities.

AROUND SIFNOS

The pretty village of **Artemonas** is a short walk or bus ride north of Apollonia. Not to be missed is the walled cliff-top village of **Kastro**, 3km from Apollonia. The former capital, it is a magical place of buttressed alleys and whitewashed houses. It has a small **archaeological museum** (☎ 2284 031 022; admission free; ⏰ 8.30am-3pm Tue-Sun).

The resort of **Platys Gialos**, 10km south of Apollonia, has a great sandy beach, entirely backed by tavernas, domatia and shops. The bus terminates at the beach's southwestern end. **Vathi**, on the west coast, is a gorgeous sandy bay with several tavernas. **Faros** is a cosy little fishing hamlet with a couple of nice beaches nearby, such as the little beach of **Fasolou**, up the steps and over the headland from the bus stop.

Sleeping & Eating

Platys Gialos has plenty of sleeping places, although most cater for package tourists.

Camping Platys Gialos (☎ 2284 071 286; camp sites per adult/tent €4/3) This reasonable site is in an olive grove, about 700m from the beach.

Platys Gialos Beach Hotel (☎ 2284 071 324; fax 2284 071 325; s/d €140/180; P ☒) In an enviable position overlooking the far end of the beach, this peaceful hotel has lovely terraces and a garden area. It has a loyal clientele, so it's wise to book well in advance.

Angeliki Rooms (☎ 2284 071 288; d/tr €45/53) Also recommended are these pleasant rooms just back from the bus terminus, and right on the beach.

There are quite a few rooms for rent by the beach in Faros: try **Margarita** (☎ 2284 071 438), **Aristi Pension** (☎ 2284 071 443) or **Villa Maria** (☎ 2284 071 421) all charging about €45 for a double.

On Platys Gialos beach **To Koutouki** (☎ 2284 071 330; dishes €4-8.50) is run by the family that has the same-name place in Appolonia. Fish is by the kilo and is lovingly prepared.

In Artemonas, on the main square, **Liotrivi** (☎ 2284 031 246) serves robust traditional fare, while **Margarita** (☎ 2284 031 058), nearby, is also worth seeking out. Both have dishes for €3 to €6.

Faros (☎ 2284 071 452; €2.50-12) is a small taverna in Faros that offers excellent fish by the kilo while **On the Rocks** (☎ 2284 031 817; dishes €3.50-6), near Fasolou, is a pleasant café serving crepes and pizzas.

SERIFOS ΣΕΡΙΦΟΣ

pop 1414

Serifos (seh-ri-fohs) is eye-catching from the start, not least because of its fabulous hora, a scribble of white houses crowning a high and rocky peak, 2km to the north of the attractive little port of Livadi and serving as a dramatic backdrop to the port. The island is fairly barren and rocky, but has a few pockets of greenery that are the result of tomato and vine cultivation. There are some pleasant paths that link various villages; the Anavasi map series *Topo 25/10.26 Aegean Cyclades/ Serifos* is quite useful for footpath details.

Getting There & Away

Three times weekly a catamaran runs to Sifnos (€10.30, 25 minutes), Milos (€12, 1¼ hours), Piraeus (€28, 2¼ hours) and Kythnos (€12.50, 45 minutes).

SERIFOS

0 — 4 km
0 — 2 miles

AEGEAN SEA

Sykamia Beach
Platys Gialos Bay
Moni Taxiarhon
Galani
Kendarhos
To Kythnos; Piraeus
Panagia
Pirgos
Serifos (582m)
Agios Ioannis Beach
Psili Ammos Beach
Avessalos
Hora
Lia Beach
(502m)
Koutalas
Livadi
Vodi
Ganema
Livadakia Beach
Megalo Livadi Beach
Vagia
Karavi Beach
To Paros; Syros
Ambeli Beach
Cape Katano
To Sifnos; Kimolos; Milos; Folegandros; Santorini; Sikinos; Ios

There is a daily ferry to Piraeus (€14.40, 4½ hours), Sifnos (€5.20, one hour), Milos (€6, two hours) and Kimolos (€7.10, 2½ hours).

Four times weekly the Piraeus ferry stops at Kythnos (€6.20, 1½ hours), and twice weekly boats go to Paros (€6.90, three hours), Syros (€8, two to four hours) and Folegandros (€9.20, five hours).

There are weekly boats to Santorini (€14.50, seven hours), Ios (€10.90, six hours) and Sikinos (€10.40, five hours).

Getting Around

There are frequent buses between Livadi and Hora (€0.90); a timetable is posted at the bus stop by the yacht marina. Vehicles can be hired from Krinas Travel (see the Livadi section for details).

LIVADI ΛΙΒΑΔΙ

pop 537

This unassuming, but endearing port is at the end of an elongated bay. It has a pleasant openness; the northern half of its waterfront road is sand, and there's a reassuring feeling that the modern world has not entirely taken over. Just over the headland that rises from the ferry quay lies the fine, tamarisk-fringed beach at **Livadakia**. **Karavi Beach**, a walk further south over the next headland, is the unofficial nudist beach. There is an Alpha Bank, with ATM, on the waterfront.

There is a **tourist information office** (☎ 2281 051 466; 10am-2pm & 6-10pm mid-Jul–Aug) on the waterfront, which has a domatia list (in Greek).

Krinas Travel (☎ 2281 051 488; sertrav@otenet.gr), just where the ferry quay joins the waterfront road, sells ferry tickets and organises car (€53 a day) and scooter (€20 a day) hire.

The **port police** (☎ 2281 051 470) are up steps from the quay.

Sleeping & Eating

Coralli Camping (☎ 2281 051 500; fax 2281 051 073; coralli@mail.otenet.gr; camp sites per adult/tent €5.50/4, d bungalows €55; P 🐕) This well-equipped site, shaded by tall eucalypts, is a step away from sandy Livadakia Beach and bungalows have mountain or sea view. There's also a restaurant and minimarket, and a minibus meets all ferries. The site's Heaven Pool Bar thinks it's in Ios.

Hotel Areti (☎ 2281 051 479; fax 2281 051 547; s/d €45/55) This light and bright hotel, is high above the ferry quay and is reached up the steps that lead on to Livadakia beach. Rooms are pleasant and airy.

Rooms to Let Marianna (☎ 2281 051 338; s/d €50/60) This place is set back from the waterfront amid a leafy garden.

Eliza (☎ 2281 051 763; fax 2281 051 763; apt €66-78; 🐕) You pay about €5 to €10 extra for air-conditioning at these reasonable rooms in a big house surrounded by a garden. It's about 100m from the beach along the turn-off road to the Hora.

Anastasia Rooms (☎ 2281 051 247; s/d/apt €45/55/65) Functional rooms that are adequate. Enquire next door at Meli café on the waterfront.

Yacht Club Serifos (☎ 2281 051 888) There may be no yachts but there's a terrific ambience at this waterfront *kafeneio*-bar (café-bar) that does breakfast for €4, or €10 for a real special breakfast, and snacks and sandwiches for €2.50 to €6. Music ranges from lounge by day, to mainstream, rock, disco and funk late into the night. Enquire at the Yacht Club about diving trips and courses.

Also recommended is the waterfront Meli where you get good sandwiches and crepes for €2.50 to €4. Most of the tavernas along the waterfront, such as Taverna Mokkas and Perseus, offer dishes for about €4 to €13.50.

HORA

The exquisite Hora, clinging to a crag above Livadi, is one of the most striking

CYCLADES

of Cycladic capitals. Ancient steps lead up from Livadi, though they are fragmented by the snaking road that links the two. You can walk up, but in the heat of summer, going up by bus may be the wiser decision. Just up from the bus terminus, steps climb into the wonderful maze of Hora proper and lead to the charming main square, watched over by the imposing neoclassical town hall. From the square, narrow alleys and more steps lead ever upwards to the remnants of the ruined 15th-century **Venetian Kastro**; an eagle's nest if ever there was one.

Back downhill, there's a post office just up from the bus turnaround.

Hora has a small **archaeological museum** (☎ 2281 051 138; admission free; ☺ 9am-2pm Tue-Sun) displaying pottery and sculpture found at the fortress. There's a **folk museum** (☺ 9am-noon & 6-9pm early Jul-early Sep) a long way down the steps to Livadi, on the lower edge of Hora.

Sleeping & Eating

Anatoli (☎ 2281 051 510; s/d €30/45) has decent rooms in a building uphill from Hora, and with wide-reaching views to the east. Head uphill from Hora for about 400m past a line of ruined and preserved windmills.

I Platia (☎ 2281 051 261; dishes €3.50-9) Just by the bus turnaround, this is an ideal place for a great night out. It has a fine bar area and an outside terrace. Delicious mezedes and local dishes are a specialty and it does an excellent choice of breakfasts. There's music in the bar, and occasional live sessions of Greek, including rembetika.

Stou Stratou (☎ 2281 052 566) In the main square are the tables of this enjoyable bar-café, with its hint of Parisian ambience. Even the stylish menu is interspersed with works of great poets, such as George Seferis.

AROUND SERIFOS

About an hour's walk north of Livadi (or a shorter drive) along a track (negotiable by motorbike) is **Psili Ammos Beach**. A path from Hora heads north for about 4km to the pretty village of **Kendarhos** (also called Kallitsos), from where you can continue by road for another 3km to the 17th-century fortified **Moni Taxiarhon**, which has impressive 18th-century frescoes. The walk from the town to the monastery takes about two hours. You will need to take food and water as there are no facilities in Kendarhos.

KYTHNOS ΚΥΘΝΟΣ

pop 1608

Kythnos (*kee*-thnos) has a muted charm, yet struggles to elicit much interest from foreign tourists. It's popular with Athenian holiday-makers for weekend breaks and draws a regular flotilla of gin palace private cruisers, whose glossy arrival makes for much enter-tainment on the evening quay. Never have so many uniformed deck crews given so much close attention to so few mooring lines.

The island's main attraction are its unique **thermal baths**.

The main settlements are the port of Merihas and the capital Hora (or Kythnos). There's an ATM on the waterfront just past the flight of steps as you come from the ferry quay. **Antonios Larentzakis Travel Agency** (☎ 2281 032 104/032 291) sells ferry tickets, can arrange accommodation and rents cars and motor-bikes. It's up the flight of steps near Ostria Taverna. Hora has the island's post office and **police** (☎ 2281 031 201). The **port police** (☎ 2281 032 290) are on the waterfront in Merihas.

KYTHNOS

0 —— 4 km
0 —— 2 miles

To Syros; Andros; Mykonos; Tinos

Cape Kefalos

AEGEAN SEA

(297m)

To Kea; Lavrio

Loutra

Kythnos

(308m)

Fikiada Beach

Apokrousi Beach

Hora (Kythnos)

Episkopi Beach

To Piraeus

Merihas

Dryopida

Cape Tzoulis

Flambouria Beach

(302m)

Kanala

To Serifos; Sifnos; Milos; Kimolos; Folegandros; Sikinos; Santorini

Dimitrios Beach

Cape Berou

LP

Getting There & Away

FAST BOAT & CATAMARAN

There are three services weekly to Piraeus (€23, 1½ hours), Sifnos (€11.20, 1¼ hours), Milos (€20, 2½ hours) and Serifos (€13, 45 minutes).

A once weekly catamaran goes to Mykonos (€19, 1¾ hours) and to Tinos (€19, 2¼ hours).

FERRY

There are at least two boats to Piraeus daily (€11.30, 2½ hours). Most services coming from Piraeus continue to Serifos (€6.50, 1½ hours), Sifnos (€7.10, 2½ hours), Kimolos (€9.10, three hours) and Milos (€9.50, 3½ hours).

There are six weekly ferries to Lavrio (€7.30, 3½ hours), three weekly to Syros (€7, two hours) and two weekly to Kea (€5.40, 1¼ hours), Folegandros (€12.90, six hours), Sikinos (€13.70, seven hours) and Santorini (€17.70, eight hours).

A ferry runs once weekly to Andros (€10, five hours).

Getting Around

There are regular buses from Merihas to Dryopida (€0.90), continuing to Kanala (€1.70) or Hora (€1). Less regular services run to Loutra (€1.70). The buses supposedly meet the ferries, but usually they leave from the turn-off to Hora in Merihas.

Taxis are a better bet, except at siesta time. It's €8 to Hora and €5 to Dryopida. There are only three taxis on the island; call ☎ 6944 743 791, ☎ 6944 276 656 or ☎ 6944 277 609.

MERIHAS ΜΕΡΙΧΑΣ

pop 289

Merihas (*meh-ree-hass*) does not have a lot going for it other than a bit of waterfront life and a slightly grubby beach. But it's a reasonable base and has most of the island's accommodation. There are better beaches within walking distance north of the quay (turn left facing inland).

Sleeping & Eating

Domatia owners usually meet the boats and there are a number of signs along the waterfront advertising rooms; alternatively enquire at Larentzakis Travel. A lot of places block book during the season and there is

an element of reluctance towards one night stopovers. You should definitely book ahead for July and August.

Kythnos Hotel (☎ 2281 032 247; d/tr €50/65) It's essential to book ahead here in high season and at weekends. It's the town's main hotel and has good rooms and a fine location above the harbour.

Ostria (☎ 2281 032 263; dishes €4-12) On the waterfront near the ferry quay, Ostria has reasonable Greek fare. Seafood is by the kilo.

Taverna to Kandouni (☎ 2281 032 220; dishes €3.50-12) Near the port police on the waterfront, Kandouni specialises in grilled meats; it also has rooms to let.

AROUND KYTHNOS

The capital, **Hora** (also known as Kythnos) is a pleasant enough place, but struggles to match the charm of many Cycladic capitals. There's a pleasant 6km walk south to **Dryopida**, a picturesque town of red-tiled roofs and winding streets that was the island's capital in the Middle Ages. You can either walk the 6km back to Merihas or catch a bus or taxi.

The best **beaches** are on the southeast coast, near the village of Kanala.

KEA KEA (TZIA)

pop 2417

Kea wears its many charms quietly. This most northerly of the Cyclades is often more associated with mainland Attica than with the main island chain and is off the major ferry routes. It's a popular weekend escape for Athenians in summer, but not many foreign tourists drop by. Kea's distant prospect of bare hills is belied by its hidden green valleys that are filled with orchards, olive groves, and almond and oak trees. The main settlements are the port of Korissia, and the delightful capital, Ioulida, 5km inland.

Getting There & Away

Services connect Kea with Lavrio (€5.30, 1¼ hours) on the mainland at least twice daily. Two weekly ferries go to Kythnos (€5.40, 1¼ hours) and on to Syros (€8.20, four hours). One weekly boat goes to Andros (€7.30, six hours).

CYCLADES

KEA

To Lavrio
To Andros
AEGEAN SEA
To Kythnos; Syros
Agia Irini
Korissia
Vourkari
Otzias
Moni Panagias Kastriani
Gialiskari Beach
Flea
Ioulida
Pera Meria
Cape Spathi
(570m)
Astra
Ellinika
Kea
Pisses Beach
Koundouros
(450m)
Havouna
Cape Tamelos

Getting Around

In July and August there are, in theory, regular buses from Korissia to Vourkari, Otzias, Ioulida and Pisses. At the time of writing, however, there was some disruption to services over internal disputes so you should consider a **taxi** (☎ 2288 021 021/021 228) to Ioulida (€5) especially. Motorcycle-rental and car-rental is well above the usual high season prices of about €20 and €45.

KORISSIA ΚΟΡΗΣΣΙΑ

pop 555

The port of Korissia (koh-ree-*see*-ah) is bland, but there are enough eateries and cafés to pass the time. There's a beach that is north-facing and tends to catch the wind.

The official **tourist information office** (☎ 2288 021 500), opposite the ferry quay, has lists of domatia in Greek, but not much more. Stefanos Lepouras and his family, next door at **Stegali Bookshop** (☎ 2288 021 435; fax 2288 021 012) are an great source of information and promote the island enthusiastically, but thoughtfully. The selection of books is very good.

Art Café (☎ 2288 021 181), on the waterfront, has Internet access (€2.50 per half hour). There is an ATM right next door to the Art Café and also near Hotel Karthea. The Piraeus Bank is behind the beach. There is a small ferry ticket office next to the car-rental agency on the waterfront.

Sleeping & Eating

Domatia owners don't meet ferries. It's wise to book in high season and at weekends.

Hotel Tzia (☎ 2288 021 305; fax 2288 021 140; s/d €45/52) This is a rather dull building owned by the municipality of Kea, but it has plain, clean rooms and an enviable location right on the beach.

Hotel Brillante Zoi (☎ 2288 022 685; kpgr2002@yahoo.it; s/d incl breakfast €90/105, apt incl breakfast €135-150) This very fine hotel has rooms with individual decor furnished handsomely. Outside areas have a garden setting. The hotel is only robbed of sea views by the presence of Hotel Tzia opposite.

Hotel Karthea (☎ 2288 021 204; fax 2288 021 417; s/d €50/60) This utterly functional hotel is convenient enough for the port. Rooms at the back overlook a quiet garden area. There's no lift to the several floors.

There are several tavernas along the waterfront, all dishing up fairly standard fare for about €3.50 to €7, but without much flair. The Art Café has a pleasant ambience and is great for people watching.

IOULIDA ΙΟΥΛΙΔΑ

pop 700

Ioulida (ee-oo-*lee*-tha) is a delightful scramble of narrow alleyways and rising lanes that lies along the rim of a natural amphitheatre among the hills. It was once a substantial settlement of ancient Greece, but few relics remain and even the Venetian kastro has been incorporated into private houses. The architecture generally is notably different from that of other Cycladic capitals – the houses have red-tiled roofs.

The bus turnaround is on a square just at the edge of town. There's a National Bank of Greece here, but no ATM. From the turnaround, an archway leads into the village. At a T-junction, a left turn leads, not too rewardingly, to what's left of the kastro. Turning right and uphill takes you into the more interesting heart of Ioulida proper. The post office is part-way up on the right.

CYCLADES

Sights

Ioulida's **archaeological museum** (☎ 2288 022 079; admission free; ☉ 8.30am-3pm Tue-Sun) is just before the post office on the main thoroughfare. It houses some intriguing artefacts, mostly from Agia Irini.

The celebrated **Kea Lion**, chiselled from a huge chunk of slate in the 6th century BC, lies on the hillside beyond the last of the houses. Keep on uphill from the museum, and pass a junction with a wooden board giving walk directions and times to Karthea, Otzias, Ellinika – and the Kea Lion, only a few hundred metres further on. Follow the track past the cemetery and the Lion, with its strange Mona Lisa smile, is just round the hillside.

Sleeping & Eating

There are a few domatia in Ioulida, and several decent tavernas. Ask about rooms at the minimarket just inside the arrival archway.

Recommended eateries are **Estiatorio I Piatsa** (☎ 2288 022 195), just inside the archway and **Kalofagadon** (☎ 2288 022 118) on the main square, both with good Greek dishes at about €3.50 to €8, with lamb and fresh fish costing more. Further uphill from the square is the colourful **To Milo Tis Eridos** (☎ 2288 022 610) offering tasty pizzas and pastas for €4 to €7.50, in a great setting.

There's an excellent bakery, just past the post office.

AROUND KEA

The beach road from Korissia leads past **Gialiskari Beach** for 2.5km to where the waterfront quay at tiny **Vourkari** is lined with yachts and cafés. **Voukariani Art Gallery** (☎ 2288 021 458) is set back mid-waterfront among the cafés and restaurants; it stages changing exhibitions of world-class art works over the summer.

The road continues for another 3km to a sandy beach at **Otzias**. A dirt road continues beyond here for another 5km to the 18th-century **Moni Panagias Kastriani** (☎ 2288 024 348), which has terrific views.

Pisses is the island's best beach and is 8km southwest of Ioulida. It is long and sandy and backed by a verdant valley of orchards and olive groves, with rugged hills rising above.

Sleeping & Eating

Kea Camping (☎ 2288 031 302; fax 2288 031 303; Pisses Beach; camp sites per adult/tent €5/5, bungalows €50) Sheltered by pines and eucalyptus trees this useful site has a shop, bar and restaurant nearby.

There are a number of domatia at Otzias charging about €40 to €45.

There are tavernas at the main beaches. **Kokka Café** (☎ 2288 021 080) at Vourkari is a cheerful place where you can watch the bustling waterfront life over great coffee or wine.

Crete Κρήτη

CRETE

Crete is Greece's largest and most southerly island, and arguably the most beautiful. A spectacular mountain chain runs from east to west, split into three ranges: the Mt Dikti Range in the east, the Mt Idi (or Mt Psiloritis) Range in the centre and the Lefka Ori (White Mountains) in the west. The mountains are dotted with plains and plateaus, and sliced by numerous dramatic gorges. Beaches speckle the coastline, and the east coast boasts Europe's only palm-tree forest.

Administratively, the island is divided into four prefectures: Lasithi, Iraklio, Rethymno and Hania. Apart from Lasithi, with its capital of Agios Nikolaos, the prefectures are named after their major cities. The island's capital is Iraklio. Nearly all Crete's major population centres are on the north coast. Most of the south coast is too precipitous to support large settlements.

Crete's size and its distance from the rest of Greece allowed an independent culture to evolve. Cretan weavings are sold in many of the towns and villages. The traditional Cretan songs differ from those heard elsewhere in Greece. Called *mantinades*, these songs are highly emotive, expressing the age-old concerns of love, death and the yearning for freedom. You will still come across men wearing the traditional dress of breeches tucked into knee-high leather boots, and black-fringed kerchiefs tied tightly around their heads.

The attractions of Crete have not gone unnoticed by tour operators, and the island has the dubious honour of hosting a quarter of Greece's tourists. Much of the north coast is packed with hastily constructed hotels for package tourists, particularly between Iraklio and Agios Nikolaos and west of Hania. Tour operators have also taken over several of the southern coastal villages that were once backpacker favourites. The rugged west coast remains untouched.

The best times to visit are from April to June and from mid-September to the end of October. Outside the major population centres, most places close down in winter.

HIGHLIGHTS

- **Wining**
  Fine wine bars in Iraklio (p214)

- **Dining**
  Romantic dinners in Hania's Old Town (p242)

- **Historical Experience**
  Knossos (p215), home of the mythical Minotaur

- **Sporting Event**
  Scuba diving in Rethymno (p233)

- **Green Haven**
  The Samaria Gorge (p244)

- **Adrenaline Rush**
  The Ha Gorge (p229)

- **Chill-Out Spot**
  Kato Zakros (p227) in far-eastern Crete

CRETE

History

Although Crete has been inhabited since Neolithic times (7000–3000 BC), as far as most people are concerned its history begins with the Minoan civilisation. The glories of Crete's Minoan past remained hidden until British archaeologist Sir Arthur Evans made his dramatic discoveries at Knossos in the early 1900s. The term 'Minoan' was coined by Evans and derived from the King Minos of Greek mythology. Nobody knows what the Minoans called themselves.

Among the ruins unearthed by Evans were the famous Knossos frescoes. Artistically, the frescoes are superlative; the figures that grace them have a naturalism lacking in contemporary Cycladic figurines, ancient Egyptian artwork (which they resemble in certain respects), and the Archaic sculpture that came later. Compared with candle-smoke-blackened Byzantine frescoes, the Minoan frescoes, with their fresh, bright colours, look as if they were painted yesterday (see the Mysterious Minoans on p206).

But no matter how much speculation the frescoes inspire about the Minoans, all we really know is that early in the 3rd millennium BC an advanced people migrated to Crete and brought with them the art of metallurgy. Many elements of Neolithic culture lived on in the Early Minoan period (3000–2100 BC), but the Middle Minoan period (2100–1500 BC) saw the emergence of a society of unprecedented artistic, engineering and cultural achievement. It was during this time that the famous palace complexes were built at Knossos, Phaestos, Malia and Zakros.

Also during this time, the Minoans began producing their exquisite Kamares pottery (see Iraklio's Archaeological Museum section, p209) and silverware, and became a maritime power trading with Egypt and Asia Minor.

Around 1700 BC all four palace complexes were destroyed by an earthquake. Undeterred, the Minoans built bigger and better palaces on the sites of the originals, as well as new settlements in other parts of the island.

CRETE

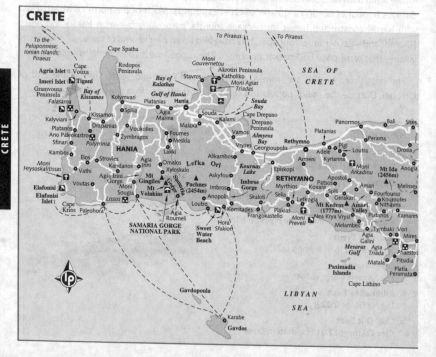

Around 1500 BC, when the Minoan civilisation was at its peak, the palaces were destroyed again, signalling the start of the Late Minoan period (1500–1100 BC). This destruction was probably caused by Mycenaean invasions, although the massive volcanic eruption on the island of Santorini (Thira) may also have been responsible. Knossos was the only palace to be salvaged. It was finally destroyed by fire around 1400 BC.

The Minoan civilisation was a hard act to follow. The war-orientated Dorians, who arrived in 1100 BC, were pedestrian by comparison. The 5th century BC found Crete, like the rest of Greece, divided into city-states. The glorious classical age of mainland Greece had little impact on Crete, and the Persians bypassed the island. It was also ignored by Alexander the Great, so was never part of the Macedonian Empire.

By 67 BC, Crete had fallen to the Romans. The town of Gortyna in the south became the capital of Cyrenaica, a province that included large chunks of North Africa. Crete, along with the rest of Greece, became part of the Byzantine Empire in AD 395.

In 1210 the island was occupied by the Venetians, whose legacy is one of mighty fortresses, ornate public buildings and monuments, and the handsome dwellings of nobles and merchants.

Despite the massive Venetian fortifications, which sprang up all over the island, by 1669 the whole of the Cretan mainland was under Turkish rule. The first uprising against the Turks was led by Ioannis Daskalogiannis in 1770. This set the precedent for many more insurrections, and in 1898 the Great Powers (Great Britain, France and Russia) intervened and made the island a British protectorate. It was not until the signing of the Treaty of Bucharest in 1913 that Crete officially became part of Greece, although the island's parliament had declared a de facto union in 1905.

The island saw heavy fighting during WWII. Germany wanted the island as an air base in the Mediterranean, and on 20 May 1941 German parachutists landed on Crete. It was the start of 10 days of fierce fighting that became known as the Battle of Crete. For two days the battle hung in the

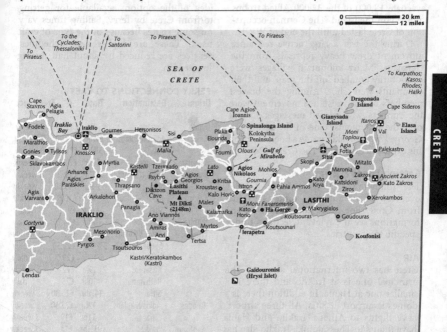

THE MYSTERIOUS MINOANS

Of the many finds at Knossos and other sites, it is the celebrated frescoes that have captured the imagination of experts and amateurs alike, shedding light on a civilisation hitherto a mystery. The message they communicate is of a society that was powerful, wealthy, joyful and optimistic.

Gracing the frescoes are white-skinned women with elaborately coiffured glossy black locks. Proud, graceful and uninhibited, these women are dressed in stylish gowns that reveal perfectly shaped breasts. The bronze-skinned men are tall, with tiny waists, narrow hips, broad shoulders and muscular thighs and biceps; the children are slim and lithe. The Minoans also seemed to know how to enjoy themselves. They played board games, boxed and wrestled, played leap-frog over bulls and over one another, and performed bold acrobatic feats.

As well as being literate, they were religious, as frescoes and models of people partaking in rituals testify. The Minoans' beliefs, like many other aspects of their society, remain an enigma, but there is sufficient evidence to confirm that they worshipped a nature goddess, often depicted with serpents and lions. Male deities were distinctly secondary.

From the frescoes it appears that women enjoyed a respected position in society, leading religious rituals and participating in games, sports and hunting. Minoan society may have had its dark side, however. There is evidence of human sacrifice being practised on at least one occasion, although probably in response to an extreme external threat.

balance until Germany won a bridgehead for its air force at Maleme, near Hania. The Allied forces of Britain, Australia, New Zealand and Greece then fought a valiant rearguard action which enabled the British Navy to evacuate 18,000 of the 32,000 Allied troops trapped on the island. The German occupation of Crete lasted until the end of WWII.

During the war a large active resistance movement drew heavy reprisals from the Germans. Many mountain villages were temporarily bombed 'off the map' and their occupants were shot. Among the bravest members of this resistance movement were the 'runners' who relayed messages on foot over the mountains. One of these runners, George Psyhoundakis, wrote a book based on his experiences entitled *The Cretan Runner*.

Getting There & Away

The following section provides a brief overview of air and boat options to and from Crete. For more comprehensive information, see the relevant sections under specific town entries.

AIR

Crete has two international airports. The principal one is at Iraklio and there is a smaller one at Hania. In addition there is a domestic airport at Sitia. All three airports have flights to Athens. Iraklio and Hania have flights to Thessaloniki; Iraklio also has flights to Rhodes and Santorini.

FERRY

Crete has ports at Iraklio, Souda (for Hania), Rethymno, Agios Nikolaos, Sitia and Kissamos.

The following table will give you some idea of the options available for getting to/from Crete by ferry. Sailing times vary on some routes because of the type of craft used. These are high-season schedules; services are reduced by about half during low season.

FERRY CONNECTIONS TO CRETE

Origin	Destination	Time	€	Frequency
Gythio	Kissamos	?hr	€19.50	weekly
Halki	Agios Nikolaos	6½hr	€12	3 weekly
	Sitia	5½hr	€11.90	3 weekly
Kalamata	Kissamos	?hr	€20.30	1 weekly
Karpathos	Agios Nikolaos	7hr	€19	3 weekly
	Sitia	5½hr	€15.50	3 weekly
Kasos	Agios Nikolaos	4hr	€10.60	3 weekly
	Sitia	4hr	€9	3 weekly
Kythira	Kissamos	4hr	€14.70	5 weekly
Piraeus	Agios Nikolaos	12hr	€27	3 weekly
	Souda (Hania)	5¾-9hr	€29.50	daily
	Iraklio	6-10hr	€29.50	daily
	Kissamos	19hr	€22	5 weekly
	Rethymno	10hr	€25	daily
	Sitia	14½hr	€25.30	3 weekly
Rhodes	Agios Nikolaos	12hr	€22.50	3 weekly
	Sitia	11hr	€19	3 weekly
Santorini	Iraklio	3¾hr	€14	3 weekly
Thessaloniki	Iraklio	23hr	€41	1 weekly

CRETE

Getting Around

A fast national highway skirts the north coast from Hania in the west to Agios Nikolaos in the east, and is being extended further west to Kissamos and east to Sitia. There are frequent buses linking all the major northern towns from Kissamos to Sitia.

Less-frequent buses operate between the north-coast towns and resorts and places of interest on the south coast, via the mountain villages of the interior. These routes are Hania to Paleohora, Omalos (for the Samaria Gorge) and Hora Sfakion; Rethymno to Plakias, Agia Galini, Phaestos and Matala; Iraklio to Agia Galini, Phaestos, Matala and the Lasithi Plateau; Agios Nikolaos to Ierapetra; and Sitia to Ierapetra, Kato Zakros, Palekastro and Vaï.

There is nothing comparable to the national highway on the south coast and parts of this area have no roads at all. There is no road between Paleohora and Hora Sfakion, the most precipitous part of the south coast; a boat (daily from June to August) connects the two resorts via Sougia and Agia Roumeli.

CENTRAL CRETE

Central Crete is occupied by the Iraklio prefecture, named after the island's burgeoning major city and administrative capital. The area's major attractions are the Minoan sites of Knossos, Malia and Phaestos. The north coast just east of Iraklio has been heavily exploited by the package tourism industry, particularly around Hersonisos.

IRAKLIO ΗΡΑΚΛΕΙΟ
pop 133,012

The Cretan capital of Iraklio (ee-*rah*-klee-oh) is a bustling modern city and the fifth largest in Greece. It doesn't captivate and seduce in the same way that Hania and Rethymno do, nor does it have the quaint postcard prettiness of its Lasithi province

partner Agios Nikolaos. Iraklio is nonetheless a dynamic lived-in city with a lively throbbing city centre, chic boutiques, quality restaurants, buzzing, student-filled cafés and a port that sees a constant procession of boats departing and arriving. Overhead, charter jets buzz the city in what seems like every few minutes, ferrying the thousands of visitors to Crete each year and who enter the island via Iraklio. Nearby the Minoan ruins of Knossos are the major drawcard, while further inland bucolic vistas of hillsides full of olive trees and vines predominate.

History

The Arabs who ruled Crete from AD 824 to 961 were the first people to govern from the site of modern Iraklio. It was known then as El Khandak, after the moat that surrounded the town, and was reputedly the slave-trade capital of the eastern Mediterranean.

El Khandak became Khandakos after Byzantine troops finally dislodged the Arabs, and then Candia under the Venetians who ruled the island for more than 400 years. While the Turks quickly overran the Venetian defences at Hania and Rethymno, Candia's fortifications proved as effective as they looked – an unusual combination. They withstood a siege of 21 years before the garrison finally surrendered in 1669.

Hania became the capital of independent Crete at the end of Turkish rule in 1898, and Candia was renamed Iraklio. Because of its central location, Iraklio became a commercial centre, and resumed its position as the island's administrative centre in 1971.

The city suffered badly in WWII, when most of the old Venetian and Turkish town was destroyed by bombing.

Orientation

Iraklio's two main squares are Plateia Venizelou and Plateia Eleftherias. Plateia Venizelou, instantly recognisable by its famous Morosini Fountain (better known as the Lion Fountain), is the heart of Iraklio. The city's major intersection is a few steps south of the square. From here, 25 Avgoustou runs northeast to the harbour; Dikeosynis runs southeast to Plateia Eleftherias; Kalokerinou runs west to the Hania Gate; 1866 (the market street) runs south; and 1821 runs to the southwest.

IRAKLIO

0 _____ 200 m
0 _____ 0.1 miles

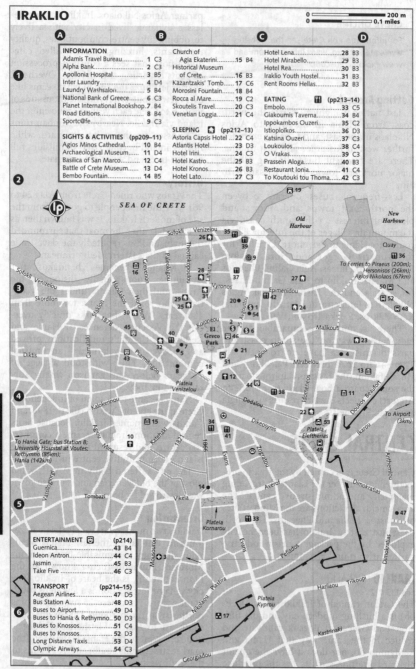

INFORMATION
Adamis Travel Bureau	1 C3
Alpha Bank	2 C3
Apollonia Hospital	3 B5
Inter Laundry	4 D4
Laundry Washsalon	5 B4
National Bank of Greece	6 C3
Planet International Bookshop	7 B4
Road Editions	8 B4
Sportc@fe	9 C3

SIGHTS & ACTIVITIES (pp209–11)
Agios Minos Cathedral	10 B4
Archaeological Museum	11 D4
Basilica of San Marco	12 C4
Battle of Crete Museum	13 D4
Bembo Fountain	14 B5

Church of Agia Ekaterini	15 B4
Historical Museum of Crete	16 B3
Kazantzakis' Tomb	17 C6
Morosini Fountain	18 B4
Rocca al Mare	19 C2
Skoutelis Travel	20 C3
Venetian Loggia	21 C4

SLEEPING (pp212–13)
Astoria Capsis Hotel	22 C4
Atlantis Hotel	23 D3
Hotel Irini	24 C3
Hotel Kastro	25 B3
Hotel Kronos	26 B3
Hotel Lato	27 C3

Hotel Lena	28 B3
Hotel Mirabello	29 B3
Hotel Rea	30 B3
Iraklio Youth Hostel	31 B3
Rent Rooms Hellas	32 B3

EATING (pp213–14)
Embolo	33 C5
Giakoumis Taverna	34 B4
Ippokambos Ouzeri	35 C2
Istioploïkos	36 D3
Katsina Ouzeri	37 C3
Loukoulos	38 C4
O Vrakas	39 C3
Prassein Aloga	40 B3
Restaurant Ionia	41 C4
To Koutouki tou Thoma	42 C3

ENTERTAINMENT (p214)
Guernica	43 B4
Ideon Antron	44 C4
Jasmin	45 B3
Take Five	46 C3

TRANSPORT (pp214–15)
Aegean Airlines	47 D5
Bus Station A	48 D3
Buses to Airport	49 D4
Buses to Hania & Rethymno	50 D3
Buses to Knossos	51 C4
Buses to Knossos	52 D3
Long Distance Taxis	53 D4
Olympic Airways	54 C3

SEA OF CRETE

Old Harbour

New Harbour

Quay

To Ferries to Piraeus (200m);
Hersonisos (26km);
Agios Nikolaos (67km)

To Airport (3km)

To Hania Gate; Bus Station B;
University Hospital at Voutes;
Rethymno (85km);
Hania (142km)

El Greco Park

Plateia Venizelou

Plateia Eleftherias

Plateia Kornarou

Plateia Kyprou

CRETE

The ferry port is 500m to the east of the old port. In between the two is Iraklio's main bus station (Bus Station A) and across the road a separate bus station for buses to Hania and Rethymno. Station B, just beyond the Hania Gate, serves Phaestos, Agia Galini and Matala. Iraklio's airport is 3km to the east of the city centre.

Information

BOOKSHOPS
Planet International Bookshop (☎ 2810 281 558; cnr Hortatson & Kydonias) Stocks most of the books recommended in this guide and has a good selection of Lonely Planet titles.
Road Editions (☎ 2810 344 610; Handakos 29) The best selection of maps in Iraklio as well as a broad range of Lonely Planet titles.

EMERGENCY
Apollonia Hospital (☎ 2810 229 713; Mousourou) Inside the old walls.
University Hospital (☎ 2810 392 111; Voutes) Located 5km south of Iraklio; the city's best-equipped medical facility.

INTERNET ACCESS
Sportc@fe (cnr 25 Avgoustou & Zotou; €2 per hr; ☻ 24 hr) Usually packed with PC gaming junkies, but machines are available for regular Internet sessions too.

LAUNDRY
There are two self-service laundrettes; both charge €6 for a wash and dry:
Inter Laundry (Mirabelou 25)
Laundry Washsalon (Handakos 18)

LEFT LUGGAGE
There are at least four handy options:
Bus Station A Left-Luggage Office (€1 per day; ☻ 6.30am-7.30pm)
Heraklion Airport Luggage Service (☎ 2810 397 349; €3.50 per day; ☻ 7.30am-11pm) Near the local bus stop.
Laundry Washsalon (Handakos 18; €1.50 per day)
Youth Hostel (Vyronos 5; €1.50 per day)

MONEY
Most of the city's banks are on 25 Avgoustou, including the **National Bank of Greece** (25 Avgoustou 35). It has a 24-hour automatic exchange machine, as does the **Alpha Bank** (25 Avgoustou 94). There is an exchange office at Bus Station A. American Express is represented by **Adamis Travel Bureau** (☎ 2810 346

202; 25 Avgoustou 23; ☻ 8am-2pm Mon-Sat). There is an ATM and exchange office in the arrivals concourse at Iraklio's airport.

POST
Central post office (Plateia Daskalogianni; ☻ 7.30am-8pm Mon-Fri, 7.30am-2pm Sat).
Mobile post office (El Greco Park; ☻ 8am-6pm Mon-Fri, 8am-1.30pm Sat Jun-Aug) Just north of Plateia Venizelou.

TOURIST INFORMATION
There is no longer an official tourist office in Iraklio but there is a useful and handy KTEL bus association tourist office inside the main Bus Station A where you will find details on local tours including the popular Samaria Gorge trek (for more information, see p244).

There's also a **tourist police office** (☎ 2810 283 190; Dikeosynis 10; ☻ 7am-11pm).

Sights
ARCHAEOLOGICAL MUSEUM
Second in size and importance only to the National Archaeological Museum in Athens, this outstanding **museum** (☎ 2810 226 092; Xanthoudidou; admission €6; ☻ 8am-7pm Tue-Sun, 12.30-7pm Mon early Apr–late Oct, 8am-5pm Tue-Sun, 12.30-5pm Mon late Oct–early Apr) is just north of Plateia Eleftherias. If you are seriously interested in the Minoans you will want more than one visit, but even a fairly superficial perusal of the contents requires half a day.

The exhibits are arranged in chronological order and include pottery, jewellery, figurines and sarcophagi as well as some famous frescoes, mostly from Knossos and Agia Triada. All testify to the remarkable imagination and advanced skills of the Minoans. Unfortunately, the exhibits are not very well explained. If they were, there would be no need to part with €6.50 for a copy of the glossy illustrated museum guide.

Room 1 is devoted to the Neolithic and Early Minoan periods. Room 2 has a collection from the Middle Minoan period. Among the most fascinating exhibits here are the tiny glazed reliefs of Minoan houses from Knossos.

Room 3 covers the same period with finds from Phaestos, including the famous **Phaestos disc**. The symbols inscribed on the disc have not been deciphered. Here also are the famous **Kamares pottery vases**, named after the sacred cave of Kamares where the pottery was first discovered. The four large vases in case 43 were part of a royal banquet set. They are of exceptional quality and are some of the finest examples of Kamares pottery.

Exhibits in Room 4 are also from the Middle Minoan period. Most striking is the 20cm black stone **Bull's Head**, which was a libation vessel. The bull has a fine head of curls, from which sprout horns of gold. The eyes of painted crystal are extremely lifelike. Also in this room are relics from a shrine at Knossos, including two fine figurines of **snake goddesses**. Snakes symbolised immortality for the Minoans.

Pottery, bronze figurines and seals are some of the exhibits displayed in Room 5. These include vases imported from Egypt and some Linear A and B tablets (see the boxed text below). The inscriptions on the tablets displayed here have been translated as household or business accounts from the palace at Knossos.

Room 6 is devoted to finds from Minoan cemeteries. Especially intriguing are two small clay models of grouped figures which were found in a tholos (Mycenaean tomb shaped like a beehive). One depicts four male dancers in a circle, their arms around each other's shoulders, possibly participating in a funeral ritual. The other model depicts two groups of three figures in a room flanked by two columns. Each group features two large seated figures being offered libations by a smaller figure. It is not known whether the large figures represent gods or departed mortals. On a more grisly level, there is a display of the bones of a horse sacrificed as part of Minoan worship.

Finds in Room 7 include the beautiful **bee pendant** found at Malia. It's a remarkably fine piece of gold jewellery depicting two bees dropping honey into a comb. Also in this room are the three celebrated vases from Agia Triada. The **Harvester Vase**, of which only the top part remains, depicts a light-hearted scene of young farm workers returning from olive picking. The **Boxer Vase** depicts Minoans indulging in two of their favourite pastimes – wrestling and bull grappling. The **Chieftain Cup** depicts a more cryptic scene: a chief holding a staff and three men carrying animal skins.

Room 8 holds finds from the palace at Zakros. Don't miss the gorgeous little crystal vase which was found in over 300 pieces and was painstakingly reconstructed by museum staff.

LINEAR B SCRIPT

The methodical decipherment of the Linear B script by English architect and part-time linguist Michael Ventris was the first tangible evidence that the Greek language had a recorded history longer than any scholar had previously believed. The decipherment demonstrated that the language disguised by these mysterious scribblings was an archaic form of Greek 500 years older than the Ionic Greek used by Homer.

Linear B was written on clay tablets that lay undisturbed for centuries until they were unearthed at Knossos in Crete. Further clay tablets were unearthed later on the mainland at Mycenae, Tiryns and Pylos on the Peloponnese and at Thebes (Thiva) in Boeotia in Central Greece.

The clay tablets, found to be mainly inventories and records of commercial transactions, consist of about 90 different signs and date from the 14th to the 13th centuries BC. Little of the social and political life of these times can be deduced from the tablets, though there is enough to give a glimpse of a fairly complex and well-organised commercial structure.

For linguists, the script did not provide a detailed image of the actual language spoken, since the symbols were used primarily as syllabic clusters designed to give an approximation of the pronunciation of the underlying language. Typically, the syllabic cluster 'A-re-ka-sa-da-ra' is the woman's name Alexandra, but the exact pronunciation remains unknown.

Importantly, what is clear is that the language is undeniably Greek, thus giving the modern-day Greek language the second-longest recorded written history, after Chinese. The language of an earlier script, Linear A, remains to this day undeciphered. It is believed to be of either Anatolian or Semitic origin, though even this remains pure conjecture.

Room 10 covers the post-palatial period (1350–1100 BC) when the Minoan civilisation was in decline and being overtaken by the warrior-like Mycenaeans. Nevertheless, there are still some fine exhibits, including a child (headless) on a swing.

Room 13 is devoted to Minoan sarcophagi. However, the most famous and spectacular of these, the **sarcophagus from Agia Triada**, is upstairs in Room 14 (the Hall of Frescoes). This stone coffin, painted with floral and abstract designs and ritual scenes, is regarded as one of the supreme examples of Minoan art.

The most famous of the Minoan frescoes are also displayed in Room 14. Frescoes from Knossos include the **Procession Fresco**, the **Griffin Fresco** (from the Throne Room), the **Dolphin Fresco** (from the Queen's Room) and the amazing **Bull-Leaping Fresco**, which depicts a seemingly double-jointed acrobat somersaulting on the back of a charging bull. Other frescoes here include the two lovely **Frescoes of the Lilies** from Amisos and fragments of frescoes from Agia Triada. More frescoes can be seen in Rooms 15 and 16. In Room 16 there is a large wooden model of Knossos.

HISTORICAL MUSEUM OF CRETE

A fascinating range of bits and pieces from Crete's more recent past is housed in this **museum** (☎ 2810 283 219; Lysimahou Kalokerinou 7; admission €3; ☺ 9am-5pm Mon-Fri, 9am-2pm Sat summer, 9am-3pm Mon-Sat winter), just back from the waterfront. The ground floor covers the period from Byzantine to Turkish rule, with plans, charts, photographs, ceramics and maps. On the 1st floor is the only **El Greco painting** on display in Crete (Domenikos Theotokopoulos, otherwise known as El Greco, was born in Iraklio). Other rooms contain fragments of 13th- and 14th-century frescoes, coins, jewellery, liturgical ornaments and vestments, and medieval pottery.

The 2nd floor has a reconstruction of the **library of author Nikos Kazantzakis**, with displays of his letters, manuscripts and books. Another room is devoted to Emmanouil Tsouderos, who was born in Rethymno and who was prime minister of Greece in 1941. There are some dramatic photographs of a ruined Iraklio in the **Battle of Crete** section. On the 3rd floor there is an outstanding **folklore collection**.

OTHER ATTRACTIONS

Iraklio burst its **city walls** long ago but these massive fortifications, with seven bastions and four gates, are still very conspicuous, dwarfing the concrete structures of the 20th century. Venetians built the defences between 1462 and 1562. At the end of the Old Harbour's jetty is another Venetian fortress, the 16th-century **Rocca al Mare** (☎ 2810 246 211; Old Harbour; admission €2; ☺ 8am-6pm Mon-Sat, 10am-3pm Sun).

Several other notable vestiges from Venetian times survive in the city. Most famous is the **Morosini Fountain** (Plateia Venizelou). The fountain, built in 1628, was commissioned by Francesco Morosini, the governor of Crete. Opposite is the three-aisled, 13th-century **Basilica of San Marco**. It has been reconstructed many times and is now an exhibition gallery. A little north of here is the attractively reconstructed 17th-century **Venetian loggia**. It was a Venetian version of a gentleman's club where the male aristocracy came to drink and gossip.

The very delightful **Bembo Fountain**, at the southern end of 1866, is shown on local maps as the Turkish Fountain, but it was actually built by the Venetians in the 16th century. It was constructed from a hotchpotch of building materials including, among other things, an ancient statue. The ornate edifice next to the fountain was added by the Turks, and now functions as a snack bar.

The former Church of Agia Ekaterini, located next to Agios Minos Cathedral, is now a **museum** (☎ 2810 288 825; Monis Odigitrias; admission €2; ☺ 9am-1.30pm Mon-Sat, 5-8pm Tue, Thu & Fri). It houses an very impressive collection of icons, most notably those painted by Mihail Damaskinos, the mentor of El Greco.

The **Battle of Crete Museum** (cnr Doukos Beaufort & Hatzidaki; admission free; ☺ 9am-1pm) chronicles this historic battle through photographs, letters, uniforms and weapons.

You can pay homage to Crete's most acclaimed contemporary writer, Nikos Kazantzakis (1883–1957; see the boxed text p212), by visiting his **tomb** at the Martinenga Bastion (the best-preserved bastion) in the southern part of town. The epitaph on his grave, 'I hope for nothing, I fear nothing, I am free', is taken from one of his works.

CRETE

NIKOS KAZANTZAKIS – CRETE'S PRODIGAL SON

Crete's most famous contemporary literary son is Nikos Kazantzakis. Born in 1883 in Iraklio, the then Turkish-dominated capital city of Crete, Kazantzakis spent his early childhood in the ferment of revolution and change that was creeping upon his homeland. In 1897 the revolution against Turkish rule finally broke out and forced him to leave Crete for studies in Naxos, Athens and later Paris. It wasn't until he was 31, in 1914, that he finally turned his hand to writing by translating philosophical books into Greek. For a number of years he travelled throughout Europe – Switzerland, Germany, Austria, Russia and Britain – thus laying the groundwork for a series of travelogues in his later literary career.

Nikos Kazantzakis was a complex writer and his early work was heavily influenced by the prevailing philosophical ideas of the time. The nihilistic philosophies of Nietzsche influenced his writings through which he is tormented by a tangible metaphysical and existential anguish. His relationship with religion was always troubling – his official stance being that of a nonbeliever, yet he always seemed to toy with the idea that perhaps God did exist. His self-professed greatest work is his *Odyssey*, a modern-day epic loosely based on the trials and travels of the ancient hero Odysseus (Ulysses). A weighty and complex opus of 33,333 seventeen-syllable iambic verses, *Odyssey* never fully vindicated Kazantzakis' aspirations to be held in the same league as the Ancient Greeks' Homer, the Romans' Virgil or the Renaissance Italians' Tasso.

Ironically it was much later in his career where Kazantzakis belatedly turned to novel writing that his star finally shone. It was through works like *Christ Recrucified* (1948), *Kapetan Mihalis* (1950) and *The Life and Manners of Alexis Zorbas* (1946) that he became internationally known. This last work gave rise to the image of the ultimate, modern Greek male 'Zorba the Greek', immortalised in the Anthony Quinn and Melina Mercouri movie of the same name, and countless restaurants throughout Crete and Greece in general.

Kazantzakis died in Freiburg, Germany on 26 October 1957 while on yet one more of his many travels. Despite resistance from the Orthodox Church, he was given a religious funeral and buried in the southernmost bastion of the old walls of Iraklio. Among the writer's more optimistic quotes is: 'Happy is the man who before dying has the good fortune to travel the Aegean Seas. Nowhere else can one pass so easily from reality to the dream'.

Tours

Iraklio's travel agents run coach tours the length and breadth of Crete. **Skoutelis Travel** (☎ 2810 280 808; 25 Avgoustou 20) is a good place to start as it does airline and ferry bookings as well car hire.

Sleeping

BUDGET

There's a reasonable range of quality backpacker accommodation in the city centre. The nearest camping grounds are 26km east of Iraklio at Hersonisos.

Iraklio Youth Hostel (☎ 2810 286 281; fax 2810 222 947; Vyronos 5; dm €9) This Greek Youth Hostel Organisation establishment is rather scruffy and rundown, but it's the cheapest option. The dorms are single-sex and the rooms are basic. Luggage storage is available for €1.50 per piece and breakfast and meals are available in the ground floor café.

Rent Rooms Hellas (☎ 2810 288 851; fax 2810 284 442; Handakos 24; dm/d €9/25) Many travellers enjoy the lively atmosphere at this de facto youth hostel which has a roof garden and a bar. Bathrooms are all shared. Luggage storage is free.

Hotel Rea (☎ 2810 223 638; hotelrheheraklion@ mail.gr; Kalimeraki-Handakos; s/d €25/30) Popular with a wide range of backpackers Rhea has an easy, friendly atmosphere. Rooms all have fans and sinks, though bathrooms are shared. There's a small communal kitchen for guests' breakfasts.

Hotel Mirabello (☎ 2810 285 052; www.mirabello -hotel.gr; Theotokopoulou 20; s/d €38/46; ✷) One of the most pleasant budget hotels in Iraklio is the relaxed Mirabello on a quiet street in the centre of town. The rooms are immaculate.

Hotel Lena (☎ 2810 223 280; www.lena-hotel.gr; Lahana 10; s/d without bathroom €30/40; ✷) Renovated extensively in 2003, Hotel Lena has comfortable, airy rooms with phones and double-glazed windows. Rooms with bathroom are also available.

MID-RANGE & TOP END

Iraklio's hotels in this range are all modern and most have been refurbished in recent years. Breakfast is normally included in the room rates.

Hotel Kronos (☎ 2810 282 240; www.kronoshotel.gr; Sofokli Venizelou 2; s/d €38/44; 🗙) This waterfront hotel, which has large rooms in excellent condition, is one of the better-value C-class hostelries. Ask for one of the 12 sea-view rooms.

Hotel Irini (☎ 2810 226 561; fax 2810 226 407; Idomeneos 4; s/d €49.50/56; 🗙) Close to the old harbour, Irini is a modern establishment with 59 large, airy rooms with TV, radio and telephone.

Hotel Kastro (☎ 2810 284 185; fax 2810 223 622; www.kastro-hotel.gr; Theotokopoulou 22; s/d €80/95; 🗙 🖳) A modern, cheery B-class hotel in the back streets, the Kastro is an excellent choice. The large rooms have fridges, TV, phones and ISDN Internet connectivity.

Hotel Lato (☎ 2810 228 103; www.lato.gr; Epimenidou 15; s/d incl breakfast €105/134; 🗙) Occupying a prominent position overlooking the old and new harbours, Lato is one of Iraklio's prime hotels. Refurbished fully in recent times, the hotel is swish and modern and most rooms have spectacular views: the penthouse suite has the best view in the city.

Atlantis Hotel (☎ 2810 229 103; www.grandhotel.gr; Ygias 2; s/d with buffet breakfast €129/144; 🗙 🖳) This A-class hotel, functioning also as a busy conference centre, offers comfortable, lavishly equipped rooms. Facilities include a health studio and sauna.

Astoria Capsis Hotel (☎ 2810 343 080; www .astoriacapsis.gr; Plateia Eleftherias 11; s/d €123/158; 🖳 🖳) This city centre A-class hotel is another top choice. Facilities include a snack bar and restaurant. A modern cinema is part of the same complex.

Eating
BUDGET

Iraklio has some excellent restaurants, and there's something to suit all tastes and budgets.

Giakoumis Taverna (☎ 2810 280 277; Theodosaki 5-8; mayirefta €2.50-5; closed Sun) Theodosaki is lined with tavernas catering to the market on 1866 and this is one of the best. There's a full menu of Cretan specialities and turnover is heavy which means that the dishes are freshly cooked.

To Koutouki tou Thoma (☎ 2810 330 533; Epimenidou 4; mains €3-5) Tucked away in a side street off 25 Avgoustou is this almost hole-in-the-wall. It's not flash, it's unassuming but the food is good and cheap. The large and filling mousakas are particularly commendable.

Restaurant Ionia (☎ 2810 283 213; Evans 3; mayirefta €3-5; closed Sun) This is the place for tasty Cretan home cooking. Choose your meal from the many pots and pans of *mayirefta* (ready-cooked meals) that are on display.

O Vrakas (☎ 6977 893 973; Plateia Anglon; mains €3-5.50) Vrakas is a small street-side ouzeri that grills fresh fish al fresco in front of the diners. It's reasonably priced and unassuming and the menu is limited, but still very popular with locals. Grilled octopus with ouzo is a delicious choice.

Katsina Ouzeri (☎ 2810 221 027; Marineli 12; mezedes €2-4.50; 🕙 dinner only, closed Mon) This is an old neighbourhood favourite. Most people come for the lamb and pork roasted in a brick oven or the excellent stewed goat.

Ippokambos Ouzeri (☎ 2810 280 240; Mitsotaki 2; mains €3.50-6) This place is as good as taverna–style eating gets. The interior is attractively decorated with cooking pots but most people prefer to squeeze onto one of the street-side tables or on the promenade across the road.

Istioploïkos (☎ 2810 228 118; Limani; fish mezedes €3-10) Housed in the huge ex-cold-store warehouses on the harbour this very low-key fish taverna belongs to the Iraklio sailing club. Fish and fish mezedes are what this busy taverna is all about and it does them well. Bookings recommended in summer.

Prassein Aloga (☎ 2810 283 429; cnr Handakos & Kydonias 21; mains €3-6) Blink and you might miss this minuscule little rustic-style café-restaurant and its associated delicatessen opposite. Taste good, generic Mediterranean food from an ever-changing menu. Good spot for lunch.

MID-RANGE & TOP END

Loukoulos (☎ 2810 224 435; Koraï 5; grills €13-16; 🕙 noon-3pm & 7pm-midnight Mon-Sat) Loukoulos offers luscious Mediterranean specialities. You can either choose the elegant interior or dine on the outdoor terrace under a lemon tree. All the vegetables are organically grown and vegetarians are well catered for.

Embolo (☎ 2810 284 244; M Miliara 7; mains €6-10) Run by former musician Giannis Stavrakakis from Anogeia, Embolo dishes up the best in Cretan food – excellent grills, *pittes* (pies) and large salads. Live music is played on Thursday, Friday and Saturday.

Entertainment

Guernica (☎ 2810 282 988; Apokoronou Kritis 2; ☯ 10am-midnight) Guernica boasts traditional decor and contemporary rock which mix well to create one of Iraklio's hippest bar-cafés.

Take Five (☎ 2810 226 564; Akroleondos 7; ☯ 10am-midnight) This is an old favourite on the edge of El Greco Park that doesn't get going until after sundown when the outside tables fill up with a diverse crowd of regulars. It's a gay-friendly place, and the music and ambience are low-key.

Jasmin (☎ 2810 288 880; Handakos 45; ☯ noon-midnight) This is a friendly bar-café with a back terrace that specialises in herbal tea but also serves alcoholic beverages. The nightly DJs play rock and world music as well as techno.

Ideon Antron (☎ 2810 242 041; Perdikari 1; ☯ 10am-1am) Off trendy Koraï with its rows of postmodern kafeneia, this is a throwback to the past. The stone interior with its shiny wood bar creates a relaxed, inviting place.

Getting There & Away

AIR

Aegean Airlines Central office (☎ 2810 344 324; fax 2810 344 330; Leof Dimokratias 11) Airport office (☎ 2810 330 475)

Olympic Airways Central office (☎ 2810 229 191; 25 Avgoustou 27; ☯ 8am-3.30pm Mon-Fri) Airport office (☎ 2810 245 644)

Domestic

Olympic Airways has at least six flights daily to Athens (€73) from Iraklio's Nikos Kazantzakis airport. It also has flights to Thessaloniki (€110, three weekly) and Rhodes (€73, two weekly).

Aegean Airlines has flights to Athens (€73, three daily) and Thessaloniki (€110, two daily).

International

Olympic Airways flies to Larnaka, in Cyprus, from Iraklio (€150, two weekly). Aegean Airlines offers direct connections to Paris and one-stop connections to Cologne/Bonn, Munich, Rome and Stuttgart.

Iraklio has lots of charter flights from all over Europe. **Skoutelis Travel** (☎ 2810 280 808; 25 Avgoustou 20) is a good place to ask.

BUS

There are buses every half-hour (hourly in winter) to Rethymno (€6.20, 1½ hours) and Hania (€11, three hours) from the Rethymno/Hania bus station opposite Bus Station A. See the table for other destinations from **Bus Station A** (☎ 2810 245 020; www.ktel.org) and Bus Station B.

BUSES FROM IRAKLIO

BUSES FROM BUS STATION A

Destination	Time	€	Frequency
Agia Pelagia	45min	€2.60	5 daily
Agios Nikolaos	1½hr	€5.25	half-hourly
Hersonisos/Malia	1hr	€2.30	half-hourly
Ierapetra	2½hr	€7.85	7 daily
Lasithi Plateau	2hr	€5.25	2 daily
Sitia	3½hr	€10.50	5 daily

BUSES FROM BUS STATION B

Destination	Time	€	Frequency
Agia Galini	2½hr	€5.75	7 daily
Matala	2hr	€5.75	9 daily
Phaestos	2hr	€4.80	8 daily

FERRY

Minoan Lines (www.minoan.gr) and **ANEK Lines** (www.anek.gr) operate ferries every evening each way between Iraklio and Piraeus (10 hours). They depart from both Piraeus and Iraklio between 7.45pm and 8pm. Fares are €29.50 deck class and €50.50 for cabins. The Minoan Lines' Highspeed boats, the F/B *Festos Palace* and F/B *Knossos Palace*, are much more modern and more comfortable than their ANEK rivals.

In summer and on weekends only, Minoan Lines runs six-hour day services on F/B *Festos Palace* and F/B *Knossos Palace*, departing Iraklio and Piraeus at 12.30pm and arriving at 6.30pm. This is by far the most convenient way to get to and from Crete.

Minoan also have three ferries weekly to Thessaloniki (€41, 23 hours) via Santorini (€14, 3¾ hours) and Mykonos (€21.50, nine hours). These services also stop at Paros

(€21.50, 7½ hours) and Tinos (€22.50, 10¼ hours) twice weekly, and at Naxos (€18.50, seven hours), Syros (€20, 10 hours) and Skiathos (€34.50, 17¾ hours) once a week.

Iraklio's port police can be contacted on ☎ 2810 244 912.

TAXI

There are **long-distance taxis** (☎ 2810 210 102/210 168) from Plateia Eleftherias, opposite the Astoria Capsis Hotel and Bus Station B, to all parts of Crete. Sample fares include Agios Nikolaos (€39), Rethymno (€47) and Hania (€81). A taxi to the airport costs around €7.

Getting Around
TO/FROM THE AIRPORT
Bus No 1 goes to and from the airport every 15 minutes between 6am and 1am (€0.70). It leaves the city from near the Astoria Capsis Hotel on Plateia Eleftherias.

BUS
Bus No 2 goes to Knossos every 10 minutes from Bus Station A (€0.95, 20 minutes). It also stops on 25 Avgoustou and 1821.

CAR & MOTORCYCLE
Most of the car- and motorcycle-rental outlets are on 25 Avgoustou. You'll get the best deal from local companies like **Ritz Rent-A-Car** (☎ 2810 223 638; hotelrheheraklion@mail.gr; Hotel Rea, Kalimeraki-Handakos), which offers discounts for hotel guests. There are also many car rental outlets at the airport.

KNOSSOS ΚΝΩΣΟΣ
Knossos (k-nos-*os*), 5km from Iraklio, was the capital of Minoan Crete. Nowadays the **site** (☎ 2810 231 940; admission €6; ✆ 8am-7pm Apr-Oct, 8am-5pm Nov-Mar) is the island's major tourist attraction.

The ruins of Knossos, home of the mythical Minotaur kept by King Minos, were uncovered in 1900 by the British archaeologist Sir Arthur Evans. Heinrich Schliemann, who had earlier uncovered the ancient cities of Troy and Mycenae, had had his eye on the spot (a low, flat-topped mound), believing an ancient city was buried there, but was unable to strike a deal with the local landowner.

Evans was so enthralled by his discovery that he spent 35 years and £250,000 of his own money excavating and reconstructing sections of the palace. Some archaeologists have disparaged Evans' reconstruction, believing he sacrificed accuracy to his overly vivid imagination. However, most nonspecialists agree that Sir Arthur did a good job and that Knossos is a knockout. Without these reconstructions it would be impossible to visualise what a Minoan palace looked like.

You will need to spend about four hours at Knossos to explore it thoroughly. There is absolutely no signage, so unless you have a travel guidebook, or hire a guide, you will have no idea what you are looking at. The café at the site is expensive – you'd do better to bring a picnic along.

History
The first palace at Knossos was built around 1900 BC. In 1700 BC it was destroyed by an earthquake and rebuilt to a grander and more sophisticated design. It is this palace that Evans reconstructed. It was partially destroyed again sometime between 1500 and 1450 BC. It was inhabited for another 50 years before it was devastated once and for all by fire.

The city of Knossos consisted of an immense palace, residences of officials and priests, the homes of ordinary people, and burial grounds. The palace comprised royal domestic quarters, public reception rooms, shrines, workshops, treasuries and storerooms, all built around a central court. Like all Minoan palaces, it also doubled as a city hall, accommodating all the bureaucracy necessary for the smooth running of a complex society.

Until 1997 it was possible to enter the royal apartments, but the area was cordoned off before it disappeared altogether under the continual pounding of tourists' feet. Extensive repairs are under way but it is unlikely to open to the public again.

Exploring the Site
Numerous rooms, corridors, dogleg passages, nooks and crannies, and staircases prohibit a detailed walk-through description of the palace. However, Knossos is not a site where you'll be perplexed by heaps of rubble, trying to fathom whether you're looking at the throne room or a workshop. Thanks to Evans' reconstruction, the most

CRETE

significant parts of the complex are instantly recognisable (if not instantly found). On your wanders you will come across many of Evans' reconstructed columns, most painted deep brown-red with gold-trimmed black capitals. Like all Minoan columns, they taper at the bottom.

It is not only the vibrant frescoes and mighty columns which impress at Knossos; keep your eyes open for the little details which are evidence of a highly sophisticated society. Things to look out for include the drainage system, the placement of light wells, and the relationship of rooms to passages, porches, light wells and verandas, which kept rooms cool in summer and warm in winter.

The usual entrance to the palace complex is across the **Western Court** and along the **Corridor of the Procession Fresco**. The fresco depicted a long line of people carrying gifts to present to the king; unfortunately only fragments remain. A copy of one of these fragments, called the **Priest King Fresco**, can be seen to the south of the Central Court.

If you leave the Corridor of the Procession Fresco and walk straight ahead to enter the site from the northern end, you will come to the **Theatral Area**, a series of steps, the function of which remains unknown. The area could have been a theatre where spectators watched acrobatic and dance performances, or the place where people gathered to welcome important visitors arriving by the Royal Road.

The **Royal Road** leads off to the west. The road, Europe's first (Knossos has lots of firsts), was flanked by workshops and the houses of ordinary people. The **Lustral Basin** is also in this area. Evans speculated that this was where the Minoans performed a ritual cleansing with water before religious ceremonies.

Entering the **Central Court** from the north, you pass the relief **Bull Fresco** which depicts a charging bull. Relief frescoes were made by moulding wet plaster, and then painting it while still wet.

Also worth seeking out in the northern section of the palace are the **Giant Pithoi**. Pithoi were large ceramic jars used for

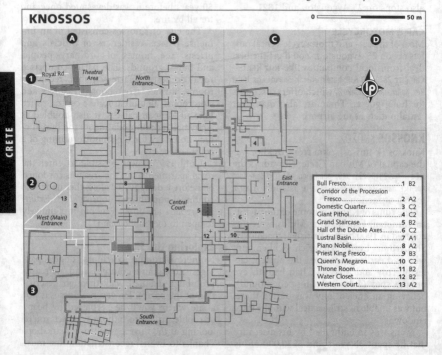

KNOSSOS

0 ———— 50 m

Bull Fresco	1	B2
Corridor of the Procession Fresco	2	A2
Domestic Quarter	3	C2
Giant Pithoi	4	C2
Grand Staircase	5	B2
Hall of the Double Axes	6	C2
Lustral Basin	7	A1
Piano Nobile	8	A2
Priest King Fresco	9	B3
Queen's Megaron	10	C2
Throne Room	11	B2
Water Closet	12	B2
Western Court	13	A2

storing olive oil, wine and grain. Evans found over 100 of these huge jars at Knossos, some 2m high. The ropes used to move them inspired the raised patterns decorating the jars.

Once you have reached the Central Court, which in Minoan times was surrounded by the high walls of the palace, you can begin exploring the most important rooms of the complex.

From the northern end of the west side of the Central Court, steps lead down to the **Throne Room**. This room is fenced off but you can still get a pretty good view of it. The centrepiece, the simple, beautifully proportioned throne, is flanked by the **Griffin Fresco**. (Griffins were mythical beasts regarded as sacred by the ancient Minoans.) The room is thought to have been a shrine, and the throne the seat of a high priestess, rather than a king. The Minoans did not worship their deities in great temples but in small shrines, and each palace had several.

On the 1st floor of the west side of the palace is the section Evans called the **Piano Nobile**, for he believed the reception and state rooms were here. A room at the northern end of this floor displays copies of some of the frescoes found at Knossos.

Returning to the Central Court, the impressive **Grand Staircase** leads from the middle of the eastern side of the palace to the royal apartments, which Evans called the **Domestic Quarter**. This section of the site is now cordoned off and is off limits to visitors. Within the royal apartments is the **Hall of the Double Axes**. This was the king's megaron, a spacious double room in which the ruler both slept and carried out certain court duties. The room had a light well at one end and a balcony at the other to ensure air circulation.

The room takes its name from the double axe marks on its light well. These marks appear in many places at Knossos. The double axe was a sacred symbol to the Minoans. *Labrys* was Minoan for 'double axe' and the origin of our word 'labyrinth'.

A passage leads from the Hall of the Double Axes to the **Queen's Megaron**. Above the door is a copy of the **Dolphin Fresco**, one of the most exquisite Minoan artworks, and a blue floral design decorates the portal. Next to this room is the queen's bathroom,

complete with terracotta bathtub and **water closet**, touted as the first ever to work on the flush principle; water was poured down by hand.

Getting There & Away

Regular buses operate from Iraklio. See Iraklio's Getting Around section (p215) for details.

GORTYNA ΓΟΡΤΥΝΑ

Conveniently, Crete's three other major archaeological sites lie close to each other forming a rough triangle some 50km south of Iraklio. It's best to visit them all together.

Lying 46km southwest of Iraklio, and 15km from Phaestos, on the plain of Mesara, is the archaeological site of **Gortyna** (Gortys; ☎ 2892 031 144; admission €4; ☼ 8am-7pm), pronounced *gor*-tih-nah. It's a vast and wonderfully intriguing site with bits and pieces from various ages strewn all over the place. The site was a settlement from Minoan to Christian times. In Roman times, Gortyna was the capital of the province of Cyrenaica.

The most significant find at the site was the massive stone tablets inscribed with the **Laws of Gortyna**, dating from the 5th century BC. The laws deal with just about every imaginable offence. The tablets are on display at the site.

The 6th-century **Basilica** is dedicated to Agios Titos, a protégé of St Paul and the first bishop of Crete.

Other ruins at Gortyna include the 2nd-century AD **Praetorium**, which was the residence of the governor of the province, a **Nymphaeum**, and the **Temple of Pythian Apollo**. The ruins are on both sides of the main Iraklio–Phaestos road.

PHAESTOS ΦΑΙΣΤΟΣ

The Minoan site of **Phaestos** (☎ 2982 042 315; admission €4; ☼ 8am-7pm May-Oct , 8am-5pm Nov-Apr), 63km from Iraklio, was the second most important palace city of Minoan Crete. Of all the Minoan sites, Phaestos (fes-*tos*) has the most awe-inspiring location, with all-embracing views of the Mesara Plain and Mt Ida. The layout of the palace is identical to Knossos, with rooms arranged around a central court.

In contrast to Knossos, the palace at Phaestos has yielded very few frescoes. It seems the palace walls were mostly covered with a layer of white gypsum. Evans didn't get his hands on the ruins of Phaestos, so there has been no reconstruction. Like the other palatial period complexes, there was an old palace here which was destroyed at the end of the Middle Minoan period. Unlike the other sites, parts of this old palace have been excavated and its ruins are partially super-imposed upon the new palace.

The entrance to the new palace is by the 15m-wide **Grand Staircase**. The stairs lead to the west side of the **Central Court**. The best-preserved parts of the palace complex are the reception rooms and private apartments to the north of the Central Court; excavations continue here. This section was entered by an imposing portal with half columns at either side, the lower parts of which are still in situ. Unlike the Minoan freestanding columns, these do not taper at the base. The celebrated Phaestos disc was found in a building to the north of the palace. The disc is in Iraklio's Archaeological Museum (p209).

Getting There & Away

There are buses to Phaestos from Iraklio's Bus Station B (€5.05, 1½ hours, eight daily). There are also buses from Agia Galini (€2, 40 minutes, six daily) and Matala (€1.35, 30 minutes, five daily). Services are halved from December to February.

AGIA TRIADA ΑΓΙΑ ΤΡΙΑΔΑ

Pronounced ah-*yee*-ah trih-*ah*-dha, **Agia Triada** (☎ 2892 091 564; admission €3; ☼ 8.30am-3pm) is a small Minoan site 3km west of Phaestos. Its principal building was smaller than the other royal palaces but built to a similar design. This, and the opulence of the objects found at the site, indicate that it was a royal residence, possibly a summer palace of Phaestos' rulers. To the north of the palace is a small town where remains of a *stoa* (long colonnaded building) have been unearthed.

Finds from the palace, now in Iraklio's Archaeological Museum, include a sarcophagus, two superlative frescoes and three vases: the Harvester Vase, Boxer Vase and Chieftain Cup.

The road to Agia Triada takes off to the right about 500m from Phaestos on the road to Matala. There is no public transport

to the site, although it is possible to catch a local cab from Phaestos, or even walk.

MATALA ΜΑΤΑΛΑ

pop 300

Matala (*mah*-tah-lah), on the coast 11km southwest of Phaestos, was once one of Crete's best-known hippie hang-outs. These days, Matala is a decidedly tacky tourist resort packed out in summer and bleak and deserted in winter. The sandy beach below the caves is, however, one of Crete's best, and the resort is a convenient base from which to visit Phaestos and Agia Triada.

It was the old **Roman Cemetery** (admission €2) situated at the northern end of the beach that made Matala famous in the 1960s. There are dozens of caves dotted over the cliff face. They were originally tombs, cut out of the sandstone rock in the 1st century AD. In the 1960s, they were discovered by irreverent hippies, who turned the caves into a modern troglodyte city – moving ever higher up the cliff to avoid sporadic attempts by the local police to evict them.

Orientation & Information

Matala's layout is easy to fathom. The bus stop is on the central square, one block back from the waterfront. There is a mobile post office near the beach. There are three ATMs in the village and you can change money at **Monza Travel** (☎ 2892 045 757). Check email at **Zafiria Internet** (☎ 2892 045 498; ☼ 10am-11pm; €4.50 per hr).

Sleeping & Eating

Matala Community Camping (☎ /fax 2892 045 340; camp sites per adult/tent €3.90/2.80) This is a reasonable, shaded, though rather uneven, site just back from the beach.

There is plenty of budget traveller accommodation in the village. The street running at right angles inland from the Hotel Zafiria is literally bristling with them. Among the myriad choices **Fantastic Rooms to Rent** (☎ 2892 045 362; fax 2892 045 292; d/tr €20/25) is one of the cheapest accommodation options along the street. The rooms are comfortable enough and each have their own bathroom.

Across the road, **Pension Antonios** (☎ 2892 045 123; fax 2892 045 690; s/d €13/19, apt €25/29) has attractively furnished rooms and apartments.

Hotel Zafiria (☎ 2892 045 366; fax 2892 045 725; s/d incl breakfast €35/46; ⊠ P) is a sprawling hotel that takes up a good portion of the northern stretch of Matala's main street. At the hotel there is a spacious lobby-bar and rooms have balconies, sea views, and telephones.

Eating in Matala is not an experience in haute cuisine, but there are plenty of choices of fairly nondescript options. About the only place worth a mention is at **Nikos** (☎ 2892 045 335; mains €4-6), which garners most of its brownie points from its position on the beach next to the Roman cemetery. The food at Nikos is a notch above that of the remaining bland and under-inspiring tourist joints scattered along the main drag.

Getting There & Away
There are buses between Iraklio and Matala (€5.75, two hours, nine daily), and between Matala and Phaestos (€1.35, 30 minutes, five daily).

MALIA ΜΑΛΙΑ
The Minoan site of **Malia** (☎ 2897 031 597; admission €4; ⏲ 8.30am-3pm), 3km east of the resort of Malia, is the only cultural diversion on the stretch of coast east of Iraklio, which otherwise has surrendered lock, stock and barrel to the package-tourist industry. Malia is smaller than Knossos and Phaestos but, like them, consisted of a palace complex and a town. Unlike Knossos and Phaestos, the palace was built on a flat, fertile plain, not on a hill.

Entrance to the ruins is from the **West Court**. At the extreme southern end of this court there are eight circular pits which archaeologists think were used to store grain. To the east of the pits is the main entrance to the palace which leads to the southern end of the **Central Court**. At the southwest corner of this court you will find the **Kernos Stone**, a disc with 34 holes around its edge. Archaeologists still don't know what it was used for.

The **Central Staircase** is at the north end of the west side of the palace. The **Loggia**, just north of the staircase, is where religious ceremonies took place.

Any bus going to or from Iraklio along the north coast can drop you at the site.

EASTERN CRETE

The eastern quarter of the island is occupied by the prefecture of Lasithi, named after the quaint plateau tucked high in the Mt Dikti Ranges rather than its busy administrative capital of Agios Nikolaos, which is becoming something of a monument to package tourism. The main attractions, apart from the Lasithi Plateau, are the palm forest and beach at Vaï and the remote Minoan palace site of Zakros.

LASITHI PLATEAU ΟΡΟΠΕΔΙΟ ΛΑΣΙΘΙΟΥ
The first view of the mountain-fringed Lasithi Plateau, laid out like an immense patchwork quilt, is quite stunning. The plateau, 900m above sea level, is a vast expanse of pear and apple orchards, almond trees and fields of crops, dotted by some 7000 windmills. These are not conventional stone windmills, but slender metal constructions with white canvas sails. They were built in the 17th century to irrigate the rich farmland but few of the original windmills are now in service. Most have been replaced by less-attractive mechanical pumps.

There are 20 villages dotted around the periphery of the plateau, the largest of which is **Tzermiado** (pop 747), with a couple of banks with ATMs and a post office. You could easily make Tzermiado your base; the **Hotel Kourites** (☎ 2844 022 194; Tzermiado; s/d €30/35) is a fairly basic hotel on the left as you enter the village from the east side. For eating the **Taverna Kri-Kri** (☎ 2844 022 170; mains €4-5.50) on Tzermiado's main street serves simple, unfussy meals.

A better option to stay might be the relaxing village of **Agios Georgios** (pop 554) where **Hotel Maria** (☎ 2844 031 209; fax 2844 031 774; s/d €20/25) on the north side of the village is the best accommodation choice. Maria has spacious stucco rooms decorated with weavings. The plant-filled enclosed garden with its attached taverna **Merastri** (☎ 2844 031 774; mains €5-6) is a great place to unwind. Run by sisters Hara and Kallia the newish taverna serves up enticing Cretan dishes made from local produce and the grape and orange spoon sweets are divine – even if you don't have a sweet tooth.

On the main street in Agios Georgios a plainer accommodation option is the **Hotel**

Dias (☎ 2844 031 207; s/d €10/15) with clean and pleasant rooms (shared bathroom) above the restaurant of the same name. Further along the street Hara and Kallia's mother runs the **Taverna Rea** (☎ 2844 031 209; mains €4-6) opposite the school. Your best bet is to ask what specials have been home-cooked that day. All ingredients are again locally produced.

The other major village is **Psyhro** (pop 301) which is handy for the Dikteon Cave. You can stay at the **Zeus Hotel** (☎ 2844 031 284; Psyhro; s/d €23/30), a modern but rather featureless D-class hotel on the west side of the village near the start of the Dikteon Cave road. Two similar restaurants opposite each other vie for business: **Stavros** (☎ 2844 031 453; mains €3-4.50) has a neat folksy interior and serves a good range of traditional Cretan dishes such as goat in lemon and rice sauce, while **Platanos** (☎ 2844 031 668; mains €3-4.50) set under a large plane tree opposite Stavros is the other one. There's a good range of vegetable-based dishes, some of which are also cooked with snails.

The plateau's rich soil has been cultivated since Minoan times. The inaccessibility of the region made it a hotbed of insurrection during Venetian and Turkish rule. Following an uprising in the 13th century, the Venetians drove out the inhabitants of Lasithi and destroyed their orchards. The plateau lay abandoned for 200 years.

Most people come to Lasithi on coach trips, but it deserves an overnight stay. Once the package tourists have departed clutching their plastic windmill souvenirs, the villages return to pastoral serenity.

Dikteon Cave Δίκταιον Αντρον

Lasithi's major sight is **Dikteon Cave** (☎ 2844 031 316; Psyhro; admission €3; ☉ 8am-4pm), just outside the village of Psyhro. Here, according to mythology, Rhea hid the newborn Zeus from Cronos, his offspring-gobbling father. The cave, which has both stalactites and stalagmites, was excavated in 1900 by British archaeologist David Hogarth. He found numerous votive offerings, indicating the cave was a place of cult worship. These finds are housed in the Archaeological Museum in Iraklio.

It is a steep 800m walk up to the cave entrance along a fairly rough track, but you can opt to take a rather expensive donkey ride (€10) instead. There is a less obvious paved trail to the cave that starts from the left side of the carpark. It is not as well-shaded as the rougher track. Walk between the two restaurants and you will see people coming down from the paved track.

Getting There & Away

Public transport to the Dikteon Cave is problematic if you don't have your own wheels. From Agios Nikolaos there's an afternoon bus to Lasithi on Monday, Wednesday and Friday (€6.30, 2½ hours) and a morning bus from Lasithi to Agios Nikolaos also on Monday, Wednesday and Friday. From Iraklio there are two buses on weekdays to Lasithi (€5.15, two hours), and three on weekdays returning to Iraklio.

All buses go through Tzermiado and Agios Georgios before terminating at Psyhro at the foot of the road leading to Dikteon Cave.

AGIOS NIKOLAOS ΑΓΙΟΣ ΝΙΚΟΛΑΟΣ

pop 10,906

Agios Nikolaos (*ah-yee-os nih-ko-laos*) is an undeniably pretty former fishing village. Today it is one of Crete's more attractive resort destinations. Boasting a fetching combination of port, lake, narrow streets and aquamarine seas, 'Agios' attracts a lot of people. By the early 1960s, it had become a chic hideaway for the likes of Jules Dassin and Walt Disney. By the end of the decade, package tourists were arriving in force. While there is superficially little to attract the independent traveller, there is reasonable accommodation, prices are not too horrendous and there is quite a bit of activity to keep all tastes catered for.

Orientation

The **bus station** (☎ 2841 022 234) is on the western side of town about 500m from the actual town centre, Plateia Venizelou. However, the most interesting part of town and the de facto town centre is the area around the picturesque Voulismeni Lake 200m from Plateia Venizelou and ringed with touristy tavernas and cafés.

Koundourou and the parallel pedestrianised 28 Oktovriou are the two main commercial thoroughfares where you'll find most banks, ATMs, travel agents and shops. The port is about 150m north east of Voulismeni Lake.

Kato Zakros (p227), Crete

PAUL HELLANDER

ALAN BENSON

Stews at a food market, Hania (p238),
Crete

Backstreets and laneways, Hania (p238), Crete

NEIL SETCHFIELD

Olives at the food market (p240), Hania, Crete

NEIL SETCHFIELD

JOHN ELK III

Minaret in Rethymno (p231), Crete

Lakki (p244), Crete

GLENN BEANLAND

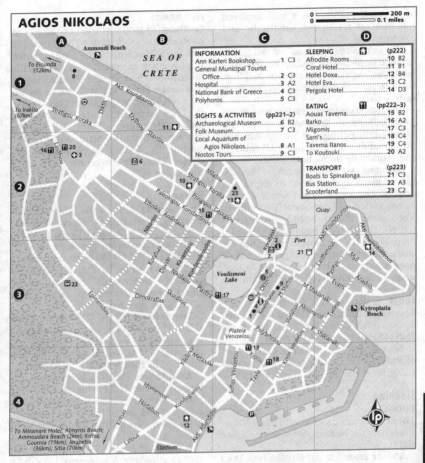

AGIOS NIKOLAOS

INFORMATION	
Ann Karteri Bookshop	1 C3
General Municipal Tourist Office	2 C3
Hospital	3 A2
National Bank of Greece	4 C3
Polyhoros	5 C3

SIGHTS & ACTIVITIES	(pp221–2)
Archaeological Museum	6 B2
Folk Museum	7 C3
Local Aquarium of Agios Nikolaos	8 A1
Nostos Tours	9 C3

SLEEPING	(p222)
Afrodite Rooms	10 B2
Coral Hotel	11 B1
Hotel Doxa	12 B4
Hotel Eva	13 C2
Pergola Hotel	14 D3

EATING	(pp222–3)
Aouas Taverna	15 B2
Barko	16 A2
Migomis	17 C3
Sarri's	18 C4
Taverna Itanos	19 C4
To Koutouki	20 A2

TRANSPORT	(p223)
Boats to Spinalonga	21 C3
Bus Station	22 A3
Scooterland	23 C2

Information

Anna Karteri Bookshop (☎ 2841 022 272; Koundourou 5) Well stocked, next to the National Bank of Greece; with maps, books in English and other languages.

General Hospital (☎ 2841 025 221; Knosou 3) On the west side of town.

Municipal Tourist Office (☎ 2841 022 357; www.forthnet.gr/internetcity/agnikola; ☼ 8am-9.30pm 1 Apr–15 Nov) Right by the bridge; changes money.

National Bank of Greece (Nikolaou Plastira) With a 24-hour automatic exchange machine.

Polyhoros (☎ 2841 024 876; 28 Oktovriou 13; €4.50 per hr; ☼ 9am-2am) For Internet access.

Post office (28 Oktovriou 9; ☼ 7.30am-2pm Mon-Fri)

Tourist police (☎ 2841 026 900; Erythrou Stavrou 47; ☼ 7.30am-2.30pm)

Sights

BEACHES

The popularity of Agios Nikolaos has little to do with its beaches. The **town beach** and **Kytroplatia Beach** are smallish and can get rather crowded.

The sandy beach at **Almyros** about 1km south of town is the best of the lot and tends to be less crowded. There's little shade but you can rent umbrellas for €2 a day. **Ammoudara Beach**, 1.5km further south along the road to Ierapetra, is a little better and has a busy restaurant and accommodation scene.

OTHER ATTRACTIONS

The **folk museum** (☎ 2841 025 093; Paleologou Konstantinou 4; admission €1; ☼ 10am-3pm Sun-Fri), next

CRETE

to the tourist office, has a well-displayed collection of traditional handicrafts and costumes.

The **archaeological museum** (☎ 2841 022 943; Paleologou Konstantinou 74; admission €2; ☺ 8.30am-3pm Tue-Sun), housed in a modern building, has a large, well-displayed collection from eastern Crete

The **Local Aquarium of Agios Nikolaos** (☎ 2841 028 030; Akti Koundourou 30; admission €4; ☺ 10am-9pm) has interesting displays of fish and information about diving (including PADI courses) and snorkelling throughout Crete.

Voulismeni Lake (Λίμνη Βουλισμένη) is the subject of many stories about its depth and origins. The locals have given it various names, including Xepatomeni (Bottomless), Voulismeni (Sunken) and Vromolimni (Dirty). The lake isn't bottomless – it is 64m deep. The 'dirty' tag came about because the lake used to be stagnant and gave off quite a pong in summer. This was rectified in 1867 when a canal was built linking it to the sea.

Tours

Travel agencies in Agios Nikolaos offer coach outings to all Crete's top attractions. **Nostos Tours** (☎ 2841 022 819; Koundourou 30) has boat trips to Spinalonga (€15) as well as guided tours of Phaestos and Matala (€30), the Samaria Gorge (€49) and the Lasithi Plateau (€34).

Sleeping

BUDGET

The nearest camping ground to Agios Nikolaos is near the Minoan site of Gournia (see p224).

Afrodite Rooms (☎ 2841 028 058; Korytsas 27; s/d €15/22) For starters these friendly rooms with mainly shared facilities and a tiny communal kitchen are a reasonable option.

Pergola Hotel (☎ 2841 028 152; fax 2841 025 568; Sarolidi 20; s/d €22/32) Rooms here are comfortable and all have fridges. There is a pleasant outdoor veranda under a pergola to relax on.

Hotel Eva (☎ 2841 022 587; Stratigou Koraka 20; s/d €24/27) A neat little place close to the centre of the action, this has smallish but quite reasonable rooms.

Hotel Doxa (☎ 2841 024 214; fax 2841 024 614; Idomeneos 7; s/d €40/55; ☒) The plant-filled lobby sets a homely tone for this hotel that also boasts an attractive terrace for breakfast or drinks. Rooms are small but inviting and are equipped with telephones, fridges and TVs.

MID-RANGE

Coral Hotel (☎ 2841 028 363; www.hermes-hotels.gr; Akti Koundourou 68; s/d €70/75; ☒ ☒) This handy and well-run B-class hotel on the northern waterfront is about as upmarket as places get in town. Rooms have satellite TV and fridges.

Miramare Hotel (☎ 2841 023 875; fax 2841 024 164; s/d €65/82; ☒ ☒ ℗) About 1km south of the town centre, Miramare Hotel has been attractively landscaped into a hillside. The skilfully decorated rooms are outfitted with satellite TV, fridges, telephones and balconies. There are also tennis courts and a fitness centre.

Eating

The lakeside restaurants, while visually tempting, all tend to be the inevitable bland tourist trap with doctored 'Greek' food. Hit the back streets for the genuine article.

Sarri's (☎ 2841 028 059; Kyprou 15; breakfast €3) Tucked away in the back streets, Sarri's is a good spot for breakfast, lunch and dinner. Check the daily changing specials board for all-in menu options.

Taverna Itanos (☎ 2841 025 340; Kyprou 1; mains €2.50-4) This is a vast place with beamed ceilings and stucco walls. It has a few tables on the pavement as well as comfortable banquettes. The food is traditional Cretan.

Aouas Taverna (☎ 2841 023 231; Paleologou Konstantinou 44; mezedes €1.80-8) This is a family-run place where dishes include such oddities as herb pies and picked bulbs. The interior is plain but the enclosed garden is refreshing and the mezedes are wonderful.

Migomis (☎ 2841 024 353; N Plastira 20; mains €5-8) Overlooking Voulismeni Lake from the high southern side, Migomis is one of the better lakeside eating places. Cuisine is Greek international and the views and ambiance are stunning. Recommended dishes are lamb chops in *mavrodaphne* (sweet dessert wine) sauce and rosemary or chicken and spinach.

Away from the tourist-oriented restaurants near the lake are a couple of 'Greek-only' eateries worth checking out. **Barko** (☎ 2841 024 610; Lasithiou 23; mezedes €4-6) is classed as an oinomayirio ('wine cook house'). Dishes are mainly Cretan meze-style and dining is in a cosy wood and stone interior.

To Koutouki (☎ 2841 026 877; Lasithiou 4a; mains €3.50-6), across the road from Barko, is a simple but popular ouzeri. Snails, mushrooms and dolmades are features on the mezedes menu. The mezedes platter is a good option for beginners.

Getting There & Away
BUS
Buses leave the Agios Nikolaos bus station for Elounda (€1.05, 20 daily), Kritsa (€1.05, 12 daily), Ierapetra (€2.60, eight daily), Iraklio (€5.25, half-hourly), Lasithi Plateau (€6.05, one daily) and Sitia (€5.25, six daily).

FERRY
LANE Lines (☎ 2841 026 465) has ferries three times a week to Piraeus (€27, 12 hours), Karpathos (€19, seven hours), Rhodes (€22.50, 10½ hours), Kasos (€10.60, four hours) and Halki (€12.90, 6½ hours). Tickets are most conveniently bought at a travel agent like **Nostos Tours** (☎ 2841 022 819; Koundourou 30).

Getting Around
You will find many car and motorcycle-hire outlets on the northern waterfront. **Scooterland** (☎ 2841 026 340; Akti Koundourou 10) has a huge range of scooters, motorcycles and cars. Prices begin at €18 a day for a scooter and go up to €50 a day for a Kawasaki EN. Cars range in price from €30 to €55.

ELOUNDA ΕΛΟΥΝΤΑ
pop 2185
There are magnificent mountain and sea views along the 11km road from Agios Nikolaos to Elounda. Formerly a quiet fishing village, Elounda is now bristling with package tourists and is only marginally calmer than Agios Nikolaos. While the setting is unquestionably attractive with its sheltered lagoon-like stretch of water formed by the Kolokytha Peninsula, the lure of the tourist euro has relegated any sense of friendliness and customer service to a distant memory. If you're looking for the Crete of yore, you won't find it in Elounda.

There's no tourist police in Elounda, but there is a **tourist office** (☎ 2841 042 464) opposite the church on the main square. Staff will help you find accommodation and change money.

Frankly, if you're looking for a place to stay and somewhere to eat in Elounda don't bother. While there are stacks of options, Elounda is neither cheap nor particularly

good value. **Hotel Aristea** (☎ 2841 041 300; fax 2841 041 302; s/d €35/50) in the town centre is one decent option and most rooms at least have a sea view.

There's an enormous range of overpriced, bland places to eat bristling with eager touts. **Nikos** (☎ 2841 041 439; mains €4-7) on the main square is as close to 'normal' as you will get. The food is cheap and honest enough, though service can be bit erratic at busy times. For a splurge you might as well place your bets on the **Ferryman Taverna** (☎ 2841 041 230; mains €7.50-11) on the pretty waterfront. It claims its moment of fame from being featured in the TV series *Who Pays the Ferryman*. The food is not cheap but it *is* admittedly good.

Up to 20 buses daily shuttle Agios Nikolaos and Elounda (€1.05, 20 minutes).

KOLOKYTHA PENINSULA ΧΕΡΣΟΝΗΣΟΣ ΚΟΛΟΚΥΘΑ
Just before Elounda (coming from Agios Nikolaos), a sign points right to ancient **Olous**, once the port of Lato. The city stood on and around the narrow isthmus (now a causeway) which joined the southern end of the Kolokytha Peninsula to the mainland. Most of the ruins lie beneath the water, and if you go snorkelling near the causeway you will see outlines of buildings and the tops of columns. The water around here appears to be a paradise for sea urchins. The peninsula is a pleasant place to stroll and there is an early Christian **mosaic** near the causeway.

There is an excellent sandy beach 1km along a narrow but graded dirt road on the east side of the peninsula. The beach is sheltered, the water pristine and few people use it, other than visitors from up to three small caïque that make the trip each day from Agios Nikolaos. These well-organised BBQ boat tours leave from Agios Nikolaos' port; expect to pay €22 per person.

SPINALONGA ISLAND ΝΗΣΟΣ ΣΠΙΝΑΛΟΓΚΑ
Spinalonga Island lies just north of the Kolokytha Peninsula. The island's massive **fortress** (admission €3; ☉ 8am-7pm) was built by the Venetians in 1579 to protect Elounda Bay and the Gulf of Mirabello. It withstood Turkish sieges for longer than any other Cretan stronghold, finally surrendering in

1715, some 30 years after the rest of Crete. The Turks used the island as a base for smuggling. Following the reunion of Crete with Greece, Spinalonga Island became a leper colony. The last leper died here in 1953 and the island has been uninhabited ever since. It is still known among locals as 'the island of the living dead'.

The island is a fascinating place to explore. It has an aura that is both macabre and poignant. The **cemetery**, with its open graves, is an especially strange place. Dead lepers came in three classes: those who saved up money from their government pension for a place in a concrete box; those whose funeral was paid for by relations and who therefore got a proper grave; and the destitute, whose remains were thrown into a charnel house.

Regular excursion boats visit Spinalonga Island from the port in Agios Nikolaos (€15) and there is a boat every half-hour from the port in Elounda (€6.50). Alternatively, you can take a cheaper boat from Plaka (5km further north). The boats from Agios Nikolaos pass Bird Island and Kri-Kri Island, one of the last habitats of the kri-kri, Crete's wild goat. Both these islands are uninhabited and designated wildlife sanctuaries.

KRITSA ΚΡΙΤΣΑ
pop 2703

The village of Kritsa (krit-*sah*), perched 600m up the mountainside 11km from Agios Nikolaos, is on every package itinerary. Tourists come in busloads to the village every day in summer. The villagers exploit these invasions to the full, and craft shops of every description line the main streets.

The tiny, triple-aisled **Church of Panagia Kera** (☎ 2841 051 525; admission €2.30; ⏰ 8.30am-3pm Mon-Fri, 8.30am-2pm Sat) is on the right, 1km before Kritsa on the Agios Nikolaos road. The frescoes that cover its interior walls are considered the most outstanding examples of Byzantine art in Crete. Unfortunately the church is usually packed with tourists.

There's very little accommodation in Kritsa, but **Rooms Argyro** (☎ 2841 051 174; s/d €25/35) is the best place to stay. Each room is immaculate and there is a little shaded restaurant downstairs for breakfast and light meals. It's on the left as you enter the village. As for eating you can have a hearty meat at **O Kastellos** (☎ 2841 051 254; mains €5-8) in the centre of the village. Oven-cooked veal and pasta in a pot is recommended.

There are 12 buses daily from Agios Nikolaos to Kritsa (€1.05, 15 minutes).

ANCIENT LATO ΑΡΧΑΙΟ ΛΑΤΩ

The ancient city of **Lato** (admission €3; ⏰ 8.30am-3pm Tue-Sun), 4km north of Kritsa, is one of Crete's few non-Minoan ancient sites. Lato (lah-*to*) was founded in the 7th century BC by the Dorians and at its height was one of the most powerful cities in Crete. It sprawls over the slopes of two acropolises in a lonely mountain setting, commanding stunning views down to the Gulf of Mirabello.

The city's name derived from the goddess Leto whose union with Zeus produced Artemis and Apollo, both of whom were worshipped here. Lato is far less visited than Crete's Minoan sites.

In the centre of the site is a deep well, which is cordoned off. As you face the Gulf of Mirabello, to the left of the well are some steps which are the remains of a **theatre**.

Above the theatre was the **prytaneion**, where the city's governing body met. The circle of stones behind the well was a threshing floor. The columns next to it are the remains of a stoa which stood in the agora. There are remains of a pebble mosaic nearby. A path to the right leads up to the **Temple of Apollo**.

There are no buses to Lato. The road to the site is signposted to the right on the approach to Kritsa. If you don't have your own transport, it's a pleasant 4km walk through olive groves along this road.

GOURNIA ΓΟΥΡΝΙΑ

The important Minoan site of **Gournia** (☎ 2841 024 943; admission €3; ⏰ 8.30am-3pm Tue-Sun), pronounced goor-*nyah*, lies just off the coast road, 19km southeast of Agios Nikolaos. The ruins, which date from 1550 to 1450 BC, consist of a town overlooked by a small palace. The palace was far less ostentatious than the ones at Knossos and Phaestos because it was the residence of an overlord rather than a king. The town is a network of streets and stairways flanked by houses with walls up to 2m in height. Trade, domestic and agricultural implements found on the site indicate Gournia was a thriving little community.

Near the Minoan site is **Gournia Moon Camping** (☎ /fax 2842 093 243; Gournia; camp sites per adult/tent €4.80/4.50; 🐾), the closest camping ground to Agios Nikolaos. The shaded and well-organised site boasts a restaurant, snack bar and minimarket. Buses to Sitia can drop you off outside.

Gournia is on the Sitia and Ierapetra bus routes from Agios Nikolaos and buses can drop you at the site.

MOHLOS ΜΟΧΛΟΣ
pop 100

Mohlos (*moh*-los) is a pretty fishing village bedecked in hibiscus, bougainvillea and bitter laurel and reached by a 6km winding road from the main Sitia–Agios Nikolaos highway. It was once joined in antiquity to the homonymous island that now sits 200m offshore and was at one time a thriving Minoan community dating back to the Early Minoan period (3000–2000 BC).

Mohlos sees mainly French and German independent travellers seeking peace and quiet from the noise and hype further west. There is a small pebble-and-grey-sand beach from which swimming is reasonable. Mohlos is an ideal travellers' rest stop with a high chill-out factor.

Mohlos is all contained within two or three blocks, all walkable within 10 minutes. There is no bank, or post office in Mohlos and very few tourist facilities at all, other than a couple of gift shops. There are two minimarkets.

There is, however, a fair bit of accommodation and eating choices. At the east side of the little harbour **Hotel Sofia** (☎ /fax 2843 094 554; d/tr €29.50/32; 🌊) offers convenient and comfortable standard rooms with TV and small fridge while downstairs the aptly named restaurant **Sofia** (☎ 2843 094 554; mains €2.50-4.50) serves a wide range of home-cooked food with some excellent vegetarian choices: artichokes with peas, or cauliflower in wine sauce are two examples.

Also on the harbour, **To Bogazi** (☎ 2843 094 200; mezedes €1.60-4.50) is one of the more popular restaurants and serves up over 30 inventive mezedes, many of which are also vegetarian. An interesting menu item worth testing is the tasty cuttlefish and pan-tossed greens.

Another decent place to stay is **To Kyma** (☎ 2843 094 177; solk@in.gr; studios €30), which is

fairly well-signposted on the west side of the village near a supermarket. The self-contained studios are spotless and good value for money.

There is no public transport travelling directly to Mohlos. Buses between Sitia and Agios Nikolaos will drop you off at the Mohlos turn-off. From there you'll need to hitch or walk the 6km to Mohlos village.

SITIA ΣΗΤΕΙΑ
pop 8748

Sitia (sih-*tee*-ah) is somewhat quieter than the prefecture capital Agios Nikolaos, though it can get quite busy in full summer with a mainly domestic crowd. It is a pleasant, traveller-friendly town and makes a good jumping-off point for the Dodecanese islands. A sandy beach skirts a wide bay to the east of town. The main part of the town is terraced up a hillside, overlooking the port. The buildings are a pleasing mixture of new and fading Venetian architecture.

Orientation & Information

The bus station is at the eastern end of Karamanli, which runs behind the bay. The town's main square, Plateia El Venizelou – recognisable by its palm trees and statue of a dying soldier – is at the western end of Karamanli.

Ferries to/from Piraeus and the Dodecanese dock about 500m north of Plateia Agnostou.

There's a **tourist office** (☑ 9.30am-2.30pm) on the main promenade and **Tzortzakis Travel** (☎ 2843 025 080; Kornarou 150) is also a good source of information. There are lots of ATMs and places to change money. The **National Bank of Greece** (Plateia El Venizelou) has a 24-hour exchange machine.

To get to the **post office** (Dimokritou) from the main square, follow El Venizelou inland and take the first left. Internet access is available at the **Itanos Hotel** (☎ 2843 022 900; Karamanli 4; €6 per hr; ☑ 9.30am-2.30pm).

The police and **tourist police** (☎ 2843 022 266; Therisou 31) are housed in the same building.

Sights

Sitia's **archaeological museum** (☎ 2843 023 917; Pisokefalou; admission €3; ☑ 8.30am-3pm Tue-Sun) houses a well-displayed collection of local finds spanning from Neolithic to Roman times,

CRETE

with emphasis on the Minoan. The museum is on the left side of the road to Ierapetra.

Festivals

Sitia produces superior sultanas, and a **sultana festival** is held in the town in the last week of August, during which wine flows freely and there are performances of Cretan dances.

Sleeping

Hotel Arhontiko (☎ 2843 028 172; Kondylaki 16; s/d €18/21) This D-class hotel, two streets uphill from the port, is beautifully maintained and spotless and has shared facilities. The owner enjoys sharing a bottle of raki with guests on the communal terrace.

Kazarma Rooms (☎ 2843 023 211; Ionias 10; d €26.50) This is a very attractive option, rooms are well cared-for with TV, fan and phone and all enjoy a communal lounge and a well-equipped kitchen. Look for the signs off Patriarhou Metaxaki.

El Greco Hotel (☎ 2843 023 133; elgreco@sit .forthnet.gr; Arkadiou 13; s/d €28/38; 🗙) For a modicum more comfort and style, the well-signposted El Greco has more character than the town's other C-class places. Rooms are very presentable and all have a fridge and phone.

Itanos Hotel (☎ 2843 022 900; www.itanoshotel .com; Karamanli 4; s/d €30/50; 🗙 🖵) The B-class Itanos has a conspicuous location on the waterfront and a popular terrace restaurant. The comfortable rooms come equipped with satellite TV, balconies and sound-proofing.

Eating

There is a string of tavernas along the quay side on El Venizelou that offer an array of mezedes and fish dishes at comparable prices.

Taverna O Mihos (☎ 2843 022 416; Kornarou 117; set menus €8.50-15.50) This taverna one block back from the waterfront has excellent charcoal-grilled souvlaki. The set menu options are a good idea if you want a complete meal package without the fuss.

Kali Kardia Taverna (☎ 2843 022 249; Foundalidou 22; mains €4-5.50) This place is excellent value and popular with locals and serves up generous sized grills and mayirefta. Walk up Kazantzaki from the waterfront, take the second right and the taverna is on the right.

Café Nato (☎ 6972 828 503; Mastropavlou 43; mezedes €1.50-2.50) Café Nato, near the ferry quay, is a laid-back little taverna with outdoor tables that serves a variety of grilled meat, artisanal cheeses and particularly good raki.

Symposio (☎ 2843 025 856; Karamanli 12; mains €5.30-6.80) Symposio utilises all-Cretan natural products such as organic olive oil from Moni Toplou. The food is top class. Rabbit in rosemary and wine sauce is recommended.

Balcony (☎ 2843 025 084; Foundalidou 18; mains €8.50-10.50) Providing the finest dining in Sitia, this has an extraordinarily creative menu that combines Greek, Italian and Mexican food. A couple of the more interesting menu items are rooster in wine with noodles or veal and rigatoni cheese.

Getting There & Away

AIR

The **Olympic Airways office** (☎ 2843 022 270) is at 4 Septemvriou 3. Sitia's now enormous and developing airport has three flights to Athens (€70, 1¼ hours), three flights a week to Thessaloniki (€125, three hours), three flights a week to Preveza (€79, 1¾ hours) and three flights a week to Alexandroupolis (€79, 1¾ hours).

BUS

There are six buses a day to Ierapetra (€4.60, 1½ hours), five buses a day to Iraklio (€10.50, 3½ hours) via Agios Nikolaos (€5.75, 1½ hours), five to Vaï (€2.20, one hour), and two to Kato Zakros via Palekastro and Zakros (€3.55, one hour). The buses to Vaï and Kato Zakros run only between May and October; during the rest of the year, the Vaï service terminates at Palekastro and the Kato Zakros service at Zakros.

FERRY

The F/B *Vitsentzos Kornaros* and F/B *Ierapetra* of LANE Lines link Sitia with Piraeus (€25.30, 14½ hours), Kasos (€9, four hours), Karpathos (€15.50, six hours), Halki (€11.90, 5½ hours) and Rhodes (€23, 10 hours) three times weekly. Departure times change annually, so check locally for latest information. Buy tickets at **Tzortzakis Travel** (☎ 2843 022 631; Kornarou 150).

Getting Around

The airport (signposted) is 1km out of town, though when the new terminal opens it will be a further 2km drive to get there. There is no airport bus; a taxi costs about €4.50.

AROUND SITIA

Moni Toplou Μονή Τοπλού

The imposing **Moni Toplou** (☎ 2843 061 226, Lasithi; admission €2.50; ✆ 9am-1pm & 2-6pm), 18km east of Sitia on the back road to Vaï, looks more like a fortress than a monastery. It was often treated as such, being ravaged by both the Knights of St John and the Turks. It holds an 18th-century icon by Ioannis Kornaros, one of Crete's most celebrated icon painters.

From the Sitia–Palekastro road it is a 3km walk. Buses can drop you off at the junction.

Vaï Βάι

The beach at Vaï, on Crete's east coast 24km from Sitia, is famous for its palm forest. There are many stories about the origin of these palms, including the theory that they sprouted from date pits spread by Roman legionaries relaxing on their way back from conquering Egypt. While these palms are closely related to the date, they are a separate species unique to Crete.

In July and August you'll need to arrive early to appreciate the setting, because the place gets packed. It's possible to escape the worst of the ballyhoo – jet skis and all – by clambering over a rocky outcrop (to the right, facing the sea) to a small secluded beach. Alternatively, you can go over the hill in the other direction to a quiet beach frequented by nudists.

There are two tavernas at Vaï but no accommodation. If you're after more-secluded beaches, head north for another 3km to the ancient Minoan site of **Itanos**. Below the site are several good swimming spots.

There are buses to Vaï from Sitia (€2.10, one hour, five daily).

ZAKROS & KATO ZAKROS
ΖΑΚΡΟΣ & ΚΑΤΩ ΖΑΚΡΟΣ
pop 955

The village of Zakros (*zah*-kros), 37km southeast of Sitia, is the nearest permanent settlement to the Minoan site of Zakros, a further 7km away (see Ancient Zakros, p228).

Kato Zakros, next to the site, is a beautiful little seaside settlement that springs to life between March and October. It is one of *the* most tranquil and friendly places to hang out for a few days in Crete.

If the weather is dry, there is an enjoyable and not-too-challenging 8km walk from Zakros to Kato Zakros through a gorge known as the Valley of the Dead because of the cave tombs dotted along the cliffs. The gorge emerges close to the Minoan site.

As far as sleeping is concerned, it's far better to stay at Kato Zakros, where there are a number places to choose from. There are three good places all under the same management which share the web address www.cretetravel.com/Hotels /Athena_Coral_Poseidon_Rooms.

The first of the three, **Poseidon Rooms** (☎ 2843 026 893; akrogiali@sit.forthnet.gr; d €18, with bathroom €25), at the southern end of the waterfront, make for a good budget alternative. Rooms are smallish but very neat and clean; some have bathrooms while others have shared facilities. **Athena Rooms** (☎ 2843 026 893; akrogiali@sit.forthnet.gr; d €35.50; 🐾) is a good-quality, more comfortable choice. These rooms are very pleasant with heavy stone walls and views of the beach from the communal balcony. **Rooms Coral** (☎ 2843 027 064; d €35.50; 🖳) below Athena Rooms is excellent, with smallish and spotlessly clean rooms equipped with Internet connectivity. All also enjoy superb sea views from the communal balcony. There's a kitchen and fridge for guests' use.

Some 800m along the old road to Zakros past the archaeological site are two other options. **George's Villas** (☎ /fax 2843 026 833; s/d €29/36) has spotless, beautifully furnished rooms with terraces. The villas are in a verdant, pine-fringed setting. Next to it the three tastefully decorated **Stella's Apartments** (☎ /fax 2843 023 739; studios €50) are all made from local stone and equipped with small lounge and kitchenette. The engaging owners welcome trekkers and walkers.

As far as food is concerned you have a few choices. In fairness all offer much the same in quality but **Taverna Akrogiali** (☎ 2843 026 893; mains €4.50-9) has a definite edge. Enjoy soothing, seaside dining here with the friendliest service from the inimitable owner Nikos Perakis. The speciality is grilled swordfish steak.

Next choice along is **Georgios Taverna Anesis** (☎ 2843 026 890; mains €3.30-5), specialising in home-cooked food and *ladera* (oven-baked dishes cooked in olive oil) dishes with oddities such as snails with onions or wild greens. Dine under shading tamarisk trees overlooking the beach. In a similar vein is the third one **Restaurant Nikos Platanakis** (☎ 2843 026 887; mains €3-3.80) where again you'll find a wide range of Greek staples as well as rarities such as rabbit, pheasant and partridge.

Up in Zakros proper, and despite its rather misleading name, **Restaurant Pizzeria Napoleon** (☎ 2843 093 152; mains €3-5) is actually a fully fledged and rather superb Cretan home-cooking restaurant. The food quality is exceptional and only locally grown and produced products are used.

There are buses to Zakros via Palekastro from Sitia (€3.65, one hour, two daily). They leave Sitia at 11am and 2.30pm and return at 12.30pm and 4pm. From June to August, the buses continue to Kato Zakros.

ANCIENT ZAKROS

The smallest of Crete's four palatial complexes, **Ancient Zakros** (☎ 2843 026 987; Kato Zakros; admission €3.50; ☉ 8am-7pm) was a major port in Minoan times, maintaining trade links with Egypt, Syria, Anatolia and Cyprus. The palace comprised royal apartments, storerooms and workshops flanking a central courtyard.

The town occupied a low plain close to the shore. Water levels have risen over the years so that some parts of the palace complex are submerged. The ruins are not well preserved, but a visit to the site is worthwhile for its wild and remote setting.

XEROKAMBOS ΞΕΡΟΚΑΜΠΟΣ
pop 25
Xerokambos (kseh-*roh*-kam-bos) is a quiet, unassuming agricultural settlement on the far southeastern flank of Crete. Its isolation has so far meant that tourism is pretty much low-key and most certainly of the unpackaged kind. Its attraction lies in its isolation, a couple of splendid beaches, a few tavernas and a scattering of studio accommodation that is ideal for people with peace and quiet in mind.

Ambelos Beach Studios (☎ /fax 2842 026 759; studios €40) has smallish, but cosy studios with kitchenettes and fridges. There is a barbecue and outdoor wood oven for guests, and

a tree-shaded courtyard. It's also handy for the sandy beaches across the road.

Akrogiali Taverna (☎ 2842 026 777; mains €3), the only beachside taverna in Xerokambos, is 50m from Ambelos Beach and near Ambelos Beach Studios. The food ranges from grills to fish, to home-cooked mayirefta.

There are no buses to Xerokambos. To get there from Zakros take the Kato Zakros road, and on the outskirts of Zakros turn left at the signpost for Livyko View Restaurant. This 8km dirt road to Xerokambos is driveable in a conventional vehicle. Otherwise there is a good paved road from Ziros. Taking a taxi is an option, albeit an expensive one.

IERAPETRA ΙΕΡΑΠΕΤΡΑ
pop 15,323
Ierapetra (yeh-*rah*-pet-rah) is Europe's most southerly major town. It was a major port of call for the Romans in their conquest of Egypt. After the tourist hype of Agios Nikolaos, the unpretentiousness of Ierapetra is refreshing, and the main business continues to be agriculture, not tourism.

Orientation & Information
The **bus station** (☎ 2842 028 237; Lasthenous) is on the eastern side of town, one street back from the beachfront. From the ticket office, turn right and after about 50m you'll come to a six-road intersection. There are signposts to the beach via Patriarhou Metaxaki, and to the city centre via the pedestrian mall section of Lasthenous.

The mall emerges after about 150m onto the central square of Plateia Eleftherias. To the north of the square is the National Bank of Greece and on the south side is Eurobank. Both banks have ATMs. If you continue straight ahead from Plateia Eleftherias you will come to Plateia Georgiou Kanoupaki.

There is no tourist office, but travel agents can usually supply localised tourist information and the Internet site www.ierapetra.net has a good range of information on the town.

You can check your email at the **Polycafé Orpheas** (☎ 2842 080 462; Koundouriotou 25; €6 per hr; ☉ 9am-11pm), or the **Net Internet Café** (☎ 2842 025 900; Koundourou 16; €5.50 per hr; ☉ 9am-midnight).

Sights

BEACHES

Ierapetra has two beaches. The main town beach is near the harbour and the other beach stretches east from the bottom of Patriarhou Metaxaki. Both have coarse, grey sand.

The beaches to the east of Ierapetra tend to get crowded. For greater tranquillity, head for **Gaïdouronisi** (Hrysi), where there are good, uncrowded sandy beaches, three tavernas and a stand of cedars of Lebanon, the only one in Europe. From June through August excursion boats (€15) leave for the islet every morning and return in the afternoon.

OTHER ATTRACTIONS

The **archaeological collection** (☎ 2842 028 721; Adrianou 2; admission €2; ☉ 8.30am-3pm Tue-Sun) is perfect for those with a short concentration span (it's one room). Pride of place is given to an exquisite statue of Persephone.

If you walk south along the waterfront from the central square you will come to the **Venetian Fortress** (Kato Meran; admission free; ☉ 8.30am-3pm Tue-Sun), built in the early years of Venetian rule and strengthened by Francesco Morosini in 1626. It's in a pretty fragile state.

Inland from the fortress is the labyrinthine **old quarter**, a delightful place to lose yourself for a while. Look out for the **Ottoman mosque** and fountain.

Some 13.5km north of Ierapetra is the **Ha Gorge**, perhaps the most challenging gorge to traverse in the whole of Europe. More of an extreme climbing experience than a hike, the Ha Gorge is a narrow rent in the imposing mountains and is visible from the main Agios Nikolaos–Ierapetra road. Reputedly fully traversed by less than a couple of dozen people, the gorge nonetheless regularly draws extreme climbers and professional gorge climbers who attempt sections of this gut-wrenching and occasionally dangerous traverse. Only experienced climbers should apply.

Sleeping

Koutsounari Camping (☎ 2842 061 213; fax 2842 061 186; Koutsounari; camp sites per adult/tent €4/3) The nearest camping ground to Ierapetra is 7km east of Ierapetra at Koutsounari. It has a restaurant, snack bar and minimarket. Ierapetra–Sitia buses pass the site.

Hotel Coral (☎ 2842 022 846; Katzonovatsi 12; s/d €18/20) It can be a bit tricky to find this place, but it's a reasonable budget option. Rooms here are well kept and apartments are comfortable. The hotel is two blocks inland close to the easily spotted church.

Katerina Rooms (☎ 2842 028 345; fax 2842 028 591; Markopoulou 95; d €25; ☒) On the seafront, Katerina has pleasant enough rooms with phone and fridge. To reach the hotel from the bus station, follow Patriarhou Metaxaki to the waterfront.

Cretan Villa Hotel (☎ /fax 2842 028 522; www .cretan-villa.com; Lakerda 16; s/d €27/30; ☒) This is a well-maintained 18th-century house with traditionally furnished rooms and a peaceful courtyard. It is a five-minute walk from the bus station.

Astron Hotel (☎ 2842 025 114; htastron@otenet.gr; Kothri 56; s/d incl breakfast €47/73; ☒) The best hotel in town is the B-class Astron at the beach end of Patriarhou Metaxaki. The rooms here are comfortably furnished with satellite TV and telephone.

Eating

Most of the souvlaki outlets are on Kyrva and there is a swathe of restaurant along the promenade.

Taverna Babis (☎ 2842 024 048; Stratigou Samouil 68; mains €3.50-5.50) Babis is one of the better tavernas along the waterfront. It has an enormous range of mezedes dishes. Ask for *kakavia* (fish soup), or *steka* (a cream cheese made from curds).

Napoleon (☎ 2842 022 410; Stratigou Samouil 26; mains €3.50-6) One of the oldest and most respected establishments is Napoleon, in the middle of the restaurant strip on the south side of town. Whatever you order is guaranteed to be of a high quality.

O Kales (To Kastro; ☎ 2842 028 254; cnr Stratigou Samouil & Kougioumtzaki; mains €4-6) At the far end of Stratigou Samouil is another locally respected and patronised fish taverna. It looks unassuming and service can be a bit gruff, but it dishes up fine fare – especially fish.

Getting There & Away

In summer, there are six buses a day to Iraklio (€7.85, 2½ hours) via Agios Nikolaos (€2.70, one hour) and Gournia; six to Sitia (€4.60, 1½ hours) via Koutsounari (for camp sites); six to Myrtos (€1.45, 30 minutes); and two a week to Ano Viannos (€3.05, one hour).

CRETE

MYRTOS ΜΥΡΤΟΣ

pop 628

Myrtos (*myr*-tos), on the coast 17km west of Ierapetra, is a sparkling village full of white-washed houses with flower-filled balconies. It is a magnet for independent travellers, many of whom come only for a day or so, yet often stay on for a week or two. The village has a cosy, lived-in ambience where everyone seems to know each other.

You'll soon find your way around as Myrtos is built on a grid system. To get to the waterfront from the bus stop, facing south, take the road to the right for 150 m.

There is no post office or bank, but there are currency exchange places around the village. Internet access is available upstairs at **Edem Café** (☎ 2842 051 551; €5 per hr; ⏰ 11am-10pm), two blocks back from the waterfront.

There's certainly no shortage of places to sleep for independent travellers. Block bookings by tour operators have made minimal inroads. **Hotel Myrtos** (☎ 2842 051 227; www.myrtoshotel.com; s/d €22/30) is a superior C-class place in the middle of the main street with large, well-kept rooms. At the eastern edge of the village **Big Blue** (☎ 2842 051 094; www.forthnet.gr/big-blue; s/d €25/50) is one of the best places to stay. You have a choice of more expensive, high-up and large airy studios with glorious beach and sea views or cheaper, cosy ground-floor rooms that require no step climbing.

Not far away **Cretan Rooms** (☎ 2842 051 427; d €26.50) are cosy, traditional-style rooms with balconies, fridges and shared kitchens. They're popular with independent travellers and are prominently signposted from the village centre. For two or more persons **Nikos House** (☎ 2842 051 116; www.nikoshouse.cz in Greek; d/tr €30/50), two blocks back from the waterfront in the thick of things, is a sensible option. These large and comfortable self-contained apartments shelter beneath the leaves of a large mulberry tree.

The waterfront is strung left to right with mostly carbon-copy eating establishments. While none distinguishes itself noticeably from its neighbour, **Myrtos Taverna** (☎ 2842 051 227; mains €3-6.50) is always busy and popular with both locals and tourists for its wide range of mezedes as well as for its vegetarian dishes. Rabbit in red wine sauce is recommended by the owner. On the waterfront itself **Taverna Akti** (☎ 2842 051

584; mains €4.50-6) at the east end offers pleasant seafood dining and better than average food. The best choices are usually on the 'daily specials' board.

There are six buses a day from Ierapetra to Myrtos (€1.45, 30 minutes). The twice-weekly Ano Viannos–Ierapetra bus also passes through Myrtos.

AROUND MYRTOS

Ano Viannos (pop 1181) 16km west of Myrtos, is a delightful village built on the southern flanks of Mt Dikti. While there used to be a folklore museum in the village, it now seems to have fallen by the wayside and the main sight is the village's tiny 14th-century **Church of Agia Pelagia** (admission free; ⏰ 9am-8pm summer). Follow the signs upwards to the top end of the village to find it. The interior walls, covered with luscious frescoes by Nikiforos Fokas, are in need of restoration but can still be appreciated.

If you choose, you can stay and eat in Ano Viannos at **Taverna & Rooms Lefkes** (☎ 2895 022 719; s/d €13/15) just downhill off the main road. While the sleeping facilities are fairly nondescript the food at the restaurant is generally well-regarded with its excellent salads and pot-baked local Cretan dishes.

Most travellers up this way are heading – usually under their own steam – for the twin mini-resorts and now contiguous villages of **Kastri** and **Keratokambos**, 13 tortuously winding kilometres downhill, where there's a pleasant tree-lined beach and better eating and sleeping choices.

Of the sleeping choices **Filoxenia Apartments** (☎ 2895 051 371; Kastri; studios €40; 🛇) is the preferred mid-range choice. The two-to-three-person studios, wrapped in a flower shaded garden, are beautiful. Equipped with kitchenette and fridge, they make for a very pleasant base for a week or so.

Decidedly more up-market are **Komis Studios** (☎ 2895 051 390; www.komisstudios.gr; Keratokambos; apt €93; 🛇). These attractively decorated three-level apartments on the sea are built from stone, wood and stucco and outfitted with many amenities. While the management has a slightly snobbish attitude to travellers, they are worth every cent.

You've got at least three places to eat in each of the two centres. In Keratokambos, **Taverna Nikitas** (☎ 2895 051 477; mains €4-5) by the sea in the centre offers up consistently high quality and delicious grills that are surprisingly inexpensive. The oven-baked roast lamb or pork is highly recommended. Over in Kastri, you have the **Morning Star Taverna** (☎ 2895 051 209; mains €4-5.50) where succulent grills and fish feature. A mixed fish grill is a good bet, while tasty artichoke stew is a good choice for vegetarians.

From Ano Viannos there are two buses weekly to Iraklio (€7.45, 2½ hours) and Ierapetra (€3.05, one hour) via Myrtos. Public transport to Kastri and Keratokambos is non-existent. You'll either need your own wheels or you'll need to rely on patchy hitching to get down to the coast.

WESTERN CRETE

The western part of Crete comprises the prefectures of Hania and Rethymno, which take their names from the old Venetian cities which are their capitals. The two towns rank as two of the region's main attractions, although the most famous is the spectacular Samaria Gorge. The south-coast towns of Paleohora and Plakias are popular resorts.

RETHYMNO PEΘYMNO
pop 28,987

Rethymno (*reh*-thim-no) is Crete's third-largest town. The main attraction is the old Venetian-Ottoman quarter that occupies the headland beneath the massive Venetian *fortezza* (fortress). The place is a maze of narrow streets, graceful wood-balconied houses and ornate Venetian monuments; several minarets add a touch of the Orient. The architectural similarities invite comparison with Hania, but Rethymno has a character of its own. An added attraction is a beach right in town.

The approaches to the town couldn't be less inviting. The modern town has sprawled out along the coast, dotted with big package hotels attracted by the reasonable beach.

History

The site of modern Rethymno has been occupied since Late Minoan times – the evidence can be found in the city's archaeological museum. In the 3rd and 4th centuries BC, the town was known as Rithymna, an autonomous state of sufficient stature to issue its own coinage. A scarcity of references to the city in Roman and Byzantine periods suggest it was of minor importance at that time.

The town prospered once more under the Venetians, who ruled from 1210 until 1645, when the Turks took over. Turkish forces held the town until 1897, when it was taken by Russia as part of the occupation of Crete by the Great Powers.

Rethymno became an artistic and intellectual centre after the arrival of a large number of refugees from Constantinople in 1923. The city has a campus of the University of Crete, bringing a student population that keeps the town alive outside the tourist season.

Orientation

Rethymno is a fairly compact city with most of the major sights and places to stay and eat within a small central area. Ethnikis Andistasis, which leads into the Old Town via the Porto Guora, is the main drag in central Rethymno, while Eleftheriou Venizelou running south of the town beach is the main beachside drag.

To the east of Eleftheriou Venizelou stretches a long sandy beach and an uninterrupted stretch of hotels, cafés, bars and restaurants. The most atmospheric places to stay and eat are all close to the centre.

Boats arrive conveniently within a couple of hundred metres of the old port, while buses arrive rather inconveniently a kilometre or so from the Old City on the western side of the city.

Information
BOOKSHOPS
Ilias Spondidakis bookshop (☎ 2831 054 307; Souliou 43) Stocks novels in English, books about Greece, tapes of Greek music and has a small second-hand section.
International Press Bookshop (☎ 2831 024 111; Petihaki 15) Stocks English novels, travel guides and history books.

INTERNET RESOURCES
Galero (☎ 2831 054 345; Plateia Rimini; €4 per hr; ⓨ 9am-1am)
Internet Café (☎ 2831 021 324; Arkadiou 186; €4.50 per hr; ⓨ 9am-midnight)

LAUNDRY
Laundry Mat self-service laundry (☎ 2831 056 196; Tombazi 45) Next door to the youth hostel; charges €7.50 for a wash and dry.

CRETE

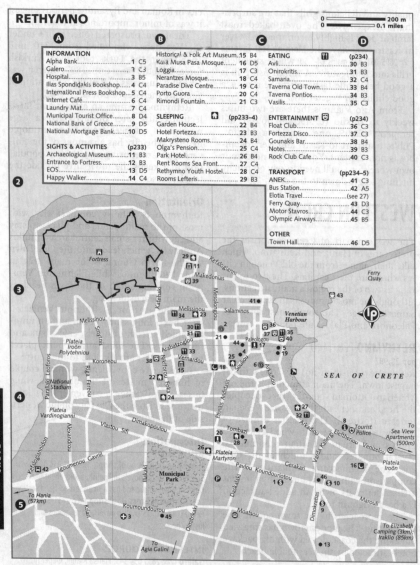

RETHYMNO

INFORMATION		
Alpha Bank	1	C5
Galero	2	C3
Hospital	3	B5
Ilias Spondidakis Bookshop	4	C4
International Press Bookshop	5	C4
Internet Café	6	C4
Laundry Mat	7	C4
Municipal Tourist Office	8	D4
National Bank of Greece	9	D5
National Mortgage Bank	10	D5

SIGHTS & ACTIVITIES	(p233)	
Archaeological Museum	11	B3
Entrance to Fortress	12	B3
EOS	13	D5
Happy Walker	14	C4

Historical & Folk Art Museum	15	B4
Kara Musa Pasa Mosque	16	D5
Loggia	17	C3
Nerantzes Mosque	18	C4
Paradise Dive Centre	19	C4
Porto Guora	20	C4
Rimondi Fountain	21	C3

SLEEPING	(pp233–4)	
Garden House	22	B4
Hotel Fortezza	23	B3
Makrysteno Rooms	24	B4
Olga's Pension	25	C4
Park Hotel	26	B4
Rent Rooms Sea Front	27	C4
Rethymno Youth Hostel	28	C4
Rooms Lefteris	29	B3

EATING	(p234)	
Avli	30	B3
Onirokritis	31	B3
Samaria	32	C4
Taverna Old Town	33	B4
Taverna Pontios	34	B3
Vasilis	35	C3

ENTERTAINMENT	(p234)	
Float Club	36	C3
Fortezza Disco	37	C3
Gounakis Bar	38	B4
Notes	39	B3
Rock Club Cafe	40	C3

TRANSPORT	(pp234–5)	
ANEK	41	C3
Bus Station	42	A5
Elotia Travel	(see 27)	
Ferry Quay	43	D3
Motor Stavros	44	C3
Olympic Airways	45	B5

OTHER		
Town Hall	46	D5

MONEY
Banks are concentrated in one area.
Alpha Bank (Pavlou Koundouriotou 29) With a 24-hour automatic exchange machine and ATM.
National Bank of Greece On the far side of the square opposite the town hall.
National Mortgage Bank Next to the town hall; with a 24-hour automatic exchange machine and ATM.

POST
Mobile post office (Eleftheriou Venizelou; May-Sep) About 200m southeast of the tourist office.
Post office (Moatsou 21)

TOURIST INFORMATION
Municipal tourist office (☎ 2831 029 148; Eleftheriou Venizelou; 9am-2pm Mon-Fri) Very convenient.

Tourist police (☎ 2831 028 156; ☺ 7am-10pm) In the same building as the tourist office.

Sights

Rethymno's 16th-century **fortress** (fortezza; ☎ 2831 028 101; Paleokastro Hill; admission €3; ☺ 8am-8pm) is the site of the city's ancient acropolis. Within its massive walls a great number of buildings once stood, of which only a church and a mosque survive intact. The ramparts offer good views, while the site has lots of ruins to explore.

The **archaeological museum** (☎ 2831 029 975; Fortezza; admission €1.50; ☺ 8.30am-3pm) is opposite the entrance to the fortress. The finds displayed here include an important coin collection. Rethymno has an excellent **Historical & Folk Art Museum** (☎ 2831 023 398; Vernardou 28-30; admission €3; ☺ 9.30am-2.30pm Mon-Sat) which gives an excellent overview of the region's rural lifestyle with a collection of old clothes, baskets, weaving and farm tools.

Pride of place among the many vestiges of Venetian rule in the old quarter goes to the **Rimondi Fountain** with its spouting lion heads, and the 16th-century **loggia**.

At the southern end of Ethnikis Andistasis is the well-preserved **Porto Guora**, a remnant of the Venetian defensive wall. Turkish legacies in the old quarter include the **Kara Musa Pasa Mosque** near Plateia Iroön and the **Nerantzes Mosque**, which was converted from a Franciscan church.

Activities

The Happy Walker (☎ 2831 052 920; www.happywalker .com; Tombazi 56) runs a varied programme of country walks in the region. Most walks start in the early morning and finish with lunch and cost from about €25 upwards. Complete walking holidays are also organised for the really enthusiastic walker. There is also an **Ellinikos Orivatikos Syndesmos** (EOS, Greek Alpine Club; ☎ 2831 057 766; Dimokratias 12) in Rethymno.

The **Paradise Dive Centre** (☎ 2831 026 317; pdcr@otenet.gr; Eleftheriou Venizelou 76) has diving activities and PADI courses for all grades of divers. The dive centre's programme usually consists of a visit to a beach on the south coast of Crete at Shinaria. Divers are taken there in 45 minutes by bus and here they can experience either a cave dive or a wall dive. Operations run from 30 April to 30 October and cost €32 for experience divers and up to €80 for novices.

Festivals

Rethymno's main cultural event is the annual **Renaissance Festival** which runs during July and August. It features dance, drama and films as well as art exhibitions.

Some years there's a **Wine Festival** in mid-July held in the municipal park. Ask the tourist office for details.

Sleeping

BUDGET

Elizabeth Camping (☎ 2831 028 694; camp sites per adult/tent €6.30/4.20) The nearest camping ground is near Mysiria Beach 3km east of Rethymno. The site has a taverna, snack bar and minimarket. There is a communal fridge, iced water 24 hours a day and free beach umbrellas and loungers. An Iraklio-bound bus can drop you at the site.

Rethymno Youth Hostel (☎ 2831 022 848; www.yh rethymno.com; Tombazi 41; dm €7) Friendly and well run with free hot showers. Breakfast is available and there's a bar in the evening. There is no curfew and the place is open all year.

Rent Rooms Sea Front (☎ 2831 051 981; www.forth net.gr/elotia; Arkadiou 159; s/d €25/38; 🕄) This is a delightful pension with six very clean and sizeable rooms. Most rooms have attached bathrooms, though one or two have private outside bathrooms.

Sea View Apartments (☎ 2831 051 981; www.forth net.gr/elotia; Sofokli Venizelou 44; apt €40; 🕄) Ideal for longer-stay guests, these neat, self contained apartments all have kitchen, bathroom, TV and balcony. Call in at Elotia Travel on the seafront for details.

Olga's Pension (☎ 2831 028 665; Souliou 57; s/d €25/35; 🕄) The friendly Olga's is tucked away on the touristy but colourful Souliou. A network of terraces, all bursting with greenery, connects a wide range of rooms, some with bathroom and sea views and others without.

Rooms Lefteris (☎ 2831 023 803; Kefalogianni 25-26; s/d €25/35) To the west side of the harbour, all rooms at Lefteris are pleasant, but the front rooms have stunning sea views, although they can be noisy at night.

Makrysteno Rooms (☎ 2831 055 465; fax 2831 050 011; Nikiforou Foka 56; s/d €20/30; 🕄) This set of rooms is a good, quiet choice. Spread over three floors all rooms have a kitchenette and fan (some have aircon) and there's a pleasant relaxing communal area.

Garden House (☎ 2831 028 586; Nikiforou Foka 82; d/tr €35/40) On a quiet street in the Old Town, this is an impeccably maintained 600-year-old Venetian house retaining many of its original features including a gorgeous grape-arboured garden. The rooms are spacious, comfortable and tasteful.

MID-RANGE

Park Hotel (☎ 2831 029 958; Igoumenou Gavriil 9; s/d incl breakfast €38/4; ❄) The only missing ingredient is an elevator to take you to rooms that are spread over two floors. The rooms are comfortable with TV, telephone, sound-proofing and balconies with park views.

Hotel Fortezza (☎ 2831 055 551; www.fortezza.gr; Melissinou 16; s/d incl breakfast €55/67; ❄ P ▣) Housed in a refurbished old building in the heart of the old town, these tastefully furnished rooms have TVs and telephones.

Eating

The waterfront along Eleftheriou Venizelou is lined with amazingly similar tourist restaurants staffed by fast-talking waiters eagerly cajoling passers-by into eating at their establishments. The situation is much the same around the Venetian Harbour, except the setting is better and the prices higher.

To find cheaper food and a more authentic atmosphere, wander inland down the little side streets.

Taverna Pontios (☎ 2831 057 624; Melissinou 34; mains €3-4.50) This place proves once again that some of the best Cretan food comes from unassuming places. A convivial group of locals comes here for the delicious cheese-stuffed calamari, among other dishes.

Samaria (☎ 2831 024 681; Eleftheriou Venizelou 39-40; mains €3.50-8) When the choice is enormous and all places look the same, it's hard to stand out. Samaria, sandwiched in among a bunch of look-alike eating venues is one of the better options. There's a large range of *mayirefta* including vegetables from the owner's own plot plus excellent soups.

Taverna Old Town (☎ 2831 026 436; Vernardou 31; 2-person set menus €14) Spilling out over a quiet back street the traditional Cretan food here is well prepared and well regarded and there are good-value, set-price menus with wine.

Vasilis (☎ 2831 022 967; Nearhou 10; mains €5-8) The enticing display of fish is no mere show. It's top-quality stuff and of the harbourside fish taverns this is one of the better ones. Fish mezedes are also a good option, as is *kakavia* (a kind of Cretan bouillabaisse).

Onirokritis (☎ 2831 058 440; Radamanthyos 16; mains €4-7) Dine on classic Greek cuisine in an Art-Deco interior or al fresco on the street in this subtly romantic venue. The Greek dishes feature a house salad based on avocado, plus you will find sun dried tomatoes and roast aubergine for vegetarians.

Avli (☎ 2831 026 213; cnr Xanthoudidou 22 & Radamanthyos; mains €5-10) One of the prettiest restaurants in Rethymno the Avli (Garden) with its flower garlanded dining area is as good as it looks. Peddling generic Mediterranean cuisine infused with Cretan elements the food is rich and filling. There are excellent sweets and a large wine list.

Entertainment

Gounakis Bar (☎ 2831 028 816; Koroneou 6; ☽ 8pm-1am) If you love drinking cheap wine and listening to live Cretan folk music, this is the place to go. There's music and impromptu dancing most nights.

Rock Club Café (☎ 2831 031 047; Petihaki 8; ☽ 9pm-dawn) For a while now one of Rethymno's trendiest hang-outs. A crowd of young professionals fills the club nightly.

Fortezza Disco (Nearhou 20; ☽ 11pm-dawn) This is the town's showpiece disco. It's big and flashy with three bars, a laser show and a well-groomed international crowd that starts drifting in around midnight.

Float Club (☎ 2831 027 205; Nearhou 26) One of the newer crop of night spots in Rethymno, the Float Club throbs to techno and electronic music while strobe lights flicker. Jump the trampoline if the mood grabs you.

Notes (☎ 2831 029 785; Himaras 27; ☽ 10am-midnight) Notes (*noh-tez*), a quiet bar-café, was opened by a musician who has an excellent selection of Greek music. It's a good place to escape the crowds along El Venizelou.

Getting There & Away

BUS

There are services to Hania (€5.80, one hour) and Iraklio (€6.20, 1½ hours). There's a bus in each direction every half-hour in summer, every hour in winter. In summer there are also four buses a day to Plakias (€3.45, one hour), four to Agia Galini (€4.60, 1½ hours), three to Moni Arkadiou (€2.10, 30 minutes), one to Omalos (€10.70, two hours) and two to Preveli (€3.45). The morning bus to Plakias continues to Hora Sfakion (€5.35, two hours). Services are reduced in winter.

CRETE

FERRY
ANEK (☎ 2831 029 221; www.anek.gr; Arkadiou 250) operates a daily ferry between Rethymno and Piraeus (€25, 10 hours) leaving both Rethymno and Piraeus at 8pm. Tickets are available from the company's office.

Getting Around
Most of the car-rental firms are near Plateia Iroön. **Motor Stavros** (☎ 2831 022 858; Paleologou 14) has a wide range of motorcycles and also rents bicycles for around €4 per day.

AROUND RETHYMNO
Moni Arkadiou Μονή Αρκαδίου
Surrounded by attractive hill country, the 16th-century **Moni Arkadiou** (Arkadi; monastery free, small museum €2; ☽ 8am-1pm & 3.30-8pm) is 23km southeast of Rethymno. The most impressive of the buildings is the Venetian baroque church. Its striking facade has eight slender Corinthian columns and an ornate triple-belled tower.

In November 1866 the Turks sent massive forces to quell insurrections which were gathering momentum throughout the island. Hundreds of men, women and children who had fled their villages used the monastery as a safe haven. When 2000 Turkish soldiers attacked the building, rather than surrender, the Cretans set light to a store of gunpowder. The explosion killed everyone, Turks included, except one small girl, who lived to a ripe old age in a village nearby. Busts of the woman, and the abbot who lit the gun powder, stand outside the monastery.

There are buses from Rethymno to the monastery (€2.10, 30 minutes) at 6am, 10.30am and 2.30pm, returning at 7am, noon and 4pm.

Rethymno to Spili
Heading south from Rethymno, there is a turn-off to the right for the **Late-Minoan cemetery** of Armeni 2km before the modern village of **Armeni**. The main road south continues through woodland, which gradually gives way to a bare and dramatic landscape. After 18km there is a turn-off to the right for **Selia** and Frangokastello (see p247) and, a little beyond, another turn-off for Plakias (this turn-off is referred to on timetables as the Koxare junction or Bale). The main road continues for 9km to Spili.

SPILI ΣΠΗΛΙ
pop 706
Spili is a gorgeous mountain town with cobbled streets, rustic houses and plane trees. Its centrepiece is a unique Venetian fountain which spurts water from 19 lion heads. Tourist buses hurtle through but Spili deserves an overnight stay.

The post office and bank are on the main street. The huge building at the northern end of town is an ecclesiastic conference centre. The bus stop is just south of the square. Spili is on the Rethymno–Agia Galini bus route.

Sleeping and eating choices are of a good quality. **Green Hotel** (☎ 2832 022 225; d €25) across from the police station on the main street is a homely place with attractive rooms, and is practically buried under plants and vines that also fill the interior. A little further along and signposted from the main road **Heracles Rooms** (☎ 2832 022 111; fax 2832 022 411; s/d €23.50/30) are very good value. All rooms are sparkling, beautifully furnished and equipped with fly screens.

Further east still **Costas Inn** (☎ 2832 022 040; fax 2832 022 043; d/tr €35/44) on the left has well-kept, ornate rooms with satellite TV, radio and the use of a washing machine and is located over **Taverna Costas** (☎ 2832 022 040; mains €2.50-4.50) where most dishes, including the wine, are organic Cretan. Try the traditional sweets for dessert.

Finally, **Taverna Stratidakis** (☎ 2832 022 006; mains €2.50-5), opposite Costas Inn, serves excellent traditional Greek dishes the best of which are visible for inspection in cooking pots at the back of the room.

AROUND SPILI
Most people come to the alluring little village of **Patsos** to visit the nearby **Church of Agios Antonios** in a cave above a picturesque gorge. You can drive here from Rethymno, or you can walk from Spili along a scenic 10km dirt track.

To reach the track, walk along 28 Oktovriou, passing the lion fountain on your right. Turn right onto Thermopylon and ascend to the Spili–Gerakari road. Turn right here and eventually you'll come to a sign for Gerakari. Take the dirt track to the left, and at the fork bear right. At the crossroads turn right, and continue on the main track for about 1.5kms to a T-junction on the outskirts of Patsos. Turn left to get to the cave.

Heading west of Spili, then south towards the coast at Plakias you will pass through the dramatic **Kourtaliotis Gorge** through which the river Megalopotamos rumbles on its way to the sea at **Preveli Beach**. About 8km before Plakias there is a turn-off to the left for Preveli Beach and Moni Preveli (see Around Plakias p237).

PLAKIAS ΠΛΑΚΙΑΣ
pop 139

The south-coast town of Plakias was once a tranquil fishing village before it became a retreat for adventurous backpackers. Plakias offers a good range of independent accommodation, some pretty decent eating options, a brace of good regional walks, a large sandy beach and enough nightlife to keep the party animals raging until dawn. All in all, Plakias is one of the better choices for independent travellers looking for a hangout in Crete.

Orientation & Information

It's easy to find your way around Plakias. One street skirts the beach and another runs parallel to it one block back. The bus stop is at the middle of the waterfront.

There are now a few places in the village to access the Internet. **Youth Hostel Plakias** (☎ 2832 032 118; €4.50 per hr) offers connectivity to guests and nonguests alike, while the **Ostraco Bar** (☎ 2832 031 710; ☻ 9am-midnight; €4.50 per hr) is another, more convenient choice.

Plakias has two ATMs while **Monza Travel Agency** (☎ 2832 031 882) near the bus stop offers currency exchange. There is a modern post office down the street next to Monza Travel.

Sleeping

Camping Apollonia (☎ 2832 031 318; camp sites per adult/tent €4.50/3; ☁) On the right of the main approach road to Plakias, this place has a restaurant, minimarket and bar. While the site is at least shaded, it all looks rather scruffy and run-down.

There is a wide range of sleeping choices on offer. Most are signposted on a communal wooden sign board next to Monza Travel.

Youth Hostel Plakias (☎ 2832 032 118; www.yh plakias.com; dm €7; ☐) For independent travellers this is the place to stay in Plakias. Manager Chris from the UK has created a very traveller-friendly place with spotless dorms,

green lawns and a volleyball court. Follow the signs from the waterfront.

Ippokambos (☎ 2832 031 525; studios €30) The large, clean rooms here have balconies covered with flowers, a fridge but no cooking facilities other than an electric kettle to make coffee or tea.

Morfeas Rent Rooms (☎ /fax 2832 031 583; s/d €25/30; ☒) Close to the bus stop and above a supermarket, Morfeas has light, airy and attractively furnished rooms with fridge and phone.

Pension Thetis (☎ 2832 031 430; fax 2832 031 987; studios €35; ☒) Thetis is a very pleasant, family-oriented set of studios. Rooms have fridge, cooking facilities, coffee maker and TV. Relax in the cool and shady garden, which is also a small play park for kids.

Pension Kyriakos (☎ 2832 031 307; fax 2832 031 631; d €35) 'If you don't like raki, stay away from here', says owner Kyriakos. His small, clean rooms have only coffee-making facilities, but that is made up for by ample raki, supplied by Kyriakos.

Castello (☎ /fax 2832 031 112; studios €36; ☒ ☐) It is the relaxed owner Christos and his leafy and shady garden that makes this place a happy haven. All rooms are cool, clean and fridge-equipped and have cooking facilities.

Eating

Nikos Souvlaki (☎ 2832 031 921; grills €4-5) Popular with travellers and just inland from Monza Travel Agency, this is a good souvlaki place, where an enormous mixed grill of *gyros* (Greek-style doner kebabs), souvlaki, sausage, hamburger and chips is a solid diet-buster meal in itself.

Taverna Sofia (☎ 2832 031 333; mains €3-6) In business since 1969, Sofia's is a solid choice. Check the meals on display from the trays in the window from which the lamb in yogurt is one of the most delicious items.

Siroko (☎ 2832 032 055; mains €3.50-6.50) On the far west side of the village, Siroko is an excellent family-run place popular with travellers. Try the lamb in egg and lemon sauce or a mixed seafood grill while vegetarians are also catered for with a range of enticing daily *ladera* (oven-baked dishes cooked on oil) dishes.

Getting There & Away

Plakias has good bus connections in summer, but virtually none in winter. A timetable is displayed at the bus stop. In Summer there are seven buses a day to Rethymno (€3.30, one hour) and a seasonal bus to Hora Sfakion.

Getting Around

Easy Ride (☎ 2832 020 052; www.easyride.reth.gr) is a newish outfit close to the post office that rents out modern bicycles (€6 to €9) and scooters (€9 to €11).

AROUND PLAKIAS

Moni Preveli Μονή Πρέβελη

Standing in splendid isolation high above the Libyan Sea, 14km east of Plakias, is the well-maintained **Moni Preveli** (☎ 2832 031 246; Preveli; admission €2; ⏱ 8am-7pm mid-Mar–May, 8am-1.30pm & 3.30-7.30pm Jun-Oct). Like most of Crete's monasteries, it played a significant role in the islanders' rebellion against Turkish rule. It became a centre of resistance during 1866, causing the Turks to set fire to it and destroy surrounding crops. After the Battle of Crete in 1941, many Allied soldiers were sheltered here by Abbot Agathangelos before their evacuation to Egypt. In retaliation the Germans plundered the monastery. The monastery's **museum** contains a candelabra presented by grateful British soldiers after the war.

From the road to the monastery, a road leads downhill to a large car park from where a steep foot track leads down to Preveli Beach.

From June through August there are two buses daily from Rethymno to Moni Preveli (€3.45).

Beaches

Preveli Beach (Paralia Finikodasous, Palm Beach), at the mouth of the Kourtaliotis Gorge, is one of Crete's most photographed and popular beaches. The river Megalopotamos meets the back end of the beach before it conveniently loops around its assorted bathers and empties into the Libyan Sea. The beach is fringed with oleander bushes and palm trees and used to be popular with freelance campers before camping was officially outlawed.

A steep path leads down to it from a large car park below Moni Preveli, or you can get to within several hundred metres of the beach by following a signposted 5km rough dirt road from a stone bridge to the left just off the Moni Preveli main road. You can also get to Preveli Beach from Plakias by boat from June through August for €9 return, or by taxi boat from Agia Galini for €18 return.

Between Plakias and Preveli Beach there are several secluded coves popular with freelance campers and nudists. Some are within walking distance of Plakias, though ideally you are going to need some transport to get to them without too much effort.

Damnoni Beach is the first one and the largest, and if you like crowds then go no further. About 1km further east are two little **coves** patronised by both clothed and naked bathers and most easily accessible via a dirt road from the somewhat larger **Ammoudi Beach**. Here, apart from a pleasant coarse sand beach, you will find some welcome shade at the rear end under large tamarisk trees where freelance campers and vanners sometimes set up temporary home. At all of these beaches the water is clear, clean and generally surf-free during the summer months. Snorkellers will particularly enjoy the **skin diving**.

AGIA GALINI ΑΓΙΑ ΓΑΛΗΝΗ

pop 1273

Agia Galini (ah-yee-ah ga-lee-nee) is another picturesque erstwhile fishing village which really has gone down the tubes due to an overdose of tourism. Hemmed in against the sea by large sandstone cliffs and phalanxes of hotels and domatia, Agia Galini is rather claustrophobic – an ambience which is not ameliorated by an ugly, cement-block-littered harbour. Still, it does boast 340 days of sunshine a year, and some places remain open out of season. It's a convenient base from which to visit Phaestos and Agia Triada, and although the town beach is mediocre, there are boats to better beaches (see Taxi Boat, p238).

Orientation & Information

The bus station is at the top of Eleftheriou Venizelou, which is a continuation of the approach road. The central square, overlooking the harbour, is downhill from the bus station. You'll walk past the post office on the way. There is no bank but there are lots of travel agencies with currency exchange. Check your email at **Cosmos Internet** (☎ 2832 091 262; €3.50 per hr; ⏱ 9am-late).

CRETE

Sleeping

Agia Galini Camping (☎ 2832 091 386; camp sites per adult/tent €4/3.50) This camping ground is next to the beach, 2.5km east of the town. It is signposted from the Iraklio–Agia Galini road. The site is well shaded and has a restaurant, snack bar and minimarket.

Candia Rooms (☎ 2832 091 203; s/d €17/20) This place has very basic rooms, but the price does include a private bathroom. To get there take the first left opposite the post office.

Areti (☎ 2832 091 240; s/d €17.60/29.50) This place with pleasant rooms is on the road to town and again the price includes a private bathroom.

Stohos Rooms (☎ 2832 091 433; d/tr €36/40) This is the only accommodation on the beach and is in standard studio-style with kitchenette and fridge.

Eating

Medousa Taverna (☎ 2832 091 487; grills €4.50-6) In the town centre, this taverna is owned by a German/Greek couple and presents a menu of specialities from both countries.

Onar (☎ 2832 091 288; mezedes €2-5.50) Onar (meaning 'dream' in Homeric Greek) overlooks the harbour and is a good place to come for breakfast, mezedes or cocktails.

Faros (☎ 2832 091 346; fish €10-15) Right on the harbour, Faros is one of the oldest and best fish tavernas and has a cult following. The owner dishes up fresh fish as well as a range of grills and mayirefta.

Madame Hortense (☎ 2832 091 215; mains €6-12) The most elaborate restaurant-bar in town is on the top floor of the three-level Zorbas complex on the harbour. Cuisine is Greek Mediterranean, with a touch of the East.

Getting There & Away

BUS

The story is the same as at the other beach resorts: heaps of buses in summer, skeletal services in winter. In peak season there are seven buses a day to Iraklio (€5.75, 2½ hours), four to Rethymno (€4.60, 1½ hours), six to Matala (€2.40, 45 minutes) and six to Phaestos (€1.70, 40 minutes).

TAXI BOAT

In summer there are daily taxi boats from the harbour to the beaches of Agios Giorgios, Agios Pavlos and Preveli (Palm Beach). These beaches, which are west of Agia Galini, are difficult to get to by land. All three are less crowded than, and far superior to, the Agia Galini beach. Departures are between 9.30am and 10.30am

HANIA XANIA

pop 53,373

Hania (hahn-*yah*; also spelt Chania) is Crete's second city and former capital. The beautiful, crumbling Venetian quarter of Hania that surrounds the Old Harbour is one of Crete's best attractions. A lot of money has been spent on restoring the old buildings. Some of them have been converted into very fine accommodation while others now house chic restaurants, bars and shops.

The Hania district gets a lot of package tourists, but most of them stick to the beach developments that stretch out seemingly endlessly to the west. The Old Town has to be one of the best places to hang out for a few days in the whole of Crete and Hania is a main transit point for trekkers heading for the Samaria Gorge.

History

Hania is the site of the Minoan settlement of Kydonia, which was centred on the hill to the east of the harbour. Little excavation work has been done, but the finding of clay tablets with Linear B script (see the boxed text p210) has led archaeologists to believe that Kydonia was both a palace site and an important town.

Kydonia met the same fiery fate as most other Minoan settlements in 1450 BC, but soon re-emerged as a force. It was a flourishing city-state during Hellenistic times and continued to prosper under Roman and Byzantine rule.

The city became Venetian at the beginning of the 13th century, and the name was changed to La Canea. The Venetians spent a lot of time constructing massive fortifications to protect the city from marauding pirates and invading Turks. This did not prove very effective against the latter, who took Hania in 1645 after a two-month siege.

The Great Powers made Hania the island capital in 1898 and it remained so until 1971, when the administration was transferred to Iraklio.

Hania was heavily bombed during WWII, but enough of the old town survives for it to be regarded as Crete's most beautiful city.

Orientation

The town's bus station is on Kydonias, two blocks southwest of Plateia 1866, one of the city's main squares. From Plateia 1866 to the Old Harbour is a short walk north down Halidon.

The main hotel area is to the left as you face the harbour, where Akti Koundourioti leads around to the old fortress on the headland. The headland separates the Venetian port from the crowded town beach in the quarter called Nea Hora.

Zambeliou, which dissects Halidon just before the harbour, was once the town's main thoroughfare. It's a narrow street, lined with craft shops, small hotels and tavernas.

Information

BOOKSHOPS
News Stand (☎ 2821 095 888; Skalidi 8) Sells foreign-language newspapers, books and maps and has a few Lonely Planet titles as well.

INTERNET RESOURCES
Manos Internet Café (☎ 2821 094 156; Zambeliou 24; €3 per hr; ☺ 10am-midnight)
Vranas Studios (☎ 2821 058 618; Agion Deka 10; €3 per hr; ☺ 9am-2am)

LAUNDRY
Afroditi Laundry (Agion Deka 18) A wash and dry costs €6.
Laundry Fidias (Sarpaki 6) A wash and dry costs €6.

LEFT LUGGAGE
Luggage can be stored at the bus station for €1.50 per day.

MONEY
Most banks are concentrated around the New City while there are some stand-alone ATMs in the Old City including a **Citibank ATM** (Halidon) and a **Commercial Bank ATM** (Food market). The **National Bank of Greece** (cnr Tzanakaki & Giannari) and the **Alpha Bank** (cnr Halidon & Sakalidi) have 24-hour automatic exchange machines. There are numerous places to change money outside banking hours.

POST
Central post office (Tzanakaki 3; ☺ 7.30am-8pm Mon-Fri, 7.30am-2pm Sat)

TOURIST INFORMATION
Hania's **Tourist Information Office** (☎ 2821 036 155; chania@atcrete.gr; Plateia 1866 16-18; ☺ 8am-2.30pm)
is a well-organised and considerably more helpful office than most and dishes up lots of practical and helpful data. Their office may have moved to Kydonias 29 by 2004. The Municipality of Hania's website www.chania.gr is also worth a look for more background information.

The **tourist police** (☎ 2821 073 333; Iraklion 23; ☺ 8am-2.30pm) are a bit of a hike from the centre.

Sights

MUSEUMS
In the 16th-century Venetian Church of San Francisco is the **archaeological museum** (☎ 2821 090 334; Halidon 21; admission €2; ☺ 8.30am-3pm Tue-Sun). The Turkish fountain in the grounds is a relic from the building's days as a mosque. The museum houses a well-displayed collection of finds from western Crete dating from the Neolithic to the Roman era. Exhibits include statues, pottery, coins, jewellery, three splendid floor mosaics and some impressive painted sarcophagi from the Late-Minoan cemetery of Armeni.

The **naval museum** (☎ 2821 091 875; Akti Koundourioti; admission €2; ☺ 9am-4pm) has an interesting collection of model ships, naval instruments, paintings and photographs. It is housed in the fortress on the headland overlooking the Venetian port.

Hania has an interesting **folklore museum** (☎ 2821 090 816; Halidon 46b; admission €1.50; ☺ 9am-3pm & 6-9pm Mon-Fri).

OTHER ATTRACTIONS
The area to the east of the Old Harbour, between Akti Tombazi and Karaoli Dimitriou, is the site of **Ancient Kydonia**. The search for Minoan remains began in the early 1960s and excavation work continues sporadically. The site can be seen at the junction of Kanevaro and Kandanoleou, and many of the finds are on display in the archaeological museum.

Kydonia has been remodelled by a succession of occupiers. After ejecting the Arabs, the Byzantines set about building their *kastelli* (castle) on the same site, on top of the old walls in some places and using the same materials. It was here, too, that the Venetians first settled. Modern Kanevaro was the corso of their city. It was this part of town that bore the brunt of the bombing in WWII.

HANIA

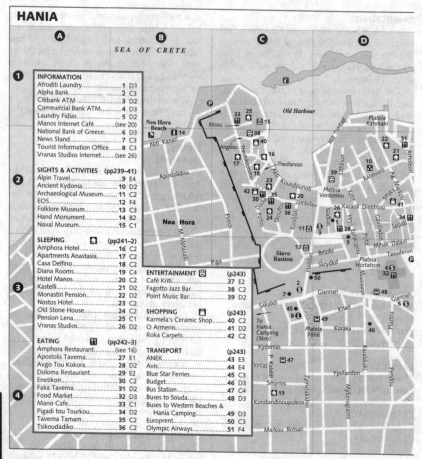

INFORMATION
Afroditi Laundry.................. 1 D3
Alpha Bank.......................... 2 C3
Citibank ATM....................... 3 D2
Commercial Bank ATM........ 4 D3
Laundry Fidias..................... 5 D2
Manos Internet Café...........(see 20)
National Bank of Greece....... 6 D3
News Stand.......................... 7 C3
Tourist Information Office..... 8 C3
Vranas Studios Internet........(see 26)

SIGHTS & ACTIVITIES (pp239–41)
Alpin Travel......................... 9 E4
Ancient Kydonia................. 10 D2
Archaeological Museum....... 11 C2
EOS..................................... 12 F4
Folklore Museum................ 13 C3
Hand Monument................. 14 B2
Naval Museum.................... 15 C1

SLEEPING (pp241–2)
Amphora Hotel.................. 16 C2
Apartments Anastasia......... 17 C2
Casa Delfino...................... 18 C2
Diana Rooms...................... 19 C4
Hotel Manos...................... 20 C2
Kastelli.............................. 21 D2
Monastiri Pension.............. 22 D2
Nostos Hotel...................... 23 C2
Old Stone House................ 24 C2
Pension Lena..................... 25 C1
Vranas Studios................... 26 C2

EATING (pp242–3)
Amphora Restaurant...........(see 16)
Apostolis Taverna............... 27 E1
Avgo Tou Kokora................ 28 D2
Doloma Restaurant............. 29 E2
Enetikon............................ 30 C2
Faka Taverna...................... 31 D2
Food Market....................... 32 D3
Mano Cafe......................... 33 C1
Pigadi tou Tourkou............. 34 D2
Taverna Tamam.................. 35 C2
Tsikoudadiko...................... 36 C2

ENTERTAINMENT (p243)
Café Kriti........................... 37 E2
Fagotto Jazz Bar................. 38 C2
Point Music Bar.................. 39 D2

SHOPPING (p243)
Karmela's Ceramic Shop...... 40 C2
O Armenis.......................... 41 D2
Roka Carpets...................... 42 C2

TRANSPORT (p243)
ANEK................................. 43 E3
Avis................................... 44 E4
Blue Star Ferries................. 45 C3
Budget............................... 46 D3
Bus Station........................ 47 C4
Buses to Souda.................. 48 D3
Buses to Western Beaches &
 Hania Camping................ 49 D3
Europrtent.......................... 50 C3
Olympic Airways................. 51 F4

The massive **fortifications** built by the Venetians to protect their city remain impressive today. The best-preserved section is the western wall, running from the fortezza to the **Siavo Bastion**. It was part of a defensive system begun in 1538 by engineer Michele Sanmichele, who also designed Iraklio's defences. You can walk up to the top of the rather overgrown bastion for some good views of the Old Town.

The **lighthouse** at the entrance to the harbour is the most visible of the Venetian monuments. It looks in need of tender loving care these days, but the 1.5km walk around the sea wall to get there is worth it.

You can escape the crowds of the Venetian quarter by taking a stroll around the **Splantzia quarter** – a delightful tangle of narrow streets and little squares.

Whether you are self-catering or not you should at least feast your eyes on Hania's magnificent covered **food market**. It makes all other food markets look like stalls at a church bazaar. Unfortunately, the central bastion of the city wall had to be demolished to make way for this fine cruciform creation, built in 1911.

Activities

Alpin Travel (☎ 2821 053 309; Boniali 11-19; ◷ 9am-2pm Mon-Fri) offers many trekking programmes. The owner, George Andonakakis, helps run the **EOS** (☎ 2821 044 647; Tzanakaki 90) and is the person to talk to about serious climbing

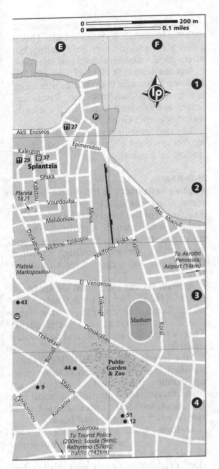

in the Lefka Ori mountains. George can provide information on Greece's mountain refuges, the E4 trail, and climbing and trekking in Crete in general.

Trekking Plan (☎ 2821 060 861; Agia Marina), on the main road next to Santa Marina Hotel, offers treks (around €25) to the Agia Irini Gorge and climbs of Mt Gingilos, among other destinations. It also offers a full programme of mountain-bike tours (from €28) at varying levels of difficulty.

Tours

British historian **Tony Fennymore** (☎ 2821 087 139; www.fennyscrete.ws) runs walking tours (a two-hour walk costs €12) which begin at the 'Hand' monument on Plateia Talo at the

bottom of Theotokopoulou. Sheffield-born photographer **Steve Outram** (☎ 2821 032 201; www.steveoutram.com) runs photography tours in Crete twice a year for amateurs and more advanced photographers alike.

Sleeping
BUDGET
The best accommodation in town is around the Venetian port, where a swathe of small boutique hotels, studios and simple rooms offer a large range of options to suit all budgets.

Hania Camping (☎ 2821 031 138; fax 2821 033 371; Hrysi Akti; camp sites per adult/tent €5/3.50) This facility, 3km west of town on the beach, is the nearest camping ground to Hania. It is shaded and has a restaurant, bar and minimarket. Take the Hania–Stalos bus (€21, every 20 minutes) from the southeast corner of Plateia 1866.

Monastiri Pension (☎ 2821 054 776; Ag Markou 18; d €32.50) This pension has a great setting right next to the ruins of the Moni Santa Maria de Miracolioco in the heart of the old kastelli. Rooms are fair value; they're simple with shared bathrooms but some have a sea view. There's a convenient communal kitchen.

Diana Rooms (☎ 2821 097 888, P Kelaïdi 33; s/d €25/40; 🖳) If you want to hop straight out of bed and onto an early morning bus bound for the Samaria Gorge, these are the most convenient rooms for the bus station. They are light, airy and clean.

Pension Lena (☎ 6932 829 788; www.travelling-crete .com/lena; Ritsou 3; s/d €28/50; 🖳) This friendly pension is in an old Turkish building. Rooms are tastefully decorated and there is a communal kitchen for guests.

Apartments Anastasia (☎ 2821 088 001; Theotokopoulou 21; studios €42; 🖳) These are stylish, well-equipped and spacious studios right on busy Theotokopoulou.

Hotel Manos (☎ 2821 094 156; www.manoshotel.gr; Zambeliou 24; s/d €45/55; 🖳) Located over its own Internet café, Hotel Manos has largish, open and airy rooms and is very central so can get a fair bit of evening noise.

Old Stone House (☎ 6932 829 788; www.travelling -crete.com/lena; Ritsou 3; house €60; 🖳) Hamburg-born Lena from Pension Lena also offers a small, two storey, fully equipped house to rent in the back streets of the old town.

Kastelli (☎ 2821 057 057; Kanevaro 39; s/d €35/40; apt €60-90; 🖳) At the quieter, eastern end of the harbour, Kastelli has renovated apartments with high ceilings, white walls and pine floors.

MID-RANGE

Most places in this category are renovated Venetian houses.

Nostos Hotel (☎ 2821 094 743; fax 2821 094 740; Zambeliou 42-46; s/d €46/75) Mixing Venetian style and modern fixtures, this is a 600-year-old building which has been modelled into classy split-level rooms and units, some with kitchenettes. Try to get a room in front for the harbour view.

Vranas Studios (☎ /fax 2821 058 618; Agion Deka 10; studios €50; ⌨ 🖥) This place is on a lively pedestrian street and has spacious, immaculately maintained studios which come with kitchenettes. All the rooms have polished wooden floors, balconies and TV. There's a handy Internet café downstairs.

TOP END

Amphora Hotel (☎ 2821 093 224; www.amphora.gr; Akti Koundourioti 49; s/d €65/75; ⌨) This is Hania's most historically evocative hotel. With its rambling wooden staircases it is located in an immaculately restored Venetian mansion with rooms around a courtyard. There's no elevator but the rooms are elegantly decorated and several have premium views of the harbour.

Casa Delfino (☎ 2821 093 098; www.casadelfino.com; Theofanous 7; s/d €117/205; ⌨) This modernised 17th-century mansion features a splendid courtyard of traditionally patterned cobblestones and 19 individually decorated suites. All have satellite TV, telephones, hair dryers, minibars and safes. The top-floor suites have their own harbour-view terraces.

Eating

BUDGET

The most atmospheric places to eat are on the harbour, but most restaurants here are over-priced, low-quality tourist traps. There are some good finds in the back streets and on the east side of the harbour. Unless noted, all places open for lunch and dinner.

Doloma Restaurant (☎ 2821 051 196; Kalergon 8; mains €3-4.70; ⌚ dinner Mon-Sat) You'll find very similar fare to the market restaurants here. This place is a great favourite with students from the nearby university.

Mano Café (☎ 2821 072 265; Theotokopoulou 62; continental breakfast €3.70; ⌚ 8am-midnight) This is a tiny place and has very little seating, but offers good-value breakfasts and snacks.

Avgo tou Kokora (☎ 2821 055 776; cnr Agion Deka & Kallinikou Sarpaki; mains €3-6) The 'Rooster's Egg' is a restaurant cum snack bar. Pasta, fish, crepes and salads all feature on the mouthwatering menu. Good for lunch.

The two no-frills restaurants in the food market are good places to seek out cheap, traditional cuisine.

MID-RANGE

Amphora Restaurant (☎ 2821 093 224; Akti Koundourioti 49; mains €4.50-7) By local consent the Amphora (in the hotel of the same name) is the best harbourside restaurant. There's no streetside touting and the quality food and service are outstanding. Excellent pasta dishes are suggested for an unfussy lunch.

Apostolis Taverna (☎ 2821 045 470; Akti Enoseos 6-10; mains €4-7.50) Over on the far eastern side of the harbour far from the tourist traps, this low-key taverna is a local favourite. There's fresh fish and grills and good value mayirefta.

Faka Taverna (☎ 2821 042 341; Enetiko Limani; mains €5.50-8.50) This is another of those quiet unassuming places that doesn't dish up bland tourist fare. The cuisine is solid and genuine. Good local choices include Cretan rice or artichokes and broad beans.

Enetikon (☎ 2821 088 270; Zambeliou 57; mains €4-6.50) If you're looking for no-nonsense, simple grills and cooked dishes, Enetikon does it right. You'd easily miss this low-key taverna if you weren't looking. Chicken in curry sauce and the spicy *fileto diavola* (devil's fillet) are two of the chef's more exotic specials.

Taverna Tamam (☎ 2821 096 080; Zambeliou 49; mains €4-6.50) An old Turkish *hamam* (bathhouse) has been converted into this taverna, where you'll find tasty soups and a good range of well-prepared main dishes.

Tsikoudadiko (☎ 2821 072 873; Zambeliou 31; mains €4-7.50) Tsikoudadiko offers among its many Cretan dishes a good *kouneli stifado* (rabbit in tomato sauce) or *fava* (yellow lentil puree). Dine in a splendid old plant-filled courtyard in a building with no roof.

Pigadi tou Tourkou (☎ 2821 054 547; Sarpaki 1; mains €5.80-8; ⌚ 7pm-midnight Wed-Mon) This is in the heart of the old Turkish residential district and has a wide range of Middle Eastern dishes, as well as occasional live music.

Entertainment

Many visitors are content to sit around the old harbour and drink beer. Party animals head west to Agia Marina and Platanias. There are a few joints in the Old City worth checking out.

Café Kriti (Lyrakia; ☎ 2821 058 661; Kalergon 22; 6pm-1am) This is a rough-and-ready dive but it's the best place in Hania to hear live Cretan music and to have a drink. Music starts after 8.30pm.

Fagotto Jazz Bar (☎ 2821 071 887; Angelou 16; 7pm-2am mid-Jul–Oct) Black-and-white photographs of jazz greats line the walls here. It's housed in a restored Venetian building and offers the smooth sounds of jazz and light rock.

Point Music Bar (☎ 2821 057 556; Sourmeli 2; 9.30pm-2am) This is a good rock bar for those allergic to techno. When the interior gets steamy you can cool off on the 1st-floor balcony overlooking the harbour.

Shopping

Roka Carpets (☎ 2821 074 736; rokacarpets@hotmail .com; Zambeliou 61) Watch the welcoming Mihalis Manousakis weave his wondrous rugs on a 400-year-old loom using methods that have remained essentially unchanged since Minoan times. This is one of the few places in Greece where you can buy the genuine item.

O Armenis (☎ 2821 054 434; Sifaka 29) Knife maker Apostolos Pahtikos has been making and selling traditional Cretan knives since he was 13. You can watch him work as he matches the blade to the carefully carved handle. A decent-sized, handmade knife will cost around €50.

Karmela's Ceramic Shop (☎ 2821 040 487; Angelou 7) Karmela's produces ceramics using ancient techniques and also displays unusual jewellery handcrafted by young Greek artisans.

Getting There & Away

AIR

Olympic Airways has at least four flights a day to Athens (€73 to €83, one hour). There are also two flights a week to Thessaloniki (€110, 1½ hours). Buy tickets from the **Olympic Airways office** (☎ 2821 057 701; Tzanakaki 88) or from any travel agent.

Aegean Airlines (☎ 2821 063 366; fax 2821 063 669) has up to six daily flights to Athens and two to Thessaloniki with the same flying times and prices as Olympic Airways. Its office is at the airport on the Akrotiri Peninsula, 14km from Hania.

BUS

Buses depart from Hania's bus station for the following destinations:

BUSES FROM HANIA

Destination	Time	€	Frequency
Elafonisi	2hr	€8.40	1 daily
Falasarna	1½hr	€5.75	2 daily
Hora Sfakion	2hr	€5.65	3 daily
Iraklio	2½hr	€11	half-hourly
Kissamos	1hr	€3.55	16 daily
Moni Agias Triadas	30min	€1.80	3 daily
Omalos	1hr	€5.25	4 daily
(for Samaria Gorge)			
Paleohora	2hr	€5.65	4 daily
Rethymno	1hr	€5.80	half-hourly
Sougia	2hr	€5.35	1 daily
Stavros	30min	€1.55	6 daily

FERRY

Hania's main port is at Souda, about 7km east of town. In summer there are two ferries a day to/from Piraeus. ANEK has a daily boat at 8.30pm (€21, nine hours) while Blue Star Ferries has a superior daily high speed service departing at 11.30pm (€25, 5¾ hours).

The **ANEK office** (☎ 2821 027 500; www.anek.gr; cnr N Plastira & Apokoronou) and the **Blue Star Ferries** (☎ 2821 075 444; www.bluestarferries.com; Plateia 1826 14) are both in the New City. Souda's port police can be contacted on ☎ 2821 089 240.

Getting Around

There is no airport bus. A taxi to the airport costs about €13.

Local buses (blue) for the port of Souda leave from outside the food market. Buses for the western beaches leave from Plateia 1866.

Most motorcycle-rental outlets are on Halidon. Car rental outlets include:

Avis (☎ 2821 050 510; Tzanakaki 58)

Budget (☎ 2821 092 778; Karaïskaki 39)

Europrent (☎ 2821 040 810; Halidon 87)

CRETE

AKROTIRI PENINSULA
ΧΕΡΣΟΝΗΣΟΣ ΑΚΡΩΤΗΡΙ

The Akrotiri (ahk-ro-*tee*-rih) Peninsula, to the east of Hania, has a few places of fairly minor interest, as well as being the site of Hania's airport, port and a military base. There is an immaculate **military cemetery** at Souda, where about 1500 British, Australian and New Zealand soldiers who lost their lives in the Battle of Crete are buried. The buses to Souda port from outside the Hania food market can drop you at the cemetery.

If you haven't yet had your fill of Cretan monasteries, there are three on the Akrotiri Peninsula. The impressive 17th-century **Moni Agias Triadas** (☎ 2821 063 310; admission €1.50; ⏱ 8am-7pm) was founded by the Venetian monks Jeremiah and Laurentio Giancarolo. The brothers were converts to the Orthodox faith.

The 16th-century **Moni Gouvernetou** (☎ 2821 063 319; ⏱ 8am-2pm & 4-8pm) is 4km north of Moni Agias Triada. The church inside the monastery has an ornate sculptured Venetian facade. Both Moni Agias Triadas and Moni Gouvernetou are still in use.

From Moni Gouvernetou, it's a 1km walk on the path leading down to the coast to the ruins of **Moni Ioannou Erimiti**, known also as **Moni Katholikou**. The monastery is dedicated to St John the Hermit who lived in the cave behind the ruins. It is 1km to reach the sea.

There are three buses daily (except Sunday) at 6.30am and 1pm to Moni Agias Triadas from Hania's bus station (€1.80, 30 minutes).

HANIA TO XYLOSKALO
ΧΑΝΙΑ ΠΡΟΣ ΞΥΛΟΣΚΑΛΟ

While the mountains and slopes of the Samaria Gorge are home to many species of Crete's wildlife, spotting them can be quite a challenge as the thousands of walkers who trek the gorge each year are something of disincentive for the animals to make an appearance. The gorge is the protected habitat of the wild ibex – the kri-kri – though the only ones you are likely to encounter are a few curious semi-domesticated samples that hang around the halfway point of the walk looking for handouts.

The road from Hania to the beginning of the Samaria Gorge is one of the most spectacular routes on Crete. It heads through orange groves to the village of **Fournes** where a left fork leads to **Meskla**. The main road continues to the village of **Lakki**, 24km from Hania. This unspoilt village in the Lefka Ori Mountains affords stunning views wherever you look. The village was a centre of resistance during the uprising against the Turks, and during WWII.

From Lakki, the road continues to **Omalos** and Xyloskalo, start of the Samaria Gorge. A number of visitors choose to stay at Omalos in order to make the earliest start possible on the Samaria Gorge. The friendliest hotel in Omalos is the **Hotel Gigilos** (☎ 2825 067 181; s/d €17/25) where rooms are rather barely furnished, but are quite large and very clean. Across the road the **Hotel Exari** (☎ 2825 067 180; fax 2825 067 124; s/d €20/25) has been renovated in recent times and has pleasant, well-furnished rooms as well as an attached restaurant. The owners give walkers lifts to Xyloskalo.

Then there is always the **Kallergi Hut** (☎ 2825 033 199; dm €6) maintained by the EOS in the hills between Omalos and the Samaria Gorge. It has 45 beds, electricity (no hot water) and makes a good base for exploring Mt Gingilos and surrounding peaks.

SAMARIA GORGE
ΦΑΡΑΓΓΙ ΤΗΣ ΣΑΜΑΡΙΑΣ

It's a wonder the stones and rocks underfoot haven't worn away completely, given the number of people who tramp through the **Samaria Gorge** (☎ 2825 067 179; admission €5; ⏱ 6am-3pm 1 May–mid-Oct). Despite the crowds, a trek through this stupendous gorge is still an experience to remember.

At 18km, the Samaria (sah-mah-rih-*ah*) Gorge is supposedly the longest in Europe. It begins just below the Omalos Plateau, carved out by the river that flows between the peaks of Avlimaniko (1858m) and Volakias (2147m). Its width varies from 150m to 3m and its vertical walls reach 500m at their highest points. The gorge has an incredible number of wild flowers, which are at their best in April and May.

It is also home to a large number of endangered species. They include the Cretan wild goat, the kri-kri, which survives in the wild only here and on the islet of Kri-Kri, off the coast of Agios Nikolaos. The gorge was made a national park in 1962 to save the kri-kri from extinction. You are unlikely to see too many of these shy animals, which show a marked aversion to trekkers.

An early start (before 8am) helps to avoid the worst of the crowds, but during July and August even the early bus from Hania to the top of the gorge can be packed. There's no spending the night in the gorge so you are going to have to complete the hike in the time allocated.

The trek from **Xyloskalo**, the name of the steep stone pathway with wooden rails that gives access to the gorge, to **Agia Roumeli** takes from between 4½ hours for the sprinters to six hours for the strollers. Early in the season it's sometimes necessary to wade through the stream. Later, as the flow drops, it's possible to use rocks as stepping stones.

The gorge is wide and open for the first 6km, until you reach the abandoned settlement of **Samaria**. The inhabitants were relocated when the gorge became a national park. Just south of the village is a small church dedicated to **Saint Maria of Egypt**, after whom the gorge is named.

The gorge then narrows and becomes more dramatic until, at the 11km mark, the walls are only 3.5m apart – the famous **Iron Gates** (Sidiroportes). Here a rickety wooden pathway leads trekkers the 20m or so over the water and through to the other side.

The gorge ends at the 12.5km mark just north of the almost abandoned village of Old Agia Roumeli. From here it's a further uninteresting 2km hike to the welcoming seaside resort of Agia Roumeli, with its much-appreciated fine pebble beach and sparkling sea, where most hikers can be seen between 1pm and 3pm stripping off boots and bathing sore and aching feet or taking a full, refreshing dip.

What to Bring

Rugged footwear is *absolutely essential* for walking on the uneven ground covered by sharp stones. Don't attempt the walk in unsuitable footwear – you will regret it. Even soft sports shoes are unsuitable. You'll also need a hat and sunscreen. There's no need to take water. While it's inadvisable to drink water from the main stream, there are plenty of springs along the way spurting delicious cool water straight from the rock. There is nowhere to buy food until

you reach either entrance to the gorge, so bring some energy food to snack on.

Getting There & Away

There are excursions to the Samaria Gorge from every sizable town and resort on Crete. Most travel agents have two excursions: 'Samaria Gorge Long Way' and 'Samaria Gorge Easy Way'. The first comprises the regular trek from the Omalos Plateau to Agia Roumeli; the second starts at Agia Roumeli and takes you as far as the Iron Gates.

Obviously it's cheaper to trek the Samaria Gorge under your own steam. Hania is the most convenient base. There are buses to Xyloskalo (Omalos, €4.70, one hour) at 6.15am, 7.30am, 8.30am and 1.45pm. There's also a direct bus to Xyloskalo from Paleohora (€4.75, 1½ hours) at 6am.

AGIA ROUMELI ΑΓΙΑ ΡΟΥΜΕΛΗ
pop 125

Agia Roumeli is a pleasant enough stopover for a day or two; however, it is hemmed in by heat-trapping mountains and can get very hot and stifling. The fine pebbled beach is OK, but gets exceptionally hot and thus impossible to sit on unless you hire a beach umbrella and sun lounger.

If you've just trekked through the gorge and you're in no hurry to leave, there are now quite a few places to stay in the village and lots of decent places to eat. There are even a few cars around even though there are hardly any roads.

You might park your weary bones at **Hotel Agia Roumeli** (☎ 2825 091 232; fax 2825 091 232; s/d €20.50/26) a D-class hotel with reasonable rooms and you could always treat yourself to a welcoming lunch at the **Farangi Restaurant** (☎ 2825 091 225; mains €3-5) where a pot-baked mousakas and a large draft beer taste like manna from heaven after the 15km of hard slog down the gorge. If you're too bushed to move far after your meal, there are some tidy **rooms** (d €27) above the restaurant where you can crash until the following day.

There are three boats daily from Agia Roumeli to Hora Sfakion (€5, 1¼ hours) via Loutro (€2.70, 45 minutes). They connect with the bus back to Hania. There's also a boat from Agia Roumeli to Paleohora (€6.80) at 4.45pm, calling at Sougia (€3.20).

CRETE

AROUND AGIA ROUMELI

The small but rapidly expanding fishing village of **Loutro** (Λουτρό) lies between Agia Roumeli and Hora Sfakion. Loutro doesn't have a beach, but there are rocks from which you can swim. There are stacks of waterside restaurants of which **Ilios** (☎ 2825 091 160; mains €4-6) at the eastern end of the harbour is the best at dishing up fish and the generic traditional Cretan dishes. You might need to book a table in August as demand can get high.

An extremely steep path leads up from Loutro to the village of **Anopolis** (Ανώπολη) or you can get in and out of Loutro much more easily by taking the thrice-daily ferry along the south coast to Hora Sfakion, or even making the 7km coastal trek. On the way you will pass the celebrated **Sweet Water Beach**, named after freshwater springs which seep from the rocks. Freelance campers spend months at a time here. Even if you don't feel inclined to join them, you won't be able to resist a swim in the translucent sea.

The Hania–Skaloti bus runs via Anopolis. It leaves Hania at 2pm and returns the following morning, calling in at Anopolis at 7am.

HORA SFAKION ΧΟΡΑ ΣΦΑΚΙΩΝ

pop 351

Hora Sfakion (ho-rah sfah-kee-on) is a small coastal port where hordes of walkers from the Samaria Gorge spill off the boat and onto the bus. As such, in high season it can seem like Piccadilly Circus at rush hour. Most people pause only long enough to catch the next bus out. That said it is pleasant enough in its own right with its fair share of sleeping and eating options and it's convenient spot for heading westwards to other south coast resorts or even taking a ferry to the island of Gavdos.

Hora Sfakion played a prominent role during WWII when thousands of Allied troops were evacuated by sea from the town after the Battle of Crete.

Orientation & Information

The ferry quay is at the eastern side of the harbour. Buses leave from the square up the hill on the eastern side. There is one ATM. The post office is on the square, and the police station overlooks it. There is no tourist office or tourist police.

Sleeping & Eating

Accommodation in the village is of a reasonable quality and value. Some of the better accommodation is on the waterfront. **Rooms Stavris** (☎ 2825 091 220; stavris@chania-cci.gr; s/d €24/26; ❄), up the steps at the western end of the port, has clean rooms with bathrooms and kitchenettes while **Hotel Samaria** (☎ 2825 091 261; fax 2825 091 161; s/d €20/28; ❄) is a reasonably decent waterfront hotel. Finally the **Livikon** (☎ 2825 091 211; fax 2825 091 222; s/d €30/40; ❄) has large, brightly decorated rooms with stone floors and sea views.

These last two hotels both have restaurants downstairs that have a good selection of mayirefta and vegetarian dishes.

Getting There & Away

BUS

There are four buses a day from Hora Sfakion to Hania (€5.65, two hours) – the last one leaves at 7pm. In summer only there are two daily buses to Plakias (€3.65, 1¼ hours) via Frangokastello, leaving at 10.30am and 5.30pm.

BOAT

From June through August there is one daily boat from Hora Sfakion to Paleohora (€8.50, three hours) via Loutro, Agia Roumeli and Sougia. The boat leaves at 1.15pm. There are also an additional two boats a day to Agia Roumeli (€4.60, one hour) via Loutro (€2.80, 15 minutes). From 1 June there are boats (€9.50) to Gavdos Island (p250) on Friday, Saturday and Sunday leaving at 10.30am and returning at 5pm.

AROUND HORA SFAKION

The road from Vryses to Hora Sfakion cuts through the heart of the Sfakia region in the eastern Lefka Ori. The inhabitants of this region have long had a reputation for fearlessness and independence – characteristics they retain to this day. Cretans are regarded by other Greeks as being immensely proud and there is none more so than the Sfakiot.

One of Crete's most celebrated heroes, Ioannis Daskalogiannis, was from Sfakia. In 1770, Daskalogiannis led the first Cretan insurrection against Ottoman rule. When help promised by Russia failed to materialise, he gave himself up to the Turks to save his followers. As punishment the Turks skinned him alive in Iraklio. Witnesses related that

Daskalogiannis suffered this excruciating death in dignified silence.

The Turks never succeeded in controlling the Sfakiots, and this rugged mountainous region was the scene of fierce fighting. The story of their resistance lives on in the form of folk tales and *rizitika* (local folk songs).

The village of **Imbros**, 23km from Vryses, is at the head of the beautiful 8km **Imbros Gorge** (admission €2), which is far less visited than the Samaria Gorge. To get there, take any bus bound for Hora Sfakion from the north coast and get off at Imbros. Walk out of the village towards Hora Sfakion and a path to the left leads down to the gorge. The gorge path ends at the village of **Komitades**, from where it is an easy walk by road to Hora Sfakion. You can of course do the trek in reverse, beginning at Komitades. The Happy Walker organises treks through this gorge (see Activities in the Rethymno section, p233).

FRANGOKASTELLO ΦΡΑΝΚΟΚΑΣΤΕΛΛΟ

Frangokastello is a magnificent fortress on the coast 15km east of Hora Sfakion. It was built by the Venetians in 1371 as a defence against pirates and rebel Sfakiots, who resented the Venetian occupation as much as they did the Turkish.

It was here in 1770 that Ioannis Daskalogiannis surrendered to the Turks. On 17 May 1828 many Cretan rebels, led by Hadzi Mihalis Dalanis, were killed here by the Turks. Legend has it that at dawn each anniversary their ghosts can be seen marching along the beach (see the boxed text below).

The castle overlooks a gently sloping, sandy beach. Domatia and tavernas are springing up rapidly here, but it's still relatively unspoilt.

Buses between Hora Sfakion and Plakias go via Frangokastello.

SOUGIA ΣΟΥΓΙΑ
pop 262

It's surprising that Sougia (*soo*-yah) hasn't yet been commandeered by the package-tour crowd. With a wide curve of sand-and-pebble beach and a tree-lined coastal road, Sougia's tranquillity has been preserved only because it lies at the foot of a narrow, twisting road that would deter most tour buses.

If you arrive by boat, walk about 150m along the coast to the town centre. If you arrive by bus, the bus will drop you on the coastal road in front of Santa Irene Hotel. The only other road intersects the coastal road by Santa Irene Hotel and runs north to the Agia Irini Gorge and Hania.

Sougia doesn't have a post office or bank, but you can change money at several places, including **Polifimos Travel** (☎ 2823 051 022) and **Roxana's Office** (☎ 2823 051 362). Both are just off the coastal road on the road to Hania. Check your email at **Internet Lotos** (☎ 2823 051 191; €4 per hr; ☑ 10am-11pm).

There's no camping ground, but the eastern end of the long, pebbled beach is popular with freelance campers. There are quite a few options for room/studio accommodation though, most of the choices being clustered towards the east end of the promenade. These include **Rooms Maria** (☎ 2823 051 337; s/d €25/30) with plain but clean rooms, **Rooms Ririka** (☎ 2823 051 167; s/d €25/30) next door to Rooms Maria and in a similar style and also with rooms overlooking the sea.

CRETE

RESTLESS SPIRITS

The Frangokastello bloodshed of 17 May 1828 gave rise to the legend of the *drosoulites*. On the anniversary of the decisive battle (or in late May around dawn) it's said that a procession of ghostly figures – the ghosts of Hadzi Mihalis Dalanis and his followers – materialises around the fort and marches to the sea. The phenomenon has been verified by a number of independent observers. The name 'drosoulites' comes from the Greek word *drosia* meaning 'moisture', which could refer to the dawn moisture that is around when the ghosts are said to appear, or the watery content of the spirits themselves. Although locals believe the figures are the ghosts of the slaughtered rebels, others theorise that it may be an optical illusion created by certain atmospheric conditions and that the figures may be a reflection of camels or soldiers in the Libyan Desert. When questioned about the ghostly phenomenon, locals are understandably a little reticent, but remain convinced that something does in fact happen. Most claim that the older residents of Frangokastello have seen the apparitions. Whether you will depends on your luck – or belief in ghosts.

Inland, on the road to Hania you'll find **Aretousa Rooms to Rent** (☎ 2823 051 178; fax 2823 051 178; s/d €25/35; 🍴), which has lovely rooms with wood-panelled ceilings and balconies and next door the **Pension Galini** (☎ /fax 2823 051 488; s/d €26/32) with equally beautiful rooms.

The smartest accommodation is **Santa Irene Hotel** (☎ 2823 051 342; www.sougia.info/hotels/santairene; s/d €36/45; 🍴) on the seafront with well-furnished standard hotel rooms.

Restaurants line the waterfront and there are more on the main street. Just on the seafront as you enter town, **Kyma** (☎ 2823 051 670; fish dishes €18-25) has a good selection of ready made food as well as fresh fish dishes, while just up on the Hania road **Taverna Rembetiko** (☎ 2823 051 510; mains €3-5) serves various Cretan specialities such as *boureki* (small pastry pies) and stuffed zucchini flowers.

There's a daily bus travelling from Hania to Sougia (€5.35, 2½ hours) at 1.30pm. Buses going from Sougia to Hania leave at 7am.

Sougia is also on the Paleohora–Hora Sfakion boat route. Boats leave at 10.15am for Agia Roumeli (€3.20, one hour), Loutro (€5.60, 1½ hours) and Hora Sfakion (€5.90, two hours). For Paleohora (€4.30, one hour) to the west there is a departure at 5.15pm. There is also a boat on Tuesdays at 9am for the island of Gavdos (€8.50, three hours)

PALEOHORA ΠΑΛΑΙΟΧΩΡΑ
pop 2553

Paleohora (pah-le-*oh*-hora) was discovered by hippies back in the 60s and from then on its days as a tranquil fishing village were numbered. However, the resort operators have not gone way over the top – yet. The place retains a laid-back feel. It is also the only beach resort on Crete that does not close down in winter.

The little town is set on a narrow peninsula with a long, curving sandy beach exposed to the wind on one side and a sheltered pebbly beach on the other. On summer evenings the main street is closed to traffic and the tavernas move onto the road.

It's worth clambering up the ruins of the 13th-century **Venetian castle** for the splendid view of the sea and mountains. The most picturesque part of Paleohora is the area of narrow streets huddled around the castle.

From Paleohora, an 18km walk along a scenic coastal path leads to Sougia, passing the ancient site of Lissos.

Orientation

Paleohora's main street is Eleftheriou Venizelou, which runs north to south. Buses arrive at the northern end of this street from where it is quick 400m to the centre of the village. To the west of Eleftheriou Venizelou is the large and sandy Pahia Ammos beach while to the north east is the more pebbly Oriental Bay beach. Coastal excursion boats and ferries depart from a small jetty located on the east side of the village.

Information

Citibank ATM (Eleftheriou Venizelou)

Erato Internet (☎ 2823 083 010; Eleftheriou Venizelou; €4.50 per hr; 🕒 5.30pm-1am)

Municipal tourist office (☎ 2823 041 507; Eleftheriou Venizelou; 🕒 10am-1pm & 6-9pm Wed-Mon May-Oct) More or less in the village centre.

National Bank of Greece (Eleftheriou Venizelou) With an ATM.

Notos Internet (☎ 2823 042 110; Eleftheriou Venizelou; €4.50 per hr; 🕒 8am-1pm & 5.30-10pm)

Post office At the northern end of Pahia Ammos beach.

Tours

Various travel agents around town offer excursions to ancient Lissos (€22) and dolphin-watching trips (€14). A good travel agent is **Tsiskakis Travel** (☎ 2823 042 110; notosgr@yahoo.gr; Eleftheriou Venizelou).

Sleeping

Camping Paleohora (☎ 2823 041 225; camp sites per adult/tent €4/2.50) This ground is 1.5km northeast of the town, near the pebble beach. The site has a taverna but no minimarket.

Homestay Anonymous (☎ 2823 041 509; s/d €14/17) This is a great place for backpackers, with clean, simply furnished rooms set around a small, beautiful garden. There is a communal kitchen. The owner, Manolis speaks good English and is full of useful information for travellers.

Spamandos Rooms (☎ 2823 041 197; d/tr €30/35) In the old quarter, Spamandos has spotless, nicely furnished rooms right on the waterfront.

Poseidon Hotel (☎ 2823 041 374; www.c-v.net/hotel/paleohora/poseidon; s/d €22/30; 🍴) The studios at this friendly, breezy place right on Pahia Ammos beach come equipped with fridges and kitchenettes and all have a little balcony.

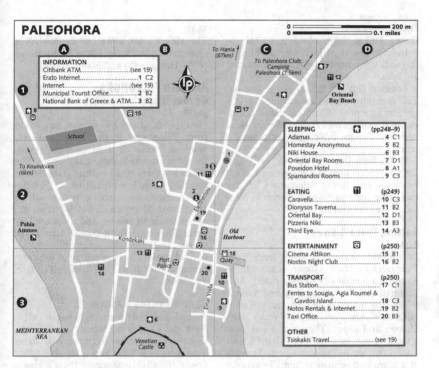

PALEOHORA

0 — 200 m
0 — 0.1 miles

INFORMATION
Citibank ATM.............................(see 19)
Erato Internet.................................1 C2
Internet...(see 19)
Municipal Tourist Office................2 B2
National Bank of Greece & ATM....3 B2

To Hania (87km)
To Paleohora Club; Camping Paleohora (1.5km)
Oriental Bay Beach

School

To Koundoura (6km)

Pahia Ammos

Kondekaki

Old Harbour

Port Police

Quay

Einai Yreba

MEDITERRANEAN SEA

Venetian Castle

SLEEPING (pp248–9)
Adamas..4 C1
Homestay Anonymous.....................5 B2
Niki House.......................................6 B3
Oriental Bay Rooms.........................7 D1
Poseidon Hotel...............................8 A1
Spamandos Rooms..........................9 C3

EATING (p249)
Caravella.......................................10 C3
Dionysos Taverna..........................11 B2
Oriental Bay..................................12 D1
Pizzeria Niki..................................13 B3
Third Eye.......................................14 A3

ENTERTAINMENT (p250)
Cinema Attikon..............................15 B1
Nostos Night Club..........................16 B2

TRANSPORT (p250)
Bus Station....................................17 C1
Ferries to Sougia, Agia Roumel & Gavdos Island.............................18 C3
Notos Rentals & Internet...............19 B2
Taxi Office.....................................20 B3

OTHER
Tsiskakis Travel...........................(see 19)

Oriental Bay Rooms (☎ 2823 041 076; s/d €35/38) This place occupies the large modern building at the northern end of the pebble beach. The owner keeps the rooms immaculate. There's also a shaded terrace-restaurant overlooking the sea (see Eating below).

Adamas (☎ 2823 041 848; adamas@chania-cci.gr; s/d €47; ❂) Amidst a flower-bedecked garden these modern rooms with TVs and large balconies are a little overpriced, but are unquestionably comfortable and make for a pleasant stay.

Niki House (☎ 2823 041 374; www.c-v.net/hotel/paleohora/niki-houses; apt €50) In the shade of the castle walls are these two large and fully equipped apartments, sleeping up to six people. They are ideal for self-caterers on extended stays.

Eating

The whole eastern seafront is chockablock full of eating choices while there are a few other options further inland.

Dionysos Taverna (☎ 2823 041 243; mains €4-7) The very popular Dionysos is a bit more expensive than other places but does serve top-grade food as well as a good range of vegetarian dishes. It has a roomy interior and a few tables outside under the trees.

Pizzeria Niki (☎ 2823 041 534; pizzas €4.50-7; ❂ dinner only) Just off Kondekaki, this place has superior pizzas cooked in a wood-fired oven and served on a spacious outdoor terrace.

Third Eye (☎ 2823 041 234; mains €4-6) Vegetarians flock to the Third Eye, just inland from Pahia Ammos. The fully vegetarian menu includes curries and a tempting range of Greek-Asian fusion dishes.

Caravella (☎ 2823 041 131; mains €5-6) Caravella has a prime position overlooking the old harbour and offers an array of fresh and competitively priced Greek dishes as well as fresh seafood.

Oriental Bay (☎ 2823 041 322; mains €6.50-9) Part of Oriental Bay Rooms, this beachside taverna is one of the best on this side of the village. Apart from a range of cheap vegetarian choices such as green beans and potatoes there are items such as 'rooster's kiss' (chicken fillet with bacon) and 'drunk cutlet' (pork chop in red wine).

CRETE

Entertainment

Cinema Attikon (tickets €5) Most visitors to Paleohora spend at least one evening at this well-signposted cinema. Showings start at 10pm.

Paleohora Club (☎ 2823 042 230; ⏰ 11pm-late) This is another option for a night out. It is next to Camping Paleohora 1.5km northeast of the village on Keratidies Beach. Head here for all-night full-moon parties once a month.

Nostos Night Club (☎ 2823 042 145; ⏰ 6pm-2am) If you've seen the movie and don't fancy the trek to the Paleohora Club, try this place right in town, between El Venizelou and the Old Harbour.

Getting There & Away

BOAT

In summer there is a daily ferry from Paleohora to Hora Sfakion (€8.50, three hours) via Sougia (€3.80, one hour), Agia Roumeli (€6.50, two hours) and Loutro (€7.90, 2½ hours). The ferry leaves Paleohora at 9.45am, and returns from Hora Sfakion at 1.15pm. There's also one boat a week in summer to Gavdos (€9.40, four hours) that leaves Paleohora every Tuesday at 8.30am and returns at 3pm. Tickets for all of these boats can be bought at **Tsiskakis Travel** (☎ 2823 042 110; Eleftheriou Venizelou) or any other travel agent selling tickets.

BUS

In summer there are five buses a day from the small **bus station** (☎ 2823 041 914) to Hania (€5.65, two hours). There is also one daily service to Omalos (€5.25, 1½ hours) – for the Samaria Gorge – that departs at 6.15am.

Getting Around

CAR, MOTORCYCLE & BICYCLE

All three can be hired from **Notos Rentals** (☎ 2823 042 110; notosgr@yahoo.gr; Eleftheriou Venizelou). Cars rent for around €25 to €35, a scooter for €16 and bicycle for €5.

EXCURSION BOAT

The M/B *Elafonisos* gets cranked into action in mid-April ferrying people to the west-coast beach of Elafonisi (€4.50, one hour). The service builds up from three times a week to daily in June through September. It departs at 10am and returns at 4pm.

TAXI

The village's **taxi office** (☎ 2823 041 128) is close to the port. Sample fares are Kissamos (€30), Hania (€45) and Elafonisi (€40).

AROUND PALEOHORA

Gavdos Island Νήσος Γαύδος

pop 98

Gavdos Island, in the Libyan Sea 65km from Paleohora, is the most southerly place in Europe. It is an excellent choice for those craving isolation and peace. The island has three small villages and pleasant beaches. There is a post office, OTE (telecommunications carrier), police officer and doctor. There are no hotels but several of the locals let rooms, and there are tavernas. Fishermen from Gavdos Island take tourists to the remote, uninhabited island of **Gavdopoula**. The best source of information about the island is Tsiskakis Travel in Paleohora.

GETTING THERE & AWAY

A small post boat operates between Paleohora and Gavdos on Monday and Thursday all year, weather permitting. It leaves Paleohora at 8.30am and takes about four hours (€9.40). In summer there's also a Tuesday boat. The boats turn around from Gavdos almost immediately.

There are also four boats a week from Hora Sfakion to Gavdos (€8) and a weekly boat from Sougia (€7).

Elafonisi Ελαφονήσι

As one of the loveliest sand beaches in Crete it's easy to understand why people enthuse so much about Elafonisi, at the southern extremity of Crete's west coast. The beach is long and wide and is separated from Elafonisi Islet by about 50m of knee-deep water on its northern side. The islet is marked by low dunes and a string of semi-secluded coves that attract a sprinkling of naturists.

All sleeping and eating choices are set back from the beach on the bluff. **Rooms Elafonissos** (☎ 2822 061 548; s/d studios €24/30) is comfortable enough and has a taverna overlooking the sea from its commanding position on a bluff. Not far away **Rooms Elafonissi** (☎ 2822 061 274; fax 2821 097 907; s/d €20/25) offers rooms with fridge, an outdoor patio and again, an attached restaurant.

Innahorion (☎ 2822 061 111; fax 2822 051 551; s/d €23.50/29.50; ☒) is perhaps the least attractive of the three options. The 15 rooms each have a fridge and kitchenette, but are set back a fair way from the beach. However, the restaurant is the best of the three, offering tasty food.

There is one boat daily from Paleohora to Elafonisi (€4.50, one hour) from mid-June through September, as well as daily buses from Hania (€8.40, 2½ hours) and Kissamos (€3.55, 1½ hours). The buses leave Hania at 7.30am and Kissamos at 8.30am, and both depart from Elafonisi at 4pm.

KISSAMOS ΚΙΣΣΑΜΟΣ
pop 3909

If you find yourself in the north-coast town of Kissamos, you've probably arrived by ferry from the Peloponnese or Kythira. Kissamos is a quiet town that neither expects nor attracts much tourism, but is worth much more than a passing glance. The huge Kissamos Bay has some fine pebble and sand beaches and the almost bucolic feel to the region is a welcome antidote to the bustling Crete further east. Kissamos is good base for walking, touring and generally unwinding. See the Gramvousa Peninsula section (p252) for information on cruises there from Kissamos.

In antiquity, its name was Kissamos and it was the main town of the province of the same name. When the Venetians came along and built a castle here, the place became known as Kastelli. The name persisted until 1966 when authorities decided that too many people were confusing this Kastelli with Crete's other Kastelli, 40km southeast of Iraklio. The official name reverted to Kissamos, and that's what appears on bus and shipping schedules. Local people still prefer Kastelli, and many books and maps agree with them. An alternative that is emerging is to combine the two into Kissamos-Kastelli, which leaves no room for misunderstanding.

Orientation & Information

The port is 3km west of town. From June through August a bus meets the boats; otherwise a taxi costs around €3.50. The bus station is on the main square, Plateia Tzanakaki, and the main commercial street, Sakalidi, runs east from Plateia Tzanakaki.

Kissamos has no tourist office, but has a reasonably informative website www.kissamos.net. The post office is on the main through road while there are a number of banks with ATMs along Sakalidi. The beach annexe is separated (still) by open fields through which it is a 200m walk to reach the foreshore promenade.

Sleeping

There are a couple of worthwhile camping grounds to choose from. Both are to the east of Kissamos.

Camping Mithymna (☎ 2822 031 444; fax 2822 031 000; camp sites per adult/tent €5/2.90) This is an excellent shaded camping ground 6km east of town, abutting the best stretch of beach on Kissamos Bay. Facilities include a restaurant, bar and shop. Getting there involves a bus trip to the village of Drapanias and a 1km walk through olive groves to the site.

Camping Nopigia (☎ 2822 031 111; www.camping nopigia.gr; camp sites per adult/tent €4.50/3; ☒) This is also a good site, 2km west of Camping Mithymna. While the beach is not the best for swimming, the swimming pool here makes up for that. Take a Hania-bound bus and get off at the signposted turnoff.

Bikakis Family (☎ 2822 024 257; www.family bikakis.gr; Iroön Polemiston 1941; s/d €20/25, studios €30; ☒) This would have to be the best budget option in the whole of Kissamos Town. The 15 rooms and five studios sparkle and most have garden and sea views. Owner Giannis not only makes guests feel very welcome, he is also an expert in herbal teas and local knowledge.

Argo Rooms for Rent (☎/fax 2822 023 563; Plateia Teloniou; s/d €23/32) The C-class Argo on the seafront has spacious rooms many of which directly overlook the beach promenade. It's about 300m from Plateia Tzanakaki.

Thalassa (☎ 2822 031 231; www.thalassa-apts.gr; Paralia Drapanias; studios €40-50; ☒ ☐) Thalassa is one of the best accommodation choices along the whole Kissamos coast and is an ideal spot to retreat to with a stack of books. All studios are immaculate and airy and have ISDN computer ports. They are no more than 30m from the beach and just a 100m walk east from Camping Mythimna.

CRETE

Christina Beach Hotel (☎ 2822 083 333; studios €65-75; Ⓟ 🗙 🖳) New in 2002 this very smart studios complex on the west side of Kissamos represents the upper end of accommodation in town. Right on the foreshore, the modern studios are large and airy and all have ISDN Internet connectivity.

Eating

Papadakis Taverna (☎ 2822 022 340; Paralia Kissamou) Opposite Argo Rooms for Rent, Papadakis is one of the oldest tavernas in town and well patronised by locals. It has a very relaxing setting overlooking the beach and serves well-prepared fish dishes such as oven-baked fish, or fish soup.

Restaurant Kastell (☎ 2822 022 144; mains €4-6) The second of the two oldest and best-respected tavernas in Kissamos, the Kastell is not flash-looking, but is reliable and of good quality and repute. Opposite the KTEL bus station on the square, you'll find dishes like satisfying *hirino kapamas* (pork stew) and other delicious mayirefta to tempt you.

O Stimadoris (☎ 2822 022 057; Fishing Harbour; mains €4-7) About the best-respected fish taverna is 2km west of town, just before the small fishing harbour. Fish is the freshest – naturally – and you can try an unusual salad made of seaweed in vinegar – *salata tou yialou*.

Getting There & Away

BUS

From Kissamos' **bus station** (☎ 2822 822 035), there are 16 buses a day travelling to Hania (€3.55, one hour), where you can then change for Rethymno and Iraklio; and two buses a day going to Falasarna (€2.50, 30 minutes) at 10am and 5.30pm. There is one bus a day heading to Paleohora (€3.55, 1½ hours).

FERRY

ANEN Ferries operates the F/B *Myrtidiotissa* on a route that takes in Antikythira (€8.50, two hours), Kythira (€14.70, four hours), Gythio (€19.50, seven hours), Kalamata (€20.30, 10 hours) and Piraeus (€22, 19 hours). It leaves Kissamos five times a week between 9am and 10.30am. You can buy tickets from **Horeftakis Tours** (☎ 2822 023 250) and the **ANEN Office** (☎ 2822 022 009), both

of which are located on the right side of Skalidi, east of Plateia Tzanakaki.

Getting Around

Cars can be hired from **Hermes** (☎ 2822 022 98; Skalidi), and motorcycles from **Moto Fun** (☎ 2822 023 400; www.motofun.info; Plateia Tzanakaki). Car hire rates are €30 to €50 per day, while for motorbikes and scooters they are from €15 to €25.

AROUND KISSAMOS

Falasarna Φαλάσαρνα

Falasarna, 16km west of Kissamos, was a Cretan city-state in the 4th century BC. There's not much to see, and most people are here for the superb beach, which is long, sandy and interspersed with boulders. There are several domatia at the beach.

From June through August there are three buses daily from Kissamos to Falasarna (€2.50) as well as buses from Hania (€5.75).

Gramvousa Peninsula Χερσόνησος Γραμβούσα

North of Falasarna is the wild and remote Gramvousa Peninsula. There is a wide track, which eventually degenerates into a path, along the east-coast side to the sandy beach of **Tigani**, on the west side of the peninsula's narrow tip. The beach is overlooked by the two islets of **Agria** (wild) and **Imeri** (tame) Gramvousa. To reach the track, take a west-bound bus from Kissamos and ask to be let off at the turn-off for the village of **Kalyviani** (5km from Kissamos). Walk the 2km to Kalyviani, then take the path that begins at the far end of the main street. The shadeless walk is around 3kms – wear a hat and take plenty of water.

You don't have to inflict this punishment upon yourself to see the beautiful peninsula. From June through August there are daily cruises in the **Gramvousa** (☎ 2822 024 344; www.gramvousa-balos.com.gr). The trip goes around the tip of the peninsula to the island of Imeri Gramvousa and onto an incredibly idyllic beach opposite on the peninsula itself. Tickets cost €20 and can be bought on the day at Kissamos port. Departures are at 10.05am and return at 5.30pm.

Ennia Horia Εννιά Χωριά

Ennia Horia (Nine Villages) is the name given to the highly scenic mountainous region south of Kissamos, renowned for its chestnut trees. If you have your own transport you can drive through the region en route to Moni Hrysoskalitissas and Elafonisi or, with a little backtracking, to Paleohora. Alternatively, you can take a circular route, returning via the coast road. The village of **Elos** (pop 326) stages a **chestnut festival** on the third Sunday of October when sweets made from chestnuts are eaten. The road to the region heads inland 5km east of Kissamos.

Polyrrinia Πολυρρηνία

The ruins of the ancient city of Polyrrinia (po-lih-reh-*nee*-ah) lie 7km south of Kissamos, above the village of Ano Paleokastro (which is sometimes called Polyrrinia). It's a steep climb to reach the ruins but the views are stunning.

The city was founded by the Dorians and was continuously inhabited until Venetian times. There are remains of city walls, and an aqueduct built by Hadrian. It's a scenic walk from Kissamos to Polyrrinia, otherwise there is a very infrequent bus service – ask at the Kissamos bus station.

Dodecanese
Δωδεκάνησα

Strung out along the coast of western Turkey like jewels upon the aquamarine sea, the Dodecanese archipelago is closer to Asia Minor than mainland Greece. Because of their strategic and vulnerable position, the Dodecanese have encountered a greater catalogue of invasions and occupations than the rest of Greece.

The name Dodecanese (*dodeka* means 12 in Greek) derives from the time of the Ottoman Empire when 12 of the 18 islands were granted special privileges for having willingly submitted to the new Ottoman overlords, a rule that began in earnest in 1478. Intriguingly, the original Dodecanese did not include the largest and richest islands of Rhodes and Kos, as they had unwillingly been subjugated to the Ottomans; they consisted only of Patmos, Lipsi, Leros, Kalymnos, Astypalea, Nisyros, Tilos, Symi, Halki, Karpathos, Kasos and Kastellorizo.

The islands' chequered history has endowed them with a wealth of diverse archaeological remains, but these are not their only attractions. The highly developed resorts of Rhodes and Kos have beaches and bars galore, while Lipsi and Tilos have appealing beaches, but without the crowds. The far-flung islands of Agathonisi, Arki, Kasos and Kastellorizo await Greek-island aficionados in pursuit of traditional island life, while everyone gapes at the extraordinary landscape that geological turbulence has created on Nisyros.

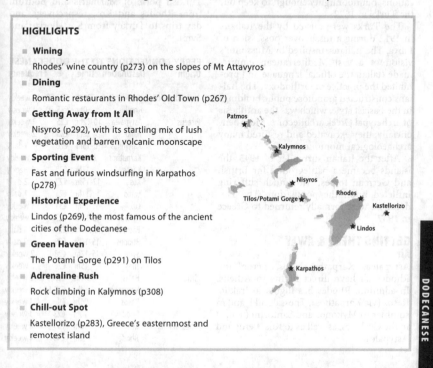

HIGHLIGHTS

■ **Wining**
Rhodes' wine country (p273) on the slopes of Mt Attavyros

■ **Dining**
Romantic restaurants in Rhodes' Old Town (p267)

■ **Getting Away from It All**
Nisyros (p292), with its startling mix of lush vegetation and barren volcanic moonscape

■ **Sporting Event**
Fast and furious windsurfing in Karpathos (p278)

■ **Historical Experience**
Lindos (p269), the most famous of the ancient cities of the Dodecanese

■ **Green Haven**
The Potami Gorge (p291) on Tilos

■ **Adrenaline Rush**
Rock climbing in Kalymnos (p308)

■ **Chill-out Spot**
Kastellorizo (p283), Greece's easternmost and remotest island

Patmos
Kalymnos
Nisyros
Rhodes
Tilos/Potami Gorge
Kastellorizo
Lindos
Karpathos

DODECANESE

HISTORY

The Dodecanese have been inhabited since pre-Minoan times; by the archaic period Rhodes and Kos had emerged as the dominant islands of the group. Distance from Athens gave the Dodecanese considerable autonomy and they were, for the most part, free to prosper unencumbered by subjugation to imperial Athens. Following Alexander the Great's death, Ptolemy I of Egypt ruled the Dodecanese.

The Dodecanese islanders were the first Greeks to become Christians. This was through the tireless efforts of St Paul, who made two journeys to the archipelago, and through St John, who was banished to Patmos, where he had his revelation.

The early Byzantine era saw the islands prosper, but by the 7th century AD they were plundered by a string of invaders. By the early 14th century it was the turn of the crusaders – the Knights of St John of Jerusalem, or Knights Hospitallers. The knights eventually became rulers of almost all the Dodecanese, building mighty fortifications, but not mighty enough to keep out the Turks in 1522.

The Turks were ousted by the Italians in 1912 during a tussle over possession of Libya. The Italians, inspired by Mussolini's vision of a vast Mediterranean empire, made Italian the official language and prohibited the practice of Orthodoxy. The Italians constructed grandiose public buildings in the Fascist style, which was the antithesis of archetypal Greek architecture. More beneficially, they excavated and restored many archaeological monuments.

After the Italian surrender of 1943, the islands became a battleground for British and German forces, with much suffering inflicted upon the population. The Dodecanese were formally returned to Greece in 1947.

GETTING THERE & AWAY

Air

Astypalea, Karpathos, Kos, Leros and Rhodes all have direct flights to Athens. In addition, Rhodes has flights to Iraklio, Kasos (via Karpathos), Thessaloniki, and in summer to Mykonos and Santorini (Thira) in the Cyclades, as well as to Kos, Leros and Astypalea.

Ferry & Hydrofoil

DOMESTIC

Ferry schedules to the Dodecanese are fairly complex, but they do follow a predictable and rarely varying pattern. Departure times in both directions tend to be geared to an early morning arrival at both Piraeus and Rhodes. This means that island hopping southwards can often involve some anti-social hours.

The 'Ferry Connections to the Dodecanese' table gives an overall view of ferry connections to the Dodecanese from the mainland and Crete in the high season. The services from Alexandroupolis are subject to seasonal demand, so always check the schedule before committing yourself to the trip.

Kyriacoulis Hydrofoils operates daily services from the Northeastern Aegean island of Samos to the northern Dodecanese, and occasional services from Ikaria.

INTERNATIONAL

There are ferries and hydrofoils to the Turkish ports of Marmaris and Bodrum from Rhodes and Kos, respectively, and day trips to Turkey from Kastellorizo and Symi.

FERRY CONNECTIONS TO THE DODECANESE

Origin	Destination	Time	€	Frequency
Alexandroupolis	Kos	26hr	€33.50	1 weekly
	Rhodes	30hr	€35.50	1 weekly
Piraeus	Astypalea	10-12hr	€25	3 weekly
	Halki	22hr	€33	2 weekly
	Kalymnos	10-13hr	€26	1 daily
	Karpathos	18½hr	€29	4 weekly
	Kasos	17hr	€28	4 weekly
	Kos	12-15hr	€27	2 daily
	Leros	11hr	€23	1 daily
	Lipsi	16hr	€31	1 weekly
	Nisyros	13-15hr	€27	2 weekly
	Patmos	8-9½hr	€21	1 daily
	Rhodes	15-18hr	€29	2 daily
	Symi	15-17hr	€28	2 weekly
	Tilos	15hr	€26	2 weekly
Sitia	Halki	5½hr	€17	2 weekly
	Karpathos	4hr	€15.50	4 weekly
	Kasos	2½hr	€9	4 weekly
	Rhodes	10hr	€23	3 weekly
Thessaloniki	Kos	18hr	€39	1 weekly
	Rhodes	21hr	€45	1 weekly

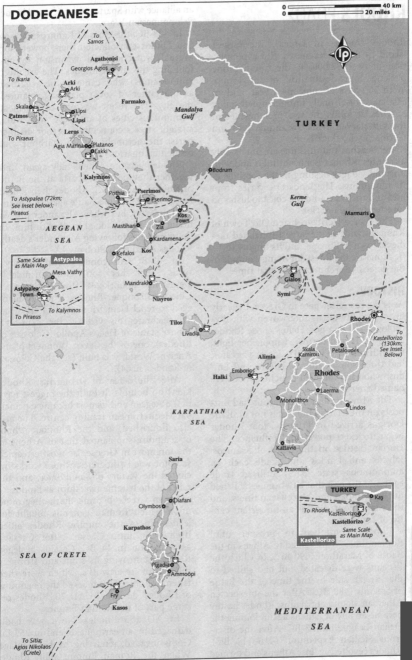

DODECANESE

0 ——— 40 km
0 ——— 20 miles

To Samos

Agathonisi
Georgios Agios

Arki
Arki

To Ikaria

Skala
Patmos
Lipsi
Lipsi

To Piraeus

Farmako

Mandalya Gulf

TURKEY

Leros
Agia Marina
Platanos
Lakki

Kalymnos
Pothia
Pserimos
Pserimos

Bodrum

To Astypalea (72km;
See Inset below);
Piraeus

AEGEAN
SEA

Mastihari
Kos Town
Zia
Kardamena

Kerme
Gulf

Marmaris

Same Scale
as Main Map
Astypalea
Mesa Vathy

Astypalea
Town

To Piraeus
To Kalymnos

Kefalos
Kos

Mandraki
Nisyros

Gialos
Symi

Rhodes

To
Kastellorizo
(130km;
See Inset
Below)

Tilos
Livadia

Alimia
Skala
Kamirou
Petaloudes

Halki
Emborios
Monolithos
Rhodes
Laerma
Lindos

KARPATHIAN
SEA

Kattavia

Saria

Cape Prasonisi

TURKEY
Kaş

To Rhodes
Kastellorizo
Kastellorizo
Same Scale
as Main Map
Kastellorizo

Olymbos
Diafani

Karpathos

SEA OF CRETE

Pigadia
Ammoöpi

Fry
Kasos

MEDITERRANEAN
SEA

To Sitia;
Agios Nikolaos
(Crete)

DODE

RHODES ΡΟΔΟΣ

Rhodes (ro-dos in Greek), the largest island in the Dodecanese, with a population of over 98,000, is the number one package tour destination of the group. With 300 days of sunshine a year, and an east coast of virtually uninterrupted sandy beaches, it fulfils the two prerequisites of the sun-starved British, Scandinavians and Germans who flock here.

But beaches and sunshine are not its only attributes. Rhodes is a beautiful island with unspoilt villages nestling in the foothills of its mountains. The landscape varies from arid and rocky around the coast to lush and forested in the interior.

The World Heritage–listed Old Town of Rhodes stands as the largest inhabited medieval town in Europe, and its mighty fortifications are the finest surviving example of the defensive architecture of that time.

HISTORY

As is the case elsewhere in Greece, the early history of Rhodes is interwoven with mythology. The sun god Helios chose Rhodes as his bride and bestowed upon her light, warmth and vegetation. Their son, Cercafos, had three sons, Camiros, Ialysos and Lindos, who each founded the cities that were named after them.

The Minoans and Mycenaeans had outposts on the islands, but it was not until the Dorians arrived in 1100 BC that Rhodes began to exert power and influence. The Dorians settled in the cities of Kamiros, Ialysos and Lindos and made each an autonomous state. They utilised trade routes to the east that had been established during Minoan and Mycenaean times, and the island flourished as an important centre of commerce.

Rhodes continued to prosper until Roman times. It was allied to Athens in the Battle of Marathon (490 BC), in which the Persians were defeated, but had shifted to the Persian side by the time of the Battle of Salamis (480 BC). After the unexpected Athenian victory at Salamis, Rhodes hastily became an ally of Athens again, joining the Delian League in 477 BC. After the disastrous Sicilian Expedition (416–412 BC), Rhodes revolted against Athens and formed an alliance with Sparta, which it aided in the Peloponnesian Wars.

In 408 BC, the cities of Kamiros, Ialysos and Lindos consolidated their powers for mutual protection and expansion by co-founding the city of Rhodes. The architect Hippodamos, who came to be regarded as the father of town planning, planned the city. The result was one of the most harmonious cities of antiquity, with wide, straight streets connecting its four distinct parts: the acropolis, agora, harbour and residential quarter.

Rhodes became Athens' ally again, and together they defeated Sparta at the Battle of Knidos, in 394 BC. Rhodes then joined forces with Persia in a battle against Alexander the Great, but when Alexander proved invincible, hastily allied itself with him. In the skirmishes following Alexander's death, Rhodes sided with Ptolemy I.

In 305 BC, Antigonus, one of Ptolemy's rivals, sent his son, the formidable Demetrius Poliorketes (the Besieger of Cities), to conquer Rhodes. The city managed to repel Demetrius after a long siege. To celebrate this victory, the 32m-high bronze statue of Helios Apollo (Colossus of Rhodes), one of the Seven Wonders of the Ancient World, was built (see the Colossus of Rhodes, p264).

After the defeat of Demetrius, Rhodes knew no bounds. It built the biggest navy in the Aegean and its port became a principal Mediterranean trading centre. The arts also flourished, and the Rhodian school of sculpture supplanted that of Athens as the foremost in Greece. Its most esteemed sculptor was Pythocretes, whose works included the Victory of Samothrace, and the relief of the trireme (warship) at Lindos.

When Greece became the battleground upon which Roman generals fought for leadership of the empire, Rhodes allied itself with Julius Caesar. After Caesar's assassination in 44 BC, Cassius besieged Rhodes, destroying its ships and stripping the city of its artworks, which were then taken to Rome. This marked the beginning of Rhodes' decline. In AD 70, Rhodes became part of the Roman Empire.

In AD 155 Rhodes Town was badly damaged by an earthquake, and in 269 the Goths invaded, rendering further damage. When the Roman Empire split, Rhodes

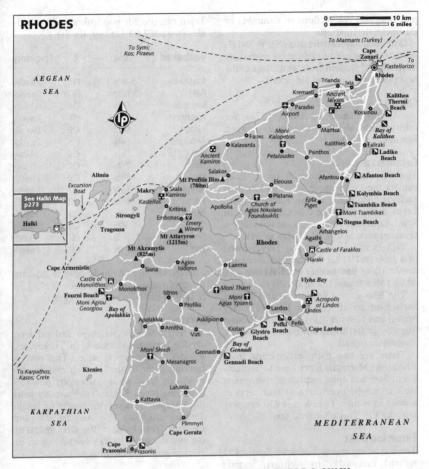

RHODES

became part of the Byzantine province of the Dodecanese. Raid upon raid followed: by the Persians in 620, the Saracens in 653, then the Turks. When the crusaders seized Constantinople, Rhodes was given independence. Later the Genoese gained control. The Knights of St John arrived in Rhodes in 1309 and ruled for 213 years until they were ousted by the Ottomans. Rhodes suffered several earthquakes during the 19th century, but greater damage was rendered to the city in 1856 by an explosion of gunpowder that had been stored and forgotten – almost 1000 people were killed and many buildings were wrecked. In 1947, after 35 years of Italian occupation, Rhodes became part of Greece along with the other Dodecanese islands.

GETTING THERE & AWAY

All the addresses listed in this section are in Rhodes Town.

Air

Olympic Airways has at least five flights daily travelling to Athens (€90), two daily to Karpathos (€28), one daily to Kastellorizo (€25), six weekly to Santorini (€125), four weekly to Iraklio (€79.50), three weekly to Kasos (€34) and two weekly each to Thessaloniki (€117) and Mykonos (€126). Direct inquiries to **Olympic Airways** (Map p266; ☎ 2241 024 571; Ierou Lohou 9).

Aegean Airlines (Map p266; ☎ 2241 024 400; Ethelondon Dodekanision 20) offers flights to Athens, Thessaloniki and Iraklio at similar rates, plus one-stop connections to a number of European destinations.

Castellania Travel Service (Map p263; ☎ 2241 075 860; castell@otenet.gr; Plateia Ippokratous) specialises in youth and student fares, and is one of the best places for low-cost air tickets.

Caïque

See Getting There & Away (p273), for information about the caïque between Rhodes and Halki.

Catamaran

The *Dodekanisos Express* starts its daily run up the Dodecanese at around 8.30am each day, stopping at Kos, Kalymnos and Leros daily, with stops at other times in Symi, Lipsi and Patmos. There is usually a seasonal service to Kastellorizo as well.

Tickets can be bought at **Skevos Travel** (Map p266; ☎ 2241 022 461; skeyos@rho.forthnet.gr; Amerikis 11) or **Dodekanisos Naftiliaki** (Map p263; ☎ 2241 070 590; www.12ne.gr; Afstralias 3).

The Tilos-owned *Sea Star* departs Rhodes each morning at 9am for Tilos (€27, 1½ hours) and Nisyros (€33). See **Triton Holidays** (Map p266; ☎ 2241 021 690; www.tritondmc.gr; Plastira 9, Mandraki) for tickets.

There are two daily catamarans from Rhodes to Marmaris from June to September at 8am and 4pm, respectively, dropping back to maybe only three or four services a week in winter. Tickets cost €30 one way plus the €15 Turkish arrival tax.

Excursion Boat

There are excursion boats to Symi (€22 return) every day in summer, leaving Mandraki Harbour at 9am and returning at 6pm. You can buy tickets at most travel agencies, but it is better to buy them at the harbour, where you can check out the boats and haggle. Look for shade and the size and condition of the boat, as these vary greatly. You can buy an open return if you want to stay on Symi.

Ferry
DOMESTIC

Rhodes is the main port of the Dodecanese and offers a complex array of departures. The following table lists scheduled domestic ferries from Rhodes to other islands in the Dodecanese in the high season. The EOT and the municipal tourist office in Rhodes

Town can provide you with current schedules (see p262 for contact details).

Destination	Time	€	Frequency
Astypalea	8-10hr	€19	2 weekly
Halki	1½-2hr	€8	9 weekly
Kalymnos	5½hr	€16	1 daily
Karpathos	3½hr	€16	3 weekly
Kasos	6½hr	€20	2 weekly
Kastellorizo	2-4hr	€15	2 weekly
Kos	3½hr	€15	1 daily
Leros	7½hr	€20	1 daily
Lipsi	9½hr	€20	1 weekly
Nisyros	3-5hr	€11	3 weekly
Patmos	8½hr	€23	1 daily
Piraeus	15-18hr	€29	2 daily
Sitia	10hr	€23	3 weekly
Symi	2hr	€8	1 daily
Tilos	2-3hr	€11	4 weekly

The weekly ferry from Rhodes to Alexandroupolis also stops at Samos (€27, nine hours) in the Northeastern Aegean.

INTERNATIONAL

There is a weekly passenger and car ferry service between Marmaris in Turkey and Rhodes on Friday at 4pm. The cost of ferrying a car to the Turkish mainland is €180 one way, while passengers pay €55, including taxes. Return rates usually work out cheaper. This service is offered by the Turkish shipping line Aegean Shipping. Contact **Triton Holidays** (Map p266; ☎ 2241 021 690; www.tritondmc.gr; Plastira 9, Mandraki) upon arrival to arrange a crossing.

Hydrofoil

Kyriacoulis Hydrofoils (Map p266; ☎ 2241 024 000; Plateia Neoriou 6) on the quay operates the following services from Rhodes in the high season:

Destination	Time	€	Frequency
Astypalea	5½hr	€37	1 weekly
Kalymnos	3½hr	€31	1 weekly
Kos	2hr	€25	2 daily
Leros	3½hr	€34	3 weekly
Patmos	3½hr	€39	3 weekly
Symi	50min	€13	2 weekly

Tickets are available from **Triton Holidays** (Map p266; ☎ 2241 021 690; www.tritondmc.gr;

Plastira 9, Mandraki). There is an additional daily hydrofoil, the *Aegli*, run and owned by Symi island, with a daily service (€11) to and from Gialos on Symi.

GETTING AROUND
To/From the Airport
The airport is 16km southwest of Rhodes Town, near Paradisi. There are 21 buses daily between the airport and Rhodes Town's west side bus station (€1.50). The first leaves Rhodes Town at 5am and the last at 11pm; from the airport, the first leaves at 5.55am and the last at 11.45pm. Buses from the airport leave from the main road outside the airport perimeter.

Bicycle
Bicycle Centre (Map p266; ☎ 2241 028 315; Griva 39; €5 per day) has a range of bicycles for hire.

Boat
There are excursion boats to Lindos (€15 return) every day in summer, leaving Mandraki Harbour at 9am and returning at 6pm.

Car & Motorcycle
There are numerous car and motorcycle rental outlets in Rhodes' New Town. Shop around and bargain because the competition is fierce.

Public Transport
Rhodes Town has two bus stations. From the **east side bus station** (Map p266; Plateia Rimini) there are 18 buses daily to Faliraki (€1.62), 14 to Lindos (€3.67), three to Kolymbia (€2.30), nine to Gennadi (€4.24) via Lardos, and four to Psinthos (€1.78).

From the **west side bus station** (Map p266), next to the New Market, there are buses every half-hour to Kalithea Thermi (€1.62), 10 to Koskinou (€1.62), five to Salakos (€3.14), two to ancient Kamiros (€3.98), one to Monolithos (€5.86) via Skala Kamirou, and one to Embonas (€4.40). The main tourist office gives out schedules.

City buses all charge a flat €0.94.

Taxi
Rhodes Town's main **taxi rank** (Map p266) is east of Plateia Rimini. There are two zones on the island for taxi meters: Zone One is Rhodes Town and Zone Two (slightly higher) is everywhere else. Rates are a little higher between midnight and 6am. Sample fares are: airport €13, Filerimos €10, Petaloudes €16, ancient Kamiros €22, Lindos €27 and Monolithos €40. Taxi company contact phone numbers include ☎ 2241 064 712, ☎ 2241 064 734 and ☎ 2241 064 778.

RHODES TOWN
pop 53,709

The heart of Rhodes Town is the Old Town, enclosed within massive walls. Avoid the worst of the tourist hordes by beginning your exploration early in the morning. But at any time, away from the main thoroughfares and squares, you will find deserted labyrinthine alleyways. Much of the New Town to the north is dominated by package tourism, but it does have a few places of interest to visitors.

Orientation
The Old Town is nominally divided into three sectors: the Kollakio, or Knights' Quarter; the Hora; and the Jewish Quarter. The Kollakio comprises the northern sector and is roughly bordered by Agisandrou and Theofiliskou which run east to west. The Kollakio contains most of the medieval historical sights of the Old Town. The Hora, often known as the Turkish Quarter, is primarily the commercial sector and contains most of the shops and restaurants. Sokratous and its northerly extension, Orfeos, are the Hora's main thoroughfares. The sector is bordered to the east by Perikleous, beyond which is the quieter, mainly residential Jewish Quarter. The Old Town is accessed by nine main gates *(pyles)* and two rampart-access portals. The whole town is a mesh of Byzantine, Turkish and Latin architecture with quiet, twisting alleyways punctuated by lively squares. While you will inevitably get lost at some point, it will never be for long.

The commercial centre of the New Town lies north of the Old Town and is easily explored on foot. Most commercial activity is centred on two blocks surrounding Plateia Kyprou. The hotel district is centred on a large sector bordered by 28 Oktovriou and G Papanikolaou. The main square of the New Town is Plateia Rimini, just north of the Old Town. The tourist offices, bus stations and main taxi rank are on or near this square.

The commercial harbour, for international ferries and large inter-island ferries, is east of the Old Town. Excursion boats, small ferries, hydrofoils and private yachts use Mandraki Harbour, further north.

Information

EMERGENCY
Emergency first aid & ambulance (☎ 2241 025 555, 2241 022 222)

INTERNET ACCESS
Mango Cafe Bar (Map p263; ☎ 2241 024 877; kare las@hotmail.com; Plateia Dorieos 3; €3 per hr; ☾ 7am-1am) In the Old Town.
Rock Style Internet Café (Map p266; ☎ 2241 027 502; info@rockstyle.gr; Dimokratias 7; €3 per hr; ☾ 7am-1am) Just south of the Old Town.

INTERNET RESOURCES
www.rodos.gr A good introduction to things happening in Rhodes.

LAUNDRY
Express Laundry (Map p266; Kosti Palama 5) Service washes for €3.50.
Express Servis (Map p266; Dilberaki 97) Around €3 a load.
Lavomatique (Map p266; 28 Oktovriou 32) Around €3 a load.

LEFT LUGGAGE
Planet Holidays (Map p266; ☎ 2241 035 722; Gallias 6; €2.60 per 2-hr period, €3.50 up to 2 days) Prices can be negotiated for longer periods.

MEDICAL SERVICES
General Hospital (Map p266; ☎ 2241 080 000; Papalouka El Venizelou) Just northwest of the Old Town.
Krito (☎ 2241 030 020; krito@rho.forthnet.gr; Ioannou Metaxa 3) Private medical provider offering a 24-hour service.

MONEY
All the banks listed have ATMs.
Alpha Credit Bank (Map p266; Plateia Kyprou) In the New Town.
American Express (Map p266; ☎ 2241 021 010; Ammohostou 18) Represented by Rhodos Tours.
Commercial Bank of Greece (Map p263; Plateia Mousiou) In the Old Town.
National Bank of Greece New Town (Map p266; Plateia Kyprou) Old Town (Map p263; Plateia Mousiou)

POST
Main post office (Map p266) On Mandraki Harbour.
Post office branch (Map p263) Old Town, open seven days.

TOURIST INFORMATION
Ellinikos Organismos Tourismou (EOT; Map p266; ☎ 2241 035 226; cnr Makariou & Papagou; ☾ 7.30am-3pm Mon-Fri) Supplies brochures and maps of the city, and will help find accommodation. Has the *Rodos News*, a free English-language newspaper.
Municipal Tourist Office (Map p266; ☎ 2241 035 945; Plateia Rimini; ☾ 8am-8pm Mon-Sat, 8am-noon Sun summer only) Provides the same service as the EOT in summer.
Port Police (Map p266; ☎ 2241 022 220; Mandraki)
Tourist Police (Map p266; ☎ 2241 027 423; ☾ 24hr) Next door to the EOT.

TRAVEL AGENCIES
Triton Holidays (Map p266; ☎ 2241 021 690; www.tritondmc.gr; Plastira 9, Mandraki) Perhaps the best overall travel agency in Rhodes. The exceptionally helpful staff provide a wide range of services catering to individual needs, as well as air, sea and land tickets.

Sights

The following sights are all on the Rhodes Old Town map, opposite.

OLD TOWN
In medieval times, the Knights of St John lived in the Knights' Quarter and other inhabitants lived in the Hora. The 12m-thick city walls are closed to the public, but you can do **guided walks** (☎ 2241 023 359; tours €6; ☾ 2.45pm Tue & Sat), starting at the courtyard of the Palace of the Grand Masters.

Knights' Quarter
An appropriate place to begin an exploration of the Old Town is the imposing cobblestone **Avenue of the Knights** (Ippoton), where the knights lived. The knights were divided into seven 'tongues' or languages, according to their place of origin – England, France, Germany, Italy, Aragon, Auvergne and Provence – each responsible for protecting a section of the bastion. The Grand Master, who was in charge, lived in the palace, and each tongue was under the auspices of a bailiff. The knights were divided into soldiers, chaplains and ministers to the sick.

To this day the street exudes a noble and forbidding aura, despite modern offices now occupying most of the inns. Its lofty buildings stretch in a 600m-long unbroken wall of honey-coloured stone blocks, and its flat facade is punctuated by huge doorways and arched windows. The inns reflect the Gothic styles of architecture of the knights' countries of origin. They form a harmonious whole in their bastion-like structure, but on closer inspection each possesses its own graceful and individual embellishments.

First on the right, if you begin at the eastern end of the Avenue of the Knights, is the **Inn of the Order of the Tongue of Italy** (1519); next to it is the **Palace of Villiers de**

l'Île Adam. After Sultan Süleyman had taken the city, it was Villiers de l'Île who had the humiliating task of arranging the knights' departure from the island. Next along is the **Inn of France**, the most ornate and distinctive of all the inns. On the opposite side of the street is a wrought-iron gate in front of a Turkish garden.

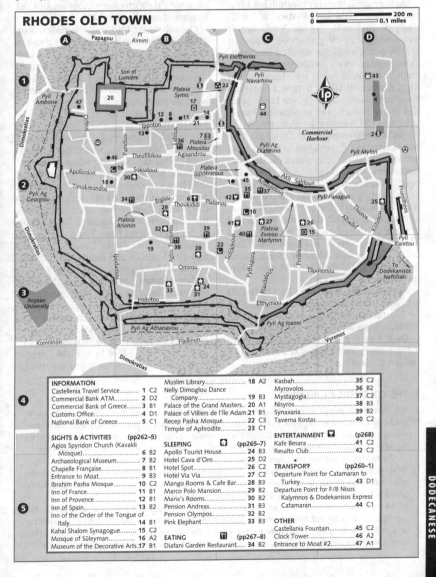

RHODES OLD TOWN

0 — 200 m
0 — 0.1 miles

INFORMATION	
Castellania Travel Service	1 C2
Commercial Bank ATM	2 D2
Commercial Bank of Greece	3 B1
Customs Office	4 D1
National Bank of Greece	5 C1

SIGHTS & ACTIVITIES	(pp262–5)
Agios Spyridon Church (Kavakli Mosque)	6 B2
Archaeological Museum	7 B2
Chapelle Française	8 B1
Entrance to Moat	9 B3
Ibrahim Pasha Mosque	10 C2
Inn of France	11 B1
Inn of Provence	12 B1
Inn of Spain	13 B2
Inn of the Order of the Tongue of Italy	14 B1
Kahal Shalom Synagogue	15 C2
Mosque of Süleyman	16 A2
Museum of the Decorative Arts	17 B1
Muslim Library	18 A2
Nelly Dimoglou Dance Company	19 B3
Palace of the Grand Masters	20 A1
Palace of Villiers de l'Île Adam	21 B1
Recep Pasha Mosque	22 C3
Temple of Aphrodite	23 C1

SLEEPING	(pp265–7)
Apollo Tourist House	24 B3
Hotel Cava d'Oro	25 D2
Hotel Spot	26 C2
Hotel Via Via	27 C2
Mango Rooms & Cafe Bar	28 B3
Marco Polo Mansion	29 B2
Maria's Rooms	30 B2
Pension Andreas	31 B3
Pension Olympos	32 B2
Pink Elephant	33 B3

EATING	(pp267–8)
Diafani Garden Restaurant	34 B2

Kasbah	35 C2
Myrovolos	36 B2
Mystagogia	37 C2
Nisyros	38 B3
Synaxaria	39 B2
Taverna Kostas	40 C2

ENTERTAINMENT	(p268)
Kafe Besara	41 C2
Resalto Club	42 C2

TRANSPORT	(pp260–1)
Departure Point for Catamaran to Turkey	43 D1
Departure Point for F/B Nisos Kalymnos & Dodekanisos Express Catamaran	44 C1

OTHER	
Castellania Fountain	45 C2
Clock Tower	46 A2
Entrance to Moat #2	47 A1

Back on the right side is the **Chapelle Française** (Chapel of the Tongue of France), embellished with a statue of the Virgin and Child. Next door is the residence of the Chaplain of the Tongue of France. Across the alleyway is the **Inn of Provence**, with four coats of arms forming the shape of a cross, and opposite is the **Inn of Spain**.

On the right is the truly magnificent 14th-century **Palace of the Grand Masters** (☎ 2241 023 359; Ippoton; admission €6; ☼ 8.30am-3pm Tue-Sun). It was destroyed in the gunpowder explosion of 1856 and the Italians rebuilt it in a grandiose manner, with a lavish interior, intending it as a holiday home for Mussolini and King Emmanuel III. It is now a museum, containing sculpture, mosaics taken from Kos by the Italians, and antique furniture.

In the 15th-century knights' hospital is the **archaeological museum** (☎ 2241 027 657; Plateia Mousiou; admission €3; ☼ 8am-5.40pm Tue-Sun). Its most famous exhibit is the exquisite Parian marble statuette, the *Aphrodite of Rhodes*, a 1st-century BC adaptation of a Hellenistic statue. Less charming to most is the 4th-century BC *Afroditi Thalassia* in the next room. However, writer Lawrence Durrell was so enamoured of it that he named his book *Reflections on a Marine Venus* after it. Also here is the 2nd-century BC marble *Head of Helios*, found near the Palace of the Grand Masters where the Temple of Helios once stood.

The **Museum of the Decorative Arts** (☎ 2241 072 674; Plateia Argyrokastrou; admission €2; ☼ 8.30am-3pm Tue-Sun), further north, houses a collection of artefacts from around the Dodecanese.

On Plateia Symis, there are the remains of a 3rd-century BC **Temple of Aphrodite**, one of the few ancient ruins in the Old Town.

Hora

The Hora has many Ottoman legacies. During Turkish times, churches were converted to mosques, and many more were built from scratch. Most are now dilapidated. The most important one is the renovated, pink-domed **Mosque of Süleyman**, at the top of Sokratous. It was built in 1522 to commemorate the Ottoman victory against the knights, then rebuilt in 1808.

Opposite is the 18th-century **Muslim library** (Plateia Arionos; Sokratous; admission free; ☼ 9.30am-4pm Mon-Sat). It was founded in 1794 by Turkish Rhodian Ahmed Hasuf and houses a small collection of Persian and Arabic manuscripts and a collection of Korans written by hand on parchment.

Jewish Quarter

The Jewish Quarter is an almost forgotten sector of Rhodes Town, where life continues at an unhurried pace and where local residents live almost oblivious to the hubbub of the Hora, no more than a few blocks away. This area of quiet streets and sometimes dilapidated houses was once home to a thriving Jewish community. Descendants of Sephardic Jews from Spain, the Jewish community here spoke Ladino (a dialect based on Spanish) and numbered over 2000 people at the height of its prosperity.

Kahal Shalom synagogue (www.rhodesjewish museum.org; Dosiadou) has a commemorative plaque to the many members of Hora's large Jewish population who were sent to Auschwitz during the Nazi occupation. Jews still worship here and it is usually open in the morning. Close by is Plateia Evreon Martyron (Square of the Jewish Martyrs).

THE COLOSSUS OF RHODES

Whether the famous *Colossus of Rhodes* ever actually existed can never be proven, since there are no remains and no tangible evidence other than the reports of ancient travellers. The statue was apparently commissioned by Demetrius Poliorketes in 305 BC after he finally capitulated to Rhodian defiance following his long and ultimately failed siege of Rhodes in that same year.

The bronze statue was built over 12 years (294–282 BC) and when completed stood 32m high. What is not clear is where this gargantuan statue stood. Popular medieval belief has it astride the harbour at Mandraki (as depicted on today's T-shirts and tourist trinkets), but it is highly unlikely that this is the case and it's also technically unfeasible.

An earthquake in either 225 or 226 BC toppled the statue, most likely on land, where the remains lay undisturbed for 880 years. In AD 654 invading Saracens had the remains broken up and sold for scrap to a Jewish merchant in Edessa (in modern-day Turkey). The story goes that after being shipped to Syria, it took almost 1000 camels to convey it to its final destination.

NEW TOWN

The following sights are all on the Rhodes Town map, p266.

The **Acropolis of Rhodes**, southwest of the Old Town on Monte Smith, was the site of the ancient Hellenistic city of Rhodes. The hill is named after the English admiral Sir Sydney Smith, who watched for Napoleon's fleet from here in 1802. It has superb views.

The site's restored 2nd-century **stadium** once staged competitions in preparation for the Olympic Games. The adjacent **theatre** is a reconstruction of one used for lectures by the Rhodes School of Rhetoric. Steps above here lead to the **Temple of Pythian Apollo**, with four re-erected columns. The unenclosed site can be reached on city bus No 5.

North of Mandraki, at the eastern end of G Papanikolaou, is the graceful **Mosque of Murad Reis**. In its grounds are a Turkish cemetery and the Villa Cleobolus, where Lawrence Durrell lived in the 1940s, writing *Reflections on a Marine Venus*.

The town **beach** begins north of Mandraki and continues around the island's northernmost point and down the west side of the New Town. The best spot is on the northernmost point, where it's not quite as crowded.

Activities
GREEK DANCING LESSONS

The **Nelly Dimoglou Dance Company** (Map p263; ☎ 2241 020 157; Folk Dance Theatre, Andronikou; admission €10.30 group, €7.40 per person; ☼ performances 9.30pm Mon, Wed & Fri) gives lessons and stages performances.

SCUBA DIVING

Three diving schools operate out of Mandraki: **Waterhoppers Diving Centre** (Map p266; ☎ /fax 2241 038 146, ☎ 6932 963 173; water-hoppers@rodos.com; Perikleous 29), **Diving Centres** (Map p266; ☎ 2241 061 115; fax 2241 066 584; Lissavonas 33) and **Scuba Diving Trident School** (Map p266; ☎ /fax 2241 029 160; S Zervou 2). All offer a range of courses including a 'One Day Try Dive' for €40 to €50. You can get information from their boats at Mandraki. Kalithea Thermi is the only site around Rhodes where diving is permitted.

Sleeping
BUDGET

The Old Town has a reasonable selection of budget accommodation.

Apollo Tourist House (Map p263; ☎ 2241 032 003; www.apollo-touristhouse.com; Omirou 28c; s/d €29/35) This is a small, cosy pension, with shared bathrooms and kitchen, a small courtyard and an engaging Spanish-Chilean owner who occasionally cooks barbecues for guests.

Maria's Rooms (Map p263; ☎ 2241 022 169; Menekleous 147; d €35) This establishment, just off Sokratous, has pleasant, clean-smelling rooms. Rooms with shared bathroom are a little cheaper.

Hotel Spot (Map p263; ☎ 2241 034 737; www.rodos island.gr; Perikleous 21; s/d €32.30/35.20; ☒ ☐) The Spot has exceptionally clean, pleasant and tastefully decorated rooms. There is also a small book exchange and left-luggage facilities.

Pink Elephant (Map p263; ☎ 2241 022 469; www .pinkelephantpension.com; Irodotou 42; s/d €34/40; ☒) Despite the name, this hotel's attractive decor is blue and white. The fan-equipped and very presentable rooms have large bathrooms, though there are some cheaper rooms with shared bathrooms.

Pension Olympos (Map p263; ☎ /fax 2241 033 567; Agiou Fanouriou 56; s/d €35/45; ☒) This pension has pleasant rooms with fridge and TV, and an attractive little courtyard.

Most of the New Town's hotels are modern and characterless, but there are a couple of exceptions.

New Village Inn (Map p266; ☎ 2241 034 937; new villageinn@rho.forthnet.gr; Konstantopedos 10; s/d €24/35) This inn has tastefully furnished rooms with refrigerator and fan, and a traditional stone-walled courtyard festooned with plants.

Hotel Anastasia (Map p266; ☎ 2241 028 007; www.anastasia-hotel.com; 28 Oktovriou 46; s/d incl breakfast €35/41) This old-style hotel, in a former Italian mansion, is set back from the road and is reasonably quiet. The high-ceilinged rooms with tiled floors are spotless. The lush garden sports a tortoise and cat family.

MID-RANGE

Mango Rooms (Map p263; ☎ 2241 024 877; www .karelas.com; Plateia Dorieos 3; s/d €30/45) This place has clean, nicely furnished rooms with bathroom, TV, ceiling fan, safety box and refrigerator. It's open all year and has heating in winter.

Hotel Via Via (Map p263; ☎ 2241 077 027; www .hotel-via-via.com; Lisipou 2; d/tr €32/47) located just

DODECANESE

RHODES TOWN

0 — 300 m
0 — 0.2 miles

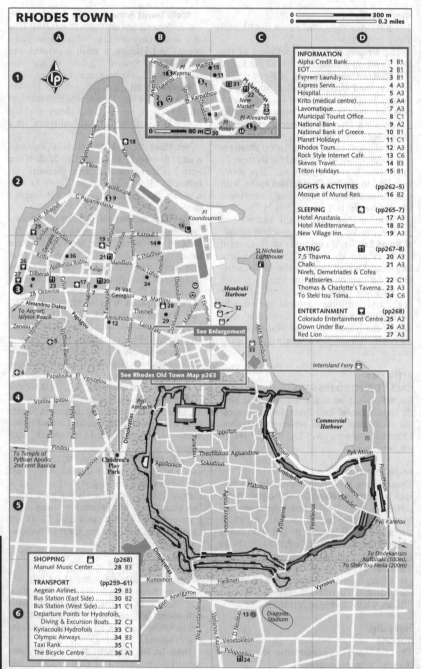

New Market

St Nicholas Lighthouse

Mandraki Harbour

See Enlargement

Interisland Ferry

Commercial Harbour

See Rhodes Old Town Map p263

Pyli Amboise

Ippoton

Pyli Milon

Children's Play Park

To Temple of
Pythian Apollo;
2nd cent Basilica

Pyli Karetou

To Dodekanisos
Naftiliaki (100m);
To Steki tou Heila (200m)

Diagoras Stadium

off Pythagora, this pristine hotel has tastefully furnished rooms – some have fridges – and is open in winter.

Pension Andreas (Map p263; ☎ 2241 034 156; www .hotelandreas.com; Omirou 28d; s/d €60/70) In one of the quietest parts of the Old Town this exceptionally friendly small boutique hotel with ever-helpful staff has tastefully decorated and comfortable rooms. There is a very social breakfast bar with terrific views across the Old Town.

Hotel Cava D'Oro (Map p263; ☎ 2241 036 980; hotel@cavadoro.com; Kistiniou 15; s/d €60/90; ⊠ P) Michael Palin stayed in one of the very tasteful old stone rooms during the series *Pole to Pole*. Rooms have TV and telephone and are very handy for the main ferry port.

TOP END

Rhodes is full of top-end resort-style accommodation. Among the more eclectic choices are the following.

Marco Polo Mansion (Map p263; ☎ 2241 025 562; www.marcopolomansion.web.com; Agiou Fanouriou 40-42; s/d €80/100) Featured in glossy European magazines is this old-fashioned Anatolian inn decorated in rich Ottoman-era colours. This cool and shady lodging, right in the heart of the Old Town, is run by the effervescent Effie Dede.

Hotel Mediterranean (Map p266; ☎ 2410 024 661; www.mediterranean.gr; s/d €90/110; ⊠ P) Renovated in 1999, this luxurious waterside hotel is one of the better upmarket establishments. Fronting the more sheltered east beach, it offers all the creature comforts you would expect from a hotel of this kind.

Eating
BUDGET
Old Town

Avoid the touts and tack along Sokratous and around Plateia Ippokratous. Hit the backstreets to find less touristy places to eat.

Taverna Kostas (☎ 2241 026 217; Pythagora 62; mains €5-7) Popular Kostas is good value and has stood the test of time with its good grills and fish dishes. It can't be beaten on quality.

Diafani Garden Restaurant (☎ 2241 026 053; Plateia Arionos; mayirefta €4-5) In the backstreets of the Old Town, this restaurant on a quiet square serves home-style, reasonably priced dishes. Try the excellent mousakas (sliced eggplant and mincemeat arranged in layers

and baked) or *stifado* (meat, game or seafood cooked in a tomato purée).

Synaxaria (☎ 2241 036 562; Aristofanous 47; mains €3-5.50) Commonly known as Maria's – after the owner – this is a cosy little eatery serving up excellent mezedes and *mayirefta* (ready-cooked meals). The traditional pork and lamb are worth an honourable mention.

Myrovolos (☎ 2241 038 693; Lahitos 13; mains €4.50-6) Minuscule Myrovolos is a welcome antidote to Rhodes' rather tacky tourist restaurants. Excellent, imaginative food is served up and there is live music from 6pm to 8pm. Sample the seafood with ouzo special.

New Town

The New Town has some surprisingly good places to eat, as long as you are prepared to look. The following places are all on the Rhodes Town map, opposite.

Chalki (☎ 2241 033 198; Kathopouli 30; mezedes €2.50-5) Chalki is a down-to-earth and thoroughly idiosyncratic eatery. Choose from an enticing display of mezedes, and down them with excellent draught wine.

To Steki tou Heila (☎ 2241 029 337; Hatziangelou & Hatzigeorgiou; mains €3-6; ⏰ dinner only) This is a totally unpretentious fish restaurant on the commercial harbour and patronised primarily by Greeks. It's not flash, but it's cheap and cheery.

Thomas & Charlotte's Taverna (☎ 2241 073 557; Georgiou Leondos 8; mains €5-9) This taverna serves a wide selection of standard Greek dishes. Try the tasty *kleftiko*, a slow-cooked mixture of meat and vegetables served wrapped in greaseproof paper.

MID-RANGE & TOP END
Old Town

The following places are all on the Rhodes Old Town map, p263.

Nisyros (☎ 2241 031 741; Agiou Fanouriou 45-47; mains €6.50-11) A beautiful and tastefully decorated restaurant with impeccable service and a wide range of Greek dishes. Dining is in a leafy, secluded courtyard.

Mystagogia (☎ 2241 032 981; Themistokleous 5; mezedes €3-10) Mystagogia draws its charm as much from the open fireplace for winter meals as from its carefully cooked dishes. Bekri meze or 'drunkard's meze' (spicy pork or beef cubes in tomato sauce) is recommended for the curious and hungry.

DODECANESE

Kasbah (☎ 2241 078 633; Platonos 4-8; mains €11.20; ☾ dinner only, closed Mon) If you crave something other than Greek food, Kasbah serves excellent Moroccan dishes. Couscous dishes predominate, with one especially for vegetarians. Ambience is Middle Eastern and piped world music entertains you as you dine.

New Town
The following places are all on the Rhodes Town map, p266.

7,5 Thavma (☎ 2241 039 805; Dilberaki 15; mains €5.50-7.50) This Swedish-influenced diner has Greek and Swedish dishes alternating on an inventive fusion menu. Recommended dishes are tiger prawns and salmon.

To Steki tou Tsima (☎ 2241 074 390; Peloponisou 22; mezedes €4.50-6) To Steki is an unpretentious and totally untouristy fish restaurant on the south side of New Town. Sample from an imaginative and occasionally unusual array of fish (such as *yermanos*) and shellfish-based mezedes – try *fouskes*.

CAFÉS
Feverish touting reaches its acme at the patisseries for people watching, with names like Nirefs, Demetriades and Cofea, bordering the New Market. Nevertheless, they're convivial meeting places.

Entertainment
OLD TOWN
The following places are all on the Rhodes Old Town map, p263.

Kafe Besara (☎ 2241 030 363; Sofokleous 11-12) This Aussie-owned place is one of the Old Town's liveliest bars, and a great place to hang out.

Mango Cafe Bar (☎ 2241 024 877; Dorieos 3) This bar claims to have the cheapest drinks in the Old Town, as well as Internet access, and is the preferred haunt of local expats, scuba divers and die-hard travellers.

Resalto Club (☎ 2241 020 520; Plateia Damagitou; ☾ 11pm-late) This Greek music centre features live music on weekends. The repertoire ranges from *entehno* (artistic compositional) to *laïko tragoudi* (popular) to rembetika.

The impressive **Sound & Light Show** (☎ 2241 021 9220; www.hellenicfestival.gr; admission €6) takes place from Monday to Saturday next to the walls of the Old Town off Plateia Rimini.

English-language sessions are staggered but in general begin at either 9.15pm or 11.15pm. Other languages offered are French, German and Swedish.

NEW TOWN
There is a plethora of discos and bars in New Town. The two main areas are Top Street (Alexandrou Diakou) and the Street of Bars (Orfanidou), where a cacophony of Western music blares from every establishment. The following places are all on the Rhodes Town map, p266.

Down Under Bar (☎ 2241 032 982; Orfanidou 37) For a wild night of dancing on the bar, make for this Aussie-influenced watering hole.

Red Lion (Orfanidou 9) For something more subdued, this bar has the relaxed atmosphere of a British pub. Ron and Vasilis will gladly answer questions about Rhodes for the price of a drink.

Colorado Entertainment Centre (☎ 2241 075 120; cnr Akti Miaouli & Orfanidou 57) The Colorado consists of three venues in one – the Dancing Club, the Heaven Night Club and a live band venue. There is more than enough fun for a week in this enormous palace of hype.

Shopping
Good buys in Rhodes' Old Town are gold and silver jewellery, leather goods and ceramics (although leather goods are cheaper in Turkey).

Manuel Music Center (Map p266; ☎ 2241 028 266; 25 Martiou 10-13) For good-quality Greek music – ie, not 'Zorba the Greek does Syrtaki' tourist music – all the latest Greek CDs and more are on sale here.

Getting Around
Local buses leave from Mandraki. Bus No 2 goes to Analipsi, No 3 to Rodini, No 4 to Agios Dimitrios and No 5 to Monte Smith. You can buy tickets at the kiosk on Mandraki.

EASTERN RHODES
Rhodes' best beaches are on the east coast. There are frequent buses to Lindos, but some beaches are a bit of a trek from the road. It's possible to find uncrowded stretches of coast even in the high season.

Kalithea Thermi, 10km from Rhodes Town, is a derelict Italian-built spa. Within the complex are crumbling colonnades, domed ceilings and mosaic floors. Buses from Rhodes Town stop opposite the turn-off to the spa. The beach is used by Rhodes' diving schools (see Activities, p265). To the right there's a small sandy beach (with a snack bar); take the track that veers right from the turn-off to the spa. Kalithea is currently being restored.

Ladiko Beach, touted locally as 'Anthony Quinn Beach', is in fact two back-to-back coves with a pebbly beach on the north side and volcanic rock platforms on the south. The swimming is good and development is relatively low-key.

At Kolymbia, further down the coast, a right turn leads in over 4km of pine-fringed road to the **Epta Piges** (Seven Springs), a beautiful cool, shady valley where a lake fed by springs can be reached either along a path or through a tunnel. This is a popular tourist attraction in its own right. There are no buses around here, so take a Lindos bus and get off at the turn-off.

Back on the coast, **Kolymbia** and **Tsambika** are good but crowded beaches. A steep road (signposted) leads in 1.5km to **Moni Tsambikas**, from where there are terrific views. The monastery is a place of pilgrimage for childless women. On 18 September, the monastery's festival day, women climb up to it on their knees and then pray to conceive.

Arhangelos, 4km further on and inland, is a large agricultural village with a tradition of carpet weaving and making goatskin boots by hand. Just before Arhangelos there is a turn-off to **Stegna Beach**, and just after to the lovely sandy cove of **Agathi**; both are reasonably quiet. The **Castle of Faraklos** above Agathi was a prison for recalcitrant knights and the island's last stronghold to fall to the Turks. The fishing port of **Haraki**, just south of the castle, has a pebbled beach. There are more beaches between here and Vlyha Bay, 2km from Lindos.

Lindos Λίνδος
pop 1091

Lindos village, 47km from Rhodes, lies below the Acropolis of Lindos and is a showpiece of dazzling white 17th-century houses, many with courtyards with black-and-white *hohlakia* (pebble mosaic) floors. Once the dwellings of wealthy admirals, many have been bought and restored by foreign celebrities. The main thoroughfares are lined with tourist shops and cafés, so you need to explore the labyrinthine alleyways to fully appreciate the place.

Lindos is the most famous of the ancient cities of the Dodecanese, receiving 500,000 visitors a year, and was an important Doric settlement because of its excellent vantage point and good harbour. It was first established around 2000 BC and is overlaid with a conglomeration of Byzantine, Frankish and Turkish remains.

After the founding of the city of Rhodes, Lindos declined in commercial importance, but remained an important place of worship. The ubiquitous St Paul landed here en route to Rome. The Byzantine fortress was strengthened by the knights, and also used by the Turks.

The 15th-century **Church of Agia Panagia** (Acropolis) is festooned with 18th-century frescoes.

ORIENTATION & INFORMATION

The town is pedestrianised. All vehicular traffic terminates on the central square of Plateia Eleftherias, from where the main drag, Acropolis, begins. The donkey terminus is a little way along here.

Commercial Bank of Greece With an ATM, it's by the donkey terminus.

Internet cafés There are two in Lindos, both near the post office.

Lindos Lending Library (Acropolis) Privately owned and well stocked with English books. It also has a laundrette (€7.30 per load).

Lindos Sun Tours (☎ 2244 031 333; Acropolis) Has room-letting services and also rents cars and motorcycles.

Municipal Tourist Office (☎ 2244 031 900; Plateia Eleftherias; ☒ 7.30am-9pm) Helpful although overworked.

National Bank of Greece On the street opposite the Church of Agia Panagia.

Pallas Travel (☎ 2244 031 494; Acropolis) Has room-letting services.

Post office Turn right at the donkey terminus to reach it.

THE ACROPOLIS OF LINDOS

Spectacularly perched atop a 116m-high rock is the **Acropolis** (☎ 2244 031 258; admission €6; ☒ 8.30am-2.40pm Tue-Sun Sep-May, 8.30am-6pm Jun-Aug). It's about a 10-minute climb to the well-signposted entrance gate. Once inside, a flight of steps leads to a large square. On the left (facing the next flight of steps) is

DODEC

a trireme (warship) hewn out of the rock by the sculptor Pythocretes. A statue of Hagesandros, priest of Poseidon, originally stood on the deck of the ship. At the top of the steps ahead, you enter the Acropolis by a vaulted corridor. At the other end, turn sharp left through an enclosed room to reach a row of storerooms on the right. The stairway on the right leads to the remains of a 20-columned **Hellenistic stoa** (200 BC). The Byzantine **Church of Agios Ioannis** is to the right of this stairway. The wide stairway behind the stoa leads to a 5th-century BC propylaeum, beyond which is the 4th-century **Temple to Athena**, the site's most important ancient ruin. Athena was worshipped on Lindos as early as the 10th century BC, so this temple has replaced earlier ones on the site. From its far side there are splendid views of Lindos village and its beach.

Donkey rides to the Acropolis cost €3.50 one way.

SLEEPING & EATING

Accommodation is expensive and reservations are essential in summer. The following two places are near each other on the north side of the village. Follow the donkeys heading to the Acropolis for about 150m to find them.

Lindos Pension (☎ 2244 031 369; s/d €33/40) This is the cheapest option. Rooms are small and plain, but clean and pleasant.

Pension Electra (☎ 2244 031 266; s/d €40/50; 🔀) Electra has a roof terrace with superb views and a beautiful shady garden. Rooms all have fridges.

Kalypso (☎ 2244 031 669; mains €7-7.50) Set in one of Lindos' historic buildings, Kalypso is open for lunch and dinner. Try either sausages in mustard, chicken in coconut sauce or rabbit stew in red wine with pearl onions.

WESTERN RHODES

Western Rhodes is greener and more forested than the east coast, but it's more exposed to winds so the sea tends to be rough, and the beaches are mostly of pebbles or stones. Nevertheless, tourist development is rampant, and consists of the suburb resorts of Ixia, Trianda and Kremasti. Paradisi, despite being next to the airport, has retained some of the feel of a traditional village.

Ancient Ialysos Αρχαία Ιαλυσός

Like Lindos, Ialysos, 10km from Rhodes, is a hotchpotch of Doric, Byzantine and medieval remains. The Doric city was built on Filerimos Hill, which was an excellent vantage point, attracting successive invaders over the years. The only ancient remains are the foundations of a 3rd-century BC temple and a restored 4th-century BC fountain. Also at the site are the **Monastery of Our Lady** and the **Chapel of Agios Georgios**.

The ruined **fortress** (adult €4; 🕙 8am-5pm Tue-Sun) was used by Süleyman the Magnificent during his siege of Rhodes Town. No buses go to ancient Ialysos. The airport bus stops at Trianda, on the coast. Ialysos is 5km inland from here.

Ancient Kamiros Αρχαία Κάμειρος

The extensive **ruins** (adult €4; 🕙 8am-5pm Tue-Sun) of the Doric city of Kamiros stand on a hillside above the west coast, 34km from Rhodes Town. The ancient city, known for its figs, oil and wine, reached the height of its powers in the 6th century BC. By the 4th century BC it had been superseded by Rhodes. Most of the city was destroyed by earthquakes in 226 and 142 BC, but the layout is easily discernible.

From the entrance, walk straight ahead and down the steps. The semicircular rostrum on the right is where officials made speeches to the public. Opposite are the remains of a **Doric temple** with one standing column. The area next to it, with a row of intact columns, was probably where the public watched priests performing rites in the temple. Ascend the wide stairway to the ancient city's main street. Opposite the top of the stairs is one of the best preserved of the **Hellenistic houses** that lined the street. Walk along the street, ascend three flights of steps and continue ahead to the ruins of the 3rd-century **great stoa**, which had a 206m portico supported by two rows of Doric columns. It was built on top of a huge 6th-century cistern that supplied the houses with rainwater through an advanced drainage system. Behind the stoa, at the city's highest point, stood the **Temple to Athena**, with terrific views inland.

Buses from Rhodes Town to Kamiros stop on the coast road, 1km from the site.

Ancient Kamiros to Monolithos
Αρχαία Κάμειρος προς Μονόλιθος

Skala Kamirou, 13.5km south of ancient Kamiros, is a fairly unremarkable place sporting a few market gardens, a scattering of tavernas and a petrol station. More importantly, it serves as the access port for travellers heading to and from the island of Halki (p273). The road south from here to Monolithos has some of the island's most impressive scenery. From Skala Kamirou, the road winds uphill with great views across to Halki. This is just a taste of what's to come at the ruined 16th-century **Castle of Kastellos**, reached along a rough road from the main road, 2km beyond Skala Kamirou. There is a left fork to Embonas (p273) 8km further on. The main road continues for another 9km to **Siana**, a picturesque village below Mt Akramytis (825m), famed for its honey and *souma*, a brew made from seasonal fruit, and similar to Cretan *raki*.

The village of Monolithos, 5km beyond Siana, has the spectacularly sited **Castle of Monolithos** perched on a sheer 240m-high rock and reached along a dirt track. Continuing along this track, at the fork bear right for **Moni Agiou Georgiou** and left for the very pleasant shingled **Fourni Beach**.

There is little accommodation along this stretch of coast, but the fairly standard **Hotel Thomas** (☎ 2246 061 291; Monolithos; d €33) is one option; while you won't go far wrong taking a seafood lunch at **Althemeni Restaurant** (☎ 2246 031 303; fish €40 per kg) right on the harbourfront at Skala Kamirou. It offers a wide range of fish, as well as grills and mayirefta.

SOUTHERN RHODES
South of Lindos, Rhodes becomes progressively less developed. Although **Pefki**, 2km south of Lindos, does attract package tourists, it's still possible to get out of earshot of other tourists, away from the main beach.

Lardos is a pleasant village 6km west of Lindos and 2km inland from Lardos Beach. From the far side of Lardos a right turn leads in 4km to **Moni Agias Ypsenis** (Monastery of Our Lady) through hilly, green countryside.

Heading south from Lardos, don't miss the almost hidden **Glystra Beach**, 4km south along the coast road. This diminutive bay is one of the best swimming spots along the whole eastern coastline.

The well-watered village of **Laerma** is 12km northwest of Lardos. From here it's another 5km to the beautifully sited 9th-century **Moni Tharri**, the island's first monastery; it has been re-established as a monastic community. It contains some fine 13th-century frescoes.

Asklipion, 8km north of Gennadi, is an unspoilt village with the ruins of yet another castle and the 11th-century **Church of Kimisis Theotokou**, which has fine Byzantine wall paintings.

Gennadi Γεννάδι
pop 655

Gennadi (ye-*nah*-dhi), 13km south of Lardos, is an attractive, largely untouched agricultural village masquerading as a holiday centre. For independent travellers it is probably the best base for a protracted stay in the south. The village itself, a patchwork of narrow streets and whitewashed houses, is set several hundred metres back from the beach.

Sleeping and eating offer a few choices. At this one you can do both. **Effie's Dreams Apartments** (☎ 2244 043 410; www.effiesdreams.com; d/tr €40/50; 🅿 😊 🖳) is right by an enormous 800-year-old mulberry tree and has modern, spotlessly clean studios with lovely rural and sea vistas from the communal balcony. The friendly Greek-Australian owners will meet you if you call ahead. Below the apartments, **Effie's Dream Cafe Bar** (☎ 2244 043 410; snacks €2.50-4) serves drinks and tasty snacks such as country-style sausage with onions and peppers.

I Kouzina tis Mamas (☎ 2244 043 547; pasta €4-5) in the main street specialises in pizza and pasta as well as a wide range of Greek grills.

Gennadi to Prasonisi
Γεννάδι προς Πρασονήσι

From Gennadi an almost uninterrupted beach of pebbles, shingle and sand dunes extends down to **Plimmyri**, 11km south. It's easy to find deserted stretches.

From Plimmyri the main road continues to **Kattavia**, Rhodes' most southerly village. The 11km dirt road north to Messanagros winds through terrific scenery. From Kattavia a 10km road leads south to remote **Cape Prasonisi**, the island's southernmost point, once joined to Rhodes by a narrow sandy isthmus now split by encroaching seas. It's a popular spot for windsurfing.

A good place to sleep is at **Lahania**, signposted 2km off the main highway, in **Studios Alonia** (☎ 2244 046 027; studios €30), where each fan-cooled studio has a kitchenette and fridge. These are owned by the proprietors of **Taverna Platanos** (☎ 2244 046 027; mains €3-5), a relaxed little taverna that makes for a popular Sunday outing. You dine on the tiny village square amid running water in the company of ducks. The food served is wholesome and filling village fare; try chickpeas, or locally produced pork chops.

Down on Prasonisi beach **Faros Taverna** (☎ 2244 091 030; d €30; mains €4-7) is one of two tavernas on the beach. The food is uncomplicated and features grills and fish, while the comfortable rooms attract a mainly windsurfer crowd.

South of Monolithos

Rhodes' southwest coast doesn't see as many visitors as other parts of the island. It is lonely and exposed and has only recently acquired a sealed road, completing the network around this southern quadrant of the island. Forest fires in recent years have devastated many of the west-facing hillsides and there is a general end-of-the-world feeling about the whole region.

The beaches south of Monolithos are prone to strong winds. From the important crossroads village of **Apolakkia**, 10km south of Monolithos, a road crosses the island to Gennadi, passing through the unspoilt villages of **Arnitha** and **Vati** with an optional detour to **Istrios** and **Profilia**. A turn-off to the left 7km south of Apolakkia leads to the 18th-century **Moni Skiadi**. It's a serene place with terrific views down to the coast, and there is free basic accommodation for visitors.

THE INTERIOR

The east–west roads that cross the island have great scenery and very little traffic. If you have transport they're well worth exploring. It's also good cycling territory if you have a suitably geared bicycle.

Petaloudes Πεταλούδες

Known as Valley of the Butterflies, **Petaloudes** (adult €1-3; 8.30am-sunset 1 May–30 Sep) is one of the more popular 'sights' on the package tour itinerary. It is reached along a 6km turn-off from the west coast road, 2.5km south of Paradisi.

The so-called 'butterflies' are in fact strikingly coloured moths *(Callimorpha quadripunctarea)* that are lured to this gorge of rustic footbridges, streams and pools by the scent of the resin exuded by the styrax trees. Regardless of what you may see other tourists doing, do not make any noises to disturb the butterflies; their numbers are declining rapidly, largely due to noise disturbance. Better still, don't visit and leave them alone. If you must, there are buses to Petaloudes from Rhodes Town.

Around Petaloudes

From Petaloudes a winding cross-island road leads to the 18th-century **Moni Kalopetras** built by Alexander Ypsilandis, the grandfather of the Greek freedom fighter. This same road leads across the central mountain spine of roads through a rather dry landscape full of olive trees to the pretty village of **Psinthos**, which makes for a very pleasant lunch break.

From Psinthos you can choose to loop back to Rhodes Town (22km) via a fast but undistinguished direct route passing through **Kalythies**, or head further south and pick up the very pretty cross-island route from **Kolymbia** to **Salakos**.

If you wish to sleep the night in the country then **Artemidis Restaurant & Rooms** (☎ 2241 051 735; d €33;) in Psinthos is a decent choice. The fairly ordinary rooms are above the restaurant, which serves tasty traditional Greek fare including grills and *mayirefta*.

Also in Psinthos is the well-regarded **Pigi Fasouli Estiatorio** (☎ 2241 050 071; mains €4.50-6), where you dine under cool plane trees next to running water – all to the sound of incessant cicadas. Good dishes on offer are goat and chickpeas, pork and lima beans and *pitaroudia* (small pites). Look for signs from the main square in Psinthos to find it.

Salakos & Mt Profitis Ilias

Σάλακος & Προφήτης Ηλίας

This route to Mt Profitis Ilias (pro-*fee*-tis ee-*lee*-as) and Salakos (*sah*-la-kos) across the north central highlands of Rhodes is perhaps the most scenic of all the day-trip drives or rides. It can be tackled from either the west or the east coast of Rhodes, though the most attractive way is from east to west.

Start at the signposted turn-off near **Kolymbia**. Shortly beyond, you may wish to stop briefly to visit beautiful **Epta Piges** (p269). Heading up and inland you will next come to the villages of **Arhipoli** and **Eleousa**, once used by the Italians as hill stations. The road now climbs through a landscape that becomes more and more forested. Two kilometres from Eleousa you will pass the small Byzantine church of **Agios Nikolaos Foundouklis** with its faded frescoes. This is a good picnic spot – there are tables, chairs and spring water.

It is a further 6km along a winding, pine-shrouded road to the summit of **Mt Profitis Ilias** (780m). The surrounding forest is lush and cool and a pleasant relief for cyclists.

It is downhill from here and a further 12km of winding cruising will bring you to the village of **Salakos**. If you are on foot you can walk down on an established track that begins near the easy-to-find **Moni Profiti Ilia**. It will take you about 45 minutes to walk down to Salakos. The village is a cheery place, with a small square and fountain and several cafés for coffee or cold beers. From Salakos it is only 9.5km downhill to the west coast village of Kalavarda.

Wine Country

From Salakos you may detour to **Embonas** on the slopes of Mt Attavyros (1215m), the island's highest mountain. Embonas is the wine capital of Rhodes and produces some of the island's best tipples. The red Cava Emery, or Zacosta and white Villare are good choices. You can taste and buy them at **Emery Winery** (☎ 2246 029 111; admission free; ☒ 9.30am-3pm Mon-Fri) in Embonas.

Embonas village is no great shakes itself, despite being touted by the tourism authorities as a 'traditional village'. However, **Bakis** (☎ 2246 041 247; mains €3.50-6) on the main square is a good spot to try some home-produced grills. The *païdakia* (spare rib chops), or the *kondosouvli* (Cypriot-style spit-roast kebabs) are particularly succulent, while for dessert the grape preserve is divine.

You may nonetheless wish to detour around Mt Attavyros to **Agios Isidoros**, 14km south of Embonas, a prettier and still unspoilt wine-producing village that you can visit en route to Siana (p271).

HALKI ΧΑΛΚΗ

pop 313

Halki is an unquestionably pretty little island just 16km off the west coast of Rhodes. But it's an island with a difficult past and a curious present. Once home to a buoyant sponge-fishing economy, a fishing fleet and a large supporting population, the island was all but abandoned when the sponge industry took a nose dive and the depredations of two wars forced many Halkiots to emigrate to the USA (particularly Florida). Now it's enjoying a quiet, though somewhat sanitised, revival with a steady flow of villa rental vacationers looking for that ideal island in the sun, but without the tack and excess that sometimes mars its larger neighbour Rhodes. Halki is ideal for a quiet holiday, for book lovers, writers, poets and incurable romantics.

Getting There & Away

CAÏQUE & BUS

Halki has a daily link to Skala Kamirou (€9, 1½ hours) on Rhodes. A bus to Rhodes Town connects at Skala Kamirou, except on Sunday.

FERRY

LANE Lines serves Halki three times weekly in either direction with services to Rhodes (€6.80, two hours), Pigadia on Karpathos (€9.50, three hours), Sitia on

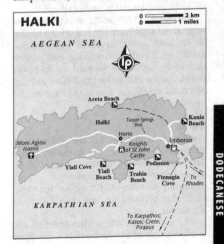

HALKI

AEGEAN SEA

Areta Beach

Halki   Tarpon Springs Blvd   Kania Beach

Horio

Moni Agiou Ioanni

Knights of St John Castle   Emborios

Yiali Cove   Yiali Beach   Trahia Beach   Podamos   Ftenagia Cove   To Rhodes

KARPATHIAN SEA

To Karpathos; Kasos; Crete; Piraeus

Crete (€17, 7½ hours) and Piraeus (€33, 22 hours). There is an occasional summer link to Santorini (€20, 15 hours).

Getting Around

There are no buses and just one taxi on the island. There are no rental cars or motorcycles, but there are water taxis to the main beaches and excursions to the island of Alimnia (€30).

EMBORIOS ΕΜΠΟΡΕΙΟΣ

The picturesque port village of Emborios resembles Gialos on Symi, but on a smaller scale. The port is draped around a horseshoe bay, and former sea captains' mansions – some renovated, others still in a state of disrepair – rise up around the bay in a colourful architectural display. Cars are all but banned from the harbour, so the Emborios waterside enjoys a tranquil, motor-free setting.

Orientation & Information

Boats arrive at the middle of the small village harbour. All commercial services are within 200m of the disembarkation point. Accommodation is further back, scattered among the restored and partially restored houses. One road leads away from Emborios as far as Moni Agiou Ioanni 8km away at the far end of the island.

There is no official tourist office on Halki but the website www.halkivisitor.com is a useful reference point, as is the free quarterly English and Greek newspaper *The Halki Visitor,* available on the island.

Zifos Travel (☎ 2246 045 082; zifos-travel@rho.forth net.gr) and **Chalki Tours** (☎ 2246 045 281; fax 2246 045 219) both assist travellers with accommodation, travel or excursions, and money exchange, as there is no bank or ATM on Halki. An on-call **doctor** (☎ 2246 045 206) can be contacted. There is a post office on the harbour.

Sights

Halki's main features are the old **captains' mansions** that festoon the harbour. Many have been restored to their former glory or are being restored. Others are in a complete state of disrepair. Either way they give Halki that picturesque look that visitors so appreciate.

The impressive stone **clock tower** at the southern side of the harbour is a gift from the Halkiots of Florida. While the clock tower may look good, don't rely on it for the time. Each of the four faces is stuck on a different hour of the day.

The **Church of Agios Nikolaos** has the tallest belfry in the Dodecanese and boasts a particularly well-made and impressive hohlaki courtyard on the east side. There is a small upstairs **museum** (adult €1; ☉ 6-7pm Mon & Fri, 11am-noon Sun) with ecclesiastical exhibits.

Sleeping & Eating

Most villa and studio accommodation is block-booked by foreign tour companies. What little private accommodation there is can be in high demand. Bookings are essential. There is no hotel as such on the island.

Captain's House (☎ 2246 045 201; d €35) This beautiful 19th-century mansion with period furniture and a tranquil, tree-shaded garden is the most pleasant place to stay. It is owned by a retired Greek sea captain, Alex, and his British wife Christine.

Mouthouria (☎ 2246 045 071; francesm@otenet.gr; house €70) Rent a whole renovated captain's house that can accommodate up to six people. It's fully equipped and ideal for longer stays, but there's a minimum two-night booking rule.

Mavri Thalassa (☎ 2246 045 021; mains €4-5) This restaurant at the end of the harbour is well regarded by locals and does good fish dishes. The whole grilled *kalamaria* (calamari), when available fresh, is delicate and soft, and the Symi prawns are well recommended.

Giannis (☎ 6945 148 196; mains €4-6) Lacking a sign at research time, Giannis is a newer Georgian-run taverna with fast, efficient service and a limited, but genuinely good menu selection. Symi shrimps are a good bet and go well with the draught wine.

AROUND HALKI

Podamos Beach is the closest and the best beach. It is 1km from Emborios in the direction of Horio. The narrowish beach is sandy and the water is rather shallow – not the best for snorkelling. For food you can try the somewhat pricey **Podamos Beach Taverna** (☎ 2246 045 295; ☉ lunch only). **Ftenagia Beach**, past the headland and 500m to the south of Emborios, doesn't have much sand, but there is excellent rock swimming and the snorkelling is far better. The **Ftenagia Beach Taverna** (☎ 6945 998 333; ☉ lunch & dinner in summer) is a cosy waterside eatery with friendly service and top-class dishes on offer.

Horio, a 30-minute walk along Tarpon Springs Blvd from Emborios, was once a thriving community of 3000 people, but it's now derelict and uninhabited. A path leads from Horio's churchyard to a Knights of St John **castle**.

Moni Agiou Ioanni is a two-hour, 8km unshaded walk along a concrete road from Horio. The church and courtyard, protected by the shade of an enormous cypress tree, is a quiet, tranquil place, but it comes alive each year from 28–29 August during the feast of the church's patron, St John.

KARPATHOS ΚΑΡΠΑΘΟΣ

pop 6084

If ever there was a Greek island that combined the right proportions of size, attractiveness, remoteness, water activities and general good feel, it might just be the elongated island of Karpathos (*kar*-pah-thos), midway between Crete and Rhodes. Karpathos has rugged mountains, numerous beaches – among the best in the Aegean – and unspoilt villages. So far, it has not succumbed to the worst excesses of mass tourism.

The island is traversed by a north–south mountain range. For hundreds of years the north and south parts of the island were isolated from one another and so they developed independently. It is even thought that the northerners and southerners have different ethnic origins. The northern village of Olymbos is of fascination to ethnologists for the age-old customs of its inhabitants.

Karpathos has a relatively uneventful history. Unlike almost all other Dodecanese islands, it was never under the auspices of the Knights of St John. It is a wealthy island, receiving more money from emigrants living abroad (mostly in the USA) than any other Greek island.

Getting There & Away

AIR

There are five flights weekly to and from Athens (€68 to €78), up to two daily to Rhodes (€28) and three weekly to Kasos (€22). **Olympic Airways** (☎ 2245 022 150) is on the central square in Pigadia. The airport is 13km southwest of Pigadia.

KARPATHOS

0 ——— 4 km
0 ——— 2 miles

Karpathos Strait

Cape Paraspori

Saria islet

Excursion Boat

Cape Vroukounda
Moni Agiou Ioanni
Vroukounda

Avlona
Moni Agiou Konstantinou
Diafani
Vananda Beach
To Halki; Rhodes

Mt Profitis Ilias ▲ (716m)
Olymbos

SEA OF CRETE

Agios Minas

Spoa

Mesohori
Agios Nikolaos

Apella Beach

Sokastro

Excursion Boat

Karpathos
Mertonas
Kyra Panagia Beach
Lefkos
Kato Lakos Beach
Kali Limni (1215m)
Aperi
Ahata Beach
Volada
Adia
Othos
Pyles
Cape Proni
Vrondi Bay

Pigadia

Menetes
Agios Nikolaos Beach
Finiki
Ammoopi
Arkasa
Cape Volakas

Cape Agios Theodoros

Afiartis Bay
Cape Akrotiri
Airport
Cape Liki

To Kasos; Crete; Piraeus

Cape Kastello

DODECANESE

FERRY
LANE Lines of Crete provides three services weekly to Rhodes (€15.60, four hours) via Halki (€9.50, three hours), as well as to Piraeus (€29, 18½ hours) via Milos (€30.80, 13 hours). Kasos (€6.50, 1½ hours) is also served by the same three-weekly services.

Note that these ferries also serve the ports of Sitia (€15.50, 4¼ hours) and Agios Nikolaos (€18.50, seven hours) in Crete. Tickets can be bought from **Possi Travel** (☎ 2245 022 148; possitvl@hotmail.com) in Pigadia.

Getting Around
TO/FROM THE AIRPORT
There is no airport bus. Travellers must take a taxi (€11) or seek independent transport.

BUS
Pigadia is the transport hub of the island; a schedule is posted at the **bus station** (☎ 2245 022 192). Buses serve most of the settlements in southern Karpathos. The fare is between €1.15 and €1.57. There is no bus between Pigadia and Olymbos or Diafani in the north, but a bus meets the excursion boats from Pigadia at Diafani and transports people to Olymbos.

CAR, MOTORCYCLE & BICYCLE
Gatoulis Car Hire (☎ 2245 022 747; fax 2245 022 814), on the east side of Pigadia on the road to Aperi, rents cars, motorcycles and bicycles. **Possi Travel** (☎ 2245 022 148; possitvl@hotmail.com) also arranges car and motorcycle hire.

The precipitous and at times hairy 19.5km stretch of road from Spoa to Olymbos is unsurfaced, but you can drive it, with care. Do not tackle this road by motorcycle or scooter. If you rent a vehicle, make it a small jeep and fill up your tank before you leave.

EXCURSION BOAT
In summer there are daily excursion boats from Pigadia to Diafani (€10 to €15 return, including the bus to Olymbos). One-way tickets can be purchased (€6). There are also frequent boats to the beaches of Kyra Panagia and Apella (€9). Tickets can be bought at the quay.

From Diafani, excursion boats go to nearby beaches and occasionally to the uninhabited islet of Saria, where there are some Byzantine remains.

TAXI
Pigadia's **taxi rank** (☎ 2245 022 705; Dimokratias) is near the bus station. A price list is displayed. Sample taxi fares from Pigadia are as follows: Amoöpi (€5), Arkasa (€11), Pyles (€11), Kyra Panagia (€15), Olymbos (€70) and Diafani (€75).

PIGADIA ΠΗΓΑΔΙΑ
pop 1692

After the charms of Symi, Chalki and Kastellorizo, at first sight Pigadia (pi-gha-dhi-ya), the island's capital and main port, does not immediately charm. It's a modern town and is attractive enough in its own way, but without any eminent buildings or sites. Much of the cement-based architecture was erected during a boom in the 1960s and '70s. Upon further investigation, Pigadia is a pleasant and busy town. The town is built on the edge of **Vrondi Bay**, a 4km-long sandy beach where you can rent water-sports equipment, while on the beach are the remains of the early Christian **Basilica of Agia Fotini**.

Orientation & Information
The ferry quay is at the northern end of the wide harbour. It's a short walk to the centre of Pigadia, which is punctuated by the main street, Apodimon Karpathion. This in turn leads to the central square of Plateia 5 Oktovriou. The bus station is one block up from the waterfront on Dimokratias.

Caffe Galileo Internet 2000 (☎ 2245 023 606; Apodimon Karpathion; 🕙 9am-2pm & 6pm-1am; €4 per hr) Offers Internet access.

Enter Café (☎ 2245 029 053; 28 Oktovriou; €4 per hr; 🕙 9am-2pm & 6.30pm-1am) Offers Internet access.

Laundro Express (Mitropolitou Apostolou)

National Bank of Greece (Apodimon Karpathion) Has an ATM.

Police (☎ 2245 022 224) Near the hospital at the western end of town.

Possi Travel (☎ 2245 022 148; possitvl@hotmail.com) The main travel agency for ferry and air tickets.

Post office Also near the hospital.

Tourist Information Office (☎ 2245 023 835; 🕙 Jul-Aug) In a kiosk in the middle of the seafront.

www.inkarpathos.com Provides tourist information.

www.karpathos.com Provides tourist information.

Sleeping
There's plenty of accommodation, and some owners meet the boats.

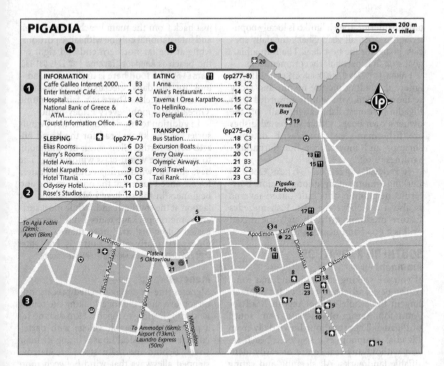

PIGADIA

0 — 200 m
0 — 0.1 miles

INFORMATION	
Caffe Galileo Internet 2000......1	B3
Enter Internet Café.................2	C3
Hospital..............................3	A3
National Bank of Greece &	
ATM................................4	C2
Tourist Information Office......5	B2

SLEEPING ⏏	(pp276–7)
Elias Rooms.......................... 6	D3
Harry's Rooms.....................7	C3
Hotel Avra..........................8	C3
Hotel Karpathos 9	D3
Hotel Titania 10	D3
Odyssey Hotel....................11	D3
Rose's Studios....................12	D3

EATING 🍴	(pp277–8)
I Anna..............................13	C2
Mike's Restaurant................14	C3
Taverna I Orea Karpathos.....15	C3
To Helliniko.......................16	C2
To Perigiali.......................17	C2

TRANSPORT	(pp275–6)
Bus Station........................18	C3
Excursion Boats..................19	C1
Ferry Quay.........................20	C1
Olympic Airways..................21	B3
Possi Travel.......................22	C3
Taxi Rank..........................23	C3

Vrondi Bay

Pigadia Harbour

To Agia Fotini (2km); Aperi (8km)

M Matthcou

Ethnikis Andistasis

Georgiou Loizou

Plateia 5 Oktovriou

Mitropoleos Apostolou

28 Oktovriou

Dimokratias

Apodimon Karpathion

To Ammoöpi (6km); Airport (13km); Laundro Express (50m)

Harry's Rooms (☎ 2245 022 188; Kyprou 2l; s/d €19/22) These rooms, just off 28 Oktovriou, are spotless.

Elias Rooms (☎ 2245 022 446; www.eliasroomstrip od.com; s/d €21/25; 🖥) Owner Ilias Hatzigeorgiou is a mine of local information and maintains these friendly rooms with great views in a quiet part of town.

Rose's Studios (☎ /fax 2245 022 284; studios €23.50) Fairly high up behind Pigadia are these well-kept studios with bathroom and kitchen.

Hotel Karpathos (☎ 2245 022 347; s/d with bathroom €23.50/25) This C-class hotel has light, airy rooms.

Hotel Avra (☎ 2245 022 388, 2245 023 486; 28 Oktovriou 50; d €29.50) This E-class hotel has small but comfortable rooms with ceiling fan, fridge and a small common kitchen.

Hotel Titania (☎ 2245 022 144; www.titania karpathos.gr; s/d €35/50; 🐾) This C-class hotel, opposite Hotel Karpathos, has spacious, pleasant rooms equipped with fridge, phone and TV, and is open all year.

Odyssey Hotel (☎ 2245 023 240; www.odyssey -karpathos.gr; studios €46/65) One of the friendliest and most charming hosts in town runs this

small complex of studios. Each one has a kitchenette, phone, music, TV, fridge, room safe and balcony, and fans are available on demand.

Eating

Eating in town can be a hit and miss affair with many of the waterfront restaurants serving bland and tourist-oriented dishes. There is some hope, with a sprinkling of genuinely good eating places scattered in among the mediocre ones.

Mike's Restaurant (☎ 2245 022 727; grills €4.20-8) One of the longer-standing and more popular eateries, Mike's serves up consistently good, solid fare at reasonable prices. Among the specials are chicken spaghetti and stuffed zucchini flowers.

Taverna I Orea Karpathos (☎ 2245 022 501; mains €3.50-5) Near the quay, I Orea Karpathos serves a wide range of consistently well-prepared traditional Karpathian dishes and reputedly the best *makarounes* (local pasta cooked with cheese and fried onions) in Pigadia.

To Helliniko (☎ 2245 023 932; daily specials €3-9) Boasting a pleasant outdoor terrace and a

DODECANESE

tasteful interior, the Helliniko is locally popular and is open all year. Check the daily specials board for the best deal. The Karpathian goat *stifado* is particularly commendable.

I Anna (☎ 2245 022 820; fish €35 per kg) If you ignore the fading picture menus and tacky restaurant sign, you will be rewarded with Pigadia's freshest fish, caught daily off the owner's own boats. Other suggested dishes are fisherman's macaroni with octopus, shrimps and mussels, or the Karpathian sardines in oil.

To Perigiali (☎ 2245 022 334; mains €2.50-7.50) Lurking unobtrusively among its more boisterous neighbours this little ouzeri-taverna is also a cut above the rest. Fish mezedes feature predominantly, though the mixed grill is a good and hearty alternative.

SOUTHERN KARPATHOS

Ammoöpi Αμμοοπή

If you are seeking sun and sand and some of the best and clearest water for snorkelling in the whole of the Aegean head for Ammoöpi (amm-oh-oh-*pee*), 8km south of Pigadia. There are four buses daily from Pigadia. Ammoöpi is a scattered beach resort without any real centre or easily identifiable landmarks. All sleeping and eating recommendations are at the northern (more accessible) end of Ammoöpi.

There is a large choice of accommodation and eating options, though much gets prebooked by tour operators. **Ammoöpi Beach Rooms** (☎ 2245 081 123; Mikri Ammoöpi; d €15) with spotless, simply furnished rooms is the cheapest place to stay. The rooms are at the far northern end of Ammoöpi adjoining Ammoopi Taverna.

A more expensive place is **Hotel Sophia** (☎ /fax 2245 081 078; d/tr €40/47), a quiet and comfortable mid-range hotel at the northern end of the settlement. Just in front of it, **Blue Sea Hotel** (☎ 2245 081 036; huguette@hellasnet.gr; d €44) has 27 comfortable double rooms, each with fridge and ceiling fan.

For a really quiet choice try **Vardes** (☎ 2245 081 111; hotelvardes@yahoo.com; studios €45; ✖), a small block of very tasteful, spacious and airy studios set back against the hillside among a lush olive grove and a few banana palms. All have largish rooms and a shaded balcony as well as a phone.

There is a rather scattered range of places to eat. **Taverna Ilios** (☎ 2245 081 148; mains €5-6.50),

just back from the main beach, offers Greek and international cuisine with large portions, while at the far northern end and right on the beach is **Ammoopi Taverna** (☎ 2245 081 138; mains €4-6). The food here is uniformly good – look for the daily specials (the clove-laced mousakas excels). There is a fairly genuine 'Greek music night' every Friday night.

In addition to snorkelling, die-hard windsurfers in the know head for the broad **Afiartis Bay**, a further 8km south of Ammoöpi, to enjoy some world-class windsurfing. The bays support windsurfing centres and caters for advanced surfers at the northern end and beginners in the sheltered Makrygialos Bay lagoon at the southern end. While most surfers come on package tours from Germany, casual 'blow-ins' are more than welcome. One particularly good outfit is **Pro Center** (☎ 2245 091 062; www.windsurfen-karpathos.com).

Menetes Μενετές

Menetes (me-ne-*tes*) is perched precariously on top of a sheer cliff overlooking the rolling landscape leading to Pigadia 8km distant. It's a picturesque, unspoilt village with pastel-coloured neoclassical houses lining its main street. Behind the main street are narrow, stepped alleyways that wind between more modest whitewashed dwellings. The village has a small but well-presented **museum** (admission free; ☺ upon request) on the right as you come from Pigadia. The owner of Taverna Manolis will open it up for you.

There is only one place to stay and that's **Mike Rigas Domatia** (☎ 2245 081 269; d/tr €18/22). These domatia are in a traditional flower-bedecked Karpathian house on the north side of Menetes.

Stop by **Taverna Manolis** (☎ 2245 081 103; mains €4.50-7) for generous helpings of grilled meat, or take a break at **Fiesta Dionysos** (☎ 2245 081 269; mains €4-6), specialising in local dishes, including omelette made with artichokes and Karpathian sausages.

Arkasa & Finiki Αρκάσα & Φοινίκι

Arkasa (ar-*ka*-sa), 9km further on, straddles a ravine. It is changing from a traditional village into a holiday resort. Turn right at the T-intersection to reach the authentic village square.

A turn-off left, just before the ravine, leads after 500m to the remains of the 5th-century **Basilica of Agia Sophia**. Two chapels stand amid mosaic fragments and columns. **Agios Nikolaos Beach** is just south across the headland from here.

The serene fishing village of Finiki (fi-*ni*-ki) lies 2km north of Arkasa. There is no decent swimming here as in Arkasa, but it is a pretty diversion while on your way north.

One of the more alluring places to sleep is **Glaros Studios** (☎ 2245 061 015, 2245 061 016; Agios Nikolaos; studios €44-50), right on Agios Nikolaos Beach. Done out in Karpathiot style, these studios have raised sofa-style beds and large terraces with sun beds and enjoy a cool sea breeze.

Further along and on the left on the road to Finiki, **Eleni Studios** (☎ /fax 2245 061 248; Arkasa; apt €44; 🏊) has fully equipped and very neat apartments. The nearby beach is no great shakes however.

Locals come from Pigadia to eat at **Dimitrios Fisherman's Taverna** (☎ 2245 061 294; Finiki; fish platters €14.70) Of the several eating choices in the little harbour, this place consistently gets the thumbs-up for the quality and freshness of its food.

Some 9km north of Finiki and just before the road winds uphill to Lefkos are the secluded **Pine Tree Studios** (☎ 6977 369 948; Adia; d €35). These comfortable fridge- and kitchenette-equipped studios with views over to Kasos make for a quiet rural retreat and include an excellent restaurant.

Lefkos Λεύκος

Lefkos (*lef*-kos), 13km north of Finiki and 2km from the coast road, is a burgeoning resort centred around a little fishing quay. It is a beach lover's paradise with five superb sandy beaches. In summer Lefkos gets crowded, but at other times it still has a rugged, off-the-beaten-track feel about it.

Local boat owners sometimes take visitors to the islet of **Sokastro** where there is a ruined castle. Another diversion from the beaches is the ancient **catacombs**, reached by walking inland and looking for the brown-and-yellow signpost to the catacombs.

Accommodation tends to be block-booked by tour companies in Lefkos, but you can call the following places before you arrive. New in 2002, the three separate blocks of **Aegean View Studios** (☎ /fax 2245 071 462; studios €45), run by a Greek-Australian, are a good bet. All are very close to the beach, are airy and have modern kitchenettes. High up is **Sunset**

Studios (☎ 2245 071 171; harokopos_sunsethotel@hotmail .com; studios €38-45) where the rooms all have sea views and are immaculate.

For eating, head to the little harbour where the first of the three tavernas, **Tou Kalymniou to Steki** (☎ 2245 071 449; mains €4.50-6), is a notch more authentic than the other two. Fish features prominently, but there's a batch of daily *mayirefta* on offer. Out on the approach road, **Small Paradise Taverna** (☎ 2245 071 184; mayirefta €3-6) offers diners a vine-shaded terrace and a range of uncomplicated, but home-cooked mayirefta. Stuffed zucchini flowers are one of the owner's recommendations.

GETTING THERE & AROUND

There are two buses weekly to Lefkos and a taxi costs €20.50. Hitching is dicey as there is not much traffic.

Lefkos Rent A Car (☎ /fax 2245 071 057) is a reliable outlet with competitive prices. The owner will deliver vehicles free of charge to anywhere in southern Karpathos.

NORTHERN KARPATHOS
Diafani Διαφάνι

Diafani is Karpathos' small northern port, where scheduled ferries stop six times weekly. It's not the most attractive of places with a rash of cement buildings somewhat detracting from its rather lush and green environment, but it's laid-back and is a popular port of entry for travellers planning to visit Olymbos and then move on south.

There's no post office, but there is a freestanding Commercial Bank ATM. **Orfanos Travel Holidays** (☎ 2245 051 410) will exchange money. There is the usual scattering of cardphones.

Serious back-to-nature lovers can camp at the quirky **Vananda Camping** (☎ 2245 051 288; camp sites per adult/tent €3.50/2.50), 3km north of the port. It's a well-watered site next to a pebbly beach and has a hippy-style kafeneio run by the rather revolutionary-looking Minas.

Close to where the road enters Diafani from Olymbos, **Nikos Hotel** (☎ 2245 051 289; s/d €22/27) is pleasant enough, though it's a short hike to the waterfront. **Balaskas Hotel** (☎ 2245 051 320; www.balaskashotel.gr; d incl breakfast €30) is a more modern option where rooms have a fridge, TV and phone.

Eating gives you a smattering of choices. **Chrysi Akti Taverna** (☎ 2245 051 215; mains €3.80-5.50)

DODECANESE

on the waterfront is an ever-popular restaurant with stock fish and *mayirefta* dishes and where the service comes with a smile.

Olymbos Ολυμπος
pop 330

Clinging to the ridge of barren Mt Profitis Illas and 4km from Diafani, Olymbos is a living museum. Women wear bright, embroidered skirts, waistcoats, headscarves and goatskin boots. The interiors of the houses are decorated with embroidered cloth and their facades feature brightly painted, ornate plaster reliefs. The inhabitants speak in a vernacular that contains some Doric words, and some of the houses have wooden locks of a kind described by Homer. The women still grind corn in windmills and bake bread in outdoor communal ovens.

Olymbos, alas, is no longer a pristine backwater caught in a time warp. Tourism has taken hold in a big way and is the village's main money spinner. The 'traditional' village is finding it ever harder to remain traditional and is in danger of becoming a kind of kitsch eco-Disney for day-trippers from Pigadia. Olymbos is still fascinating, but sadly rather overrated for what it ultimately has to offer.

There are a few unpretentious places to stay. **Mike's Rooms** (☎ 2245 051 304; d €21) are the first you will come across. They are just beyond the bus stop before you enter the village proper. There's a restaurant downstairs. Within the village, **Hotel Aphrodite** (☎ 2245 051 307; d €30) is very close to the central square, and has immaculate rooms and impressive west-looking sea views.

Makarounes is served up in Olymbos in most restaurants. The best place to eat would have to be the delightfully sited **Taverna O Mylos** (☎ 2245 051 333; mains €2-6) on the north side of the village. Built in and around a restored and working windmill, the truly excellent food is cooked in a wood oven and features organic meat and vegetable produce. Dishes to try are goat in red wine sauce, artichokes or the filling pittes, some with sweet cottage cheese others with silver beet. At the south side of the village and on the main street **Olymbos Taverna** (☎ 2245 051 252; mains €3-4) is a good place for *makarounes*, though the table service can be tediously slow.

KASOS ΚΑΣΟΣ

pop 990

Kasos, 11km south of Karpathos, is really the end of the line. It's the last Dodecanese island before Crete, and looking south, it is the last Greek island before Egypt. It is neither particularly easy to get to, nor to get away from, if the weather in these parts is inclement. Kasos is a rocky little island with prickly pear trees, sparse olive and fig trees, drystone walls, sheep and goats.

History

Despite being diminutive and remote, Kasos has an eventful history. During Turkish rule it flourished, and by 1820 it had 11,000 inhabitants and a large mercantile fleet. Mohammad Ali, the Turkish governor of Egypt, regarded this fleet as an impediment to his plan to establish a base on Crete from which to attack the Peloponnese and quell the uprising. So, on 7 June 1824, Ali's men landed on Kasos and killed around 7000 inhabitants. This massacre is commemorated annually on the anniversary of the slaughter, and Kasiots return from around the world to participate.

During the late 19th century, many Kasiots emigrated to Egypt and around 5000 of them helped build the Suez Canal. Last century many emigrated to the USA.

Getting There & Away
AIR

There are six flights weekly to Rhodes (€40) and Karpathos (€22). **Olympic Airways** (☎ 2245 041 555; Kritis) is in Fry. The airport is 800m west along the coast road from Fry.

EXCURSION BOAT

In summer the *Athina* **excursion boat** (☎ 2245 041 047) travels from Fry to uninhabited Armathia Islet (€7 return) where there are sandy beaches.

FERRY

LANE Lines of Crete includes Kasos on its long run to/from Rhodes and Piraeus via Karpathos, Crete and Milos. Sample fares are: Piraeus (€28, 17 hours), Rhodes (€18.50, 6½ hours) and Sitia (€9, 2½ hours).

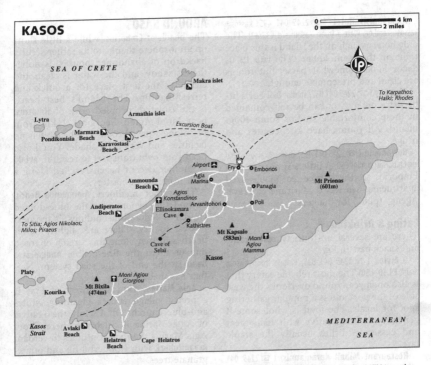

KASOS

SEA OF CRETE

Makra islet

To Karpathos;
Halki; Rhodes

Lytra
Armathia islet

Excursion Boat

Marmara Beach
Pondikonisia
Karavostasi Beach

Airport
Agia Marina
Fry
Emborios

Ammounda Beach
Agios Konstandinos
Panagia
Mt Prionas (601m)

Andiperatos Beach
Ellinokamara Cave
Arvanitohori
Poli

To Sitia; Agios Nikolaos;
Milos; Piraeus
Kathistres
Mt Kapsalo (583m)
Moni Agiou Mamma

Cave of Selai
Kasos

Platy
Moni Agiou Giorgiou

Kourika
Mt Bixila (474m)

MEDITERRANEAN SEA

Kasos Strait
Avlaki Beach
Helatros Beach
Cape Helatros

Getting Around

There is no bus on Kasos. There are just two **taxis** (☎ 2245 041 158, 2245 041 278) on the island. Motorcycles can be rented from **Frangiskos Moto Rentals** (☎ 2245 041 746) for around €12 per day.

FRY ΦΡΥ

Fry (pronounced free) is the island's capital and port. It can be thoroughly explored in under an hour. It's a pleasant, ramshackle kind of place with little tourism. Its narrow whitewashed streets are usually busy with locals in animated discussion. The town's focal point is the very picturesque old fishing harbour of Bouka. The suburb of Emborios is located 1km east of Fry.

Orientation & Information

Fry's large new harbour complex abuts the settlement 500m from its main square, Plateia Iroön Kasou. Turn left from the harbour to get to Emborios. Fry's main street is Kritis. Kasos does not have an EOT or tourist police.

Commercial Bank ATM This stand alone ATM is on the south side of Fry next to the port entrance.
Co-Operative Bank of the Dodecanese Has a branch in Fry.
Kasos Maritime & Travel Agency (☎ 2245 041 495; kassos@kassos-island.gr; Plateia Iroön Kasou) Emmanuel Manousos here is helpful. Will also exchange money.
Kasosnet (☎ 2245 041 705; kasos@kasosnet.gr; €4.50 per hr; ☻ 10am-10pm) Near Bouka. Has Internet access.
Police (☎ 2245 041 222) Just beyond the post office.
Port police (☎ 2245 041 288) Behind the Church of Agios Spyridon.
Post office Near the Commercial Bank ATM.

Sleeping

There is very little accommodation in Kasos, but with the exception of the days on either side of 7 June – Holocaust Memorial Day – a room can normally be found quite easily. It is recommended you book ahead in the high season.

Flisvos Rooms (☎ 2245 041 284; Hohlakoulia; d €32) These tidy, seafront rooms are on the left 300m along the road to Emborios. They are fairly plain but there is a communal kitchen for guests' use.

DODECANESE

Anagennisis Hotel (☎ 2245 041 495; kassos@
kassos-island.gr; Plateia Iroön Kasou; s/d €32/42) The
only hotel as such on the island is this place
right on the main square. The late 1970s
decor looks somewhat passé, but rooms
are clean and presentable enough.

Blue Sky (☎ 2245 041 047; studios €60) For a little extra outlay you can be self-contained
in these comfortable studios some 400m
inland. All rooms have kitchenettes and
fridge.

Borianoula (☎ 2245 041 495; kassos@kassos-island
.gr; Emborios; studios €60) A little way out of Fry in
Emborios are these three reasonable-sized
apartments. See Kasos Maritime & Travel
Agency (p281) for the keys.

Eating & Drinking

There are several un-touristy restaurants
and snack bars in Fry.

O Mylos (☎ 2245 041 825; Plateia Iroön Kasou;
mains €3.50-4.50) The most reliable eatery that
is also open year-round overlooks the west
side of the port and is a popular gathering
spot for locals. The food is wholesome if
generally unimaginative with fish, meat
and casserole dishes usually the staple
fare.

Restaurant Mihail Karagiannis (☎ 2245 041
390; mains €4-5) Somewhat downmarket, but
also open year-round, this dependable
eating place opposite Kasos Maritime and
Travel Agency is rough and ready but fine
for a solid no-frills grill dinner and other
staple fare.

Apangio (☎ 2245 041 880; Bouka; mezedes €3-5)
Enjoying a very atmospheric Bouka harbour location, the Apangio, new in 2003,
is a pleasant ouzeri-cum-café serving select
mezedes, drinks, snacks and coffee.

Zivaeri (☎ 2245 041 747; Bouka; mains €4.50-5.50)
This neat taverna also has neat location,
overlooking the west side of Bouka harbour.
The food is predictably stock Greek, but is
well prepared and of good quality.

Cafe Zantara (☎ 2245 041 880; Bouka) Kasiots
congregate at this trendy café that overlooks
Bouka harbour. Mihalis, the owner, makes
excellent cappuccinos and cocktails.

Entertainment

Perigiali Bar (☎ 2245 041 767; Bouka) This diminutive bar between Bouka and Plateia
Iroön Kasou is Kasos' nightclub. The music
played is predominantly Greek.

AROUND KASOS

The beach at **Emborios**, while a little short
on atmosphere thanks to its rather scruffy
backdrop of abandoned houses, is nonetheless sandy, and the water is clean and
clear. It's the best place for a quick and
refreshing dip. The island's best beach
is the isolated, pebbled cove of **Helatros**,
near Moni Agiou Georgiou, 11km from
Fry along a paved road. The beach has no
facilities and very little shade. You'll also
need your own transport to reach it. **Avlaki**
is another decent beach reached along a
path from the monastery.

The rather mediocre **Ammounda Beach**,
beyond the airport near the blue-domed
church of Agios Konstandinos, is the next
nearest to Fry. There are slightly better
beaches further along this stretch of coast,
one of them the fine-pebble **Andiperatos
Beach** at the end of the road system. Neither has shade.

Agia Marina, 1km southwest of Fry, is
a pretty village with a gleaming white-
and-blue church. On 17 July the Festival
of Agia Marina is celebrated here. From
Agia Marina the road continues to verdant
Arvanitohori, with wonderful fig and pome-
granate trees.

Poli, 3km southeast of Fry, is the former
capital, built on the ancient acropolis.
Panagia, between Fry and Poli, has fewer
than 50 inhabitants. Its once-grand sea
captains' and ship owners' mansions are
now derelict.

Monasteries

The island has two monasteries: **Moni
Agiou Mamma** and **Moni Agiou Georgiou**. The
uninhabited Moni Agiou Mamma, on the
south coast, is a 1½-hour walk from Fry.
Take the Poli road and turn left just before the village (signposted 'Ai Mammas').
The road winds uphill through a dramatic,
eroded landscape of rock-strewn mountains, crumbling terraces and soaring
cliffs. Eventually you will come to a sharp
turn right (signposted again). From here
the track descends to the blue-and-white
monastery.

There are no monks at Moni Agiou
Georgiou, but there is a resident caretaker
for most of the year. Free accommodation
may be available for visitors, but don't
bank on it.

KASTELLORIZO (MEGISTI)
ΚΑΣΤΕΛΛΟΡΙΖΟ (ΜΕΓΙΣΤΗ)

pop 430

It takes a certain amount of decisiveness and a sense of adventure to come to tiny, rocky Kastellorizo (kah-stel-*o*-rih-zo), a mere speck on the map 118km east of Rhodes, its nearest Greek neighbour, yet only 2.5km from the southern coast of Turkey and its nearest neighbouring town, Kaş. Kastellorizo is so-named for the 'red castle' that once dominated the main port, but is also known as 'Megisti' (the largest), for it is the largest of a group of 14 islets that surround this isolated Hellenic outpost. Tourism is low-key, yet there are more Australian-Greek Kastellorizians here in summer than there are locals. There are no stunning beaches, but there are rocky inlets from where you can swim and snorkel.

The island featured in the Oscar-winning Italian film *Mediterraneo* (1991), which was based on a book by an army sergeant.

History

Kastellorizo has suffered a tragic history. Once a thriving trade port serving Dorians, Romans, crusaders, Egyptians, Turks and Venetians, Kastellorizo came under Ottoman control in 1552. The island was allowed to preserve its language, religion and traditions, and its cargo fleet became the largest in the Dodecanese, allowing the islanders to achieve a high degree of culture and education.

Kastellorizo lost all strategic and economic importance after the 1923 Greece–Turkey population exchange. In 1928 it was ceded to the Italians, who severely oppressed the islanders. Many islanders chose to emigrate to Australia, where today a disproportionate number still live.

During WWII, Kastellorizo suffered bombardment, and English commanders ordered the few remaining inhabitants to abandon the island. Most fled to Cyprus, Palestine and Egypt. When they returned they found their houses in ruins and re-emigrated. The island has never fully recovered from its population loss. In recent years, returnees have been slowly restoring buildings and the island now enjoys a tenuous, but pleasant resurgence of resettlement.

Getting There & Away

AIR

In July and August there are daily flights to and from Rhodes (€25), dropping to three weekly at all other times. You can buy tickets from **Dizi Tours & Travel** (☎ 2246 049 241; dizivas@otenet.gr) or **Papoutsis Travel** (☎ 2246 070 830; www.greeklodgings.gr) located in Kastellorizo Village. You must take a taxi (€4) to get from the airport to the main settlement.

CATAMARAN & FERRY

Kastellorizo is the least well-connected island in the whole of the Dodecanese archipelago. Ferry links are subject to seasonal changes and the only direct domestic destination is Rhodes (€15, four hours). Call in at Papoutsis Travel for the latest details and tickets.

At the time of research the *Dodekanisos Express* catamaran was running to/from Kastellorizo every Wednesday (€28, 2¼ hours). Contact **Dodekanisos Naftiliaki** (☎ 2241 070 590; info@12ne.gr) in Rhodes for the current schedules.

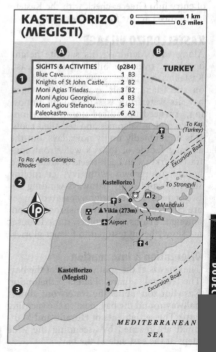

KASTELLORIZO (MEGISTI)

SIGHTS & ACTIVITIES	(p284)
Blue Cave	1 B3
Knights of St John Castle	2 B2
Moni Agias Triados	3 B2
Moni Agiou Georgiou	4 B3
Moni Agiou Stefanou	5 B2
Paleokastro	6 A2

TURKEY

To Kaş (Turkey)

Excursion Boat

To Ro; Agios Georgios; Rhodes

Kastellorizo

To Strongyli

▲Vikla (273m)

Airport

Mandraki

Horafia

Kastellorizo (Megisti)

Excursion Boat

MEDITERRANEAN SEA

EXCURSION BOAT

Excursion boats go to the islets of **Ro**, **Strongyli** and the spectacular **Blue Cave** (Parasta), famous for its brilliant blue water produced by refracted sunlight. Visitors are transferred from a larger caïque to a small motorised dingy in order to enter the very low cave entrance. Claustrophobics be warned. Bring your bathing gear as the boatman usually allows visitors a quick dip in the cave itself.

The trip to the cave costs €8, and the longer trip to Ro, Strongyli and round Kastellorizo costs €15. All leave at around 8.30am daily.

Excursion Boat to Turkey

Islanders go on frequent shopping trips to Kaş in Turkey, and day trips (€15) are also offered to tourists. Look for the signs along the waterfront.

Note that in 2003 one-way travellers could still not legally enter Greece via Kastellorizo, though there was no restriction on exiting Greece and entering Turkey legally at Kaş. By 2004 Kastellorizo should be a legal port of entry into Greece: check with the Kastellorizo travel agents for the latest news.

KASTELLORIZO VILLAGE

Along with Mandraki, its satellite neighbourhood over the hill and to the east, Kastellorizo Village is the only settlement on the island. Built around a U-shaped bay, its waterfront is skirted with imposing, spruced-up, three-storey mansions with wooden balconies and red-tiled roofs. It is undoubtedly pretty nowadays, but the alluring façade of today's waterfront contrasts starkly with backstreets of abandoned houses overgrown with ivy, crumbling stairways and stony pathways winding between them. Newer, brightly painted houses are emerging like gaudy mushrooms from among the ruins, while older, ruined houses are slowly being restored to former glories.

Orientation & Information

The quay is at the southern side of the bay. The central square, Plateia Ethelondon Kastellorizou, abuts the waterfront almost halfway round the bay, next to the yachting jetty. The settlements of Horafia and Mandraki are reached by ascending the wide steps at the east side of the bay.

There are a couple of cardphones and all Greek mobile service providers can be picked up on the island as well as several Turkish mobile networks.

Athina Restaurant Internet access is provided for free at this waterfront eatery.

National Bank of Greece On the eastern waterfront has an ATM.

Police station (☎ 2246 049 333) On the bay's western side.

Port police (☎ 2246 049 333) At the eastern tip of the bay.

Post office On the bay's western side.

Sights

The **Knights of St John Castle** stands above the quay. A rickety metal staircase leads to the top from where there are splendid views of Turkey. Signs advise you not to climb up, but it's OK – just. Lower down the castle grounds, a well-displayed collection is held at the **museum** (☎ 2246 049 283; admission free; ⏱ 7am-2.30pm Tue-Sun). Beyond the museum, steps lead down to a coastal pathway, from where more steps go up the cliff to a 3rd- to 4th-century BC **Lycian tomb** with a Doric façade. There are several along the Anatolian coast in Turkey, but this is the only known one in Greece.

Moni Agiou Georgiou is the largest of the monasteries that dot the island. Within its church is the subterranean Chapel of Agios Haralambos, reached by steep stone steps. Greek children were given religious instruction here during Turkish times. The church is kept locked; ask around the waterfront for the whereabouts of the caretaker. To reach the monastery, ascend the conspicuous zigzagging white stone steps behind the village and at the top follow the prominent path.

Moni Agiou Stefanou, on the north coast, is the setting for one of the island's most important celebrations, Agios Stefanos Day on 1 August. The path to the little white monastery begins behind the post office. From the monastery, a path leads to a bay where you can swim.

Paleokastro was the island's ancient capital. Within the city's Hellenistic walls are an ancient tower, a water cistern and three churches. Concrete steps, just beyond a soldier's sentry box on the airport road, mask the beginning of the pretty steep path to Paleokastro.

Sleeping

Accommodation runs the gamut from simple and small to traditional and spacious. The trouble is there's not too much of it. Book ahead in peak times to be sure of a bed.

I Anaviosi (☎ 2246 049 302; s/d €18/20) Right above the Sydney Restaurant are these fairly basic small rooms, which constitute Kastellorizo's budget-entry sleeping choice.

Villa Kaserma (☎ 2246 049 370; fax 2246 049 365; d/tr €28/34; ☒) Set back high on the western side of the harbour, this red-and-white coloured pension has oldish, fridge-equipped rooms with perhaps the best views of Kastellorizo harbour.

Pension Palameria (☎ 2246 049 282; fax 2246 049 071; d/tr €30/45) This converted building on the small square at the northwest corner of the waterfront has spotless rooms with kitchen and dining area. Inquire about them at To Mikro Parisi (see Eating below).

Panorama Studios (☎ /fax 2246 049 098; Mandraki; d €45) Somewhat removed from the main drag in the harbour are these roomy, fridge-equipped studios. Some have balconies and views across to Kaş.

Pension Mediterraneo (☎ 2246 049 007; s/d €59) At the far western tip of the harbour are these well-appointed rooms housed in the same building as the one used in *Mediterraneo* where Vasilissa traded her comely wares.

Kastellorizo Hotel Appartments (☎ 2246 049 044; www.kastellorizohotel.gr; s/d €74/100; ☒ ☒ ☒) The best accommodation is right here. All of these airy rooms have satellite TV, phone and fridge. The pint-sized pool is mainly for sitting in, but you can jump into the decidedly more capacious harbour from directly in front of the hotel.

Eating

Eating in Kastellorizo is generally a pleasant experience as restaurateurs have to please demanding Greek tastes before catering to travellers' sometimes more accommodating expectations. Most places to eat are strung out along the waterfront.

To Mikro Parisi (☎ 2246 049 282; mains €4.50-5) To Mikro Parisi has been going strong since 1974 and still serves generous helpings of grilled fish and meat. Fish soup is the house speciality, but the rich *stifado* is also good.

Sydney Restaurant (☎ 2246 049 302; mayirefta €3.50-4) Dishing up hearty home-cooked dishes and grilled fish, the Sydney, a little

further around from To Mikro Parisi, is a popular low-key eatery with a couple of tables teetering precariously on the harbour's edge. Handy for feeding the fish on leftovers.

Tis Ypomonis (☎ 2246 049 224; mains €4-6; ☽ dinner only) This corner *psistaria* (restaurant serving grilled food) does a nightly roaring trade in souvlaki, sausage and steaks, all cooked on a little streetside charcoal barbecue grill. Dine inside or on the busy street corner.

Akrothalassi (☎ 2246 049 052; mains €3-5) It's a good sign when Greeks congregate to feed at a particular establishment. Dine under the vines at this relaxed taverna on the southwest side of the harbour, where succulent grills and fish are served up, as well as the odd daily *mayirefta* such as green beans in *skordalia* (garlic and potato dip).

Restaurant Platania (☎ 2246 049 206; Mandraki; mains €3-5) Check out this out-of-the-way, unpretentious eatery that appeared in *Mediterraneo*. Haul yourself uphill to Mandraki for good breakfasts, or its *revithokeftedes* (chickpea rissoles).

Entertainment

There are several easy-going cafeterias on the waterfront. Kaz Bar is a good place to kick off. Next door, Meltemi has tempting waterside chairs and cold beers while the gaudily painted Mythos Bar is another popular watering hole on the east side of the harbour.

SYMI ΣΥΜΗ

pop 2606

Symi is a rocky, dry island 24km north of Rhodes. It lies within the geographical embrace of Turkey, 10km from the Turkish peninsula of Datça. The island has a scenic rocky interior, with pine and cypress woods. It has a deeply indented coast with precipitous cliffs and numerous small bays with pebbled beaches, and is enormously popular with day-trippers from Rhodes. Symi has good accommodation and eating choices and enjoys excellent transport links to the outside world. However, the island suffers from a severe water shortage and the day-tripper crowds can get a bit overwhelming at times. The main town is Gialos.

History

Symi has a long tradition of both sponge diving and shipbuilding. During Ottoman times it was granted the right to fish for sponges in Turkish waters. In return, Symi supplied the sultan with 1st-class boat builders and top-quality sponges scooped straight off the ocean floor.

These factors, and a lucrative shipbuilding industry, brought prosperity to the island. Gracious mansions were built and culture and education flourished. By the beginning of the 20th century the population was 22,500 and the island was launching some 500 ships a year. But the Italian occupation, the introduction of the steamship and Kalymnos' rise as the Aegean's principal sponge producer put an end to Symi's prosperity.

The treaty surrendering the Dodecanese islands to the Allies was signed in Symi's Hotel (now Pension) Catherinettes on 8 May 1945.

Getting There & Away
EXCURSION BOAT

There are daily excursion boats running between Symi and Rhodes. The Symi-based *Symi I* and *Symi II* (☎ 2246 071 444; anes1@otenet.gr) are the cheapest (€12 return) and tickets can be bought on board.

Symi Tours (☎ 2246 071 307; fax 2246 072 292) has excursion trips to Datça in Turkey (€31, including Turkish port taxes).

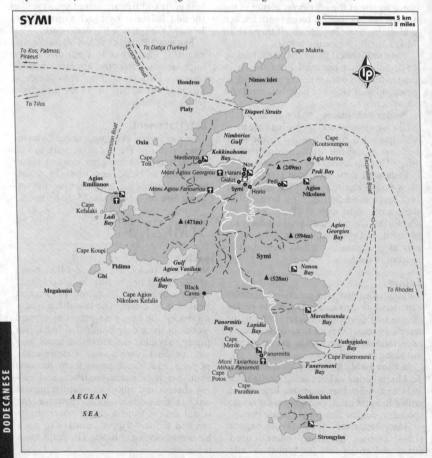

SYMI

0 — 5 km
0 — 3 miles

To Kos; Patmos; Piraeus
To Datça (Turkey)
Cape Makria
Hondros
Nimos islet
To Tilos
Platy
Diapori Straits
Oxia
Nimborios Gulf
Cape Koutsoumpos
Cape Toli
Nimborios
Kokkinohoma Bay
Nos
Agia Marina
Moni Agiou Georgiou
Harani
Pedi Bay
Agios Emilianos
Moni Agiou Fanouriou
Gialos
Symi
Horio
Pedi
Agios Nikolaos
Cape Kefalaki
Ladi Bay
(249m)
(471m)
Agios Georgios Bay
Cape Koupi
(594m)
Pidima
Gulf Agiou Vasiliou
Symi
Nanou Bay
Ghi
Kefalos Bay
(528m)
Megalonisi
Black Caves
To Rhodes
Cape Agios Nikolaos Kefalis
Panormitis Bay
Lopidia Bay
Marathounda Bay
Cape Merde
Panormitis
Vathygialos Bay
Cape Faneromeni
Moni Taxiarhou Mihail Panormiti
Faneromeni Bay
Cape Potos
Cape Parathiras
Sesklion islet
AEGEAN SEA
Strongylos

FERRY, CATAMARAN & HYDROFOIL

Symi has up to four ferries a week heading north to other Dodecanese islands and Piraeus. Additional links are provided by the F/B *Nisos Kalymnos*.

The *Dodekanisos Express* catamaran services the island at least twice a week with a connection to Rhodes (€12, 50 minutes) and islands further north.

Symi is connected by hydrofoil to Kos (€15.40, one hour), Kalymnos (€21.30, 1½ hours) and Rhodes (€9.80, 50 minutes). The Symi-owned *Aigli* hydrofoil also connects Symi with Rhodes.

Getting Around

BUS & TAXI

The bus stop and taxi rank are on the south side of the harbour in Gialos. The green minibus makes frequent runs between Gialos and Pedi Beach (via Horio). The flat fare is €0.73. Taxis depart from a stop 100m west of the bus stop.

EXCURSION BOAT

Several excursion boats do trips to Moni Taxiarhou Mihail Panormiti and Sesklion Islet where there's a shady beach. Check the boards for the best-value tickets.

TAXI BOAT

The small boats *Katerina I* and *Katerina II* do trips (€7.50 to €12) to many of the island's beaches.

GIALOS ΓΙΑΛΟΣ

Gialos, Symi's port town, is a Greek treasure. Neoclassical mansions in a harmonious medley of colours are heaped up the hills flanking its harbour. Behind their strikingly beautiful facades, however, many of the buildings are derelict. The town is divided into two parts: Gialos, the harbour, and Horio, above, crowned by the kastro.

Gialos' beach is the crowded, minuscule **Nos Beach**. Turn left at the Italian-era clock tower at the northeastern end of the harbour.

Orientation & Information

Arriving ferries, hydrofoils and the catamaran dock just to the left of the quay's clock tower. Excursion boats dock a little further along. The centre of activity in Gialos is the promenade at the centre of the harbour.

Kali Strata, a broad stairway, leads from here to hill-top Horio.

There is no official tourist office in Symi Town. The *Symi Visitor* is a free English- and Greek-language newspaper sold by portside newspaper vendors.

ATMs At both banks.

Police (☎ 2246 071 111) By the ferry quay.

Port police (☎ 2246 071 205) By the ferry quay.

Post office By the ferry quay.

Roloï bar (☎ 2246 071 595; €3.50 per hr; ☺ 9am-3am) Access the Internet here, a block back from the waterfront.

www.symivisitor.com A useful source of island information and gossip.

Sights

Horio consists of narrow, labyrinthine streets crossed by crumbling archways. As you approach the **Knights of St John Kastro** dominating Horio, the once-grand 19th-century neoclassical mansions give way to the modest stone dwellings of the 18th century. The castle incorporates blocks from the ancient acropolis, and the **Church of Megali Panagia** is within its walls.

On the way to the kastro, archaeological and folklore exhibits are held in the **Museum of Symi** (adult €1.50; ☺ 10am-2pm Tue-Sun). Signposting to the museum is almost impossible to follow, so head upwards and rely on pot luck to find it.

Activities

Symi Tours (☎ 2246 071 307; fax 2246 072 292) has multilingual guides who lead **guided walks** around the island. The publication *Walking on Symi* by Francis Noble (€7) is on sale at Kalodoukas Holidays at the beginning of Kali Strata while the *Symi Map & Walking Book* can be ordered from the author Lance Chilton at marengowalks@aol.com.

Foodies may care to participate in organised **Greek cooking** classes. See the 'Cooking with Stavros' website at www.laskarina.co.uk.

Sleeping

Most accommodation is in studios or a few private domatia. There are a couple of good hotels as well.

Hotel Kokona (☎ 2246 071 549; fax 2246 072 620; s/d €35/41) On the street to the left of the large church, this small and basic hotel has comfortable rooms.

Pension Catherinettes (☎ /fax 2246 072698; marina -epe@rho.forthnet.gr; d €30-48) The historic Catherinettes (see History, p286) is on the north side of the harbour. The pink-stuccoed pension has wrought–iron balconies and some of the rooms have magnificent painted high ceilings.

Hotel Fiona (☎ 2246 072 755; www.symivisitor.com; s/d €43/53) This hotel in Horio has lovely rooms with wood-panelled ceilings and great views and is a shade cooler than accommodation in Gialos as it catches welcome breezes. To reach it, turn left at the top of the stairs and walk for 50m.

Hotel Nireus (☎ 2246 072 400; nireus@rho.forth net.gr; s/d €47/80; 🖳) One of the two regular hotels in Gialos, the prominently sited Nireus, by the clock tower, has elegant, traditional rooms and suites with fridge, TV and phone.

Opera House Hotel (☎ 2246 072 034; operasym@ otenet.gr; studios €85-100; 🖳) Named after the Sydney (Australia) Opera House, these spacious studios in a peaceful garden are well signposted 150m back from the harbour and are fully self-contained.

Eating

There's a wide variety of places to eat in Gialos and Horio. Steer clear of the obvious picture menu tourist traps and try the following.

GIALOS

Taverna Neraïda (☎ 2246 071 841; mains €4-5) You can't go wrong with the unpretentious and solid Greek dishes at this excellent, low-priced option, a block back from the waterfront. Fish souvlaki features on the menu, as does a range of vegetarian dishes. Walk into the kitchen and select from the dishes on display.

Estiatorio Mythos (☎ 2246 071 488; mezedes €3.60-10) This is a neat little eatery serving imaginative food. At lunch time Mythos serves mainly pasta dishes, while mezedes feature in the evening. For palate pleasing consider chicken with gorgonzola cheese, or mussels in white-wine sauce with garlic and saffron. Mythos is on the far south side of the harbour.

Manos (☎ 2246 072 429; fish €13-24) While there is a wide choice of fish taverna in Gialos, Manos just pips most at them to the post with its unpretentious setting and

honest fresh, home-cooked fish. This is a good place to try Symi's own minuscule 'Symi shrimps'.

Ellinikon (☎ 2246 072 455; set menu €9) Serving up generic Mediterranean cuisine, the Ellinikon on the central waterfront makes dining easy with a choice of imaginative set menus. Some dishes use ingredients such as coriander, cardamom and fennel – not often found in standard Greek cooking. Excellent wine cellar.

HORIO

Giorgos (☎ 2246 071 984; mains €6-9) There is an always-changing and enticing *mayirefta* menu with such mouth-watering dishes as chicken stuffed with rice, herbs and pine nuts, lamb in vine leaves, or stuffed onions.

Restaurant Syllogos (☎ 2246 072 148; mains €5-7) Similar in style, though not quite as popular, the Syllogos still offers imaginative fare such as chicken with prunes and pork with leek, fish with rosemary and tomato and vegetarian options such as artichokes in egg and lemon sauce, or *spanakopita* (spinach pie).

Entertainment

There are several lively bars in the streets behind the south side of the harbour.

Vapori Bar (☎ 2246 072 082) Drop by here during the day to read the free papers and in the evenings for schmoozing, drinks and cruising.

Roloï Bar (☎ 2246 071 595) A busy, happening little watering hole one block inland from the south side of the port, open most of the day and a large part of the night.

AROUND SYMI

Pedi is a little fishing village and busy mini-holiday resort in a fertile valley 2km downhill from Horio. It has some sandy stretches on its narrow beach. There are domatia, hotels and tavernas. Walking tracks down both sides of the bay lead to **Agia Marina** beach on the north side and **Agios Nikolaos** beach on the south side. Both are sandy, gently shelving beaches and thus suitable for children.

Nos Beach is the closest beach to Gialos. It's a 500m walk north of the campanile. There is a taverna, bar and sun beds (€3 per person).

Nimborios is a long, pebbled beach 2km west of Gialos. It has some natural shade as well as sun beds and umbrellas. Water quality can be a shade slimy. You can walk there from Gialos along a scenic path. Take the road by the east side of the central square and continue straight ahead; the way is fairly obvious. Just bear left after the church and follow the stone trail.

Taxi boats are the only convenient way to get to **Agios Georgios Bay** and the more developed **Nanou Beach**, which has sun beds, umbrellas and a taverna.

The remoter **Marathounda** beach can be reached by road, while **Agios Emilianos** beach on the far west side of Symi is best reached by excursion boat.

Moni Taxiarhou Mihail Panormiti
Μονή Ταξιάρχου Μιχαήλ Πανορμίτη
An often winding but now good sealed road leads you across the island through scented pine forests, before dipping in spectacular zigzag fashion to the expansive, but protected Panormitis Bay. This is the site of Symi's principal attraction – the large Moni Taxiarhou Mihail Panormiti (Monastery of Archangel Michael of Panormitis). The large monastery complex with its ornate Italianate campanile occupies most of the foreshore of the bay and is open to visitors all day.

A monastery was first built here in the 5th or 6th century, but the present building dates from the 18th century. The *katholikon* (principal church of a monastic complex) contains an intricately carved wooden iconostasis, frescoes, and an icon of St Michael that supposedly appeared miraculously where the monastery now stands. St Michael is the patron saint of Symi, and protector of sailors.

The monastery is also a magnet for hoards of day-trippers who commonly arrive at around 10.30am on excursion boats so it is a good idea to visit early or after they have left.

The monastery complex comprises a **Byzantine museum** and **folkloric museum** (adults €1.50 for both), a bakery with excellent bread and apple pies, and a basic restaurant-cafeteria to the north side that usually entices customers with loudspeaker appeals to visit for coffee and beer.

Accommodation is also available at the **guest house** (☎ 2246 072 414; r €15-35) where reservations in July and August are mandatory.

TILOS ΤΗΛΟΣ

pop 533
Tilos is one of the few islands left in the Dodecanese that retains something of its traditional character and where tourism has not widely impacted on the slow and carefree lifestyle of the islanders. Most foreign visitors tend to be gentrified walkers from the UK's villa holiday specialist Laskarina, Italians in search of tranquillity and a mixed bag of lost yachties.

Tilos lies 65km west of Rhodes, has good, uncrowded beaches, two abandoned, evocative villages, and a well-kept monastery at the end of a spectacularly scenic road. It's a terrific island for walkers, with vistas of high cliffs, rocky inlets and sea, valleys of cypress, walnut and almond trees, and bucolic meadows. The island's rich agricultural potential is little utilised nowadays, since, rather than work the land for a pittance, young Tiliots have long preferred to leave for the mainland or emigrate to Australia or the USA.

History
Mastodon bones – midget elephants that became extinct around 4600 BC – were found in a cave on the island in 1974. The cave, **Harkadio** (closed), is signposted from the Livadia–Megalo Horio road and brilliantly illuminated at night. Erinna, one of the least known of ancient Greece's female poets, lived on Tilos in the 4th century BC.

Elephants and poetry aside, Tilos' history shares the same catalogue of invasions and occupations as the rest of the archipelago.

Getting There & Away
CATAMARAN
The Tilos-owned **Sea Star** (☎ 2246 077 048) connects Tilos daily with Nisyros and Rhodes. *Sea Star* departs Tilos for Nisyros daily in the mid-morning (€10, 35 minutes) and for Rhodes in the late afternoon (€27.55, 1½ hours).

EXCURSION BOAT
There are a number of excursions advertise around Livadia. One is an all-inclusive bea barbecue excursion for €25 (food and wir

DODEC

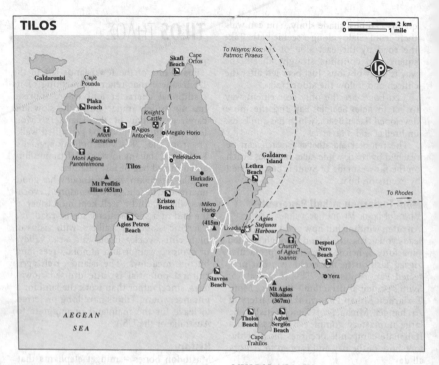

TILOS

0 — 2 km
0 — 1 mile

To Nisyros; Kos; Patmos; Piraeus

Galdaronisi
Cape Pounda
Plaka Beach
Skafi Beach
Cape Ortos
Knight's Castle
Moni Kamariani
Agios Antonios
Megalo Horio
Moni Agiou Panteleimona
Tilos
Pelekitados
Galdaros Island
Lethra Beach
Mt Profitis Illias (651m)
Harkadio Cave
Eristos Beach
Mikro Horio (415m)
Agios Petros Beach
Livadia
Agios Stefanos Harbour
Church of Agios Ioannis
Despoti Nero Beach
Yera
Stavros Beach
Mt Agios Nikolaos (367m)
To Rhodes

AEGEAN SEA

Tholos Beach
Agios Sergios Beach
Cape Trahilos

is included) and another is a multi beach island tour for the same price. Look for posters around Livadia for details.

FERRY
Tilos is served by G&A Ferries, DANE Sealines and the Kalymnos-based F/B *Nisos Kalymnos*, with up to almost daily services in high season. Sample fares are Rhodes (€10, 3½ hours), Kos (€7.60, three hours) and Piraeus (€26, 15 hours). Tickets are sold at **Stefanakis Travel** (☎ 2246 044 310; stefanakis@rho.forthnet.gr) in Livadia.

Getting Around
Tilos' public transport consists of a bus that ploughs up and down the island's main road on a fairly regular basis. The current timetable is posted at the bus stop in Livadia. The fare is €1.67 to Megalo Horio or Eristos. On Sunday there is a special excursion bus to Moni Agiou Panteleimona (€4 return), which leaves Livadia at 11am and gives you one hour at the monastery. Tilos currently has only one **taxi** (☎ 6944 981 727), owned by Nikos Logothetis.

LIVADIA ΛΙΒΑΔΕΙΑ
Livadia is the main town and port, though not the capital: that honour belongs to Megalo Horio, situated 8km north of the port. Livadia is a sleepy, pleasant enough place, though it can be a bit more hot and humid than other parts of the island. In the town you will find most services and shops as well as the bulk of the island's accommodation.

Orientation & Information
All arrivals are at Livadia. The small port is 300m southeast of the town centre. Tilos has no official tourist bureau and no banks.

Kosmos (☎ 2246 044 074; www.tilos-kosmos.com; €6 per hr; 9am-1.30pm & 7.30-11.30pm) Has Internet access. Its website is a useful source of information on Tilos and includes the local ferry timetables. An accurate local map of Tilos produced by Barry 'Paris' Ward is available here for €3.

Port police (☎ 2246 044 322) In the white Italianate building at the quay.
Regular police (☎ 2246 044 222).
Post office On the central square.

Stefanakis Travel (☎ 2246 044 310; stefanakis@rho
.forthnet.gr) Between the port and the village; has helpful
staff.
Tilos Travel (☎ 2246 044 294; www.tilostravel.co.uk)
At the port; has helpful staff. Credit card withdrawals and
money exchange can be made here.

Walks
There are a number of popular walks that
can easily be made from Livadia. The most
popular is to **Lethra Beach**, an undeveloped
pebble and sand cove with limited shade,
3km north of Livadia. The trail starts at the
far north side of the port and is fairly easy.
Return via the less easy, but very picturesque, oleander-strewn and goat-inhabited
Potami Gorge, which will bring you to the
main island highway.

Another is a return hike to **Stavros Beach**,
an hour's steady walk along a well-marked
trail that starts from near the Tilos Mare
Hotel in Livadia. This is another easy and
accessible walk, and the lure of a dip at the
fine-pebble beach is enough to attract a
steady line of walkers.

A third walk is a longer return track to
the small abandoned settlement of **Yera** and
its accompanying beach access at **Despoti
Nero**. From Livadia follow the road past
Agios Stefanos, on the east side of the bay,
and keep walking. Allow half a day for this
hike.

Sleeping
Accommodation on the island is generally of a high standard, though much of it
gets block-booked by low-key foreign tour
operators. An information kiosk at the harbour opens whenever a ferry arrives and has
photos and prices of some of the island's
accommodation options.

Paraskevi Rooms (☎ 2246 044 280; d €30) There
are a couple of basic places on the waterfront
in Livadia. This one has clean, simply furnished rooms with well-equipped kitchens.

Apollo Studios (☎ 2246 044 379; www.apollostudios
.com; d €57) Here you'll find seven double
rooms with kitchenette and fan. They are
smallish but spotless, with sparkling tiled
floors and are in a very central location.

Olympus Studios (☎ 2246 044 365; d €60) Close
by the Apollo Studios but with a little
more space, these fully equipped studios
are a better, though slightly more expensive, option.

Hotel Eleni (☎ 2246 044 062; elenihtl@otenet.gr; s/d
€50/60 incl breakfast) This airy hotel, 400m along
the beach road, has beautiful, tastefully
furnished double rooms with refrigerator
and telephone.

Marina Beach Rooms (☎ 2246 044 066; marina
room@otenet.gr; d €55) These immaculate and
compact rooms with sea-view balconies
are on the bay's eastern side, 1km from
the quay.

Irini Hotel (☎ 2246 044 193; www.tilosholidays.gr;
s/d €45/60 incl breakfast) Catering mainly to the
packaged travellers, the neat Irini also welcomes independents. The hotel is set back a
little from the waterfront in a citrus garden
and the rooms are very well appointed.

Eating
Joanna's Cafe Bar (☎ 2246 044 145; pizzas €6.50-9.50)
This café-bar is a popular breakfast and
brunch hang-out, serving excellent coffee
(ask for the Tilos coffee – a caffeine hit
with a zing), yogurt and muesli, pizza and
delicious home-made cakes.

Sofia's Taverna (☎ 2246 044 340; mayirefta €3-5)
This taverna, 100m along the beach road,
serves delicious, home-cooked food where
you can guarantee the freshness of the local
product.

Restaurant Irina (☎ 2246 044 206; mayirefta €4-5)
With its relaxing waterside location, Irina
does great home-made food, including
excellent mousakas and *papoutsaki* (aubergine slippers) and a rich, beefy *stifado*.

Taverna Blue Sky (☎ 2246 044 259; mezedes
€1.80-3.20) Blue Sky, on the harbour, is good
for grilled fish and vegetarian mezedes. It
is now run by Italians so has a slight Italian spin on the food, with pasta featuring
prominently on the menu.

Calypso (☎ 2246 044 382; mains €3.50-7) For a
slightly unusual twist, the daily changing
menu at Calypso showcases dishes such as
shark with basmati rice or organic salads,
combining elements from Greek, French
and Vietnamese cuisines.

Entertainment
There are a few summer bars on Livadia's
waterfront, such as Ino and Bozi, but seri-
ous ravers head for the abandoned village of
Mikro Horio, 3km from Livadia, where **Mikro
Horio Music Bar** (☎ 2246 044 081; ◷ midnight-5am Jul
& Aug) belts out music most of the night. A
minibus ferries ravers to and from the port.

MEGALO HORIO ΜΕΓΑΛΟ ΧΩΡΙΟ

Megalo Horio, the island's capital, is a serene whitewashed village. Its alleyways are fun to explore, and the village makes a great alternative base if you are looking for a taste of rural life in Tilos. There are domatia, a restaurant and at least one atmospheric bar to keep visitors bedded, fed and suitably watered. From here you can visit the **Knight's Castle**, a taxing 40-minute upwards walk along a track starting at the north end of the village. Along the way you will pass the **ancient settlement** of Tilos precariously built in its time on rocky ledges overlooking Megalo Horio.

The little **museum** on the main street houses finds from Harkadio Cave. It's locked, but if you ask at the town hall on the 1st floor someone will show you around.

Sleeping gives you two choices. **Elefantakia Studios** (☎ 2246 044 242; d €30) on the main street is fairly uncomplicated. All rooms have little kitchenettes and fridges. Next door and up a notch are the secluded studios of **Miliou Rooms & Apartments** (☎ 2246 044 204; d €35), sequestered in a tree-shaded garden including a couple of banana palms.

To Kastro (☎ 2246 044 232; mains €4.56) on the village's south side overlooking the Eristos plain below is the best place to eat. The fare features charcoal-grilled meats that feature organic goat and locally raised pork as well as fresh fish and a range of daily *mayirefta*.

After-dinner happenings take place at **Anemona** (☎ 2246 044 090), well illuminated by night and perched at the northeastern side of the village near the start of the castle track. Greek music predominates.

AROUND MEGALO HORIO

Just before Megalo Horio, a turn-off to the left leads after 2.5km to the pleasant, tamarisk-shaded **Eristos Beach**, a mixture of gritty sand and shingle. A signposted turn-off to the right from the junction leads to the quiet settlement of **Agios Antonios**, where the small Elpida Restaurant is the only reliable source of food and drink. The undeveloped **Plaka Beach**, 3km further west, is backed by shady trees and is clean and uncluttered.

The 18th-century **Moni Agiou Panteleimona** is 5km beyond here along a scenic road. It is uninhabited but well maintained, with fine 18th-century frescoes. The island's minibus driver takes groups of visitors here on Sunday. A well-attended and lively three-day **festival** takes place at the monastery, beginning on 25 July.

You can camp unofficially on Eristos Beach, but facilities are pretty basic. The municipality's plans to formalise the site seen to have fallen on stony ground for the moment.

The best place to stay is at the expansive grounds and studios of **Eristos Beach Hotel** (☎ /fax 2246 044 024; d €32) abutting the northern end of the beach. Here you'll find excellent, airy studios for up to four people with fridge and kitchenette. A new complex complete with restaurant should be ready by 2004. Meanwhile, the only real eating option is **Tropicana Taverna** (☎ 2246 044 020; mains €2.60-3.30) on the Eristos road, where the owner serves up locally produced meat and vegetables and scrumptious *revithokeftedes* (chickpea rissoles).

NISYROS ΝΙΣΥΡΟΣ

pop 948

Nisyros (*nee-sih-ros*) is one of those quirky Greek islands that is not on the usual island-hopping circuit. It has no stunning sandy beaches and supports a rather low-key tourist infrastructure that favours individuals, yachties and lost souls. Nisyros is an almost round island and has something that no other Greek island has – its own volcano. The landscape is at the same time rocky, lush and green, yet it has no natural water.

The lunar landscape of the interior is offset by craggy peaks and rolling hillsides leading down to brown pebbly beaches that see relatively few visitors. The island's settlements are the main port of Mandraki, the fishing village of Pali and the crater-top villages of Emborios and Nikea.

Getting There & Away

Nisyros is linked by almost daily ferries to Rhodes (€6, three to five hours), Kos (€6, 1¾ hours) and Patmos (€12, four hours). The caïque *Chrysoula* links Mandraki with Kardamena on Kos (€6, two hours) daily.

The island is serviced by a catamaran service to Tilos and Rhodes about three times a week. In summer there are daily excursion boats from Kardamena, Kefalos and Kos Town on Kos (€13 to €18).

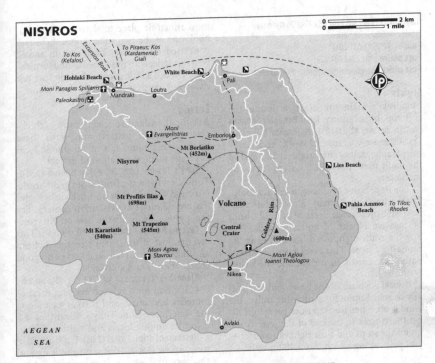

NISYROS

0 — 2 km
0 — 1 mile

To Kos (Kefalos)
Excursion Boat
To Piraeus; Kos (Kardamena); Giali
Hohlaki Beach
White Beach
Pali
Moni Panagias Spilianis
Loutra
Mandraki
Paleokastro
Moni Evangelistrias
Emborios
Mt Boriatiko (452m)
Nisyros
Lies Beach
Mt Profitis Ilias (698m)
Volcano
Caldera Rim
Pahia Ammos Beach
To Tilos; Rhodes
Mt Karariatis (540m)
Mt Trapezina (545m)
Central Crater
(600m)
Moni Agiou Stavrou
Moni Agiou Ioanni Theologou
Nikea
Avlaki
AEGEAN SEA

Getting Around

BUS
There are two companies that run up to 10 excursion buses every day to the volcano (€7.33 return) with around 40 minutes waiting time between 9.30am and 3pm. These are in addition to the three daily buses that travel to Nikea (€1.67) via Pali. You'll find the bus stop is located at the quay.

EXCURSION BOAT
From June to September there are excursion boats (€8 return) to the pumice-stone islet of Giali where there is a good sandy beach.

MOTORCYCLE
There are three motorcycle-rental outlets on Mandraki's main street.

TAXI
There are two taxis on Nisyros: **Babis Taxi** (☎ 6945 639 723) and **Irene's Taxi** (☎ 6973 371 281). Sample fares include the volcano €20 return, Nikea €11 and Pali €5.

MANDRAKI ΜΑΝΔΡΑΚΙ

Mandraki is the sleepy port and capital of Nisyros. It has just the right amount of somnolence to make it great for a spot of aimless wandering. Its two-storey houses have brightly painted wooden balconies. Some are whitewashed but many are painted in bright colours, predominantly ochre and turquoise. The web of streets huddled below the monastery and the central square are especially captivating, and you can easily get lost for a while in their narrow confines.

Orientation & Information

The port is 500m northeast of the centre of Mandraki. Take the road right from the port and you will hit the centre. A shoreline road and an inner street both lead eventually to the tree-shaded Plateia Ilikiomeni, Mandraki's focal point.

Co-operative Bank of the Dodecanese Offers currency exchange and credit card withdrawals, but has no ATM. Travel agents will usually exchange money for a commission.

Enetikon Travel (☎ 2242 031 180) On the main street. Provides tourist information.

Nisyrian Travel (☎ 2242 031 204) On the quay. Provides tourist information.
Police (☎ 2242 031 201)
Port police (☎ 2242 031 222)
Post office Shares premises opposite the quay.

Sights

Mandraki's main tourist attraction is the cliff top 14th-century **Moni Panagias Spilianis** (Virgin of the Cave; ☎ 2242 031 125; admission by donation; ⏰ 10.30am-3pm), crammed with ecclesiastical paraphernalia. Turn right at the end of the main street to reach the steps up to the monastery.

The impressive Mycenaean-era acropolis, **Paleokastro** (Old Kastro), above Mandraki, has well-preserved Cyclopean walls built of massive blocks of volcanic rock. Follow the route signposted 'kastro', near the monastery steps. This eventually becomes a path. At the road, turn right and the kastro is on the left.

Hohlaki is a black-stone beach and can usually be relied upon for swimming unless the wind is up, when the water can get rough. To get there, walk to the end of the waterfront, go up the steps and turn right onto a stone-laid path, along which it is a 400m walk.

Sleeping

Mandraki has a fair amount of accommodation, though owners do not usually meet incoming ferries.

Hotel Romantzo (☎ /fax 2242 031 340; s/d €25/35) Turn left from the quay to find this hotel with its clean, well-kept rooms. The rooms are above a snack bar and there is a large communal terrace with a refrigerator, tables and chairs.

Three Brothers Hotel (☎ 2242 031 344; fax 2242 031 640; s/d €23/33) Opposite Romantzo, this pleasant option overlooks the sea.

Iliovasilema Rooms (☎ 2242 031 159; d €25) Occupying one of the few central Mandraki spots, these fairly basic but well-sited rooms do cop a fair bit of noise from the waterfront tourist traffic.

Haritos Hotel (☎ 2242 031 322; hharitos@otenet.gr; d/tr €40/50; ⌘ ▨) Overall, this is one of the better all-round good choices. The rooms are well appointed and have fridge, TV and telephone. Take the Pali road from the port and you'll find them after 200m on the right.

Ta Liotridia (☎ 2242 031 580; liotridia@yahoo.com; suites €150; ▨) For the absolute classiest and most romantic place to sleep in Mandraki, book one of the two suites above these two converted oil presses. Done out in classic Nisyriot style, with raised beds, solid furnishings, TV and a little cooker, the suites are not cheap but worth it for the sea views alone.

Eating

Ask for the island speciality *pitties* (chick-pea and onion patties) and wash them down with *soumada*, a nonalcoholic local beverage made from almond extract.

Tony's Tavern (☎ 2242 031 460; mains €3.50-5) Tony's, on the waterfront, does great breakfasts and superb meat and fish dishes, and has a wide range of vegetarian choices. Try the gyros – probably the best on Nisyros.

Taverna Nisyros (☎ 2242 031 460; grills €4-5) This taverna, just off the main street, is a cheap and cheerful little place and serves up good charcoal grills and souvlakia.

Kleanthes Taverna (☎ 2242 031 484; mezedes €3-4.50) Good for a relaxed evening meal of mezedes and ouzo, and further east along the waterfront from Tony's, Kleanthes is a favourite among locals and visitors alike.

Restaurant Irini (☎ 2242 031 365; Plateia Ilikiomeni; mayirefta €2.50-4) Irini's, on the leafy and shady central square, is recommended for its low-priced, no-nonsense and very good quality home cooking.

Taverna Panorama (☎ 2242 031 185; grills €3-5) Heading towards Plateia Ilikiomeni, this is another commendable option. Try suckling pig or goat, or even the Cypriot-style *seftelies* (herb-laced sausages).

AROUND NISYROS
The Volcano Το Ηφαίστειο

Nisyros is on a volcanic line that passes through the islands of Aegina, Paros, Milos, Santorini, Nisyros, Giali and Kos. The island originally culminated in a mountain of 850m, but the centre collapsed 30,000 to 40,000 years ago after three violent eruptions. Their legacy are the white-and-orange pumice stones that can still be seen on the northern, eastern and southern flanks of the island, and the large lava flow that covers the whole southwest of the island around Nikea village. The first eruption partially blew off the top of the ancestral cone, but the majority of the sinking of the central part of the island came about as a result of the removal of magma from within the reservoir underground.

Another violent eruption occurred in 1422 on the western side of the caldera depression (called Lakki), but this, like all others since, emitted steam, gases and mud, but no lava. The islanders call the volcano Polyvotis, because during the Great War between the gods and the Titans, the Titan Polyvotis annoyed Poseidon so much that Poseidon tore off a chunk of Kos and threw it at Polyvotis. This rock pinned Polyvotis under it and the rock became the island of Nisyros. The hapless Polyvotis from that day forth has been groaning and sighing while trying to escape – hence the volcano's name.

There are five craters in the **caldera** (adult €1.20; 🕙 9am-8pm). A path descends into the largest one, **Stefanos**, where you can examine the multicoloured fumaroles, listen to their hissing and smell their sulphurous vapours. The surface is soft and hot, making sturdy footwear essential.

The easiest way to visit the volcano is by tourist bus, but you will share your experience with hoards of day-trippers. Better still, walk in from Nikea, or even Mandraki, or take a taxi before 10.30am.

Emborios & Nikea Εμπορειός & Νίκαια

Emborios and Nikea perch on the volcano's rim. From each, there are stunning views down into the caldera. Only a handful of inhabitants linger on in Emborios. You may encounter a few elderly women sitting on their doorsteps crocheting, and their husbands at the kafeneio. But generally, the winding, stepped streets are empty, the silence broken only by the occasional braying of a donkey or the grunting of pigs. There's one place to eat, the seasonal **To Balkoni** (☎ 2242 031 607; mains €3-4) where you can enjoy the view of the crater over lunch.

In contrast to Emborios, picturesque Nikea, with 50 inhabitants, buzzes with life. It has dazzling white houses with vibrant gardens and a central square with a lovely pebble mosaic. The bus terminates on Plateia Nikolaou Hartofyli. Nikea's main street links the two squares. The simple **Community Hostel** (☎ 2242 031 401; Plateia Nikolaou Hartofyli; d €22) is your only choice of a place to stay.

The steep path down to the volcano begins from Plateia Nikolaou Hartofyli. It takes about 40 minutes to walk it one way. Near the beginning you can detour to the signposted **Moni Agiou Ioanni Theologou**.

Pali Πάλοι

Pali is a small yachtie port with some simple accommodation and plenty of places to eat. The island's best beaches are here and at **Lies**, 5.5km further on. **Pahia Ammos** beach is a further 1km from Lies along a coastal track.

If you decide to stay, the basic **Hotel Ellinis** (☎ 2242 031 453; d €30) will see you through. Rooms are small and fairly basic, but are OK for a night or two's stay. For an extra €20 you can rent a fully equipped studio.

Perhaps the best of the bunch of Pali's five eateries is **Afroditi Restaurant** (☎ 2242 031 242; grills €5-6), where home cooking and grills are the order of the day. The rich fish soup is worth splashing onto your palate. Dining is waterside, though motorcycles and cars weave between tables.

KOS ΚΩΣ

pop 17,890

Kos is the third-largest island of the Dodecanese and one of its most fertile and well watered. It is second only to Rhodes in its wealth of archaeological remains and its tourist development, with most of its beautiful beaches wall-to-wall with sun beds and parasols. It's a long, narrow island with a mountainous spine, lying only 5km from the Turkish peninsula of Bodrum.

Pserimos is a small island between Kos and Kalymnos. It has a good sandy beach, but occasionally becomes overrun with day-trippers from its larger neighbours.

History

Kos' fertile land attracted settlers from the earliest times. So many people lived here by Mycenaean times that it sent 30 ships to the Trojan War. During the 7th and 6th centuries BC, Kos flourished as an ally of the powerful Rhodian cities of Ialysos, Kamiros and Lindos. In 477 BC, after suffering an earthquake and subjugation to the Persians, it joined the Delian League and flourished.

Hippocrates (460–377 BC), the father of medicine, was born and lived on the island. After Hippocrates' death, the Sanctuary of Asclepius and a medical school were built, which perpetuated his teachings and made Kos famous throughout the Greek world.

Ptolemy II of Egypt was born on Kos, thus securing it the protection of Egypt,

DODECANESE

under which it became a prosperous trading centre. In 130 BC Kos came under Roman domination, and in the 1st century AD it was administered by Rhodes, with which it came to share the same vicissitudes, right up to the tourist deluge of the present day.

Getting There & Away
AIR
There are three flights daily to Athens (€83, 55 minutes) and three flights a week each to Rhodes (€52, 40 minutes), Leros (€53, 20 minutes) and Astypalea (€45, one hour 10 minutes). **Olympic Airways** (☎ 2242 028 330; Vasileos Pavlou 22) is in Kos Town. The **airport** (☎ 2242 051 229) is 27.5km from Kos Town near the village of Antimahia.

FERRY
Domestic
Kos is well connected with all the islands in the Dodecanese and with Piraeus, with additional connections to the Cyclades. In summer there is a weekly ferry service to Samos and Thessaloniki. Services are offered by four major companies: **Blue Star Ferries** (☎ 2242 028 914), **DANE Sealines** (☎ 2242 027 311), **G&A Ferries** (☎ 2242 028 545) and the **F/B Nisos Kalymnos** (☎ 2242 029 900).

Sample fares are Rhodes (€13, 3½ hours), Piraeus (€27, 12 to 15 hours), Patmos (€10, four hours). **NEL** (☎ 2242 049 930) runs the more expensive *Aiolos Kenteris* express from Kos to Rhodes and Piraeus throughout the high season.

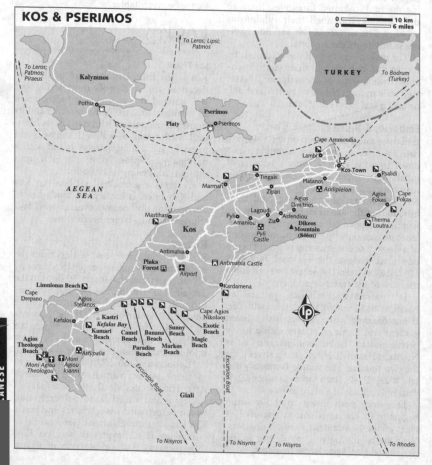

KOS & PSERIMOS

Local ferries run from both Mastihari (€3, one hour, three daily) and Kos Town (€5, 1½ hours, two daily) to Pothia on Kalymnos.

International

There are daily excursions boats in summer travelling from Kos Town to Bodrum in Turkey (one hour, €34 return). Boats leave at 8.30am and return at 4.30pm. Cars can be shipped across to Bodrum on a 4pm Turkish ferry for a rather steep €100 one way. Many travel agents around Kos Town sell tickets; **Exas Travel** (☎ 2242 028 545) is a good bet.

HYDROFOIL & CATAMARAN

Kos is served by Kyriacoulis Hydrofoils and the *Dodekanisos Express* catamaran. In the high season there are daily shuttles to and from Rhodes (€24, two hours), with good connections to all the major islands in the group, as well as Samos (€22.60, four hours), Ikaria (€23, 3½ hours) and Fourni (€26, 3½ hours) in the Northeastern Aegean.

Information and tickets are available from the many travel agents in Kos Town.

Getting Around
TO/FROM THE AIRPORT

An Olympic Airways bus (€3.14) leaves the airline's office two hours before the main Olympic flights. The airport is 26km southwest of Kos Town. Kefalos buses stop at the big roundabout near the airport entrance. A taxi to/from the airport will cost €17.

BUS

The **bus station** (☎ 2242 022 292; Kleopatras 7) is just west of the Olympic Airways office. Buses regularly serve all parts of the island as well as the all-important beaches on the south side of Kos.

CAR, MOTORCYCLE & BICYCLE

There are numerous car, motorcycle and moped rental outlets. You'll be tripping over bicycles to rent. Prices range from €4 for an old bone-shaker to €10 for a top-notch mountain bike.

EXCURSION BOAT

From Kos Town there are many boat excursions around the island and to other islands. Examples of return fares are: Kalymnos €9; Pserimos, Kalymnos and Platy €18; and Nisyros and Giali €19. There is also a daily excursion boat from Kardamena to Nisyros (€12 return) and from Mastihari to Pserimos and Kalymnos. These boats line the southern arm of Akti Koundourioti.

TOURIST TRAIN

You can take a guided tour of Kos in the city's (vehicular) Tourist Train (€2, 20 minutes), which runs 10am to 2pm and 6pm to 10pm starting from the Municipality Building. Or take a train to the Asklipieion and back (€3 return), departing on the hour from 9am to 6pm Tuesday to Sunday.

KOS TOWN

Kos Town, on the northeast coast, is the island's capital and main port. The Old Town was destroyed by an earthquake in 1933. The New Town, although modern, is picturesque and lush, with an abundance of palms, pines, oleander and hibiscus. The Castle of the Knights dominates the port, and Hellenistic and Roman ruins are strewn everywhere. It's a pleasant enough place and can easily be covered on foot in half a day.

Orientation

The ferry quay is north of the castle. The central square of Plateia Eleftherias is south of Akti Koundourioti along Vasileos Pavlou. Kos' so-called Old Town is on Ifestou; its souvenir shops, jewellers and boutiques denude it of any old-world charm, though.

Southeast of the castle, the waterfront is called Akti Miaouli. It continues as Vasileos Georgiou and then G Papandreou, which leads to the beaches of Psalidi, Agios Fokas and Therma Loutra.

Information

Alpha Bank (Akti Koundourioti) Has a 24 hour automatic exchange machine. Most banks have ATMs, including the easy-to-find National Bank of Greece.

Cafe Del Mare (☎ 2242 024 244; www.cybercafe.gr; Megalou Alexandrou 4; €4.50 per hr; ☽ 9am-1am) Has Internet access.

Dr Konstantinos Lambrianidis (☎ 6944 533 440; Tingaki) A private practitioner who deals primarily with tourists needing on-the-spot medical services.

Happy Wash (Mitropolis 20) Charges around €8 for a full wash and dry.

Laundromat Center (Alikarnassou 124) Charges around €8 for a full wash and dry.

Hospital (☎ 2242 022 300; Ippokratous 32) In the centre of town.

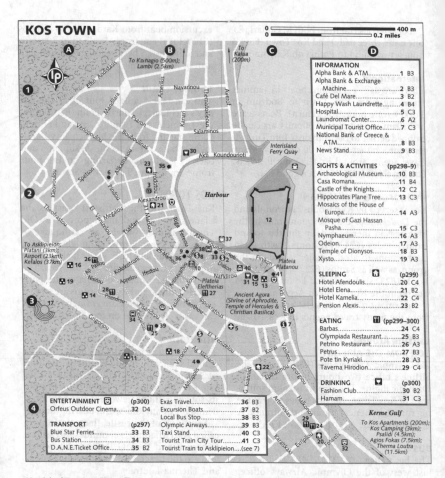

KOS TOWN

| 0 | | 400 m |
| 0 | | 0.2 miles |

INFORMATION
Alpha Bank & ATM.................1 B3
Alpha Bank & Exchange
 Machine...........................2 B3
Café Del Mare.....................3 B2
Happy Wash Laundrette.......4 B4
Hospital.............................5 C3
Laundromat Center..............6 A2
Municipal Tourist Office........7 B3
National Bank of Greece &
 ATM...............................8 B3
News Stand........................9 B3

SIGHTS & ACTIVITIES   (pp298-9)
Archaeological Museum........10 B3
Casa Romana.....................11 B4
Castle of the Knights...........12 C2
Hippocrates Plane Tree........13 C3
Mosaics of the House of
 Europa............................14 A3
Mosque of Gazi Hassan
 Pasha..............................15 C3
Nymphaeum......................16 A3
Odeion.............................17 A3
Temple of Dionysos.............18 B3
Xysto...............................19 A3

SLEEPING   ☐   (p299)
Hotel Afendoulis.................20 C4
Hotel Elena.......................21 B2
Hotel Kamelia....................22 C4
Pension Alexis....................23 B2

EATING   ☐   (pp299-300)
Barbas.............................24 C4
Olympiada Restaurant..........25 B3
Petrino Restaurant..............26 A3
Petrus..............................27 B3
Pote tin Kyriaki..................28 A3
Taverna Hirodion.................29 C4

DRINKING   ☐   (p300)
Fashion Club......................30 B2
Hamam.............................31 C3

Kerme Gulf

To Kos Apartments (200m);
Kos Camping (3km);
Psalidi (4.5km);
Agios Fokas (7.5km);
Therma Loutra
(11.5km)

ENTERTAINMENT ☐   (p300)
Orfeus Outdoor Cinema.......32 D4

TRANSPORT   (p297)
Blue Star Ferries.................33 B3
Bus Station........................34 B2
D.A.N.E.Ticket Office...........35 B2

Exas Travel........................36 B3
Excursion Boats..................37 B2
Local Bus Stop...................38 B3
Olympic Airways.................39 B3
Taxi Stand.........................40 C3
Tourist Train City Tour..........41 C3
Tourist Train to Asklipieion....(see 7)

Municipal Tourist Office (☎ 2242 024 460; www.hippo
crates.gr; Vasileos Georgiou 1; ☼ 8am-8pm Mon-Fri, 8am-
3pm Sat May-Oct) Delivers general information on Kos Town.
The staff are efficient and helpful.

News Stand (☎ 2242 030 110; Riga Fereou 2) Sells
foreign-language newspapers and publications.

Tourist police (☎ 2242 022 444)

Regular police (☎ 2242 022 222) Shares the Municipality Building with tourist police.

Sights

ARCHAEOLOGICAL MUSEUM

There's a fine 3rd-century AD mosaic in
the vestibule of the **archaeological museum**
(☎ 2242 028 326; Plateia Eleftherias; adult/student €3/2;
open 8am-2.30pm Tue-Sun). The most renowned
statue is that of Hippocrates.

ARCHAEOLOGICAL SITES

The **ancient agora** (admission free) is an open
site south of the castle. A massive 3rd-
century BC stoa, with some reconstructed
columns, stands on its western side. On the
north side are the ruins of a **Shrine of Aphrodite**, **Temple of Hercules** and a 5th-century
Christian basilica.

North of the agora is the lovely cobblestone Plateia Platanou, where you can pay
your respects to the **Hippocrates Plane Tree**,
under which Hippocrates is said to have
taught his pupils. Plane trees don't usually
live for more than 200 years – so much for
the power of the Hippocratic oath – though
in all fairness it is certainly one of Europe's
oldest. This once-magnificent tree is held

up with scaffolding, and looks to be in its death throes. Beneath it is an old sarcophagus converted by the Turks into a fountain. Opposite the tree is the well-preserved 18th-century **Mosque of Gazi Hassan Pasha**, its ground-floor loggia now converted into souvenir shops.

From Plateia Platanou a bridge leads across Finikon (called the Avenue of Palms) to the **Castle of the Knights** (☎ 2242 027 927; Leof Finikon; admission €2.40; 8am-2.30pm Tue-Sun). Along with the castles of Rhodes Town and Bodrum, this impregnable fortress was the knights' most stalwart defence against the encroaching Ottomans. The castle, which had massive outer walls and an inner keep, was built in the 14th century. Damaged by an earthquake in 1495, it was restored by the Grand Masters d'Aubuisson and d'Amboise (each a master of a 'tongue' of knights) in the 16th century. The keep was originally separated from the town by a moat (now Finikon).

The other ruins are mostly in the southern part of the town. Walk along Vasileos Pavlou to Grigoriou and cross over to the restored **Casa Romana** (☎ 2242 023 234; Grigoriou 5; 8am-2.30pm Tue-Sun), an opulent 3rd-century Roman villa that was built on the site of a larger 1st-century Hellenistic house and is now under restoration. Opposite are the scant ruins of the 3rd-century **Temple of Dionysos**.

Facing Grigoriou, turn right to reach the **western excavation site**. Two wooden shelters at the back of the site protect the 3rd-century mosaics of the **House of Europa**. The best-preserved mosaic depicts Europa's abduction by Zeus in the guise of a bull. In front of here an exposed section of the Decumanus Maximus (the Roman city's main thoroughfare) runs parallel to the modern road, then turns right towards the **nymphaeum**, which consisted of once-lavish latrines, and the **xysto**, a large Hellenistic gymnasium with restored columns. On the opposite side of Grigoriou is the restored 3rd-century **odeion**.

Sleeping

Kos Camping (☎ 2242 023 910; Psalidi; camp sites per adult/tent €4.50/2.50) This site, 3km along the eastern waterfront, is Kos' only camping ground. It's a well-kept, shaded site with a taverna, snack bar, minimarket, kitchen and laundry.

Hotel Elena (☎ 2242 022 740; Megalou Alexandrou 7; d/tr €24/31) This D-class hotel is a commendable budget option, though it looks a little tired and old at first glance.

Pension Alexis (☎ 2242 028 798; fax 2242 025 797; Irodotou 9; s/d €23/29) This convivial pension has long been a budget favourite with travellers and is run by the same manager as Hotel Afendoulis. It has clean rooms and a communal kitchen and is highly recommended.

Hotel Afendoulis (☎ 2242 025 321; afendoulis hotel@kos.forthnet.gr; Evripilou 1; s/d €29/42;) The friendly, English-speaking Alexis Zikas runs this relaxed, traveller-friendly establishment. The rooms are tastefully decorated and all have fans. Your laundry can be done here for €6 a load.

Hotel Kamelia (☎ 2242 028 983; fax 2242 027 391; kamelia_hotel@hotmail.com; s/d €25/45) On a quiet tree-lined street, the Kamelia is a pleasant C-class hotel with simple but comfortable rooms.

Eating

The restaurants lining the central waterfront are generally expensive and poor value; avoid them and head for the backstreets.

Taverna Hirodion (☎ 2242 026 634; Artemisias 27; mains €5-6) On the south side of town, this long-running taverna serves good and inexpensive food. The pork fillet in brandy sauce is considered the house speciality, though all dishes can be counted on for quality and the size of the portions.

Barbas (☎ 2240 027 856; Evripilou 6; mains €3-5) Right opposite Hotel Afendoulis is this busy little *psistaria* with streetside tables and fetching décor. The grills are the speciality and the chicken souvlaki or fillet is to die for: it's succulent and melts in your mouth. The chef also serves up a range of equally delicious *mayirefta*.

Olympiada Restaurant (☎ 2242 023 031; Kleopatras 2; mains €3.50-4) For reliable, predictable and unfussy food, this unpretentious place behind the Olympic Airways office delivers the goods, among which are a variety of stuffed dishes – tomatoes, aubergines, zucchini and vine leaves to name but a few.

Pote tin Kyriaki (☎ 2242 027 872; Pisandrou 9; mezedes €3.50-5; dinner only, closed Sun) You can't get more untouristy than this quirky, ouzeri-style restaurant with its idiosyncratic owner and menus written by hand in school exercise books. The food is topnotch too. Try the various styles of *pites* and mezedes.

Karnagio (☎ 2242 027 900; Ethelondon Polemiston & Filinou; specials €7.50-16.50) If you see the owner in a wetsuit don't be surprised. He catches the fish for the restaurant, so it's fresh. Apart from fresh fish, the specials are inventive: paella, stuffed squid, pot-baked prawns and filling fish soup.

Petrino Restaurant (☎ 2242 027 251; Plateia Ioannou Theologou; mains €7-9; ☾ dinner only) Pitched at discerning diners, the Petrino is a stylish place in a stone mansion, with outdoor eating in a romantic garden setting. Try chicken stuffed with spinach, cheese and mint sauce.

Petrus (☎ 2242 049 480; Ippokratous 3; mains €16-24) Petrus is a classy bistro–wine bar featuring a European-Greek menu with French-Swiss overtones. There's a tempting selection of cold salads, grills and specials. Memorable is the delectable stuffed chicken with ham and parmesan cheese, or the roast partridge with fresh vegetables combined tastefully with olive oil, oregano and pepper. An extensive wine list has between 30 and 40 top-class wines on offer.

Entertainment

Kos Town has two streets of bars, Diakon and Nafklirou, that positively pulsate in high season. Most bars belt out techno, but **Hamam** (Akti Koundourioti 1) plays Greek music. **Fashion Club** (☎ 2242 022 592; Kanari 2) is one of the more popular and longer-standing clubs with three bars to whet your whistle at. **Kalua** (☎ 2242 024 938; Akti Zouroudi 3), further round the north side of the harbour, serves up a mixed menu of music and includes R&B. It's an outdoor venue and also has a swimming pool.

There is also an outdoor cinema, **Orfeus** (☎ 2242 025 036; Fenaretis 3; adult €6; ☾ summer only), with a wide range of movies screened.

AROUND KOS TOWN
Asklipieion Ασκληπιείον

The island's most important ancient site is the **Asklipieion** (☎ 2242 028 763; Platani; adult/student €4/3; ☾ 8.30am-6pm Tue-Sun), built on a pine-covered hill 4km southwest of Kos Town. From the top there is a wonderful view of Kos Town and Turkey. The Asklipieion consisted of a religious sanctuary to Asclepius, the god of healing, a healing centre, and a school of medicine, where the training followed the teachings of Hippocrates.

Hippocrates was the first doctor to have a rational approach to diagnosing and treating illnesses. Until AD 554 people came from far and wide to be treated here, as well as for medical training.

The ruins occupy three levels. The **propylaea**, Roman-era public **baths** and remains of guest rooms are on the first level. On the next level is a 4th-century BC **altar of Kyparissios Apollo**. West of this is the **first Temple of Asclepius**, built in the 4th century BC. To the east is the 1st-century BC **Temple to Apollo**; seven of its graceful columns have been re-erected. On the third level are the remains of the once-magnificent 2nd-century BC **Temple of Asclepius**.

Frequent buses and the Tourist Train go to the site, but it is pleasant to cycle or walk there.

HIPPOCRATES – THE FIRST GP

Hippocrates is often called the father of medicine, yet little is known for certain about his life. He is believed to have lived between 460 and 377 BC, but 'facts' about his birth and medical practices owe more to mythology – than to hardcore evidence. The earliest known biography of him is *Life of Hippocrates* by Soranus, a Roman physician. This work was published about AD 100, more than 400 years after Hippocrates' death.

Hippocrates' fame probably resulted from about 80 anonymously written medical works that became part of the collection of the Library of Alexandria after about 200 BC. These writings became linked with Hippocrates and are known by scholars as the *Hippocratic corpus*. However, it cannot be proved that Hippocrates actually wrote any of these works.

Hippocrates' medicine challenged the methods of many physicians who used magic and witchcraft to treat disease. It taught that diseases had natural causes and could therefore be studied and possibly cured according to the workings of nature. Under Hippocratic medicine, a well-trained physician could cure illness with knowledge gained from medical writings or from experience. Modern medicine is based on this assumption.

AROUND KOS

Kos' main road runs southwest from Kos Town, with turn-offs for the mountain villages and the resorts of Tingaki and Marmari. Between the main road and the coast, a quiet road, ideal for cycling, winds through flat agricultural land as far as Marmari.

The nearest decent beach to Kos Town is the crowded **Lambi Beach**, 4km to the northwest. Further round the coast, **Tingaki**, 9km from Kos Town, has an excellent, long pale-sand beach. **Marmari Beach**, 4km west of Tingaki, is slightly less crowded. Windsurfing is popular at all three beaches.

Vasileos Georgiou (later G Papandreou) in Kos Town leads to the three crowded beaches of **Psalidi**, 3km from Kos Town; **Agios Fokas**, 7km away; and **Therma Loutra**, 11km away. The latter has hot mineral springs that warm the sea.

Mastihari Μαστιχάρι

Mastihari (mas-ti-*ha*-ri), north of Antimahia and 30km from Kos Town, is an important village in its own right. It's a resort destination, but also an arrival/departure point for ferries to Pothia on Kalymnos. It is better equipped to cater for independent travellers, with a good selection of domatia all within a hop, skip and jump of an excellent though sometimes windy beach. Mastihari is just that little bit more 'Greek' than Marmari and Tingaki. From here there are excursion boats to Kalymnos and the island of Pserimos.

There are plenty of accommodation choices in Mastihari and many cater to independent travellers. Among these options is the pleasant **Rooms to Rent Anna** (☎ 2242 059 041; d €25-35), 200m inland along the main road and on the left. **To Kyma** (☎ 2242 059 045; kokkino4@otenet.gr; s/d €28/33) is a pleasant, small, family-run hotel with smallish but present-able rooms that enjoy a good sea breeze. There is a clean and homely communal kitchen for guests' use. Overlooking the west beach, **Rooms Panorama** (☎ /fax 2242 059 145; studios €30) are tidy self-contained studios, most of which have a kitchenette.

Right on the central square, the busy **Kali Kardia Restaurant** (☎ 2242 059 289; fish €7-10) is commendable, and the fish is particularly good, as is laid-back **O Makis** (☎ 2242 059 061; mains €4-6), which serves as a taverna and grill house. There are lots of good salads on offer too.

Mountain Villages

Several attractive villages are scattered on the northern slopes of the green and wooded, alpine-like Dikeos mountain range. At **Zipari**, 10km from the capital, a road to the southeast leads to **Asfendiou**. Along the way and 3km past Zipari you will pass **Taverna Panorama** (☎ 2242 069 367; mezedes €3-3.50; ☯ evenings only), which enjoys a great night-time view with nary a tourist in sight, as most head for Zia. Enjoy good mezedes and excellent service in the company of a mainly Greek clientele.

From Asfendiou, a turn-off to the left leads to the pristine hamlets of **Agios Georgios** and **Agios Dimitrios**. The road straight ahead leads to the village of **Zia**, which is touristy but worth a visit for the surrounding countryside, honey, herbs and spices and some great sunsets. In Zia **Taverna Olympia** (☎ 2242 069 121; mains €4.50-5) is a less obvious choice – as it doesn't have the views – but it earns its good reputation based on solid, reliable local cuisine and repeat clientele.

Lagoudi is a small, unspoilt village to the west of Zia. From here you can continue to **Amaniou** (just before modern Pyli) where there is a left turn to the ruins of the medieval village of **Pyli**, overlooked by a ruined castle. The village of Pyli has a pleasant eating venue in **Palia Pygi** (☎ 2242 041 510; mains €5-6), a little taverna overlooking a lion-headed fountain just off the central square. It serves up fragrant grills and filling *mayirefta*.

Kamari & Kefalos Καμάρι & Κέφαλος

From Antimahia the main road continues southwest to the huge Kefalos Bay, fringed by a 5km stretch of sandy beaches that are divided into roughly six 'name' beaches, each signposted from the main road. The most popular is **Paradise Beach**, while the most undeveloped is **Exotic Beach**. **Banana Beach** (also known as **Langada Beach**) is a good compromise.

Agios Stefanos Beach at the far western end is dominated by a vast Club Med complex. The beach, reached along a short turn-off from the main road, is still worth a visit to see the island of **Agios Stefanos** (named after its church), which is within swimming distance, and the ruins of two 5th-century basilicas to the left of the beach as you face the sea.

Kefalos, 43km southwest of Kos Town, is a sprawling village perched high above

Kamari Beach. It's a pleasant place with few concessions to tourism. The central square, where the bus terminates, is at the top of the 2km road from the coast. There is a post office and bank with an ATM here. Daily excursion boats leave from Kamari for Nisyros (€16).

For sleeping there are a couple of little-known places worth seeking out. Walk about 150m south of Sebastian Tours to find them. **Anthoula Studios** (☎ 2242 071 904; studios €39) is a spotless set of airy and roomy studios surrounded by a flourishing vegetable garden. Closer to Sebastian Tours, **Rooms to Let Katerina** (☎ 2242 071 397; studios €38) are also a similar choice, although they are a bit smaller. There's no shortage of eating options, but most are tourist-oriented with picture menus. **Stamatia** (☎ 2242 071 245; mains €3-6) has been in business since 1935 and stands apart from the general mediocrity with a good range of well-prepared classic fish and meat dishes.

The southern peninsula has the island's most wild and rugged scenery. **Agios Theologos Beach** is on the east coast, 7km from Kefalos at the end of a good sealed road. You can't miss **Restaurant Agios Theologos** (☎ 6974 503 556; fish €9-11), which enjoys the best sunsets in Kos, as well as serving up good fish dishes such as white snapper in addition to home-made goat cheese and scrumptious home-baked bread.

ASTYPALEA ΑΣΤΥΠΑΛΑΙΑ

pop 1238

Astypalea (ah-stih-*pah*-lia), the most westerly island of the archipelago, is a butterfly-shaped hideaway that is more often than not missed by even seasoned travellers to the region. It is the kind of place you go to 'get away' and often end up staying. Treeless in the main with bare, gently contoured hills, high mountains, green valleys and sheltered coves, activity is centred upon an appealing hill-top hora, a lively port, and a couple of small and unassuming beach resorts – all peppered with an instant appeal.

Astypalea is also an island in search of a sense of belonging. Geographically and architecturally it is more akin to the Cyclades, but administratively it is a Dodecanese island. Sited more or less equidistant between its nearest Cycladic neighbour, Amorgos, to the northwest and its fellow Dodecanese island, Kos, to the east, Astypalea effectively has a foot in both camps. The island undergoes a short, sharp summer season from mid-July to mid-August when accommodation, unless prebooked, is almost impossible to find. The best time to visit is June and September.

Getting There & Away

AIR

There are five flights weekly from Astypalea to Athens (€53, 50 minutes) plus three flights weekly to Leros (€39, 20 minutes), Kos (€45, one hour) and Rhodes (€45, 1½ hours). **Astypalea Tours** (☎ 2243 061 571), in Astypalea Town, is the agent for Olympic Airways.

FERRY

Astypalea has two services a week to Piraeus (€25, 10 to 12 hours) and two a week to Rhodes (€18, seven to nine hours) via Kalymnos and Kos. The local ferry F/B *Nisos Kalymnos* calls in three times a week, linking the island with Kalymnos. Tickets are available from **Paradisos Ferries Agency** (☎ 2243 061 224; fax 2243 061 450) or from **Astypalea Tours** (☎ 2243 061 571).

Getting Around

BUS

From Skala a bus travels fairly frequently to Hora and Livadia (€0.83) and from Hora and Skala to Maltezana (€1.05) via Marmari.

EXCURSION BOAT

From June to August there are daily excursion boats to the island's less accessible beaches and to Agia Kyriaki Islet (€6). Tickets can be bought from the stalls by the boats.

SKALA & HORA ΣΚΑΛΑ & ΧΟΡΑ

The main settlement of Astypalea consists of the port of Skala and the picturesque hill-top village of Hora, crowned by an imposing 15th-century castle. Skala can get hot and noisy in peak season, but does offer a fairly reasonable sandy beach if the pressure is too much. Most head uphill to Hora where you can catch a hill-top breeze and enjoy an unparalleled view. The so-called Windmill Square in Hora is backed by several restored windmills and is the main focal point. Leading upwards from here to the castle are a series of narrow streets with dazzling-white

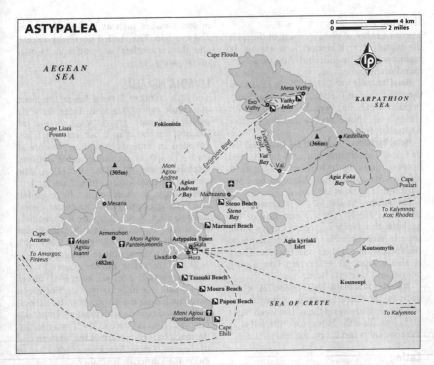

ASTYPALEA

0 — 4 km
0 — 2 miles

AEGEAN SEA

Cape Flouda

Mesa Vathy

Exo Vathy · Vathy Inlet

KARPATHION SEA

Cape Liani Pounta

Fokionisia

Kastellano

(366m)

Moni Agiou Andrea

Agios Andreas Bay

Vai Bay · Vai

Agia Foka Bay

Cape Poulari

Mesaria

(305m)

Maltezana

Steno Beach
Steno Bay

To Kalymnos; Kos; Rhodes

Marmari Beach

Cape Armeno

Armenohori

Moni Agiou Panteleimonos

Astypalea Town
Skala

Agia kyriaki Islet

Koutsomytis

To Amorgos; Piraeus

Moni Agiou Ioanni

(482m)

Livadia · Hora

Tzanaki Beach

Kounoupi

Moura Beach

Papou Beach

SEA OF CRETE

Moni Agiou Konstantinou

Cape Ehili

To Kalymnos

---

cubic houses sporting brightly painted balconies, doors and banisters.

Orientation & Information

Ferries and hydrofoils dock at the western end of the port, a 300m walk to the centre of Skala. A steep road to Hora starts from here, while a road to the right leads to the airport and the east side of the island.

Commercial Bank With an ATM, it's on the waterfront.
Municipal Tourist Office Adjoins the quayside café; open seasonally.
Police (☎ 2243 061 207)
Port police (☎ 2243 061 208) In a prominent Italianate building on the waterfront.
Post office At the top of the Skala–Hora road.
www.astypalaia.com Gives a good rundown on the island's facilities and sights.

Sights
CASTLE

Astypalea was occupied by the Venetian Quirini family, whom Giovanni built the imposing **castle** (admission free; ☼ dawn to dusk) starting in 1413. In the Middle Ages the

population lived within its walls in order to escape the depredations of piracy that was rife in the Aegean Sea, but gradually the settlement outgrew them. The last inhabitants left in 1953 following a devastating earthquake, as a result of which the stone houses collapsed. Above the tunnel-like entrance is the Church of Our Lady of the Castle and within the walls is the Church of Agios Giorgios. The castle is currently being restored.

ARCHAEOLOGICAL MUSEUM

Skala sports a small **archaeological museum** (☎ 2243 061 206; admission €2; ☼ 8am-2.30pm Tue-Sun). The whole island of Astypalea is in fact a rich trove of archaeological treasure, and many of the finds are on display here. The collection runs from the prehistoric-Mycenaean period through to the Middle Ages. Look out for a fine selection of grave offerings from two Mycenaean chamber tombs excavated at Armenohori, and the little bronze Roman statue of Aphrodite found at Trito Marmari. The museum is a little way up the Skala–Hora road on the right.

DODECANESE

Sleeping

There's a range of good sleeping options on the island, though reservations are highly recommended in July and August as demand often exceeds supply.

Hotel Australia (☎ 2243 061 275; d/tr €35/38) On the right side of the waterfront, this long-popular hotel has well-kept rooms with fridge and phone and a friendly Greek-Australian owner.

Hotel Paradisos (☎ 2243 061 224; fax 2243 061 450; s/d €35/50) This ageing but well-maintained hotel overlooking the harbour has comfortable rooms and is most likely to be open when other options are closed.

Akti Rooms (☎ 2243 061 114; aktirooms@hotmail .com; d/tr €55/65; 🐾) On the east side of the harbour this block of rooms enjoys some superb harbour views from the balconies. All rooms have fridges and phones. There is also a topnotch restaurant (see Eating below) and cafeteria here.

Aphrodite Studios (☎ 2243 061 478; fax 2243 061 087; studios €42/50) These beautiful, well-equipped studios are halfway up the hill between Skala and Hora. Take the Hora road, turn left after the shoe shop and it's on the left.

Eating

There's a decent selection of good restaurants both in Skala and up in Hora.

Karavos (☎ 2243 061 072; Skala; mains €3-4.50) Excellent home-cooked food is served at this homey and diminutive eatery on the Skala waterfront overlooking the beach. Try stuffed zucchini flowers, or *poungia* (cheese fold-overs), or any of the vegetarian choices.

Restaurant Akti (☎ 2243 061 114; mains €3-8.50) For the best harbourside dining seats in Astypalea, book the day before. Perched high up overlooking the harbour entrance, the few available tables are enormously popular. So is the food, which includes a filling squid stuffed with rice.

Maïstrali (☎ 2243 061 691; mains €4-8) Tucked away in the little street behind the harbour is this yachtie-popular eatery that has a predictably fish-based menu but occasional *mayirefta* such as succulent beef *stifado*. Service is brisk and friendly and dining is alfresco on the shaded, stepped veranda.

Barbaros (☎ 2243 061 577; mains €4-12; 🍴 dinner only) The best place to tempt your taste buds is in Hora. Many of the dishes are wok-cooked, and ginger features prominently in some dishes such as lamb with fennel and avocado. The stuffed pork with cheese and plum is another taste-bud tickler worth investigating.

LIVADIA ΛΙΒΑΔΕΙΑ

The little resort of Livadia lies in the heart of a fertile valley 2km from Hora. Its wide pebble and fine gravel beach is one of the best on the island, but can get fairly crowded in summer. Sleeping presents at least a couple of recommendable options.

Kaloudis Domatia (☎ 2243 061 318; d €33) A little way up the road leading inland on the left, these budget domatia set in a large garden and sharing a communal kitchen are a good place to start. A notch up are the smallish, but well-equipped studios at **Venetos Studios** (☎ 2243 061 490; fax 2243 061 423; studios €50-60; 🐾), set around a shady orange-tree grove.

There are a few quality places to eat. **Astropelos** (☎ 2243 061 473; mains €4-6) serves up a small, but imaginative range of menu items including the always popular *astako-makaronada* (pasta with lobster). **Trapezakia Exo** (☎ 2243 061 083; snacks €3.50-4.50) is a neat little snack bar–restaurant at the western end of the beach strip. Snack on sandwiches or enjoy the cuttlefish speciality.

EAST OF SKALA

To the east of Skala is the easterly wing of the 'butterfly' – the waist being marked by a narrow 100m isthmus that barely joins the two wings of the island. **Marmari**, 2km northeast of Skala, has three bays with pebble-and-sand beaches and is home to Astypalea's **Camping Astypalea** (☎ 2243 061 338; astropalitisa@hotmail.com; camp sites per adult/tent €4/ 2.50). Though it only operates from June to September, this shaded ground is right next to the beach. **Steno Beach**, 2km further along, is one of the better but least frequented beaches on the island. It's sandy, has shade and is well protected. This is the point where the island is barely 100m wide.

Maltezana (also known as **Analipsi**) is 7km beyond Marmari in a fertile valley on the isthmus. A former Maltese pirates' lair, it's a scattered, pleasantly laid-back settlement with a long sand and pebble beach shaded by tamarisk trees. The water is clean and shallow. There are some remains of Roman baths with mosaics on the settlement's outskirts.

Accommodation is concentrated in Maltezana. **Maltezana Rooms** (☎ 2243 061 446; fax 2243 061 370; d €30) are fairly standard rooms 50m east of the quay, just back from the beach. **Villa Varvara** (☎ /fax 2243 061 448; studios €45/54) has 14 blue-and-white painted studios overlooking a vegetable garden 100m from the beach. All have TVs and fridges. The most expansive accommodation here and perhaps on the island is **Hotel Maltezana Beach** (☎ 2243 061 558; www.maltezanabeach.gr; d/tr €80/95; P ⬚), occupying the middle section of the foreshore. The complex of cubed white studios is tastefully decorated and rooms each have satellite TV, fridge and hairdryer. The hotel's restaurant is considered one of the best on the island.

Other eating choices include **To Steki tou Manoli** (☎ 2243 061 111; mains €3.50-5), which dishes up locally caught fish at a very reasonable price as well as *kakavia* (a rich fish soup like bouillabaisse), and **Ouzeri tou Handra** (☎ 2243 061 051; mains €3-5) up on the bluff at the east side of Maltezana, which offers mezedes, fish and grills as well as café-style snacks.

KALYMNOS ΚΑΛΥΜΝΟΣ

pop 16,441
Kalymnos (*kah*-lim-nos), only 2.5km south of Leros, is a mountainous, arid island speckled with fertile valleys. Kalymnos is renowned as the 'sponge-fishing island', but with the demise of this industry it is now exploiting its tourist potential. It faces a tough job. The general diffidence of islanders towards tourists doesn't help, and while there is plenty on offer to entice travellers – good food, accommodation and rugged scenery – the pull of neighbouring Kos on the package tourism industry is just too strong. New adventure enterprises in rock climbing are drawing growing numbers of visitors, and if you do make it across to Kalymnos via the local ferry you will find an island that is still generally in touch with its traditions.

Getting There & Away
AIR
Most people wishing to fly to Kalymnos fly to Kos and transfer to the Mastihari–Pothia local ferry.

Olympic Airways is represented by **Kapellas Travel** (☎ 2243 029 265) in Pothia.

FERRY
Kalymnos is linked to Rhodes (€16, five hours) and Piraeus (€26, 10 to 13 hours) and islands in between, including a useful link to Astypalea (€10, three hours). Services are provided by **DANE Sealines** (☎ 2243 023 043), **G&A Ferries** (☎ 2243 023 700) and the **F/B Nisos Kalymnos** (☎ 2243 029 612).

Car and passenger ferries leave between three and six times daily between 7am and 8pm from Pothia to Mastihari on Kos (€3, 50 minutes) and twice daily from Pothia to Kos Town (€5, 1½ hours).

HYDROFOIL & CATAMARAN
Hydrofoils link Kalymnos with most islands in the north and south Dodecanese group, such as Rhodes (€31, 3½ hours) and Patmos (€18, 1½ hours), and Samos (€23, 3½ hours) in the Northeastern Aegean. Tickets can be bought from **Magos Travel** (☎ 2243 028 777) in Pothia.

The *Dodekanisos Express* catamaran calls in once daily during summer on its run up and down the Dodecanese chain. Fares are similar to those of the hydrofoil. Tickets are issued by **G&A Ferries** (☎ 2243 023 700).

Getting Around
BUS
In summer there is a bus on the hour from Pothia to Masouri (€0.78) via Myrties, to Emborios (€0.94) three times weekly and to Vathys (€0.94) four times daily. Buy tickets from Pilatos Minimarket in Pothia.

EXCURSION BOAT
From Myrties there is a daily excursion boat to Emborios (€7), leaving at 10am and returning at 4pm. Day trips to the **Kefalas Cave** (€18), impressive for its stalactites and stalagmites, run from both Pothia and Myrties.

MOTORCYCLE
There are several motorcycle rental outlets along Pothia's waterfront.

TAXI
Shared taxis cost a little more than buses and run from the Pothia **taxi stand** (☎ 2243 050 300; Plateia Kyprou) to Masouri. They can also be flagged down en route. A regular taxi to Emborios costs €13.50 and to Vathys €10.

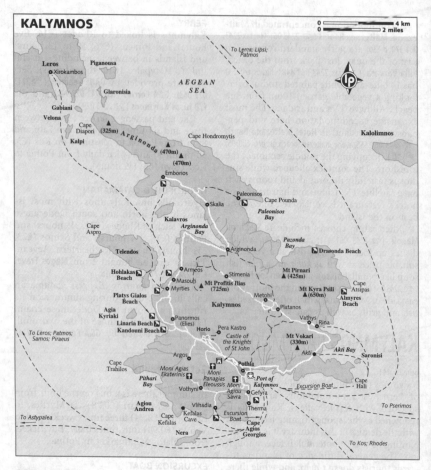

KALYMNOS

0 — 4 km
0 — 2 miles

To Leros; Lipsi; Patmos

AEGEAN SEA

Leros
Xirokambos
Piganousa
Glaronisia
Gabiani
Velona
Cape Diapori (325m)
Kalpi
Arginonda (470m)
(470m)
Cape Hondromytis
Kalolimnos

Emborios
Paleonisos
Cape Pounda
Skalia
Paleonisos Bay
Kalavros
Arginonda Bay
Cape Aspro
Pazonda Bay
Telendos
Arginonda
Drasonda Beach

Hohlakas Beach
Armeos
Stimenia
Mt Pirnari (425m)
Cape Atsipas
Masouli
Myrties
Mt Profitis Ilias (725m)
Mt Kyra Psili (680m)
Almyres Beach
Platys Gialos Beach
Metohi
Agia Kyriaki
Kalymnos
Platanos
Linaria Beach
Panormos (Elies)
Vathys
Rina
Kandouni Beach
Horio
Pera Kastro
To Leros; Patmos; Samos; Piraeus
Argos
Castle of the Knights of St John
Mt Vokari (330m)
Akti Bay
Saronisi
Cape Trahilos
Moni Agias Ekaterinis
Pothia
Akti
Moni Panagias
Port of Kalymnos
Excursion Boat
Cape Hali
Pithari Bay
Moni Eleoussis
Moni Agiou Savra
Vothyni
Gefyra
To Pserimos
Agiou Andrea
Vlihadia
Therma
Kefalas Cave
Excursion Boat
To Astypalea
Cape Kefalas
Nera
Cape Agios Georgios
To Kos; Rhodes

POTHIA ΠΟΘΙΑ

Pothia (*poth*-ya), the port and capital of Kalymnos, is a fairly large town by Dodecanese standards. It is built amphitheatrically around the slopes of the surrounding hills and valley, and its visually arresting melange of colourful mansions and houses draped over the hills makes for an incredibly photogenic sight when you first arrive. While Pothia can be a tad brash and very busy, and its narrow vehicle-plagued streets a challenge to all pedestrians, it is nonetheless the focus of the island's life, and you will be passing through here at some point in your stay even if you choose not to linger for very long.

Orientation & Information

Pothia's quay is located at the southern side of the port. Most activity, however, is centred on the main square, Plateia Eleftherias, abutting the lively waterfront. The main commercial centre is on Venizelou (more commonly known as Emboriki to the locals), along which are most of the shops.

National, Commercial & Ionian Banks With ATMs. All are close to the waterfront.

Neon Internet Cafe 1 (☎ 2243 048 318; €5 per hr; ☽ 8.30am-midnight)

Neon Internet Cafe 2 (☎ 2243 028 343; €5 per hr; ☽ 8.30am-midnight)

Police (☎ 2243 029 301; Patriarhou Maximimou) Before the post office.

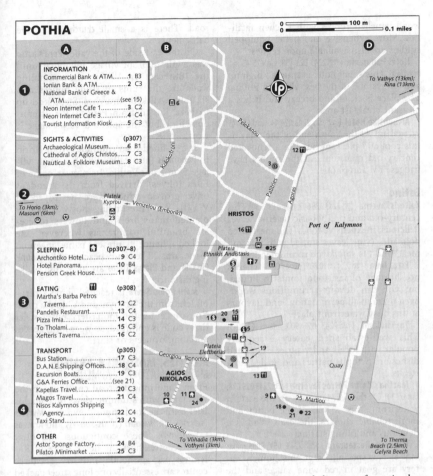

POTHIA

0 ———— 100 m
0 ———— 0.1 miles

INFORMATION
Commercial Bank & ATM........1 B3
Ionian Bank & ATM................2 C3
National Bank of Greece &
ATM...............................(see 15)
Neon Internet Cafe 1.............3 C2
Neon Internet Cafe 3.............4 C4
Tourist Information Kiosk........5 C3

SIGHTS & ACTIVITIES (p307)
Archaeological Museum.........6 B1
Cathedral of Agios Christos.....7 C3
Nautical & Folklore Museum...8 C3

SLEEPING (pp307–8)
Archontiko Hotel.....................9 C4
Hotel Panorama.....................10 B4
Pension Greek House.............11 B4

EATING (p308)
Martha's Barba Petros
Taverna..............................12 C2
Pandelis Restaurant................13 C4
Pizza Imia..............................14 C3
To Tholami............................15 C3
Xefteris Taverna....................16 C2

TRANSPORT (p305)
Bus Station............................17 C3
D.A.N.E.Shipping Offices........18 C4
Excursion Boats......................19 C3
G&A Ferries Office..............(see 21)
Kapellas Travel......................20 C3
Magos Travel.........................21 C4
Nisos Kalymnos Shipping
Agency...............................22 C4
Taxi Stand.............................23 A2

OTHER
Astor Sponge Factory.............24 B4
Pilatos Minimarket 25 C3

To Vathys (13km);
Rina (13km)

Polekanou

Kaldokotoni

Plateia
Kyprou — Venizelou (Emboriki)

To Horio (3km);
Masouri (6km)

Plfirtes

Agrras

HRISTOS

Port of Kalymnos

Plateia
Ethnikis Andistasis

Plateia
Eleftherias

Georgiou_Ikonomou

AGIOS
NIKOLAOS

Quay

25_Martiou

Irodotou

To Vlihadia (3km);
Vothyni (3km)

To Therma
Beach (2.5km);
Gefyra Beach

Port police (☎ 2243 029 304) At the eastern side of
the port.

Post office A 10-minute walk northwest of Plateia
Eleftherias.

Tourist Information Kiosk (☎ 2243 050 879;
www.kalymnos-isl.gr; ⏱ 7.30am-10pm in summer) In
the middle of the central promenade.

Sights
North of Plateia Kyprou, housed in a neoclassical mansion that once belonged to a
wealthy sponge merchant, is the **Archaeological Museum** (☎ 2243 023 113; adult/student €1/2;
⏱ 8.30am-2pm Tue-Sun). In one room there are
some Neolithic and Bronze Age objects.
Other rooms are reconstructed as they were
when the Vouvalis family lived here.

In the centre of the waterfront is the
Nautical & Folklore Museum (☎ 2243 051 361;
adult/student €2/1; ⏱ 8am-1.30pm Mon-Fri, 10am-
12.30pm Sat & Sun). Its collection is of traditional
regional dress, plus a section on the history
of sponge diving.

Sleeping
While there is a fair selection of sleeping
options in Pothia, most travellers head out
of the town to the resorts. One good reason
to take a room in Pothia is to be on hand to
catch the notoriously early morning ferry
heading south.

Pension Greek House (☎ 2243 023 752; s/d
with €16/25) This pension, inland from the
port, is a pleasant budget option with cosy

wood-panelled rooms with kitchen facilities. More expensive and better-equipped studios are also available upon request.

Hotel Panorama (☎ 2243 023 138; s/d €25/45 incl breakfast) This small hotel is situated high up and enjoys one of the best views in Pothia. The place is clean and breezy and it has a pleasant breakfast area.

Archontiko Hotel (☎ /fax 2243 024 149; s/d €35/45 incl breakfast) At the south end of the quay, is this cool and pleasant hotel in a renovated century-old mansion. All the rooms have fridges, TV and phone.

Eating

Xefteris Taverna (☎ 2243 028 642; mains €3-5.50) This century-old and pretty basic taverna serves delicious, inexpensive food. The meal-sized dolmades (vine leaves stuffed with rice and meat) and the *stifado* are recommended.

Pizza Imia (☎ 2243 050 809; pizzas €6-8) There's no shortage of fast-food joints in Pothia, but you can devour scrumptious wood-oven pizza in all permutations and flavours at this busy waterfront place.

To Tholami (☎ 2243 051 900; mains €3.50-5) This well-established eatery is equally popular with locals and visitors. Suggested dishes are octopus patties and grilled tuna steaks.

Martha's Barba Petros Taverna (☎ 2243 029 678; fish €6-11) Of the fish tavernas on the eastern waterfront, this is one of the better and more reliable choices; the crab salad is a delicious and filling starter.

Pandelis Restaurant (☎ 2243 051 508; mains €4.50-6) The specialities at this homely eatery are goat in red wine sauce and the home-made dolmades, but all food is well prepared and presented.

AROUND POTHIA

Running northwards from the port is a busy, densely populated valley with a series of almost contiguous settlements. High up on the west side of the valley you may spot the scars of Kalymnos' completed, but as yet nonfunctioning airport, widely held to be a costly white elephant. Built at the wrong angle to the prevailing winds, it is thought that the airport is too risky for use by civilian aircraft.

On the same side and nearby the ruined **Castle of the Knights of St John** (or Kastro Hrysoherias) looms to the left of the Pothia–Horio road. There is a small **church** inside the battlements.

On the east side of the valley **Pera Kastro** was a pirate-proof village inhabited until the 18th century. Within the crumbling walls are the ruins of stone houses and six tiny, well-kept churches. Steps lead up to Pera Kastro from **Horio**. It's a strenuous climb but the splendid views make it worthwhile.

A tree-lined road continues from Horio to **Panormos** (also called Elies), a pretty village 5km from Pothia. Its prewar name of Elies (olives) derived from its abundant olive groves, which were destroyed in WWII. An enterprising postwar mayor planted many trees and flowers to create beautiful panoramas wherever one looked – hence its present name, meaning 'panorama'. The sandy beaches of **Kandouni**, **Linaria** and **Platys Gialos** are all within walking distance.

Moni Agiou Savra is reached along a turn-off left from the Vothyni and Vlihadia road. You can enter the monastery but a strict dress code is enforced, so wear long sleeves and long trousers or skirt.

MYRTIES, MASOURI & ARMEOS
ΜΥΡΤΙΕΣ, ΜΑΣΟΥΡΙ & ΑΡΜΕΟΣ

From Panormos the road continues to the west coast with stunning views of Telendos Islet until the road winds down into **Myrties** (myr-*tyez*), **Masouri** (mah-*soo*-ri) and **Armeos** (ar-*me*-os). These contiguous and busy resort centres host the lion's share of Kalymnos' package holiday industry. The three centres are essentially one long street packed head to tail with restaurants, bars, souvenir shops and minimarkets. On the land side, apartments and studios fill the hillside, while on the sea side an extinct volcano plug separates the dark sand beach into two distinct sections – the Myrties beach with Melitsahas harbour and the marginally better Masouri and Armeos beaches.

Come here if you like an active holiday. There are exchange bureaus, car and motorcycle rental outlets and even an Internet café. From Myrties there's a daily caïque to Xirokambos on Leros (€6), and Emborios (€6) in the north of Kalymnos.

In recent years Kalymnos has become something of a mecca for **rock climbers**. Some spectacular limestone walls backing the resorts now attract legions of climbers looking for some seriously challenging extreme sport. There are about 21 documented climbs awaiting the adventurous. The **Municipal Athletics Organisation** (☎ /fax 2243 051 601; www.kalymnos-isl.gr/climbing) is a good place to start for the full low-down on the activity that pulls in visitors from as early as March onwards.

Most accommodation in Masouri and Myrties is block-booked by tour groups. There are a couple of places that deal with walk-ins. On the Myrties side of the resort strip are the 12 smallish, but comfy **Studios Fotini** (☎ 2243 047 016; d €30), each with a fridge and cooking ring. Each room has a view over the small harbour of Melitsahas. Over in Masouri and on the hill side of the main road are the somewhat more spacious **Tina's Studios** (☎ 2243 048 390; www.tinastudios.tripod.com; d €30; ⚡) each with kitchenette, fridge and large seaside verandas.

There's no shortage of places to eat. A top choice is **I Drosia** (☎ 2243 048 745; seafood mezedes €5-12) overlooking Melitsahas harbour. Among the excellent mezedes on offer are *kalognomones* (local mussels), *ahini* (sea urchins) and a real treat – whole squid stuffed with creamy feta cheese.

In Masouri, **To Iliovasilema** (☎ 2243 047 683; mains €4-6) distinguishes itself by its service, though its *kondosouvli* (Cypriot-style spit-roasted meat) is particularly succulent while close by, **Kelly's** (☎ 2243 048 390; mains 3-6) serves up breakfast, lunch and dinner with staples like mousakas and *stifado* and a smattering of French-influenced dishes.

TELENDOS ISLET ΝΗΣΟΣ ΤΕΛΕΝΔΟΣ

The lovely, tranquil and (almost) traffic-free islet of Telendos, with a little quayside hamlet, was part of Kalymnos until separated by an earthquake in AD 554. Nowadays it's a great escape from the busy resort strip opposite. Caïque for Telendos depart every half-hour from the Myrties quay between 8am and 1am (€1.50 one way).

If you turn right from the Telendos quay, you will pass the ruins of a Roman basilica. Further on, there are several pebble-and-sand beaches. To reach the far superior, 100m-long and fine-pebble **Hohlakas Beach**, turn left from the quay and then right at the sign to the beach. Follow the paved path up and over the hill for 10 minutes.

Telendos has quite a few rooms to stay and one hotel. All have pleasant, clean rooms with bathroom. Opposite the quay is **Pension & Telendos Taverna** (☎ 2243 047 502; d €24), while adjoining the café of the same name is **On the Rocks Cafe Rooms** (☎ 2243 048 260; www.telendos.com; studios €40) with four studios equipped with fridge, TV, iron, hairdryer and mosquito nets.

Telendos' only hotel as such is **Hotel Porto Potha** (☎ 2243 047 321; portopotha@klm.forthnet.gr; s/d €25/30; ⚡), 100m beyond On the Rocks Cafe. Rooms are airy and bright and there's a large lobby where guests come to relax and watch TV over a drink.

The best place to eat is **On the Rocks Cafe** (☎ 2243 048 260; mains €4.50-7) where Greek-Australian owner George serves well-prepared meat and fish dishes as well as vegetarian mousakas, or baked or grilled tuna and swordfish. It becomes a lively music bar at night – with over 300 cocktails to choose from – and on Friday and Monday evenings there's 'Greek Night'.

In a little lane behind the waterfront, **Barba Stathis** (☎ 2243 047 953; mains €5-6) does a great spin on octopus in red sauce *(ohtapodi stifado)*, as well as octopus patties.

EMBORIOS ΕΜΠΟΡΕΙΟΣ

The scenic west coast road winds a further 11.5km from Masouri to Emborios, where there's a pleasant, shaded sand-and-pebble beach, a minimarket and **Artistico Café** (☎ 2243 040 115) for evening entertainment that sometimes features live guitar renditions.

One of the better places to stay is **Harry's Apartments** (☎ 2243 040 062; d/tr €27/33), made all the more attractive by its lush flower garden and adjoining **Paradise Restaurant** (☎ 2243 040 062; mains €3.50-6.50) run by the charming Evdokia. She rustles up a good line in vegetarian dishes such as *revithokeftedes* and *pites* with fillings such as aubergine, vegetables and onion. Stuffed courgette flowers are another of her specialities.

VATHYS & RINA ΒΑΘΥΣ & PINA

Vathys, 13km northeast of Pothia, is one of the most beautiful and peaceful parts of the island. Vathys means 'deep' in Greek and refers to the slender fjord that cuts through high cliffs into the fertile valley, where narrow roads wind between citrus orchards. There is no beach at Vathys' harbour, Rina, but you can swim off the jetty at the south side of the harbour. **Water taxis** (☎ 2243 031 316) take tourists to quiet coves nearby.

Vathys has two places to stay, both at the little harbour of Rina. **Hotel Galini** (☎ 2243 031 241; fax 2243 031 100; d €30 incl full breakfast) is marginally better on the basis of convenience; but higher up on the hill and messier to get to with heavy luggage is **Pension Manolis** (☎ 2243 031 300; s/d €21/25) with neat basic rooms and private bathrooms enjoying the best views. The pension has a communal kitchen and is surrounded by an attractive garden.

A few harbourside tavernas ring the port: of these **Restaurant Galini** (☎ 2243 031 241; mains €4-5) is part of Hotel Galini and is a friendly place to eat. Roast local pork and grilled octopus are two of its recommended dishes. In a stone-clad building opposite is the cosy and intimate **Taverna tou Limaniou** (The Harbour's Taverna; ☎ 2243 031 206; mains €4.50-5.50). Ask for the pork and chicken special, or the garlic prawn *saganaki* (fried cheese).

LEROS ΛΕΡΟΣ

pop 8207

Travellers looking for an island that is unmistakably Greek and still relatively untouched by mass commercial tourism will find it on Leros, a destination surprisingly little known to foreign travellers, though well known for years to the discerning Greek public. Leros is a medium-sized island in the northern Dodecanese offering an attractive mix of sun, sea, rest and recreation, a stunning medieval castle and some excellent dining opportunities.

The island also offers gentle, hilly countryside dotted with small holdings and huge, impressive, almost landlocked bays, which look more like lakes than open sea. The immense natural harbour at Lakki was the principal naval base of the Italians in the eastern Mediterranean, and is now a curious living architectural museum of Italian Fascist Art Deco buildings.

Getting There & Away
AIR
There is a flight daily to Athens (€54, one hour) as well as three flights a week to Rhodes (from €41, two hours 10 minutes) via Kos (from €38, 25 minutes). There are also three flights a week to Astypalea (from €39, 20 minutes). **Olympic Airways** (☎ 2247 022 844) is in Platanos, before the turn-off for Pandeli. The **airport** (☎ 2247 022 777) is near Partheni in the north. There is no airport bus.

EXCURSION BOAT
The caïque leaves Xirokambos at 7.30am daily for Myrties on Kalymnos (€6 one way). In summer Lipsi-based caïque make daily trips between Agia Marina and Lipsi. The trip costs €15 return.

FERRY
Leros is on the main north–south route for ferries between Rhodes and Piraeus. There are daily departures from Lakki to Piraeus (€23, 11 hours), Kos (€7.20, 3¼ hours) and Rhodes (€16.30, 7¼ hours), as well as two weekly to Samos (€7.50, 3½ hours). Ferry offices are all in Lakki.

HYDROFOIL & CATAMARAN
In summer there are hydrofoils and a catamaran every day to Patmos (€9.50, 45 minutes), Lipsi (€7.20, 20 minutes), Samos (€15, two hours), Kos (€12.30, one hour) and Rhodes (€28, 3¼ hours). Hydrofoils and the catamaran leave from Agia Marina.

Getting Around
The hub for Leros' buses is Platanos. There are four buses daily to Partheni via Alinda and six buses to Xirokambos via Lakki (€0.73 flat fare).

There is no shortage of car, motorcycle and bicycle rental outlets around the island.

LAKKI ΛΑΚΚΙ
Arriving at Lakki (lah-*kee*) by boat is akin to stepping into a long abandoned Fellini film set. The grandiose buildings and wide tree-lined boulevards dotted around the Dodecanese are best (or worst) shown here, for Lakki was built as a Fascist showpiece during the Italian occupation. Very few people linger in Lakki, though it has decent accommodation and restaurants, and there are some nice and secluded swimming opportunities on the road past the port.

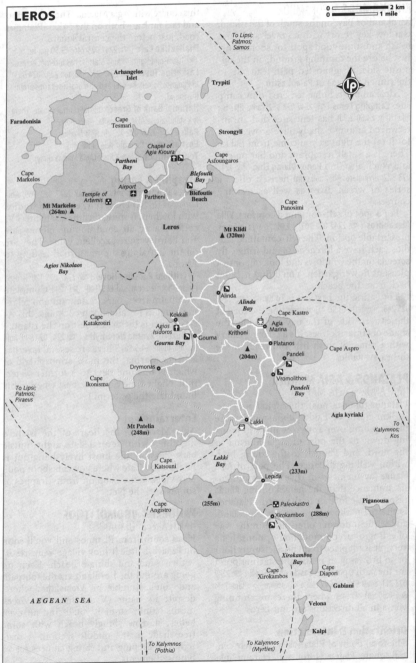

LEROS

0 _____ 2 km
0 _____ 1 mile

To Lipsi;
Patmos;
Samos

**Arhangelos
Islet**

Trypiti

Cape
Tesmari

Strongyli

Chapel of
Agia Kioura

*Partheni
Bay*

Cape
Asfoungaros

Faradonisia

Cape
Markelos

*Blefoutis
Bay*

Airport

Temple of
Artemis

Partheni

**Blefoutis
Beach**

Mt Markelos
(264m) ▲

Leros

Mt Klidi
▲ (320m)

Cape
Panosimi

*Agios Nikolaos
Bay*

Alinda

*Alinda
Bay*

Cape Kastro

Kokkali

Agia
Marina

Cape
Katakrotiri

Agios
Isidoros

Krithoni

Cape Aspro

Gourna

Platanos

Gourna Bay

(204m) ▲

Pandeli

Drymonas

Vromolithos

Cape
Ikonisma

*Pandeli
Bay*

To Lipsi;
Patmos;
Piraeus

Agia kyriaki

Mt Patelia
(248m) ▲

Lakki

To
Kalymnos;
Kos

*Lakki
Bay*

Cape
Katsouni

Lepida

▲ (233m)

Piganousa

Cape
Angistro

▲
(255m)

Paleokastro

Xirokambos

▲
(288m)

*Xirokambos
Bay*

Cape
Diapori

Cape
Xirokambos

Gabiani

AEGEAN SEA

Velona

Kalpi

To Kalymnos
(Pothia)

To Kalymnos
(Myrties)

DODECANESE

XIROKAMBOS ΞΗΡΟΚΑΜΠΟΣ

Xirokambos Bay, on the south of the island, is a low-key resort with a gravel-and-sand beach and some good spots for snorkelling. Just before the camping ground, on the opposite side, a signposted path leads up to the ruined fortress of **Paleokastro**.

Xirokambos is home to Leros' only camp site. **Camping Leros** (☎ 2247 023 372; camp sites per adult/tent €4.50/2.50) has tent sites that are interwoven among a shady olive grove. Look for it on the right as you come from Lakki. There is a small restaurant and bar on site and you'll also find **Panos Diving Club** (☎ 2247 023 372; divingleros@hotmail.com) here. It offers a series of wreck dives as well as training courses.

For a spot of self-contained comfort, **Villa Alexandros** (☎ 2247 022 202; d €48; 🗶) is a very presentable option. The self-contained studios each have a kitchenette and fridge, fly screens on the windows and look out onto a pleasant flower garden. You'll find it 150m back from the beach.

For eating the best bet is **To Kyma** (☎ 2247 025 248; mayirefta €3.50-4), straddling the road at the eastern side of the bay and under the shade of tamarisk trees. It's a relaxing eatery with a range of fresh fish and ready-made dishes available.

PLATANOS & AGIA MARINA
ΠΛΑΤΑΝΟΣ & ΑΓΙΑ ΜΑΡΙΝΑ

Platanos (*plah*-ta-nos), the capital of Leros, is 3km north of Lakki. It's a picturesque place spilling over a narrow hill and pouring down to the port of Agia Marina to the north and Pandeli to the south, both within walking distance. The port of **Agia Marina** (ay-*i*-a ma-*ri*-na) has a more authentic ambience than the neighbouring **Alinda** resort a little further to the north. Platanos is the main shopping area for the island, and while it doesn't offer much in the way of eating or accommodation options, it's a very pleasant place to spend a leisurely hour or so browsing. It is also the starting point for the path up to the **Castle of Pandeli** (☎ 2247 023 211; adult €1 castle, €2 castle & museum; 🕒 8am-1pm & 5-8.30pm), from where there are stunning views in all directions around Leros.

Orientation & Information

The focal point of Platanos is the lively central square, Plateia N Roussou. Harami links this square with Agia Marina. The bus station and taxi rank are both on the Lakki–Platanos road, just before the central square.

Enallaktiko Cafe (☎ 2247 025 746; €3.50 per hr; 🕒 10am-midnight) In Agia Marina; has Internet access.

Laskarina Tours (☎ 2247 024 550; fax 2247 024 551) In Platanos; is very helpful and also organises trips around the island.

National Bank of Greece On the central square. There is a stand-alone ATM at Agia Marina's port.

Police (☎ 2247 022 222) In Agia Marina.

Post office On the right side of Harami.

Tourist Information Kiosk (Agia Marina quay)

Sleeping & Eating

Tassos II Appartments (☎ /fax 2247 023 769; Agia Marina; d €42; 🗶) These fully equipped studios with kitchen, ironing facilities, satellite TV, coffee maker, air-conditioning, money safe and hairdryer are excellent value. They are on the left along the main road leading to Alinda.

Crithoni Paradise Hotel (☎ 2247 025 120; lerosparadise@hotmail.com; s/d €88/120; P 🗶) Complete with palm trees, bars, restaurant and relaxing lounges for afternoon cocktails, this A-class hotel is by far the best on the island.

Ouzeri-Taverna Neromylos (☎ 2247 024 894; Agia Marina; mains €4-5.50) There are several tavernas at Agia Marina, the most atmospheric of which is this one next to a former watermill. Night-time dining is best when lights illuminate the watermill.

Entertainment

Agia Marina is the heart of the island's nightlife, with several late-night music bars. Possibly the most lively hang-out is Enallaktiko Cafe where you can shoot pool, play video games, sup on frothy frappes or simply surf the Net.

PANDELI & VROMOLITHOS
ΠΑΝΤΕΛΙ & ΒΡΩΜΟΛΙΘΟΣ

Head south from Platanos and you'll soon hit **Pandeli**, a little fishing village–cum-resort with a sand-and-shingle beach. Keep on going around the headland via the footpath and you'll stumble on **Vromolithos** where, despite its name (Vromolithos in Greek means 'stinky stone'), you'll find an even better, narrow shingly beach with some tree shade in the middle section. A scattering of sleeping and eating choices serves both settlements.

At a pinch Pandeli wins in the sleeping stakes as there's a bit more concentrated daytime activity and nightlife to pull in the punters. Easy to spot for its striking blue-and-white columned facade, **Rooms to Rent Kavos** (☎ 2247 023 247; d €35) is a sensible choice. Rooms are largish, sport balconies and have fans and a fridge. Grab a front room if you want a harbour view.

Up on the hill is the ever popular **Pension Rodon** (☎ 2247 022 075; www.gotohellas.com; d €30). Open year-round it is a reliable and welcoming choice with comfortable rooms.

The eating scene is dominated by the exceptional **Mezedopoleio Dimitris** (☎ 2247 025 626; mezedes €2.50-7), which would win out on its views alone. Its delicious mezedes (40 to 50 to choose from) include cheese courgettes, stuffed calamari, and onion and cheese pies; main courses include chicken in retsina and pork in red sauce. It's next to Pension Rodon.

At Pandeli, **Psaropoula** (☎ 2247 025 200; mains €5) is right on the beach and is as good as any of the several tavernas plying their trade here. Psaropoula has a wide-ranging menu featuring fish; the prawn souvlaki with bacon is suggested.

KRITHONI & ALINDA ΚΡΙΘΩΝΙ & ΑΛΙΝΤΑ

Krithoni and Alinda are contiguous resorts on the wide Alinda Bay, running about 3km northwest from Agia Marina. Most of the action is concentrated at the Alinda end where the only real danger is from the parades of kamikaze motorcyclists who roar indiscriminately up and down the narrow beachside road, pausing only to partake of coffee and gossip at the many buzzing cafeterias. Despite the occasional racket, the beach is pebbled and the water clean. Further to the north around the bay are some quieter coves and beaches.

On Krithoni's waterfront there is a poignant, well-kept **war cemetery**. After the Italian surrender in WWII, Leros saw fierce fighting between German and British forces. The cemetery contains the graves of 179 British, two Canadian and two South African soldiers.

Not surprisingly for the island's main resort area there are plenty of sleeping choices. **Hotel Gianna** (☎ /fax 2247 024 135; s/d €30/40) is 100m up the airport road and far enough away from the 'strip' to be quiet. All

rooms are pleasantly furnished. Behind the War Cemetery, **Studios & Apartments Diamantis** (☎ 2247 022 378; d/tr €36/44) is a sparkling, pine-furnished place and is another good choice. For some comfortable self-catering **Tassos Studios I** (☎ /fax 2247 023 769; studios €42) has beautiful fully equipped mini-apartments close to Krithoni beach, run by the same owners as Tassos II in Agia Marina.

Finikas Taverna (☎ 2247 022 695; mezedes €2.50-4.20) is about the only really Greek place left. This waterfront taverna in Alinda offers 15 types of salad and 20 different mezedes. When available, the delicious fish soup is worth opting for, as is the swordfish steak.

PATMOS ΠΑΤΜΟΣ

pop 3044

Patmos could well be the ideal Greek island destination, with a beguiling mix of qualities. It appeals in equal doses to the culturally inclined, the religiously motivated, gastronomes and sun worshippers, shoppers, yachties, bookaholics and travellers simply seeking to unwind. Patmos is a place of pilgrimage for both Orthodox and Western Christians, for it was here that St John wrote his divinely inspired revelation (the Apocalypse). Patmos is the *primus inter pares* place to come and experience Orthodox Easter, when advance accommodation bookings are absolutely essential. Patmos is instantly palatable and entices the visitor to linger and to almost certainly return another time.

History

In AD 95 St John the Divine was banished to Patmos from Ephesus by the pagan Roman Emperor Domitian. While residing in a cave on the island, St John wrote the Book of Revelations. In 1088 the Blessed Christodoulos, an abbot who came from Asia Minor to Patmos, obtained permission from the Byzantine Emperor Alexis I Komninos to build a monastery to commemorate St John. Pirate raids necessitated powerful fortifications, so the monastery looks like a mighty castle.

Under the Duke of Naxos, Patmos became a semiautonomous monastic state and achieved such wealth and influence that it was able to resist Turkish oppression. In

DODE

the early 18th century a school of theology and philosophy was founded by Makarios and it flourished until the 19th century.

Gradually the island's wealth became polarised into secular and monastic entities. The secular wealth was acquired through shipbuilding, an industry that diminished with the arrival of the steam ship.

Getting There & Away

EXCURSION BOAT

The local *Patmos Express* leaves Patmos daily for Lipsi at 10am (€7 return) and returns at 4pm.

The Patmos-based **Delfini** (☎ 2247 031 995) goes to Marathi every day in the high season and Monday and Thursday at other times

(€15 return). Twice a week it also calls in at Arki. From Marathi a local caïque will take you across to Arki.

FERRY

Patmos is well connected with ferries to Piraeus (€22, eight hours), Rhodes (€19, 7½ hours) and several islands in between. Services are provided by Blue Star Ferries, DANE Sealines and G&A Ferries, while the F/B *Nisos Kalymnos* provides additional links to Arki, Agathonisi and Samos. Blue Star runs a superior, high-speed service.

HYDROFOIL & CATAMARAN

There are daily hydrofoils to Rhodes (€37.50, five hours) and destinations in between.

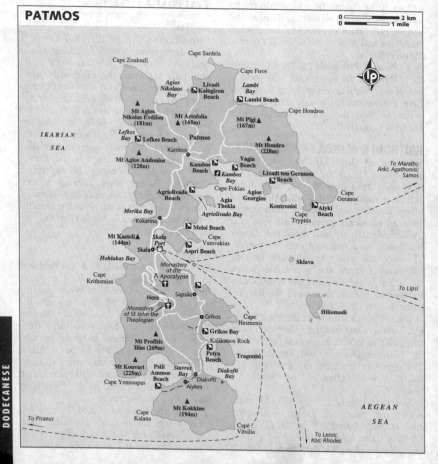

PATMOS

DODECANESE

Twice a week a hydrofoil runs to and from Agathonisi (€12, 40 minutes).

The *Dodekanisos Express* catamaran calls in at Patmos six times a week during summer. Tickets can be bought at **Dodekanisos Shipping Agency** (☎ 2247 029 303; liapi1@otenet.gr) in Skala.

Getting Around
BUS
From Skala there are 11 buses daily in July and August to Hora (€0.73), eight to Grikos (€0.78) and four to Kambos (€0.78). The frequency drops off during the rest of the year. There is no bus service to Lambi.

CAR & MOTORCYCLE
There are motorcycle and car rental outlets in Skala. Competition is fierce, so shop around. **Australis Motor Rentals** (☎ 2247 032 723) rents scooters for between €9 and €18 per day.

EXCURSION BOAT
Boats go to all the island's beaches from Skala, leaving about 11am and returning about 4pm.

TAXI
Taxis (☎ 2247 031 225) congregate at Skala's taxi rank. Sample fares include Meloï Beach €2.50, Lambi €5.50, Grikos €3.50 and Hora €3.50.

SKALA ΣΚΑΛΑ
Patmos' port town is Skala (*ska*-la), a bright and glitzy town draped around a curving bay and only visible from arriving ships once the protective headland has been rounded. It's a busy port and large cruise ships are often anchored offshore and smaller ones at Skala's harbour. Once the cruise ships and daily ferries depart, Skala reverts to being a fairly normal, livable port town. It has a wide range of good accommodation and restaurants, and all the island's major facilities are here.

Orientation & Information
Facing inland from the quay, turn right to reach the main stretch of waterfront where excursion boats and yachts dock. Further along you will reach Netia, where there are a considerable number of accommodation options. The right side of the large, white Italianate building opposite the quay overlooks the central square. For the road to Hora, turn left from the quay and right

at Taverna Grigoris. The bus terminal and taxi rank are at the large quay.

Astoria Travel (☎ 2247 031 205; fax 2247 031 975) On the waterfront near the quay; has helpful staff.

ATMs There is one ATM-equipped National Bank of Greece in Skala plus a stand alone ATM.

Blue Bay Internet Café (☎ 2247 031 165; €4 per hr; �9am-7pm) At the Hotel Blue Bay (see Sleeping, p316).

Hospital (☎ 2247 031 211) Two kilometres along the road to Hora.

Municipal Tourist Office (☎ 2247 031 666; ☉ summer only) Shares the Italianate building with the post office and police station.

Port police (☎ 2247 031 231) Behind the large quay's passenger-transit building.

Travel Point (☎ 2247 032 801; info@travelpoint.gr) Just inland from the central square; has helpful staff and a room-finding service.

Sleeping
BUDGET
Domatia owners commonly meet all arrivals at the port. Ignore suggestions by touts that places listed here are closed.

Pension Maria Pascalidis (☎ 2247 032 152; s/d €15/20) One of the better budget options is on the road leading to Hora. These simple but quite presentable rooms are set amid a leafy citrus tree garden, though the dull brown furnishings of the rooms are not the most appealing.

Yvonne's Studios (☎ 2247 033 066; www.12met.gr/yvonni; s/d €25/45; ⬛) Call into Yvonne's shop in the street behind the waterfront in quiet Hohlakas Bay to find these very pleasant self-contained studios.

Domatia Katina (☎ /fax 2247 031 327; s/d €35/45) These four tidy rooms out on the edge of Skala each has a kitchenette and a four-poster bed. Turn right at the last street on the north side of Netia to find them.

Pension Avgerinos (☎ /fax 2247 032 118; d €44) In a slightly quieter part of Netia, Pension Avgerinos is run by a welcoming Greek-Australian couple. Rooms are cosy and in an elevated part of the quarter affording good views over the bay.

MID-RANGE
Captain's House (☎ 2247 031 793; www.greekhotel net.com; s/d €53/73 incl breakfast; ⬛ ⬛) Each comfortable room here has a TV, fridge and phone. The front rooms have the best views but do get the noise from the often boisterous nightlife nearby.

Hotel Blue Bay (☎ 2247 031 165; www.bluebay.50g .com; s/d €54/68) This Australian-Greek–owned waterfront hotel has very clean, pleasantly furnished rooms and is at the quieter far southern end of Skala.

Porto Scoutari Hotel (☎ 2247 033 123; www.porto scoutari.com; d/tr €75-129 incl breakfast; P ⓛ ⓧ) The classiest and most romantic place to sleep on the island is here, just north of Skala on the hill enjoying stunning views. Each self-contained and individually named studio is impeccably decorated, with a large personal porch to sit out on.

Eating

Hiliomodi Ouzeri (☎ 2247 034 080; meze platter €8) For the freshest fish on the island head to this ouzeri for its excellent seafood and seafood-based mezedes. Open all year, the Hiliomodi is patronised as much by permanent locals as by discerning foreign visitors.

Grigoris Taverna (☎ 2247 031 515; mains €3-5) Grigoris, on the corner of the Hora road, is always very popular, and his dolmades are recommended along with his range of grills and *mayirefta*.

Loukas Restaurant (☎ 2247 031 832; grills €4-6) Succulent grill dishes are served in this leafy, shaded garden restaurant, in the backstreets 150m inland from the harbour.

Pandelis Taverna (☎ 2247 031 230; mains €2.50-4) One of the more picturesque and always thriving eateries is this busy little taverna that caters well to cruise groups and travellers alike. The service is efficient and the street dining is atmospheric.

Entertainment

Skala's music nightlife revolves around a scattering of bars and the odd club or two.
Consolato Music Club (☎ 2247 031 194; ☾ 9pm-late) A popular bar that is open year-round.

Aman (☎ 2247 032 323) Another popular spot. This is more a place to sit outside on its tree-shaded patio and relax to music while nursing a cold beer or cocktail.

MONASTERIES & HORA

The immense **Monastery of St John the Theologian**, with its buttressed grey walls, crowns the island of Patmos. A 4km sealed road leads in from Skala, but many people prefer to walk up the Byzantine path. To do this, walk up the Skala–Hora road and take the steps to the right, 100m beyond the far side

of the football field. The path begins opposite the top of these steps.

A little way along, a dirt path to the left leads through pine trees to the **Monastery of the Apocalypse** (☎ 2247 031 234; treasury €3; ☾ 8am-1.30pm daily, 4-6pm Tue, Thu & Sun), built around the cave where St John received his divine revelation. In the cave you can see the rock that the saint used as a pillow, and the triple fissure in the roof, from which the voice of God issued, and which is said to symbolise the Holy Trinity.

The finest frescoes of this monastery are those in the outer narthex. The priceless contents in the monastery's **treasury** include icons, ecclesiastical ornaments, embroideries and pendants made of precious stones.

Huddled around the monastery are the immaculate whitewashed houses of **Hora**. These houses are a legacy of the island's great wealth of the 17th and 18th centuries. Some of them have been bought and renovated by wealthy Greeks and foreigners.

There are no hotel or domatia signs in Hora. There is accommodation, but it is expensive and the best places are prebooked months in advance. Try Travel Point in Skala (see Orientation & Information, p315) which has at least 10 traditional houses for rent. For dining, **Vangelis Taverna** (☎ 2247 031 967; mains €4.50-6) on the lively central square is probably your best bet. Good menu choices include *bekri meze* (pork cubes in a spicy sauce with vegetables) and the similar *spetsofaï*.

NORTH OF SKALA

The pleasant, tree-shaded **Meloï Beach** is just 2km northeast of Skala, along a turn-off from the main road. Here you have at least a couple of sleeping choices. **Stefanos Camping** (☎ 2247 031 821; camp sites €6.50) is a fairly good camping ground by island standards, with bamboo-shaded sites, a minimarket, café-bar and motorcycle rental facilities. There's also the well-regarded and economical *psistaria* **O Barbas** (☎ 2247 031 754; grills €3-5) on site. Nearby are the unoriginally listed and fairly unadorned **Rooms to Rent** (☎ 2247 031 213; d €23), 50m back from the beach. The family also owns some newer rooms nearby, at a slightly higher price.

Two kilometres further along the main road there's a turn-off right to the relatively quiet **Agriolivado Beach**. The main road

JUDI WILLOUGHBY

Vineyards at Embonas (p273), Rhodes, Dodecanese

Bell tower in Masouri (p308),
Kalymnos, Dodecanese

WAYNE WALTON

PAUL HELLANDER

Moni Agiou Panteleimona (p292), Tilos,
Dodecanese

PAUL HELLANDER

Makrygialos beach
(p278), Karpathos,
Dodecanese

Rina (p309), Kalymnos, Dodecanese

Waterfront, Kastellorizo (p283), Dodecanese

Church of Agios Nikolaos (p274),
Halki, Dodecanese

Petaloudes (p272), Rhodes,
Dodecanese

continues to the inland village of **Kambos** and then descends to the shingle, but protected and child-friendly beach where there is a rather Greek-oriented beach scene. Eating choices include **To Agnanti** (☎ 2247 032 733; mezedes €2-3), a neat little ouzeri with a range of cheap mezedes, though for a little extra you can sample the pasta stuffed with seafood special. At the northern end of the beach is the cool **George's Place** (☎ 2247 031 881; snacks €3-5) where you can play backgammon to laid-back music while grazing on light snacks and drinks.

From Kambos you can walk to the secluded pebbled **Vagia Beach** around the headland. The main road ends at **Lambi**, 9km from Skala, where there is a beautiful beach of multicoloured pebbles and yet another well-regarded beach taverna, **Psistaria Leonidas** (☎ 2247 031 490; mayirefta €2.50-3.50). Owner Leonidas rustles up a wide range of home-made mayirefta dishes, various fish of the day plates and highly recommended *saganaki*.

SOUTH OF SKALA

Sapsila is a quiet little corner 3km south of Skala, ideal for book lovers who want space and quiet and a couple of underused beaches to read on. The best chill-out spot to bunker down with a book for a week or so is the immaculate self-contained **Matheos Studios** (☎ 2247 032 119; d/tr studios €40/45). The eight fully equipped and tastefully decorated studios are set in a quiet, leafy garden 200m from Sapsila Beach.

Grikos, 1km further along over the hill, is a relaxed low-key resort with a narrow sandy beach and shallow, clean water. A cheap and unadorned place to sleep here is **Stamatis Rooms** (☎ 2247 031 302; d €35) where the rooms are comfortable enough, if not exactly luxurious. Eating is best undertaken at two places on the southwest side of Grikos Bay. **Flisvos Restaurant** (☎ 2247 031 764; mains €3-5) is a well-shaded, modern taverna dishing up standard grills and *mayirefta*. A further 100m along is the rather exciting **Ktima Petra** (☎ 2247 033 207; mains €4-7) with its emphasis on organic and home-grown products. Its stuffed and baked goat just melts in your mouth, and the organic cheese and vegetables simply shout flavour. Wash it down with a fragrant Myliasto Spyropoulou organic wine.

Diakofti, the last settlement in the south, is reached by a roundabout sealed road or a rougher and shorter coastal track passing the startling **Kalikatsos Rock** abutting pebbly **Petra Beach**. The long, sandy, tree-shaded **Psili Ammos** beach can be reached by excursion boat or walking track; here you'll find a seasonal and quite reasonable taverna.

LIPSI ΛΕΙΨΟΙ

pop 698

Lipsi (lip-*see*), 12km east of Patmos and 11km north of Leros, is the kind of place that few people know about, and once they have discovered it feel disinclined to share their discovery with others. It's a friendly place with the right balance of remoteness and 'civilisation'. There is comfortable accommodation, a pleasing choice of quality restaurants and a good selection of underpopulated beaches. Lipsi gained national and international fame in the summer of 2002 when the alleged leader of the November 17 terrorist group was found to be living a double life among the islanders. Apart from two or three days a year in August when pilgrims and revellers descend upon Lipsi for its major festival, you can have most of it to yourself.

Getting There & Away
EXCURSION BOAT

The *Captain Makis* and *Popi Express* do daily trips in summer to Agia Marina on Leros and to Skala on Patmos (both €14 return). *Black Beauty* and *Margarita* do 'Five Island' trips for around the same price. All four excursion boats can be found at the small quay in Lipsi village and all depart at around 10am each day.

FERRY

Lipsi is not well served by ferries. The F/B *Nisos Kalymnos* calls four times a week in summer (three times weekly the rest of the year), linking Lipsi with Samos and Rhodes and islands in between. G&A Ferries provides a weekly milk-run linking Lipsi with Piraeus via a host of in-between islands such as Fourni, Samos, Ikaria and Mykonos. The Patmos-based *Patmos Express* excursion boat arrives from Patmos every morning in summer at around 11am and departs for Patmos again at around 6pm (€7, one hour).

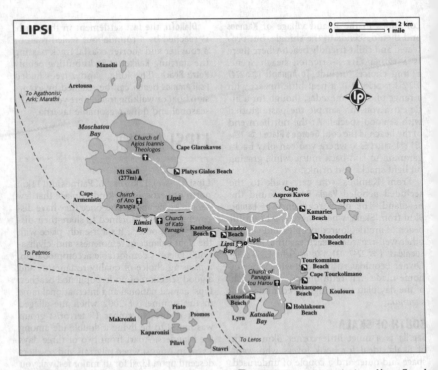

LIPSI

0 ———— 2 km
0 ———— 1 mile

Manolis

Aretousa

To Agathonisi;
Arki; Marathi

Moschatou
Bay

Church of
Agios Ioannis
Theologos

Cape Glarokavos

Mt Skafi
(277m) ▲

Platys Gialos Beach

Cape
Armenistis

Church
of Ano
Panagia

Lipsi

Cape
Aspros Kavos

Aspronisia

Kamaries
Beach

Kimisi
Bay

Church
of Kato
Panagia

Kambos
Beach

Liendou
Beach

Lipsi

Monodendri
Beach

To Patmos

Lipsi
Bay

Church of
Panagia
tou Harou

Tourkomnima
Beach

Cape Tourkolimano

Xirokampos
Beach

Kouloura

Piato

Psomos

Katsadia
Beach

Hohlakoura
Beach

Makronisi

Lyra

Katsadia
Bay

Kaparonisi

Pilavi

Stavri

To Leros

HYDROFOIL & CATAMARAN

In summer Kyriacoulis Hydrofoils calls at
Lipsi at least twice daily on its routes north
and south between Samos and Rhodes, with
further links to Patmos and Ikaria. The *Dodekanisos Express* catamaran calls in three
times a week in summer. Sample fares are
Rhodes (€36, 4½ hours) and Patmos (€9.40,
30 minutes).

Getting Around

Lipsi has three minibuses going to Platys
Gialos (€1), Katsadia and Hohlakoura (both
€1). Two taxis also operate on the island.
There are several motorcycle rental outlets.

LIPSI VILLAGE
Orientation & Information

All boats dock at Lipsi Port, where there are
two quays. The ferries, hydrofoils and catamaran all dock at the larger, outer jetty, while
excursion boats dock at a smaller jetty nearer
the centre of Lipsi village. It's a 500m walk
from the outer jetty to the village centre.

There is no organised official tourist
office to speak of, though **Laid Back Holidays**

(☎ 2247 041 141; www.lipsiweb.gr) or **Lipsos Travel**
(☎ /fax 2247 041 225), both in Lipsi village, will
be happy to help out with any queries.

The post office is on the central square,
and there is a freestanding Commercial
Bank ATM near the wide steps leading to
the main square. The **police** (☎ 2247 041 222)
and **port police** (☎ 2247 041 133) are to the right
of the wide steps.

Sights

Of macabre political interest is the **pink villa**
of alleged terrorist and leader of the ultra-
secretive November 17 terrorist group who
lived for a number of years under a pseu-
donym among the unsuspecting islanders.
The solitary-standing villa is visible high
on the bluff to the north side of the small
boat harbour (see the Terrorist Connection,
opposite). While it's not open for visitors,
the outer gate of the compound can be
reached via a cement track on the north
side of the bluff.

Lipsi's **museum** (admission free; ⏰ 11am-1pm) is
hardly earth shattering, but contains a small
collection of odd items such as pebbles and

DODECANESE

bottles of holy water from various locations around the world. It's on the main village square, opposite the large church.

Boat trips to the **offshore islands** are a popular diversion for a sail, picnic and swim (See Excursion Boat, p317).

Festivals & Events

The annual religious festival of **Panagia tou Harou** takes places on 24 August when the island fills up with visitors from all over the Dodecanese. After a religious festival and procession through the island's narrow roads with an icon of the Virgin Mary, all-night revelry takes place in the village square with live music, food and wine.

Sleeping

Studios Kalymnos (☎ 2247 041 141; www.lipsiweb.gr; d €36) One of the more appealing and certainly the most friendly places to stay is at these neat and airy studios, 800m from the quay on the east side of the village. Studios Kalymnos is set in a cool garden with a barbecue for guests, and has soothing chill-out music. Check in at the Laid Back Holidays booth on the ferry quay.

O Glaros (☎ 2247 041 360; d €28) Set back on the hill about 100m from the small boat harbour are these smallish but airy and comfortable rooms with a wide communal balcony and a well-equipped shared kitchen.

Flisvos Pension (☎ 2247 041 261; d/tr €35/42) The rooms of this simple pension at the southern end of the harbour front are equipped with fridges, but are otherwise unremarkable and probably slightly overpriced.

Hotel Calypso (☎ /fax 2247 041 420; d/tr €45/50) Opposite the excursion boat quay you'll find this D-class hotel with reasonably comfortable rooms in a good location.

Rooms Galini (☎ 2247 041 212; www.greeklodgings .gr; d €40) High up overlooking the harbour, Galini has pleasant, light rooms with refrigerator, cooking ring and balcony.

Rizos Studios (☎ 2247 041 215; fax 2247 041 225; d/tr €44/50) These exceptionally well-located studios are tastefully decorated, equipped with every kitchen utensil imaginable and enjoy a view over Liendou Bay. Contact **Lipsos Travel** (☎ /fax 2247 041 225) in the village for location details.

Eating

There are restaurants and cafés on the waterfront between the two quays, as well as one or two places up near the main square.

Yiannis Restaurant (☎ 2247 045 395; grills €5-6) The first one up of any significance is this popular *psistaria* near the main ferry quay. Grills feature in the main, though you will find the odd *mayirefta* and one or two meze-style dishes for vegetarians.

Psarotaverna Theologos (☎ 2247 041 248; fish €6-15) Next on the quay, owner Theologos

---

THE TERRORIST CONNECTION

The quiet island life of Lipsi suffered a rude shock on 17 July 2002 when agents of the Greece police special forces descended and arrested a greying sexagenarian 'professor' the moment he was about to board a hydrofoil for Patmos. Alekos Giotopoulos (known to the islanders for many years as Mihalis Oikonomou) had been pinpointed as the alleged leader of the shadowy November 17 Greek terrorist group, which for 28 years had terrorised, looted and murdered its way through Greek urban society. Not a single person had been arrested in that time, and the existence and whereabouts of the members of the group was a total mystery to Greece's security services. Following a botched bombing attempt by alleged co-terrorist Savvas Xeros in July 2002, evidence found at November 17 hideouts led police to the suspected leader of the group who had been living a quiet life as a retired 'academic' on Lipsi. Alekos Giotopoulos had been an active Marxist activist in the heady revolutionary days of the early 1970s in Paris and later in Greece, and had allegedly managed to spread his virulent form of politically motivated urban terrorism without detection throughout Greece. Meetings with international terrorist Carlos are believed to have been conducted in secret during the 1980s by Giotopoulos on islets off the coast of Lipsi. Giotopoulos and his French wife Marie-Thérèse Peignot lived in a rose-coloured villa high on a hill overlooking the port of Lipsi. The bunker-like residence now lies abandoned – attended to by the occasional cleaning lady – a silent sentinel to the day when terrorism stalked the lives of the friendly islanders of Lipsi.

only opens when he has caught his own fish to cook and that is not every day. However, the product is guaranteed to be very fresh as it comes straight off his caïque anchored in front of the taverna.

The Rock (☎ 2247 041 180; mezedes €1.50-2.50) This coffee bar and ouzeri offers some unusual mezedes such as sea urchins, while the succulent grilled octopus is a standard meze – best taken at sunset over a small glass of ouzo with ice.

Kalipso Restaurant (☎ 2247 041 060; grills €4-5) Adjoining the hotel of the same name, Kalipso serves up wholesome, low-priced food mixing a few *mayirefta* dishes with the stock fish and meat grills.

Cafe du Moulin (☎ 2247 041 416; snacks €3-4) The Moulin, up on the main square, is good for light lunches – omelettes, mousakas and the like. French is spoken by the owners.

AROUND THE ISLAND

Lipsi has quite a few beaches and all are within walking distance of Lipsi village. Some are shaded, some are not. Some are sandy, others gravelly. At least one is for nudism. Getting to them makes for pleasant walks through countryside dotted with smallholdings, olive groves and cypresses, but minibuses also go to most of them.

Liendou Beach is the most accessible and naturally the most popular beach. The water is very shallow and calm; this is the best beach for children. It's 500m from Lipsi village, just north of the ferry port over a small headland.

Next along is sandy **Kambos Beach**, a 1km walk along the same road that leads to Platys Gialos. Take the dirt road off to the left. There is some shade available.

Beyond Kambos Beach the road takes you, after a further 2.5km, to **Platys Gialos**, a lovely but narrow sandy beach with the decent **Kostas Restaurant** (☎ 6944 963 303; grills €4-5; ☺ 8am-6pm Jul-Aug, later on Wed & Sat). Owner Kostas Makris dishes up excellent fish and grill dishes as well as suckling pig. The water here is turquoise-coloured, shallow and ideal for children. The minibus runs here.

South 2km from Lipsi village is the sand-and-pebble **Katsadia Beach**, shaded with tamarisk trees and easily reached on foot, or by the hourly minibus. There are a couple of restaurants here. **Gambieris Taverna** (☎ 2247 041 087; mains €2.50-3.50) is a small,

rustic taverna, set back from the beach and owned by an elderly couple who serve simple meat and fish dishes. Their son, the English-speaking Christodoulos, runs the livelier **Dilaila Cafe Restaurant** (☎ 2247 041 041; mains €3-5), closer to the beach and caressed by an eclectic range of musical selections during the day and evening. Recommended dishes include vegetarian mousakas and chickpea patties.

The pebble **Hohlakoura Beach**, to the east of Katsadia, offers neither shade nor facilities. Further north, **Monodendri** is the island's unofficial nudist beach. It stands on a rocky peninsula, and there are no facilities. It is a 3km walk to get there, though it is reachable by motorcycle.

ARKI & MARATHI
ΑΡΚΟΙ & ΜΑΡΑΘΙ

Studded like earrings off the eastern side of Patmos these two almost forgotten satellite islands attract relatively few visitors and in the main these tend to be yachties or offbeat Greek media personalities. There are no cars and few permanent residents, and so they make for ideal hideaways for a few solitary days.

Getting There & Away
The F/B *Nisos Kalymnos* calls in once or twice a week as it goes between Patmos

ARKI & MARATHI

AEGEAN SEA

Arki

Church of Metamorfosis

Arki

Marathi

Tiganakia Bay

Church of Agios Nikolaos

Marathi Beach

To Patmos

To Lipsi

and Samos. However, this depends on the weather as the ferry is met by a small local caïque to or from which passengers must precariously transfer just outside the harbour entrance.

In summer the Lipsi-based excursion boats visit Arki and Marathi, and the Patmos-based caïque **Delfini** (☎ 2247 031 995) does frequent trips (€15 return).

ARKI ΑΡΚΟΙ
pop 50
Tiny Arki, 5km north of Lipsi, is hilly, with shrubs but few trees. Its only settlement, the little west coast port, is also called Arki. Islanders make a meagre living from fishing.

There is no post office or police on the island, but there is a cardphone. Away from its little settlement, the island seems almost mystical in its peace and stillness.

The **Church of Metamorfosis** stands on a hill behind the settlement. From its terrace are superb views of Arki and its surrounding islets. The cement road between Taverna Trypas and Taverna Nikolaos leads to the path up to the church. The church is locked but ask a local if it's possible to look inside.

Several secluded **sandy coves** can be reached along a path skirting the right side of the bay. To reach the path, walk around the last house at the far right of the bay, go through a little wooden gate in the stone wall, right near the sea, and continue ahead.

Tiganakia Bay on the southeast coast has a good sandy beach. To walk there from Arki village, take the cement road that skirts the north side of the bay. The bay is reached by a network of goat tracks and lies at the far side of the headland. You will recognise it by the incredibly bright turquoise water and the offshore islets.

Arki has three tavernas, two of which run a few basic but comfortable rooms. Bookings are necessary in August. First up, **O Trypas Taverna & Rooms** (☎ 2247 032 507; d €30; mains €4-6) is to the right of the quay, as you face inland. Suggested dishes are black-eyed beans (*fasolia mavromatika*) and *pastos tou trypa*, a kind of salted fish dish. Nearby **Taverna Nikolaos Rooms** (☎ 2247 032 477; d €24; mains €4-66) is the second option. The food is marginally better here; try the potatoes au gratin.

MARATHI ΜΑΡΑΘΙ
Marathi is the largest of Arki's satellite islets. Before WWII it had a dozen or so inhabitants, but now has only one family. The old settlement, with an immaculate little church, stands on a hill above the harbour. The island has a superb sandy beach. There are two tavernas on the island, both of which rent rooms and are owned by the island's only permanent inhabitants, who speak English. **Taverna Mihalis** (☎ 2247 031 580; d €25; meals €4-6) is the more laid-back and cheaper of the two places to eat and sleep at, while **Taverna Pandelis** (☎ 2247 032 609; d €35; mains €4-6) at the top end of the beach is a tad more upmarket and not as traveller-oriented as the former.

AGATHONISI ΑΓΑΘΟΝΗΣΙ

pop 158
Agathonisi is a sun-bleached, often ignored speck of strategic rock a couple of hours east of Patmos. The island attracts yachties, serious island-hoppers and the curious, as well as latter-day Robinson Crusoes all seeking what Agathonisi has to offer – plain peace and quiet. If you ignore the occasional low-level roar of Turkish jets playing war games, the most exciting event of the day is the departure or arrival of the daily ferry or hydrofoil. There are only three settlements of any stature on the island: the port of Agios Georgios, and the

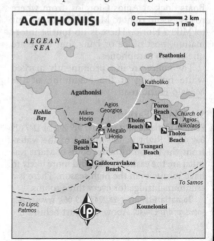

AGATHONISI

villages of Megalo Horio and Mikro Horio, which are less than 1km apart.

Getting There & Away

Agathonisi is linked to Samos (€4, one hour) and Patmos (€6, two hours) about four times a week by the F/B *Nisos Kalymnos*. A hydrofoil also links the island with Samos and destinations further south on the other three days. Ferry agent **Savvas Kamitsis** (☎ 2247 029 004) sells tickets at the harbour prior to departures.

Getting Around

There is no public transport, and it is a steep 1.5km uphill walk from Agios Giorgios to the main settlement of Megalo Horio; somewhat less to Mikro Horio. From Megalo Horio the island's eastern beach coves are all within a 2km to 3km walk.

AGIOS GIORGIOS ΑΓΙΟΣ ΓΕΩΡΓΙΟΣ

The village of Agios Giorgios (*agh*-ios ye-*or*-yi-os) is a languid settlement at the end of a protected fjord-like. It has a 100m-long curved, pebbled beach at which you can comfortably swim, but **Spilia Beach**, 900m southwest around the headland, is quieter. A track around the far side of the bay will take you there. A further 1km walk will bring you to **Gaïdouravlakos**, a small bay and beach where water from one of the island's few springs meets the sea.

Orientation & Information

Boats dock at Agios Giorgios, from where roads ascend right to Megalo Horio and left to Mikro Horio. There is no tourist information, post office or bank, but there are one or two cardphones.

The police are in a prominently marked white building at the beginning of the Megalo Horio road.

Sleeping & Eating

Pension Maria Kamitsi (☎ 2247 029 003; fax 2247 029 004; d €30) Right in the middle of the waterfront, the 13 comfortable rooms of Maria Kamitsi are the easiest to find and more likely to have vacancies in the high season. There is a communal fridge for every three rooms.

Domatia Giannis (☎ 2247 029 062; www.aegean-news.gr; d/tr €34/40) Above and just behind the

Glaros Restaurant are these five airy rooms – the best accommodation on the island. Most have harbour views, are well constructed and enjoy modern furnishings.

Glaros Restaurant (☎ 2247 029 062; mains €4.50-6) Of the few harbourside eateries, Glaros is probably the best place to eat. German- and English-speaking owners Voula and Giannis are very engaging and make *markakia* (feta cheese fingers in vine leaves with a special sauce) among standard *mayirefta*, grills and fish dishes.

George's Taverna (☎ 2247 029 101; fish €5-9) Closer to the ferry quay is the taverna of the affable George and his German staff. Food is predictably reasonable, though limited to meat and fish grills and the occasional goat in lemon sauce, but service can be a shade slow.

AROUND AGATHONISI

Megalo Horio is the only village of any size on the island. Somnolent and unhurried for most of the year, it comes to life each year with religious festivals on 26 July (Agiou Panteleimonos), 6 August (Sotiros) and 22 August (Panagias), when after church services the village celebrates with abundant food, music and dancing.

There are a series of accessible beaches to the east of Megalo Horio: pebbled **Tsangari Beach**, pebbled **Tholos Beach**, sandy **Poros Beach** and pebbled **Tholos (Agios Nikolaos Beaches)**, close to the eponymous church. All are within easy walking distance.

Further out at the end of the line is the small fishing harbour of **Katholiko** with the uninhabited and inaccessible islet of **Neronisi** just offshore.

If you prefer an even quieter stay than at the port, **Studios Ageliki** (☎ 2247 029 085; www.agathonisi.ejb.net; s/d €25/30) in Megalo Horio will serve you very well. The four basic, but quite comfortable studios all have stunning views over a small vineyard and down to the port, and are equipped with kitchenette, fridge and bathroom. Eating in the village is unfortunately limited to the reliable **Restaurant I Irini** (☎ 2247 029 054; mains €5-6) on the central square, or the **Kafeneio Ta 13 Adelfia** (mains €3-4) on the south side of the central square, serving up budget snacks and meals.

Northeastern Aegean Islands

Τα Νησιά του Βόρειοανατολικό Αιγαίου

Strewn across the northeastern corner of the Aegean Sea, most of the islands in this chapter lie closer to Turkey than to the Greek mainland. Rest assured; you're still in Greece. Turkish influence is barely visible even though the islands were part the Ottoman Empire until 1912. Far more visible are the ancient sites that recall classical Greece in all its real and mythological glory.

These islands provide more than just archaeological pleasures. Their interiors are refreshingly green and marked by forested mountains that offer stunning coastal views and occasional trekking trails. Along their indented shores you'll find everything from pebbly coves to magnificent stretches of sand. Perhaps because island-hopping is not an easy matter in these far-flung islands, they remain relatively calm when the Dodecanese and Cyclades are sagging with summer visitors. Even at the height of the summer season, it's easy to escape the crowded coastlines and head to the hills for a taste of traditional village life.

There are seven major islands in the group: Chios, Ikaria, Lesvos (Mytilini), Limnos, Samos, Samothraki and Thasos. The Fourni Islands situated near Ikaria, Psara and Inousses near Chios, and Agios Efstratios near Limnos are small, little-visited islands in the group.

Accommodation throughout the island chain tends to be a little more expensive than on some of the more touristed islands, but bear in mind that the high-season (July to August) prices quoted in this chapter are 30% to 50% cheaper out of season.

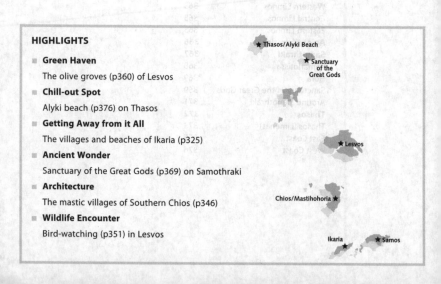

HIGHLIGHTS

- **Green Haven**
  The olive groves (p360) of Lesvos
- **Chill-out Spot**
  Alyki beach (p376) on Thasos
- **Getting Away from it All**
  The villages and beaches of Ikaria (p325)
- **Ancient Wonder**
  Sanctuary of the Great Gods (p369) on Samothraki
- **Architecture**
  The mastic villages of Southern Chios (p346)
- **Wildlife Encounter**
  Bird-watching (p351) in Lesvos

★ Thasos/Alyki Beach

★ Sanctuary of the Great Gods

★ Lesvos

Chios/Mastihohoria ★

Ikaria ★   ★ Samos

Getting There & Away

AIR

Samos, Chios, Lesvos, Limnos and Ikaria have air links with Athens. In addition, Samos, Chios, Lesvos and Limnos have flights to Thessaloniki. Lesvos is connected to both Limnos and Chios by local flights.

FERRY

Ferry schedules make it difficult to plan an itinerary that takes in all the islands, particularly in the off season. Samothraki and Thasos are particularly difficult to reach as there is no connection between these two islands. Ferry connections are much easier in the southernmost islands.

Domestic

The Ferry Connections to the Northeastern Aegean Islands table below gives an overview of the scheduled domestic ferries to this island group travelling from mainland ports during the high season. Further details and information on inter-island links can be found under individual island entries.

FERRY CONNECTIONS TO THE NORTH-EASTERN AEGEAN ISLANDS

Origin	Destination	Time	€	Frequency
Alexandroupolis	Chios	12½hr	€23.50	1 weekly
	Lesvos			
	(Mytilini)	9hr	€19.60	1 weekly
	Limnos	5hr	€14.10	2 weekly
	Samos	16hr	€28.90	1 weekly
	Samothraki	2hr	€7.80	1 daily
Kavala	Chios	16hr	€23.50	1 weekly
	Lesvos			
	(Mytilini)	10hr	€23.30	2 weekly
	Limnos	5hr	€13.20	4 weekly
	Thasos (Skala			
	Prinos)	1¼hr	€3	hourly
Keramoti	Thasos			
	(Limenas)	40min	€1.50	hourly
Piraeus	Chios	8hr	€19.50	1 daily
	Ikaria	9hr	€17.60	1 daily
	Lesvos			
	(Mytilini)	12hr	€24.20	1 daily
	Limnos	13hr	€24	3 weekly
	Samos	13hr	€23.80	2 daily
Rafina	Agios			
	Efstratios	8½hr	€15	2 weekly
	Limnos	13hr	€17	4 weekly
	Sigri	9hr	€14.38	4 weekly
Thessaloniki	Chios	18hr	€30	1 weekly
	Lesvos	13hr	€30	2 weekly
	Limnos	7hr	€19	2 weekly

International

In summer there are daily ferries from Samos to Kuşadası (for Ephesus) in Turkey and from Chios to Çeşme. Ferries from Lesvos to Ayvalık run four times weekly.

HYDROFOIL

In summer there are regular hydrofoil links between Kavala and Thasos, and some hydrofoils travelling between Alexandroupolis and Samothraki. Hydrofoils also operate out of Samos west towards Ikaria, south towards the Dodecanese, and north towards Chios and Lesvos.

IKARIA & THE FOURNI ISLANDS
IKAPIA KAI OI ΦΟΥΡΝΟΙ

area 255 sq km

Ikaria (ih-kah-*ree*-ah) is a small, rugged island with a profusion of cypress trees, pine forests, vineyards, and olive and fruit trees. Mythmakers of millennia past chose wisely in naming Ikaria as the birthplace of Dionysos, the Greek god of wine, fruitfulness and vegetation. According to myth, the Ikarians were the first people to make wine, which is why ancient Ikarian coins had a picture of Dionysus on them. Although Ikarian wine was once considered the best in Greece, a devastating phylloxera outbreak in the mid-1960s put paid to many of the vines. Production is now low-key and mainly for local consumption.

Ikaria's radioactive springs are no myth; their therapeutic powers have drawn visitors for many centuries. Most of these springs can still be visited for cures or relaxation.

Long neglected by mainland Greece, Ikaria was used as a dumping ground for dissidents and troublemakers while investment in its tourist infrastructure lagged. Inattention has had the happy effect of leaving the island's many placid beaches and idyllic coves relatively unspoiled. Ikaria's north-coast beaches, particularly Livadia and Mesahti near Armenistis, have to be rated as among the very best in Greece.

The island's capital is the port of Agios Kirykos on the south coast. Evdilos on the north coast is its second harbour and a good base to enjoy the lush and heavily indented northern coastline.

Getting There & Away

AIR

In summer there are two flights weekly to Athens (€46.50), usually departing in the early afternoon. **Olympic Airways** (☎ 2275 022 214) is in Agios Kirykos, although tickets can also be bought from **Blue Nice Agency** (☎ 2275 031 990; fax 2775 031 752) in Evdilos. There is no bus to the airport and a taxi will cost around €10 from Agios Kirykos.

CAÏQUE

A caïque leaves Agios Kirykos at 1pm on Monday, Wednesday and Friday for Fourni, the largest island in the miniature Fourni archipelago. The caïque calls at Fourni (the main settlement) and usually at Hrysomilia or Thymena, where there are domatia and tavernas. Tickets cost €4 one way. There are also day excursion boats to Fourni from Agios Kirykos and from Evdilos which cost around €15.

FERRY

Nearly all ferries that call at Ikaria's ports of Evdilos and Agios Kirykos are on the Piraeus–Samos route. Generally there are departures daily from Agios Kirykos and three to four weekly from Evdilos. There are five ferries a week to Mykonos (€11.50, 2½ hours) and Samos (€7.40, five hours) and four to Syros (€12.50, 2½ hours). Buy tickets at **Icariada Travel** (☎ 2275 023 322; ikariada@ika.forthnet.gr) and **GA Ferries agency** (☎ 2275 022 426) in Agios Kirykos or from **Blue Nice Agency** (☎ 2275 031 990; fax 2775 031 752) in Evdilos.

Chios-based **Miniotis Lines** (☎ 2271 024 670; www.miniotis.gr; Neorion 23) also runs a couple of small boats twice weekly to Chios (€18.70, 8½ hours) from Agios Kirykos via Fourni and Samos.

HYDROFOIL

Agios Kirykos handles the majority of Ikaria's hydrofoil services. There are year-round hydrofoils from Piraeus (€34, 5½ hours) that go three times daily in winter and daily from June to October, stopping either at Agios Kirykos or Evdilos and continuing on to Samos.

In summer there are two connections weekly to the Fourni Islands (€9.40, 20 minutes), two to Pythagorio on Samos (€15.45, 1¼ hours), two to Patmos (€15, 1¼ hours) and Kos (€27, 2¾ hours), and weekly services to Chios (7½ hours). There's also one boat a week each to Paros (€24, two hours) and Naxos (€21, 1½ hours). Check with **Dolihi Tours Travel Agency** (☎ 2275 023 230; fax 2275 022 346) in Agios Kirykos for the latest information.

Getting Around

BUS

Ikaria's bus services are almost as mythical as Icarus, but they do occasionally run. In summer a bus is supposed to leave Evdilos for Agios Kirykos at 8am daily and return to Evdilos at around noon. However, it's best not to count on these buses as they exist to serve the schools during term time.

Buses to the villages of Hristos Rahes (near Moni Evangelistrias), Xylosyrtis and Hrysostomos from Agios Kirykos are more elusive and depend mainly on the whims of the local drivers. It is usually preferable to share a taxi with locals or other travellers for long-distance runs.

CAR & MOTORCYCLE

Cars can be rented from **Dolihi Tours Travel Agency** (☎ 2275 023 230; fax 2275 022 346) in Agios Kirykos, **Nas Travel** (☎ 2275 071 396; fax 2275 071 397) in Evdilos and Armenistis, and **Aventura Car Rental** (☎ 2275 031 140; aventura@otenet.gr) in Evdilos and Armenistis.

TAXI BOAT

In summer there are daily taxi boats from Agios Kirykos to Therma and to the sandy beach at Faro (also known as Fanari) on the northern tip of the island. A return trip costs around €11.

AGIOS KIRYKOS ΑΓΙΟΣ ΚΉΡΥΚΟΣ
pop 1879

Agios Kirykos is Ikaria's capital and main port but it's far from a bustling metropolis. The most exciting action in town is the arrival and departure of ferries. Other than watching boats come and go, there are radioactive springs, a few decent restaurants, embryonic nightlife and a little nest of old streets to explore. The pebbled beach at Xylosyrtis, 4km to the southwest, is the best of a mediocre bunch of stony beaches near town.

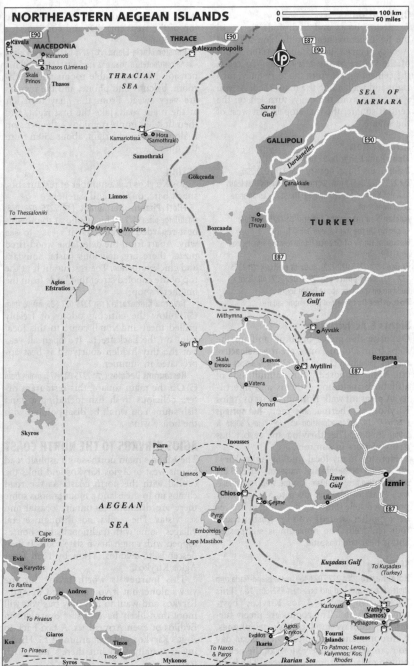

NORTHEASTERN AEGEAN ISLANDS

0   100 km
0   60 miles

Orientation

Excursion boats and hydrofoils tie up in the town centre near Dolihi Tours Travel Agency. Ferries tie up about 150m south of the centre at the ferry quay. To reach the central square from the ferry quay, turn right and walk along the main road. As you walk away from the quay, turn left on the central square; the bus stop is just west of the square.

Information

Alpha Bank Next to Dolihi Tours; has an ATM.
Dolihi Tours Travel Agency (☎ 2275 023 230; fax 2275 022 346) At the bottom of the steps that lead to Agios Kirykos' police building. The staff can arrange accommodation.
Icarian-Sea Internet Corner (☎ 2275 022 864; €6 per hr) Up the steps above Dolihi Tours.
National Bank of Greece On the central square; has an ATM.
Police (☎ 2275 022 222), **tourist police** (☎ 2275 022 222), **port police** (☎ 2275 022 207) All share a building up the steps above Dolihi Tours.
Post office On the left of the central square.

Sights & Activities

Opposite the police building and up the steps from Dolihi Tours, are the **radioactive springs** (admission €5; ☼ 7am-2.30pm & 5-9pm Jun-Oct). A dip supposedly cures a multitude of afflictions including arthritis and infertility. A pleasant walk 1km northeast of Agios Kirykos, at Therma, are more **hot springs** (☎ 6977 147 014; admission €5; ☼ 7am-2.30pm & 5-9pm Jun-Oct). This thriving spa resort has many visitors in summer.

Housing many local finds is Agios Kirykos' small **archaeological museum** (☎ 2275 031 300; admission free; ☼ 10am-3pm Tue, Wed, Fri-Sun Jul & Aug). Pride of place is given to a large, well-preserved stele (500 BC) depicting in low relief a mother (seated) with her husband and four children. The museum is signposted and is near the hospital.

Sleeping

Hotel Kastro (☎ 2275 023 480; www.island-ikaria.com /hotels/kastro.asp; s/d incl breakfast €52/60; ☒) This C-class property is Agios Kirykos' best-appointed hotel. The rooms are nicely furnished and have modern TVs, telephones, bathrooms and balconies. On a clear day you can get some lovely views of the neighbouring islands from its terraces. The hotel

is up the steps from Dolihi Tours; at the top of the steps turn left and continue for about 20m.

Pension Maria-Elena (☎ 2275 022 835; www.island -ikaria.com/hotels/mariaelena.asp; d/tr €44/53) This pension has impeccable rooms with bathroom, balcony and phone, and the owners are very sweet. From the quay turn left at the main road, take the first right, and then first left into Artemidos – the pension is along here on the right, about 250m from the quay.

Eating

Agios Kirykos has a number of restaurants, snack bars, ouzeria and kafeneia.

Filoti Pizzeria Restaurant (☎ 2275 023 088; small/large pizza €5/11) This is one of the town's best-regarded restaurants. It's easy to see why. Apart from the delectable wood-fired pizza, there are delicious pasta, souvlaki and chicken dishes. The restaurant is at the top of the cobbled street that leads from the butcher's shop.

Taverna Klimataria (☎ 2275 022 686; mains from €5) Follow the enticing odour of freshly grilled meat and you'll come to this local joint on the backstreets. It's open all year but the tiny hidden courtyard is best appreciated in summer.

Restaurant Dedalos (☎ 2275 022 473; mains from €5) On the main square, this restaurant offers delicious fresh fish including a good fish soup. You won't be disappointed with the house wine.

AGIOS KIRYKOS TO THE NORTH COAST

The island's main north–south asphalt road begins west of Agios Kirykos and links the capital with the north coast. As the road climbs up to the island's mountainous spine there are dramatic mountain, coastal and sea vistas. The road winds through several villages, some with traditional stone houses topped with rough-hewn slate roofs. It then descends to Evdilos, 41km by road from Agios Kirykos.

This journey is worth taking for the views alone, but if you are based in Agios Kirykos and want to travel by bus you will more than likely have to stay overnight in Evdilos or even Armenistis. A taxi back to Agios Kirykos will cost around €25. Hitching is usually OK, but there's not much traffic.

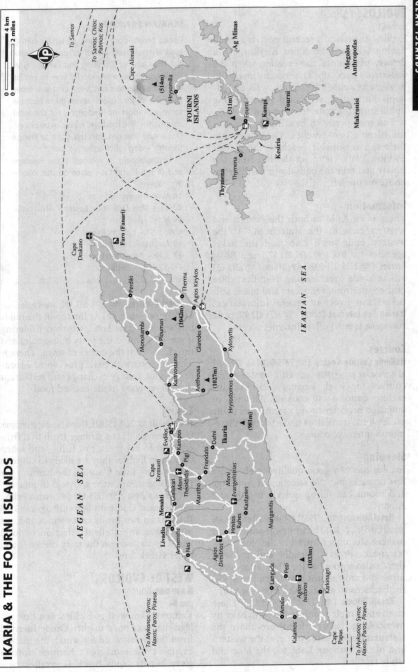

EVDILOS ΕΥΔΗΛΟΣ

pop 461

Evdilos, the island's second port, is a small fishing village. Like Agios Kirykos, it's a drowsy place until the evening, when the waterfront perks up. To see some lovely old houses and a cute little church, walk up Kalliopis Katsouli, the cobbled street leading uphill from the waterfront square.

You may prefer to head further west to the island's best beaches. There is, nonetheless, a reasonable beach to the east of Evdilos. Walk 100m up the hill from the square and take the path down past the last house on the left.

Information

There is an ATM at both the eastern and western ends of the waterfront. At the western end, you'll also find the ticket agencies for **NEL** (☎ 2275 031 572) and **Hellas Ferries** (☎ 2275 031 990). **Aventura** (☎ 2275 031 140), in a side street leading from the centre of the waterfront, rents cars and bikes, sells tickets and gives out general information. **Icarian-Sea Internet Corner** (☎ 2275 032 918; on the main square; €6 per hr) offers Internet access.

Courses

Hellenic Culture Centre (☎ 2275 061 140, 2275 061 139; www.hcc.gr; ✆ May-Oct) This centre offers courses in Greek language, culture, literature, dancing and cooking. All levels of language proficiency are catered for; many professional translators undertake the three-month intensive course.

Sleeping

Evdilos has two good-quality hotels and a few domatia but the selection is not large and rooms can fill up quickly in July and August.

Hotel Atheras (☎ 2275 031 434; www.atheras-kerame .gr; s/d €53/59; ✆ ✆) The white-on-white decor makes a stunning contrast to the blue Mediterranean. Breezy, friendly and modern, there's also a pool bar for a lazy after-beach drink and most rooms have balconies. It's in the backstreets, about 200m from the port.

Korali Rooms (☎ 2275 031 924; d €35) These clean and simple rooms (some with balcony overlooking the waterfront) are above the restaurant of the same name, at the western end of the harbour. Look for the blue and white facade.

IKARIAN PANIGYRIA

Locals break loose during *panigyria*, night-long festivals held on saints' days throughout the summer. Drinking and carousing in a village can be a wonderful way to get to know the islanders but it will cost you more than you might expect – since these festivals serve as important fundraisers for the local community, the food and wine can be pricey. Make sure you get into the spirit of things though – don't just order a salad!

Festivals held in villages in the western end of the island take place on the following dates:

14 May – Agios Isidoros
40 days after Orthodox Easter – Armenistis
14 May – Pezi
6 August – Hristos Rahes
15 August – Langada
17 July – Agios Kirykos
14–17 July – Evdilos

Hotel Evdoxia (☎ 2275 031 502; www.evdoxia.gr; d €60; ✆ year-round; ✆) At the top of the hill is this small B-class hotel, worth considering if you don't mind the petty house rules and the climb from the centre of town. There is a minimarket with basic provisions, a laundry service, money exchange and restaurant that serves good home-cooked food.

Eating

To Keïmali (☎ 2275 031 923; Plateia Evdilou; mains from €5; ✆ from 7pm) It is a strange truth that fishers tend to eat meat, not fish – and when they do in Evdilos they are likely to come to this inviting little place on the harbour for the grilled meat or the souvlaki in pita.

Cuckoo's Nest (☎ 2275 031 540; Plateia Evdilou; mezedes around €2.50, mains from €4.50; ✆ from 7pm) Ikaria is known for its saucy wines and this ouzeri has an excellent selection of local wines to wash down the tasty mezedes and other Greek fare.

WEST OF EVDILOS

Kampos Κάμπος

pop 94

Kampos, 3km west of Evdilos, is a tiny village that was once mighty Oinoe (derived from the Greek word for wine), the island's capital. Little remains of Kampos' former glory but its sandy beach is excellent and easily accessible. It also offers the possibility of relaxing country walks with stunning coastal views.

INFORMATION

Charismatic Vasilis Dionysos (who speaks English) is a fount of information on Ikarian history and walking in the mountains. You will often find him in his gloomy but well-stocked village store – it's on the right as you come from Evdilos. The village's post box is outside this shop and inside there is a metered telephone. There is a cardphone nearby.

SIGHTS & ACTIVITIES

As you enter Kampos from Evdilos, the ruins of a **Byzantine Palace** can be seen up on the right. In the centre of the village there is a small **museum** (☎ 2275 031 300; admission free). It houses Neolithic tools, geometric vases, fragments of classical sculpture, figurines and a fine 'horse head' knife sheath carved from ivory. Opening hours are irregular but Vasilis Dionysos at the village store has the key and will open it upon request.

Next to the museum is the 12th-century **Agia Irini**, the island's oldest church. It is built on the site of a 4th-century basilica, and columns standing in the grounds are from this original church. Agia Irini's frescoes are currently covered with whitewash because of insufficient funds to pay for its removal. Vasilis Dionysos also has the keys to the church.

The village is a good base for mountain walking. A one-day circular walk along dirt roads can be made, taking in the village of **Dafni**, the remains of the 10th-century Byzantine **Castle of Koskinas** and the villages of **Frandato** and **Maratho**. The trek up to the little Byzantine **Chapel of Theoskepasti**, jammed in beneath an overhanging lump of granite, is worth the effort. Inside you will be shown the skulls of a couple of macabre internees. To get to the chapel and neighbouring **Moni Theoktistis**, where there are beautiful 300-year-old frescoes, look for the signs at the village of Pigi on the road to Frandato. A lovely woman named Evangelia runs a kafeneio at the monastery.

SLEEPING & EATING

Rooms Dionysos (☎ 2275 031 300, ☎ /fax 2275 031 688; www.island-ikaria.com/hotels/dionysos.asp; d €30) Vasilis

and Yiannis Dionysos create a wonderful family atmosphere replete with excellent Greek cooking, music and hospitality. The terrace offers splendid views and is a convivial meeting place for their happy guests. You can take a variety of strolls through the surrounding countryside or head down to the nearby beach to work on your tan. From Evdilos, take the dirt road to the right from near the cardphone and follow it round to the blue and white building on your left. Alternatively, make your presence known at the village store.

Pashalia (☎ 2275 031 346; mains from €4.50) Of the two tavernas in the village, this is the better one, serving up substantial portions of Greek specialities with an emphasis on meat.

Armenistis Αρμενιστής

pop 130

Armenistis, 15km west of Evdilos, is the island's largest resort. It has two beautiful long beaches of pale golden sand, separated by a narrow headland composed of a harbour and a web of hilly streets. Tourism is the only business here, leaving the town somewhat lonely and stranded in the off season. **Dolihi Tours** (☎ 2275 071 480; fax 2275 071 340), on the road that skirts the sea, organises walking tours and jeep safaris on the island. **Aventura** (☎ 2275 071 117), by the *zaharoplasteio* (patisserie) before the bridge, rents cars and sells tickets.

Just east of Armenistis a road leads inland to **Moni Evangelistrias** and the delightful hill village of **Hristos Rahes**, surrounded by numerous trekking opportunities.

From Armenistis a road continues 3.5km west to the small and secluded pebbled beach of **Nas** at the mouth of a stream. This is Ikaria's unofficial nudist beach. Behind the beach are some scant remains of a **temple of Artemis**. Nas has in recent times witnessed a mini boom and there are now quite a few domatia and tavernas.

SLEEPING
Budget

Atsachas Rooms (☎ /fax 2275 071 226; d €33) With a superb location at the eastern end of Armenistis beach, right on the water, you won't miss a swimming pool. Rooms are clean and nicely furnished, some have kitchens and most have sea-view balconies with a refreshing breeze.

Rooms Fotinos (☎ 2275 071 235; www.island-ikaria
.com/hotels/PensionFotinos.asp; d with/without bathroom
€29/18) At the approach to the village, before
the road forks, you will see these rooms on
the left in a spiffy white building. Rooms
are light, airy and furnished in local style.
There's no air-conditioning but the rooms
come with fans and the owners are extraordinarily accommodating.

Kirki (☎ 2275 071 254; fax 2275 071 083; d/studios
€38/50; ✷) These rooms are on the right
as you approach town. They are small but
comfortably furnished and each room has a
private terrace overlooking the sea.

Pension Thea (☎ 2275 071 491; d €20-34) This
friendly pension over a large restaurant at
Nas has attractive new rooms with fridges
and outstanding sea views. The owners
speak English.

Mid-Range

Villa Dimitri (☎ /fax 2275 071 310; www.villa-dimitri
.de; 2-person studios & apt with private patios €39-62;
✷) The most exquisite accommodation on
the island is this Cycladic-inspired pension
belonging to Dimitris Ioannidopoulos. The
individual studios and apartments, 800m
west of Armenistis, spill down a cliff that
overlooks the sea amid a riotous profusion of flowers and plants. Bookings are
essential and should be for a minimum of
one week.

Hotel Daidalos (☎ 2275 071 390; www.island-ikaria
/hotels/hotelDaidalos.asp; s/d incl breakfast €58/72;
✷ ✷) This is a great place to enjoy the
Aegean good life. The interior is cool and
inviting, the rooms are tastefully furnished
and the sea-water swimming pool is best
of all.

EATING

Wherever you eat, see if you can try some of
the locally made light but potent wine.

Kafestiatorio O Ilios (☎ 2275 071 045; mains from
€6) Whether grilled or fried, the seafood
here is the best in town, and why not?
The owner is a fisherman with a talent for
plucking the lushest morsels from the sea.

Pashalia Taverna (☎ 2275 071 302; mains from €6)
After a hard day at the beach you may be
ready for rib-sticking fare such as *katsikaki*
(kid goat) or filling pasta and veal in a clay
pot. Come to this taverna, the first place
along the harbour road.

Delfini (☎ 2275 071 254; mains from €5.50) Directly opposite and below Pashalia Taverna
is this folksy restaurant offering great
grilled souvlaki (and good fish) to complement the view over the water. It often gets
crowded in summer so come early.

To Mouragio (☎ 2275 071 208; mains from €5.30)
With tender, perfectly cooked chunks of
meat, you can't find better souvlaki than at
this harbourside option. Plus, the portions
are large and the service is friendly.

FOURNI ISLANDS OI ΦOYPNOI
pop 1469

The Fourni Islands are a miniature archipelago lying between Ikaria and Samos.
Two of the islands are inhabited: Fourni and
Thymena. The capital of the group is **Fourni**
(also called Kampos), which is the port of
Fourni Island. Fourni has one other village,
tiny Hrysomilia, 10km north of the port;
the island's only road connects the two.
The islands are mountainous but rather dry
and shadeless. A good number of beaches
are dotted around the coast.

THE NIGHTOWLS OF RAHES

The hill town of Hristos Rahes, and its neighbouring villages (known collectively as Rahes), are
famous for their late hours, sometimes to 3am. What started out as a tradition – perhaps to
protect the villagers from pirate raids – has become a minor tourist attraction as visitors flock to
the area for midnight shopping. Whatever time of day, Rahes offers a unique taste of local life
and should not be missed.

Another oddity of this region is the design of the older houses. Many of them were built out
of the local stone and have a sloping, one-sided roof. There are no windows or chimneys, just a
low door that's obscured by a high wall in front. This unique design served to camouflage the
villages in the days when the threat of pirate raids was very real.

If you have the time and energy, it's best to explore the region on foot. The local community
has published a walking map with excellent notes called *The Round of Rahes on Foot*; it's available
at most tourist shops and supermarkets.

Fourni has a **doctor** (☎ 2275 051 202), and both local **police** (☎ 2275 051 222) and **port police** (☎ 2275 051 207).

Fourni is the only island with accommodation for tourists and is ideal for those seeking a quiet retreat. Other than the settlement of Fourni itself and a beach south over the headland at **Kampi**, the island offers little else besides eating, sleeping and swimming. Most of the islanders make a living from fishing, sending their catch to the Athens fish market. For accommodation bookings, it is best to go through **Dolihi Tours Travel Agency** (☎ 2275 023 230; fax 2275 022 346) in Agios Kirykos (see Information, p328).

Getting There & Away
FERRY
Fourni lies on the ferry route between Piraeus and Samos. As well as daily boats to Ikaria (€3, 40 minutes), there are four ferries weekly to Samos (€6.60, two hours), and three weekly to Piraeus (€18, 10 hours) via Paros (€9, 3¼ hours) and Naxos (€8, four hours). These ferries stop at Mykonos (€9, 4½ hours) and Syros (€13, 5½ hours) twice a week. Tickets are available from the office on the corner of the waterfront and the main shopping street.

HYDROFOIL
Hydrofoils call at Fourni on the route from Ikaria to Samos and the Dodecanese. See the Hydrofoil section (p326) for details of services.

Getting Around
There are two caïques a week to Hrysomilia and three to Thymena. The boats operate year round and leave at 7.30am.

SAMOS ΣΑΜΟΣ

pop 32,814
Only the 3km-wide Mykale Straits separates Samos from Turkey, making the island a popular transit point for travellers heading to and from Turkey. Those who rush off without stopping are missing one of Greece's most resplendent islands. Forays into Samos' hinterland reveal dense mountain greenery populated by hordes of birds. Spring brings pink flamingos,

wild flowers and the orchids that Samos grows for export. In summer the air grows heavy with the scent of flowers as the many jasmine bushes bloom. During the hottest days, cool mountain villages make an ideal escape from Samos' baking beaches and archaeological sites.

Samos has a glorious history as the legendary birthplace of Hera, wife and sister of God-of-all-Gods, Zeus. The Sanctuary of Hera, built by the tyrant Polycrates in the 6th century BC, is one of the Seven Wonders of the Ancient World and a major tourist attraction. The well-known mathematician Pythagoras was born in Samos around the same time. The island has been ruled by the Romans, Venetians and Genoese and took part in a major uprising against the Turks in the early 19th century.

Samos has three ports: Vathy (Samos) and Karlovasi on the north coast, and Pythagorio on the south coast. Nature lovers flock to the island for mountain walks and treks and package tourists fill every available hotel room in July and August.

Getting There & Away
AIR
There are at least four flights daily from Samos to Athens (€73) and two flights weekly to Thessaloniki (€149). **Olympic Airways** (☎ 2273 027 237; cnr Kanari & Smyrnis) is in Vathy (Samos). There is also an **Olympic Airways** (☎ 2273 061 213; Lykourgou Logotheti) in Pythagorio. The airport is 4km west of Pythagorio.

EXCURSION BOAT
In summer there are excursion boats four times weekly between Pythagorio and Patmos (€32 return) leaving at 8am and a local bus to take you to the monasteries of St John. Daily excursion boats also go to the little island of Samiopoula for €18 with lunch. There is also a boat tour of Samos once or twice a week, leaving from Pythagorio's harbour; it costs €40 and does not include lunch.

FERRY
Domestic
Samos is the transport hub of the Northeastern Aegean, with ferries to the Dodecanese and Cyclades as well as to the other Northeastern Aegean islands. Schedules are subject to seasonal changes, so consult

SAMOS

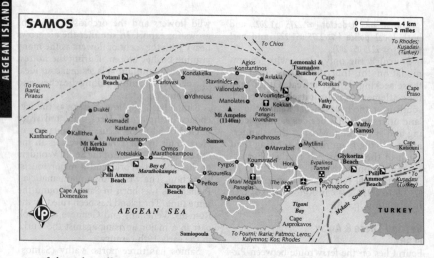

any of the ticket offices for the latest versions. **ITSA Travel** (☎ 2273 023 605; itsa@otenet.gr) is the closest agency to the ferry terminal in Vathy (Samos). Your luggage can also be stored for free whether you buy a ticket or not. Ferries depart from both Vathy (Samos) and Pythagorio.

To Piraeus there are at least two ferries daily (€23.80, 13 hours). Two ferries daily go to Ikaria (€7.80, three hours) and four boats a week go to Fourni (€6.60, two hours); two to three weekly to Chios (€10.70, four hours); and one weekly to Lesvos (€14.60, 11 hours), Limnos (€23.40, 11 hours) and Alexandroupolis (€28.90, 16 hours). At least four ferries a week go to Naxos (€18.90, seven hours) and Paros (€15.20, eight hours), with connections to Mykonos, Ios and Santorini. There are about three ferries a week to Patmos (€6.90, 2½ hours), two each to Leros (€5.50, 3½ hours) and Kalymnos (€10, four hours), and one each to Kos (€11.50, 5½ hours) and Rhodes (€27, nine hours).

The *Aeolis Express* operates from Vathy (Samos) to Piraeus (€47, seven hours, six weekly). There are also two services weekly from Vathy (Samos) to Fourni (€11.50, 1¾ hours) and Ikaria (€14.50, 2¼ hours).

International

In summer two ferries go daily from Vathy (Samos) to Kuşadası (for Ephesus) in Turkey. From Pythagorio there is one boat a week to Kuşadası. From November to March there are one to two ferries weekly. Tickets cost around €45 return (plus €21 port taxes). Daily excursions are also available from 1 April to 31 October and for an additional €23 you can visit Ephesus. Tickets are available from many outlets, but the main agent is **ITSA Travel** (☎ 2273 023 605; itsa@otenet.gr), near the ferry terminal in Vathy (Samos).

Bear in mind that the ticket office will require your passport in advance for port formalities. Turkish visas, where required, are issued upon arrival in Turkey. The fee depends upon nationality. Check with the Turkish diplomatic mission in your home country for the requirements as these change frequently. Visas are not required for daily excursions.

HYDROFOIL

In summer hydrofoils link Pythagorio twice daily with Patmos (€12.90, 1¼ hours), Leros (€15, two hours), Kos (€21, 3½ hours) and Kalymnos (€21, 2½ hours). Also from Pythagorio there are hydrofoils four times per week to Fourni (€11.50, 50 minutes) and Ikaria (€14.50, 1½ hours), daily to Lipsi (€13, 1½ hours) and once a week to Agathonisi (€9, 35 minutes) as well as Mykonos three times a week (€17.70, six hours).

Also from Vathy (Samos) there are three hydrofoils a week to Patmos (€18.50, one hour), Kos (€25.50), Leros (€22.50) and Kalymnos (€25) as well as a daily boat to Naxos (€37.20, three hours) and Paros (€29.90, four hours). Schedules are subject to frequent changes, so contact the **tourist office** (☎ 2273 061 389) or the **port police** (☎ 2273 061 225), both in Pythagorio, for up-to-date information. Tickets are available from **By Ship Travel** in Pythagorio (☎ 2273 062 285; fax 2273 061 914) and Vathy (Samos) (☎ 2273 022 116 or **ITSA Travel** (☎ 2273 023 605; itsa@otenet.gr) in Vathy.

Getting Around
TO/FROM THE AIRPORT
There are no Olympic Airways buses to the airport. A taxi from Vathy (Samos) should cost about €10. Alternatively, you can take a local bus to Pythagorio and a taxi to the airport from there for about €4.

BUS
Samos has an adequate bus service that continues till about 8pm in summer. On weekdays, there are six buses daily from Vathy (Samos) **bus station** (☎ 2273 027 262; Ioannou Lekati) to Kokkari (€1.62, 20 minutes), eight to Pythagorio (€1.08, 25 minutes), seven to Agios Konstantinos (€1.62, 40 minutes) and Karlovasi (via the north coast; €2.50, one hour), five to the Ireon (€2.16, 25 minutes) and five to Mytilinii (€1.08, 20 minutes).

In addition to frequent buses to/from Vathy (Samos) there are five buses from Pythagorio to the Ireon (€1.10, 15 minutes) and four from Pythagorio to Mytilinii (€1.10, 20 minutes). Pay for your tickets on the bus. Services are greatly reduced on Saturday, with no buses running on Sunday.

CAR & MOTORCYCLE
Samos has many car-rental outlets, including **Hertz** (☎ 2273 061 730; Lykourgou Logotheti 77) and **Europcar** (☎ 2273 061 522; Lykourgou Logotheti 65), both in Pythagorio, as well as **Pegasus** (☎ 2273 024 470) under ITSA Travel in Vathy (Samos).

There are also many motorcycle-rental outlets on Lykourgou Logotheti. Many of the larger hotels can arrange motorcycle or car rental for you.

TAXI
The **taxi rank** (☎ 2273 028 404) is in front of the National Bank of Greece in Vathy (Samos).

VATHY (SAMOS) ΒΑΘΥ (ΣΑΜΟΣ)
pop 2025
The island's capital is the large and bustling Vathy, also called Samos, on the northeast coast. The waterfront road is a string of bars, cafés and restaurants running from tacky to trendy. A harbourside walk is agreeable enough but the best part of town is the upper town of Ano Vathy, to the south, where 19th-century, red-tiled houses perch on a hillside. A string of small beaches starts at the northern end of town around the Pythagoras Hotel. The best is Gagou Beach about 1km north of the town centre.

Orientation
From the ferry terminal (facing inland) turn right to reach the central square of Plateia Pythagorou on the waterfront. It's recognisable by its four palm trees and statue of a lion. A little further along and a block inland are the shady municipal gardens. The waterfront road is called Themistokleous Sofouli. The bus station (KTEL) is on Ioannou Lekati.

Information
Commercial Bank On the east side of the square; has an ATM.
Diavlos NetCafé (☎ 2273 022 469; Themistoklous Sofouli 160; €4 per hr; ⏰ 8.30am-11.30pm) Access is fast; it closes in the afternoon from November to April.
Hospital (☎ 2273 027 407) On the waterfront, north of the ferry quay.
Municipal tourist office (☎ 2273 028 530) Just north of Plateia Pythagorou in a little side street, it only operates during the summer season. The staff may assist in finding accommodation.
National Bank of Greece On the waterfront just south of Plateia Pythagorou; has an ATM.
Police (☎ 2273 027 980; Themistokleous Sofouli 129) On the south side of the waterfront.
Port police (☎ 2273 027 890) Just north of the quay, one block back from the waterfront.
Post office (Smyrnis) Four blocks from the waterfront.
Tourist police (☎ 2273 027 980; Themistokleous Sofouli 129) On the south side of the waterfront.

Sights
Apart from the charming old quarter of Ano Vathy, which is a peaceful place to stroll, and the municipal gardens, which are a pleasant place to sit, the main attraction is the **archaeological museum** (☎ 2273 027 469; adult/student €3/2; ⏰ 8.30am-3pm Tue-Sun). Many of the fine exhibits in this well-laid-out

NORTHEASTERN AEGEAN ISLANDS

VATHY (SAMOS)

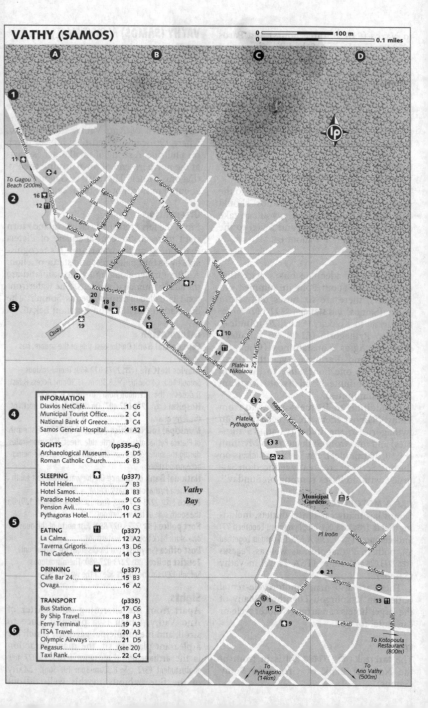

0   100 m
0   0.1 miles

Vathy Bay

INFORMATION
Diavlos NetCafé......................1 C6
Municipal Tourist Office..........2 C4
National Bank of Greece..........3 C4
Samos General Hospital..........4 A2

SIGHTS (pp335–6)
Archaeological Museum..........5 D5
Roman Catholic Church..........6 B3

SLEEPING (p337)
Hotel Helen............................7 B3
Hotel Samos..........................8 B3
Paradise Hotel........................9 C6
Pension Avli..........................10 C3
Pythagoras Hotel...................11 A2

EATING (p337)
La Calma..............................12 A2
Taverna Grigoris....................13 D6
The Garden...........................14 C3

DRINKING (p337)
Cafe Bar 24...........................15 B3
Ovaga..................................16 A2

TRANSPORT (p335)
Bus Station...........................17 C6
By Ship Travel.......................18 A3
Ferry Terminal.......................19 A3
ITSA Travel...........................20 A3
Olympic Airways....................21 D5
Pegasus............................(see 20)
Taxi Rank.............................22 C4

To Gagou Beach (200m)

To Pythagorio (14km)

To Ano Vathy (500m)

To Kotopoula Restaurant (800m)

museum are a legacy of Polycrates' time. They include a gargantuan (4.5m) *kouros* (male statue of the Archaic period) found in the Ireon (Sanctuary of Hera). In true Polycrates fashion, it was the largest standing kouros ever produced. The collection includes many statues, mostly from the Ireon, bronze sculptures, stelae and pottery.

Sleeping

Vathy does not have a camping ground. Be wary of touts who may approach you as you disembark and tell you that places listed in this guide are closed – it's usually not true.

Pension Avli (☎ 2273 022 939; Areos 2; d €28) Just up the street from the harbour, this traditional place is a former Roman Catholic convent, built around a lovely courtyard. It has loads of atmosphere. The rooms are spacious and simply but tastefully furnished.

Pythagoras Hotel (☎ 2273028422; www.pythagoras hotel.com; Kallistratou 12; s/d with phone €20/35; 🖥️) The tidy and simply furnished rooms are good but this hotel is best for its convivial atmosphere. Travellers meet and compare notes in the spacious snack bar or on the relaxing terrace with a view over the water. If you can swing a room with a sea view, you won't be disappointed.

Hotel Helen (☎ 2273 028 215; fax 2273 022 866; Grammou 2; d €40) This C-class establishment has cosy rooms with attractive furniture. Rooms have fans, fridge and TV and the English-speaking owner is friendly.

Hotel Samos (☎ 2273 028 377; www.samoshotel.gr; 11 Themistokleous Sofouli; s/d €40.50/51; 🈁 🈁) Stretch out and relax in this grand-looking establishment. You can play billiards, hit the bar or grab a bite to eat in the snack bar. From your comfortable carpeted room you can stroll out onto the balcony, which just might have a view over the water. Prices include breakfast.

Paradise Hotel (☎ 2273 023 911; samosparadise@ internet.gr; Kanari 21; s/d €35/45.50; 🈁 🈁) The well-manicured grounds are a green oasis in busy Vathy. The quiet rooms are extremely well outfitted with hairdryers, TVs and minibars. It's also very convenient to the bus station but in the high season it's likely to be booked out by tour groups.

Eating

When dining out on Samos don't forget to sample the Samian wine, extolled by Byron.

Kotopoula (☎ 2273 028 415; Vlamaris; mezedes around €4, mains around €6) Greeks escape the tourists and head for this vine-cloaked restaurant, hidden by a leafy plane tree in the backstreets. Its spit-roasted chicken (served only in the evenings) is the thing to order, but you should also try the delicious *revithokeftedes* (chickpea rissoles). Follow Ioannou Lekati inland for about 800m until you find it on your left.

The Garden (☎ 2273 024 033; Manolis Kalomiris; mains €4-9) This spot, just off Lykourgou Logotheti (entry is from the next street up to the north) has a garden setting with a vast and tree-filled outdoor terrace. The Greek standards are good, particularly the fish soup which makes a nice light meal.

La Calma (☎ 2273 022 654; Kefalopoulou 7; mains from €6; 🕖 7pm-midnight May-Sep) For a romantic evening ambience, try La Calma, which overlooks the sea. The food (pepper steak, for example) is a change from standard Greek fare – probably because the owners are from Sweden.

Taverna Grigoris (☎ 2273 022 718; Mihalis 5; appetisers €1.50-3, mains €3.50-6) This folksy place near the post office serves Greek dishes with a strong accent on grilled meat. There's also a small outdoor terrace. It's open all day.

Drinking

There are plenty of bars along the waterfront, all pretty much of a muchness. Generally, night life doesn't swing into action until people drift back from the beach and shower up. Head out about 8pm.

For something a bit more interesting, head to the bars by the water on Kefalopoulou, just past La Calma restaurant. These include Escape Music Bar, Cosy and **Ovaga** (☎ 2273 025 476; Kefalopoulou 13), which has a stunning terrace by the water.

Café Bar 24 (side street off Themistokleous Sofouli) is an intimate little outdoor bar that plays excellent music and has an underhyped candlelit ambience.

PYTHAGORIO ΠΥΘΑΓΟΡΕΙΟ
pop 1327

Pythagorio, on the southeast coast of the island, is 14km from Vathy (Samos). Today, it's a busy yet pretty tourist resort with streets lined with red hibiscus and pink oleander. It has a somewhat upmarket feel, perhaps because of the many comfortable and expensive cafés along the harbour. The nightlife is good and it's a convenient base from which to visit the ancient sights of Samos.

Pythagorio stands on the site of the now World Heritage–listed ancient city of Samos. Although the settlement dates from the Neolithic era, most of the remains are from Polycrates' time (around 550 BC). The town beach begins just beyond the jetty. All boats coming from Patmos, and other points south of Samos, dock at Pythagorio.

Orientation

From the ferry quay, turn right and follow the waterfront to the main thoroughfare of Lykourgou Logotheti, a turn-off to the left. Here there are supermarkets, greengrocers, bakers, travel agents and numerous car, motorcycle and bicycle rental outlets. The central square of Plateia Irinis is further along the waterfront.

Information

Bus stop On the south side of Lykourgou Logotheti.
Digital World (☎ 2273 062 722; Pythagora; €4 per hr; ✆ 11am-10.30pm) Has Internet access.

National Bank of Greece (Lykourgou Logotheti)
Post office (Lykourgou Logotheti)
Taxi rank (☎ 2273 061 450; cnr waterfront & Lykourgou Logotheti)
Tourist office (☎ 2273 061 389; deap5@otenet.gr; ✆ 8am-9.30pm) On the south side of Lykourgou Logotheti. The English-speaking staff is particularly friendly and helpful and give out a town map, bus timetable and information about ferry schedules. It's also a currency exchange.
Tourist police (☎ 2273 061 100; Lykourgou Logotheti) To the left of the tourist office.

Sights

Walking northeast on Polykratous from the town centre, a path left passes traces of an ancient theatre. The right fork past the theatre leads up to **Moni Panagias Spilianis** (Monastery of the Virgin of the Grotto). The city walls extend from here to the Evpalinos Tunnel (see opposite), which can also be reached along this path; take the left fork after the theatre.

Back in town, the remains of the **Castle of Lykourgos Logothetis** are at the southern end of Metamorfosis Sotiros. The castle was built in 1824 and became a stronghold of Greek resistance during the War of Independence.

PYTHAGORIO

To Evpalinos Tunnel (1km);
Moni Panagias Spilianis (1km)

To Evpalinos Tunnel (1.5km)

To Airport (4km);
The Ireon (8km)

To Psili Ammos Beach (11km);
Vathy (Samos) (14km)

Harbour

Plateia Irinis

Plateia Tarsana

AEGEAN SEA

Quay

INFORMATION	
Commercial Bank ATM	1 B1
Digital World	2 B2
National Bank of Greece	3 A1
Tourist Office	4 B2

SIGHTS & ACTIVITIES	(p338)
Castle of Lykourgos Logothetis	5 A2
Pythagorio Museum	6 C1
Ruins of Aphrodite	7 B2

SLEEPING	(p339)
Hotel Alexandra	8 B2
Hotel Elpis	9 B2
Hotel Evripili	10 C2
Polixeni Hotel	11 C2

EATING	(p339)
Poseidonas	12 D2
Restaurant Remataki	13 D2
Symposium	14 C2
Taverna ta Platania	15 C2

ENTERTAINMENT	(p339)
Mythos	16 C1

TRANSPORT	(p338)
Bus Stop	17 A1
By Ship Travel	18 B2
Ferry Quay	19 D3
Olympic Airways	20 A1
Taxi Rank	21 C2

In the town hall at the back of Plateia Irinis, is the **Pythagorio Museum** (☎ 2273 061 400; Plateia Irinis; admission free; ☼ 8.45am-2pm Tue-Sat). It has some finds from the Ireon.

Between Lykourgou Logotheti and the car park are the **ruins of Aphrodite**.

The 1034m-long **Evpalinos Tunnel** (☎ 2273 061 400; adult/student/senior €4/2/2, EU student free; ☼ 8.45am-2.45pm Tue-Sun) is a remarkable feat of precision engineering. Constructed in 524 BC to channel mountain water to the city, the diggers laboriously chopped through a mountainside, beginning at each end and finally meeting in the middle. In the Middle Ages the inhabitants of Pythagorio used the tunnel as a hide-out during pirate raids. The tunnel is, in effect, two tunnels: a service tunnel and a lower water tunnel that can be seen at various points along the narrow walkway.

The tunnel is fun to explore, though access to it is via a very constricted stairway. If you are tall, portly or suffer from claustrophobia, give it a miss!

The tunnel is most easily reached from the western end of Lykourgou Logotheti, from where it is signposted. If you arrive by road, a sign points you to the tunnel's southern mouth as you enter Pythagorio from Samos.

Sleeping

Many of Pythagorio's places to stay are block-booked by tour companies.

Polixeni Hotel (☎ 2273 061 590; fax 2273 061 359; d with balcony €65; 🖳) This homely place on the waterfront has nicely furnished, clean and comfortable rooms with balconies.

Hotel Evripili (☎ 2273 061 096; fax 2273 061 897; s/d €40/55) This is a friendly place occupying a stone building not far from the waterfront. The rooms are cosy and nicely furnished with shutters to protect against the sun. Some rooms have balconies.

Hotel Elpis (☎ 2273 061 144; fax 2273 087 774; Metamorfosis Sotiros; s/d €24/25) This neat and clean D-class hotel on a quiet street has rooms equipped with mini-kitchenettes and the owner speaks English. Most rooms have balconies.

Hotel Alexandra (☎ 2273 061 429; Metamorfosis Sotiros 22; d €25) Nearby, this well-kept establishment offers eight small but fetching rooms, some with a sea view. The enclosed garden is a treat on hot summer days.

Eating

The waterfront is packed with restaurants all offering much the same fare.

Restaurant Remataki (☎ 2273 061 104; mezedes €2-6; mains €4-7) This restaurant is at the beginning of the town beach. It has an imaginative menu of carefully prepared, delicious food – it's a miracle that a place this good has survived in a tourist enclave. Try a meal of various mezedes for a change: revithokeftedes, *piperies* Florinis (Florina peppers) and *gigantes* (lima beans) make a good combination. The artichoke soup and dolmades (aromatic rice wrapped in vine leaves) are also excellent.

Poseidonas (☎ 2273 062 530; mains €5-13) Next door to Remataki, this popular restaurant serves some interesting dishes, including Chinese-inspired seafood as well as Greek food prepared with the freshest ingredients.

Taverna ta Platania (☎ 2273 061 817; Plateia Irinis; mains €4-6) This taverna, opposite the museum, is away from the more expensive waterfront eateries. As a result, it tends to attract a relaxed, local crowd.

Symposium (☎ 2273 061 938; cnr Roikou & Egou Pelagous; mains €5-11) If you're in a meaty mood, try this upmarket restaurant which is known for its steaks and Greek classics.

Entertainment

Mythos (☼ from 12.30am Jun-Sep) This throbbing disco is the centre of the universe as far as island nightlife is concerned. They came, they saw, they danced till they dropped.

AROUND PYTHAGORIO
The Ireon Ηραίον

The Sacred Way, once flanked by thousands of statues, led from the city to the **Ireon** (☎ 2273 095 277; adult/student €3/2, EU student free; ☼ 8.30am-3pm Tue-Sun), the legendary birthplace of Hera. Every goddess needs a sanctuary and this one was built in the 6th century BC on swampy land where the River Imbrasos enters the sea. There had been a temple on the site since Mycenaean times, but the Ireon was enormous; it was four times the size of the Parthenon. As a result of plunderings and earthquakes only one column remains standing, although the extent of the temple can be gleaned from the foundations. Other remains on the site include a stoa, more temples and a 5th-century basilica.

The Ireon is now listed as a World Heritage site. It is situated on the coast 8km west of Pythagorio.

Mytilinii Μυτιληνιοί

The fascinating **palaeontology museum** (☎ 2273 052 055; admission €2.50; ☉ 9am-2pm), on the main thoroughfare of the inland village of Mytilinii, between Pythagorio and Vathy (Samos), houses skeletons of prehistoric animals. Included in the collection are remains of animals that were the antecedents of the giraffe and elephant. From the museum it's a nice walk to Agia Triada monastery, where there's an ossuary.

Beaches

Sandy **Psili Ammos** (not to be confused with a beach of the same name near Votsalakia in the west of the island) is the finest beach near Pythagorio. This lovely cove is bordered with trees and looks across the water at Turkey. The gently sloping water makes it ideal for families and it's extremely popular, so get there early to grab your spot. There are a few reasonably priced tavernas off the beach that rent rooms. The beach can be reached by car or scooter from the Vathy–Pythagorio road (signposted), or by excursion boat (€11) from Pythagorio. There are also buses from Vathy (Samos). If you arrive by road, look out for the pond on your left that hosts a bevy of pink flamingos in the spring. It's about 1km before the beach.

Glykoriza Beach, nearer Pythagorio, is dominated by a few hotels, but is a clean, public beach of pebbles and sand. It's a good alternative to Psili Ammos, but not as pretty.

SOUTHWEST SAMOS

The southwest coast of Samos remained unspoilt for longer than the north coast, but in recent years a series of resorts has sprung up alongside the best beaches. The area east of Marathokampos was ravaged by fires in 2000, and the forests are only beginning to recover.

Ormos, 50km from Vathy, has a pebble beach. From here a road leads 6km to the inland village of **Marathokampos**, which is worth a visit for the stunning view down to the immense Bay of Marathokampos. **Votsalakia**, 4km west of Ormos and known officially as Kampos, and the much nicer **Psili Ammos**, 2km beyond, have long, sandy

beaches. There are many domatia and tavernas on this stretch of coast though it has a rather scrappy feel and lacks the intimacy of smaller coastal resorts.

With your own transport you may like to continue from Psili Ammos along a stunning route that skirts mighty **Mt Kerkis**, high above the totally undeveloped and isolated west coast. The road passes through the village of **Kallithea**, and continues to **Drakeï**, where it terminates.

WEST OF VATHY (SAMOS)

The road that skirts the north coast passes many beaches and resorts. The fishing village of **Kokkari**, 10km from Vathy (Samos), is also a holiday resort with a long and narrow pebble beach. The place is very popular with tourists, and it is exposed to the frequent summer winds and for that reason is a favourite of windsurfers. Rooms, studios and tavernas abound, all offering much the same quality.

Beaches extend from here to **Avlakia**, with **Lemonaki** and **Tsamadou Beaches** being the most accessible for walkers staying in Kokkari. Clothing is optional at these two secluded beaches. Continuing west, beyond Avlakia, the road is flanked by trees, a foretaste of the scenery encountered on the roads leading inland from the coast. A turn-off south along this stretch leads to the delightful mountain village of Vourliotes, from where you can walk another 3km to **Moni Panagias Vrondianis**. Built in the 1550s, it is the island's oldest extant monastery; a sign in the village points the way.

Continuing along the coast, a 5km road winds its way up the lower slopes of Mt Ampelos through thick, well-watered woodlands of pine and deciduous trees, to the gorgeous village of **Manolates**, which is nearly encircled by forested mountains. The area is rich in bird life, with a proliferation of nightingales, warblers and thrushes whose chirpings echo through the steep old streets. **Vourliotes** is slightly larger than Manolates with multicoloured, shuttered houses surrounding a central square. It can be reached by a footpath from Kokkari. The Samians say that if you have not visited either Vourliotes or Manolates, then you have not seen Samos. We would agree.

Back on the coast, the road continues to the pretty flower-filled village of **Agios**

Konstantinos. Beyond here it winds through rugged coastal scenery to the town of **Karlovasi**, Samos' third port. The town consists of three contiguous settlements: Paleo (old), Meson (middle) and Neo (new). It once boasted a thriving tanning industry, but now it's a lacklustre place with little of interest for visitors. The nearest beach is the sand and pebble **Potami**, 2km west of town.

Sleeping

In the high season the **EOT** (National Tourism Organisation; ☎ 2273 092 217) in Kokkari will assist in finding accommodation. The bus stops on the main road at a large stone church, and the EOT is about 100m up the street next to the OTE. Along the coastal strip of Kokkari there are many hotels and pensions.

Kokkari Beach Hotel (☎ 2273 092 238; fax 2273 092 381; s/d €90/100; ☒ ☒) For a touch of class try this place, about 1km west of the bus stop. The pretty yellow building is set back from the road leaving the comfortably furnished rooms a quiet haven in this busy village.

Studio Angella (☎ 2273 094 478, 2105 059 708 in Athens, 6972 975 722; d €30) In Manolates try this studio built into the side of a hill. Rooms have balconies with spectacular views over the mountains.

Traditional Greek House (☎ 2273 094 331, 2273 094 174; d €20.50) Phone to inquire about the studio in this nice little unnamed house in Manolates. The quiet and romantic room is large and tastefully furnished. It's in the centre of the village next to Giorgidas taverna.

If you get stuck in Karlovasi there are several budget hotels and domatia, some signposted from the central square where the bus terminates.

Eating

There are many reasonably priced restaurants to be found in Kokkari, all offering 'English menus' and the usual range of bland tourist fare but the best eating is in the little mountain villages.

Grill Café (☎ 2273 093 291; mains from €5) In Vourliotes, this little taverna on the left of the main square is run by two women who very obviously appreciate their own fine cooking. The plate of mixed mezedes is excellent (and vegetarian) and the pita sandwiches with home-made sausage are not to be believed.

Paradisos Restaurant (☎ 2273 094 208; mains from €7, with wine or beer around €11) This restaurant, at the turn-off to Manolates, serves delectable dishes on a relaxing tree-shaded terrace.

Loukas Taverna (☎ 2273 094 541; mains €3-4.50) In Manolates, climb to the top of the hill to this taverna for the best and cheapest food around as well as great views. Try the stuffed courgette flowers and the special home-made *moshato* (muscat) wines. Follow the prominent signs to the back end of the village.

CHIOS ΧΙΟΣ

area 859 sq km

Chios (*hee*-os) does not feature prominently on the travel circuit. Situated rather awkwardly on the ferry routes and without a tangible international profile, the island attracts curious travellers and expat Greeks rather than hordes of package tourists, though those that do come find the island subtly rewarding in its own distinct way. The mastic villages of the south are highly original, there are some decent beaches and the glorious profusion of tulips in the spring is magnificent. The island is separated from Turkey's Karaburun Peninsula by the 8km-wide Chios Straits which makes it a convenient stepping stone to Turkey.

A large number of highly successful ship owners come from Chios and its dependencies, Inousses and Psara. This, and its mastic production, have meant that Chios has not needed to develop a large tourist industry. In recent years, however, package tourism has begun to make inroads, though it's limited to a fairly small coastal stretch south of Chios.

Getting There & Away

AIR

Chios has on average four flights daily to Athens (€69), three weekly to Thessaloniki (€149) and two weekly to Lesvos (€43). **Olympic Airways** (☎ 2271 020 359; Leof Aigaiou) is in Chios Town. The airport is 4km from Chios Town. There is no Olympic Airways bus, but a taxi to/from the airport should cost about €5.

FERRY
Domestic

In summer at least one ferry goes daily to Piraeus (€19.50, eight hours) and Lesvos (€12, three hours). There's one ferry per week to Thessaloniki (€30, 18 hours) via

CHIOS

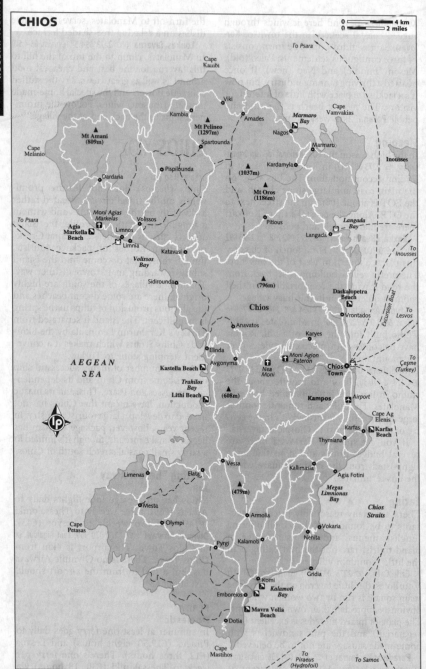

NORTHEASTERN
AEGEAN ISLANDS

Limnos (€18, 11 hours), and Alexandroupolis (€23.50, 12½ hours) via Limnos. There are three boats weekly to Samos (€10.70, four hours) and one each per week to Kos (€17.50, nine hours) and Rhodes (€27.70, 15 hours). Tickets for these routes can be bought from **NEL** (☎ 2271 023 971; fax 2271 041 319; Leof Aigaiou 16) in Chios Town.

Miniotis Lines (☎ 2271 024 670; www.miniotis.gr; Neorion 23) in Chios Town runs small boats to Karlovasi (€9, four hours) and Vathy (€11, 4½ hours) on Samos twice a week. Three times a week these boats continue on to Fourni (€17.50, 7½ hours) and Ikaria (€18.70, 8½ hours). Miniotis also has three boats weekly to Psara (€8.80, 3½ hours). Miniotis boats occasionally dock at the southern end of the harbour, at the corner of Leof Aigaiou and Kokali.

The *Oinoussai II,* another small local boat, runs to and from Inousses (€3, 1¼ hours, daily). Most days it leaves Chios in the afternoon and Inousses in the morning, so you must stay overnight. Purchase tickets on board. **Sunrise Tours** (☎ 2271 041 390; Neorion 37) also runs excursions to the island in the high season (€15) about three times a week. There are also daily water taxis between Langada and Inousses (€45, shared between the passengers).

International
Boats to Turkey run all year from Chios. From April to October there are usually two ferries weekly to Çeşme, leaving Chios at 8.30am and returning at 6.30pm. During May there is an additional sailing and from July to September there are daily sailings. The fare is €40/50 one way/return (not including the €9 port tax). Further information and tickets can be obtained from **Miniotis Lines** (☎ 2271 024 670; www.miniotis.gr; Neorion 23). The special daily excursion rates often work out cheaper. Check with local agencies offering such trips.

Travellers requiring visas for Turkey can obtain them upon arrival in Çeşme for around US$45 depending on their nationality.

HYDROFOIL
From April to September there are about three hydrofoils a week to Lesvos (€23.50, two hours) and Piraeus (€35.60, four hours).

Getting Around
BUS
From the **long-distance bus station** (☎ 2271 027 507) in Chios there are, in summer, eight buses from Monday to Friday to Pyrgi (€2.16), five to Mesta (€2.66) and six to Kardamyla (€2.16) via Langada. There are four buses a week to Volissos (€2.66). A few buses go to the main beaches of Kampia, Nagos and Lithi but the schedule may make it impractical to take day trips. Services are reduced by about half in the low season. Buses to Karfas Beach are serviced by the blue (city) bus company. Schedules are posted at both the **local bus station** (☎ 2271 022 079) and the long-distance bus station in Chios Town.

CAR & MOTORCYCLE
The numerous car-rental outlets in Chios Town include **Aegean Travel** (☎ 2271 041 277; aegeantr@otenet.gr; Leof Aigaiou 114), at the northern end of the waterfront. In summer it's a good idea to book in advance for weekends.

TAXI
There is a **taxi rank** (Plateia Vounakiou) in Chios Town. Call ☎ 2271 041 111 for a taxi.

CHIOS TOWN
pop 23,779
The town of Chios, on the east coast, is the island's port and capital. It's a large settlement, home to almost half of the island's inhabitants. Its waterfront, flanked by concrete buildings and trendy bars, is noisy in the extreme, with an inordinate number of cars and motorcycles careering up and down. The atmospheric old quarter, with many Turkish houses built around a Genoese castle, and the lively market area, are both worth a stroll. Chios doesn't have a beach; the nearest is the sandy beach at Karfas, 6km south.

Orientation
Most ferries dock at the northern end of the waterfront at the western end of Neorion. Some ferries from Piraeus arrive at the very inconvenient time of 4am – worth remembering if you are planning to find a room. The old Turkish quarter (called Kastro) is to the north of the ferry quay. To reach the town centre from here, follow the waterfront around to the left and walk along Leof

Aigaiou. Turn right onto Kanari to reach the central square of Plateia Vounakiou. To the northwest of the square are the public gardens, and to the southeast is the market area. The main shopping streets are south of the square. As you face inland, the local bus station is on the right side of the public gardens, and the long-distance bus station is on the left.

Information

Enter Internet Café (☎ 2271 041 058; Leof Aigaiou 48; €3.60 per hour) On the southern waterfront.
Mr Quick (☎ 2271 026 108; Prokymea 46; €6 per kg) Handy for doing laundry.
Municipal Tourist office (☎ 2271 044 389; infochio@otenet.gr; Kanari 18; ☻ 7am-10pm Apr-Oct,

7am-4pm Nov-Mar) Extremely helpful and friendly, it provides information on accommodation, car rental, bus and boat schedules, and more. The book *Hiking Routes on Chios* is available here for free.
National Bank of Greece This and most other banks are between Kanari and Plateia Vounakiou. There is an ATM halfway along Aplotarias.
Port police (☎ 2271 044 432) At the eastern end of Neorion.
Post office One block back from the waterfront.
Tourist police (☎ 2271 044 427) Also at the eastern end of Neorion.

Sights

The most interesting museum is the **Philip Argenti Museum** (☎ 2271 023 463; Koraïs; admission €1.50; ☻ museum & library 8am-2pm Mon-Fri, 5-7.30pm

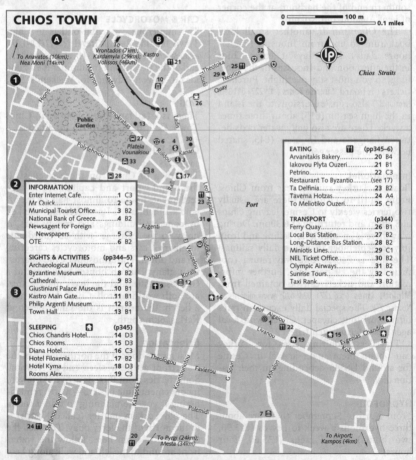

CHIOS TOWN

0 — 100 m
0 — 0.1 miles

Chios Straits

To Anavatos (10km);
Nea Moni (14km)

Vrontados (7km);
Kardamyla (29km); Kastro
Volissos (46km)

Public Garden

Plateia Vounakiou

Port

Argenti

Psyhari

To Pyrgi (24km);
Mesta (34km)

To Airport;
Kampos (4km)

INFORMATION
Enter Internet Cafe...............1 C3
Mr Quick..............................2 C3
Municipal Tourist Office........3 B2
National Bank of Greece.......4 B2
Newsagent for Foreign
  Newspapers.......................5 C3
OTE.....................................6 C3

SIGHTS & ACTIVITIES (pp344-5)
Archaeological Museum........7 C4
Byzantine Museum...............8 B2
Cathedral.............................9 B3
Giustiniani Palace Museum...10 B1
Kastro Main Gate.................11 B1
Philip Argenti Museum.........12 B3
Town Hall............................13 B1

SLEEPING (p345)
Chios Chandris Hotel............14 D3
Chios Rooms.......................15 D3
Diana Hotel.........................16 C3
Hotel Filoxenia.....................17 B2
Hotel Kyma.........................18 D3
Rooms Alex..........................19 C3

EATING (pp345-6)
Arvanitakis Bakery...............20 B4
Iakovou Plyta Ouzeri............21 B1
Petrino................................22 C3
Restaurant To Byzantio........(see 17)
Ta Delfinia...........................23 B2
Taverna Hotzas....................24 A4
To Meliotiko Ouzeri..............25 C1

TRANSPORT (p344)
Ferry Quay..........................26 B1
Local Bus Station.................27 B2
Long-Distance Bus Station....28 B2
Miniotis Lines.......................29 C1
NEL Ticket Office..................30 B2
Olympic Airways...................31 B2
Sunrise Tours.......................32 C1
Taxi Rank............................33 B2

Fri, 8am-12.30pm Sat) is in the same building as the Koraïs Library, one of the country's largest libraries. The museum, which is near the cathedral, contains embroideries, traditional costumes and portraits of the wealthy Argenti family.

The town's other museums are not so compelling. The **archaeological museum** (☎ 2271 044 239; Mihalon 10; admission €2; ⏱ 8.30am-2.45pm Tue-Sun) contains sculptures, pottery and coins dating from the Neolithic period. It sometimes has interesting temporary exhibits. The **Byzantine Museum** (☎ 2271 026 866; Plateia Vounakiou; admission free; ⏱ 10am-2pm Tue-Sun) is housed in a former mosque, the Medjitie Djami. The most worthwhile exhibit is the collection of sculptures that date from the 14th- to 15th-century Genoese occupation of Chios.

Just inside the Kastro's main gate is the tiny **Giustiniani Palace Museum** (☎ 2271 022 819; admission €2 Mon-Sat, €1 Sun; ⏱ 9am-3pm Tue-Sun). It holds a few restored wall paintings of prophets, and other Byzantine bits and pieces. The most important works are the 12 Byzantine frescoes of the prophets that date from the 13th century.

Sleeping
BUDGET
With over 30 domatia to choose from, budget accommodation is fairly plentiful in Chios. Call into the municipal tourist office for a full listing. Be aware, though, that accommodation in central Chios can be very noisy – choose carefully.

Chios Rooms (☎ 2271 020 198, 6972 833 841; Leof Aigaiou 110; s/d/tr €20/26/35) This beautifully decked-out neoclassical place is a real find. It's clean, comfortable and full of interesting artworks and old pieces of furniture. Front rooms are cooler but may be noisy. Except for the triples, rooms have shared bath.

Rooms Alex (☎ 2271 026 054; Livanou 29; d €31) This is another domatia option. Alex has six doubles and there is a relaxing roof garden festooned with flags. Alex will pick you up at your boat if you call him. He will also help with car or bike rentals and give general information on Chios.

MID-RANGE & TOP END
Hotel Kyma (☎ 2271 044 500; kyma@chi.forthnet.gr; Evgenias Chandris 1; s/d €46/60; ✾) The Kyma occupies a century-old mansion and has lots of character. Try to get one of the rooms

overlooking the sea. The breakfast is magnificent (and included in the room rate). The helpful owners can organise driving itineraries that include accommodation in Mesta and Volissos.

Diana Hotel (☎ 2271 044 180; fax 2271 026 748; El Venizelou 92; s/d incl breakfast €47/58; ✾) This place is a good hotel aimed primarily at the Greek business market. The rooms are soundproof and the service is efficient.

Hotel Filoxenia (☎ 2271 026 559; fax 2271 028 447; Voupalou 8; s/d €40/50; ✾) This is signposted from the waterfront and is above Restaurant To Byzantio. The foyer has a lovely faded decadence about it, but the rooms are standard-issue. They all have fridges and balconies and prices include breakfast.

Chios Chandris Hotel (☎ 2271025768; www.chandris .gr; Evgenias Chandris 2; s/d incl breakfast €93/120, 3-person studio & 2-person ste €200; ✾ ✾) This classy international-style hotel is the best on the island. All rooms have a balcony with sea view. There's a good restaurant and bar, full room service and many other facilities.

Eating
Petrino (☎ 2273 029 797; mains from €7) New and trendy, but with a good handle on the Greek classics, this sleek place may be a little pricier than the average, but it's well worth it.

Taverna Hotzas (☎ 2271 042 787; Kondyli 3; dishes around €4; ⏱ evening Mon-Sat year-round) This taverna at the southern end of town is an institution, with lots of ugly cats and a lovely garden littered with lemon trees. Try the *fava* (yellow split peas), the *mastelo* (grilled cheese) and the grilled fish.

Restaurant To Byzantio (☎ 2271 041 035; cnr Ralli & Roïdou; mains from €4) This bright, cheerful, unpretentious place serves good traditional Greek fare to a local crowd at low prices.

Iakovou Plyta Ouzeri (☎ 2271 023 858; Agiou Georgiou Frouriou 20; mezedes from around €3) Tucked away in the old town is this ouzeri specialising in tasty fish mezedes.

Arvanitakis Bakery (cnr Katapoka & Kountouriotou) The bread baked here is some of the best you'll find in Greece. Try the whole wheat.

To Meliotiko Ouzeri (☎ 2271 040 407; salads & vegetable dishes around €3, seafood around €7) This basic place on the waterfront near the police station dishes out huge helpings of delicious Greek salads, seafood and vegetable appetisers. Be hungry.

Ta Delfinia (☎ 2271 022 607; Leof Aigaiou 36; mains from around €4) This waterfront taverna is a bit touristy (with photo menus), but the food and service are good and it's the best place to watch the street life.

CENTRAL CHIOS

North of the town of Chios is an elongated beachside suburb leading to **Vrontados** where you can sit on the supposed stone chair of Homer, the Daskalopetra, although it is quietly accepted that it's unlikely to have been used by Homer himself. It's a serene spot however, and it is not hard to imagine Homer and his acolytes reciting epic verses to their admiring followers.

Immediately south of Chios is a warren of walled mansions, some restored, others crumbling, called the **Kampos**. This was the preferred place of abode of wealthy Genoese and Greek merchant families from the 14th century onwards. It's easy to get lost here so keep your wits about you. It's best to tour the area by bicycle, moped or car, since it is fairly extensive. Chios' main beach resort, **Karfas**, is here too, 7km south of Chios. The beach is sandy though comparatively small with some moderate development and some A-class hotels; if you like your beaches quiet, look elsewhere.

In the centre of the island is the **Nea Moni** (admission free; ☺ 8am-1pm & 4-8pm). This large, 11th-century World Heritage–listed monastery stands in a beautiful mountain setting, 14km from Chios. Like many monasteries in Greece it was built to house an icon of the Virgin Mary who appeared before the eyes of three shepherds. In its heyday the monastery was one of the richest in Greece with the most pre-eminent artists of Byzantium commissioned to create the mosaics in its katholikon.

In 1822, the buildings were set on fire and all the resident monks were massacred by the Turks. There is a macabre display of their skulls in the ossuary at the monastery's little chapel. In the earthquake of 1881 the katholikon's dome caved in, causing damage to the mosaics. Nonetheless, the mosaics, esteemed for the striking contrasts of their vivid colours and the fluidity and juxtapositions of the figures, still rank among the most outstanding examples of Byzantine art in Greece. A few nuns live at the monastery. The bus service to the monastery is poor,

but travel agents in Chios have excursions here and to Anavatos.

Ten kilometres from Nea Moni, at the end of a road that leads to nowhere, stands the forlorn village of **Anavatos**. Its abandoned grey-stone houses stand as lonely sentinels to one of Chios' great tragedies. Nearly all the inhabitants of the village perished in 1822 and today only a couple of elderly people live there, mostly in houses at the base of the village. It is a striking village, built on a precipitous cliff which the villagers chose to hurl themselves over, rather than be taken captive by the Turks. Narrow, stepped pathways wind between the houses to the summit of the village but the general decrepitude of the village makes the walk dangerous and the route is often closed. Currently, the village is being spruced up a little in the hope of attracting more tourists.

The beaches on the mid-west coast are not spectacular, but they are quiet and generally undeveloped. **Lithi Beach**, the southernmost, is popular with weekenders and can get busy.

SOUTHERN CHIOS

Southern Chios is dominated by medieval villages that look as though they were transplanted from the Levant rather than built by Genoese colonisers in the 14th century. The rolling, scrubby hills are covered in low mastic trees that for many years were the main source of income for these scattered settlements (see the Gum Mastic box, opposite).

There are some 20 Mastihohoria (mastic villages); the two best preserved villages are Pyrgi and Mesta. As mastic was a lucrative commodity in the Middle Ages, many an invader cast an acquisitive eye upon these villages, necessitating sturdy fortifications. The archways spanning the streets were to prevent the houses from collapsing during earthquakes. Because of the sultan's fondness for mastic chewing gum, the inhabitants of the Mastihohoria were spared in the 1822 massacre.

Pyrgi Πυργί
pop 1044

The fortified village of Pyrgi, 24km southwest of Chios, is the largest of the Mastihohoria and one of the most extraordinary villages in the whole of Greece. The vaulted

GUM MASTIC

'The Tear of a Shrub' is how the mastic industry describes its famous product. The resin that seeps from the mastic tree, or lentisk bush, resembles tears and the hard manual work required to harvest, dry and clean the product probably provokes them. Many ancient Greeks, including Hippocrates, proclaimed the pharmaceutical benefits of mastic, claiming that it cured stomach upsets, chronic coughs and diseases of the liver, intestines and bladder. It was also used as an antidote for snake bites. During Turkish rule Chios received preferential treatment from the sultans who, along with the ladies of the harem, were hooked on chewing gum made from mastic.

Conditions in southern Chios are ideal for the growth of the mastic tree. Until recently, mastic was widely used in the pharmaceutical industry, as well as in the manufacture of chewing gum and certain alcoholic drinks, particularly arak, a Middle Eastern liqueur. In most cases mastic has now been replaced by *raki*, a Greek firewater. But mastic production may yet have a future. Some adherents of alternative medicine claim that it stimulates the immune system and reduces blood pressure and cholesterol levels. Chewing gum, lotions, toothpaste, soaps and various other mastic products are available at **Mastihashop** (☎ 2271 081 600; Leof Aigaiou 36), in Chios Town, and chewing gum made from mastic can be bought everywhere on Chios, under the brand name Elma.

streets of the fortified village are narrow and labyrinthine, but what makes Pyrgi unique are the building facades, decorated with intricate grey and white designs. Some of the patterns are geometric and others are based on flowers, leaves and animals. The technique used, called *xysta*, is achieved by coating the walls with a mixture of cement and black volcanic sand, painting over this with white lime, and then scraping off parts of the lime with the bent prong of a fork, to reveal the matt grey beneath.

From the main road, a fork heading to the right (coming from Chios) leads to the heart of the village and the central square. The little 12th-century **Church of Agios Apostolos**, just off the square, is profusely decorated with well-preserved 17th-century frescoes. It's usually open for mass on Sunday and in the late afternoon. The facade of the larger church, on the opposite side of the square, has the most impressive xysta of all the buildings here.

SLEEPING & EATING

Rooms are few and far between but there are three tavernas on the central square. **Giannaki Rooms** (☎ 2271 025 888, 6945 959 889; fax 2271 022 846; d €55; ✷) are worth a try if you stay in town. Giannaki offers modern and renovated rooms with TV. Book ahead.

Emboreios Εμπορειός

Six kilometres south of Pyrgi, Emboreios was the port of Pyrgi in the days when mastic production was big business. These

days Emboreios is a quiet place, perfect for people who like to get away from it all. As you come from Chios, a sign points left to Emboreios, just before you arrive at Pyrgi.

Mavra Volia Beach is at the end of the road and has unusual black volcanic pebbles as its main attraction. The effect is striking but the wide beach is shadeless.

There is another more secluded beach, just over the headland along a paved track.

SLEEPING & EATING

Studio Apartments Vasiliki (☎ 2271 071 422; d €45; ✷) These comfortable studios in Emboreios are often full, but the same people also have rooms in Mavra Volia.

Porto Emborios (☎ 2271 070 025; mains from €6, appetisers €3.50) On the main square this shady place is very pleasant, with an old stone facade decorated with fishing nets and hanging strings of chillies and garlic. It has good home-cooked food, including roast lamb and a number of vegetarian dishes.

Mesta Μεστά

Mesta has a very different atmosphere from that created by the striking visuals of Pyrgi and should be on any visitor's itinerary. Nestled among low hills, the village is exquisite and completely enclosed within massive fortified walls. Entrance to the maze of streets is via one of four gates. This method of limiting entry to the settlement and its disorienting maze of streets and tunnels is a prime example of 14th-century defence architecture, as protection against pirates and marauders. The labyrinthine cobbled streets of bare stone houses and arches have a melancholy aura, though it's generally a cheerful place, with women chatting on their front steps as they shell almonds and fresh *revithia* (chickpeas) or tie bundles of sweet-smelling herbs.

The village has two churches of the Taxiarhes (archangels). The older one dates from Byzantine times and has a magnificent 17th-century iconostasis. The second one, built in the 19th century, has very fine frescoes.

ORIENTATION

Buses stop on Plateia Nikolaou Poumpaki, on the main road outside Mesta. To reach the central square of Plateia Taxiarhon, with your back to the bus shelter, turn right, and then immediately left, and you will see a sign pointing to the centre of the village.

SLEEPING & EATING

Despina Floris Rooms (☎ 2271 076 050; fax 2271 076 529; double studio around €32.50) This clearing house for renovated rooms is perhaps the best place to start if you're looking for somewhere to stay. Despina, who also runs Mesaonas restaurant on the square (and were you need to go to enquire about a room), speaks good English and is a fountain of information about the village.

Anna Floradis Rooms (☎ 2271 028 891, 2271 076 455/176; d €40) These five, very comfortable rooms are next to the church.

Karambelas Apartments (☎ 2271 022 068; 10 Ilia Mandalaka; d €65) These exquisite, spotless studios in a renovated medieval house belong to the family that runs O Morias Sta Mesta taverna. Rooms contain beautiful handmade textiles and stone wall niches. You can negotiate a much better rate outside the high season. Ask at the taverna if no-one answers the phone.

O Morias Sta Mesta (☎ 2271 076 400; Plateia Taxiarhon; mains from €4.50) Dionyssis Karambelas, the affable owner of this restaurant – one of the two on the square in romantic courtyard settings – is originally from the Peloponnese (hence the name of the restaurant: Morias was once used as a name for the Peloponnese). Dionyssis will provide you with superb country cooking. Ask to try the *hortokeftedes* (vegetable patties) and an unusual wild green, *kritamos* (rock samphire), that grows by the sea. The bread is home-made and the

unusually sweet olives taste like mastic. You may be given a glass of *souma*, an ouzo made from seasonal fruit, or a mastic firewater.

Mesaonas (☎ 2271 076 050; Plateia Taxiarhon; mains from €4.50) This restaurant on the square is also very good. It specialises in traditional recipes made with local ingredients. The wine, oil, cheese and, of course, the souma, are all from Mesta.

NORTHERN CHIOS

Northern Chios is characterised by its craggy peaks (Mt Pelineo, Mt Oros and Mt Amani), deserted villages and scrawny hillsides once blanketed in rich pine forests. The area is mainly for the adventurous and those not fazed by tortuous roads.

Volissos is the main focus for the villages of the northwestern quarter. Reputedly Homer's place of birth, it is today a quiet settlement, capped with an impressive Genoese fort. Volissos' port is **Limnia**, a workaday fishing harbour. It's not especially appealing, but has a welcoming taverna. You can continue to **Limnos**, 1km away, where caïques sometimes leave for Psara. The road onwards round the north end is very winding and passes some isolated villages.

On the eastern side a picturesque road leads out of Vrontados through a landscape that is somewhat more visitor-friendly than the western side. **Langada** is the first village, wedged at the end of a bay looking out towards Inousses. Next are **Kardamyla** and **Marmaro**, the two main settlements. If you fancy a dip, head a few kilometres further to the lush little fishing hamlet of **Nagos**. It has a nice beach with coloured pebbles.

Beyond Nagos, the road winds upwards, skirting craggy Mt Pelineo. The scenery is green enough, but settlements are fewer and more remote. **Amades** and **Viki** are two villages you will traverse before hitting the last village, **Kambia**, perched high up on a ridge overlooking bare hillsides and the sea far below. From here a mostly sealed road leads you round Mt Pelineo, past a futuristic phalanx of 10 huge wind-driven generators on the opposite side of the valley, and back to the trans-island route near Volissos.

Sleeping

Hotel Kardamyla (☎ 2272 023 353; kyma@chi.forthnet .gr; s/d €56/72; 🏊) If you choose to stay in Marmaro, try this comfortable hotel run by the

Kritamos dish (p348), Chios, Northeastern
Aegean Islands

ALAN BENSON

ALAN BENSON

Cafés in Pyrgi (p346), Chios,
Northeastern Aegean Islands

Domed church, Samos (p333), Northeastern Aegean Islands

STELLA HELLANDER

CHRIS CHRISTO

Pythagorio (p337), Samos, Northeastern
Aegean Islands

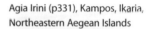

Agia Irini (p331), Kampos, Ikaria,
Northeastern Aegean Islands

STELLA HELLANDER

Lesvos (p350), Northeastern Aegean Islands

DAVID TIPLING

same management as Hotel Kyma in Chios. The sprawling establishment is right on a quiet cove just outside the village, making it an ideal spot for a holiday at the beach. If you call ahead, the owners will arrange for transport.

INOUSSES ΟΙΝΟΥΣΣΕΣ

pop 1050 / area 14 sq km

Off the northeastern coast of Chios lie nine tiny islets, collectively called Inousses. Only one of these, also called Inousses, is inhabited. Those who live here permanently make their living from fishing and sheep farming. The island has three fish farms and exports small amounts of fish to Italy and France. Inousses is hilly and covered in scrub and has good beaches.

However, these facts aside, Inousses is no ordinary Greek island. Inousses may be small, but it is the ancestral home of around 30% of Greece's ship owners. Most of these wealthy maritime barons conduct their business from Athens, London and New York, but in summer return with their families to Inousses, where they own luxurious mansions.

There is a rumour that these ship owners offer financial incentives to discourage people from opening tavernas or domatia on the island, because they don't want to attract foreign tourists. It may not be possible to vouch for the truth of this but certainly tourism is not encouraged on the island: no domatia owners come to meet the boat, there are no domatia signs and wandering around the streets fails to bring offers of accommodation. There is one overpriced hotel and a couple of nearly deserted tavernas. The place has a curiously barren and sterile air since there are few tourist facilities and even fewer visitors.

On a more positive note – and if these quirks have not discouraged you from going to Inousses – the island's town has some nice neoclassical mansions and abandoned houses, good beaches (**Kastro Beach** is the usual swimming stop for day-trippers) and no tourists. In the town of Inousses there is a large naval boarding school. If you visit during term time you may well encounter the pupils parading around town to bellowed marching orders.

Getting There & Away

The best way to visit this island is on a day-long excursion (€15). These are run regularly between June and September. Try **Sunrise Tours** (☎ 2271 041 390; Neorion 37) in Chios Town. The island is served only by the local ferry boat (€3, one hour) but the schedule is not always geared towards day trips. There are also daily **water taxis** (☎ 6944 168 104) travelling to/from Langada. The one-way fare is €45, which is split between the passengers.

Getting Around

Inousses has no public transport and nowhere to rent wheels, but there is one taxi.

PSARA ΨΑΡΑ

pop 422 / area 45 sq km

Psara (psah-*rah*) is a rocky island with little vegetation, lying off the northwest coast of Chios. During Ottoman times Greeks settled on this remote island to escape Turkish oppression. By the 19th century, many of these inhabitants, like those of Chios and Inousses, had become successful ship owners. When the rallying cry for self-determination reverberated through the country, the Psariots zealously took up arms and contributed a large number of ships to the Greek cause. In retaliation the Turks stormed the island and killed all but 3000 of the 20,000 inhabitants. The island never regained its former glory and today all of the inhabitants live in the island's one settlement, also called Psara.

Like Inousses, Psara sees few tourists but there are some domatia and a couple of tavernas.

Getting There & Away

Ferries leave Chios for Psara (€8.80, 3½ hours) at 7am or 8am three times weekly but the schedule may mandate an overnight stay. Call **Miniotis Lines** (☎ 2271 024 670) in Chios or check with a local agent for current departure days since these change from year to year. Local caïques also run from Limnos (€5, three hours) on the west coast of Chios about once a week, but departure times are unpredictable and often depend on the prevailing weather conditions.

LESVOS (MYTILINI)
ΛΕΣΒΟΣ (ΜΥΤΙΛΗΝΗ)

pop 93,428 / area 1637 sq km

Lesvos (Mytilini) is the third-largest island in Greece, after Crete and Evia, and one of the most interesting. Scenically, culturally, historically and gastronomically, the Lesvos experience is hard to rival. The island is predominantly mountainous, with wonderful opportunities for trekking and bird-watching, while the fertile south and east of the island are carpeted with olive groves producing the best olive oil in Greece. The terrain is ideal for grazing and the sheep's milk cheese of Lesvos (*ladotyri*) is justifiably prized. The Gulf of Kalloni produces pungent sardines, eaten salted with local ouzo.

The artistic side of Lesvos is no less developed than its hedonistic side. Terpander, the musical composer, and Arion, the poet, were both born on Lesvos in the 7th century BC. A few centuries later, Aristotle and Epicurus taught at an exceptional school of philosophy which flourished on Lesvos. Perhaps the island's most famous progeny was Sappho, one of the greatest poets of ancient Greece, who was born on Lesvos around 630 BC. Unfortunately little of her poetry is extant, but what remains reveals a genius for combining passion with simplicity and detachment, in verses of beauty and power. More recently, the primitive painter Theophilos (1866–1934) and the Nobel Prize–winning poet Odysseus Elytis (1911–96) were born on Lesvos. The island is to this day a spawning ground for innovative ideas in the arts and politics, and is the headquarters of the University of the Aegean.

Lesvos is becoming a popular package-holiday destination, but is large enough to absorb tourists without seeming to be overrun. Still, it's best to visit outside the peak tourist months of July and August. Early spring and late autumn are ideal for trekking. There's a lot to see here; you could easily spend two weeks taking in the sights and still feel you've run out of time to see everything.

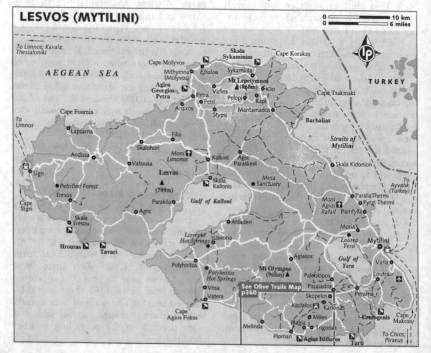

LESVOS (MYTILINI)

Trekking

Lesvos has some nice trekking trails in the north and south. Some of these were once marked with colour-coded signs, but these days only a few signs are left; nonetheless, the trails are easy to follow. These walks can be taken in sections, or over a few days, stopping off along the way where appropriate. They are a mixture of dirt vehicle tracks and pedestrian trails. The main trails are Vatera–Yera, Petra–Lapsarna, Kapi–Sykaminia and Sigri–Eresos. There are many other walking trails on the island, including those in the olive-growing region around Plomari (see Olive Trails, p360). Of these, the Skopelos–Karionas–Kastelos–Trigonas/Plagia day-trek is the most popular.

Bird-Watching

Bird-watching is big business in Lesvos. The island is the transit point and home to over 279 species of birds ranging from raptors to waders. As a result, Lesvos is attracting an ever-increasing number of visitors – human and feathered – particularly in spring. There are four main observation areas centred on Eresos, Petra, Skala Kallonis and Agiasos. The major aim of birders seems to be spotting the elusive cinereous bunting and Kruper's nuthatch.

Festivals & Events

Throughout summer, villages hold festivals on the name day of their church. These two-day festas with very ancient origins usually involve the racing of beautifully decorated horses and the sacrifice of a bull. For a list of dates and villages, see Festival Time on the next page.

If you're visiting the island in February, don't miss **carnival** in the town of Agiasos – among other things, the locals perform hilariously vulgar comedies.

Getting There & Away

AIR

Olympic Airways (☎ 2251 028 659; Kavetsou 44) in Mytilini (Kavetsou is a southerly continuation of Ermou) has at least four flights daily from Lesvos to Athens (€78) and one daily to Thessaloniki (€87), as well as two flights weekly to Chios (€28) and five weekly to Limnos (€46). **Aegean Airlines** (☎ 2251 061 120; fax 2251 061 801) flies between Lesvos and Athens three times a day and Thessaloniki

once a day; they have an office at the airport. Note that Lesvos is always referred to as Mytilene on air schedules. The airport is 8km south of Mytilini. A taxi to/from the airport will cost about €7.

FERRY

Domestic

In summer there is at least one ferry daily to Piraeus (€24.20, 12 hours) via Chios (€12, three hours) and three weekly high-speed services (€50, six hours). There are two ferries weekly to Kavala (€23.30, 10 hours) via Limnos (€15.80, six hours), two weekly to Thessaloniki (€30, 13 hours) via Limnos and one weekly to Alexandroupolis (€19.60, nine hours). Ferry ticket offices line the eastern side of Pavlou Kountourioti in Mytilini. Get tickets from **Maritime Company of Lesvos** (NEL; ☎ 2251 028 480; fax 2251 028 601; Pavlou Kountourioti 67) or **Samiotis Tours** (☎ 2251 042 574; fax 2251 041 808; Pavlou Kountourioti 43).

Samiotis Tours also handles tickets for the high-speed *Aeolis Express,* which sails three times weekly to Chios (€23.50, 1½ hours) and Piraeus (€47, six hours).

Lesvos has a very strict anti-drug policy, and the port police sometimes conduct searches of ferry passengers who look 'suspect'. Heavy penalties are imposed for possession of any drugs.

International

Ferries to Ayvalık in Turkey run roughly four times a week in high season. One-way and return tickets cost €39 (including port taxes). Tickets are available from **Aeolic Cruises** (☎ 2251 023 266; aeolic@les.forthnet.gr; Pavlou Kountourioti 47).

HYDROFOIL

In summer there are around three hydrofoils a week to Chios (€23.50, two hours).

Getting Around

BUS

Lesvos' transport hub is the capital, Mytilini. In summer, from the **long-distance bus station** (☎ 2251 028 873) there are three buses daily to Skala Eresou (€6.76, 2½ hours) via Eresos, five buses daily to Mithymna (€4.67, 1¾ hours) via Petra, and two buses daily to Sigri (€6.76, 2½ hours). There are no direct buses between Eresos, Sigri and Mithymna.

If you wish to travel from one of these villages to another, change buses in Kalloni, which is 48km from Eresos and 22km from Mithymna. There are five buses daily to the south coast resort of Plomari (€3, 1¼ hours). There are about half as many buses in the off season, with a schedule that may not allow day trips. A timetable is posted in the window at the bus station.

CAR & MOTORCYCLE

The many car-hire outlets in Mytilini include **Hertz** (☎ 2251 037 355, 6936 880 422; Pavlou Kountourioti 87) and **Egeon Rent a Car** (☎ 2251 029 820, 6977 653 583; Chiou 2), but it's best to shop around.

Many motorcycle-rental firms are located along the same stretch of waterfront. You will, however, be better off hiring a motorcycle or scooter in Mithymna or Skala Eresou, since Lesvos is a large island and an underpowered two-wheeler is not really a practical mode of transport for getting around.

FERRY

In summer there are hourly ferries (€1, five minutes) between Perama and Koundouroudia, near Loutra. Buses to Mytilini meet all ferries.

FESTIVAL TIME

One of the best times to be in Lesvos is during July and August when the days and nights are given over to wild bacchanals in honor of patron saints. There's usually a lot of food, drink, live music and dancing, as well as horse races and the sacrifice of a bull, which is then cooked overnight with wheat and eaten the next day. This traditional dish is known as *keskek*. On 6 August Skala Kalloni holds a sardine festival, which is not to be missed.

Major festival dates are as follows:
1 July – Agia Paraskevi
20 July – Agiasos, Eresos, Plomari, Vrisa
22 July – Skopelos
24 July – Eresos
25 July – Skala Kalloni
26 July – Paleokipos, Plomari
27 July – Eresos, Gavathas, Perama, Plomari
6 August – Eresos, Andissa, Skala Kalloni
15 August – Agiasos, Kerami
30 August – Vafios

MYTILINI TOWN ΜΥΤΙΛΗΝΗ

pop 27,247

Mytilini, the capital and port of Lesvos, is a large workaday town. If you are enthralled by pretty towns like Mykonos you won't necessarily find the same ambience in Mytilini. However, this town has its own attractions, including a lively harbour and nightlife, once-grand 19th-century mansions (that are gradually being renovated), and jumbled streets. You will love Mytilini if you enjoy seeking out traditional kafeneia and little backstreet ouzeria, or if you take pleasure in wandering through unfamiliar towns. With a large university campus and a year-round population, Mytilini – unlike most island towns – is also lively in winter.

The northern end of Ermou, the town's main commercial thoroughfare, is a wonderful ramshackle street full of character. It has old-fashioned zaharoplasteia, grocers, fruit and vegetable stores, bakers, and antique, embroidery, ceramic and jewellery shops.

Orientation

Mytilini is built around two harbours (north and south) that occupy both sides of a promontory and are linked by the main thoroughfare of Ermou. East of the harbours is a large fortress surrounded by a pine forest. All passenger ferries dock at the southern harbour. The waterfront here is called Pavlou Kountourioti and the ferry quay is at its southern end. The northern harbour's waterfront is called Navmahias Ellis.

Information

Commercial Bank The booth on Pavlou Kountourioti has an ATM, near the ferry terminal.

EOT (☎ 2251 042 511; 6 Aristarhou; ⏰ 9am-1pm Mon-Fri) Has brochures about the island.

National Bank of Greece (Pavlou Kountourioti) Has an ATM. Other banks can also be found along Pavlou Kountourioti.

Port police (☎ 2251 028 827) Next to Picolo Travel on the east side of Pavlou Kountourioti.

Post office (Vournazon) West of the southern harbour.

Sfetoudi Bookshop (☎ 2251 022 287; Ermou 51) Sells good maps, postcards and books on Lesvos. Look for *39 Coffee Houses and a Barber's Shop*, a beautifully produced book of photos by Jelly Hadjidimitriou.

Sponda (☎ 2251 041 007; Komniaki; €3 per hr) Has Internet access.

Tourist police (☎ 2251 022 776) At the entrance to the quay.

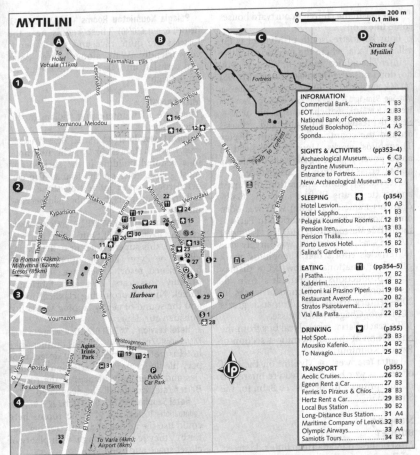

MYTILINI

INFORMATION	
Commercial Bank	1 B3
EOT	2 B3
National Bank of Greece	3 B3
Sfetoudi Bookshop	4 A3
Sponda	5 B2

SIGHTS & ACTIVITIES	(pp353–4)
Archaeological Museum	6 C3
Byzantine Museum	7 A3
Entrance to Fortress	8 C1
New Archaeological Museum	9 C2

SLEEPING	(p354)
Hotel Lesvion	10 A3
Hotel Sappho	11 B3
Pelagia Koumiotou Rooms	12 B1
Pension Iren	13 B3
Pension Thalia	14 B2
Porto Lesvos Hotel	15 B2
Salina's Garden	16 B1

EATING	(pp354–5)
I Psatha	17 B2
Kalderimi	18 B2
Lemoni kai Prasino Piperi	19 B4
Restaurant Averof	20 B2
Stratos Psarotaverna	21 B4
Via Alla Pasta	22 B2

DRINKING	(p355)
Hot Spot	23 B3
Mousiko Kafenio	24 B2
To Navagio	25 B2

TRANSPORT	(p355)
Aeolic Cruises	26 B2
Egeon Rent a Car	27 B3
Ferries to Piraeus & Chios	28 B3
Hertz Rent a Car	29 B3
Local Bus Station	30 B2
Long-Distance Bus Station	31 A4
Maritime Company of Lesvos	32 B3
Olympic Airways	33 A4
Samiotis Tours	34 B2

www.greeknet.com Information on Mytilini, and Lesvos in general.

Sights & Activities

Mytilini's imposing **fortress** (adult/student €2/1; 8.30am-3pm Tue-Sun) was built in early Byzantine times, renovated in the 14th century by Fragistco Gatelouzo, and subsequently enlarged by the Turks. The surrounding pine forest is a pleasant place for a picnic.

One block north of the quay and hotused in a neoclassical mansion is the **archaeological museum** (2251 022 087; adult/senior €3/2 both museums; 8.30am-3pm Tue-Sun). It has a large array of impressive finds from Neolithic to Roman times. It's a fascinating collection, with interesting ceramic figurines,

including some somersaulting women, and gold jewellery. There are excellent notes in Greek and English. There is also a **new archaeological museum** (8 Noemvriou; 8.30am-3pm Tue-Sun), 400m away, with impressive displays, including spectacular mosaics – whole housefuls – laid out under glass so that you can walk over them. Admission is included in the ticket for the other archaeological museum.

The dome of the **Church of Agios Therapon** can be spotted from almost anywhere on the southern waterfront. The church has a highly ornate interior with a huge chandelier, an intricately carved iconostasis and priest's throne, and a frescoed dome. The **Byzantine Museum** (2251 028 916; admission €2;

9am-1pm) in the church's courtyard houses some fine icons.

Four kilometres south of Mytilini is the village of **Varia**, where the prolific primitive painter Theophilos was born. Whatever you do, don't miss the **Theophilos Museum** (☎ 2251 041 644; admission €2; ☽ 9am-2.30pm & 6-8pm Tue-Sun May-Sep, 9am-1pm & 4-6pm Tue-Sun Oct & Apr, 9am-2pm Tue-Sun Nov-Mar), which houses his works. Several prestigious museums and galleries around the country now proudly display Theophilos' works. However, he lived in abject poverty, painting the walls of kafeneia and tavernas in return for sustenance.

Next door, commemorating the artist and critic Stratis Eleftheriadis (he Gallicised his name to Teriade) who was born on Lesvos but lived and worked in Paris, is the **Teriade Museum** (☎ 2251 023 372; adult/student €2/1; ☽ 9am-5pm Tue-Sun). It was largely due to Teriade's efforts that Theophilos' work gained international renown. On display are reproductions of Teriade's own illustrations and his collection of works by 20th-century artists, including such greats as Picasso, Chagall and Matisse.

To reach Varia, take a local bus from the bus station at the northernmost section of Pavlou Kountourioti.

Loutra Yera, west of Mytilini on the Gulf of Yera, is worth a visit if you're interested in hot springs – for details see Balm for the Soul, p356.

Sleeping
BUDGET
Most of these domatia are in little side streets off Ermou, near the northern harbour.

Salina's Garden (☎ 2251 024 073; cnr Fokeas & Kinikiou; s/d €25/28) These cosy and clean rooms are in a delightful garden, and guests can use the lovely kitchen to prepare their own meals. The rooms are signposted from the corner of Ermou and Adramytiou.

Pension Iren (☎ 2251 022 787; Komninaki 41; d/tr incl breakfast €30/35) This place has the nearest domatia to the quay. It has clean and simply furnished rooms. Komninaki is one block behind the eastern section of Pavlou Kountourioti.

Pension Thalia (☎ 2251 024 640; Kinikiou 1; d/tr €26/30) Coming from Ermou, if you turn right opposite Salina's Garden (belonging to the same owners) you will reach these clean, bright rooms in a large family house.

Pelagia Koumiotou Rooms (☎ 2251 020 643; Tsertseti 6; d/tr €30/40) These rooms near the fortress are quite nice and the owner is very friendly. Walk along Mikras Asias and turn left into Tsertseti; the rooms are on the right.

MID-RANGE
There are a few interesting choices in this price range.

Porto Lesvos Hotel (☎ 2251 022 510; www.portolesvos.gr; Komninaki 21; s/d €60/90; ☒) This new hotel in a restored building is the slickest and most stylish hotel on the island. The carpeted rooms sport interesting stone walls, toiletries, hairdryers, bathrobes, slippers and minibars.

Hotel Votsala (☎ 2251 071 231; www.votsalahotel .com; Pyrgi Thermi; d €63-75) Only 11km north of Mytilini, this superb hotel near the fishing village of Pyrgi Thermi offers a simple but refined resort experience. The hotel proudly forswears TVs and fabricated 'Greek Nights', promising classical music and the sound of gently lapping waves just outside your door.

Hotel Lesvion (☎ 2251 022 037; lesvion@otenet.gr; Kountourioti 27a; s/d €50/70; ☒) This business-like hotel is not a charmer but you do get coppery tile floors and a full selection of toiletries and other conveniences in the rooms. Better rates can usually be negotiated.

Hotel Sappho (☎ 2251 022 888; fax 2251 024 522; Kountourioti 31; s/d €35/54; ☒) The rooms here could use the advice of an interior decorator but they're large enough, with plenty of closet space and good beds.

Eating
You will eat well on Lesvos whether you enjoy fish dishes, traditional Greek food, international cuisine or vegetarian meals. You might wish to avoid the restaurants on the western section of the southern waterfront where the waiters tout for customers. These restaurants are atypical of Mytilini as they pander to tourists and serve bland, overpriced food.

Restaurant Averof (☎ 2251 022 180; Ermou 52; mains from €4) This place, in the middle of the southern waterfront, is a no-nonsense traditional restaurant serving hearty Greek staples like *patsas* (tripe soup). Despite its earthy cuisine it has a classy romantic ambience and excellent service.

Kalderimi (☎ 2251 046 577; Thasou 3; appetisers €2-4, mains around €6) Also near the main harbour, locals congregate at this little ouzeri with tables that spill out into the street. The food is excellent (try the grilled sardines) in contrast to the service, which can be slow.

I Psatha (☎ 2251 045 922; Hrysostomou; mains €4.50; ☺ evenings only) If you want some good-value meat dishes such as souvlaki, check out this place off Ermou. There is an old jukebox that actually works.

Stratos Psarotaverna (☎ 2251 021 739; Hristougennon 1944; mains from €8) Head to this place at the bottom end of the main harbour for top-quality fish dishes. Tables from all the surrounding restaurants take over the road in summer.

Lemoni kai Prasino Piperi (☎ 2251 024 014; cnr Pavlou Kountourioti & Hristougennon 1944; mains €6-12) If you're looking for a change, check out this classy Italian-Mediterranean place. It's upstairs, above a souvlaki joint, and has tables on a large balcony that overlooks the port.

Via Alla Pasta (☎ 2251 037 717; Mitropoleos 22; mains €7-12) The Italian food here is the real thing with excellent pasta and sauces made from the freshest ingredients.

Drinking
Mousiko Kafenio (cnr Mitropoleos & Vernardaki; ☺ 7.30am-2am) This is a hip place – arty without being pretentious. Drinks are mid-price range rather than cheap, but worth it for the terrific atmosphere.

Hot Spot (Kountourioti; ☺ 10am-midnight) On the east side of the harbour, this joint is known for its good music, and you can borrow board games here. It's a nice place to be at sunset.

To Navagio (☎ 2251 021 310; Arhipelagos 23) This upmarket yet casual place in the centre of the waterfront serves a good variety of alcoholic beverages as well as fresh juices, hearty breakfasts and great coffee.

Getting There & Away
Mytilini has two bus stations: the long-distance bus station is just beyond the southwestern end of Pavlou Kountourioti; the local bus station is on the northernmost section of Pavlou Kountourioti. For motorists, there is a large free parking area just south of the main harbour.

NORTHERN LESVOS
Northern Lesvos is dominated economically and physically by the exquisitely preserved traditional town of Mithymna, of historical, and modern, importance in Lesvos' commercial life. The neighbouring beach resort of Petra, 6km south, receives low-key package tourism, and the villages surrounding Mt Lepetymnos are authentic, picturesque and worth a day or two of exploration. Sykaminia, Mantamados and Agia Paraskevi in particular, are very pretty and worth a visit. Moni Taxiarhon, near Mantamados, is also worth a visit. Skala Sykaminias is a nice beach for a swim.

Mithymna Μήθυμνα
pop 1497
Although this town has officially reverted to its ancient name of Mithymna (Methymna), most locals still refer to it as Molyvos. It is 62km from Mytilini and is the principal town of northern Lesvos. A one-time rival to Mytilini, picturesque Mithymna is nowadays the antithesis of the island capital. Its impeccable stone houses with brightly coloured shutters reach down to the harbour from a castle-crowned hill. Its two main thoroughfares of Kastrou and 17 Noemvriou are winding, cobbled and shaded by vines. In contrast to Mytilini, Mithymna's pretty streets are lined with souvenir shops.

ORIENTATION
From the bus stop, walk straight ahead towards the town. Where the road forks (at the Medical Station sign), take the right fork into 17 Noemvriou. At the top of the hill, the road forks again; the right fork is Kastrou and the left fork is a continuation of 17 Noemvriou.

INFORMATION
Central Internet Café (€4.40 per hr) On the road to the port.
Commercial Bank A booth directly opposite National Bank of Greece; has an ATM.
Municipal tourist office (☎ 2253 071 347) A small office on the left of Kastrou between the bus stop and the fork in the road.
National Bank of Greece Next to the tourist office; it has an ATM.
Post office (Kastrou) Along the left of the street.

SIGHTS & ACTIVITIES

One of the most pleasant things to do in Mithymna is to stroll along its flower-shaded streets. If you have the energy, the ruined 14th-century **Genoese castle** (☎ 2253 071 803; admission €2; ◷ 8.30am-7pm Tue-Sun) is worth clambering up to for fine views of the coastline and over the sea to Turkey. From this castle in the 15th century, Onetta d'Oria, wife of the Genoese governor, repulsed an onslaught by the Turks by putting on her husband's armour and leading the people of Mithymna into battle. In summer the castle is the venue for a **drama festival**; ask for details at the tourist office.

The beach at Mithymna is pebbled and crowded, but in summer **excursion boats** leave at 10.30am daily for the superior beaches of Eftalou, Skala Sykaminias and Petra. Trips cost around €17 and up, depending on the itinerary; sunset cruises and boat 'safaris' are also available. Contact **Faonas Travel** (☎ 2253 071 630; tekes@otenet.gr), down at the port, for more information.

Eftalou's **hot spring** is an entrancing place on the beach – don't miss it (see below).

BALM FOR THE SOUL

Lesvos has many mineral springs, most dating back to ancient times. The baths are usually housed in old whitewashed buildings that look like sunken church domes. Small holes in the roof let in rays of sunlight, creating a magical dappled effect on the water. The pools are usually made of marble.

In times past, before houses had their own bathrooms, these communal baths were the places people came to bathe and talk.

With the exception of the ramshackle abandoned hot springs at Thermi, which are worth a visit (if you like faded grandeur), it's possible to take a dip at all of the baths. There are springs at Loutra Yera (near Mytilini) and Eftalou (near Mithymna) and two in the vicinity of Polyhnitos. The properties of the waters are outlined in the following text.

Loutra Yera

These **springs** (admission €2.50; ◷ 8am-6pm) are 5km west of Mytilini on the Gulf of Yera. It's thought that there was once a temple to Hera at this site, where ancient beauty pageants took place. The springs contain radium and are 39.7°C. They are recommended for infertility, rheumatism, arthritis, diabetes, bronchitis, gall stones, dropsy and more. The cool, white marble interior is steamy and dreamy.

Polyhnitos

Southeast of Polyhnitos, these **springs** (☎ 2252 041 449; fax 2252 042 678; admission €2; ◷ 7am-10am & 4-6pm) are in a pretty, renovated Byzantine building. They are some of the hottest springs in all of Continental Europe, with a temperature of 87.6°C, and are recommended for rheumatism, arthritis, skin diseases and gynaecological problems.

Lisvorio

About 5km north of the Polyhnitos springs, these **springs** (☎ 2253 071 245; admission €3; ◷ 8am-1pm & 3-8pm) are just outside the little village of Lisvorio. There are two quaint little baths here, situated on either side of a stream, with pretty vegetation all around. Ask in the village for directions as the baths are unmarked. The buildings are in disrepair but one of the baths is in reasonable condition and it's possible to have a soak. The temperature and the properties of the waters are similar to those at Polyhnitos.

Eftalou

These **baths** (admission €3.50-5; ◷ 9am-1pm & 2-7pm) on the beach not far from Mithymna are idyllic with perfectly clear 46.5° water. You can choose between the old bathhouse in an old whitewashed vault with a pebbled floor or a recently constructed new bathhouse that provides individual tubs for bathing. These springs are recommended for rheumatism, arthritis, neuralgia, hypertension, gall stones and gynaecological and skin problems.

SLEEPING
Budget
There are over 50 official domatia in Mithymna; most consist of only one or two rooms. All display domatia signs and most are of a high standard. The municipal tourist office will help you if you can't be bothered looking; otherwise, the best street to start at is 17 Noemvriou.

Camping Mithymna (☎ 2253 071 169; camp sites per adult/tent €3.50/2.70; ✆ Jun-Oct) This excellent and refreshingly shady camping ground is 1.5km from town and signposted from near the tourist office. Although it opens in early June, you can usually camp if you arrive a bit earlier than that.

Nassos Guest House (☎ 2253 071 022; Arionos; d/t €25/30) Among the first signposted rooms you will come to are those in this old Turkish house run by the lovely Betty Katsaris. Arionos leads off 17 Noemvriou to the right. The rooms are simply furnished and most have a panoramic view. Stop by Betty's restaurant (see Eating) if there's no-one at the rooms.

Mid-Range
Molyvos Hotel I (☎ 2253 071 556; fax 2253 071 640; d €73; ✆) This pleasant hotel has spacious, clean rooms and friendly staff. There's a lovely terrace overlooking the water, and a good breakfast is included in the price. It's down near the beach.

Amfitriti Hotel (☎ 2253 071 741; fax 2253 071 744; s/d incl breakfast €60/95; ✆ ✆) The exterior is traditional stone but the interior is classy and comfortable. This very lux-looking place is down near the old olive press, not far from the town beach and its cluster of bars.

Hotel Olive Press (☎ 2253 071 205; fax 2253 071 647; s/d €60/90; ✆ ✆) This converted olive-oil factory on the beach is often full, but call ahead and you might be in luck. The rooms have a whimsical charm and the staff is friendly.

Hotel Sea Horse (☎ 2253 071 630; www.seahorse -hotel.com; d €73.50; ✆) Down at the fishing harbour, this hotel has bright breezy rooms with balcony and all mod cons such as hairdryers and fridges in all rooms. Prices include breakfast.

Hotel Delfinia (☎ 2253 071 315; www.hoteldelfinia .com; s €51-97, d €75-126, with sea view & breakfast; ✆ ✆) This older but superior hotel caters mainly to packages, but is very accommodating to independent travellers. It's 1km out of

Mithymna on the road to Petra. Try to get a room with a sea view.

EATING
The streets 17 Noemvriou and Kastrou have a wide range of restaurants serving typical Greek fare.

Betty's (☎ 2253 071 421; 17 Noemvriou; mains from €5.50) If you're looking for a lovely atmosphere try this place which occupies an old bordello. All the food is cooked fresh every day and there are plenty of fish and vegetarian dishes. The elegant rooms upstairs provide a view of the water. To get there, take the downhill fork after passing uphill through the tunnel.

Captain's Table (☎ 2253 071 241; appetisers €2-6, mains €5-10; ✆ from 4.30pm) For more of a fishing-village ambience, head down to the far end of the little harbour where there is a clutch of restaurants, the best of which is this Australian-Greek place. The mezedes are exquisite: try *adjuka* (a Ukrainian-inspired spicy aubergine dish) or the spinach salad. There is live bouzouki music once a week.

Taverna tou Ilia (☎ 2253 071 536; mains from €4.50) For a change of scenery and a meal with a view, head up to this taverna at Vafios, 8km inland from Mithymna. The food is topnotch. *Pikilia* (a plate of mixed appetisers) costs around €4 per person, while lamb dishes are around €6. All of the meat is local and the food is very traditional.

O Gatos (☎ 2253 071 661; 17 Noemvriou; mains from €5.50) With a sleeping cat on its doorstep, this little place has a homely feel and a great view from its giant balcony. Heading uphill, it's on the left as you come out of the tunnel.

Petra Πέτρα
pop 1246
Petra, 5km south of Mithymna, is a popular coastal resort with a long sandy beach shaded by tamarisk trees. Despite a substantial number of souvenir shops, it remains an attractive village retaining some traditional houses. Petra means 'rock', and looming over the village is an enormous, almost perpendicular rock that looks as if it has been lifted from Meteora in Thessaly. The rock is crowned by the 18th-century **Panagia Glykophilousa** (Church of the Sweet Kissing Virgin). You can reach it by climbing the 114 rock-hewn steps – worth it for the view.

Petra, like many settlements on Lesvos, is a 'preserved' village. It has not and will not make any concessions to the concrete monstrosities that characterise tourist development elsewhere in Greece. The nearby village of **Petri**, to the east, has some nice old kafeneia and provides an excellent vantage point from which you can survey Petra and its surrounding landscape.

Petra has a post office, OTE, bank, medical facilities and bus connections. There's an interesting refurbished Turkish mansion, known as **Vareltzidaina's House** (admission free; ☺ 8am-7pm Tue-Sun), between the rock and the waterfront. It can be difficult to find, but the locals can point you in the right direction.

For accommodation, excursions, boat and air tickets, head to **Petra Tours** (☎ 2253 041 390; petratours@otenet.gr) in the centre of town.

SLEEPING

Women's Agricultural Tourism Collective (☎ 2253 041 238; fax 2253 041 309; s/d around €15/21) There are about 120 private rooms available in Petra, but your best bet for accommodation is to head straight for this women's collective, Greece's first. They can arrange for you to stay with a family in the village. The office is on the central square, upstairs in the restaurant above Cantina; enter from the street behind the waterfront.

Hotel Mediteraneo (☎ 2253 041 778; fax 2253 041 880; d €40; ❄) If you want to stay in the centre of things, try this simply furnished hotel, so close to the sea that you can practically dive in from the balcony of your room.

EATING

Syneterismos (☎ 2253 041 238; fax 2253 041 309; mains €4) This very popular and friendly place, belonging to the Women's Agricultural Tourism Collective, has mouth-watering mousakas and Greek salad. It's upstairs on the waterfront square, above Cantina; enter from the street running one block behind the waterfront.

To Tyhero Petalo (☎ 2253 041 755; mains from €5) This taverna, towards the eastern end of the waterfront, has attractive decor and sells ready-made food.

O Rigas (☎ 2253 041 405; mains from €5; ☺ 7pm) For something very authentic, head up to the old village to this wisteria-swathed taverna, which is the oldest in Petra. It

has a very laid-back feel and the music is excellent. To get there walk uphill around the rock and keep going straight ahead for about 500m.

WESTERN LESVOS

Western Lesvos is different from the rest of the island and this becomes apparent almost immediately as you wind westward out of Kalloni. The landscape becomes drier and barer and there are fewer settlements, although they look very tidy and their red-tiled roofs add vital colour to an otherwise mottled green-brown landscape. The far western end is almost devoid of trees other than the petrified kind. Here you will find Lesvos' 'petrified forest' on a windswept and barren hillside. One resort, a remote fishing village, and the birthplace of Sappho are what attract people to western Lesvos.

Eresos & Skala Eresou Ερεσός & Σκάλα Ερεσού
pop 1560
Eresos, 90km from Mytilini, is a workaday inland village without a great deal to detain the visitor. Beyond the village a riotously fertile agricultural plain leads to Eresos' beach annexe, Skala Eresou`, which is 4km away

on the west coast. It is a popular resort linked to Eresos by an attractive, very straight tree-lined road. A new sealed road links Eresos with Kalloni via Parakila and Agra.

Skala Eresou is built over ancient Eresos, where Sappho (c. 630–568 BC) was born. Although it gets crowded in summer it has a good, laid-back atmosphere. It is also a popular destination for lesbians who come on a kind of pilgrimage in honour of the poet. The whole island is very gay-friendly, with most businesses being lesbian-owned (including the bars). If you're a beach-lover you should also certainly visit – there is almost 2km of coarse silvery-brown sand.

ORIENTATION & INFORMATION
From the bus turnaround at Skala Eresou, walk towards the sea to reach the central square of Plateia Anthis & Evristhen-ous abutting the waterfront. The beach stretches to the left and right of this square. Turn right at the square onto Gyrinnis and just under 50m along you will come to a sign pointing left to the post office; the OTE is next door. Neither Skala Eresou nor Eresos has a bank but there is an ATM outside Sappho Travel in Skala Eresou.

Krinellos Travel (☎ 2253 053 246, 2253 053 982; krinellos@otenet.gr), close to the main square, is helpful. It can arrange accommodation, car, motorcycle and bicycle hire, and treks on foot or on horses and donkeys.

SIGHTS
Eresos' **archaeological museum** (admission free; ☽ 8.30am-3pm Tue-Sun) houses archaic, classical Greek and Roman finds including statues, coins and grave stelae. The museum, in the centre of Skala Eresou, stands near the remains of the early Christian Basilica of Agios Andreas.

The **petrified forest** (☎ 2253 054 434; admission €1.50; ☽ 8am-4pm), as the EOT hyperbolically refers to this scattering of ancient tree stumps, is near the village of Sigri, on the west coast north of Skala Eresou. Experts reckon the petrified wood is at least 500,000, but possibly 20 million, years old. If you're intrigued, the forest is easiest to reach on an excursion from Skala Eresou; enquire at travel agencies. If you're making your own way, the turn-off to the forest is signposted 7km before the village of Sigri.

Sigri itself is a beautiful, peaceful fishing port with a delicious edge-of-the-world feeling. The **Natural History Museum of the Lesvos Petrified Forest** (☎ 2253 054 434; admission €1.50; ☽ 8am-4pm) is a very swish place with background information on the forest and, of course, a few tree stumps.

SLEEPING
There are a few domatia in Eresos but most people head for Skala Eresou, where there are a number of domatia, pensions and hotels.

Sappho Hotel (☎ 2253 053 233; www.sapphohotel .com; s/d incl breakfast & sea view €31/52, d without view €44; ☒) This C-class property is a small women-only hotel on the waterfront. It can be noisy here and the rooms are somewhat charm-challenged.

Hotel Galini (☎ 2253 053 137/174; fax 2253 053 155; d €52) This C-class property has small but airy rooms with private balcony. It is clearly signposted.

Pete Metaxas Studios (☎ 2253 053 506; d €40) These small studios are at the northwest end of the waterfront, one block back from the beach.

EATING & DRINKING
The shady promenade of Skala Eresou offers many eating options, most with beach and sea views across to Chios and Psara.

Soulatso (☎ 2253 052 078; appetisers & salads around €2.50; mains around €5) Fresh fish (from €6) and a nice array of appetisers (including a decent ladotyri) are served at this place in the middle of the waterfront.

Gorgona (☎ 2253 053 320; appetisers €3-5, mains €5.50-8) Gorgona, with its stone-clad facade, is as good a place as any to start. It's at the southeastern end of the promenade.

Margaritatari (☎ 2253 053 042) For a good and fortifying breakfast or afternoon tea, head straight for this waterfront café to sample scrumptious Austrian pastries, including very delectable apple strudel (€6.50).

Popular watering holes include Tenth Muse, on the square, which is a favourite lesbian bar that serves excellent fruit drinks; Parasol, on the waterfront, with a funky tropical feel and exotic cocktails; and Notorious, at the far southeastern end of the promenade, in an isolated, romantic spot overlooking the water. During summer (June to September) most of these places are open from 10am to 1am.

SOUTHERN LESVOS

Southern Lesvos is dominated by Mt Olympus (968m). Pine forests and olive groves decorate its flanks.

The large village of **Agiasos** on the northern flank of Mt Olympus features prominently in local tourist publications and is a popular day-trip destination. Agiasos is picturesque but not tacky, with artisan workshops making everything from handcrafted furniture to pottery. Its winding, cobbled streets lead you to the church of the Panagia Vrefokratousa with its **Byzantine Museum** and **Popular Museum** in the courtyard.

Plomari on the south coast is a pleasant, crumbling resort town. A large, traditional village, it also has a laid-back beach settlement. Most people stay at **Agios Isidoros**, 3km to the east where there is a narrow, overcrowded beach. **Tarti**, east of Agios Isidoros, is

---

OLIVE TRAILS

The most delightful way to experience the Plomari region is to walk. Old paths linking the hill villages have been restored and offer magical glimpses of the region's natural beauty. You'll pass through lush dells filled with old oaks, wild pears and pistachios, plane trees, pink hollyhocks, miscellaneous wild flowers and herbs, as well as higher, drier forests of pine and juniper. The wildlife is watered by a wealth of springs, fountains, rivers and streams that also served the olive mills and presses that dot the landscape. As you traverse the olive groves, you'll notice old *setia* (dry-walled terraces) and *damia* (small one-storey stone houses). To top it off, there are startling views down to the sea. In general, it's best to walk these paths in spring or autumn before or after the heat kicks in. The trails are clearly signposted, and there are maps in villages and at the airport.

The major routes are as follows:

Melinda–Paleohori

Distance: 1.2km. Duration: 30 minutes. This trail starts at the fishing village of Melinda and follows the Selandas River for 200m. It ascends to the living village of Paleohori, passing a spring with potable water along the way. The trail ends at one of the village's two olive presses, where there is now a museum.

Paleohori–Rahidi

Distance: 1km. Duration: 30 minutes. The path here is 2m to 4m wide and paved with white stone. It ascends to Rahidi, which used to be the summer residence of the villagers from Paleohori. There are two springs along the way, and vineyards. There are about 40 nice old houses in Rahidi and a kafeneio that opens in summer. Rahidi, which now has a population of about five,

---

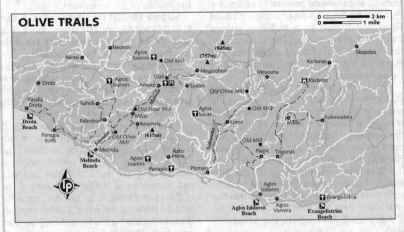

OLIVE TRAILS

a much nicer beach. West of Plomari, **Melinda** is a very pretty, serene fishing village with a beach. There are three tavernas in Melinda, all offering rooms and cheap hearty food.

About one hour's walk from Melinda, west along the coast, is the **Panagia Krifti**, a little church built in a cave near a hot spring.

The family resort of **Vatera**, over to the east, has an 8km stretch of beach that never seems to fill up with visitors. It is reached via the inland town of **Polyhnitos** where there are hot springs (see Balm for the Soul, p356).

Sleeping & Eating

Camping Dionysos (☎ 2252 061 151; dionyso@otenet.gr; camp sites per adult/tent €6.50/6.50; ⏳ 1 May–Oct). This is the only camping ground, at Vatera. It's quite good, if somewhat small, and has a pool, minimarket, restaurant and cooking facilities. It is set back 100m from the beach.

---

first received electricity in 2001. There are stunning views from here. If you like, you can continue to Agios Ioannis along the same path.

Melinda–Kournela

Distance: 1.8km. Duration: 40 minutes. An old stone path climbs from the beach at Melinda to Kournela, a village of about 50 houses, with a population of three to four people. There are big shady plane trees, a triple-spouted fountain where people used to wash clothes, and an old steam-driven olive mill. There are good views across to Paleohori and Rahidi.

Kournela–Milos

Distance: 800m. Duration: 20 minutes. This trail descends to Milos, where there's an old flour mill. The village is at a crossroads, with paths leading to Paleohori, Melinda, Kournela and Megalohori.

Melinda–Milos

Distance: 2km. Duration: one hour. This level trail follows the Selandas River and passes a few houses, some ruined olive mills, one spring and two bridges. There is some unusual vegetation, including orange and mandarin trees. It's a shady trail, good for summer.

Milos–Amaxo

Distance: 1.75km. Duration: one hour. This very level trail follows the Melinda River, through vineyards and plane, poplar and pine forests. There are springs and fountains with good drinking water along the way. Nice wooden bridges made of chestnut cross the river. It's possible to start this walk from Amaxo, after driving from Plomari. If you're a good rider, you can mountain bike all the way from Amaxo down to Melinda.

Amaxo–Giali–Spides

Distance: 1.5km. Duration: 45 minutes. This trail follows a dirt road for about 500m to Giali, then ascends to Spides on a path. Halfway between Amaxo and Giali there's a little church with a picnic table that makes a nice spot for lunch.

Skopelos–Karionas–Kastelos–Trigonas/Plagia

Distance: 8km. Duration: three hours. This route follows a dirt road from Skopelos to Karionas, but there are cobbled paths the rest of the way. At the ruined castle known as Kastelos, there's now a small church. It's possible to take a detour to the village of Milies, where there is a fountain and some nice old houses. A path from Milies continues to Kolimvatera.

Plomari–Mesouna

Distance: 6km. Duration: three hours. The trail follows the Sedoundas River past many old houses. There's an olive processing plant in the village of Limni and about 4km upriver there's an old watermill that used to crush olives.

FASCINATING FOSSIL FIND

Lesvos is hardly the kind of place that you would associate with great excitement in the musty and dusty world of palaeontology. Nonetheless, the island has been thrust onto centre stage with the extraordinary discovery of fossils of animals, fish and plants at Vatera, a sleepy beach resort on the south coast, hitherto more associated with sun and sand than fossilised fish.

Among the fossils found in the Vatera region are elephants, mastodons, giraffes, bones of rhinoceros and hippopotamus, deer, tortoises, snails, fish, and pieces of a gigantic prehistoric horse. Dated up to 5.5 million years old, the fossils are being displayed at the **Museum of Natural History** in the neighbouring village of Vrisa, just 2km from the excavation sites.

Hotel Vatera Beach (☎ 2252 061 212; www.vatera beach.gr; d €80; ✖) This friendly establishment offers a delightful resort experience that includes rooms with views of the sea, a spacious restaurant and bar, English-language newspapers and help with car rental and sightseeing.

LIMNOS ΛΗΜΝΟΣ

pop 15,224 / area 482 sq km

Limnos has a unique and understated appeal resting on a gently undulating landscape dotted with little farms and a coastline graced with fine beaches. In spring vibrant wild flowers dust the hills, and in autumn purple crocuses sprout in profusion. Flocks of flamingos wade through the placid lakes of eastern Limnos, the tranquillity only broken by the roar of fighter jets overhead. The garrison is due to Limnos' sensitive position near the Straits of the Dardanelles, midway between the Mt Athos Peninsula and Turkey.

Coming up a loser in the geographic sweepstakes, Limnos has suffered through a traumatic history. During the Peloponnesian Wars, Limnos sided with Athens and suffered many Persian attacks. After the split of the Roman Empire in AD 395 it became an important outpost of Byzantium. In 1462 it came under the rule

of the Genoese. The Turks succeeded in conquering the island in 1478 and Limnos remained under Turkish rule until 1912. Moudros Bay was the Allies' base for the disastrous Gallipoli campaign of WWI.

The far-from-ubiquitous military presence adds a certain edge to an island seemingly ready to slip into eternal sleep. Tourist hubbub is minimal and mainly confined to northern Greeks in July and August. The relative scarcity of museums, archaeological sites and other culturally uplifting must-sees encourages long, guilt-free days of dozing in the sun.

Getting There & Away

AIR

There is a daily flight to Limnos from Athens (€65), four weekly from Thessaloniki (€65) and five flights weekly to Lesvos (€46). **Olympic Airways** (☎ 2254 022 214; Nikolaou Garoufalidou) is opposite Hotel Paris, in Myrina.

The airport is 22km east of Myrina. A taxi will cost about €14.

EXCURSION BOAT

Every Sunday in July and August, the *Aiolis* does a round trip to the small island of Agios Efstratios. The boat usually leaves at about 8am and returns from Agios Efstratios at 5pm. Tickets cost €15.

FERRY

In summer four ferries weekly go from Limnos to Kavala (€13.20, five hours). In the high season there is usually one boat per week to Sigri in Lesvos (€19.30, six hours). There are also three to four boats weekly to Chios (€18.60, 11 hours) and Piraeus (€24, 13 hours) via Lesvos. There are two boats weekly to Thessaloniki (€19, eight hours) and one to two to Alexandroupolis (€14.10, five hours) via Samothraki (€10.50, three hours).

In addition, the *Aiolis*, a small local ferry, does the run to Agios Efstratios (€5.90, two hours) five times weekly. Tickets can be bought at **Myrina Tourist & Travel Agency** (☎ 2254 022 460; root@mirina.lim.forthnet.gr) on the harbour front in Myrina.

Getting Around

BUS

Bus services on Limnos are poor. In summer there are two buses daily from Myrina

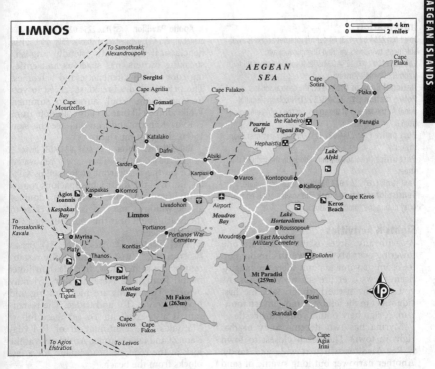

LIMNOS

0 ——— 4 km
0 ——— 2 miles

To Samothraki;
Alexandroupolis

*AEGEAN
SEA*

Cape
Plaka

Sergitsi

Cape Agrilia

Cape Falakro

Cape
Mourtzeflos

Gomati

Cape
Sotira

Plaka

Cape
Mourtzeflos

Katalako

*Pournia
Gulf*

Sanctuary of
the Kabeiroi

Tigani Bay

Panagia

Dafni

Hephaistia

Atsiki

*Lake
Alyki*

Sardes

Karpasi

Varos

Kontopouli

Kaspakas

Kornos

Kalliopi

Cape Keros

**Agios
Ioannis**

Livadohori

Airport

**Keros
Beach**

*Kaspakas
Bay*

*Moudros
Bay*

To
Thessaloniki;
Kavala

Limnos

Portianos

*Lake
Hortarolimni*

Myrina

Portianos War
Cemetery

Moudros

Roussopouli

Platy

Kontias

East Moudros
Military Cemetery

Thanos

Poliohni

Nevgatis

*Kontias
Bay*

▲
Mt Paradisi
(259m)

Cape
Tigani

Mt Fakos
▲ (263m)

Fisini

Cape
Stavros

Cape
Fakos

Skandali

Cape
Agia
Irini

To Agios
Efstratios

To Lesvos

---

to most of the villages but you may need to stay overnight in order to catch a bus back. Check the schedule (scribbled on a blackboard in Greek) at the **bus station** (☎ 2254 022 464; Plateia Eleftheriou Venizelou).

CAR & MOTORCYCLE
In Myrina, cars and jeeps can be rented from **Myrina Rent a Car** (☎ 2254 024 476; fax 2254 022484; P Kyda-Karatza), near the waterfront. Prices range from €30 to €45 for a small car or jeep, depending on the season. There are several motorcycle-hire outlets on P Kyda-Karatza.

MYRINA MYPINA
pop 5107
Myrina is the capital and port of Limnos. Surrounded by massive hunks of volcanic rock, it is not immediately perceived as a picturesque town, but it is animated, full of character and unfettered by establishments pandering to tourism. With two wonderful, sandy beaches on either side of the town, it's easy to spend a relaxing week here without stepping inside a car or bus.

The main thoroughfare of P Kyda-Karatza is a charming paved street with clothing stores, traditional shops selling nuts and honey, old-fashioned kafeneia and barber shops – the latter are testimony to the island's military presence. Down the side streets you'll see – interspersed with modern buildings – little whitewashed stone dwellings, decaying neoclassical mansions and 19th-century wattle-and-daub houses with overhanging wooden balconies. A Genoese castle looms dramatically over the town.

Orientation
From the end of the quay turn right onto Plateia Ilia Iliou. Continue along the waterfront passing Hotel Lemnos and the town hall. A little further along you will see the run-down Hotel Aktaion, set back from the waterfront. Turn left here, then immediately veer half-left onto P Kyda-Karatza. Proceeding up here you will reach the central square. Walk up P Kyda-Karatza and you will come to Plateia Eleftheriou Venizelou where you will see the bus station.

Information

Joy (☎ 2254 025 453; €4 per hr) Internet access is available here, two doors up from Olympic Airways.

Laundrette (☎ 2254 024 392; Nikolaou Garoufallidou) Opposite Olympic Airways.

National Bank of Greece On the central square.

Police station (☎ 2254 022 201; Nikolaou Garoufallidou) At the far end of the street, on the right coming from P Kyda-Karatza.

Port police (☎ 2254 022 225) On the waterfront near the quay.

Post office (Nikolaou Garoufallidou) On the right of the street.

Taxi rank (☎ 2254 023 033) On the central square.

Tourist information kiosk This small kiosk is on the quay during the summer season.

Sights & Activities

As with any Greek-island **castle**, the one towering over Myrina is worth climbing up to. From its vantage point there are magnificent views over the sea to Mt Athos. As you walk from the harbour, take the first side street to the left by an old Turkish fountain. A sign here points you to the castle.

Myrina has two decent sandy **beaches** right in town. The beach closest to town is Rea Maditos which is wide and sandy. Another narrower but long swathe of sand begins on the other side of the castle as Romeïkos Gialos which can be reached by walking along P Kyda-Karatza from the harbour, and taking any of the streets off to the left. It continues on to Riha Nera (shallow water), so named because of its gently shelving beach that is ideal for children. Most of the nightlife is along this stretch.

In Myrina, and housed in a neoclassical mansion, is the **archaeological museum** (admission €2; ☉ 9am-3pm Tue-Sun). Worth a visit, it contains finds from all the three sites on Limnos, exhibited in chronological order. The museum overlooks the beach, next to Hotel Kastro.

Tours

Theodoros Petrides Travel Agency (☎ 2254 022 039; www.petridestravel.gr; ☉ Jun-Sep) This travel agency organises round-the-island boat trips (€40) which include stops for swimming and lunch.

Sleeping

Budget accommodation is thin on the ground in Myrina.

Apollo Pavillion (☎ /fax 2254 023 712; apollo47@ otenet.gr; dm €11 per person, d studios €50; ☒) This neoclassical place, with friendly English-speaking owners, has spacious and enticing rooms with kitchenette and balconies. The price includes breakfast served to you in your room. Book ahead in summer. Walk along Nikolaou Garoufallidou from P Kyda-Karatza and you will see the sign 150m along on the right.

Blue Waters Hotel (☎ 2254 024 403; bwkon@ otenet.gr; s/d €60/80; ☒) This newly renovated place on the beachfront at Romeïkos Gialos, north of the Kastro, has spacious rooms with brand-new tile bathrooms, double-glazed windows and fridges. It's so close to the beach you'll hear the sound of waves as you fall asleep.

Hotel Filoktitis (☎ /fax 2254 023 344; Ethnikis Antistaseos 14; s/d €50/60; ☒) Above the restaurant of the same name, this pleasant hotel inland from Riha Nera has very friendly owners. The rooms are nice and big and have balconies, TV and fridge. The restaurant is also excellent. To get there follow Maroulas (the continuation of P Kyda-Karatza and take Ethnikis Antistaseos at the fork in the road, or head inland for a few blocks from the beach.

Arion Beach Apartments (☎ 2254 022 144; fax 2254 022 147; d/tr €55/65; ☒) Thirty metres from the Riha Nera beach is this lovely homely place with friendly English-speaking owners. The rooms are huge with small kitchenettes and have big shady balconies. To get there, take Seferi, the first street on your right as you walk over the hill to Riha Nera from Romeïkos Gialos. Look for the Arion's sign just a few doors up.

Hotel Lemnos (☎ 2254 022 153; fax 2254 023 329; d €60; ☒) This harbourside place has an ideal location, especially if you are stumbling off the ferry in the middle of the night. The rooms are relatively large and have TV, phone, and balconies with views of the port.

Hotel Sevdadi (☎ 2254 022 303; fax 2254 025 429; Nikolaou Garoufallidou; d €63; ☒) The rooms here are somewhat drab but the bathrooms are large and many rooms have balconies overlooking the street.

Eating

Restaurants are of a high standard on Limnos. Several restaurants line the waterfront, all offering freshly caught fish and seafood.

Taverna Glaropoula (☎ 2254 024 069; mains from €6) Locals give top marks to this cosy little taverna with a nice harbourside location.

O Platanos Taverna (☎ 2254 022 070; mains from €5) Halfway along P Kyda-Karatza is this small taverna with an emphasis on meat. You'll find it on the left as you walk from the waterfront on a small square under a couple of huge plane trees. It makes an attractive alternative to the waterfront establishments but the menu is limited.

WESTERN LIMNOS

North of Myrina, turn left just past the little village of **Kaspakas** and a narrow road leads down to the beach at **Agios Ioannis**. The beach is pleasant enough, but Agios Ioannis consists of a few desultory fishing shacks, scattered beach houses and a couple of tavernas, one of which has its tables set out in the embrace of a large volcanic rock.

Inland from Kaspakas, the barren hilly landscape dotted with sheep and rocks (particularly on the road to Katalako via Sardes and Dafni) looks more like the English Peak District than an Aegean island. The villages themselves have little to cause you to pause and you will certainly be an object of curiosity if you do. There is a remote and completely undeveloped beach at **Gomati** on the north coast and it can be reached by a good dirt road from Katalako.

Heading 3km south from Myrina you will reach **Platy**. It's a fairly scrappy little resort, but the beach is OK.

Back on the beach road, if you continue past Lemnos Village Resort Hotel, you will come to a sheltered sandy cove with an islet in the bay. The beach here is usually less crowded than Platy. **Thanos Beach** is the next bay around from Platy; it is also less crowded, and long and sandy. To get there, continue on the main road from Platy to the cute little village of Thanos, where a sign points to the beach. **Nevgatis**, the next bay along, is deserted but a trifle windy. Continuing along the coast road you'll come to the almost picturesque village of **Kontias**, marked by a row of old windmills.

CENTRAL LIMNOS

Central Limnos is flat and agricultural with wheat fields, small vineyards, and cattle and sheep farms. The island's huge air-force base is ominously surrounded by endless

barbed-wire fences. The muddy and bleak Moudros Bay cuts deep into the interior, with **Moudros**, the second-largest town on the island, positioned on the eastern side of the bay. Moudros does not offer much for the tourist other than a couple of small hotels with tavernas on the waterfront. The harbour has none of Myrina's picturesque qualities.

One kilometre out of Moudros on the road to Roussopouli, you will come across the **East Moudros Military Cemetery**, where Commonwealth soldiers from the Gallipoli campaign are buried. Limnos, with its large protected anchorage, was occupied by a force of Royal Marines on 23 February 1915 and was the principal base for this ill-fated campaign. A metal plaque, inside the gates, gives a short history of the Gallipoli campaign. A second Commonwealth cemetery, **Portianos War Cemetery**, is at Portianos, about 6km south of Livadohori on the trans-island highway. The cemetery is not as obvious as the Australian-style blue and white street sign with the name 'Anzac St'. Follow Anzac St to the church and you will find the cemetery off a little lane behind the church.

EASTERN LIMNOS

Eastern Limnos has three **archaeological sites** (admission free; ☉ 8am-7pm). The Italian School of Archaeologists has uncovered four ancient settlements at **Poliohni**, on the island's east coast. The most interesting was a sophisticated pre-Mycenaean city, which predated Troy VI (1800–1275 BC). The site is well laid out and there are good descriptions in Greek, Italian and English. However, there is nothing too exciting to be seen; the site is probably of greater interest to archaeological buffs than casual visitors.

The second site is that of the **Sanctuary of the Kabeiroi** (Ta Kaviria) in northeastern Limnos on the shores of remote Tigani Bay. This was originally a site for the worship of Kabeiroi gods predating those of Samothraki (see Sanctuary of the Great Gods, p369). There is little of the splendour of Samothraki's sanctuary, but the layout of the site is obvious and excavations are still being carried out.

The major site, which has 11 columns, is that of a Hellenistic sanctuary. The older site is further back and is still being excavated. Of additional interest is the cave of Philoctetes, the hero of the Trojan War, who was abandoned here while a gangrenous leg (the result of snakebite) healed. The sea cave can be reached by a path that leads down from the site. The cave can actually be entered by a hidden, narrow entrance (unmarked) to the left of the main entrance.

You can reach the sanctuary easily, if you have your own transport, via a road that was built for the expensive tourist enclave, Kaviria Palace. The turn-off is 5km to the left, after the village of **Kontopouli**. From Kontopouli you can make a detour along a rough dirt track to the third site, **Hephaistia** (Ta Ifestia), once the most important city on the island. Hephaestus was the god of fire and metallurgy and, according to mythology, was thrown here from Mt Olympus by Zeus. The site is widely scattered over a scrub-covered, but otherwise desolate, small peninsula. There isn't much to see of the ancient city other than low walls and a partially excavated theatre. Excavations are still under way.

The road to the northern tip of the island is worth exploring. There are some typical Limnian villages in the area and the often deserted beach at **Keros** is popular with windsurfers. Flocks of flamingos can sometimes be seen on shallow **Lake Alyki**. From the cape at the northeastern tip of Limnos you can see the islands of Samothraki, and Imvros (Gökçeada) in Turkey.

AGIOS EFSTRATIOS
ΑΓΙΟΣ ΕΥΣΤΡΑΤΙΟΣ

pop 371

The little-known island of Agios Efstratios, called locally Aï-Stratis, merits the title of perhaps the most isolated island in the Aegean. Stuck more or less plumb centre in the North Aegean some distance from its nearest neighbour Limnos, it has few cars and fewer roads, but sees a steady trickle of curious foreign island-hoppers seeking to find some peace and quiet.

Large numbers of political exiles were sent here for enforced peace and quiet before and after WWII. Among the exiled guests were such luminaries as composer Mikis Theodorakis and poets Kostas Varnalis and Giannis Ritsos.

The little village of Aï-Stratis was once picturesque, but in the early hours of the morning of 21 February 1968 a violent earthquake, with its epicentre in the seas between Limnos and Aï-Stratis, virtually destroyed the vibrant village in one fell swoop. Many people emigrated as a result and there are now large numbers of islanders living in Australia and elsewhere.

Ham-fisted intervention by the then ruling junta saw the demolition of most of the remaining traditional homes and in their place, cheaply built concrete boxes were erected to house the islanders. Needless to say, the islanders are still pretty miffed more than 30 years after the event, and the remaining hillside ruins stand silent sentinel over a rather lacklustre village.

Still, if you yearn for serenity and traffic-free bliss, and enjoy walking, Aï-Stratis is a great place. It has some fine beaches – though most are only accessible by caïque – some accommodation, simple island food and a nightlife. There are some 100 rooms available that can be booked through **Myrina Tourist & Travel Agency** (☎ 2254 022 460; root@mirina .lim.forthnet.gr) or **Theodoros Petrides Travel Agency** (☎ 2254 022 039; www.petridestravel.gr), both in Myrina, or fax the community fax machine at ☎ 2254 093 210 to make a booking.

There is a post office, one cardphone and one metered phone for the public.

Getting There & Away

Agios Efstratios is on the Kavala–Rafina ferry route, which includes Limnos. There are five services weekly to Limnos (€5.90, two hours) and one per week to Kavala (€13.50, 6¾ hours).

In addition, the small local ferry *Aiolis* putters to and from Limnos every morning from Monday to Friday. But the harbour is exposed to the west winds, causing ferry services to often be cancelled or delayed. The island makes a good excursion; travel agencies in Limnos sell tickets for €15.

Beaches

Apart from the reasonable **village beach** of dark volcanic sand, the nearest beach worth making the effort to visit is **Alonitsi** on the northeast side of the island. It is a long, totally undeveloped, pristine strand and it can be all yours if you are prepared to walk the 90 minutes to reach it. To get there take the little track from the northeast side of the village, starting by a small bridge, and follow it up towards the power pylons. Halfway along the track splits; take the right track for Alonitsi, or the left track for the **military lookout** for great views. **Lidario**, a beach on the west side, can be reached – with difficulty – on foot, but is better approached by sea if you can get someone to take you there.

Sleeping & Eating

Accommodation options in Agios Efstratios are now pretty good. There is no hotel on the island but there are currently about 100 beds available and you will always find somewhere to stay unless you turn up at the height of the summer season without a reservation.

Xenonas Aï-Strati (☎ 2254 093 329; d €40) This spotless and airy place is run by Julia and Odysseas Galanakis. The rooms are in one of the few buildings that survived the earthquake on the northeastern side of the village.

Malama Panera Domatia (☎ 2254 093 209; d €35) These domatia, on the south side of the village, are as equally well appointed as Xenonas Aï-Strati.

Places to eat are fairly inexpensive, though fish tends to be a bit on the steep side.

Thanasis Taverna (☎ 2254 093 269; mains around €5.50) This fairly obvious community-run taverna stands overlooking the harbour.

Tasos Ouzeri (mains around €4.50; ☽ summer only) This place is diagonally opposite Thanasis Taverna and offers similar fare.

SAMOTHRAKI
ΣΑΜΟΘΡΑΚΗ

pop 2723 / area 176 sq km

Strange and beautiful Samothraki is 32km southwest of Alexandroupolis. Cursed with awkward transportation links, few visitors make their way here but those who do are richly rewarded. Samothraki's natural attributes are dramatic, big and untamed, culminating in the mighty peak of Mt Fengari (1611m), the highest mountain in the Aegean. Homer related that Poseidon watched the Trojan War from Mt Fengari's summit.

The jagged, boulder-strewn mountain looms over valleys of massive gnarled oak and plane trees, thick forests of olive and pine, dense shrubbery and damp, dark glades where waterfalls plunge into deep, icy pools. On the gentler, western slopes of the island there are corn fields studded with poppies and other wild flowers in spring. Samothraki is also rich in fauna. Its springs are the habitat of a large number of frogs, toads and turtles; in its meadows you will see swarms of butterflies and may come across the occasional lumbering tortoise.

Samothraki's ancient site, the Sanctuary of the Great Gods, at Paleopolis evokes an epoch when Samothraki was a major religious centre. The mysterious cult of the Great Gods was brought to the island by the Thracians around 1000 BC, and by the 5th century BC luminaries from far and wide came to the site to be initiated. With the outlawing of paganism in the 4th century AD, the cult died out and the island dwindled into insignificance. Historians are unable to ascertain the nature of the rites performed here, but its aura of potent mysticism prevails over the whole island.

Getting There & Away

FERRY

Samothraki has daily ferry connections with Alexandroupolis (€7.80, two hours) and in summer there are at least two per week to Kavala (€14, four hours) and two to Limnos (€10.50, three hours). There are also a couple of boats a week to Sigri (Lesvos) in peak season. Outside the high season, boats to/from Kavala are nonexistent. Schedules are listed on the window of the **ticket kiosk** (☎ 2551 041 505) opposite the pier. Ferry tickets can be bought at **Niki Tours** (☎ 2551 041 465; fax 2551 041 304), in Kamariotissa, and from the kiosk.

HYDROFOIL

In summer there are two to three hydrofoils daily between Samothraki and Alexandroupolis (€14.70, one hour). For departure details contact **Niki Tours** (☎ 2551 041 465; fax 2551 041 304) or the **ticket kiosk** (☎ 2551 041 505).

Getting Around

BUS

In summer there are at least four buses daily from Kamariotissa to Hora (€0.75) and Loutra (Therma), via Paleopolis. Some of the Loutra buses continue to the nearby camping grounds. There are four buses daily to Profitis Ilias (via Lakoma).

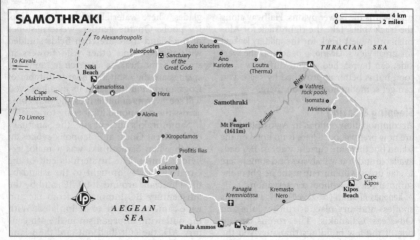

SAMOTHRAKI

To Alexandroupolis
To Kavala
Niki Beach
Cape Makrivrahos
To Limnos
Kamariotissa
Paleopolis
Kato Kariotes
Sanctuary of the Great Gods
Ano Kariotes
Loutra (Therma)
THRACIAN SEA
Hora
Samothraki
River
Fonias
Vathres rock pools
Isomata
Mnimoria
Alonia
Mt Fengari (1611m)
Xiropotamos
Profitis Ilias
Lakoma
Cape Kipos
Kipos Beach
Panagia Kremniotissa
Kremasto Nero
AEGEAN SEA
Pahia Ammos
Vatos

0 — 4 km
0 — 2 miles

CAR & MOTORCYCLE

Cars and small jeeps can be rented from **X Rentals** (☎ 2551 042 272) on the harbour and **Kyrkos Rent a Car** (☎ 2551 041 620, 6972 839 231). A small car is about €50. Motorcycles can be rented from **Rent A Motor Bike** (☎ 2551 041 057), opposite the ferry quay.

EXCURSION BOAT

Depending on demand, caïques do trips from the Kamariotissa jetty to Pahia Ammos and Kipos Beaches, and the Samothraki excursion boat does trips around the island.

TAXI

For a taxi, call ☎ 2551 041 733, 2551 041 341 or 2551 041 077.

KAMARIOTISSA ΚΑΜΑΡΙΩΤΙΣΣΑ

pop 963

Kamariotissa, on the northwest coast, is Samothraki's port and largest town although, peculiarly, not its capital. As the transport hub of the island, you may wish to use it as a base for further explorations. It's not the most captivating of towns but the long, exposed pebbly beach to the east is good for a contemplative stroll. Tourism is extremely low-key here. Speaking German is a big asset since the town has a great deal of people-traffic to and from Germany.

Orientation & Information

The bus station is on the waterfront just east of the quay (turn left when you disembark).

There is no EOT or tourist police, and the regular police are in Hora. There are two ATMs on the waterfront, but no post office or OTE – those also are in Hora.

Café Aktaion (☎ 2551 041 056; €4 per hr) Internet café at the end of the harbour.

Niki Tours Opposite the bus station; it is marginally helpful.

Port police (☎ 2551 041 305) East along the waterfront.

www.samothraki.com Has general information about the island, including boat schedules.

X Rentals Also opposite the bus station, and helpful to travellers; the English-speaking owner can provide a lot of information about the island.

Festivals & Events

Humble little Samothraki has been hosting Greece's largest electronic dance party since 2002. The **Samothraki Dance Festival** (www.samoth rakidancefestival.com) commandeers the Multilary Camping grounds and surrounding area for seven days of electronica at the end of August. Some 7000 fans arrive to dance and chill on the island of the Great Mother. Tickets cost from €70 to €135 (the earlier you buy, the cheaper it is) and are on sale in outlets throughout Europe.

Sleeping

Domatia owners often meet ferries in Kamariotissa, and domatia are easy to find in the compact port.

Niki Beach Hotel (☎ 2551 041 545; fax 2551 041 461; s/d €40/60) It's a zoo in here – practically. The unpaying animal guests include five monstrous goldfish, an overweight turtle and a splendid white cockatoo as well as the usual assortment of dogs and cats. After ogling the menagerie you can retire to large rooms with TV or walk across the street to a pebble beach. This spacious C-class hotel, just past Hotel Kyma, also has a lovely garden and is fronted by poplar trees.

Hotel Kyma (☎ 2551 041 263; d €45; 🛱) The friendly German-speaking owner takes good care of her guests and the small, simply furnished rooms represent good value. The hotel is along the coastal road, about 300m from the port.

Aeolos Hotel (☎ 2551 041 595; fax 2551 041 810; s/d incl breakfast €60/70; 🛋 🛱) Behind Niki Beach Hotel, this B-class property has a commanding position on a hill overlooking the sea. The rooms, which come with bathroom, fridge, TV, telephone and air-con, are comfortable enough but nothing special.

Eating

Despite an abundance of café-bars, breakfast joints and ouzeria, Kamariotissa's eating establishments are all pretty run-of-the-mill.

If you are just looking for a quick bite, try one of the gyros stands on the waterfront. A souvlaki or gyros costs about €4.50.

Klimataria Restaurant (☎ 2551 041 535; mains from €4.50) At the eastern end of the waterfront road, this pleasant restaurant serves an unusual speciality called *gianiotiko* (an oven-baked dish of diced pork, potatoes, egg and other goodies; €6). It also serves a good *pastitsio* (layers of buttery macaroni and seasoned lamb; €5).

I Synantisi (☎ 2551 041 308; fish from €5) For simple fresh fish, try this ouzeria on the waterfront between the ferry dock and the bus stop. The food is straightforward but excellent.

Psistaria Pizzeria Skorpios (☎ 2551 041 920; pizzas €6-9, grilled meat dishes from €4.50) A few doors up from Klimataria, Skorpios serves decent home-made pizzas (takeaway available) and grilled meat in no-frills surroundings.

HORA XOPA

Hora is the island's capital, probably chosen more for its beauty than any practical reason. Concealed in a fold of the mountains above Kamariotissa it occupies a striking site. The crumbling red-tiled houses – some of grey stone, others whitewashed – are stacked up two steep, rocky mountainsides cloaked with pine trees. The twisting cobbled streets resound with cockerels crowing, dogs barking and donkeys braying, rather than the ubiquitous roar of motorcycles. The village is totally authentic with no concessions to tourism. The ruined kastro at the top of the main thoroughfare offers sweeping vistas down to Kamariotissa but part of the site is closed due to the instability of the structure.

Orientation & Information

To get to Hora's narrow winding main street, follow the signs for the kastro from the central square where the bus turns around. Here on the main street, which is nameless (as are all of Hora's streets; houses are distinguished by numbers), are the OTE, the Agricultural Bank and the post office. The **police station** (☎ 2551 041 203) is in the ruined castle. Further up on the main street, on the right, a fountain gushes refreshing mountain water.

Sleeping & Eating

There are no hotels in Hora but if you ask in one of the kafeneia you will be put in touch with a room owner.

Taverna-Ouzeri I Plateia (mains from €3) This taverna on the central square offers grilled meat and a couple of vegetarian options. The tomato-and-feta *saganaki* (fried cheese traditionally served as a meze) is not bad.

SANCTUARY OF THE GREAT GODS
ΤΟ ΙΕΡΟ ΤΩΝ ΜΕΓΑΛΟΝ ΘΕΩΝ

Next to the little village of Paleopolis, 6km northeast of Kamariotissa, is the **Sanctuary of the Great Gods** (admission free; 🕑 8.30am-8.30pm Tue-Sun). The extensive site, lying in a valley of luxuriant vegetation between Mt Fengari and the sea, is one of the most magical in the whole of Greece. The Great Gods were of greater antiquity than the Olympian gods worshipped in the official religion of ancient Greece. The principal deity, the Great Mother (Alceros Cybele), was worshipped as a fertility goddess.

When the original Thracian religion became integrated with the state religion, the Great Mother was merged with the Olympian female deities Demeter, Aphrodite and Hecate. The last of these was a mysterious goddess associated with darkness, the underworld and witchcraft. Other deities worshipped here were the Great Mother's consort, the virile young Kadmilos (god of the phallus), who was later integrated with the Olympian god Hermes; as well as the demonic Kabeiroi twins, Dardanos and Aeton, who were integrated with Castor and Pollux (the Dioscuri), the twin sons of Zeus and Leda. These twins were invoked by mariners to protect them against the perils of the sea. The formidable deities of Samothraki were venerated for their immense power. In comparison, the Olympian gods were a frivolous and fickle lot.

Initiates were sworn on punishment of death not to reveal what went on at the sanctuary; so there is only very flimsy knowledge of what the initiations involved. All that the archaeological evidence reveals is that there were two initiations, a lower and a higher. In the first initiation, gods were invoked to bring about a spiritual rebirth within the candidate. In the second initiation the candidate was absolved of transgressions. There was no prerequisite for initiation – it was available to anyone.

The site's most celebrated relic, the Winged Victory of Samothrace (now in the Louvre in Paris), was found by Champoiseau, the French consul, at Adrianople (present-day Edirne in Turkey) in 1863. Sporadic excavations followed in the late 19th and early 20th centuries, but did not begin in earnest until just before WWII when the Institute of Fine Arts, New York University, under the direction of Karl Lehmann and Phyllis Williams Lehmann, began digging.

Exploring the Site

The site is labelled in Greek and English. If you take the path that leads south from the entrance you will arrive at the rectangular **anaktoron**, on the left. At the southern end was a **sacristy**, an antechamber where candidates put on white gowns ready for their first (lower) initiation. The initiation ceremony took place in the main body of the anaktoron. Then one at a time each initiate entered the holy of holies, a small inner temple at the northern end of the building, where a priest instructed them in the meanings of the symbols used in the ceremony. Afterwards the initiates returned to the sacristy to receive their initiation certificate.

The **arsinoein**, which was used for sacrifices, to the southwest of the anaktoron, was built in 289 BC and was at that time the largest cylindrical structure in Greece. It was a gift to the Great Gods from the Egyptian queen Arsinou. To the southeast of here you will see the **sacred rock**, the site's earliest altar, which was used by the Thracians.

The initiations were followed by a celebratory feast which probably took place in the **temenos**, to the south of the arsinoein. This building was a gift from Philip II. The next building is the prominent Doric **hieron**, which is the most photographed ruin on the site; five of its columns have been reassembled. It was in this temple that candidates received the second initiation.

On the west side of the main path (opposite the hieron) are a few remnants of a **theatre**. Nearby, a path ascends to the **Nike monument** where the magnificent Winged Victory of Samothrace once stood. The statue was a gift from Demetrius Poliorketes (the 'besieger of cities') to the Kabeiroi for helping him defeat Ptolemy II in battle. To the northwest are the remains of a massive **stoa**, which was a two-aisled portico where pilgrims to the sanctuary sheltered. Names of initiates were recorded on its walls. North of the stoa are the ruins of the **ruinenviereck**, a medieval fortress.

Retrace your steps to the Nike monument and walk along the path leading east; on the left is a good plan of the site. The path continues to the southern **necropolis** which is the most important ancient cemetery so far found on the island. It was used from the Bronze Age to early Roman times. North of the cemetery was the **propylon**, an elaborate Ionic entrance to the sanctuary; it was a gift from Ptolemy II.

MUSEUM

The site's **museum** (☎ 2551 041 474; admission €2, free Sun & public holidays; ☼ 8.30am-3pm Tue-Sun) is well laid out, with English labels. Exhibits include terracotta figurines, vases, jewellery and a plaster cast of the Winged Victory.

Sleeping & Eating

There are several domatia at Paleopolis, all of which are signposted from near the museum.

Kastro Hotel (☎ 2551 089 400; www.kastrohotel.gr; s/d incl breakfast €50/86; ☒ ☒) Just west of Paleopolis, above the coast road, this spacious hotel offers simple but comfortable rooms with a sea view.

I Asprovalta (☎ 2551 098 250; fish from around €5)
Overlooking the sea, this serene little taverna in Kato Kariotes, just past Paleopolis, serves delicious fresh seafood.

AROUND SAMOTHRAKI
Loutra (Therma) Λουτρά (Θέρμα)
Loutra, also called Therma, is 14km east of Kamariotissa and a short walk inland from the coast. It's in an attractive setting with a profusion of plane and horse-chestnut trees, dense greenery and gurgling creeks. While not an authentic village, it is the nearest Samothraki comes to having a holiday resort. Many of its buildings are purpose-built domatia, and most visitors to the island seem to stay here. If you visit before mid-May, be prepared to find most places closed.

The village takes both its names from its therapeutic, sulphurous, mineral springs. Whether or not you are arthritic you may enjoy a **thermal bath** (☎ 2551 098 229; admission €1.50; ☽ 6-11am & 5-7pm Jun-Sep). The baths are in the large white building by the bus stop. Alternatively, take the road to the right of the bathhouse and about 50m up on the right you'll see another small structure containing a thermal bath which is free. About 20m up the hill there are two other small baths outdoors.

SLEEPING
Samothraki's two official camping grounds are both near Loutra, on the beach, and both are signposted 'Multilary Campings'. Rest assured, the authorities mean municipal, not military, camping grounds.

Multilary Camping (Camping Plateia; ☎ 2551 041 784; camp sites per adult/tent €3/3; ☽ Jun-Aug) This site is to the left of the main road, 2km beyond the turn-off for Loutra, coming from Kamariotissa. It is shady, with toilets and cold showers but no other amenities.

Multilary Camping (☎ 2551 041 491; camp sites per adult/tent €3/3; ☽ Jun-Aug) This second site is 2km further along the road. It has a minimarket, restaurant and hot showers, but is a rather dry camping ground.

Domatia owners meet the buses at Loutra.

Mariva Bungalows (☎ 2551 098 230; fax 2551 098 374; d €60; ☒) These spacious bungalows, set on a hillside in a secluded part of the island, near a waterfall, are perhaps the loveliest

place to stay on Samothraki. Rooms are airy and the bungalows are surrounded by lush foliage. Prices include breakfast. To reach the hotel take the first turn left along the road that leads from the coast up to Loutra. Follow the signs to the hotel, which is 600m along this road.

Kaviros Hotel (☎ 2551 098 277; fax 2551 098 278; s/d €40/50) This B-class hotel is bang in the middle of Loutra, just beyond the central square. It looks like a concrete bunker but is a pleasant family-run place surrounded by greenery. Although there is no air-con, the hotel will provide fans.

EATING
In Loutra there are a number of restaurants and tavernas scattered throughout the upper and lower village.

Paradisos Restaurant (☎ 2551 095 267; mains from €4) In the upper village try this restaurant, which plies its trade under the welcome shade of a huge plane tree. Take the road to the right from the bus stop to find it.

Fengari Restaurant (☎ 2551 098 321; mains from €4) This restaurant cooks its food in traditional Samothraki ovens. It is hidden away on a backstreet – it's the road to the right just before reaching Kaviros Hotel.

Kafeneio Ta Therma (☎ 2551 098 325) Next to the bus stop and baths, this place serves excellent coffee, drinks and mezedes, as well as superb home-made sweets. Try the figs in syrup.

Fonias River
Visitors to the north coast should not miss the walk along the Fonias River to the **Vathres** rock pools. The walk starts at the bridge over the river 4.7km east of Loutra where there are a couple of ticket booths. The admission price of €1 is largely theoretical as the site is unfenced and the ticket booths are only open in the summer season. After an easy 40-minute walk along a fairly well-marked track you will come to a large rock-pool fed by a dramatic 12m-high waterfall. The water is pretty cold but very welcome on a hot day. Locals call the river the 'Murderer' – winter rains can transform the waters into a raging torrent. Although there are a total of six waterfalls, marked paths only run to the first two; after that, the walk becomes dangerously confusing.

Beaches

The gods did not overendow Samothraki with good beaches. However, its one sandy beach, **Pahia Ammos**, on the south coast, is superb. You can reach this 800m stretch of sand along an 8km winding road from Lakoma. In summer there are caïques from Kamariotissa to the beach. Around the headland is the equally superb **Vatos Beach**, used mainly by nudists.

Opposite Pahia Ammos, on a good day, you can see the mass of the former Greek island of Imvros (Gökçeada), ceded to the Turks under the Treaty of Lausanne in 1923.

Samothraki's other decent beach is the pebbled **Kipos Beach** on the southeast coast. It can be reached via the road skirting the north coast. However, there are no facilities here other than a shower and a freshwater fountain, and there is no shade. It pales in comparison to Pahia Ammos. Kipos Beach can also be reached by caïque from Kamariotissa. In summer, there are boat excursions that take in both beaches for about €15.

Other Villages

The small villages of **Profitis Ilias**, **Lakoma** and **Xiropotamos** in the southwest, and **Alonia** near Hora, are serene, unspoilt and all worth a visit. The hillside Profitis Ilias, with many trees and springs, is particularly delightful and has several tavernas, of which **Vrahos** (☎ 2551 095 264) is famous for its delicious roast kid. Asphalt roads lead to all of these villages.

THASOS ΘΑΣΟΣ

pop 13,530 / area 375 sq km

Thasos lies 10km southeast of Kavala. The EOT brochures tout it as the 'emerald isle', and despite bad fires it is indeed a marvel of lushness and greenery. Villages are shaded by huge oaks and plane trees watered by streams and springs. The main attractions of Thasos, aside from its villages and forests, are its many excellent white-sand beaches and the archaeological remains in and around the capital, Thasos (Limenas). A good asphalt road goes around the island, so all the beaches are easily accessible.

Where there are beaches, tourists soon follow and they have come to Thasos in droves, mostly on package tours. Tourism

is not all that Thasos relies upon, however. The island was once known for its gold. The Parians who founded the ancient city in 700 BC struck gold at Mt Pangaion and it became the foundation for Thasos' lucrative export trade. With money came military power in the form of a navy as well as a number of notable painters and sculptors. Subsequent rulers from Athenians, Macedonians and Romans to the 18th-century Turks and 19th-century Egyptians couldn't keep their hands away from Thasos' pot of money, taxing the island into penury. In recent years Thasos has once again struck 'gold'. This time it is 'black gold', in the form of oil, and oil derricks can now be spotted at sea at various locations around Thasos. Thasos is also a major provider of very white marble – the quarries are fast creating huge holes in the island's mountainsides.

Getting There & Away

FERRY

There are ferries every one or two hours depending on the season between Kavala, on the mainland, and Skala Prinos (€3, 1¼ hours). Ferries direct to Limenas leave every hour or so in summer from Keramoti (€1.50, 40 minutes), 46km southeast of Kavala. If you are coming from Kavala airport, catch a taxi (€9, 15 minutes) to the ferry at Keramoti instead of Kavala – it's much closer, the ferries go direct to Thasos (Limenas), and the ferry ride itself is much quicker. Ferry schedules are posted at the **ticket sales booths**

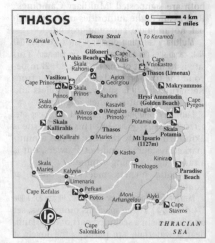

THASOS

0 ___ 4 km
0 ___ 2 miles

To Kavala

Thasos Strait

To Keramoti

Glifoneri
Pahis Beach
Skala Rahoni
Cape Pahis
Cape Vriokastro
Thasos (Limenas)

Vasiliou
Cape Prinos
Agios Georgiou

Skala Prinos
Makryammos

Skala Prinos
Rahoni

Skala Sotira
Kasaviti
Hrysi Ammoudia (Golden Beach)
Cape Pyrgos

Mikros Prinos
Megalos Prinos
Panagia

Skala Kallirahis
Potamia
Skala Potamia

Thasos
Mt Ipsario (1127m)

Kallirahi
Maries

Skala Maries
Kastro
Kinira

Kalyvia
Theologos
Paradise Beach

Cape Kefalas
Limenaria
Pefkari

Potos
Moni Arhangelou
Alyki
Cape Stavros

Cape Salonikios
THRACIAN SEA

(☎ 2593 022 318) and **port police** (☎ 2593 022 106) in Limenas and Skala Prinos.

The dock for the ferries to Keramoti is 150m west of the town centre.

HYDROFOIL
There are three hydrofoils every day between Limenas and Kavala (€9, 40 minutes).

Getting Around
BICYCLE
Bicycles can be hired from **Babis Bikes** (☎ 2593 022 129), on a side street between 18 Oktovriou and the central square in Limenas.

BUS
Thasos (Limenas) is the transport hub of the island. There are at least seven buses daily to Limenaria via the west coast villages (€3) and many to Skala Potamia at the south end of Hrysi Ammoudia (Golden Beach) via Panagia and Potamia. There are five buses a day to Theologos and three to Alyki (€2.50). Five buses daily journey in a clockwise direction all the way around the island (€7.10, 3½ hours) and another five go anticlockwise. Timetables are available from the **bus station** (☎ 2593 022 162).

CAR & MOTORCYCLE
Cars can be hired from **Avis Rent a Car** (☎ 2593 022 535; fax 2593 023124) on the central square in Limenas or in Skala Prinos (☎ 2593 072 075) and Potamia (☎ 2593 061 735). There are many other agencies, so you may want to shop around. In Limenas you can hire motorcycles and mopeds from **Billy's Bikes** (☎ 2593 022 490), opposite the foreign-language newspaper agency, and **2 Wheels** (☎ 2593 023 267), on the road to Prinos.

The coast road is about 100km all up, but due to winding mountain sections a full circuit with stops takes about a day.

EXCURSION BOAT
The **Eros 2 excursion boat** (☎ 2593 022 285) makes trips around the island three to four times a week, with stops for swimming and a barbecue. The boat leaves from the old harbour at 10am (but you should be there at 9.30am) and returns at 6pm. The price is €28, including barbecue. There are also a couple of water taxis running regularly to Hrysi Ammoudia (Golden Beach) and Makryammos beach.

THASOS (LIMENAS) ΘΑΣΟΣ (ΛΙΜΕΝΑΣ)
pop 2610
Thasos (also known as Limenas or Limin), on the northeast coast, is the main port and capital of the island. As the island's transport hub, it makes a great base for exploring coastal resorts and villages. Others have come to the same conclusion though, leaving the little town inundated with visitors all summer. Amid the uninspiring modern buildings lie a scattering of ancient ruins and there's a sandy beach just beyond the old harbour.

Orientation & Information
The town's main thoroughfare is 18 Oktovriou, which is packed with souvenir shops and tavernas.
Ferry ticket booths (☎ 2593 022 318)
Laundry Express (☎ 2593 022 235)
Millennium Internet Café (☎ 2593 058 089; ☯ 8.30am-midnight; €3 per hr) Has Web access.
National Bank of Greece On the waterfront; it has an ATM.
Newsagent (Theogenous) Sells English-language newspapers.
Port police (☎ 2593 022 106)
Tourist police (☎ 2593 023 111) Will assist in finding accommodation if necessary.

Sights
Thasos' **archaeological museum** (☎ 2593 022 180), next to the ancient agora at the small harbour, has been closed for years and, unfortunately, is not expected to reopen.

The **ancient agora** (admission free) next to the museum was the bustling marketplace of ancient and Roman Thasos – the centre of its civic, social and business life. It's a pleasant, verdant site with the foundations of stoas, shops and dwellings.

The **ancient theatre**, nearby, stages performances of ancient dramas and comedies (see Festival & Events, p374). The theatre is signposted from the small harbour.

From the theatre a path leads up to the **acropolis** of ancient Thasos where there are substantial remains of a medieval fortress built on the foundations of the ancient walls that encompassed the entire city. From the topmost point of the acropolis there are magnificent views. From the far side of the acropolis, steps carved into the rock lead down to the foundations of the ancient wall. From here it's a short walk to the Limenas–Panagia road at the southern edge of town.

THASOS (LIMENAS)

0 — 100 m
0 — 0.1 miles

INFORMATION	
ATM..................................1	C2
Laundry Express...................2	C2
National Bank of Greece........3	B2
Newsagent.........................4	C2

SIGHTS & ACTIVITIES	(p373)
Ancient Agora 5	D2
Archaeological Museum.........6	D1
Sanctuary of Hercules..........7	C3

SLEEPING	(pp374–5)
Amfipolis Hotel....................8	C2
Hotel Akropolis....................9	B3
Hotel Angelica...................10	C1
Hotel Mironi......................11	B3
Hotel Victoria....................12	A3

EATING	(p375)
Da Remo...........................13	C1
I Pigi Grill Room.................14	B2
Simi................................15	D1
Stamatis...........................16	B2
Toxotis............................17	B3

DRINKING	(p375)
Anonymous........................18	C2
Full Moon.........................19	C2
Platea Bar.........................20	B2
The Drift Chill Out Café.......21	D1
To Karanti........................22	D1

TRANSPORT	(pp372–3)
Avis Rent a Car..................23	B2
Babis Bikes.......................24	B2
Billy's Bikes......................25	C2
Bus Station.......................26	B2
Ferries to Kavala................27	B2
Ferry Tickets.....................28	B2
Taxis..............................29	B2
Tickets for Eros 2 Excursion Boat...............................30	D1

Thasos Strait

To Syrtaki (100m); Karnagio (150m)

Old Harbour

To Ancient Theatre; Acropolis (100m)

Quay

18 Oktovriou

Central Square

Pavlou Mela

M. Alexandrou

Street of French Archaeological School

K. Dimitriadi

To Millennium Internet Cafe (100m); Ferries to Keramoti (150m); Hotel Tarsanas; Taverna Tarsanas (1km)

To Prinos (24km)

To I Kokkinia (100m); Makryammos Bungalows (2km); Panagia (14km)

Festivals & Events

In July and August, performances of various ancient plays are held in the ancient theatre as part of the **Kavala Festival of Drama**. Not to be missed is the annual **Full Moon concert** that takes place each year in August. Admission is free and singers come from all over Greece to participate. Information and tickets can be easily obtained from the **EOT** (☎ 2510 222 425) in Kavala or from the **tourist police** (☎ 2593 023 111) on Thasos.

Sleeping

BUDGET

Limenas has many reasonably priced domatia. If you are not offered anything when you arrive, look for signs around the small harbour and the road to Prinos.

Hotel Akropolis (☎/fax 2593 022 488; s/d €45/55; ❄) This well-maintained, century-old mansion has a lovely garden out the front and a foyer filled with wondrous family heirlooms. The rooms are somewhat pokey and cramped but comfortable enough and the prices include breakfast.

Hotel Tarsanas (☎ 2593 023 933; fax 2593 022 333; d €60; ❄) This little hotel is 1km west of town on a quiet beach. The cheerful rooms have TVs and kitchenettes and there is a very good restaurant and bar.

Hotel Victoria (☎ 2593 022 556; fax 2593 022 132; d €30) This comfortable place is next door to Hotel Mironi and is run by the same owner.

Hotel Mironi (☎ 2593 023 256; fax 2593 022 132; s/d €35/40; ❄) This is a modern and spacious hotel with lots of cool marble. The rooms are basic but in good condition and have fridges.

Hotel Angelica (☎ 2593 022 387; fax 2593 022 160; Old Harbour; d €50; ❄) This box-like structure has good-size rooms and is conveniently close to the town beach.

MID-RANGE & TOP END

Makryammos Bungalows (☎ 2593 022 101; www .makryammos-hotel.gr; s/d incl breakfast €88/117; ❄ ⚏ P) This attractive, slightly hippieish resort was the first on the island and is situated on an idyllic beach 2km southeast of Limenas. There are around 200 bungalows hidden in the forest behind the beach, all very private and furnished in an elegant, traditional style. Incorporated into the complex is a restaurant, taverna, tennis court, swimming pools and water-sports equipment. Excellent child-minding facilities are provided free of charge. For an additional charge, guests (and others) may participate in courses that include yoga, tai chi etc.

Amfipolis Hotel (☎ 2593 023 101; fax 2593 022 110; cnr 18 Oktovriou & Theogenous; s/d/ste with buffet breakfast €60/90/135; 🖳 ❄) This A-class hotel occupies a grand old tobacco factory. Rooms are elegantly furnished and have interesting wood-panelled ceilings. The hotel has two bars and an excellent restaurant.

Eating
You can eat well in Limenas although too many restaurants are dumbing down their menus with poorly prepared versions of international standards.

Toxotis (☎ 2593 022 720; mains from €4.50) This is not a pizza/schnitzel/fish-and-chips kind of place. The Greek food here is particularly well prepared and, consequently attracts a discerning local crowd. It would be impossible to find a better *kleftiko* (slow, oven-baked lamb or goat).

I Pigi Grill Room (☎ 2593 022 941; central square; mains €4-6; 🕒 from 7pm) This restaurant is an inviting, unpretentious place next to a spring. The food is good and the service friendly and attentive. Try *stifado* (stew in tomato sauce) or mussel saganaki.

Simi (☎ 2593 022 517; Old Harbour; mains €4-7.50) With nicely set tables and white tablecloths, this place has a classy look that carries over to its cuisine. The fish is of the freshest and the preparation is excellent.

I Kokkinia (☎ 2593 023 729; appetisers €2.50, mains €4.50-6.50) This little taverna is on the Street of the French Archaeology School, on the outskirts of Limenas, on the way to Panagia and Makryammos. Fish is the speciality (the owner's father is a fisherman), but chargrilled meat and other traditional dishes are also offered.

Syrtaki (☎ 2593 023 353; mains from €5) Just beyond the old harbour, along the beach, this place serves good traditional Greek fare. Try the lamb kleftiko or the *stamnato* (pork and vegetables in a clay pot).

Da Remo (☎ 2593 022 890; 18 Oktovriou; pizzas €4-12) This pizza place is a cut above the usual Greek pizzerias; home delivery is an option.

Taverna Tarsanas (☎ 2593 023 933; mezedes €2.50, mains €3-20) This lovely place, 1km west of Thasos on the site of a former boatbuilders, serves the most exquisite seafood on the island. There are lots of interesting seafood mezedes that you won't find anywhere else. Fresh lobster (€44 per kg) – difficult to find on Thasos – is always available. Traditional meat dishes are also served.

Stamatis (☎ 2593 022 131; 18 Oktovriou) This zaharoplasteio has been going since 1958. It's the best place for coffee and sweets.

Drinking
The nightlife is young and active, with the latest in techno bursting from a variety of slicked-up establishments.

Platea Bar (☎ 2593 022 144) This earthy, quirky little bar with shaman-style handcrafted decor is a local favourite. It's known for its reliably good music and casual, welcoming atmosphere. Look for it on the central square.

To Karanti (☎ 2593 024 014) This outdoor ouzeri next to the fishing boats on the old harbour has one of the most beautiful settings in Thasos. Its relaxed atmosphere is enhanced by excellent Greek music. Aside from a full bar, breakfast and mezedes are available.

The Drift Chill Out Café (Old Harbour) With a nice laid-back outdoor setting by the water northeast of the Old Harbour, this bar is a refreshing option.

Karnagio (☎ 2593 023 170) Beyond the Old Harbour this is a lovely place to have a drink at sunset. Sited where wooden boats are still built, it has a dramatic locale at the end of the promontory.

Anonymous (☎ 2593 022 847; 18 Oktovriou) This bar serves English-style snacks and Guinness in a can, as well as many other beers.

Full Moon Bar (☎ 2593 023 230; 18 Oktovriou) Next door to Anonymous café, this watering hole has an Australian owner and is also very popular.

EAST COAST
The hillside villages of **Panagia** and **Potamia** are a bit touristy but very picturesque. Both are 4km west of Hrysi Ammoudia (Golden Beach). The Greek-American artist Polygnotos Vagis was born in Potamia in 1894 and some of his work can be seen in the **Polygnotos Vagis Museum** (☎ 2593 061 400;

admission €3; ⊙ 8.30am-noon & 6-8pm Tue-Sat, 8.30am-noon Sun & holidays) in the village next to the main church. (The Municipal Museum of Kavala also has a collection of Vagis' work – see p297.)

It may get a trifle crowded, but the long and sandy **Hrysi Ammoudia** (Golden Beach) is one of the island's best beaches. Roads from both Panagia and Potamia lead to it, and the bus from Limenas calls at both villages before continuing to the southern end of the beach, which is known as Skala Potamia.

The next beach south is at the village of **Kinira**, and just south of here is the very pleasant **Paradise Beach**. The little islet just off the coast here is also called Kinira. **Alyki**, on the southeast coast, is a magical, spectacular place consisting of two quiet beaches back to back on a headland and some quaint old houses. The southernmost beach is the better of the two. There is a small **archaeological site** near the beach and an ancient, submerged **marble quarry**. Here marble was cut and loaded on ships from the 6th century BC to the 6th century AD.

The road linking the east side of the island with the west side runs high across the cliffs, providing some great views of the bays to the south. Along here you will come to **Moni Arhangelou**, an old monastery built on top of cliffs directly opposite Mt Athos on the mainland. It's possible to visit, and the nuns sell some hand-painted icons, crosses and other paraphernalia.

Sleeping & Eating

Thassos Inn (☎ 2593 061 612; fax 2593 061 027; d €45; ⊙ summer & winter) This lovely hotel in Panagia is up the hill, in the cool of the forest. Built in traditional style, it has views over the slate rooftops of the village. Rooms have TVs and balconies. From the bus stop, follow the small street leading from the fountain. Turn right at the sign to the hotel about 20m up the street, just past the honey shop, and follow the babbling brook.

Golden Beach Camping (☎ 2593 061 472; fax 2593 061 473; camp sites per adult/tent €3.25/2.60) This place, smack in the middle of Hrysi Ammoudia, is the only camping ground on this side of the island; it's only a stone's throw from the inviting water. Facilities are good and include a minimarket.

Hotel Emerald (☎ 2593 061 979; fax 2593 061 451; self-contained 2-/4-person studios with kitchen €65/80; 🐾) This hotel up the hill at the northern end of Hrysi Ammoudia has a pool and other facilities and very nice rooms; it's often prebooked by package tours.

Apartments Kavouri (☎ 2593 062 031; 2 3-person apt €60) These spacious studios have balconies and fully equipped kitchens. They are at the far southern end of Skala Potamia, near the bus turn-around.

Hotel Elvetia (☎ 2593 061 231; fax 2593 061 451; d €40) This hotel in Panagia has pleasant doubles with fridges. With your back to the fountain in the central square of Panagia (where the bus stops), turn left and take the first main road to the left; the hotel is on the left.

Hotel Hrysafis (☎ /fax 2593 061 451; d €45) This vine-covered hotel is just beyond Hotel Elvetia, on the right, and has the same owners as the Elvetia.

There are domatia at both Kinira and Alyki.

Drosia/Platanos (☎ 2593 062 172, 2593 061 340; salads €2-4, mains €4-5) This popular taverna is on Panagia's central square and serves pizza and spaghetti as well as traditional Greek dishes.

Fedra (☎ 2593 061 474; mains €4-10) In the middle of Hrysi Ammoudia, this was one of the first restaurants on Thasos and is deservedly popular.

Avalon (☎ 2593 062 060; mains €4-10) In an imposing old monastery at the southern end of Hrysi Ammoudia in Skala Potamia, this establishment serves traditional fare as well as pizza and fish.

Taverna Captain (☎ 2593 061 160; fish €5.50-10) In Skala Potamia, this somewhat touristy place right off the beach offers decent fish.

WEST COAST

The west coast consists of a series of beaches and seaside villages, most with Skala (literally 'step' or 'ladder', but also meaning 'little pier') before their names. Roads lead from each of these to inland villages with the same name (minus the 'skala'). Travelling from north to south the first beach is **Glifoneri**, closely followed by **Pahis Beach**. The first village of any size is **Skala Rahoni**, a favourite of the package-tour companies. It has an excellent camping ground and the inland village of **Rahoni** remains unspoilt.

A wide range of water-sports equipment can be hired from **Skala Rachoni Watersports** (☎ 2593 081 056).

Skala Prinos, the next coastal village and Thasos' second port, is nothing special. There is an ATM at the port and a few small hotels along the waterfront in case you get stuck. **Vasiliou**, about 1km south of the port, is a very nice beach backed by trees. The hillside villages of Mikros Prinos and Megalos Prinos, collectively known as **Kasaviti**, are gorgeous and lush, with excellent tavernas (see Eating, below).

Skala Sotira and **Skala Kallirahis** are pleasant and both have small beaches. Kallirahi, 2km inland from Skala Kallirahis, is a peaceful village with steep narrow streets and old stone houses. It has a large population of skinny, anxious-looking cats and word has it that the locals are scared of dogs. Judging by the graffiti and posters, there are also a lot of communists (though not as many as in Skala Potamia).

Skala Maries is a delightful fishing village and one of the least touristy places around the coast. It was from here, early in the 20th century, that the German Speidel Metal Company exported iron ore from Thasos to Europe. There are beaches at both sides of the village, and between here and Limenaria there are stretches of uncrowded beach. **Maries**, Skala Maries' inland sister village, is very pretty and has a lovely square.

Limenaria is Thasos' second-largest town. It's a crowded though pleasant resort with a narrow sandy beach. The town was built in 1903 by the Speidel Metal Company. There are slightly less-crowded beaches around the coast at **Pefkari** and **Potos**.

From Potos a scenic 10km road leads inland to **Theologos**, which was the capital of the island in medieval and Turkish times. This is one of the island's most beautiful villages and the only mountain settlement served by public transport. The village houses are of whitewashed stone with slate roofs. It's a serene place, still unblemished by mass tourism.

Sleeping

Camping Perseus (☎ /fax 2593 081 242; camp sites per adult/tent €3/2; ☾ May-Oct) This facility, at Skala Rahoni, is a pleasant, grassy camping ground among olive trees.

Camping Prinos (☎ 2593 071 171; camp sites per adult/tent around €3.50/2.75) This EOT-owned site, at Skala Prinos, is well maintained with lots of greenery and shade and is about 1km or so south of the ferry quay, in Vasiliou.

Camping Daedalos (☎ /fax 2593 058 251; camp sites per adult/tent around €3.50/2.25) This camping ground is just north of Skala Sotira right on the beach. It has a minimarket, restaurant and bar. Sailing, windsurfing and waterskiing lessons are also on offer.

Camping Pefkari (☎ 2593 051 190; camp sites per adult/tent around €3.50/3.90; ☾ Apr-Oct) This nifty camping ground is at Pefkari Beach, south of Limenaria. It requires a minimum three-night stay.

All of the seaside villages have hotels and domatia and the inland villages have rooms in private houses. For information about these enquire at kafeneia or look for signs.

Alexandra Beach Hotel (☎ 2593 052 391; www .alexandrabeach.gr; d €148; ☒ ☒ Ⓟ) Rates are considerably less outside high season. This resort-like complex is near Potos and is one of the island's best hotels. Aside from the very nice beach there's a restaurant, bar, tennis court and more. Breakfast and dinner are included in the room rate.

Eating

Taverna Glifoneri (mains from €4.50) At Glifoneri Beach, on the way from Thasos (Limenas) to Skala Rahoni, this place is on a small beach with a freshwater spring. Try the excellent home-made mussel saganaki with feta.

Pefkospilia (☎ 2593 081 051; appetisers €2-3, mains €4-18) This cute, traditional, family-run taverna by the water at Pahis Beach, just off the road between Thasos (Limenas) and Skala Rahoni, is in a beautiful spot under a large pine tree. It serves delectable local specialities, including the sought-after fish known as *mourmoures* (€25 per kg), *kravourosalata* (crab salad; €4) and *htapodokeftedes* (octopus rissoles; €3.50).

Taverna Drosia (☎ 2593 081 270; mains €3-5) This taverna in a grove of plane and oak trees on the outskirts of Rahoni features live bouzouki on Friday, Saturday and Sunday evenings. Chargrilled meat is the speciality of the house, though it also has fresh seafood and precooked dishes.

Taverna O Andreas (☎ 2593 071 760; mains from €3) This homespun taverna on Kasaviti's serene central square shaded by ancient plane trees, serves excellent soup, vegetable dishes, meat and oven-cooked foods. The whole family participates in cooking, and, judging by the food, they're passionate about it. Chirping birds, and cute cats chasing each other around the plane tree, will entertain you as you quietly savour your meal.

Vasilis (☎ 2593 072 016; mains from €4) This beautiful, traditional wooden place on the road into Kasaviti has very good local food but is worth visiting for its stunning old-world architecture alone.

Taverna Orizontes (☎ 2593 031 389; mains from €4; ☙ from 7pm) This taverna, the first on the left

as you enter Theologos, features rembetika nights.

Augustus (mains €4-7.50; ☙ from 7pm) Specialising in grilled meat, including goat and lamb, this bouzouki joint is also in Theologos. The bouzouki action takes place on Friday, Saturday and Sunday nights. Strangely passive ducks swim around in a floodlit pond – just one of the kitschy highlights that await you.

Ciao Tropical Beach Bar (☎ 2593 081 136) More Hawaiian than Hawaii, this beach bar in Pahis is quite a work of art. The owner has created everything by hand, from the umbrellas to the wood-carved lamps and furniture. You have to see it to believe it.

Evia & the Sporades
Εύβοια & Οι Σποράδες

CONTENTS

Hugging the coastline of mainland Greece, the large island of Evia provides Athenians with a convenient destination for a weekend break. Much of the island, however, is relatively undeveloped and remains undiscovered by foreign tourists. To the north, Loutra Edipsou and Limni draw Greeks in search of mineral spas and sandy beaches. In central Evia, trekkers head to the creek-side village of Steni at the foot of Mt Dirfys. To the south, the landscape changes from mountainsides carpeted in pine and poplar to arid hillsides dotted with olive trees and cut by rocky gorges. Above the coastal resort of Karystos, you can visit the dragon houses, ancient Stonehenge-like landmarks set in seemingly impossible positions.

The Sporades lie northeast of Evia and southeast of the Pelion Peninsula, to which they were joined in prehistoric times. Indeed, with their dense vegetation and mountainous terrain, the islands seem like a continuation of this peninsula. There are 11 islands in the archipelago, four of which are inhabited. Skiathos claims the best beaches of the bunch and a throbbing tourist scene and nightlife, while Skopelos kicks back with an inviting postcard waterfront, sandy bays and lush forest trails. Alonnisos and Skyros, although by no means remote, are far less visited and retain more local character. The National Marine Park of Alonnisos encompasses seven islands, of which Alonnisos is the largest. The marine park is home to the endangered Mediterranean monk seal, and much of the island seems dedicated to preserving the region's delicate ecology.

HIGHLIGHTS

▪ **Wining**

Wine & Cultural Festival in Karystos (p385), Evia

▪ **Dining**

The fish tavernas at Steni Vala (p398), Alonnisos

▪ **Sporting Event**

The half-marathon (p401) across Skyros in September

▪ **Wildlife**

Dolphin watching tours (p394) in the National Marine Park of Alonnisos

▪ **Adrenaline Rush**

Diving (p389) off Nostos Bay, Skiathos

▪ **Chill-out Spot**

Little Banana Beach (p389) on Skiathos

Getting There & Away

AIR

Skiathos airport receives charter flights from northern Europe and there are also domestic flights to Athens (see the Skiathos Getting There & Away section, p386). Skyros airport has domestic flights to Athens (see Getting There & Away under Skyros, p400), as well as occasional charter flights from the Netherlands.

BUS

From the Terminal B bus station in Athens (Liossion St) there are buses every half-hour to Halkida from 5.30am to 9pm (€4.80, one hour), two daily to Paralia Kymis (€10.45, four hours) and three daily to Loutra Edipsou (Edipsos; €9.30, 3½ hours). From the Mavromateon terminal in Athens (located opposite Aeros Park)there are buses every 45 minutes to Rafina (for Karystos and Marmari; one hour, €1.65).

FERRY

There are daily ferries to the Sporades from both Agios Konstantinos and Volos. In addition, there are ferries twice weekly from Thessaloniki to the Sporades, as well as five ferry routes connecting Evia to the mainland.

The table on this page lists ferries to this island group from mainland ports in high season. Further details and interisland links can be found under each island entry in this chapter. Summer ferry timetables are usually available in late April. The main companies are

GA Ferries (☎ 2104 582 640; fax 2104 510 001; www .gaferries.com; Akti Miaouli & 2 Kantharou, Piraeus GR-185 37)

Minoan Lines (☎ 2104 082 495; fax 2104 080 015; www.minoan.gr; 6-19 Thermopylon, Piraeus GR-185 45)

Hellas Ferries (☎ 2104 199 000; fax 2104 131 111; www .hellasferries.gr; Akti Kondyli & 2 Etolikou, Piraeus GR-185 45)

HYDROFOIL

There are frequent daily hydrofoil links from both Agios Konstantinos and Volos to the Northern Sporades (including Skiathos, Skopelos and Alonnisos). However, there is no longer a hydrofoil service to Skyros or Evia. The table on this page lists all hydrofoil connections during the high season. Also, further details and interisland links can be found under each island entry in this chapter. The summer hydrofoil timetable is usually available in late April from **Hellas Flying Dolphins** (☎ 2104 199 100; fax 2104 110 047; www.dolphins.gr; Akti Kondyli & 2 Etolikou, Piraeus GR-185 45). The Athens office (☎ 2103 244 600) is at Filellinon 3. The timetable is also available from local hydrofoil booking offices located in Volos and Agios Konstantinos. You'll find that slightly cheaper return fares apply on most hydrofoil services.

FERRY CONNECTIONS TO EVIA & THE SPORADES

Origin	Destination	Time	€	Frequency
Agia Marina	Evia (Nea Styra)	1hr	€1.90	5 daily
Agios Konstantinos				
(jet ferry)	Alonnisos	4hr	€28.40	2 daily
(jet ferry)	Skiathos	2½hr	€20.80	2 daily
(jet ferry)	Skopelos	3½hr	€28.40	2 daily
Arkitsa	Evia (Loutra Edipsou)	1hr	€1.90	12 daily
Evia (Paralia Kymis)	Skyros	2hr	€6.90	2 daily
Evia (Marmari)	Rafina	1hr	€4.50	5 daily
Glifa	Evia (Agios Kampos)	30min	€1.20	hourly
Skala Oropou	Evia (Eretria)	30min	€1.30	half-hourly
Thessaloniki	Skiathos	6hr	€16	2 weekly
Volos	Alonnisos	4hr	€15.70	2 daily
	Skiathos	2½hr	€11.60	2 daily
	Skopelos	4hr	€15.10	2 daily

HYDROFOIL CONNECTIONS TO EVIA & THE SPORADES

Origin	Destination	Time	€	Frequency
Agios Konstantinos				
	Alonnisos	2¾hr	€28.40	3 daily
	Skiathos	1½hr	€20.80	3 daily
	Skopelos	2½hr	€28.40	3 daily
Volos	Alonnisos	2½hr	€26.60	4 daily
	Skiathos	1¼hr	€19.80	4 daily
	Skopelos	2¼hr	€25.20	4 daily

TRAIN

There are hourly train services from Athens' Larissa station to Halkida from 4.40am to 11pm (€3.55, 1½ hours), and five express trains to Volos from 10.53am to 5.05pm (€19.40, 4½ hours).

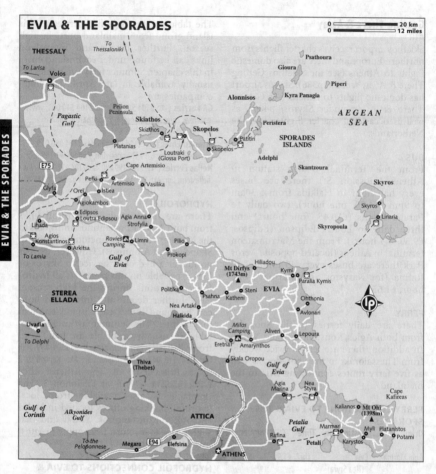

EVIA EYBOIA

The island of Evia (*eh*-vih-ah), a prime holiday destination for Greeks, remains less charted by foreign tourists. If you're in Athens with a few days to spare and (preferably) your own transport, a foray into Evia is well worthwhile for its scenic mountain roads (the best in Greece), its good trekking destinations, unusual archaeological finds, and its (mostly) uncrowded beaches. A mountainous spine runs north-south; the east coast consists of precipitous cliffs, whereas the gentler west coast has a string of beaches, resorts and spas. A number of ferry connections, as well as a bridge over the Evripous Channel to the

island's capital, Halkida, connect the island to the mainland.

At the mention of Evia, many Greeks will eagerly tell you that the current in this narrow channel changes direction around seven times daily, which it does, if you are prepared to hang around long enough to watch. The next bit of the story – that Aristotle became so perplexed at not finding an explanation for this mystifying occurrence that he threw himself into the channel and drowned – can almost certainly be taken with a grain of salt.

Getting Around

Halkida is the transport hub of Evia. There are buses to Kymi Town (€5.80, 2½ hours, nine daily) via Eretria, two of which continue to Paralia Kymis to link up with the ferry arrivals/departures. There are also buses to Steni (€2.80, one hour, two daily), Limni (€5.40, 2½ hours, four daily), Loutra Edipsou (€8.20, 3½ hours, two daily) and Karystos (€8, 3½ hours, three daily) via Eretria. The port of Marmari (for ferry connections to/from Rafina) is 11km from Karystos, and can be reached by bus (€1.10) or taxi (€10).

HALKIDA ΧΑΛΚΙΔΑ

pop 53,584

Halkida (also Halkis) was an important city-state in ancient times, with several colonies dotted around the Mediterranean. The name derives from the bronze manufactured here in antiquity (*halkos* means 'bronze' in Greek). Today it's a lively industrial and agricultural town, but with nothing of sufficient note to warrant an overnight stay. However, if you have an hour or so to spare between buses, have a look at the **Archaeological Museum** (☎ 2221 060 944; Leof Venizelou 13; admission €2; ☼ 8.30am-3pm Tue-Sun); it's worth a mosey around. It houses finds from Evia's three ancient cities of Halkida, Eretria and Karystos, including a chunk from the pediment of the Temple of Dafniforos Apollo at Eretria.

The Halkida train station is on the mainland side of the bridge. To reach central Halkida, turn right outside the train station, walk over the bridge, turn left and you will find Leof Venizelou, Halkida's main drag, off to the right. For emergencies, call the Halkida **tourist police** (☎ 2221 077 777).

Diving

The **Sport Apollon Scuba Diving Centre** (☎ 2221 086 369) in Halkida offers a range of diving activities for all grades. The dives take place off the Alikes coast, north of Evia. A one-day dive costs about €45.

CENTRAL EVIA

Steni Στενή

pop 926

From Halkida, it's 31km to the lovely mountain village of Steni, with its gurgling springs and shady plane trees.

Steni is the starting point for the climb up **Mt Dirfys** (1743m), Evia's highest mountain.

The EOT-owned **Dirfys Refuge** (☎ 2228 051 285), at 1120m, can be reached along a 9km dirt road. From the refuge it's 7km to the summit. You should not attempt this walk unless you are an experienced trekker. A reliable trekking guidebook is also essential. For further information contact the **EOT** (☎ 2221 025 230; Angeli Gyviou 22, Halkida). A good road continues from Steni to **Hiliadou**, on the north coast, where there is a fine pebble-and-sand beach, along with a few domatia and two tavernas. Campers can find shelter near the big rocks at the northern end of the beach.

SLEEPING & EATING

Hotel Dirfys (☎ 2228 051 217; s/d €28/35) This is the best value of Steni's two hotels, and is 50m uphill from the bus terminal. It has comfortable, carpeted rooms with great views from the balconies.

Mouria Taverna (☎ 2228 051 234; mains €3-7) This taverna on the central square serves generous portions of tender chargrilled chicken (€4.50) and lamb chops (€7) and very palatable local wine.

Ouzeri Vrachos (☎ 2228 051 546; mains €2.50-6.50) Next door to Mouria Taverna on the central square, this little eatery offers a huge helping of fried *gavros* (sardines) and Greek salad for €5.90.

Taverna Kissos (☎ 2228 051 226; mains €3.50-7) This brookside taverna offers non-vegetarian favourites like *kokoretsi* (lamb offal or organ meat) for €7, and spanikopita for €3.50.

Kymi Κύμη

pop 3037

The untouristy, workaday town of Kymi is built on a cliff 250m above the sea. Things perk up at dusk when the town square comes to life. The port of Kymi (called Paralia Kymis), 4km downhill, is the only natural harbour on the precipitous east coast, and the departure point for ferries to Skyros. Hook up to the only Internet service on the waterfront at **Café 1887** (☎ 2222 024 424).

The **Folklore Museum** (☎ 2222 022 011; admission €1.50; ☼ 10am-1pm & 5.30-8pm), on the road to Paralia Kymis, has an impressive collection of local costumes and historical photos, including a display commemorating Kymi-born Dr George Papanikolaou, inventor of the Pap smear test.

SLEEPING & EATING

Hotel Beis (☎ 2222 022 604; fax 2222 029 113; s/d €35/55; ☒) This waterfront hotel has comfortable, well-maintained rooms and is just across from the ferry dock.

Hotel Carali (☎ 2222 022 212; fax 2222 023 353; s/d €36/50; ☒) It's a 300m walk from the ferry dock to this quiet hotel run by two sisters, Sofia and Evangelia.

Chalkidou Domatia (☎ 2222 023 896; Athinon 14, Kymi; s/d/tr €25/35/40) These well-kept domatia, 100m south of the central square, have great balcony views down to Paralia Kymis.

Taverna Mouria (☎ 22220 22629; Galani 34; mains €3-6.50) Around 100m north of the church on the main square, this family eatery specialises in grills (chicken and potatoes €5.50) and pasta (*pastitsio*; €4.50).

In Paralia Kymis a string of tavernas and ouzeri lines the waterfront.

NORTHERN EVIA

From Halkida a road heads north to **Psahna**, the gateway to the highly scenic mountainous interior of northern Evia. The road climbs through pine forests to the beautiful agricultural village of **Prokopi**, 52km from Halkida. The inhabitants are descendants of refugees who, in 1923, came from Prokopion (present-day Ürgüp) in Turkey, bringing with them the relics of St John the Russian. On 27 May (**St John's Festival**), hordes of pilgrims come to worship his relics in the Church of Agios Ioannis Rosses.

At Strofylia, 14km beyond Prokopi, a road heads southwest to **Limni**, a picturesque and busy fishing village with whitewashed houses and a beach. With your own transport or a penchant for walking, you can visit the 16th-century **Convent of Galataki**, 8km southeast of Limni. Its katholikon has fine frescoes. Limni has several hotels and domatia. There's one camping ground, **Rovies Camping** (☎ 2227 071 120), on the coast, 13km northwest of Limni.

Loutra Edipsou Λουτρά Αιδηψού
pop 3600

The road continues to the sedate spa resort of **Loutra Edipsou** (119km from Halkida), whose therapeutic sulphur waters have been celebrated since antiquity. Many luminaries, including Aristotle, Plutarch and Plinius, sang the praises of these waters. Today

the town has Greece's most up-to-date hydrotherapy and physiotherapy centre; contact the **EOT Hydrotherapy-Physiotherapy Centre** (☎ 2226 023 501) in Loutra Edipsou. Even if you don't rank among the infirm you may enjoy a visit to this resort with its attractive port and beach tavernas.

For charm and value, you can't beat the **Hotel Aegli** (☎ 2226 022 215; fax 2226 022 886; Paraliakis 18; s/d/tr €30/45/50), 200m south of the ferry dock. This well-managed neoclassic holdover from the 1930s is decorated with framed autographs of luminaries who spent an evening here, including Greta Garbo, Aristotle Onassis and Winston Churchill. Like most of the hotels in town, this one offers hydrotherapy baths for about €5, far less than the up-market spas nearby.

SOUTHERN EVIA

Eretria Ερέτρια
pop 3156

As you head east from Halkida, Eretria is the first major place of interest. Ancient Eretria was a major maritime power and also had an eminent school of philosophy. The city was destroyed in AD 87 during the Mithridatic War, fought between Mithridates (king of Pontos) and the Roman commander Sulla. The modern town was founded in the 1820s by islanders from Psara fleeing the Turkish. Despite its modern package-tourist patina, it remains one of Evia's major archaeological sites.

SIGHTS

From the top of the **ancient acropolis**, at the northern end of town, there are splendid views over to the mainland. West of the acropolis are the remains of a palace, temple and theatre with a subterranean passage once used by actors. Close by, the **Museum of Eretria** (☎ 2229 062 206; admission €2; ☒ 8am-3pm Tue-Sun) contains well-displayed finds from ancient Eretria. In the centre of town are the remains of the **Temple of Dafniforos Apollo** and a mosaic from an ancient bath.

SLEEPING & EATING

Eretria has loads of hotels and domatia, and one camping ground.

Dreams Island Bungalows (☎ 2229 061 224; www .dreams-island.gr; s/d €45/55, 4-bed r incl breakfast €90) Tucked away on an islet 100m from Eretria's main promenade, this collection of bright bungalows among scattered pines is family-friendly. Kids can indulge in ping-pong and mini-golf, or play in the sand while mum and dad sip a cool one at the beach bar.

Milos Camping (☎ 2229 060 460; fax 2211 060 360; adult/tent €4/6) This clean camping ground on the coast 1km west of Eretria has good shade, and a restaurant, bar and decent beach.

Taverna Ligouris (☎ 2229 062 352; Ammarisias Artemidos; mains €3.50-8) Opposite the ferry dock, is the very best of the waterfront eateries. Come early for reasonably priced fresh fish.

Karystos Κάρυστος
pop 4960

Continuing east from Eretria, the road branches at Lepoura: the left fork leads to Kymi, the right to Karystos (*kah*-ris-tos). Set on the wide Karystian Bay, below Mt Ohi (1398m), Karystos is the most attractive of southern Evia's resorts and is flanked by two sandy beaches. The town was designed by the Bavarian architect Bierbach, who was commissioned by King Othon. If you turn right from the quay you will come to the central square of Plateia Amalias (named after the king's wife), which abuts the waterfront. Further along the waterfront is the remains of a 14th-century Venetian castle, the **Bourtzi**, which has marble from a temple dedicated to Apollo incorporated into its walls, along with some contemporary graffiti to liven it up. Karystos is the starting point for treks to Mt Ohi and the Dimosari Gorge. In August and September, the town hosts a carnival and wine festival.

SIGHTS
Karystos is mentioned in Homer's *Iliad*, and was a powerful city-state during the Peloponnesian Wars. The **Karystos Museum** (☎ 2224 025 661; admission €2; 🕒 9am-3pm Tue-Sun), just opposite the Bourtzi, documents the town's archaeological heritage, from tiny Neolithic clay lamps to an exhibit of 6th-century *drakospita* (dragon houses), which includes a stone plaque written in the Halkidian alphabet.

TOURS
With helpful English-speaking staff, **South Evia Tours Travel Agency** (☎ 2224 025 700; fax 2224 029 011) offers a range of services including car hire, accommodation and excursions. The latter include walks in the foothills of Mt Ohi, the

6th-century BC Roman-built *drakospita* near Skyra, and a cruise around the Petali Islands. The agency also provides do-it-yourself maps with graded walking trails.

FESTIVALS
Karystos hosts a summer **Wine & Cultural Festival** every July and August, with music and dancing, wine-tasting and theatre. Festival schedules are available at the museum (see Sight on this page) Karystos.

SLEEPING & EATING
Hotel Karystion (☎ 2224 022 391; fax 2224 022 727; Kriezotou 2; s/d incl breakfast €45/55; 🗏) Starting with the homemade breakfast muffins, you get your money's worth at this modern hotel 100m east of the Bourtzi, with carpeted rooms, satellite TV and sea-view balconies.

Hotel Galaxy (☎ 2224 022 600; fax 2224 022 463; cnr Kriezotou & Odysseos; s/d incl breakfast €35/50; 🗏) This well-managed waterfront hotel has simple rooms with TV, music channels and balconies.

Cavo d'Oro (☎ 2224 022 326; mains €3-7) Join the locals in this cheery little alleyway restaurant one block west of the main square, where tasty oil-based dishes (*ladera*, or fasting food) cost from €2.80 and a generous plate of lamb *yuvetsi* (claypot pasta) fetches a modest €6.50.

For evening drinks and sounds, walk west about 200m beyond the Galaxy Hotel to a string of late-night bars, such as **Club Arhipelagos** (☎ 2224 025 040), which features a healthy collection of reggae tunes and an open-air bar facing the sea.

Around Karystos
The ruins of **Castello Rossa** (Red Castle), a 13th-century Frankish fortress, are a short walk from **Myli**, a delightful, well-watered village 4km inland from Karystos. The aqueduct behind the castle once carried water from the mountain springs, and a tunnel led from this castle to the Bourtzi in Karystos. A little beyond Myli there is an **ancient quarry** scattered with fragments of the once-prized Karystian marble.

With your own transport you can explore the nearby dragon houses of Mt Ohi and Styra. The discovery of these Stonehenge-like slab dwellings hewn from rocks weighing up to several tons has spawned a number of theories regarding their origin, ranging from slave-built temples for Zeus and Hera to UFO overnight getaways.

Hikers can head north from Karystos to the summit of Mt Ohi where a footpath leads to the Dimosari Gorge and **Lenosei village** with views down to the coastal village of **Kalianos**. For less strenuous walks, explore the sleepy villages nestling in the foothills east of Mt Ohi. From the charming village of **Platanistos**, a 5km dirt road (driveable) passes a chestnut forest before reaching the coastal village of **Potami** with a sand-and-pebble beach. Contact South Evia Tours in Karystos (p385) for trail conditions.

SKIATHOS ΣΚΙΑΘΟΣ

pop 6160

The good news is that much of the pine-covered coast of Skiathos is blessed with exquisite beaches. The bad news is that in July and August the island is overrun with package tourists and everything is expensive. Despite the large presence of sun-starved northern Europeans, and the ensuing tourist excess, Skiathos is still a beautiful island and one of Greece's premier resorts.

The island has only one settlement, the port and capital of Skiathos Town, on the southeast coast. The rest of the south coast is one long chain of holiday villas and hotels, plus a number of sandy beaches with pine trees for a backdrop. The north coast is precipitous and less accessible; in the 14th century the Kastro Peninsula served as a natural fortress against invaders. Today, most people come to the island for the sun and nightlife, but the truly curious will discover inviting walks, picturesque monasteries, hilltop tavernas and even quiet beaches.

Getting There & Away

AIR

As well as the numerous charter flights from northern Europe to Skiathos, during summer there is one flight daily to Athens (€47). **Olympic Airways** (☎ 2427 022 200) has an office at the airport, not in town.

FERRY

In summer, there are ferries from Skiathos to Volos (€11.60, 2½ hours, two to three daily), Agios Konstantinos (€20.80, 2½ hours by jet ferry, two daily) and Alonnisos (€7.80,

two hours, two daily) via Skopelos (€5.50, 1¼ hours).

From mid-June to late September, there is twice-weekly service north to Thessaloniki (€16.80, six hours), and weekly service south to Tinos (€11, 7½ hours), Mykonos (€15, 8½ hours), Paros (€18, 10 hours), Santorini (€22, 13½ hours) and Iraklio (€27, 18 hours). Heading east, there is weekly service to Limnos (€14, 5½ hours).

Tickets can be purchased from **Skiathos Travel** (☎ 2427 022 029; fax 2427 022 750) at the bottom of Papadiamanti in Skiathos Town.

HYDROFOIL

In summer, there are hydrofoils from Skiathos to Volos (€19.80, 1¼ hours, four daily) and Alonnisos (€13, one hour, six daily) via Glossa on Skopelos (€5.60, 20 minutes) and Skopelos Town (€9.10, 35 minutes). There are also hydrofoils to Agios Konstantinos (€20.80, 1½ hours, three daily), and there is daily service to Pefki (€9) in northern Evia. Hydrofoil tickets can be purchased from Skiathos Travel (see above).

Getting Around

BUS

Crowded buses leave Skiathos Town for Koukounaries Beach (€1.10, 30 minutes) every half-hour between 7.30am and 11pm. The buses stop at all the access points to the beaches along the south coast.

CAR & MOTORCYCLE

Reliable car-hire outlets in Skiathos Town include **Heliotropio Tourism & Travel** (☎ 2427 022 430) and **Euronet** (☎ 2427 024 410). There are also heaps of motorcycle-hire outlets all along the town's waterfront.

SKIATHOS TOWN

Skiathos Town, with its red-roofed, white-washed houses, is built on two low hills. Opposite the waterfront lies inviting **Bourtzi Islet** (reached by a causeway) between the two harbours. The town is a major tourist centre, with hotels, souvenir shops, travel agents, tavernas and bars dominating the waterfront and main thoroughfare.

Orientation

The quay (wharf) is in the middle of the waterfront, just north of Bourtzi Islet. To the right (as you face inland) is the straight,

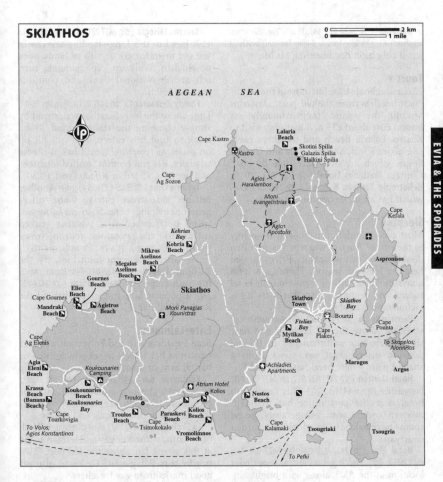

SKIATHOS

AEGEAN SEA

Cape Kastro
Lalaria Beach
Kastro
Skotini Spilia
Galazia Spilia
Halkini Spilia
Cape Ag Sozon
Agios Haralambos
Moni Evangelistrias
Cape Kefala
Kehrias Bay
Kehria Beach
Agios Apostolis
Mikros Aselinos Beach
Megalos Aselinos Beach
Gournes Beach
Skiathos
Aspronisos
Elies Beach
Cape Gournes
Mandraki Beach
Agistros Beach
Skiathos Town
Skiathos Bay
Cape Ag Elenis
Moni Panagias Kounistras
Bourtzi
Cape Pounta
Agia Eleni Beach
Koukounaries Camping
Ftelias Bay
Mytikas Beach
Cape Plakes
To Skopelos; Alonnisos
Krassa Beach (Banana Beach)
Koukounaries Beach
Koukounaries Bay
Atrium Hotel
Kolios
Achladies Apartments
Maragos
Argos
Troulos
Troulos Beach
Paraskevi Beach
Kolios Beach
Nostos Beach
Cape Tourkovigia
Cape Tsimokokalo
Vromolimnos Beach
Cape Kalamaki
Tsougriaki
Tsougria
To Volos; Agios Konstantinos
To Pefki

0 — 2 km
0 — 1 mile

new harbour; to the left, and with more character, is the curving old harbour used by local fishing and excursion boats. The main thoroughfare of Papadiamanti strikes inland from opposite the quay. The central square of **Plateia Trion Ierarhon** is just back from the middle of the old harbour, next to a large church. The bus terminus is at the northern end of the new harbour.

Information

EMERGENCY

Port police (☎ 2427 022 017)

Tourist police (☎ 2427 023 172; ⏰ 8am-9pm) Opposite the regular police station about halfway along Papadiamanti, next to the high school; open daily during the summer season.

INTERNET ACCESS

Internet Zone Café (☎ 2427 0227671; Evangelistrias 28) This café is 30m from the post office.

MONEY

The National Bank of Greece and several ATMs are on Papadiamanti. There are also ATMs along the waterfront.

TOURIST INFORMATION

The OTE office is on Papadiamanti.

Museum

Skiathos was the birthplace of popular Greek short-story writer and poet Alexandros Papadiamantis, as well as novelist Alexandros Moraïtidis. Papadiamantis' house is now a **museum** (☎ 2427 023 843; Plateia Papadiamantis; admission €1; ⊕ 9am-1pm & 5-8pm Tue-Sun) with a small collection documenting his life.

Tours

Excursion boats travel to most of the south-coast beaches from the old port. Day trips around the island (approximately six hours) cost about €15 and include a visit to Kastro, Lalaria Beach and the three caves of Halkini Spilia, Skotini Spilia and Galazia Spilia, which are only accessible by boat. Contact **Mathinos Travel** (☎ 2427 021 729) or **Heliotropio Tourism & Travel** (☎ 2427 022 430), which has an office opposite the quay.

Sleeping

Most accommodation is booked from July to the end of August, when prices are often double those of low season. Prices quoted here are for high season. There's a helpful quayside kiosk with information on hotel rooms and domatia. Also worth trying is Heliotropio (see above).

Pension Koula (☎ 24270 22025; koula@mathinos.gr; s/d €50/60) Above the old harbour and near the church, this well-managed traditional pension offers great sea views from a shaded patio where breakfast is served.

Hotel Marlton (☎ 2427 022 552; fax 2427 022 878; Evangelistrias 10; s/d €41/55; ⊠) This family-run hotel near the post office has well-kept modern rooms with refrigerators. Some rooms have balconies overlooking a garden courtyard.

Hotel Akti (☎ 2427 022 024; fax 2427 022 430; s/d €26/52; ⊠) You'll get a central waterfront location at the Akti, along with bright airy rooms.

Eating

Many eateries in Skiathos are geared to the tourist trade and are expensive. The following offer better value than most.

Psaradika Ouzeri (☎ 2427 023 412; mains €3.50-10) This busy waterfront eatery at the far end of the old port specialises in fresh fish at decent prices. If you're on a limited budget, go for a hearty bowl of fish soup at €5.50, or *gavros* (sardines) at €4.50.

O Kavouras (☎ 2427 021 094; opposite hydrofoil dock) Greeks come here for the tasty and reasonably priced mezedes; the *tarama-salata* (fish-roe dip) and dolmades (rice-stuffed vine leaves) are staples.

Taverna Misogia (☎ 2427 021 440; Grigoriou; mains €3-7) Head to this long-standing taverna in the old town for good grills of lamb, pork or chicken. Walk up Papadiamanti, turn left at the National Bank and continue another 150m.

Family Restaurant (☎ 2427 021 439; mains €6-14) Dine above the busy Skiathos waterfront by simply climbing the stairs behind Alpha Bank to find this eatery. You can fill up on plates of *tyropitaki* (small baked cheese triangles, €3) and *gemista* (stuffed tomatoes and peppers, €5.80) or *stifado* (veal, €8.80).

Taverna Cuba (☎ 2427 022 638; Pigadia) Another reliable side-street eatery, Cuba offers generous helpings of ready-to-eat *katsarolas* (oven pot), baked fish, *pastitsio* (baked macaroni) and potatoes *fourno* (oven potatoes; €4 each). It's off Papadiamanti.

To satisfy late-night munchies, try the 24-hour **Crepali** (☎ 2427 023 840; Papadiamanti) for fresh crêpes, or **Maria's Pizza** (☎ 2427 022 292), a popular hole-in-the-wall behind the Rock & Roll Bar.

Entertainment

Scan Papadiamanti and Polytehniou (better known as Bar Street) to see which disco or bar takes your fancy.

Kentavros Bar (☎ 2427 022 980; off Plateia Papadiamantis) The long-established Kentavros promises rock, soul, jazz and blues, and gets the thumbs up from locals and expats.

La Skala Bar (☎ 2427 023 102; Polytehniou) Check out Skiathos' low-key gay and lesbian scene at this swank bar above the old port. Two nearby bars, Adagio and De Facto, also get good marks from gay travellers.

Kahlua Bar (☎ 2427 023 205; Polytehniou) Like several clubs along the waterfront, this popular bar pulses with mainstream DJ sets and dancing drinkers.

Cinema Attikon (☎ 2427 022 352; Papadiamanti; admission €7) You can catch recent English-language movies at this outdoor cinema, and practice speed-reading your Greek subtitles at the same time.

Shopping

Loupos & his Dolphins (☎ 2427 023 777) This high-end gallery shop sells original icons and fine ceramics and jewellery. It's adjacent to the museum.

Natura Traditional Products (☎ 2427 024 383; Papadiamanti 28) You can find delicate olive-wood boxes and handcrafted paper products at this pleasant shop.

AROUND SKIATHOS
Beaches

With some 65 beaches to choose from, beach-hopping on Skiathos can become a full-time occupation. Many are only accessible by caïque and the ones that are more easily accessible tend to get crowded. All the south-coast beaches have water-skiing and windsurfing outlets, and motorboats are available for hire at Koukounaries Beach.

Buses ply the south coast stopping at numbered beach access points. The ones nearest town are extremely crowded; the first one worth getting off the bus for is the pine-fringed, long and sandy **Vromolimnos Beach**. Further along, **Platanias** and **Troulos** beaches are also good but both, alas, are very popular. The bus continues to **Koukounaries Beach**, backed by pine trees and a lagoon and touted as the best beach in Greece. But nowadays it's best viewed at a distance, from where the 1200m long sweep of pale gold sand does indeed look beautiful.

Krassa Beach, at the other side of a narrow headland, is more commonly known as **Banana Beach**, because of its curving shape and soft yellow sand. It is nominally a nudist beach, though the skinny-dippers tend to abscond to **Little Banana Beach** (which also gets the big thumbs up from gay and lesbian sunbathers) around the corner if things get too crowded.

Just west of Koukounaries, and 500m from bus stop No 23, **Agia Eleni Beach** is a favourite with windsurfers. The northwest coast's beaches are less crowded but are subject to the strong summer meltemi winds. From Troulos (look for bus stop No 17), a road heads north to sandy **Moni Panagias Kounistras**; as you pass Moni Kounistra, the sealed road turns to a well-maintained dirt road. A right fork continues 300m to **Mikros Aselinos Beach** and 5km further on to secluded **Kehria Beach**.

Lalaria Beach, a tranquil strand of pale grey, egg-shaped pebbles on the northern coast, is easily the fairest of them all. It is much featured in tourist brochures, but only reached by excursion boat from Skiathos Town.

Kastro Κάστρο

Kastro, perched dramatically on a rocky headland above the north coast, was the fortified pirate-proof capital of the island from 1540 to 1829. It consisted of some 300 houses and 20 churches and the only access was by a drawbridge. Except for two churches, it is now in ruins. Access is by steps, and the views from it are tremendous. Excursion boats come to the beach below Kastro, from where it's an easy clamber up to the ruins.

Moni Evangelistrias Μονή Ευαγγελίστριας

The most appealing of the island's monasteries is the 18th-century **Moni Evangelistrias** (☎ 2427 022 012; 🕒 8am-9pm). It is in a delightful setting, poised above a gorge, 450m above sea level, and surrounded by pine and cypress trees. The monastery was a refuge for freedom fighters during the War of Independence, and the islanders claim the first Greek flag was raised here in 1807. Once home to 70 monks, two monks now do the chores, which include wine-making. You can sample the tasty results of their efforts in the museum shop. An adjacent shed of old presses and vintage barrels recalls an earlier era, long before the satellite dish was installed above the courtyard. The monastery is signposted off the Skiathos Town ring road, a 4km walk or drive up the hill.

Trekking

A 6km-long trekking route begins at Moni Evangelistrias and passes the deserted monastery of Agios Haralambos, eventually reaching **Cape Kastro**, before circling back through Agios Apostolis. Kastro is a spring mecca for bird-watchers who may catch glimpses of Mediterranean shags, crested larks and singing thrushes.

Diving

Dolphin Diving (☎ 2427 021 599; www.ddiving.gr; Nostos Beach, bus stop No 12) This is the only sanctioned diving school in the Sporades. Both the beginners and advanced dives cost €40. The Discovery Dive, which explores locations 30m deep, is €50.

Sleeping & Eating

Koukounaries Camping (☎ /fax 2427 049 250; camp sites per adult/tent €6.50/3) This excellent site (with a car park) at the eastern end of

Koukounaries Beach is the only officially recognised camping ground in the Sporades. It has clean toilets and showers, a minimarket and a taverna. There is also a decent, if unofficial, **camping ground** (camp sites per adult/tent €4/2) at Megalos Aselinos Beach. Inquire at the beach **cantina** (☎ 2427 049 554).

Achladies Apartments (☎ 2427 022 486; d/tr €50/65 2-night minimum) Look for the small yellow hand-painted sign to find this hidden gem, 3km from Skiathos Town. In addition to the self-catering rooms with ceiling fans, this family-friendly establishment sports a tortoise sanctuary and a succulent garden winding down to a sandy beach, from where a water-taxi makes 20-minute runs back and forth to Skiathos Town.

Atrium Hotel (☎ 2427 049 345; d €130; ❄ ❂) This well-appointed property is perched on a pine-covered hillside overlooking Paraskevi Beach and offers balconied rooms with sea views and satellite TV. Facilities include a game lounge with and billiards, and a snack bar.

Taverna Agnantio (☎ 2427 022 016; mains €4-9) Among the best restaurants on Skiathos is family-run Agnantio, attracting locals and tourists alike. Come early to catch house specialities like *yuvetsi* (claypot pasta) with shrimp (€8), or chicken in wine sauce (€7.50). It's 400m off the ring road, with superb views down to Skiathos Town.

For brick-oven pizza with a Greek touch, follow the locals uphill to **Panorama Pizza** (☎ 6944 192 066; ☽ from 7pm), where the views match the food. It's 2.4km from the ring road. A pizza for two averages €7.

SKOPELOS ΣΚΟΠΕΛΟΣ

pop 4700
Skopelos is less commercialised than Skiathos, but until recently seemed to be following hot on its tourism trail. In recent years, however, locals have worked to keep the island's traditions and character intact. Skopelos is a beautiful island of pine forests, vineyards, olive groves and fruit orchards. It is noted for its plums and almonds, which are used in many local dishes.

Like Skiathos, the northwest coast is exposed, with high cliffs. The sheltered southeast coast harbours many beaches but, unlike Skiathos, most are pebbled. There are

two large settlements: the capital and main port of Skopelos Town on the east coast; and the lovely, unspoilt hill village of Glossa, the island's second port, 3km north of Loutraki on the west coast.

In 1936 Skopelos yielded an exciting archaeological find, a royal tomb dating to ancient times when the island was an important Minoan outpost ruled by Staphylos, the son of Ariadne and Dionysos in Greek mythology. Staphylos means grape in Greek and the Minoan ruler is said have introduced wine-making to the island.

Getting There & Away
FERRY
In summer there are several daily ferries to Alonnisos from Skopelos Town (€4.10, 30 minutes, two or three daily) and to Skiathos (€5.50, 1½ hours, three to four daily). There are also ferries to Volos (€15.10, four hours, two to three daily) and to Agios Konstantinos (€28.40, 3½ hours, two jet ferries daily). Tickets are available from **Skopelos Ferry Office** (☎ 2424 022 767; fax 2424 023 060) next to the French bakery opposite the new quay.

HYDROFOIL
Skopelos has two hydrofoil ports, one at Skopelos Town and a secondary one at Glossa to the northwest; boats from Glossa depart from nearby Loutraki. During summer the main hydrofoil services from Skopelos Town are to Alonnisos (€6.90, 20 minutes, five daily) and Skiathos (€9.10, 45 minutes, eight to 10 daily). From Glossa, there are services to Skopelos Town (€7.40, 30 minutes, five daily), to Skiathos (€5.60, 20 minutes, four daily) and to Alonnisos (€10.70, 55 minutes, five daily).

There are also hydrofoils that go to Volos (€25.20, 2¼ hours, three daily) and to Agios Konstantinos (€28.40, 2½ hours, three daily). You can purchase tickets from **Skopelos Ferry Office** (☎ 2424 022 767; fax 2424 023 060).

Getting Around
BUS
There are eight buses a day from Skopelos Town all the way to Glossa/Loutraki (€2.90, one hour), a further three that go only as far as Panormos (€1.50, 25 minutes) and Milia (€2, 35 minutes) and another two that go

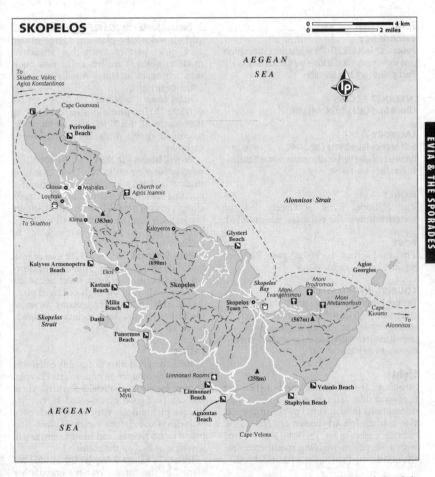

SKOPELOS

0 — 4 km
0 — 2 miles

AEGEAN
SEA

To Skiathos; Volos; Agios Konstantinos

Cape Gourouni

Perivoliou Beach

Glossa ○ ○ Mahalas
Loutraki

Church of Agios Ioannis

To Skiathos

Klima ▲ (383m)

Kaloyeros ○

Glysteri Beach

Alonnisos Strait

Kalyves Armenopetra Beach

Elios

▲ (690m)

Kastani Beach

Skopelos

Milia Beach

Skopelos Bay

Skopelos Strait

Dasia

Panormos Beach

Skopelos Town

Moni Evangelismou

Moni Prodromou

Agios Georgios

Moni Metamorfosis

(567m) ▲

Cape Kiourto

To Alonnisos

AEGEAN
SEA

Limnonari Rooms

(258m) ▲

Cape Myti

Limnonari Beach

Velanio Beach

Staphylos Beach

Agnontas Beach

Cape Velona

EVIA & THE SPORADES

only as far as Agnontas (€0.90, 15 minutes) and Stafylos (€0.90, 15 minutes).

CAR & MOTORCYCLE

There are a fair number of car and motorcycle rental outlets in Skopelos Town, mostly at the eastern end of the waterfront. Among them is the reliable **Motor Tours** (☎ 2424 022 986; fax 2424 022 602) next to Hotel Eleni.

SKOPELOS TOWN

Skopelos Town is one of the most captivating towns in the Sporades. It skirts a semicircular bay and clambers in tiers up a hillside, culminating in a ruined fortress. Dozens of churches are interspersed among

tall, dazzlingly white houses with brightly shuttered windows and flower-adorned balconies. Traditionally, roofs in Skopelos Town were tiled with beautiful rough-hewn bluestone, but these are gradually being replaced with mass-produced red tiles.

Orientation

Skopelos Town's waterfront is flanked by two quays. The old quay is at the western end of the harbour and the new quay is at the eastern end. All ferries and hydrofoils now use the new quay. From the ferry, turn right to reach the bustling waterfront lined with cafés, souvenir shops and travel agencies. The bus stop is to the left of the new quay.

Information

EMERGENCY
Police (☎ 2424 022 235) The regular police station (there is no tourist police office) is above the National Bank.
Port police (☎ 2424 022 180)

INTERNET ACCESS
Click & Surf Café (☎ 2424 023 093)

LAUNDRY
Self-service laundrette (☎ 2424 023 123) Head up the street opposite the bus station, turn right at Platanos Taverna and it's on the left.

MONEY
The National Bank of Greece, on the waterfront near the old quay, has an ATM.

POST
The post office is 100m past Platanos Square, on the right.

TOURIST INFORMATION
Thalpos Leisure & Services (☎ 2424 022 947; thalpos@otenet.gr) The staff at this privately owned agency on the waterfront are helpful, offering a wide range of services including booking accommodation and tours around the island.

Sights
Strolling around town and sitting at the waterside cafés might be your chief occupations in Skopelos Town, but there is also a small **Folk Art Museum** (☎ 2424 023 494; Hatzistamati; admission free; ☒ 11am-1.30pm & 7-9pm) with a Skopelean wedding room, complete with traditional costumes and bridal bed.

Sleeping
Skopelos Town is still a place where you have a good chance of renting a room in a family house, and people with rooms to offer meet the ferries and hydrofoils. There are no camping grounds on the island. Hotel prices quoted are for the August high season, but are often reduced by 30% to 50% at other times.

Sotos Pension (☎ 2424 022 549; fax 2424 023 668; s/d €35/50) The delightful pine-floor rooms at this well-managed pension in the middle of the waterfront are each a bit different; an old brick oven serves as a handy shelf in one. There's a little courtyard and well-equipped communal kitchen. In low season, doubles cost only €23.

Pension Soula (☎ 2424 022 930; d/tr with bath €45/55) This welcoming place, in a large garden in a quiet part of town, has attractive, modern rooms. Turn left at the new quay, turn left again at Hotel Amalia and after 200m bear right.

Hotel Adonis (☎ 2424 022 231; fax 2424 023 239; s/d €70/90; ☒) In a prime location overlooking the waterfront, this hotel offers comfortable, balconied rooms with big old-fashioned bathtubs.

Perivoli Studios (☎ 2424 022 640; fax 2424 023 668; perivoli@otenet.gr; d/tr €60/70; ☒) These charming studios occupy a single-storey traditional building about 100m from the new quay, along the ring road. Each studio is simply but stylishly furnished with a well-equipped kitchen and a terrace overlooking an orchard.

Hotel Dionyssos (☎ 2424 023 210; www.dionyssos hotel.gr; s/d €95/105; ☒ ☒) This elegant, low-key hotel occupies a quiet street below the ring road. Many of the high-ceilinged pine-and-marble rooms offer balcony views of the harbour below. Rates include a generous breakfast.

Eating
You'll find a good choice of quality eateries in Skopelos. Several are on or near Tria Platania, known locally as Souvlaki Square, where you can find good gyros, souvlaki, *tyropita* (cheese pie) and *spanikopita* (spinach pie). Skopelos is known for a variety of plum- and prune-based recipes, and most tavernas will have one or two on the menu.

Taverna Ta Kimata O Angelos (☎ 2424 022 381) Started by the current owner's grandfather in 1928, this traditional-style taverna is the oldest on the island. The ready-to-eat *fourno* (oven) dishes include hearty staples like moussaka, *yuvetsi* (claypot pasta) and stuffed zuchini (€5.50). It's a short walk to the end of the old quay, opposite a small marina.

Taverna Peparithos (☎ 2424 023 670; mains €4-8) This low-key courtyard eatery is on the ring road between the Aperiton and Denise hotels. The rabbit *stifado* (€7.50) is first-rate, and a hearty plate of mackerel and *horta* (wild greens), along with bread and beer will cost you €9.

Ouzeri Anatoli (☎ 2424 022 851; mains €2.50-8) Open summer only. For mezedes and live music, head to this ouzeri, high above the Kastro. From 11pm onwards you will hear rembetika music sung by Skopelos' own exponent of the Greek blues, Georgos Xindaris. The easiest though most strenuous way to get there is to follow the path up past the church (Agio Apostolis) at the northern end of the quay.

Perivoli Taverna (☎ 2424 023 758; North of Souvlaki Sq; mains €6-12.50) Have a splurge under the vine arbour at this sophisticated taverna, 50m inland from Platanos Square. The Greek and international menu includes fresh sole with spinach in wine sauce (€8.20), a number of vegetarian dishes plus a good selection of Greek wines.

Alpha-Pi supermarket (Doulidi) This is a well-stocked supermarket, just inland from the bus station, toward the post office.

Entertainment

Oionos Blue Bar (☎ 2424 023 731) This cool little bar near OTE in a traditional Skopelean house offers jazz, blues, soul and world beat music. It serves 17 types of beer, 25 malt whiskies and a wide range of cocktails.

Platanos Jazz Bar (☎ 2424 023 661) You can hear jazz, blues and salsa at this long-established atmospheric place on the old quay. It's open all day and serves breakfast on its shady terrace – an ideal place to recover from a hangover, or to prepare for one.

Babalos Bouzoukia (☎ 2424 024 158; admission €3) Follow the late-night locals to this courtyard club featuring live rembetika music. The drinks are pricey and things don't get going here until after 11pm. It's on the ring road, 50m west of Denise Hotel.

For more entertainment there is a strip of clubs along Doulidi, toward the post office and Internet café. Each attracts its own following; poke your nose in to see if you fit in.

Dancing Club Kounos (☎ 2424 023 623; Doulidi) The DJ spins soul and hard rock, and a little Greek music.

Metro Club (☎ 2424 024 478; Doulidi) This popular bar plays mostly high-volume Greek pop.

GLOSSA ΓΛΩΣΣΑ

Glossa, Skopelos' other major settlement, is considerably quieter than the capital. Another whitewashed delight, it has miraculously managed to retain the feel of a pristine Greek village.

The bus stops in front of a large church at a T-junction. As you face the church, the left road winds down to the port of Loutraki and the right to the main thoroughfare of Agiou Riginou. Along here you'll find a bank and a few small stores. There are also places to stay and tavernas at Loutraki, but there's not a lot to do other than hang around while waiting for a hydrofoil connection to Skiathos or Skopelos Town.

Sleeping & Eating

Pension Platanas (☎ 24240 33602; s/d €20/30) This small pension, opposite the church, has clean and simple rooms and a welcoming owner.

Agnanti Taverna & Bar (☎ 2424 033 076; Agiou Riginou; opposite bakery; mains €4-9) It's worth a trip to Glossa just to eat at this superb taverna, where local produce is used to create imaginative Greek dishes. Garlic feta with sweet red peppers (€5) is just one of the many perfect starters. Other offerings include pork with plums (€7.50) and chicken with okra (€6). There are sweeping views over to Evia from the taverna's roof terrace.

AROUND SKOPELOS
Monasteries

Skopelos has several monasteries that can be visited on a scenic, if strenuous, one-day trek from Skopelos Town. Facing inland from the waterfront, turn left and follow the road (Monastery Rd), which skirts the bay and then climbs inland. Continue beyond the signposted Hotel Aegeon until you reach a fork. Take the left fork for the 18th-century **Moni Evangelismou** (now a convent). From here there are breathtaking views of Skopelos Town, 4km away. The monastery's prize piece is a beautiful and ornately carved and gilded iconostasis in which there is an 11th-century icon of the Virgin Mary.

The right fork leads to the uninhabited 16th-century **Moni Metamorfosis**, the island's oldest monastery. From here the track continues to the 18th-century **Moni Prodromou** (now a convent), 8km from Skopelos Town.

Beaches

Skopelos' beaches are mostly pebbled, and almost all are on the sheltered southwest and west coasts. All buses stop at the beginning of paths that lead down to the beaches. The first beach you come to is the crowded sand-and-pebble **Staphylos Beach** (site of Staphylos' tomb), 4km southeast of Skopelos Town. From the eastern end of the beach a path leads over a small headland to the quieter **Velanio Beach**, the island's official nudist beach and the best spot for some snorkelling. **Agnontas**, 3km west of Staphylos, has a small pebble-and-sand beach and from here caïques sail to the superior and sandy **Limnonari Beach**, in a sheltered bay flanked by rocky outcrops. Limnonari is also a 1km walk from Agnontas.

From Agnontas the road cuts inland through pine forests before re-emerging at the sheltered **Panormos Beach**. The next beach, **Milia**, is considered one of the island's best with a long swathe of tiny pebbles, and the only beach that has organised water sports, including parasailing, windsurfing, water-skiing and sea kayaking.

Tours

If you can't tell a green bush cricket from a Cleopatra butterfly, join one of Heather Parson's **guided walks** (☎ 2424 024 022; www .skopelos-walks.com). Her three-hour walk (€15) above Skopelos Town follows an old path into the hills, and offers views to Alonnisos and Evia. Her book, *Skopelos Trails*, contains graded walking trail descriptions, maps and illustrations, and is available in waterfront stores (€16).

Day-long **cruise boats** depart from the new quay at 10am, and usually take in the Marine Park of Alonnisos (p398), pausing along the way for lunch and a swim. There's a good chance of spotting dolphins (striped, bottlenose and common), though the endangered Mediterranean monk seal is seldom seen. Most excursions start at €20, and include a full lunch. For bookings, contact **Thalpos Travel** (☎ 2424 022 947) on the waterfront.

Sleeping & Eating

There are hotels, domatia and tavernas at Staphylos, Limnonari, Panormos and Milia.

Limnonari Rooms (☎ 2424 023 046; lemonisk@ otenet.gr; d €60) This attractive domatia is in a peaceful setting behind Limnonari Beach. Rooms are airy and nicely furnished, plus there's a well-equipped communal kitchen and a large terrace.

Taverna Pavios (☎ 2424 022 409; Agnontas; mains €2.50-6.50) The most popular of the three

waterside tavernas, the Pavlos specialises in fresh fish, priced by the kilo. A plate of *gavros* is €4, and grilled red mullet around €12.

ALONNISOS ΑΛΟΝΝΗΣΟΣ

pop 2700

Alonnisos is an island of profuse greenery and its residents have high regard for the delicate ecology of the region. Thick stands of pine and oak cover the island, along with mastic and arbutus bushes, and fruit trees. The west coast is mostly precipitous cliffs but the east coast is speckled with pebble-and-sand beaches. The water around Alonnisos has been declared a national marine park, and is the cleanest in the Aegean. Every house has a cesspit, so no sewage enters the sea.

Starting in the 1950s, Alonnisos had its share of bad luck. A flourishing cottage wine industry came to a halt in 1952, when the vines were struck with the disease phylloxera. Robbed of their livelihood, many islanders moved away. Then, in 1965, an earthquake destroyed the hilltop capital of Alonnisos Town. The inhabitants were subsequently re-housed in hastily assembled concrete dwellings at Patitiri. In the past decade, island life has returned to normal, and many of the derelict houses in the capital have been renovated.

Getting There & Away
FERRY

There are ferries from Alonnisos to Skopelos Town (€4.10, 30 minutes, four daily), to Skiathos (€7.80, 1½ hours, five daily), to Volos (€15.70, four hours, two daily) and to Agios Konstantinos (€28.40, four hours by jet ferry, one daily).

Tickets can be purchased from **Alonnisos Travel** (☎ 2424 065 198; fax 2424 029 033) in Patitiri.

HYDROFOIL

As with Skiathos and Skopelos, there are frequent connections in summer. Hydrofoils connect Alonnisos to Skopelos Town (€6.90, 20 minutes, five daily), to Glossa (€10.70, 55 minutes, four daily), to Skiathos (€13, one hour, six daily), to Volos (€26.60, 2½ hours, three daily) and to Agios Konstantinos (€28.40, 2½ hours, three daily).

There is less frequent service to Pefki in northern Evia (€12.40, 1½ hours, one

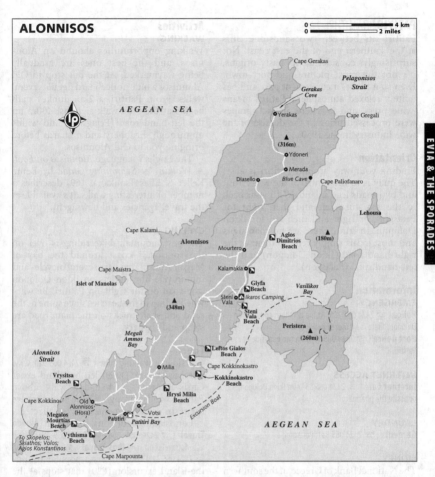

ALONNISOS

AEGEAN SEA

Cape Gerakas

Pelagonisos Strait

Gerakas Cove

Yerakas

Cape Gregali

(316m)

Ydoneri

Merada

Diasello

Blue Cave

Cape Paliofanaro

Lehousa

Cape Kalami

Alonnisos

Agios Dimitrios Beach

(180m)

Mourtero

Cape Maistra

Kalamakia

Islet of Manolas

Glyfa Beach

Vasilikos Bay

Steni Vala

Ikaros Camping

(348m)

Steni Vala Beach

Peristera

(260m)

Megali Ammos Bay

Leftos Gialos Beach

Alonnisos Strait

Milia

Cape Kokkinokastro

Vrysitsa Beach

Kokkinokastro Beach

Cape Kokkinos

Old Alonnisos (Hora)

Hrysi Milia Beach

Megalos Mourtias Beach

Patitiri

Votsi

Excursion Boat

Vythisma Beach

Patitiri Bay

AEGEAN SEA

To Skopelos; Skiathos; Volos; Agios Konstantinos

Cape Marpounta

---

daily). Tickets may be purchased from **Ikos Travel** (☎ 2424 065 320; fax 2424 065 321), opposite the quay in Patitiri.

Getting Around

BOAT

The easiest way to get to the east coast beaches is by the taxi boats that leave from the quay in Patitiri every morning.

Water-taxi rates are €6 for a return trip. Alonnisos Travel rents out four-person 15-horsepower motorboats. The cost is €60 per day in August.

BUS

In summer, one bus plies the route between Patitiri (from opposite the quay)

and Old Alonnisos (€0.90) more or less upon the hour. There is also a service to Steni Vala from Old Alonnisos via Patitiri (€1.30) three times a day.

MOTORCYCLE

Several motorcycle-hire outlets can be found on Pelasgon, in Patitiri. Be wary when riding down to the beaches since some of these sand and shale tracks are steep and slippery. Motorbike accidents along these tracks are not uncommon.

TAXI

The four taxis on the island tend to congregate opposite the quay. It's €3 to Old Alonnisos and €15 to Steni Vala.

PATITIRI ΠΑΤΗΤΗΡΙ

Patitiri sits between two sandstone cliffs at the southern end of the east coast. Not surprisingly, considering its hasty origins, it's not the most picturesque port town. Even so it makes a convenient base and has quite a relaxed atmosphere. Patitiri means 'wine press' and is where, in fact, grapes were processed prior to the demise of the wine industry in the 1950s.

Orientation

Finding your way around Patitiri is easy. The quay is in the centre of the waterfront and two roads lead inland. With your back to the sea, turn left and then right for Pelasgon, or right and then left for Ikion Dolopon. In truth, there are no road signs and most locals simply refer to them as the right-hand road (Ikion Dolopon) and the left-hand road (Pelasgon).

Information
EMERGENCY
Police (☎ 2424 065 205) At the northern end of Ikion Dolopon; there is no tourist police office.
Port police (☎ 2424 065 595) On the quayside at Patitiri.

INTERNET ACCESS
Internet Café (☎ 2424 065 834) On Ikion Dolopon, opposite the pharmacy.

LAUNDRY
Gardenia (☎ 2424 065 831; Pelasgon)

MONEY
The National Bank of Greece, at the southern end of Ikion Dolopon, has an ATM.

POST & TELEPHONE
The post office is on Ikion Dolopon. There is no OTE but there are cardphones in Patitiri, Old Alonnisos and Steni Vala.

Museum
Historical & Folklore Museum of Alonnisos & the Northern Sporades (☎ 2424 066 250; admission €3; ⓧ 11am-7pm) The long name says it all; nothing is left to chance in detailing the heritage and customs of the island's proud residents. The private collection is largely a labour of love by one family, and includes century-old furnishings, a horseshoe shop and antique nautical maps.

Activities
WALKING
Walking opportunities abound on Alonnisos, and the best ones are gradually being waymarked. At the bus stop in Old Alonnisos a blue noticeboard details several walks. From Patitiri, a 2km donkey path begins at the blue walk signpost 400m up the left-hand road (Pelasgon), and winds up through shrubbery and orchards before bringing you to Old Alonnisos.

The English-language *Alonnisos on Foot: A Walking & Swimming Guide* by Bente Keller & Elias Tsoukanas (€9) describes a number of interesting walks. It's available at the travel agencies and newsagent.

CYCLING
The best mountain-bike riding is over on the southwest coast around the bay of Megali Amos. There are several bicycle- and motorcycle-hire outlets on Ikion Dolopon (the road on the right) in Patitiri. Be wary when riding to the beaches since some of the sand and shale tracks off the main road are steep and slippery.

Tours
Consider a **walking tour** (☎ 2424 065 910; www .alonnisoswalks.co.uk; €10-20) led by island expat Chris Browne. A half-day walk above Patitiri winds through a pine forest where the resin used in retsina wine is collected.

For island excursions inquire at **Albedo Travel** (☎ 2424 065 804; fax 2424 065 806; www .albedotravel.com) or **Ikos Travel** (☎ 2424 065 320; fax 2424 065 321). Ikos offers a popular round-the-island excursion (€20) that stops at the **Blue Cave** on the northeast coast. Albedo runs regular snorkelling and swimming excursions (€35) to **Skantzoura** and other islets aboard the newest sailing vessel in the harbour.

Sleeping
Accommodation standards are high on Alonnisos and good value. Book ahead if you plan to visit during the first two weeks of August. The efficient **Rooms to Let Service** (☎ 2424 066 188; fax 2424 065 577; ⓧ 9.30am-2pm & 6.30-10pm), opposite the quay, will help you find a room on any part of the island from June to August.

Pension Pleiades (☎ 2424 065 235; pleiades@inter net.gr; s/d €35/45; ⓧ) This bright and cheerful

SALLY WEBB

Church near beach on Kythira (p442), Ionian Islands

JOHN ELK III

Fresh fruit and vegetables in Corfu's old town (p409), Ionian Islands

Alfresco dining, Zakynthos (p437), Ionian Islands

VERONICA GARBUTT

SALLY WEBB

Hora (p443), Kythira, Ionian Islands

Skyros (p399), Sporades

Livestock, Gioura (p399),
Alonnisos, Sporades

Pefkos beach (p404) at Skyros, Sporades

budget option offers views of Patitiri Bay. There are nine immaculate, balconied rooms, plus a family-sized studio with kitchen.

Ilias Rent Rooms (☎ 2424 065 451; fax 2424 065 972; Pelasgon 27; d €33, 2-/3-bed studios €45/50) The pleasant rooms and studios here are very clean. The rooms have a communal kitchen with kettle and sink, and the studios have a well-equipped kitchen area.

Liadromia Hotel (☎ 2424 065 521; liadromia@alonnisos.com; d/tr €60/75) This impeccably maintained hotel was Patitiri's first. All the rooms have a bit of character, from hand-embroidered curtains and old lamps to stone floors and traditional wood furnishings. From the port, take the steps just before the Internet café on the right, follow the path around and the hotel is on the left, next to the Paradise.

Paradise Hotel (☎ 2424 065 213; fax 2424 065 161; s/d €62/77) Wood ceilings and stone tiled floors give a rustic feel to the rooms here, most of which overlook the sea or harbour at Patitiri. Room prices include a buffet breakfast served next to the pool. Take the stairway up the hill opposite the National Bank.

Eating

To Kamaki Ouzeri (☎ 2424 065 245; Ikion Dolopon; mains €4-10) Start off with mezedes like taramasalata (€2.70) and ouzo at this traditional island eatery, then check the ready-to-eat dishes in the open kitchen. Try the stuffed calamari and peppers (€9.50), or splurge on grilled red mullet (€49 per kilo). It's next to the bank.

Café Flisvos (☎ 2424 065 307) Among the waterfront restaurants, this is the pick of the bunch. In the summer, sit under the canopy opposite the dock. It's not the quietest place, but the food and the homemade sweets are first rate. A light lunch of *yemistes* (stuffed tomatoes and peppers) with a beer will fetch €7.

Entertainment

Symvolo Bar (☎ 2424 066 156) You can enjoy jazz, blues, techno and rock at Symvolo, two doors down from the National Bank. The atmospheric interior is a medley of traditional north African and Greek furnishings.

Enigma Disco (☎ 2424 065 333; waterfront) Enigma rocks from midnight on when the tourist season kicks in.

Mythos Bar (☎ 2424 066 273) This local favourite next to the Health Centre plays mostly Greek music, and serves an assortment of wines, beer and coffee.

Shopping

Ikos Traditional Products (☎ 2424 066 270; ✆ 9am-2.30pm & 6-9.30pm) This delightful low-key cooperative is run by the Women's Association of Alonnisos and sells handmade soaps and fresh herbs, along with local honey and tempting *glyka* (sweets). Walk 200m up the right-hand road from the dock, and it's on the left.

OLD ALONNISOS

Old Alonnisos (also known as Hora or Palio Horio or Old Town) with its winding stepped alleys is a tranquil, picturesque place with lovely views. From the main road just outside the village an old donkey path leads down to pebbled Megalos Mourtias Beach and other paths lead south to Vythisma and Marpounta Beaches.

Sleeping

There are no hotels in Old Alonnisos, but there are a number of well-managed domatia.

Fantasia House (☎ 2424 065 186; Plateia Hristou; s/d €30/40) Tucked away between the church and the square, the attractive modern rooms with exposed-beam ceilings offer good value, and there is a snack bar in the courtyard.

Rooms & Studios Hiliadromia (☎ /fax 2424 065 814; Plateia Hristou; d €45, 2-bed studios €65) Several of the pine- and stone-floor rooms at the Hiliadromia come with balcony views, and the studios have well-equipped kitchens.

Eating

Astrofengia (☎ 2424 065 182; mains €5-12) This sophisticated restaurant, signposted from the bus stop, offers exquisite mezedes such as *tzatziki* (cucumber and garlic yogurt; €1.50) and *saganaki* (fried cheese; €3). Distinctive mains include vegetarian cannelloni (€6.50), and ostrich stroganoff (€12). On summer evenings, stick around until Nick, the owner and a professional musician, picks up his bouzouki.

Nappo (☎ 2424 065 579; mains €5-7.50) The Italian owner, Paolo, serves top-rate pizzas at this restaurant, signposted from the main street.

Megalos Mourtias Taverna (☎ 2424 065 737) This welcoming beachside taverna serves traditional Greek fare and fresh fish by the kilo, and is open from morning to night. From Old Alonnisos, take the 1km donkey trail south, or drive 2km on the signposted road, past Agios Panagia church, to Megalos Mourtias Beach. If you decide to never leave Greece, inquire about the reasonable domatia next door.

AROUND ALONNISOS

There are no organised water sports on Alonnisos, but several good swimming beaches can be found on the east coast, which means they avoid the strong summer meltemi winds and the flotsam that can accumulate on the west coast beaches. Apart from the road from Patitiri to Old Alonnisos, there are only three roads on the island. One goes north to the tip of the island and is driveable and sealed all the way though to the last settlement, Yerakas (19km), home to a marine research station. Dirt tracks lead off to the beaches. Six kilometres north of Patitiri, another sealed road branches off to the fishing port of Steni Vala, and follows the shore past Kalamakia for 5km. The last takes you from Patitiri to Megalos Mourtias.

The first beach of note once you leave Patitiri is the clean and gently shelving **Hrysi Milia Beach**, a great beach for children. The next one up is **Kokkinokastro**, a beach of red pebbles. This is the site of the ancient city of Ikos (once the capital); there are remains of city walls and a necropolis under the sea.

Steni Vala is a small fishing village with a permanent population of no more than 40 and a good beach, **Glyfa**, just over the headland. There are three tavernas opposite the small marina and 30-odd rooms in domatia, as well as modest **Ikaros Camping** (☎ 2424 065 772), next to the beach and decently shaded by olive trees. Try **Ikaros Café & Market** (☎ 2424 065 390) for food and lodging information. It's also a good perch from which to watch the fashionable yachties coming and going.

Kalamakia, 2km further north, is near a good beach and has a few domatia and tavernas. When the boats arrive at Steni Vala with the morning catch, they tie up directly in front of **Margarita's Taverna** (☎ 2424 065 738), where the fresh fish seem to jump from boat to plate.

Beyond Kalamakia, the sealed road continues 3km to a wetland marsh and **Agios Dimitrios Beach**, a long stretch of sand beyond which the road dwindles to a footpath heading inland.

ISLETS AROUND ALONNISOS

Alonnisos is surrounded by eight uninhabited islets, all of which are rich in flora

---

ALONNISOS MARINE PARK

The National Marine Park of Alonnisos – Northern Sporades is an ambitious but belatedly conceived project begun in May 1992. Its prime aim was the protection of the endangered Mediterranean monk seal (Monarchus monarchus), but also the preservation of other rare plant and animal species threatened with extinction.

The park is divided into two zones, A and B. Zone A, east of Alonnisos, is less accessible and comprises the islets of Kyra Panagia, Gioura, Psathoura, Skantzoura and Piperi. Restrictions on human activities apply on all islands in Zone A. In the case of Piperi, visitors are banned altogether, since the island is home to around 33 species of bird, including 350 to 400 pairs of Eleanora's falcon. Other threatened sea birds found on Piperi include the Mediterranean shag and Audouin's gull. Visitors may approach other islands with private vessels or on day trips organised from Alonnisos.

Zone B comprises Alonnisos itself and the nearer islands of Peristera, Lehousa, and Dio Adelfi (Two Brothers) off the southeast coast. Most nautical visitors to Alonnisos base themselves at the small yacht port of Steni Vala.

For the casual visitor the Alonnisos Marine Park is somewhat inaccessible since tours to the various islands are limited and run during summer only. Bear in mind also that the park exists for the protection of marine animals and not for the entertainment of human visitors, so do not be surprised if you see very few animals at all. In a country not noted in its recent history for long-sightedness in the protection of its fauna, the Alonnisos Marine Park is a welcome innovation.

and fauna. The largest remaining population of the monk seal, a Mediterranean sea mammal faced with extinction, lives in the waters around the Sporades. These factors were the incentive behind the formation of the national marine park in 1992, which encompasses the sea and islets around Alonnisos (see the Alonnisos Marine Park opposite). Its research station is on Alonnisos, near Gerakas Cove.

Piperi, the furthest island northeast of Alonnisos, is a refuge for the monk seal and it is forbidden to set foot there without a licence to carry out research.

Also northeast of Alonnisos, **Gioura** has many rare plants and a rare species of wild goat known for the crucifix-shaped marking on its spine. **Kyra Panagia** has good beaches and two abandoned monasteries. **Psathoura** boasts the submerged remains of an ancient city and the brightest lighthouse in the Aegean.

Peristera, just off Alonnisos' east coast, has several sandy beaches and the remains of a castle. Nearby **Lehousa** is known for its stalactite-filled sea caves.

Skantzoura, to the southeast of Alonnisos, is the habitat of the Eleanora's falcon and the rare Audouin's seagull. The eighth island in the group, situated between Peristera and Skantzoura, is known as **Dio Adelphi** (Two Brothers); each 'brother' is actually a small island, both home to vipers, according to local fishermen who refuse to step foot on either.

SKYROS ΣΚΥΡΟΣ

pop 2602

Skyros is the largest of the Sporades islands, with rolling, cultivated hills and pine forests covering much of its northern half, and barren hills and a rocky shoreline making up the sparsely populated southern section. The island is some distance from the rest of the northern Sporades and gets a modest number of visitors. Solo women travellers are increasingly drawn to Skyros because of its reputation as a safe, hassle-free island, and a number of expats, particularly English and Dutch, have made Skyros their home.

In Byzantine times, rogues and criminals from the mainland exiled on Skyros entered

SKYROS CARNIVAL

In this wild pre-Lenten festival, which takes place on the last two Sundays before Kathara Deftera (Clean Monday – the first Monday in Lent, seven weeks before Easter), young men don goat masks, hairy jackets and dozens of copper goat bells. They then proceed to clank and dance around town, each with a partner (another man), dressed up as a Skyrian bride but also wearing a goat mask. During these revelries there is singing and dancing, performances of plays, recitations of satirical poems and much drinking and feasting. Women and children join in, wearing fancy dress as well. These strange goings-on are overtly pagan, with elements of Dionysian festivals, including goat worship. In ancient times, as today, Skyros was renowned for its goat's meat and milk.

The transvestism evident in the carnival seems to derive from the cult of Achilles associated with Skyros in Greek mythology. According to legend, the island was the childhood hiding place for the boy Achilles, whose mother, Thetis, feared a prophecy requiring her son's skills in the Trojan War. The boy was given to the care of King Lykomides of Skyros, who raised him disguised as one of his own daughters. Young Achilles was outwitted, however, by Odysseus who arrived with jewels and finery for the girls, along with a sword and shield. When the maiden Achilles alone showed interest in the weapons, Odysseus discovered his secret, then persuaded him to go to Troy where he distinguished himself in battle. This annual festival is the subject of Joy Koulentianou's book *The Goat Dance of Skyros*.

into a mutually lucrative collaboration with invading pirates. The exiles became the elite of Skyrian society, furnishing and decorating their houses with items brought by seafarers or looted by pirates from merchant ships: elaborately hand-carved furniture, plates and copper ornaments from Europe, the Middle East and East Asia. Today, almost every Skyrian house is decorated with similar items.

In Greek mythology, Skyros was the hiding place of young Achilles. See Skyros Carnival above for more information about the

EVIA & THE SPORADES

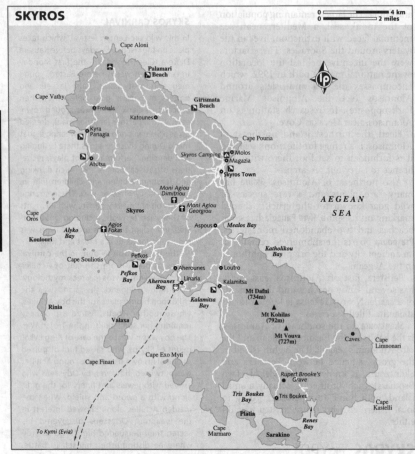

SKYROS

Cape Aloni

Palamari
Beach

Cape Vathy

Frokala

Girismata
Beach

Katounes

Kyra
Panagia

Cape Pouria

Atsitsa

Skyros Camping
Molos
Magazia

Skyros Town

Moni Agiou
Dimitriou

Moni Agiou
Georgiou

*AEGEAN
SEA*

Cape
Oros

Skyros

*Alyko
Bay*

Agios
Fokas

Aspous

Mealos Bay

Koulouri

*Katholikou
Bay*

Pefkos

Cape Souliotis

Aherounes

Loutro

*Pefkos
Bay*

Aherounes
Bay

Linaria

Kalamitsa

Mt Dafni
(734m)

*Kalamitsa
Bay*

Rinia

Mt Kohilas
(792m)

Valaxa

Mt Vouva
(727m)

Caves

Cape
Limnonari

Cape Finari

Cape Exo Myti

*Rupert Brooke's
Grave*

*Tris Boukes
Bay*

Tris Boukes

Cape
Kastelli

Platia

*Renes
Bay*

To Kymi (Evia)

Cape
Marmaro

Sarakino

Skyros Lenten Carnival and its traditions, which allude to Achilles' heroic feats.

Skyros was also the last port of call for the English poet Rupert Brooke (1887–1915), who died of septicaemia at the age of 28 on a hospital ship off the coast of Skyros en route to Gallipoli.

Getting There & Away
AIR
In summer there are only two flights weekly (Wednesday and Sunday) between Athens and Skyros (€36, 35 minutes). Between Thessaloniki and Skyros, there are three flights weekly (€57, 40 minutes). For tickets go to the **Skyros Travel Agency** (☎ 2222 091 600).

FERRY
There are ferry services at least twice daily in summer, provided by F/B *Lykomidis*, between the port of Kymi (Evia) and Skyros (€7.50, two hours). You can buy tickets from **Lykomidis ticket office** (☎ 2222 091 789; fax 2222 091 791), near the bank on Agoras in Skyros Town. There is also a ferry ticket kiosk at the dock in Linaria.

Skyros Travel Agency sells tickets for the Kymi–Athens bus (€10.45, 3½ hours), which meets the ferry on arrival at Paralia Kymis (the port of Kymi).

Getting Around
In addition to the options listed here, it is also possible to join a boat trip to sites

around the island. See Tours in the Skyros Town section (p402).

BUS & TAXI

In high season there are five buses daily from Skyros Town to Linaria (€0.90) and to Molos (via Magazia). Buses for both Skyros Town and Molos meet the boats at Linaria. However, outside of high season there are only two buses to Linaria (to coincide with the ferry arrivals) and none to Molos. Occasional bus services to Kalamitsa and Atsitsa are organised on an ad hoc basis during summer. Contact Skyros Travel (see below) for full details.

A taxi from Skyros Town to Linaria is €8.

CAR & MOTORCYCLE

Cars and 4WD vehicles can be rented from **Theseus Rentals** (☎ 2222 091 459) or **Skyros Travel Agency** (☎ 2222 091 600), near the bus stop. A small car will run cost about €35 per day, and a 4WD about €50. Motorcycles can be rented from nearby **Vayos Motorbikes** (☎ 2222 092 957).

SKYROS TOWN

Skyros' capital is a striking, dazzlingly white town of flat-roofed Cycladic-style houses draped over a high rocky bluff and topped by a 13th-century fortress and the monastery of Agios Georgios. It is a gem of a place and a wander around its labyrinthine, whitewashed streets will often produce an invitation to admire a traditional Skyrian house by its proud owner.

Orientation

The bus stop is at the southern end of town on the main thoroughfare (Agoras) – an animated street lined with tavernas, snack bars and grocery shops and flanked by narrow winding alleyways. To reach the central square, known simply as the **Plateia**, walk straight ahead up the hill; the narrow road soon becomes even narrower, marking the beginning of the town's pedestrian zone. Motorbikes still squeeze through, but cars must park in the nearby car park.'

About 100m beyond the Plateia, the main drag of Agoras forks. The right fork leads up to the **fortress** and **Moni Agiou Georgiou**, with its fine frescoes and sweeping views. The left fork zig-zags to **Plateia Rupert Brooke**, where a simple bronze statue of a nude Rupert

Brooke faces the sea. The frankness of the statue caused an outcry among the islanders when it was first installed in the 1930s. From this square the cobbled steps descend to Magazia Beach, 1km away.

Information

EMERGENCY

Police (☎ 2222 091 274) Take the first right after Skyros Travel Agency, and turn right at the T-junction; there is no tourist police.

INTERNET ACCESS

Meroi Café Bar (☎ 2222 091 016; Agoras; ✆ 9am-11pm)

MONEY

The National Bank of Greece is on Agoras next to the central square. It sports an ATM.

POST

The post office is on the westside of the square.

TOURIST INFORMATION

Skyros Travel Agency (☎ 2222 091 600; www.skyros travel.com; Agoras) Has most of the information you'll need and handles room bookings.

Sights & Activities

Skyros Town has two museums.

The **Archaeological Museum** (☎ 2222 091 327; Plateia Rupert Brooke; admission €2; ✆ 8.30am-7.30pm Tue-Sun) features an impressive collection of artefacts from Mycenaean to Roman times, as well as a traditional Skyrian house interior, transported in its entirety from the home of the benefactor.

The **Faltaïts Museum** (☎ 2222 091 232; Plateia Rupert Brooke; admission €2; ✆ 10am-2pm & 6-9pm) is a private museum housing the outstanding collection of a Skyrian ethnologist, Manos Faltaïts. The collection includes Skyrian costumes and furniture, antique ceramics, vintage books and photographs. You can join an evening tour and lecture (€5, wine included!) detailing the mythology and folklore of Skyros.

Every year about mid-September, Skyros is host to a **half-marathon** (☎ 2222 092 789), which starts in Atsitsa and ends on the Plateia in Skyros Town. A mini-marathon for the children sets the tone, and the whole event is all followed by a concert on the square.

There are no organised water sports on Skyros.

Courses

Reiki Centre (☎ 2222 029 039; janetinskyros@ hotmail.com) Reiki Master Janet Smith (English co-owner of the Internet café opposite) offers small five-day residential classes in Reiki technique to visitors and locals alike.

Skyros Centre (☎ 2222 093 193; www.skyros.com) This holistic-based centre runs courses on a range of subjects, from Hatha yoga and Greek dancing to T'ai Chi and windsurfing. There is a branch in Skyros Town, but the main complex is at Atsitsa Beach, on the west coast. Contact the centre for detailed information on its fortnightly programmes.

Tours

A day-long **boat excursion** (€29) to Sarakiniko Islet and the Gerania sea caves includes lunch and a swim. Contact **Skyros Travel** (☎ 2222 091 600) for details.

A range of **walking tours** (☎ 2222 092 158) are led by the versatile Niko Sikkes (€10 to €15) around Skyros. A visit to his shop (Argos) will get a you a map and free advice as well.

Sleeping

Accommodation in Skyros Town varies from conventional small hotels and domatia to individual rooms in traditional Skyrian houses. Finding one of the latter, however, usually requires an agent. For starters, try the domatia run by the women who usually meet the bus from Linaria. Prices should be in the €20 to €35 range for a single/double. Failing that, head for Skyros Travel Agency (p400). Prices quoted here are for the higher summer season.

Hotel Elena (☎ 2222 091 738; s/d €25/45; 🏋) This newly refurbished hotel has 10 large rooms, each with a balcony and mini-bar. A new rooftop terrace and bar is a good spot to enjoy sunset. It's less than 100m north of the bus stop.

Domatia Evangelia (☎ 2222 091 115; s/d €20/30) This simple but welcoming bougainvillaea-laden domatia is a bargain and just off the main drag, opposite Liakos Restaurant.

Pension Nikolas (☎ 2222 091 778; fax 2222 093 400; r €40/50) This pension has attractive, well-maintained rooms on the quiet edge of Skyros Town. From the bus stop, walk south (toward the Hotel Nefeli) about 50m until the road splits. Take the track to the right, and continue another 50m. The pension is on the right side.

Hotel Nefeli & Dimitrious Studios (☎ 2222 091 964; fax 2222 092 061; s/d/studios €70/86/122; 🏊) This well-managed and recently refurbished hotel on the edge of town has modern well-appointed rooms with vintage photographs depicting traditional Skyrian life. The adjacent three- and four-bed studios are actually a large remodelled Skyrian house with traditional furnishings. Both properties share a swimming pool and pool bar.

Eating

Skyros gets a steady number of Athenians and other mainland visitors, with the pleasant result that island cooks do not cater to touristy tongues. On the contrary, you can find a number of authentic Skyrian dishes in the smallest taverna, including several made with goat's milk or meat.

O Pappous kai Ego (☎ 2222 093 200; Agoras; mains €4.50-7) The name of this small taverna means 'my grandfather and me'. Mezedes are excellent, especially the Skyrian dolmades made with a touch of strained goat's milk (€3.80). Tasty mains include seafood pilaf and Skyrian squid with aniseed (both €5.50).

Orestes Taverna (☎ 2222 091 311; Agoras; mains €7.50-16) Orestes sports a large menu, including *kleftiko* (goat in parchment paper, €9) and grilled red mullet and sea bream (€40 a kilo), either of which go nicely with *skordalia* (garlic dip, €3).

Liakos Café (☎ 2222 093 509; mains €5-8.50) During the day you can have a drink or meal in the Liakos' serene interior where botanical prints grace the walls. In the evening, head to the roof terrace, where an imaginative fusion menu includes cold octopus salad (€7), chicken with yogurt and dill (€6.20) and fava beans with sun-dried tomatoes (€3). To get there turn right after Skyros Travel Agency.

Anatolikos Anemos Café & Ouzeri (☎ 2222 092 822; mains €4-7; ⏰ 10am-3pm & 6pm-1am) This out-of-the-way spot near Plateia Rupert Brooke touts an 'endless blue view', and it's easy to enjoy a morning coffee or evening meal from the terrace overlooking Magazia and the sea beyond. Wines include regional favourites from around Greece. You can work up a good thirst or appetite if you walk from the main square, so heed the hours.

Anemos Snack (☎ 2222 092 155) Start the day with made-to-order eggs or just coffee and a roll at this snappy eatery opposite Orestes on Agoras.

Entertainment

Nightlife centres mostly around the bars on Agoras, all of which are tastefully decorated.

Artistiko Bar (☎ 2222 091 864; Agoras) The music is all Greek all night under the beamed ceilings at little Artistiko, a hole-in-the-wall that buzzes till dawn.

Akamatra (☎ 2222 029 029; Plateia) The DJs here put out a mellow mix of reggae, rock and blues; the rooftop terrace is a good place to nurse a cold beer.

Kalypso (☎ 2222 092 696) The further north you go along Agoras the more mellow the sounds. Classy little Kalypso plays mostly jazz and blues.

Neoptolemos (☎ 2222 092 484) Mellow like its neighbour, this attractive bar plays lots of Greek sounds. As well as breakfasts, coffees and juices, it offers 70 different cocktails.

Stone (☎ 2222 092 355) Stone rocks till the wee hours with disco, pop and funk dance tunes.

Skyropoula Disco (☎ 2222 091 180) On the ring road, Skyropoula draws a slightly older crowd than Stone, but still manages to belt out a danceable mix of pop European and Greek sounds.

MAGAZIA & MOLOS ΜΑΓΑΖΙΑ & ΜΩΛΟΣ

The resort of Magazia is at the southern end of a splendid, long sandy beach, situated a short distance north of Skyros Town; quieter Molos is at the northern end of the beach. Although the two are contiguous, Magazia is a compact and attractive place of winding alleys, whereas, with the exception of its windmill and the adjacent rock-hewn Church of Agios Nikolaos, arid Molos seems to go on for no particular reason.

Sleeping

Skyros Camping (☎ 2222 092 458; adult €5) In Magazia, opposite the steps up to Skyros Town, is this unofficial camping ground, Skyros' only one. It's clean, if rather run-down, with some thirsty-looking olive trees offering shade.

Ferogia Domatia (☎ 2222 091 828; Magazia; s/d/tr €28/40/65) These modern and balconied rooms opposite the beach are good value; the beautifully furnished apartment contains lovely antique Skyrian ceramics displayed on carved wooden shelves.

Angela Bungalows (☎ 2222 091 764; fax 2222 092 030; s/d €60/75; 🛱) Never mind that there's not a bungalow in sight at this Molos oasis 100m from the beach; the welcoming Angela still offers modern spacious rooms, a breakfast courtyard and a bus stop to Skyros Town, 2km away.

Georgia Tsakami Rooms (☎ 2220 91 357; s/d €30/35) You can't get much closer to the sand and sea than at these cosy domatia 20m from Magazia Beach. Follow the Magazia Beach road and you'll find them on the left opposite a handy car park.

Eating & Drinking

Taverna Stefanos (☎ 2222 091 272; mains €3.50-7) This traditional eatery, at the southern end of Magazia Beach, offers a range of ready-to-eat oven dishes, along with grilled meat and fresh fish.

Anemomilos Ouzeri & Bar (☎ 2222 093 373; mains €3.50-10) In a splendid setting at Molos' 19th-century windmill near the little rock-hewn Church of Agios Nikalaos, the Anemomilos serves well-prepared food during the day, and in the evening metamorphoses into a lively bar. Mezedes include fava (€2.60), squid (€2.60) and calamari (€3.50). Mains feature chicken souvlaki (€5.30) and shrimp in tomato sauce (€7.30).

Shopping

Latiri Shop (☎ 2222 092 555; Agoras) You'll find a variety of quality, if non-Skyrian, icons, jewellery and ceramic masks at this appealing shop.

Argos Shop (☎ 2222 092 158; Agoras) Argos specialises in high-quality copies of ceramics from the Faltaïts Museum.

Andreou Woodcarving (☎ 2222 092 926; Agoras) Get a close look at the intricate designs that distinguish traditional Skyrian furniture at this handsome shop on the main drag.

AROUND SKYROS

Linaria Λιναριά

Linaria, the port of Skyros, is tucked into a small bay filled with bobbing fishing boats and lined with tavernas and ouzeri. Things perk up briefly whenever the Lykomidis ferry comes in, announcing its arrival with the impressive sound of Richard Strauss' *Also Sprach Zarathustra* blasting from huge speakers. The bus to Skyros Town coincides with the ferry's arrival and departure.

SLEEPING & EATING

Linaria Bay Hotel (☎ 2222 093 274; fax 2222 093 275; s/d €35/50) You won't miss your ferry connection at this attractive 11-room spot above the port at Linaria. Though quiet, it's just a few minutes' walk to the dock, and a good alternative to staying in Skyros Town.

Taverna Psariotis (☎ 2222 093 250; Linaria; mains €4-11) This busy fish taverna, located opposite the ferry dock, serves up lobster along with traditional ready-to-eat oven dishes like *briami* (roasted veggies) and *pastitsio* (baked macaroni).

Kavos Bar (☎ 2222 093 213; Linaria) This laid-back Linaria bar pulls in Skyrians from across the island for drinks and evening gossip.

Beaches

At **Atsitsa**, on the west coast, there's a tranquil pebble beach shaded by pines. The beach attracts freelance campers, and there's the main outdoor centre of the Skyros Centre and a taverna with domatia here. Just to the north is the even less crowded beach of **Kyra Panagia** (also with freelance campers).

At **Pefkos**, 10km southeast of Atsitsa, there is another good but small beach and a taverna. If you don't have transport take a Skyros Town–Linaria bus and ask to be dropped at the turn-off. It's a 3km walk to the beach. Nearby **Aherounes Beach** has a gentle sandy bottom, very nice for children. There are two taverna opposite the road, next to a small hotel.

Skinny-dippers can leave it all behind at the nudist beach of **Batakouma** next to Magazia. **Palamari**, near the airport, is a long stretch of sandy beach that does not get crowded.

Rupert Brooke's Grave

Rupert Brooke's well-tended grave is in a quiet olive grove just inland from Tris Boukes Bay in the south of the island. The actual grave is marked with a rough wooden sign in Greek on the roadside, but you can hardly miss it. The gravestone is inscribed with some verses of Brooke's among which is the following apt epitaph:

> If I should die think only this of me:
> That there's some corner of a foreign field
> That is forever England.

From Kalamitsa, a good scenic road (built for the navy) passes the village of Nifi, and brings you to Brookes' simple tomb. However, no buses come here, and travel is carefully restricted beyond this southernmost corner of the island that is dominated by the Greek Naval station on Tris Boukes Bay.

Ionian Islands
Τα Επτάνησα

IONIAN ISLANDS

It's not hard to fall under the spell of the idyllic Ionian group of islands, comprising Corfu, Paxi, Lefkada, Kefallonia, Ithaki, Zakynthos Kythira. Anchored in the Ionian Sea off the west coast of mainland Greece and the Peloponnese, these mountainous islands are more reminiscent of Corfu's neighbour Italy, not least in light, and their colours are mellow and green compared with the stark brightness of the barren Aegean islands.

Each Ionian island has idiosyncrasies of culture and cuisine, and differing dollops of Mediterranean European and British influences. Nowhere is this better exemplified than in the group's largest settlement, Corfu Town – home to a cricket ground, arcaded buildings inspired by Paris' Rue de Rivoli, and backstreets and alleyways resembling those of Venice or Naples.

There's no denying that some parts of the Ionians have been scarred by insensitive tourism development, but away from these eyesore areas the islands' charms are legendary. There are mountainside monasteries, museums displaying archaeological treasures, unspoilt villages, ancient olive groves, laid-back harbourside restaurants, white-sand beaches and unbelievable blue-heaven waters, along with great literary connections. Plus there's no shortage of activities for holiday-makers seeking more than a sun lounge parked on a glorious beach. Go cycling or bushwalking to get off the beaten track, try underwater sightseeing with a diving operator, explore islets and sheltered coves by motorboat, or join the pros at one of the world's top windsurfing locations. You'll definitely want to return.

HIGHLIGHTS

■ **Architecture**

Wandering the narrow streets of Corfu's old town and admiring the fine Venetian buildings (p413)

■ **Getting Away From It All**

Walking the ancient olive groves of Paxi (p421) and swimming in the crystal-clear water of Antipaxi (p424)

■ **Scenic Splendours**

Travelling the dramatic west coast of Lefkada, with its stunning beaches and exquisite blue water (p424)

■ **Beauty Spot**

Unwinding on beautiful Myrtos Beach in Kefallonia (p429), then exploring the gorgeous village of Assos (p433)

■ **Live Music**

Being entertained by the exuberant singers at Arekia restaurant in Zakynthos Town (p439)

■ **Remote Retreat**

Visiting the tranquil inland villages of Kythira, and swimming at the island's lovely undeveloped beaches (p442)

GETTING THERE & AWAY

Air

Corfu, Kefallonia, Zakynthos and Kythira have airports; Lefkada has no airport, but Aktion airport, near Preveza on the mainland, is about 20km away. These four airports have frequent flights to/from Athens. **Olympic Airways** (www.olympic-airways.gr) has introduced a useful service linking the Ionians: three times a week there are return flights from Corfu to Zakynthos, stopping en route at Aktion and Kefallonia.

From May to September, many charter flights come from northern Europe and the UK to Corfu, Kefallonia, Zakynthos and Aktion.

Bus

KTEL (www.ktel.org) long-distance buses connect each major island with Athens and Thessaloniki, and usually also with Patra. Buses to Corfu, Lefkada, Kefallonia and Zakynthos depart from Athens' intercity bus station (Terminal A) at Kifissou 100, 7km northwest of Omonia.

Ferry

DOMESTIC

The Peloponnese has several departure ports for the Ionian Islands: Patra for ferries to Corfu, Kefallonia and Ithaki; and Kyllini for ferries to Kefallonia and Zakynthos; and Piraeus, Kalamata, Neapoli and Gythio for Kythira. Epiros has one port, Igoumenitsa, for Corfu and Paxi;

and Sterea Ellada has one, Astakos, for Ithaki and Kefallonia (although this service is limited to the high season). There are numerous websites offering information on ferry timetables; among the best is www.ferries.gr.

The following table gives an overall view of the scheduled domestic ferries to the Ionians from mainland ports in the high season.

DOMESTIC FERRY CONNECTIONS TO THE IONIAN ISLANDS

Origin	Destination	Time	€	Frequency
Astakos	Sami (Kefallonia)	3hr	€7	1 daily
	Piso Aetos (Ithaki)	4hr	€6.50	1 daily
Gythio	Diakofti (Kythira)	2½hr	€8.90	5 weekly
Igoumenitsa	Corfu Town	1¼hr	€5.10	14 daily
	Lefkimmi (Corfu)	1hr	€2.80	6 daily
	Gaïos (Paxi)	1¾hr	€6.10	5 weekly
Kyllini	Zakynthos Town	1¼hr	€5.10	6 daily
	Argostoli (Kefallonia)	2½hr	€10.50	1-2 daily
	Poros (Kefallonia)	1½hr	€6.50	2-3 daily
Neapoli	Agia Pelagia (Kythira)	1hr	€5.20	1-4 daily
Patra	Corfu Town	6hr	€21-25.50	1-3 daily
	Sami (Kefallonia)	2½hr	€11.50	2 daily
	Vathy/Piso Aetos (Ithaki)	3¾hr	€11.70	2 daily
Piraeus	Diakofti (Kythira)	6½hr	€19.30	2 weekly

Within the Ionian group, Corfu and Paxi are well connected by ferry and hydrofoil, but unfortunately there are no services from either Corfu or Paxi to Lefkada. Travellers may be able to sail one way on hydrofoil day trips from Corfu to Kefallonia (offered twice weekly).

Within the southern Ionians, Lefkada, Kefallonia and Ithaki are well connected by ferry, and there's a twice-daily service between southern Kefallonia and northern Zakynthos (an alternative is to sail from Argostoli to Kyllini in the Peloponnese, and from there to Zakynthos Town).

WWW.PLANNING YOUR TRIP.COM

There's loads of websites devoted to the Ionians – here are some of the best we've found:

Ionian Islands www.ionianislands.gr, www.visit-ionianislands.com

Corfu www.terrakerkyra.gr, kerkyra.net, www.corfuhomepage.com

Paxi www.paxos-greece.com, paxos.tk

Lefkada www.lefkas.net, www.lefkada-greece.biz

Kefallonia www.kefaloniathewaytogo.com, www.kefalonia.net.gr

Kythira www.kythira.com

Ithaki www.ithaca.ionichost.co

Zakynthos www.zakynthos-net.gr, www.zanteweb.gr

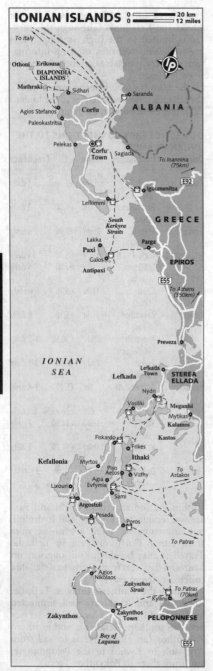

There are no direct connections between the main Ionians and Kythira.

Further details can be found under each island entry.

INTERNATIONAL
Corfu has regular connections with four ports in Italy (Brindisi, Bari, Trieste and Venice), operated by a handful of ferry companies sailing between Italy and Igoumenitsa and/or Patra. (Travellers can also sail between Ancona and Igoumenitsa, then transfer to a local ferry.) Crossings are most frequent in July and August, but there are year-round services at least weekly between Corfu and Brindisi, Bari and Venice.

From Corfu it's also possible to cross to Albania (or to visit on a day trip).

ANEK Lines (www.anek.gr) From Trieste and Ancona to Corfu, Igoumenitsa and Patra.

Blue Star Ferries (www.bluestarferries.com) From Ancona, Venice and Brindisi to Corfu, Igoumenitsa and Patra.

Fragline (www.fragline.gr) From Brindisi to Corfu and Igoumenitsa.

Hellenic Mediterranean Lines (HML; www.hml.gr) From Brindisi to Corfu, Igoumenitsa and Patra (and also high-season services connecting Brindisi with Paxi, Kefallonia and Zakynthos).

Italian Ferries (www.italianferries.it) High-season, high-speed catamaran services between Brindisi, Corfu and Paxi.

Med Link (www.ferries.gr/medlink) From Brindisi to Igoumenitsa and Patra (and also between Brindisi and Kefallonia in high season).

Minoan Lines (www.minoan.gr) From Venice and Ancona to Corfu, Igoumenitsa and Patra.

My Way Maritime (www.ferries.gr/myway) From Brindisi to Corfu, Igoumenitsa and Patra (calling at Kefallonia in high season).

Superfast Ferries (www.superfast.com) From Ancona and Bari to Igoumenitsa and Patra.

Ventouris (www.ventouris.gr) From Bari to Corfu and Igoumenitsa.

HISTORY & MYTHOLOGY

The origin of the name Ionian is obscure but is thought to derive from the goddess Io. Yet another of Zeus' paramours, Io, while fleeing the wrath of a jealous Hera (in the shape of a heifer), happened to pass through the waters now known as the Ionian Sea.

If we are to believe Homer, the islands were important during Mycenaean times; however, no magnificent palaces or even modest villages from that period have been revealed, though Mycenaean tombs have been unearthed. Ancient history lies buried beneath tonnes of earthquake rubble – seismic activity has been constant on all Ionian Islands, including Kythira.

By the 8th century BC, the Ionian Islands were in the clutches of the mighty city-state of Corinth, which regarded them as stepping stones on the route to Sicily and Italy. A century later, Corfu staged a successful revolt against Corinth, which was allied to Sparta, and became an ally of Sparta's archenemy, Athens. This alliance provoked Sparta into challenging Athens, thus precipitating the Peloponnesian Wars (431–404 BC). The wars left Corfu depleted, as they did all participants, and Corfu became little more than a staging post for whoever happened to be holding sway in Greece. By the end of the 3rd century BC, Corfu, along with the other Ionian Islands, had become Roman. Following the decline of the Roman Empire, the islands saw the usual waves of invaders that Greece suffered. After the fall of Constantinople, the islands became Venetian.

Corfu was never part of the Ottoman Empire. Paxi, Kefallonia, Zakynthos, Ithaki and Kythira were variously occupied by the Turks, but the Venetians held them longest. The exception was Lefkada, which was Turkish for 200 years. The Ionian Islands fared better under the Venetians than their counterparts in the Cyclades.

Venice fell to Napoleon in 1797. Two years later, under the Treaty of Campo Formio, the Ionian Islands were allotted to France. In 1799 Russian forces wrested the islands from Napoleon, but by 1807 they were his again. By then, the all-powerful British couldn't resist meddling. As a result, in 1815, after Napoleon's downfall, the islands became a British protectorate under the jurisdiction of a series of Lord High Commissioners.

British rule was oppressive but, on a more positive note, the British constructed roads, bridges, schools and hospitals, established trade links, and developed agriculture and industry. However, the nationalistic fervour in the rest of Greece soon reached the Ionian Islands, and a call for *enosis* (political union with Greece) was realised in 1864 when Britain relinquished the islands to Greece.

In WWII the Italians invaded Corfu as part of Mussolini's plan to resurrect the mighty Roman Empire. Italy surrendered to the Allies in September 1943 and, in revenge, the Germans massacred thousands of Italians who had occupied the island. The Germans also sent some 5000 Corfiot Jews to Auschwitz.

The islands saw a great deal of emigration after WWII, and again following the earthquakes of 1948 and 1953 that devastated the region. But while Greeks left the islands, the foreign invasion has never really stopped, and these days takes the form of package tourism from northern Europe, especially to Corfu, Zakynthos, Kefallonia and, to a lesser extent, Lefkada.

CORFU ΚΕΡΚΥΡΑ

pop 109,540

Corfu is the second-largest, greenest Ionian island, and also the best known. In Greek, the island's name is Kerkyra (*ker*-kih-rah). It was Homer's 'beautiful and rich land', and Odysseus' last stop on his journey home to Ithaca. Shakespeare reputedly used it as a background for *The Tempest*. In the 20th century, the Durrell brothers, among others, extolled its virtues.

With its beguiling landscape of wildflowers and cypress trees rising out of shimmering olive groves, Corfu is considered by many as Greece's most beautiful island. With the nation's highest rainfall, it's also a major vegetable garden and produces scores of herbs, and the mountain air is heavily scented.

Getting There & Away

AIR

Olympic Airways (Map p412; ☎ 2661 038 694; www.olympic-airways.gr; Iakovou Polyla 11, Corfu Town) has a central office as well as a desk at the airport. The national airline has three flights to/from Athens daily (from €78), and four flights a week to/from Thessaloniki (€63). You can also fly three times weekly to Preveza (€35), Kefallonia (€35) and Zakynthos (€45).

Aegean Airlines (☎ 2661 027 100; www.aegeanair.com) has two or three flights daily between Athens and Corfu. Its office is located at the airport.

BUS
KTEL (☎ 2661 039 985) runs buses two or three times daily between Corfu Town and Athens (€29.50, 8½ hours) – some services go via Lefkimmi in the island's south. There's also a twice-daily service to/from Thessaloniki (€28.50, eight hours); for both destinations budget an additional €5.10 for the ferry between Corfu and the mainland. Long-distance tickets should be purchased in advance; the bus station is on Avramiou, between Plateia San Rocco and the new port.

FERRY
Domestic
Hourly ferries travel daily between Corfu and Igoumenitsa (€5.10, 1¼ hours). Car ferries go to Paxi (€6.10, three hours) two or three times weekly (the hydrofoil is a better option as it's much more frequent). You can travel to/from Patra on one of the frequent international ferries that call at Corfu daily (€21.50 to €25, six hours) en route to/from Italy.

There are also half a dozen ferries daily between Lefkimmi in the island's south and Igoumenitsa (€3, one hour).

International
Corfu is on the Patra–Igoumenitsa ferry route to Italy (Brindisi, Bari, Ancona, Trieste and Venice), although at the time of research ferries from Ancona weren't stopping at Corfu (passengers will need

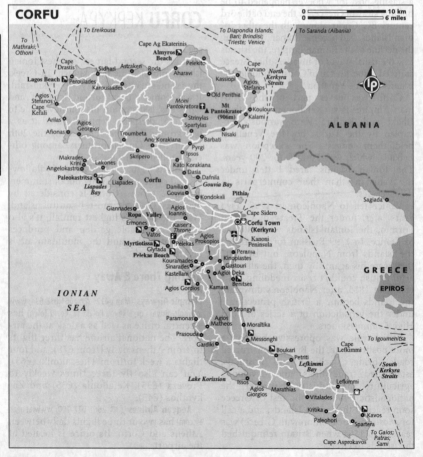

to disembark at Igoumenitsa and cross to Corfu on a local ferry).

Ferries go a few times daily to Brindisi (€40 to €50 depending on which company you travel with, eight hours), and in the summer usually once daily to Bari (€56, 10 hours), Trieste (€86, 26 hours) and Venice (€77 to €96 depending on the company, 28 hours). The fares listed here are for airline-style seats (and are not for cabin berths), one-way passage in the high season; there are sizable reductions in price in the low- and mid-seasons, and also for return tickets.

Italian Ferries (www.italianferries.it) operates high-speed catamaran services between Corfu and Brindisi daily from July to mid-September. The journey takes only 3¼ hours and fares are either €57 or €85 depending on the date of travel (passengers aged under 26 receive a substantial discount).

Shipping agencies selling tickets are found mostly along Xenofondos Stratigou and Ethnikis Antistasis. **Alsi Travel & Shipping** (Map p412; ☎ 2661 080 030; Ethnikis Antistasis 1), directly across from Corfu's new port, can help with information on most international shipping lines – the assortment of companies, routes and prices can get confusing.

For more information regarding Italian ferries to Corfu, see the international section under Ferries in Getting There & Away on p408.

HYDROFOIL
Domestic
Petrakis Lines (Map p412; ☎ 2661 031 649; Ethnikis Antistasis 4) operates passenger-only hydrofoils between Corfu, Igoumenitsa and Paxi from May until mid-October. There are one to three services daily, except on Thursdays, between Corfu and Paxi (€12.90, one hour), but there's only one service weekly between Corfu and Igoumenitsa (€10.20, 35 minutes) – on this particular route the ferries are definitely a much better option.

Petrakis Lines also operates day trips to Kefallonia (Sami and its surrounds) twice weekly. The cost of the day trip is €47, but travellers can often use the hydrofoil for one-way passage for €38. This is the only sea link between the northern and southern Ionian Islands.

International
Less popular than the Italy-bound ferries are the hydrofoil services connecting Corfu and Albania, operated by **Petrakis Lines** (Map p412; ☎ 2661 031 649; Ethnikis Antistasis 4). There are daily sailings to/from the town of Saranda (€15, 25 minutes), plus twice-weekly services to/from Himara (€25, 1¼ hours) and Vlora (€38, 2½ hours). Some travellers to Albania need a visa, so it's best to investigate this before you leave home. Alternatively, Petrakis Lines offers regular day trips to the historic areas around Saranda for €70, and no visa is required for this trip.

Getting Around
TO/FROM THE AIRPORT
There's no bus service between Corfu Town and the airport. Bus Nos 6 and 10 from Plateia San Rocco in Corfu Town stop on the main road about 800m from the airport (en route to Benitses and Ahillion). A taxi between the airport and Corfu Town will set you back around €10.

BUS
KTEL buses (green-and-cream) travel from Corfu Town's **long-distance bus station** (Map p412; ☎ 2661 030 627; Avramiou) to the following destinations.

LONG-DISTANCE BUSES FROM CORFU TOWN

Destination	Via	Time	Frequency
Agios Gordios	Sinarades	40min	5 daily
Agios Stefanos	Sidhari	1½hr	6 daily
Aharavi	Roda	1¼hr	4 daily
Glyfada	Vatos	45min	6 daily
Kavos	Lefkimmi	1½hr	10 daily
Kassiopi		1hr	6 daily
Messonghi	Benitses	45min	4 daily
Paleokastritsa	Gouvia	45min	7 daily
Pyrgi	Ipsos	30min	10 daily

Fares cost €1 to €3.80. Sunday and holiday services are reduced considerably, and some routes don't run at all.

The numbers and destinations of local buses (dark blue) from the **local bus station** (Map p415; ☎ 2661 031 595; Plateia San Rocco), in Corfu Town, include those places mentioned in the table 'Local Buses in Corfu Town' on p413.

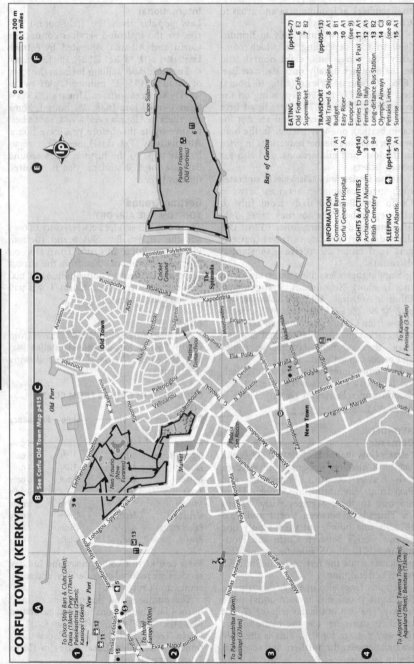

CORFU TOWN (KERKYRA)

0 _____ 200 m
0 _____ 0.1 miles

See Corfu Old Town Map p415

Old Town

New Port

Old Port

The Spianada

Cricket Ground

New Town

Palaio Frourio
(Old Fortress)

Bay of Garitsa

Cape Sidero

New Frourio
(New Fortress)

Market

To Disco Strip Bars & Clubs (2km);
Dasia (13km); Pyrgi (17km);
Paleokastritsa (26km);
Kassiopi (36km)

To Hotel Europe (100m)

To Airport (1km); Taverna Tripa (7km);
Aqualand (9km); Benitses (13km)

To Paleokastritsa (26km);
Kassiopi (37km)

To Kanoni Peninsula (3.5km)

LOCAL BUSES IN CORFU TOWN

Destination	Via	Time	Frequency
Agios Ioannis &	Afra	20min	13 daily
	Aqualand (8)		
Ahillion (10)	Gastouri	20min	6 daily
Kanoni (2)		20min	half-hourly
Kastellani (5)	Kourmades	25min	13 daily
Kontokali &	Gouvia	30min	half-hourly
	Dasia (7)		
Pelekas (11)		30min	7 daily
Perama (6)	Benitses	30min	13 daily

Tickets are either €0.55 or €0.75 depending on the length of journey. They can be bought on board or from the booth on Plateia San Rocco.

CAR & MOTORCYCLE

Car- and motorbike-rental outlets are plentiful in Corfu Town and most of the resort towns on the island. Shop around to get a good deal. Most international car-rental companies are represented in Corfu Town and at the airport, and there are numerous local companies. Most have offices along the northern waterfront, including the following companies.

Budget (Map p412; ☎ 2661 028 590; Eleftheriou Venizelou 32)

Easy Rider (Map p412; ☎ 2661 043 026) Opposite the new port, rents scooters and motorbikes from €15 per day.

Europcar (Map p412; ☎ 2661 046 931; Eleftheriou Venizelou 32)

Ocean (Map p415; ☎ 2661 032 351; Eleftheriou Venizelou 22)

Sunrise (Map p412; ☎ 2661 026 511; Ethnikis Antistasis 16)

CORFU TOWN

pop 28,200

The island's capital is beautiful Corfu Town (Kerkyra), built on a promontory, and it's a gracious medley of many occupying influences. The Spianada (Esplanade) is green, gardened and boasts Greece's only cricket ground, a legacy of the British. The Liston, a row of arcaded buildings flanking the northwestern side of the Spianada and housing upmarket cafés, was built during the French occupation and modelled on Paris' Rue de Rivoli. Georgian mansions and Byzantine churches complete the picture. The Venetian influence prevails, particularly in the old town, wedged between two fortresses.

Narrow alleyways of 18th-century shuttered tenements in muted ochres and pinks are more reminiscent of Venice or Naples than Greece.

Orientation

The town is separated into northern and southern sections. The old town is in the northern section between the Spianada and the New Fortress. The Old Fortress is east of here and projects out to sea, cut off from the town by a moat. The southern section is the new town.

The old port is north of the old town, and the new port is west. Between them is the hulking New Fortress. The long-distance bus station is off Avramiou between Plateia San Rocco and the new port. The local bus station is on Plateia San Rocco.

Information

EMERGENCY

Tourist police (Map p415; ☎ 2661 030 265; 3rd fl, Samartzi 4) Off Plateia San Rocco.

INTERNET ACCESS

The going rate for Internet access is €4 to €5 per hour.

Netoikos (Map p415; Kaloxairetou 14) Between Church of Agios Spyridon and the Liston.

On Line Internet Café (Map p415; Kapodistria 28) Opposite the Spianada.

MEDICAL SERVICES

Corfu General Hospital (Map p412; ☎ 2661 088 200; I Andreadi)

MONEY

Alpha Bank (Map p415; Kapodistria, behind the Liston)

Banks & ATMs Around Plateia San Rocco, on G Theotoki and by both ports.

National Bank of Greece (Map p415; Voulgareous)

POST

Post office (Map p415; Leof Alexandras)

TELEPHONE

OTE (Map p415; Mantzarou 9)

TOURIST INFORMATION

Showing its disregard for the thousands of tourists that flood into Corfu, EOT closed its Corfu tourist office in the early summer of 2003. Although the old office was hard to find, understaffed and open erratic hours, it was better than nothing. There were unconfirmed rumours of a new office (maybe opening in 2004), but don't hold your breath.

THE CORFIOT

In the absence of any official tourist literature, pick up a copy of the *Corfiot* (€2), an English-language newspaper published monthly. It's available at many kiosks around Corfu Town, and although some articles are geared to long-term residents, it also contains details of island events and services, plus practical information like bus timetables and emergency telephone numbers.

Sights & Activities

The star exhibit of the **Archaeological Museum** (Map p412; ☎ 2661 030 680; P Vraïla 5; admission €3; 8.30am-3pm Tue-Sun) is the Gorgon Medusa sculpture, one of the best-preserved pieces of Archaic sculpture found in Greece. It was part of the west pediment of the 6th-century-BC Temple of Artemis at Corcyra (the ancient capital), a Doric temple that stood on the Kanoni Peninsula south of the town. The petrifying Medusa is depicted in the instant before she was beheaded by Perseus. Note the disturbing snakes that emerge from Medusa's hair.

Just north of the cricket ground is the **Museum of Asian Art** (Map p415; ☎ 2661 030 443; admission €2; 8.30am-3pm Tue-Sun), containing an impressive collection that includes Chinese and Japanese porcelain, bronzes, screens and sculptures. It's housed in the Palace of Sts Michael & George, built in 1819 as the British Lord High Commissioner's residence.

Inside the Church of Our Lady of Antivouniotissa is the **Byzantine Museum** (Map p415; ☎ 2661 038 313; off Arseniou; admission €2; 8.30am-3pm Tue-Sun). It has an outstanding collection of Byzantine and post-Byzantine icons dating from the 13th to the 17th centuries.

Apart from the pleasure of wandering the narrow streets of the old town and the gardens of the Spianada, you can explore the two fortresses, Corfu Town's most dominant landmarks. The hilltop on which the **Neo Frourio** (Map p412; New Fortress; admission €2; 9am-9pm May-Oct) stands was first fortified in the 12th century. The existing remains date from the late 15th and early

16th centuries. The ruins of the **Palaio Frourio** (Map p415; Old Fortress; ☎ 2661 048 310; admission €4; 8.30am-3pm, 8.30am-7pm Jun-Aug) date from the mid-12th century.

In Corfu, many males are christened Spyros after the island's miracle-working patron St Spyridon. His mummified body lies in a silver, glass-fronted coffin in the 16th-century **Church of Agios Spyridon** (Map p415; Agiou Spyridonos). It's paraded on Palm Sunday, Easter Sunday, 11 August and the first Sunday in November.

For something completely different and to contrast the old with the new, visit the heavily promoted **Aqualand** (Map p412; ☎ 2661 052 963; www.aqualand-corfu.com; adult/child under 12 €17/11, discounted entry after 3pm; 10am-6pm May-Oct, 10am-7pm Jul-Aug). This huge waterpark is 9km west of town in Agios Ioannis, and is chock-full of waterslides, pools and family-oriented attractions (all included in the entry price).

Another family-friendly activity is to take a one-hour cruise on the **Kalypso Star** (Map p415; ☎ 2661 046 525; adult/child €12/6), which departs hourly (10am to 6pm) from the old port. The boat has an underwater viewing area, and passengers are treated to a show featuring performing sea lions.

There are a number of **day trips** offered from Corfu Town, including an interesting excursion to Saranda and the World Heritage-listed ruins at Butrint in Albania (€70); a boat trip taking in Paxi, Antipaxi and Parga (€34); and a trip to Sami and surrounds in Kefallonia (€47). Contact **Petrakis Lines** (Map p412; ☎ 2661 031 649; Ethnikis Antistaseos 4) for details and bookings.

Sleeping

Budget accommodation choices in Corfu Town are disappointing, and campers will need to head to the coastal resorts (the nearest camping ground is 8km north). There are, however, some excellent mid-range options – these can fill up quickly with businesspeople and holiday-makers, so bookings are advised.

We list high-season prices here (mid-July to August, and at Easter), but it's worth noting that low-season prices (October to April) can be drastically reduced and mid-season prices (May to mid-July, and September) are usually good value. All hotels in Corfu Town are open year-round.

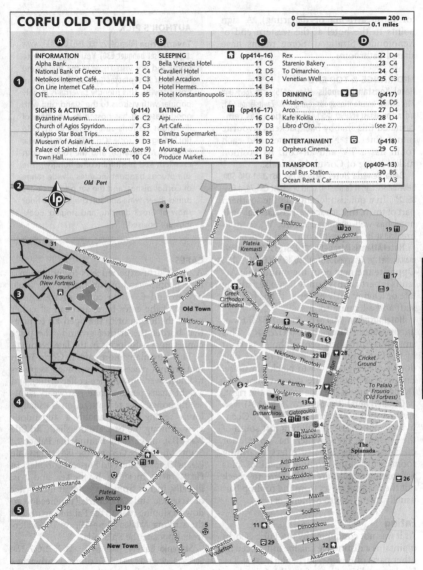

CORFU OLD TOWN

0 — 200 m
0 — 0.1 miles

INFORMATION	
Alpha Bank	1 D3
National Bank of Greece	2 C4
Netoikos Internet Café	3 C3
On Line Internet Café	4 D4
OTE	5 B5

SIGHTS & ACTIVITIES	(p414)
Byzantine Museum	6 C2
Church of Agios Spyridon	7 C3
Kalypso Star Boat Trips	8 B2
Museum of Asian Art	9 D3
Palace of Saints Michael & George	(see 9)
Town Hall	10 C4

SLEEPING	(pp414–16)
Bella Venezia Hotel	11 C5
Cavalieri Hotel	12 D5
Hotel Arcadion	13 C4
Hotel Hermes	14 B4
Hotel Konstantinoupolis	15 B3

EATING	(pp416–17)
Arpi	16 C4
Art Café	17 D3
Dimitra Supermarket	18 B5
En Plo	19 D2
Mouragia	20 D2
Produce Market	21 B4
Rex	22 D4
Starenio Bakery	23 C4
To Dimarchio	24 C4
Venetian Well	25 C3

DRINKING	(p417)
Aktaion	26 D5
Arco	27 D4
Kafe Koklia	28 D4
Libro d'Oro	(see 27)

ENTERTAINMENT	(p418)
Orpheus Cinema	29 C5

TRANSPORT	(pp409–13)
Local Bus Station	30 B5
Ocean Rent a Car	31 A3

IONIAN ISLANDS

BUDGET
Locals who let rooms often meet the boats. It's a good idea to ask to see the location of their accommodation on a map.

Hotel Hermes (Map p415; ☎ 2661 039 268; G Markora 14; s/d with shared bathroom €28/33, s/d with private bathroom €36/44) The Hermes is in an atmospheric if noisy location, directly opposite one end of

the bustling daily fruit and vegetable market. It has basic, timeworn rooms and is popular with backpackers, but it's still quite pricey for what you get.

Hotel Europi (Map p412; ☎ 2661 039 304; d €45) Small, scruffy and basic, the Europi has little to recommend it other than being cheap and near the new port (convenient for those arriving or departing). A sign points to the hotel at the western end of Xenofondos Stratigou. Some rooms have shared bathroom.

MID-RANGE & TOP END

Hotel Konstantinoupolis (Map p415; ☎ 2661 048 716; www.konstantinoupolis.com.gr; K Zavitsianou 11; s/d incl breakfast €60/90; 🕮) Renovation has reincarnated this shabby backpacker's favourite into a fine Art Nouveau hotel, and each room has a TV and air-con. Its position makes it one of Corfu's best deals.

Bella Venezia Hotel (Map p415; ☎ 2661 046 500; belvenht@hol.gr; N Zambeli 4; s incl breakfast €58-74, d €65-85; 🕮) In a quietish location in the southern part of town, this attractive, neoclassical-style hotel has well-equipped rooms. Wake up to breakfast in the pretty courtyard garden.

Hotel Atlantis (Map p412; ☎ 2661 035 560; atlanker@ mail.otenet.gr; Xenofondos Stratigou 48; s/d €72/87; 🕮) Opposite the new port, the monolithic Atlantis is particularly handy if you're arriving late or leaving early by ferry. It has friendly staff and adequate rooms.

Hotel Arcadion (Map p415; ☎ 2661 037 670; www .arcadionhotel.com; Kapodistria 44; d €122; 🕮) This smartly refurbished central hotel is right by the Liston and offers elegant rooms, plus double-glazed windows to block out noise. Entrance is not via the ground-floor McDonald's, but on the side street to the right.

Cavalieri Hotel (Map p415; ☎ 2661 039 041; www .cavalieri-hotel.com; Kapodistria 4; d €180; 🕮) Occupying a 300-year-old building just south of the Spianada, the Cavalieri has an interior of classical elegance. It offers charming rooms with all the required amenities, plus welcoming public areas (be sure to check out the magical views from the rooftop bar, usually open June to September).

Eating

As it was not conquered by the Turks, Corfu maintains a distinctive cuisine influenced by other parts of Europe, particularly Italy. Try local specialities like *sofrito* (beef, lamb or veal with garlic, vinegar and parsley), *pastitsada* (beef in red sauce stewed with spices and served with macaroni) or *bourdeto* (a spicy casserole of fish in tomato sauce).

Stroll around pretty Plateia Dimarchiou (Town Hall Square) and along Guilford to investigate the menus of some of Corfu Town's most tempting restaurants.

AUTHOR'S PICK

Tavern Tripa (Map p412; ☎ 2661 056 333; www .tripas.gr; set banquet €30) You can't come to Corfu and not visit Tripa, in the tiny inland village of Kinopiastes (about 7km south of Corfu Town). This friendly taverna is hugely popular with visitors to the island, and with good reason. It has hosted its fair share of illustrious patrons since opening in 1936 (including Aristotle Onassis, Jane Fonda, François Mitterrand), and the food is both excellent and plentiful (come hungry!). The sumptuous banquet includes a wide range of Corfiot dishes, and the set price includes drinks (beer, wine and soft drink) and a floor show of Greek dancing and singing. Bookings are advised.

CAFÉS

A true Corfu experience is to indulge in a little people-watching on the Liston. You'll pay around €3 for a coffee or fresh juice at any of the cafés here, and can sit either under the loggia or in the open-air terraces that border the cricket ground. The place comes alive with locals in the late evening.

There are many more cafés in Corfu Town that are not places to eat so much as places to linger over a *frappé* (ice-coffee drink), and a light snack perhaps, and rest weary sightseeing bones. The real attraction is usually a lovely setting and invariably a stupendous view. Among the best are the shady **Art Café** (Map p415), in gardens behind the Palace of Saints Michael & George; the **Old Fortress Café** (Map p412), inside the Old Fortress complex; **En Plo** (Map p415), meaning 'by the sea' and it is, literally, inches from the water at the corner of Arseniou and Kapodistria (you need to go down a sloping road to the Faliraki area); and the striking **Aktaion** (Map p415), on the waterfront opposite the Spianada.

Starenio Bakery (Map p415; ☎ 2661 047 370; Guildford 59; snacks under €2) offers sandwiches plus homemade pies (the usual cheese and spinach, plus more unusual fare like zucchini, leek or eggplant). It also sells an array of cakes, pastries and gooey baklava.

RESTAURANTS

To Dimarchio (Map p415; ☎ 2661 039 031; Plateia Dimarchiou; mains €7-20) Highly regarded, To Dimarchio has an extensive menu of fine

Greek, Italian and French dishes. There are pricey but delicious seafood creations, as well as cheaper pasta and salad dishes.

Arpi (Map p415; ☎ 2661 027 715; Giotopoulou 10; mains €6-12) The more casual Arpi is located in a small alley off Plateia Dimarchiou, but also offers seating on the square. Its speciality is crepes (savoury and sweet), but there are also local favourites on the menu (eg pastitsada, sofrito, mousakas).

Rex (Map p415; ☎ 2661 039 649; Kapodistria 66; mains €9-20) Rex has operated behind the Liston since 1932. It's now a popular, upmarket eatery offering carefully prepared dishes of quality seafood and grilled meats, plus traditional Greek and Corfiot choices (including bourdeto). Check the daily specials for creations using fresh seasonal produce.

Venetian Well (Map p415; ☎ 2661 044 761; Plateia Kremasti; mains €14-20) For an upmarket treat, head inland from the old port to this well-hidden eatery (turn left past the cathedral and look for the signs). The romantic setting includes outdoor tables set around a decorative Venetian well. Meals are pricey, but the food is excellent and includes creative dishes such as duck fillet served with dried fruit or wild boar with frangelico and vegetables.

Mouragia (Map p415; ☎ 2661 033 815; Arseniou 15; mezedes €2-4, mains €4.50-12) It doesn't offer absolute waterfront seating like its neighbours, but Mouragia is the pick of the trio of restaurants here due to its great range of mezedes perfect for sharing. It also offers well-priced local dishes like mousakas, pastitsada and sofrito (priced around €5 to €6), plus grilled fish and meat.

SELF-CATERING
Head to the colourful stalls of the bustling **produce market** (Map p415), open morning to early afternoon daily except Sunday, for fresh fruit, vegetables and fish. It's north of Plateia San Rocco, by the southern wall of the New Fortress. **Dimitra supermarket** (Map p415; G Markora), next to Hotel Hermes, supplies the groceries you can't pick up at the nearby produce market, and there's another **supermarket** (Map p415) by the long-distance bus station.

Drinking
Evenings in Corfu consist of strolling around the town centre or nursing a drink at a café or bar, with many young locals then heading out to a club (see Entertainment, p418). Popular bars include **Kafe Koklia** (Map p415), **Arco** (Map p415) and **Libro d'Oro** (Map p415) on the Liston; nearby **Aktaion** (Map p415), opposite the Spianada; and the classy roof-top bar at the **Cavalieri Hotel** (Map p415; ☎ 2661 039 041; www.cavalieri-hotel.com; Kapodistria 4).

CORFU ACTIVITIES

Obviously the best activities in this part of the world are centred on, under or around water. If you're not fortunate enough to be **sailing** around the Ionians in your own private yacht, there are companies based at Gouvia marina that offer yacht-charter services and flotilla holidays. **Corfu Sea School** (UK ☎ 01273 263828; Corfu ☎ 2661 099 470; www.corfuseaschool.com), also at Gouvia marina, offers sailing lessons. There are also excellent opportunities, especially in the villages of Corfu's northeast, to rent a motorboat and explore the coastal coves.

You can dive in the crystal-clear waters off Corfu, and there are half-a-dozen **diving** operators on the island (in Kassiopi, Agios Gordis, Agios Giorgios, Ipsos, Gouvia and Paleokastritsa).

For land-lubbers, **walking** is extremely popular. Heading off the main roads allows you to see so much more of the countryside and enjoy the unspoilt villages. Keen walkers should purchase *The Second Book of Corfu Walks* by Hilary Whitton Paipete, available in bookshops around town. By the same author is *The Companion Guide to the Corfu Trail*; it's written to guide walkers tackling the recently developed **Corfu Trail**, which traverses the island and should take between eight and 12 days to complete. See www.travelling.gr/corfutrail for more information.

Given Corfu's hilly terrain, it's not surprising that **mountain-biking** is becoming popular. **Corfu Mountainbike Shop** (☎ 2661 093 344; www.mountainbikecorfu.gr) is based in Dasia and rents bikes for independent exploration, as well as organising day trips and cycling holidays.

Not far from Ermones on the island's west coast is the **Corfu Golf Club** (☎ 2661 094 220; www.corfugolfclub.com), one of the few courses in Greece. Or you can go **horse riding** through olive groves with **Trailriders** (☎ 2663 023 090), based in the small inland village of Ano Korakiana.

IONIAN ISLANDS

Entertainment

Corfu's disco strip is 2km northwest of the new port, along Ethnikis Antistasis. Here, high-tech places cater mainly to locals and to holidaying Greeks and Italians in the high season (holidaying northern Europeans tend to stay and party in their resort areas), and there are numerous bars and restaurants.

Don't expect an evening at any of the clubs along here to be a cheap night out. Drinks cost around €5 and you usually pay a sizable cover charge to get in. The big, flashy Hippodrome and long-established Apokalipsis are very popular with holidaying Italians. Privilege is a fashionable new player, and the latest haunt of the city's cool crowd is Au Bar (Ω in Greek) – it's the first bar you'll encounter on the disco strip, heading out of Corfu Town. Home is the place to go late (after 3am), with an 'after-club' feel and a good mix of music.

If it's visual entertainment you want, Corfu Town has the **Orpheus cinema** (Map p415; ☎ 2661 039 768; G Aspioti), which screens English-language films with Greek subtitles for €6. Many restaurants and bars in resort towns screen recent DVDs for their patrons.

NORTH OF CORFU TOWN

Most of the coast of northern Corfu is package-tourist saturated, though once you venture beyond the main package resorts (ending at Pyrgi) you enter some of Corfu's most privileged scenery.

Dasia and **Ipsos** are brash tourist strips full of bars and restaurants. The beach is narrow and a busy road separates the sea from the entertainment. More or less extending out of Ipsos is **Pyrgi**, where a road continues east around the base of **Mt Pantokrator** (906m), the island's highest peak. From Pyrgi, another road snakes north and inland over the western flank of the mountain to the north coast. A detour can be made to the picturesque village of **Strinylas**, from where a road leads through stark terrain to the mountain's summit and stupendous views.

Heading west around the winding coastal road you will first hit **Barbati**, a developing resort with a long pebbled beach downhill from the main road, and then **Nisaki**, little more than a small cove with a pebble beach, a couple of tavernas and some rooms. The tiny cove of **Agni** is considered by many to be the gourmet heart of Corfu, with three excellent tavernas (and little else). The next village of interest is **Kalami**, where the White House was the home of the Durrell brothers (see the boxed text below). The building (now a restaurant) is perched right on the water's edge and must have been idyllic during the writers' sojourn here. Just round the next headland is the pretty little harbour of **Kouloura**. From both Kalami and Kouloura the buildings in neighbouring Albania can be seen quite clearly.

Kassiopi is the next major port of call. It's an agreeable resort town with good facilities,

---

THE BROTHERS DURRELL

The name Durrell is synonymous with Corfu, though it's perhaps surprising that of the two brothers – Lawrence (1912–90) and Gerald (1925–95) – it is the naturalist Gerald rather than the poet and novelist Lawrence who has so inextricably linked the name of this famous duo with the island of Corfu and the little village of Kalami on Corfu's northeast coast.

Gerald Durrell was born in India and gained considerable repute among conservationists for his role in breeding endangered animal species for eventual release in the wild. Durrell's love of animals started when living in Corfu in the 1930s. He was a prolific author, producing more than 35 informative yet amusing books about animals. His best-known books were *The Overloaded Ark* (1953), *Three Singles to Adventure* (1953), *My Family and other Animals* (1956), *A Zoo in My Luggage* (1960) and *Birds, Beasts and Relatives* (1969).

Brother Lawrence, also born in India, was the dedicated writer in the family. He was at once a novelist, poet, writer of topographical books, verse plays and farcical short stories. He is best known for the *Alexandria Quartet*, a series of four interconnected novels. His Greek trilogy included *Prospero's Cell* (1945), in which he describes his life in Corfu during 1937 and 1938, *Reflections on a Marine Venus* (1953), for which he spent two years in Rhodes in 1945–46 as press officer for the Allied government, and *Bitter Lemons of Cyprus* (1957), where he spent 1952–56 as a teacher and government official – latterly during the Cypriot insurgency.

set around an attractive circular harbour. The main road continues inland from the long (and surprisingly under-developed) beach of **Almyros** to the busy resorts of **Aharavi** and **Roda**, both rather uninspiring after the arresting scenery of the northeast coast. **Sidhari**, also a rather tacky tourist resort, is not much better.

Pleasant **Agios Stefanos**, further around the coast (and not to be confused with the village of Agios Stefanos in the northeast), has a long sandy beach extending under the lee of high sand cliffs. Regular boats to the Diapondia islands (see the boxed text this page) leave from the small harbour 1.5km from the village centre.

Sleeping & Eating
Dionysus Camping Village (☎ 2661 091 417; www .dionysuscamping.gr; camp sites per adult/tent €5/3.50, huts per person €9; 🏊) There are a handful of camping grounds along the northeast coast; Dionysus is the closest to Corfu Town, signposted between Dafnila and Dasia and well served by bus. It's a large, shady place boasting good facilities, including a pool, shop and restaurant. Simple huts contain two or four beds and no facilities; tents can also be hired. It's open from late April to mid-October.

At the opposite end of the spectrum, if you want to holiday like the British moneyed classes (who regularly visit Corfu's northeast), contact UK-based **CV Travel** (☎ 020-7591 2800; www.cvtravel.net), which rents out luxurious villas in the region on a weekly basis. Villas can accommodate small and large groups, and many have swimming pools.

Manessis Apartments (☎ 2661 034 990; diana@ otenet.gr; apt €82.50) By Aleka's lace shop at the end of Kassiopi's picturesque harbour are these appealing two-bedroom apartments (sleeping up to four) surrounded by bougainvillea. The owner is an Irish woman with great information about the area.

If you're after a memorable dining experience, a visit to Agni is highly recommended. Here you can take your pick from three highly regarded restaurants and enjoy the lovely setting. Alternatively, if you're a Durrell fan you can have a nostalgic meal at Kalami's **White House** (☎ 2661 091 251; mains €7-12), the Durrell family's former home, and ponder the view as you search for your own literary inspiration.

THE DIAPONDIA ISLANDS

Scattered like forgotten stepping stones to Puglia in Italy lie the Diapondia islands, a cluster of little-known and even less-visited satellite islands belonging administratively to Corfu. Of the five islands only three are inhabited, though many of their original residents have long since departed for the lure of New York City and only return in the summer months to renew their ties.

Ereikousa (pop 700) is the closest Diapondia island to Corfu and therefore the easiest to visit. Wild and wooded **Mathraki** (pop 300) is the least developed of the trio, but offers solitude and fine walking. **Othoni** (pop 650) is the largest of the group and also the furthest from Corfu; it's popular with Italian yachties.

Often isolated by tricky seas, the islands require effort to visit. Development is proceeding slowly, but all offer a few places to stay and eat. Most people visit on day trips from Sidhari or Agios Stefanos on Corfu's northwest coast, though regular ferries do link the islands with both Agios Stefanos and Corfu Town.

If you're keen to visit the Diapondia, your best bet is to contact **San Stefano Travel** (☎ 2663 051 910; www.corfudirect.f9.co.uk) in Agios Stefanos. Friendly Noula will give you the lowdown on the ferry options from Agios Stefanos and the various accommodation possibilities on each island, as well as offering travel services in and around Agios Stefanos itself.

SOUTH OF CORFU TOWN
The Kanoni Peninsula, 4km south of Corfu Town, was the site of the ancient capital, Corcyra, but little has been excavated. **Mon Repos Villa**, at its northeast tip, was the birthplace of Prince Philip (Queen Elizabeth II's husband). The beautiful wooded **grounds** (admission free; 🕐 8am-5pm Sep-May, 8am-7pm Jun-Aug) can be explored, and the residence has been restored to its former glory and houses the excellent **Museum of Palaeopolis** (☎ 2661 030 680; admission €3; 🕐 8.30am-3pm Tue-Sun), with displays on the history of the Mon Repos estate as well as information about the ancient city.

The coast road continues south with a turn-off to **Ahillion Palace** (☎ 2661 056 245; admission €6; 🕐 9am-2.30pm Sep-May, 9am-7pm Jun-Aug), near the village of Gastouri and well sign-posted. In the 1890s it was the summer palace of Austria's Empress Elizabeth (King Otho of Greece was her uncle), and she dedicated the villa to Achilles. The beautifully landscaped garden is guarded by kitsch statues of the empress' other mythological heroes.

The resort of **Benitses** used to be the play-ground of holiday hooligans, but in recent times has made strenuous efforts to get its act together. Still, the excesses of too much package tourism have taken the sheen off the place, but the narrow winding streets of the old village maintain an air of authenticity.

Heading further south you'll hit **Moraïtika** and **Messonghi**, two busy resorts that have merged into one. The beach scene, while not ideal, is better than that of Benitses. The winding coastal road between Messonghi and **Boukari** is decidedly more appealing and is dotted with a few well-situated tav-ernas and small pebbly beaches.

There's accommodation aplenty around Benitses and further south along the coast, but there's not a lot here to hold the inde-pendent traveller for long. For a peaceful break away from the resort crowds, un-wind at **Golden Sunset Hotel** (☎ 2662 051 853; www.corfusunset.gr; s/d €38/50), a friendly, family-run place in tiny Boukari, with a restaurant attached. Rooms are bright and spacious and have balconies with sea views.

THE WEST COAST

Corfu's best beaches are on the west coast, and **Paleokastritsa**, 26km from Corfu Town, is the largest resort, with development along a 3km stretch of road. Built around coves with a green mountain backdrop, Paleokas-tritsa is incredibly beautiful – but while the water looks enticing, it's generally consider-ably colder than at other parts of the island. At the beaches here you'll find small **excur-sion boats** (€8, 30min per person) to take you out exploring nearby beaches and grottoes.

Perched on the rocky promontory above Paleokastritsa is picturesque **Moni Theotokou** (admission free; ☽ 7am-1pm & 3-8pm Apr-Oct), a mon-astery founded in the 13th century (but the present building dates from the 18th cen-tury). There are wonderful views from here, and a taverna from which to enjoy them.

From Paleokastritsa a path ascends to the unspoilt village of **Lakones**, 5km inland by road. There are superb views along the

6km road west to **Makrades** and **Krini**; the res-taurants along the way extol the views from their terraces. From Krini you can explore the ruins of the 13th-century Byzantine fortress of **Angelokastro**.

Further south, the beach at **Ermones** is near **Corfu Golf Club**, among the largest in Europe. Hilltop **Pelekas**, 4km away, is a good base for exploring. This friendly village can be as busy as the coast, but with independ-ent travellers rather than package tourists. It's renowned for its spectacular sunsets – a popular spot to watch them is **Kaiser's Throne**, a lookout high above Pelekas village.

Pelekas is close to three excellent sandy beaches, **Glyfada**, **Pelekas** (marked on some maps as Kontogialos) and **Myrtiotissa**. The first two are quite developed, with sun lounges, watersports and large hotels; the last is an unofficial nudist beach at the bot-tom of a steep unsealed road (don't drive down – it's best to park in the olive grove at the top of the hill and walk).

Agios Gordios is a popular backpacker hang-out south of Glyfada. It's a laid-back place with a long sandy beach and will ap-peal to travellers interested primarily in the booze-and-beach scene.

Sleeping & Eating
Paleokastritsa Camping (☎ 2663 041 204; camp sites per adult/tent €4.40/3) You'll find this camping ground on the right of the main approach road to town. It's a shady and well-organised place, with a restaurant on site and conveni-ences close by (eg minimarket, swimming pool), but is a fair way back from the main beaches (about 2.5km).

Paleokastritsa also has many hotels, stu-dios and domatia. At the end of the main road, before the climb to the monastery, are some good options.

Hotel Zefiros (☎ 2663 041 244; hotelzef@otenet.gr; d/ tr €62/78) This eye-catching hotel has friendly owners, attractive decor, some larger rooms suitable for families (with kitchenette), plus a café downstairs.

Hotel Apollon (☎ 2663 041 211; apollon1@hol.gr; d incl breakfast €65) Next door to Hotel Zefiros, the Apollon has comfortable rooms (all with sea view) above its restaurant and bakery.

La Grotta (☎ 2663 041 006) In Paleokastritsa, be sure to seek out this cool café-bar set in a gorgeous rocky cove perfect for swimming (there's even a diving board). It's a little tough to find (down a long flight of steps opposite the driveway up to Hotel Paleokastritsa on the main road), but once you're here you may not want to leave.

Golden Fox (☎ 2663 049 101; www.goldenfox.gr; d €54-64; 🏊) High up overlooking Paleokastritsa and just beyond the village of Lakones is this scenic spot with breathtaking views. The Golden Fox has terraces on three levels, and includes a restaurant, snack bar and swimming pool (open to the public and free of charge). This complex also has a few well-maintained studios to rent.

Levant Hotel (☎ 2661 094 230; www.levanthotel .com; d €110; 🏊 🏊) Near Kaiser's Throne lookout, this stylish, neoclassical building, once a private house, is one of the most elegant hotels on the island. It has helpful staff, superb rooms with all mod-cons, a swimming pool set in gardens and a restaurant terrace with awesome views.

Jimmy's Restaurant & Rooms (☎ 2661 094 284; jimmyspelekas@hotmail.com; mains €4-10; d €35; 🏊) At the intersection of the roads to Pelekas Beach, Kaiser's Throne and Corfu Town is Jimmy's, a popular hang-out with friendly staff. Its menu features Corfiot dishes such as sofrito, pastitsada and bourdeto, Greek favourites like calamari, souvlaki and mousakas, and decent choices for vegetarians. Jimmy's also has pleasant, good-value rooms for rent above the restaurant.

Sunrock (☎ 2661 094 637; www.geocities.com /sunrock_corfu; r per person €18, with private bathroom, incl breakfast & dinner per person €24; 🏊 🖥) At the southern end of Pelekas Beach is family-run Sunrock (formerly known as Vrachos), with excellent facilities (pool, restaurant, bar, Internet access, large terrace, path down to beach, resident masseuse, organised excursions) that have earned it the status of backpacker favourite. Pick up from the port can be arranged. The bar and taverna are open to the public. Sunrock is open year-round, with a capacity of 80 to 100 people.

Mirtiotisa (☎ 2661 094 113; sks_mirtia@hotmail.com; d €35) A 10-minute walk uphill from Myrtiotissa beach is this busy eatery, in an idyllic garden setting and serving the usual taverna fare. It also has simple, agreeable rooms that are very popular, and the shady grounds double as an unofficial beach car park (parking costs €1.50).

PinkPalace (☎ 2661 053 103; www.thepinkpalace.com; A-/B-class r incl breakfast & dinner per person €25/32; 🖥) You'll either love or hate this huge, garish complex on the main road into Agios Gordis. It's considered a 'must do' by many on the Europe backpacker circuit (especially Americans), and it's designed for under-25s who want fun and sun without the hassles of having to look for it. There are two categories of accommodation: A-class rooms are equivalent to those of a modern hotel (with air-con); B-class is hostel-style rooms that can sleep up to four people. The drawcard is the debauchery for which it is (in)famous, so it's not to everyone's liking (female travellers in particular might feel uneasy). There's a nightly disco, theme parties and watersports. A big pink bus will pick you up from the port. The Palace is open year-round, with a capacity of 900 people.

PAXI ΠΑΞΟΙ

pop 2380

At only 10km long and 4km wide, Paxi (pahx-*ee*), also commonly referred to as Paxos, is the smallest main Ionian island. It has a captivating landscape of dense, centuries-old olive groves, snaking drystone walls, derelict farmhouses and abandoned stone olive presses. There are only three coastal settlements and a few inland villages. Paxi's gentle east coast has small pebble beaches, while the west coast has awesome vistas of precipitous cliffs, punctuated by several grottoes only accessible by boat.

Paxi has escaped the mass tourism of Corfu and caters for small, discriminating tour companies. People come here because they have fallen in love with Paxi's cosy feel, or have heard about its friendly islanders and its captivating scenery. Paxi is a must for any serious island-hopper and is worth the extra effort needed to travel here.

The best way to get to know Paxi, and a favourite pastime of many visitors, is to walk the island. Pick up a copy of the excellent *Bleasdale Walking Map of Paxos* (€10.50), available at most travel agencies around the island.

Getting There & Away
BUS

There's a twice weekly direct bus service between Athens and Paxi (€29, plus €6.10 for ferry ticket between Paxi and Igoumenitsa, 7½ hours). Buses from Athens depart from **Hotel Vienni** (☎ 2105 249 143; Pireos 20, Athens), near Plateia Omonias. Information and tickets on Paxi are available from **Bouas Travel** (☎ 2662 032 401), on the Gaïos waterfront.

FERRY
Domestic
Two car ferries operate five services weekly between Paxi, Corfu and Igoumenitsa on the mainland. The Paxi–Igoumenitsa trip takes 1¾ hours; Paxi–Corfu (via Igoumenitsa) can take three to five hours (depending on the stopover in Igoumenitsa); tickets for either trip cost €6 and can be obtained from most travel agencies on the island.

Ferries dock at Gaïos' new port 1km east of the central square, though excursion boats dock by the central square and along the quay towards the new port.

International
You can reach Corfu and Igoumenitsa from the major ports in Italy, then transfer to a local ferry to Paxi.

Hellenic Mediterranean Lines (www.hml.gr) has high-season (late June to August) connections a few times a week between Brindisi and Paxi (from €40, 10 hours). **Italian Ferries** (www.italianferries.it) operates a high-speed catamaran service between Brindisi and Paxi (€73 or €110 depending on date of travel, 4¾ hours), via Corfu, daily from July to early September. Tickets and information can be obtained from **Paxos Magic Holidays** (☎ 2662 032 269; www.paxosmagic.com) in Gaïos.

HYDROFOIL
Popular passenger-only hydrofoils link Corfu and Paxi (and occasionally Igoumenitsa) from May until mid-October. There are one to three services daily, except Thursday, between Corfu and Paxi (€12.90, one hour), but only one service weekly between Paxi and Igoumenitsa (€11.70, 45 minutes) – on this route ferries are a much better option.

For detailed information in Paxi contact **Bouas Travel** (☎ 2662 032 401), or **Petrakis Lines** (☎ 2661 031 649) in Corfu.

Getting Around
The island's bus links Gaïos and Lakka via Longos up to five times daily in either direction (€1.50). A taxi from Gaïos to Lakka or Longos costs €8 to €10; the taxi rank in Gaïos is on the waterfront by the main square.

Alfa Hire (☎ 2662 032 505) in Gaïos rents cars, and **Rent a Scooter Vassilis** (☎ 2662 032 598), opposite the bus stop in Gaïos, has the biggest range of scooters and mopeds on the island. Most travel agencies offer the option of renting a small boat – this is another great way to get around.

GAÏOS ΓΑΪΟΣ
pop 560
Gaïos, on a wide, east-coast bay, is the island's capital. It's a delightfully photogenic place with crumbling, 19th-century pink, cream and whitewashed buildings. The fortified Agios Nikolaos Islet almost fills its harbour. Panagia Islet, named after its monastery, lies at the northern entrance to the bay.

The town's main square abuts the central waterfront, and the main street of Panagioti Kanga runs inland from here to another square where you'll find the bus stop (and the post office just beyond it). There are a couple of banks and ATMs in town; the only Internet café is Akis Bar (p424) in Lakka.

PAXI & ANTIPAXI

To Corfu
To Igoumenitsa

South
Kerkyra
Straits

Lakka
Kastanitha
Cave
Longos

To Parga

Fontana
Magazia
Paxi
Panagia Islet
Agios Nikolaos
Islet
Excursion Boat
Gaïos
Ortholithos
Stack
Bogdanatika
Agrilas Bay
Agrilas
Vellianitatika
Ozias
Trypitos
Mongonisi

Excursion Boat

Antipaxi
Vrika Beach
Voutoumi
Beach

Vigla
Agrapidia

IONIAN
SEA

There's no tourist office, but staff at **Paxos Magic Holidays** (☎ 2662 032 269; www.paxosmagic .com) are helpful and organise a number of excursions on the island, including walking tours and round-the-island boating trips.

The **Cultural Museum of Paxi**, in a former school on the southern waterfront, has an eclectic collection of local history, but unfortunately its hours are erratic – it's a case of dropping by to see if it's open (you're more likely to meet with success in the evening).

Sleeping

Accommodation in Paxi mostly consists of prebooked apartments and villas; all the island's agencies can help with bookings, and all produce glossy brochures detailing the properties on their books. Independent travellers can usually find somewhere private to stay, but advance bookings are advised in July and August.

San Giorgio Rooms to Rent (☎ 2662 032 223; d €55-60) This is the first accommodation option you'll encounter if you're walking from the new port towards the town centre. The large pension has bright and airy rooms, as well as studios with kitchenettes. It's up a set of steps above the waterfront (signposted), halfway between the port and the central square.

Clara Studios (☎ 2662 032 313; d €65; 🔀) Possibly the best-value accommodation in Gaïos is run by delightful Thekli. Her immaculate and well-equipped studios have everything you could need: kitchen, air-con, TV, balconies and wonderful views. They're tricky to find (up two sets of steps behind the museum) – call ahead and Thekli will meet you at the port.

Paxos Beach Hotel (☎ 2662 032 211; www.paxos beachhotel.gr; s/d/tr from incl breakfast & dinner €80/114/145; 🔀) This hillside bungalow complex, 1.5km south of Gaïos and overlooking the sea, has tastefully furnished rooms in a pretty setting. The complex has a private jetty, tennis court, beach, bar and restaurant.

Eating

Restaurant Mambo (☎ 2662 032 670; mains €6-12.50) Gaïos has a glut of good eating places, but countless locals and return visitors will tell you that this waterfront restaurant is the top choice for an evening meal, and the always-full outdoor tables attest to its popularity. There's the added attraction of perhaps the best baked feta in all of Greece, but other menu favourites include chicken souvlaki, grilled squid and meatballs.

Taverna Dodos (☎ 2662 032 265; mains €4.50-13) Tucked away in a colourful, lamp-lit courtyard garden in the southern part of town (back from the waterfront – follow the signs) is this friendly and informal family taverna. All the usual suspects are featured on the menu, and there are good choices for vegetarians.

George's Corner (sandwiches & pittas €1-5, mains €8) Cheap and cheerful, this no-frills spot is on the main square and offers great gyros ('to spin', Greek version of doner kebab) and pittas, plus an array of good-value snacks such as omelettes, burgers and pizza.

Self-catering supplies can be picked up at the Paxos Market & Delicatessen on the central square. There's a bakery next door to Café Kalimera Espresso Bar (the latter serves excellent coffee), just west of the central square on Panagioti Kanga.

LONGOS ΛΟΓΓΟΣ

The small fishing village-cum-resort of Longos is 5km north of Gaïos, and has a few beaches nearby. It's much smaller than Gaïos and has a more intimate feel. The village consists of little more than a cramped square and a winding waterfront, and it's a great base if you want a quieter stay.

Arthur House (☎ 2662 031 330; d €60, apt €80) Most of the accommodation in Longos is monopolised by tour companies, but if you follow the waterfront signs to Julia's Boat & Bike Hire (behind the village proper), you'll find this agreeable option, attached to the rental agency. The double rooms are studios, each with kitchen facilities and balconies, and the apartment has two bathrooms and two bedrooms that sleep up to five people.

Vassilis (☎ 2662 031 587; mains €6-13) Smart, waterfront Vassilis has upmarket menu offerings (including roast suckling pig) that have been widely praised, and indeed it's tough to get an outside table without prebooking.

I Gonia (☎ 2662 031 060; mains €5-12) Many locals recommend you head here for authentic, home-style fare, including good-value grilled meats.

Taxidi (☎ 2662 031 325) Right at the end of the Longos harbour, in a whitewashed building with two seafront terraces, is this inviting bar run by friendly Spiros. Even if you don't fancy one of his fresh melon and vodka mega-cocktails, it's worth calling in for some local advice. He usually knows several individuals who have private rooms to rent.

LAKKA ΛΑΚΚΑ

The picturesque harbour of Lakka lies at the end of a deep, narrow bay on the north coast and is a popular yachtie call. There are a couple of decent beaches around either side of the bay's headland, including Harami Beach (take the steps by Akis Bar to access the path), and there are some great walks in the area.

Routsis Holidays (☎ 2662 031 807; www.forthnet.gr /routsis-holidays) This helpful waterfront agency is the agent for many well-appointed apartments and villas in and around Lakka; most bookings are for weekly stays (but shorter stays can be accommodated). Properties include the following two reasonably priced hotels in the centre of the village.

Lefkothea (d per week €203) This hotel has simple rooms with shared bathroom and communal kitchen, and feels a little like a hostel.

Ilios (d per week €259) Similar to Lefkothea, but all rooms have private bathrooms.

La Rosa di Paxos (☎ 2662 031 471; mains €8-16) On the eastern side of the waterfront is this fine choice, with tables spilling over two terraces and surrounded by flowering plants. The international menu features well-prepared Greek cuisine but there's also a heavy Italian influence, including tiramisu for dessert. Plus there's lots of fresh seafood (priced per kilogram), and grilled vegetables in local olive oil.

In the evening, there are a number of central waterside bars perfectly placed for a drink or three. **Akis Bar** (☎ 2662 031 665) offers good meals, a pool table and seating out over the water, plus has the distinction of being the only place on Paxi where you can access the Internet (€4.50/7.50 per 30/60 minutes).

ANTIPAXI ΑΝΤΙΠΑΞΟΙ
pop 64

The diminutive satellite island of Antipaxi, 2km south of Paxi, is covered with grape vines from which excellent wine is produced. Caïques and tourist boats run daily from Gaïos and Lakka, and usually pull in at a couple of beaches offering swimming in exquisitely clear water.

Vrika Beach is sandy and gently sloping. Two **restaurants** serve the beachgoers, plus provide beach umbrellas for hire.

Spiros (☎ 2662 031 172, 2662 032 417) From Spiros Taverna, Spiros has accommodation on the island for those who like isolation. He offers a fully equipped villa sleeping up to six people for €180 per night.

A path links Vrika Beach with Voutoumi Beach, further south around a couple of headlands. **Voutoumi Beach** is very pretty, but is made up of large pebbles. A taverna set back from the beach serves hungry bathers. If you don't fancy just beach bumming, take a walk up to the scattered settlement of **Vigla**.

Boats (€6 return) to Antipaxi leave Gaïos at 10am and return from Vrika Beach around 5pm (they will pick up from Voutoumi Beach if requested). Boats run more often in the high season.

LEFKADA ΛΕΥΚΑΔΑ

pop 22,500

Lefkada, also referred to as Lefkas, is the fourth-largest island in the Ionians. Joined to the mainland by a narrow isthmus until the occupying Corinthians dug a canal in the 8th century BC, its 25m strait is spanned from the mainland by a causeway.

Lefkada is mountainous with several peaks over 1000m. It's also fertile, with cotton fields, dense olive groves, vineyards, fir and pine forests. There are 10 satellite islets off the heavily developed east coast, while the west coast boasts spectacular beaches.

Once a very poor island, Lefkada's beauty is also in its people, who display intense pride in their island. Many of the older women wear traditional costume.

Getting There & Away
AIR

Lefkada has no airport but Aktion airport, near Preveza on the mainland, is about 20km away. There are daily flights between Athens and Preveza (€50), and flights three times a week to Corfu (€35) and Kefallonia (€30). Contact **Olympic Airways** (☎ 2645 022 881; Dorpfeld 1, Lefkada Town) for bookings and information.

BUS

From Lefkada Town's **KTEL bus station** (☎ 2645 022 364; Golemi), on the main waterfront road, there are buses to Athens (€22.50, 5½ hours, four or five daily), Patra (€11, three hours, two weekly), Thessaloniki (€28.10, nine hours, at least two weekly) and Preveza (€2.10, 30 minutes, six daily).

FERRY

Four Islands Ferries runs a useful daily ferry service that sails to a complex, ever-changing schedule between Nydri (Lefkada), Frikes (Ithaki), Fiskardo (Kefallonia) and Vasiliki (Lefkada). Information and tickets can be obtained from **Borsalino Travel** (☎ 2645 092 528; Nydri) and **Samba Tours** (☎ 2645 031 520; Vasiliki). Nydri to Frikes costs €4.20 and takes 1½ hours. Sailing from Nydri to Fiskardo (€5) takes 2½ hours as the ferry goes via Frikes; Vasiliki to Fiskardo (€5, one hour) is a direct route.

Getting Around

There's no reliable bus connection between Lefkada and Aktion airport, near Preveza. Taxis are costly (around €30); a cheaper option is to take a taxi to Preveza and then a bus to Lefkada.

From Lefkada Town, frequent buses ply the east coast, with up to 15 services daily to Nydri and Vlyho, and four daily continuing to Vasiliki. West-coast services are not so good – three per day to Agios Nikitas, and limited high-season services to Kalamitsi and Athani. There are seven daily services to the inland village of Karya. Other villages are served by one or two buses daily. Sunday services are reduced.

Cars can be hired from **Europcar** (☎ 2645 022 538) and its neighbour, **Budget** (☎ 2645 025 274), both at Panagou 16 in Lefkada Town. Rent a bike or moped from nearby **Santas Motorcycle Rental** (☎ 2645 025 250), next to the Ionian Star Hotel. There are countless car- and bike-rental companies in Nydri.

LEFKADA TOWN

pop 6900

The island's main town is built on a promontory at the southeastern corner of a salty lagoon, which is used as a fish hatchery. It's not overly touristy, but visitors can spend a pleasant hour or two wandering the pretty, narrow alleys. The town was devastated by earthquakes in 1867 and 1948. After 1948 many houses were rebuilt in a unique style, with upper floors of painted sheet metal or corrugated iron that is strangely attractive, constructed in the hope they would withstand future earthquakes (damage from the 1953 earthquake was minimal).

A large earthquake shook Lefkada in August 2003, almost 50 years to the day after the one that devastated neighbouring Kefallonia and killed about 500 people. The 2003 earthquake measured 6.4 on the Richter scale but thankfully only caused minor damage.

Lefkada Town is a popular port of call for yachties, and a large new marina on the southern waterfront should be fully functional by the time you read this.

Orientation & Information

The vibrant main thoroughfare, Dorpfeld, starts just south of the causeway at Hotel Nirikos. This street is named after 19th-century archaeologist Wilhelm Dorpfeld, who is held in high esteem for postulating that Lefkada, not Ithaki, was the home of Odysseus. Dorpfeld leads to Plateia Agiou Spyridonos. After the square the thoroughfare's name changes to Ioannou Mela, and it's lined with interesting shops and cafés. Visitors will find essentials such as banks with ATMs and the post office on Ioannou Mela. There's no tourist office. The bus station is on the southern waterfront.

Check your email at the large **Internet Café** (Koutroubi), just off 8th Merarchias (next to the Commercial Bank of Greece). It's a few minutes' walk southwest of the bus station.

Sights

Housed in the modern Cultural Centre at the western end of Sikelianou is the **Archaeological Museum** (☎ 2645 021 635; admission €2; ☾ 8.30am-3pm Tue-Sun). It has a well-displayed and labelled collection of artefacts found on the island. One of the earliest objects, dating from the late 6th century BC, is a delicate terracotta figurine of nymphs dancing around a flute player. There's also extensive information on the archaeologist Dorpfeld and his theories.

Works by icon painters from the Ionian school are held in a **collection of post-Byzantine icons** (☎ 2645 022 502; Rontogianni; admission €1.50; ☾ 8.30am-1.30pm Tue-Sat, 6-8.15pm Tue & Thu). It's housed above the public library in a late-19th-century building off Ioannou Mela.

LEFKADA & ITS SATELLITES

0 ——— 4 km
0 ——— 2 miles

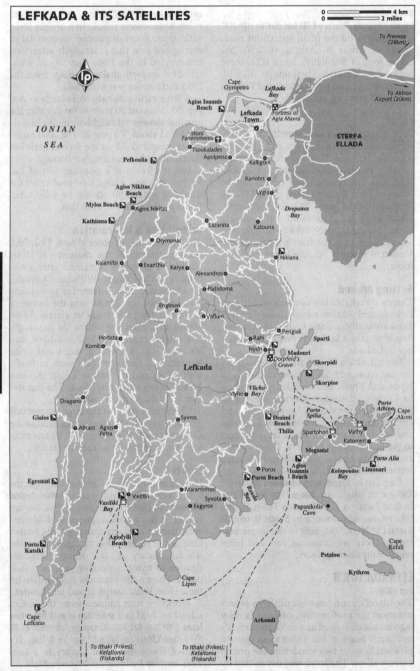

IONIAN ISLANDS

*IONIAN
SEA*

To Preveza
(28km)

To Aktion
Airport (20km)

STEREA
ELLADA

Cape
Gyropetra

Agios Ioannis
Beach

*Lefkada
Bay*

Lefkada
Town

Fortress of
Agia Mavra

Moni
Faneromenis

Tsoukalades

Apolpena

Kalligoni

Pefkoulia

Kariotes

Agios Nikitas
Beach

Lygia

*Drepanos
Bay*

Mylos Beach

Agios Nikitas

Kathisma

Lazarata

Katouna

Drymonas

Nikiana

Kalamitsi

Exanthia

Karya

Alexandros

Platistoma

Englouvi

Vafkeri

Hortata

Komili

Rahi

Perigiali

Sparti

Nydri

Madouri

*Dorpfeld's
Grave*

Skorpidi

Skorpios

*Porto
Athina*

Cape
Akoni

Dragano

*Vlicho
Bay*

Vlyho

*Porto
Spilia*

Gialos

Athani

Agios
Petra

Syvros

Desimi
Beach

Thilia

Spartohori

Vathy

Katomeri

Meganisi

Porto Alia

Egremni

Marantohori

Syvota

Poros

Poros Beach

Agios
Ioannis
Beach

*Kolopoulos
Bay*

Limonari

Vasiliki

*Vasiliki
Bay*

Evgyros

Papanikolis
Cave

Agiofylli
Beach

Petalou

Cape
Kefali

Kythros

Porto
Katsiki

Cape
Lipso

Cape
Lefkatas

Arkoudi

To Ithaki (Frikes);
Kefallonia
(Fiskardo)

To Ithaki (Frikes);
Kefallonia
(Fiskardo)

Lefkada

Skorpios

The 14th-century Venetian **Fortress of Agia Mavra** is just across the causeway, north of the town. It was first established by the crusaders but the remains mainly date from the Venetian and Turkish occupations of the island. **Moni Faneromenis**, 3km west of town, was founded in 1634, destroyed by fire in 1886 and rebuilt. The views of the lagoon and town are worth the ascent.

Sleeping

Hotel Santa Maura (☎ 2645 021 308; s/d incl breakfast €55/65; ☒) The nicest place to stay in Lefkada Town is this bright and breezy place off Dorpfeld, halfway between the main square and the waterfront. The immaculate rooms are large and airy, and each has a balcony, TV, fridge and air-con; you can enjoy breakfast in the courtyard garden. The owner speaks little English.

Pension Pirofani (☎ 2645 022 270; Dorpfeld; d €60; ☒) Opposite the Santa Maura, this modern pension has equally well-appointed and good-value rooms in the heart of town.

Ionion Star Hotel (☎ 2645 024 762; www.ionion star.gr; d €112; ☒ ☐ ☒) This is the most upmarket choice in Lefkada Town – a smartly refurbished hotel with facilities laid on thick, including pool, pool bar, café, restaurant and even a hairdressing salon. Rooms are modern and well equipped, if a little bland.

Eating

Regantos Taverna (☎ 2645 022 855; Vergioti 17; mains €3-10) Tucked away west of Dorpfeld (look for the sign near Plateia Agiou Spyridonos) is this atmospheric little place, painted an eye-catching combination of blue and yellow. The well-priced menu features authentic grilled and baked Greek standards, plus well-prepared seafood dishes.

The western side of the waterfront is lined with bars and cafés frequented by stylish Lefkadians; Il Posto, at the end of Dorpfeld, is a fashionable place to hang out. The cafés of Plateia Agiou Spyridonos are also well sited for people-watching. Look out for development on Golemi, as the new marina brings more visitors to the area.

Self-caterers can pick up supplies at the **supermarket** (Golemi) next to the bus station. There's a good **bakery** (Ioannou Mela 182) on the main street selling pies, pastries, cakes and bread.

NYDRI & SURROUNDS ΝΥΔΡΙ

A sleepy fishing village until not so long ago, Nydri, 16km south of Lefkada Town, has fallen hook, line and sinker to the lure of the tourist trade. Now it's a busy, commercialised town from where you can cruise around the islets of **Madouri**, **Sparti**, **Skorpidi** and **Skorpios**, plus visit **Meganisi**. Take an evening stroll along the harbourfront and shop around for the full range of **excursions** – a day trip taking in Meganisi and Skorpios costs €12 to €20 (€20 will get you a full-day excursion that visits Ithaki and Fiskardo on Kefallonia as well), and some operators include lunch in the price. If you'd prefer to explore the islets independently, motorboats can be hired from a number of agencies, including **Trident** (☎ 2645 092 978) on the main drag; the price is from €30 per day.

The privately owned Madouri islet, where the Greek poet Aristotelis Valaoritis (1824–79) spent his last 10 years, is off limits. It's not officially possible to land on Skorpios, where Aristotle, sister Artemis and children Alexander and Christina Onassis are buried in a cemetery visible from the sea, but you can swim off a sandy beach on the northern side of the island.

Sleeping & Eating

There are loads of rooms and studios in and around Nydri, though many are block-booked by tour companies. Try **Borsalino Travel** (☎ 2645 092 528) on the main street for assistance with accommodation and other tourist services.

Poros Beach Camping & Bungalows (☎ 2645 095 452; www.porosbeach.com.gr; camp sites per adult/tent €6/3.50, bungalows sleeping 2/4 €44/90; ☒) About 12km south of Nydri is this large, popular complex with accommodation for most budgets. It's at pretty Poros Beach (also known as Mikros Gialos), below the village of Poros, and facilities are excellent – there's a restaurant, minimarket, bar and swimming pool. Your own transport will be an asset.

Back in Nydri, get off the hectic main thoroughfare to find the more calming accommodation options, such as the following hotel.

Gorgona Hotel (☎ 2645 092 268; d €60) On a side street opposite the Avis car-rental office you'll find this friendly, family-run place set in a flower-filled garden, which offers simple, spotlessly clean rooms.

IONIAN ISLANDS

Ta Kalamia (☎ 2645 092 983; mezedes €5-7, mains €7-20) There are loads of eateries in Nydri catering to unadventurous tourist palates, but one of the most interesting is this place, on the main street and with a large alfresco dining area out the back. There's a great selection of mezedes to build a meal from, plus traditional Greek favourites, pricier seafood selections and some good vegetarian options.

VASILIKI ΒΑΣΙΛΙΚΗ

Purported to be *the* best windsurfing location in Europe, Vasiliki is a pretty fishing village with a below-average beach (but that's OK as most visitors are here to engage in more active pursuits than sunbathing and paddling). It attracts a largely youthful crowd, and to add to its appeal you can easily hop over to Kefallonia and Ithaki. Caïques take visitors to swim at the best beaches on the west coast, and a boat will also take you to unspoilt **Agiofylli Beach**, south of Vasiliki.

Sleeping & Eating

It's worth booking ahead for high-season travel. **Samba Tours** (☎ 2645 031 520), on the main road in the village, can help with accommodation and other travel services.

Pension Holidays (☎ 2645 031 426; d €50; ✍) Friendly Spiros offers simply furnished but well-equipped rooms with air-con, TV, fridge and balcony at reasonable prices. Head down the main street to the waterfront, turn left and you'll reach the pension.

Vasiliki Bay Hotel (☎ 2645 023 567; s/d €53/82; ✍) A smart hotel set 50m back from Alexander Restaurant on the harbour front, with well-equipped, bright and airy rooms.

Alexander Restaurant (☎ 2645 031 858; mains €4-11) Busy, popular Alexander, on the waterfront, has a wide-ranging menu that offers grilled meats and seafood, as well as loads of salad, pasta and oven-baked-pizza options.

WEST COAST

Beach lovers should skip Lefkada's east coast and head straight for the west. The sea here is possibly the best in the Ionian – an incredible pale turquoise blue that is almost iridescent – and most beaches feature pale golden or white sand. The best beaches include the long stretches of **Pefkoulia** and **Kathisma** in the north (the latter beach is becoming more developed and there are a few studios for rent here), and remote **Egremni** and breathtaking **Porto Katsiki**. These final two are a long drive south, signposted off the road leading to the island's southwestern promontory (a sanctuary of Apollo once stood at **Cape Lefkatas**). You'll pass roadside stalls set up by locals selling olive oil, honey and wine.

The town of **Agios Nikitas** is hardly Lefkada's best-kept secret, but it is the island's most picturesque and sophisticated resort. Most people staying here head to lovely **Mylos Beach** just around the headland (inaccessible by road – take a taxi boat from the tiny Agios Nikitas beach).

There are good accommodation options in Agios Nikitas.

Pension Elena (☎ 2645 097 385; d €50) Well situated (it's above the enticing Elena patisserie in the heart of the village), rooms are simple, comfortable and excellent value.

Hotel Agios Nikitas (☎ 2645 097 460; www.agios nikitas.com; d from €70, 4-person apt €95) A more

---

GET MOVING!

Many of the active-holiday companies in Vasiliki organise all-inclusive package trips from the UK or Germany that include flights and accommodation, plus tuition and/or equipment rental for sports such as windsurfing, sailing and mountain-biking. In the quieter periods, if these companies are not already booked solid, you might be able to rent equipment for a day or two or take a couple of lessons. Priority is, understandably, given to people who have come on one of their organised holidays, but it's worth a try if you're keen. The following companies have representation in town – walk along the beach and you'll spot their base.

Club Vass (UK ☎ 01920-484121; www.clubvass.com) Windsurfing instruction and equipment rental.

Happy Surf (Germany ☎ 030-3260 1733; www.happy-surf.de) German-based windsurfing company; more likely to offer day rental of boards to independent travellers.

Neilson Holidays (UK ☎ 0870-333 3356; www.neilson.co.uk) Windsurfing and mountain-biking packages.

Wildwind (UK ☎ 01920-484516; www.wildwind.co.uk) Catamaran rental and instruction.

Pottery at a market stall, Zakynthos (p437), Ionian Islands

SALLY WEBB

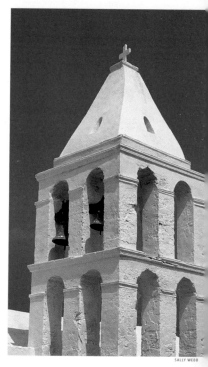

SALLY WEBB

Bell tower of the Church of Panagia (p445) in Hora, Kythira, Ionian Islands

Sidari, Corfu (p409), Ionian Islands

JOHN ELK III

Traditional house in Hora (p443),
Kythira, Ionian Islands

Beach near Lakka (p424), Paxi,
Ionian Islands

Painted house on Kefallonia (p429), Ionian Islands

upmarket option is this classy hotel on the coastal road just north of the village. You'll find tasteful rooms, studios and apartments in a pretty complex of whitewashed buildings set around a central courtyard.

Panorama (☎ 2645 033 476; d €35) In the village of Athani, Panorama makes a great pitstop en route to the southwestern beaches. Enjoy the views from the terrace and sample the taverna fare, or opt to make its cosy, no-frills rooms a low-key base for a few days of blissful beach-bumming.

MEGANISI ΜΕΓΑΝΗΣΙ

pop 1090

Meganisi has the largest population of Lefkada's three inhabited satellite islets. It's tranquil, with a verdant landscape and deep bays of turquoise water, fringed by pebbled beaches. It's visited primarily by yachties and is untouched by package-tour operators. It's well worth a visit and is easily accessible on a day trip, either independently or on one of the excursion boats from Nydri.

Meganisi has only three settlements: quiet **Spartohori**, with narrow laneways and pretty, flower-bedecked houses, perches on a plateau above Porto Spilia (where the ferry docks). A road ascends steeply to Spartohori or you can walk the 1km there up steps. **Vathy** is the island's second port, and beyond here the road climbs to **Katomeri**, about 1km away.

Sleeping & Eating

Hotel Meganisi (☎ 2645 051 240; d incl breakfast €67; ❄ ▣) The island's only hotel is the friendly, family-run Meganisi in Katomeri (well signposted from Vathy). It offers spotless, modern rooms with air-con, a lovely outdoor area, plus a restaurant serving traditional dishes.

Kiki's Corner (☎ 2645 051 134; vathi_blues@hotmail .com; ▣) This welcoming spot in Vathy offers superb pizza, pasta and gelati in a shady garden. There's a computer set up for Internet access, as well as currency exchange and a book exchange. In quieter periods, Kiki, the friendly, English-speaking owner, can usually help travellers find private accommodation in Vathy and surrounds.

Other dining options on the island include **Taverna Porto Vathy**, an idyllic fish taverna right next to the ferry quay in Vathy, and **Taverna Porto Spilia**, a sprawling, bustling waterside eatery down in the ferry-docking area below

Spartohori. **Taverna Lakis**, on Spartohori's square, offers home-style Greek fare and also features evenings of traditional music and dance (often attended by tourists from Nydri, brought over by excursion boat).

Getting There & Away

The Meganisi ferry boat runs about six times daily between Nydri (the southern end of the quay) and Meganisi (€1.70, 25 to 40 minutes). It usually calls in first at Porto Spilia and then into Vathy before heading back to Nydri.

Whether you're visiting for a day or plan to stay longer, you may want to bring over a bicycle or moped on the ferry from Nydri, as there's nowhere to rent transport on the island. Alternatively, rent a small motorboat from Nydri for your visit.

KEFALLONIA ΚΕΦΑΛΛΟΝΙΑ

pop 35,600

Kefallonia, the largest of the Ionian Islands, has highlights including rugged, towering mountains, pretty villages and some great beaches. The highest point, Mt Enos (1627m), is the Mediterranean's only mountain with a unique fir forest species, Abies Cephalonica. While not as tropical as Corfu, Kefallonia has many species of heavily scented herbs and wildflowers.

Kefallonia's capital is Argostoli but the main port is Sami, 25km northeast (useful ferry services also run from Poros and Fiskardo). As the island is so big and mountainous, travelling between towns can be time-consuming.

Getting There & Away

AIR

There's at least one daily flight between Kefallonia and Athens (€65), and connections to other Ionian Islands, including Zakynthos (€28) and Corfu (€35). **Olympic Airways** (☎ 2671 028 808; R Vergoti 1, Argostoli) can help with information and bookings.

BUS

There are a few options for the bus journey between Athens and Kefallonia (via Patra), utilising the various ferry services to the mainland: daily buses ply the Argostoli–Poros–Kyllini–Patra–Athens route; the

IONIAN ISLANDS

Argostoli–Kyllini–Patra–Athens route; and the Argostoli–Sami–Patra–Athens route. All cost around €27 and take around seven hours (prices include ferry tickets). For information contact the **KTEL bus station** (☎ 2671 022 276) on the southern waterfront in Argostoli.

FERRY
Domestic

There are frequent ferry services to Kyllini in the Peloponnese from both Poros (€6.50, 1½ hours, two to three daily) and Argostoli (€10.50, 2½ hours, one or two daily).

Blue Star Ferries (www.bluestarferries.com) has two ferries daily connecting Sami with Patra (€11.50, 2½ hours) and Vathy or Piso Aetos on Ithaki (€4.50, one hour).

Four Islands Ferries runs a daily ferry in the high season linking Sami with Piso Aetos (€2.50, 40 minutes), and Astakos on the mainland (€7, three hours direct from Astakos to Sami, 3½ hours from Sami to Astakos via Piso Aetos). The same company operates a useful daily ferry service that sails to a complex, ever-changing schedule between Nydri (Lefkada), Frikes (Ithaki), Fiskardo (Kefallonia) and Vasiliki (Lefkada). Sailing from Fiskardo to Frikes (€3) takes just under an hour; Fiskardo–Vasiliki (€5) takes one hour; Fiskardo–Nydri (€5) takes 1½ hours direct, or 2½ hours via Frikes. Information and tickets for these routes can be obtained from **Blue Sea Travel** (☎ 2674 023 007; Sami) and **Nautilus Travel** (☎ 2674 041 440; Fiskardo).

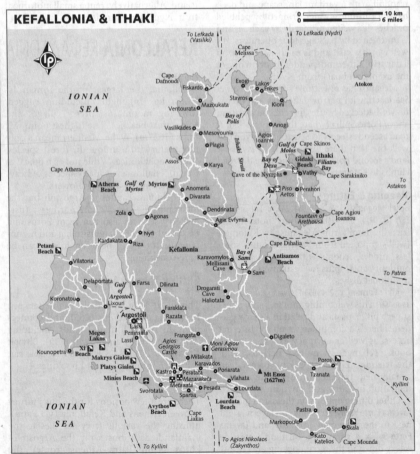

KEFALLONIA & ITHAKI

From Pesada in the south there are two high-season services daily travelling to Agios Nikolaos (€4, 1¼ hours), on the northern tip of Zakynthos. There's no bus to the remote port of Pesada, and few buses from Agios Nikolaos, making crossing without your own transport difficult (and costly if you rely on taxis). Another option is to travel from Argostoli or Poros to Kyllini, then catch a ferry from Kyllini to Zakynthos Town.

International
In the high season there are regular ferries plying the route between Patra, Sami, Igoumenitsa and Brindisi in Italy (Kefallonia–Brindisi costs €50 and takes around 14 hours). To get to other ports in Italy, you need to take the ferry first from Sami to Patra.

Tickets and information can be obtained from **Vassilatos Shipping** (☎ 2671 022 618; Metaxa 54, Argostoli), opposite the port authority, and from helpful **Blue Sea Travel** (☎ 2674 023 007; Sami), on the waterfront.

Getting Around
TO/FROM THE AIRPORT
The airport is 9km south of Argostoli. There's no airport bus; a taxi costs around €10.

BUS
From Argostoli's **bus station** (☎ 2671 022 276) on the southern waterfront there are nine buses daily to the Lassi Peninsula (€1), three buses to Sami (€2.50), two to Poros (€3.50), two to Skala (€3) and two to Fiskardo (€4). There's a daily east-coast service linking Kato Katelios with Skala, Poros, Sami, Agia Evfymia and Fiskardo. No buses operate on Sunday.

CAR & MOTORCYCLE
The major resorts have loads of places offering cars and bikes for rent. In Argostoli, cars can be hired from **Reliable Rent a Car** (☎ 2671 023 613; R Vergoti 3) and **CBR Travel** (☎ 2671 022 770; Vallianou 3) at the southern end of the central square. Rent motorcycles from **Sunbird** (☎ 2671 023 723; Antoni Tritsi 139), with branches in a number of resorts.

FERRY
Car ferries run hourly from about 7.30am to 10.30pm between Argostoli and Lixouri, on the island's western peninsula. The journey takes 30 minutes, and tickets (€1.10/3.60/1 per person/car/bike) are sold on board.

ARGOSTOLI ΑΡΓΟΣΤΟΛΙ
pop 8900
Argostoli, unlike Zakynthos Town, was not restored to its former Venetian splendour after the 1953 earthquake. It's a modern, lively port set on a peninsula, and offers good accommodation and eating options, plus shopping and nightlife.

Orientation & Information
The bus station is on the southern waterfront near the causeway; the main ferry quay is at the waterfront's northern end. The centre of Argostoli's activity is Plateia Vallianou, the huge palm-treed central square up from the waterfront off 21 Maïou, and its surrounding streets. Other hubs are the waterfront (Antoni Tristi, which becomes Ioannou Metaxa to the south), and pedestrianised Lithostrotou, two blocks inland, lined with smart shops and cafés.

The **EOT** (☎ 2671 022 248; ☾ 8am-2.30pm Mon-Fri) is on the northern waterfront beside the port police. In the high season (July and August) it also usually opens 5pm to 9.30pm weekdays, and in August it often opens on weekends.

There are banks with ATMs along the northern waterfront and on Lithostrotou. The post office is on Lithostrotou, and **Excelixis** (Minoos), signposted just off Lithostrotou (behind the Greek Orthodox Church), offers Internet access.

Sights & Activities
Argostoli's **Archaeological Museum** (☎ 2671 028 300; R Vergoti; admission €3; ☾ 8.30am-3pm Tue-Sun) has a well-displayed collection of island relics, including Mycenaean finds from tombs. The **Korgialenio History & Folklore Museum** (☎ 2671 028 835; R Vergoti; admission €3; ☾ 9am-2pm Mon-Sat) has a worthwhile collection of traditional costumes, furniture and tools, items that belonged to British occupiers, and photographs of pre- and post-earthquake Argostoli.

KTEL (☎ 2671 022 276) organises good-value **day tours** of the island (taking in Drogarati Cave, Mellisani Cave, a subterranean lake, and Fiskardo; entrance fees not included) for €20, and day trips to Ithaki (€33) and Zakynthos (€34). Popular **glass-bottom boat trips** (☎ 2671 023 956) leave daily from just south of Argostoli's port (€50/35 adult/child for a full day, including beach barbecue lunch). Book ahead.

The town's closest sandy beaches are **Makrys Gialos** and **Platys Gialos**, 5km south in the package-resort area of Lassi. Regular buses serve the area.

Sleeping

The EOT should be able to give you a list of locals offering inexpensive rooms for rent.

Vivian Villa (☎ 2671 023 396; villaviv@otenet.gr; Deladetsima 9; d €50-59, 4-person apt €100; ☒) The nicest, most welcoming place in town is this small complex, run by super-friendly, English-speaking Vivian and Nick. They offer spacious, spotless accommodation (including studios) in the northern part of town, and if they're full, they'll always attempt to find you somewhere else to stay.

Kyknos Studios (☎ 2671 023 398; M Geroulanou 4; d €45) These pleasant, simple studios are a good-value option. They're set behind a garden in a reasonably quiet street – you'd never know Plateia Vallianou was only two minutes' walk away.

There's a string of hotels along the waterfront and some around the bustling Plateia Vallianou, with prices to suit most budgets.

Hotel Ionian Plaza (☎ 2671 025 581; Plateia Vallianou; s/d €54/78; ☒) Argostoli's smartest hotel is the landmark Ionian Plaza on Plateia Vallianou. The marble-decorated lobby and public areas are impressively stylish; the rooms have balconies overlooking the square and offer all you'll need for a comfortable stay.

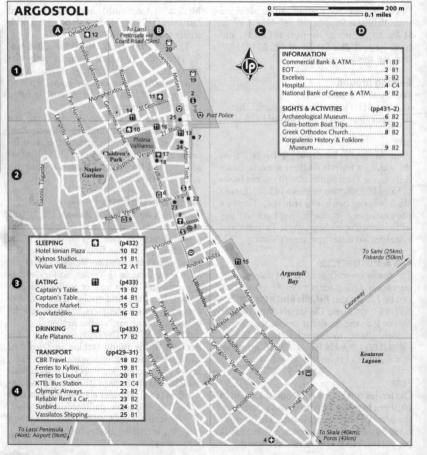

ARGOSTOLI

0 ——— 200 m
0 ——— 0.1 miles

INFORMATION
Commercial Bank & ATM...............1 B3
EOT...2 B1
Excelixis...3 B2
Hospital..4 C4
National Bank of Greece & ATM.......5 B2

SIGHTS & ACTIVITIES (pp431–2)
Archaeological Museum....................6 B2
Glass-bottom Boat Trips..................7 B2
Greek Orthodox Church....................8 B2
Korgialenio History & Folklore
    Museum.....................................9 B2

SLEEPING ☐ (p432)
Hotel Ionian Plaza 10 B2
Kyknos Studios.............................11 B1
Vivian Villa..................................12 A1

EATING ☐ (p433)
Captain's Table.............................13 B2
Captain's Table.............................14 B1
Produce Market............................15 C3
Souvlatzidiko................................16 B2

DRINKING ☐ (p433)
Kafe Platanos...............................17 B2

TRANSPORT (pp429–31)
CBR Travel...................................18 B2
Ferries to Kyllini...........................19 B1
Ferries to Lixouri..........................20 B1
KTEL Bus Station..........................21 C4
Olympic Airways...........................22 B2
Reliable Rent a Car.......................23 B2
Sunbird.......................................24 B2
Vassilatos Shipping.......................25 B1

To Lassi Peninsula (4km); Airport (9km)

To Sami (25km); Fiskardo (50km)

Argostoli Bay

Koutavos Lagoon

To Skala (40km); Poros (43km)

Eating & Drinking

Captain's Table (☎ 2671 023 896; Rizospaston 3; mains €5-20) Just off Plateia Vallianou (behind Hotel Ionian Plaza), upmarket Captain's is the place to go for a splurge, and there's live Greek music nightly. Choosing seafood or fish can inflate the bill considerably – you'll do well with any of the meat dishes (including surprising offerings like ostrich fillet), as well as the reasonably priced salads, pastas and Greek classics. There's a sister restaurant, also called the **Captain's Table** (☎ 2671 027 170; 21 Maïou; mains €5-15), on the waterfront. This place is open all day and also offers high-quality food, but there's a more casual feel and more casual prices. Both restaurants have good kids' menus.

Among the pricey cafés on Plateia Vallianou is the popular Souvlatzidiko, next to Hotel Aeon, offering quick and tasty gyros for about €1.50. Pick up self-catering supplies from the huge waterfront produce market. Opposite are bakeries and grocery stores.

The main hub for nightlife is Plateia Vallianou, with plenty of café-bars, tables spilling out onto the road and music pumping until late. Fashionable **Kafe Platanos** (☎ 2671 028 282; Plateia Vallianou) is the classiest of the bunch, with chandeliers inside and tables and wicker chairs scattered around a large plane tree outside.

SAMI & SURROUNDS ΣΑΜΗ

pop 1220

Sami, 25km northeast of Argostoli and the main port of Kefallonia, was also devastated by the 1953 earthquake. It now has undistinguished buildings, but its setting is pretty, nestled in a bay and flanked by steep hills. It's worth an overnight stay to visit the nearby caves and beach. All facilities, including a post office and banks, are in town. Buses for Argostoli usually meet ferries.

Be sure to visit gorgeous **Antisamos Beach**, 4km northeast of Sami. The long, stony beach is in a lovely green setting backed by hills. The drive here is also a highlight, offering dramatic views.

Spectacular **Mellisani Cave** (admission incl boat trip €5; ☼ 9am-7pm) is a subterranean sea-water lake. When the sun is overhead its rays shine through an opening in the cave ceiling, lighting the water's many shades of blue. The cave is 2.5km from Sami, well signposted

beyond the seaside village of Karavomylos. The large **Drogarati Cave** (admission €3.50; ☼ 9am-8pm) is worth a visit for its impressive stalactites. It's signposted from the Argostoli road, 4km from Sami.

The fishing village of **Agia Evfymia**, is 10km north of Sami, and en route there are coves ideal for swimming. Agia Evfymia is a popular yachting stop, and there are a few hotels and studios here, as well as motorboat hire and a diving operator.

Sleeping & Eating

Karavomylos Beach Camping (☎ 2674 022 480; www.camping-karavomilos.gr; camp sites per adult/tent €6/3.50; ⌨) This well-kept beachfront camping ground is 800m west of Sami – if you're walking, turn right from the quay and follow the coast. It's a large, shady place and offers all manner of facilities: minimarket, laundry, restaurant, playground and Internet access.

Hotel Melissani (☎ 2674 022 464; d €53) This quirky, older-style hotel is in a quiet part of Sami, signposted from the eastern end of the waterfront. Rooms are smallish but comfortable and eclectically decorated; all offer comforts such as balcony or terrace, TV, fridge and fan (some have air-con).

Riviera (☎ 2674 022 777; mains €3.50-8.50) Riviera is a welcoming waterfront café-pizzeria in Sami where you can while away an hour or so with good coffee, breakfast or a light meal (salad, pizza, pasta etc). Simple, inexpensive rooms are offered above the café for €45. Rooms at the front enjoy harbour views, but rooms at the rear are quieter.

ASSOS ΑΣΟΣ

Tiny Assos is a gem of whitewashed and pastel houses, straddling the isthmus of a peninsula on which stands a Venetian fortress. Assos was damaged in the 1953 earthquake, but sensitively restored with the help of a donation from the city of Paris. There's good accommodation along the road into town, much of it block-booked by upmarket tour operators.

Linardos Studios (☎ 2674 051 563; d €65) At the base of the road, Linardos is home to immaculate double studios enjoying views over the village.

Pension Gerania (☎ 2674 051 526; www.pension gerania.gr; d €65; ▨) Set in lush gardens at the back of the village (look for the small sign on the right as you come into town – it also

THE CULT OF CAPTAIN CORELLI

Kefallonia has always seen its fair share of package tourists, but not on the same scale as Corfu and Zakynthos – until recently. The island has received unprecedented publicity in the past few years thanks to Louis de Bernières' novel *Captain Corelli's Mandolin*, some high-profile visitors and heavy Hollywood exposure. It was on a package holiday to Kefallonia that de Bernières, a former soldier, received his inspiration for the story. Instead of relaxing on the beach he spent his holiday learning about the island's history, and the resulting book tells the emotional story of a young Italian army officer sent to Kefallonia during WWII and his relationships with the locals, his fellow soldiers and German commanders. Copies of the book are available in almost every minimarket and bookshop on the island.

Publicity for the island reached fever pitch in the summer of 2001 with the release of the movie based on the book, starring Nicholas Cage as Corelli and co-starring Penelope Cruz and John Hurt (plus hundreds of Kefallonian extras). The movie was filmed entirely on location in Kefallonia in 2000, largely in and around the town of Sami. You'll be disappointed if you see the film then visit Sami hoping to marvel at its pretty Venetian architecture. Sami was largely reduced to rubble in the 1953 earthquake that devastated most of the island, and the town you see in the movie was a cleverly constructed set.

indicates parking), this is an excellent option. Rooms are spotless and well equipped, with fridge, air-con, balconies and great views.

AROUND ASSOS

One of Greece's most breathtaking beaches can be found at **Myrtos**, 13km south of Assos. Pull off the hair-raising stretch of road north to Fiskardo to admire and photograph the white sand and exquisite blue water set between tall limestone cliffs. There are minimal facilities at the beach itself (just a kiosk selling basic food and drinks), and you may want to take your own beach mat and umbrella – renting a sunlounge and umbrella costs a hefty €9. Be aware that the water here becomes deep quite quickly and there can be a strong undercurrent.

FISKARDO ΦΙΣΚΑΡΔΟ
pop 225

Fiskardo, 50km north of Argostoli, was the only Kefallonian village not devastated by the 1953 earthquake. Framed by cypress-mantled hills and with fine Venetian buildings, it's a delightful place, even if it is a little dolled up for the tourists. It's especially popular with yachties (and the higher prices reflect its popularity and chi-chi status).

The **Fiskardo Nautical and Environmental Club** (☎ 2674 041 182; www.fnec.gr) is a nonprofit organisation active in the community (volunteers welcome), running a small local museum (up the stairs next to the church) and environ-

mental information centre, as well as offering a variety of scuba-diving activities.

Sleeping & Eating

Again, most accommodation is block-booked by upmarket British tour companies. It will be tough to find accommodation in the high season if you haven't prebooked. At other times it's OK, but prices are higher than other parts of the island. **Pama Travel** (☎ 2674 041 033; pamatvl@otenet.gr; 🖳) can help with travel services including, car and boat hire.

Regina's Rooms (☎ 2674 041 125; d €50-60) Behind the waterfront, by the car park area, is this reasonably priced place run by friendly Regina. Rooms are newly renovated and offer simple, comfortable furnishings. There's a communal kitchen, and some rooms have kitchenettes and/or balconies enjoying views over the water.

Stella Apartments (☎ 2674 041 211; www.stella-apartments.gr; d €79; apt €162; 🔀) There's excellent accommodation on offer at this yellow-and-green complex about 800m from the harbourfront. Stella's immaculate studios are spacious and well equipped; each has kitchen, TV, phone, air-con and balcony. There are also large apartments perfect for families, sleeping up to five. Across from the apartments are steps leading down to a cove for swimming.

You can't miss the **Captain's Cabin** (☎ 2674 041 007; mains €6.50-14) on the seafront, a popular watering hole for visiting yachties. There's a short menu offering a few Greek favourites (meatballs, mousakas), as well as pizza, pasta and seafood. Next door is an excellent bakery. For more authentic choices, try **Lagoudera** (☎ 2674 041 275; mains €5-9), in a pretty setting just back from the harbourfront. It's known for its grilled meat and serves well-priced gyros, souvlaki, steaks and lamb chops.

Getting There & Away
You can get to Fiskardo by ferry from Lefkada and Ithaki or by bus from Argostoli. The bus will drop you off on the road that bypasses Fiskardo. Walk across the car park, descend the steps to the left of the church and continue ahead to Fiskardo's central square and waterfront.

ITHAKI IΘAKH

pop 3080
Ithaki, or ancient Ithaca, was Odysseus' long-lost home, the island where his wife, the stoical Penelope, patiently awaited her husband's return. She told her suitors, who believed Odysseus was dead, that she would choose one of them once she had completed the shroud she was weaving. Cunningly, she unravelled it every night in order to keep her suitors at bay.

Ithaki comprises two large peninsulas joined by a narrow isthmus, and is separated from Kefallonia by a narrow strait. Its interior is mountainous and rocky, with pockets of pine forest, stands of cypresses, olive groves and vineyards. Because of its lack of good beaches, Ithaki doesn't attract large crowds, but it's a fine place to spend a quiet holiday.

Getting There & Away
Blue Star Ferries (www.bluestarferries.com) has two ferries daily connecting Vathy or Piso Aetos with Patra (€12.20, 3½ hours) via Sami (€4.50, one hour) on Kefallonia. (Piso Aetos, on Ithaki's west coast, has no settlement; taxis usually meet boats.)

Four Islands Ferries runs a daily ferry in the high season between Piso Aetos, Sami and Astakos on the mainland (€6.50, 2¾ hours direct from Piso Aetos to Astakos, four hours from Astakos to Piso Aetos via Sami). It also operates a useful daily ferry service that sails to a complex, ever-changing schedule between Nydri (Lefkada), Frikes

(Ithaki), Fiskardo (Kefallonia) and Vasiliki (Lefkada). Sailing from Frikes to Fiskardo (€3) takes just under an hour; Frikes–Vasiliki (€4.20) goes via Fiskardo and takes two hours; Frikes–Nydri costs €4.20 and takes 1½ hours. Information and tickets for these routes can be obtained from **Delas Tours** (☎ 2674 032 104) on the main square in Vathy.

Getting Around
The island's one bus runs twice daily (Monday to Friday only) between Kioni and Vathy via Stavros and Frikes (€2). It's primarily a bus for getting children to/from school (and it doesn't run in the summer school holiday period) so its limited schedule is not well suited to travellers on day trips. Taxis are expensive (eg €20 for the Vathy–Frikes trip), so your best bet is to hire a moped or car (or a motorboat) to get around. In Vathy, **Rent a Scooter** (☎ 2674 032 840) is down the laneway opposite the port authority, and **AGS Rent a Car** (☎ 2674 032 702) is on the western waterfront beside the town hall.

VATHY BAΘY
pop 1820
Old mansions rise up from the seafront of Vathy, also known as Ithaki Town. Its centre is small, with a few twisting streets, a large central square, cafés, restaurants and a few tourist shops.

The ferry quay is on the western side of the bay. To reach the central square of Plateia Efstathiou Drakouli, turn left and follow the waterfront.

Ithaki has no tourist office, but there are travel agencies on the main square that can help with tourist information. Banks with ATMs are also on the main square, as is the post office. Kafe Steki, next to the Fuji photo shop on the main square, offers Internet access.

Sights & Activities
Behind Hotel Mentor is a small **archaeological museum** (☎ 2674 032 200; admission free; ☼ 8.30am-3pm Tue-Sun). The charming **nautical & folklore museum** (admission €1; ☼ 9am-1pm Tue-Sat) is housed in an old generating station just back from the waterfront (signposted), and displays clothing (including traditional dress), household items and furniture, as well as shipping paraphernalia.

Boat excursions leave from Vathy harbour in the summer months and include a trip around Ithaki and to Fiskardo (€30), and a day trip to Lefkada and Meganisi (€30). There's also a taxi boat to **Gidaki Beach**, north-east of Vathy and inaccessible by road.

Sleeping

Dimitrios Maroudas Rooms & Apartments (☎ 26/4 032 751; d €35, 4-person apt €60) Just off the eastern waterfront, this place is sign-posted 180m beyond the OTE (two blocks behind Century Music Club). It's a family-run place providing clean, simple budget rooms (with shared bathroom), plus apartments with private kitchen and bathroom.

Captain Yiannis Hotel (☎ 2674 033 311; d €70-80; ❄ ❄) This sprawling complex is on the opposite side of the harbour to the ferry dock, about 1km from town. You'll know you've reached it by the smart swimming pool and bar area (there's also a tennis court). There's a feeling of space, as the clean, comfortable rooms and well-equipped apartments are well spread out over the property.

Hotel Omirikon (☎ 2674 033 596; www.omirikon hotel.com; d €100; ❄) On the eastern waterfront, about 10 minutes' walk from the centre of town, is this small, sophisticated hotel. It's home to high-quality studio apartments, each with modern furnishings, kitchen and living area, plus balcony overlooking the water. There's also a Jacuzzi for guests.

Eating

Try the sweet, gooey *rovani,* the local speciality made with rice, honey and cloves, at one of the patisseries on or near the main square.

Sirens (☎ 2674 033 001; mains €6-15) This classy place is tucked away well back from the waterfront, not far from the bank. It's run by locals who have returned to Ithaki after migrating to New York and their imaginative menu offers lots of great small dishes you can make a meal from. Baked cheese dishes are the speciality – try the delicious baked fetta with tomato and peppers, or baked artichokes with cheese. There are also tempting pasta, seafood and vegetarian dishes.

Kantouni (☎ 2674 032 918; mains €4-15) Make your selection from a kitchen full of freshly prepared, authentic home-style fare at this restaurant on the waterfront. There's a great selection of cheap, hearty, oven-baked cas-

serole dishes (€4 to €7) such as lamb with potatoes and beef in red sauce, plus pricier grilled meats and seafood.

Drakouli Café (☎ 2674 033 435) Young locals meet at this stylish café-bar in a waterfront mansion, which was the home of George Drakoulis, a wealthy Ithakan shipowner. It's a pleasant spot for a drink, but the snack menu is limited.

Other popular café-bars line the eastern harbour front.

AROUND ITHAKI

Ithaki has a few sites associated with the Homer tale, *The Odyssey.* Though none is terribly impressive, you may enjoy (or endure) the scenic walks to them. The most renowned is the **Fountain of Arethousa**, in the island's south, where Odysseus' swineherd, Eumaeus, brought his pigs to drink and where Odysseus, on his return to Ithaca, went to meet him disguised as a beggar after receiving directions from the goddess Athena. The walk takes 1½ to two hours; take a hat and plenty of water.

A shorter trek is to the **Cave of the Nymphs**, where Odysseus concealed the gifts of gold, copper and fine fabrics that the Phaeacians had given him. The cave is signposted from the town. Below the cave is the **Bay of Dexa** (good for swimming), thought to be ancient Phorkys where the Phaeacians disembarked and laid the sleeping Odysseus on the sand.

The location of Odysseus' palace has been much disputed and archaeologists have been unable to find conclusive evidence; present-day archaeologists speculate it was on a hill near **Stavros**.

Homeric legends aside, 14km north of Vathy is sleepy **Anogi**, the old capital. The restored 12th-century church of **Agia Panagia** has beautiful Byzantine frescoes. The church is usually locked; visit the neighbouring kafeneio, where there's often a local happy to show you inside.

There's not much to the laid-back fishing village of **Frikes**, set in among windswept cliffs. There are a couple of accommodation options, a few waterfront restaurants, a popular bar and that's it.

Kioni ΚΙΌΝΙ

Four kilometres southeast of Frikes is Kioni, one of Ithaki's best-kept secrets. It's a small village draped around a verdant hillside

ODYSSEUS & ITHAKI

Ithaki (Ithaca) has long been the symbolic image for the end of a long journey. For mythical hero Odysseus (Ulysses), Ithaki was the home he left to fight in the Trojan War. According to the often wild tales recounted in Homer's *The Iliad*, though more specifically in *The Odyssey*, it took the wily hero Odysseus 10 long years to return home to Ithaki from Troy on the Asia Minor coast.

Tossed by tempestuous seas, attacked by sea monsters, delayed by a cunning siren yet helped on his way by friendly Phaeacians, Odysseus finally made landfall on Ithaki. Here, disguised as a beggar, he teamed up with his son Telemachus and his old swineherd Eumaeus, and slayed a castleful of conniving suitors who had been eating him out of home and fortune while trying unsuccessfully to woo the ever-patient and faithful Penelope, Odysseus' long-suffering wife who had waited 20 years for him to return.

Despite Ithaki owing its fame to such illustrious classical connections, no mention of the island appears in writings of the Middle Ages. As late as AD 1504 Ithaki was almost uninhabited following repeated depredations by pirates. The Venetians were obliged to induce settlers from neighbouring islands to repopulate Ithaki. Yet the island is described in considerable detail in *The Odyssey*, which matches in many respects the physical nature of the island today. The 'Fountain of Arethousa' has been identified with a spring rising at the foot of a sea cliff in the south of the island and the 'Cave of the Nymphs' with a fairly nondescript cave up from the Bay of Phorkys. However, many Homerists have been hard-pressed to ascribe other locales described in *The Odyssey* – particularly Odysseus' castle – to actual places on the islands since scant archaeological remains assist the researcher.

spilling down to a picture-perfect little harbour where yachties congregate. There are tavernas and a couple of bars, though it's not the best place to swim. Instead, seek out the little bays between Kioni and Frikes.

Maroudas Apartments (☎ 2674 031 691; d €44) This place, opposite the doctor's surgery on the narrow road into the village, offers some of Kioni's cheapest accommodation – and it's in a great location, so book ahead (or inquire in person at the nearby souvenir store, across from the small supermarket). Look past the slightly tired decor and you'll find well-maintained, well-equipped studios.

Captain's Apartments (☎ 2674 031 481; www .captains-apartments.gr; d €60, 4-person apt €80) Signposted as you enter Kioni are these excellent studios and apartments owned by the friendly Dellaporta family. Each of the tastefully furnished and spacious units has a phone, satellite TV and outdoor terrace or private balcony.

Kalipso (☎ 2674 031 066; mains €6-12) Sit right beside the colourful small boats lining this tiny harbour and enjoy inviting Kalipso's house speciality, onion pie. There's also a selection of seafood, grilled meats, pastas and traditional dishes, such as rabbit stifado, lamb *kleftiko* (lamb in a clay pot) to enjoy.

ZAKYNTHOS ΖΑΚΥΝΘΟΣ

pop 39,020

Zakynthos (*zahk*-in-thos), also known as Zante, has inspired many superlatives. The Venetians called it Fior' di Levante (Flower of the Orient); the poet Dionysios Solomos wrote that 'Zakynthos could make one forget the Elysian Fields'. Indeed, it is an island of exceptional natural beauty and outstanding beaches. Unfortunately, in many coastal areas it has been the victim of the worst manifestations of package tourism. Even worse, tourism is endangering the loggerhead turtle, or Caretta caretta (for more details see the boxed text 'At Loggerheads' on p441). Still, if you're travelling outside of the high season and avoid resorts such as Laganas, you can enjoy a relaxing holiday here.

Getting There & Away

AIR

There's at least one daily flight between Zakynthos and Athens (€74), and connections to other Ionian Islands including Kefallonia (€28) and Corfu (€45). **Olympic Airways** (☎ 2695 028 611; Alexandrou Roma 16, Zakynthos Town) can assist with information on flights and bookings.

BUS

KTEL (☎ 2695 022 255; Filita 42) operates five buses daily between Zakynthos Town and Patra (€5.20, 3½ hours), and five daily connections to/from Athens (€22.60, six hours). There's also a twice-weekly service to Thessaloniki (€32.80). Budget an addition €5.10 for the ferry fare between Zakynthos and Kyllini.

FERRY
Domestic

Depending on the season, between three and six ferries operate daily between Zakynthos Town and Kyllini in the Peloponnese (€5.10, 1¼ hours). Tickets can be obtained from the **Zakynthos Shipping Cooperative** (☎ 2695 041 500;

Lombardou 40) in Zakynthos Town, next to the Hertz car-rental outlet.

From the northern port of Agios Nikolaos a car ferry shuttles across to Pesada in southern Kefallonia twice daily from May to October (€4, 1¼ hours). There's no bus from Pesada to anywhere else on Kefallonia, and few buses to Agios Nikolaos, making crossing without your own transport quite difficult – not to mention costly if you rely on taxis.

International

Hellenic Mediterranean Lines (www.hml.gr) has high-season (July and August) connections once or twice a week between Brindisi and Zakynthos (€54 to €64, about 18 hours).

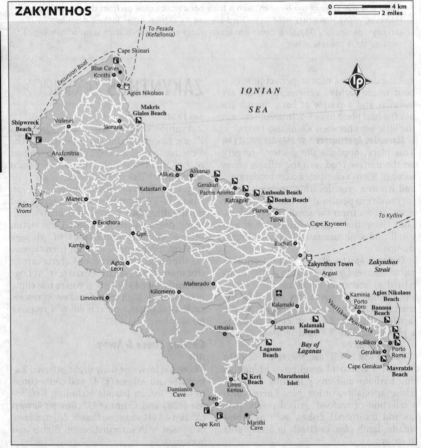

ZAKYNTHOS

Getting Around

There's no bus service between Zakynthos Town and the airport, 6km to the southwest. A taxi costs €8 to €10.

Frequent buses go from Zakynthos Town's **bus station** (☎ 2695 022 255; Filita 42), one block back from the waterfront, to the developed resorts of Alikes, Tsilivi, Argasi, Laganas and Kalamaki (€1). Bus services to other villages are poor (one or two daily).

You'll be tripping over car- and moped-rental places in the larger resorts. Many international car-rental companies have offices at the airport as well as in Zakynthos Town, including **Hertz** (☎ 2695 045 706; Lombardou 38) and **Avis** (☎ 2695 027 512), just south of Plateia Agiou Markou. **BesTour** (☎ 2695 024 808; Lombardou 92) is a helpful agency offering car rental, accommodation assistance and other travel services.

ZAKYNTHOS TOWN

pop 11,200

Zakynthos Town is the capital and port of the island. The town was devastated by the 1953 earthquake, but was reconstructed with its former layout preserved in wide arcaded streets, imposing squares and gracious neoclassical public buildings. It's hardly cosy, given its strung-out feel, but it's a reasonable place for an overnight stop and there's at least a semblance of Greekness in comparison to many of the overtouristed parts of the island. The northern area (around Plateia Solomou) is of most interest to visitors, with hotels and restaurants clustered around here.

Orientation & Information

Plateia Solomou is on the northern waterfront of Lombardou, opposite the ferry quay. Another large square, Plateia Agiou Markou, is behind it. The bus station is on Filita, one block back from the waterfront and south of the quay. The main thoroughfare is Alexandrou Roma, parallel to the waterfront and several blocks inland.

The **tourist police** (☎ 2695 027 367; Lombardou 62) have one or two brochures for visitors. There are banks with ATMs along Lombardou and just west of Plateia Solomou. The **post office** (Tertseti 27) is one block west of Alexandrou Roma. **Top's** (Filita 34), near the bus station, offers Internet access. Zakynthos Town has no tourist office.

Sights & Activities

The **Byzantine museum** (☎ 2695 042 714; Plateia Solomou; admission €3; ☼ 8am-2.30pm Tue-Sun) houses an impressive collection of ecclesiastical art, rescued from churches razed in the earthquake. The nearby **Museum of Solomos** (☎ 2695 028 982; Plateia Agiou Markou; admission €3; ☼ 9am-2pm) is dedicated to Dionysios Solomos (1798–1857), who was born on Zakynthos and is regarded as the father of modern Greek poetry. His work *Hymn to Liberty* became the stirring Greek national anthem. The museum houses memorabilia associated with his life.

If you're feeling energetic, the peaceful, shady **Kastro** (☎ 26950 48099; admission €3; ☼ 8am-8pm), a ruined Venetian fortress high above Zakynthos Town, is a good place to hike to. It's about 2.5km from town in the village of Bochali (take Dionysiou Roma north and turn left at Kapodistria, following the signs for Bochali); once here you can enjoy the views and maybe elect to dine at one of Bochali's well-sited restaurants (some have live traditional music of an evening).

Sleeping

Hotel Egli (☎ 2695 028 317; Lombardou 14; d €44) Tucked in beside the waterfront Strada Marina behemoth is this good-value, low-key hotel, offering clean, simple rooms with TV, fridge and fan; it's just a pity about the unhelpful management!

Hotel Diana (☎ 2695 028 547; Plateia Agiou Markou; s/d incl breakfast €45/80; ✻) The plush lobby hints at the high standards of accommodation here, so the reasonable prices are somewhat surprising. This pleasant hotel is in a great location at the rear of Plateia Agious Markou, close to all the action. Rooms are well appointed and comfortable.

Hotel Strada Marina (☎ 2695 042 761; strada marina@aias.gr; Lombardou 14; s/d €60/90; ✻ 🖳) This large, central, newly renovated hotel is among the plushest accommodation options in town. The modern rooms are well equipped with TV, phone and air-con; prices include buffet breakfast; and the icing on the cake is the inviting rooftop pool and bar area.

Eating & Drinking

Cafés selling *mandolato*, a local nougat sweet, are found along Alexandrou Roma,

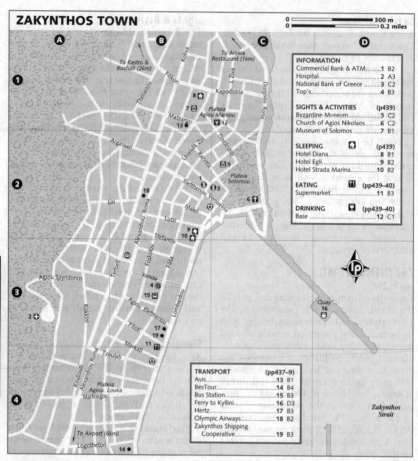

ZAKYNTHOS TOWN

0 — 300 m
0 — 0.2 miles

INFORMATION
Commercial Bank & ATM........1 B2
Hospital............................2 A3
National Bank of Greece 3 C2
Top's................................4 B3

SIGHTS & ACTIVITIES (p439)
Byzantine Museum...............5 C2
Church of Agios Nikolaos......6 C2
Museum of Solomos 7 B1

SLEEPING (p439)
Hotel Diana........................8 B1
Hotel Egli..........................9 B2
Hotel Strada Marina...........10 B2

EATING (pp439–40)
Supermarket......................11 B3

DRINKING (pp439–40)
Base 12 C1

TRANSPORT (pp437–9)
Avis.................................13 B1
BesTour............................14 B4
Bus Station.......................15 B3
Ferry to Kyllini..................16 D3
Hertz...............................17 B3
Olympic Airways................18 B2
Zakynthos Shipping
  Cooperative....................19 B3

*Zakynthos
Strait*

---

as are good gyros places. Street vendors on Plateia Solomou sell barbecued corn on the cob, while spruikers at the decent (but somewhat overpriced) restaurants of Plateia Agious Markou compete for your custom.

Arekia (☎ 2695 026 346; mains under €10) There's no menu at this popular, non-touristy place in Kryoneri, a 10- to 15-minute walk north of Plateia Solomou along the waterfront. The owner tells you what's been made that day and you choose, and although the food is hearty Greek fare and very reasonably priced, it's not what you come for. The attraction is the wonderful live music – *kantades* and the *arekia* of the restaurant's name – most nights from about 10pm. You'll probably have as much fun as

the singers, even if you don't understand a word of the songs.

Base (☎ 2695 042 409; Plateia Agiou Markou) This hip bar is a good choice for an alfresco daytime coffee or evening drink. It's particularly popular with young Zantiots as a nighttime hang-out, and there's often a DJ playing music.

There's a well-stocked supermarket on the corner of Filioti and the waterfront.

AROUND ZAKYNTHOS

Loggerhead turtles come ashore to lay their eggs on the golden-sand beaches of the huge Bay of Laganas, on Zakynthos' south coast. Laganas is a highly developed, tacky resort and is a pretty dreadful place to spend a holiday. **Kalamaki** is not much quieter than Laganas and it's tough to find accommodation that hasn't been block-booked by tour operators. **Keri Beach** (follow the sign off the main road indicating Limni Keriou) is a far more pleasant option, although its narrow, stony beach is not much to write home about. There's also a scuba diving centre here.

The **Vasilikos Peninsula**, southeast of Zakynthos Town beyond the busy resort of Argasi, offers a number of small, beachfront settlements off the main road, and there are tavernas and accommodation options at all these places. The first decent place to stop is **Kaminia**, followed by the sandy cove of **Porto Zoro**. Virtually at the tip of the east coast, **Banana Beach** is a pleasant place to hang out with a long (albeit narrow) strip of golden sand. There are plenty of watersports, umbrellas and sun lounges. **Agios Nikolaos** at the very end of the peninsula (not to be confused with Agios Nikolaos in the northeast) also has watersports facilities.

Beyond Mavratzis (dominated by the over-the-top Zante Palace Hotel) is the more pleasant beach of **Porto Roma**, although this narrow strip of sand can get crowded.

On the other side of the peninsula, facing Laganas Bay, is Zakynthos' best beach, the long and sandy **Gerakas**. This is one of the main turtle-nesting beaches (see the boxed text below) and access to the beach is strictly forbidden between dusk and dawn during the breeding season.

You can semi-escape from the tourist hype by visiting the accessible west-coast coves, such as lovely **Limnionas** or **Kambi** (the latter has tavernas ideally positioned for sunset-watching), or head to the quieter northeast coast around **Agios Nikolaos**, where development is proceeding slowly.

Sleeping & Eating

Tartaruga Camping (☎ 2695 051 967; www.tartaruga -camping.com; camp sites per adult/tent €4.80/3.50, r per person €15) If you're travelling on the road from Laganas to Keri, you'll pass the well-signposted turn-off to this camping ground, with a wonderful setting amid terraced olive groves and vineyards and a trail down to the beach. There's also a small store and café, plus a few rooms for rent (usually need to be booked in advance).

Seaside Apartments (☎ 2695 043 297; www.seaside .net.gr; d €44, 4-person apt €73) These delightful,

---

AT LOGGERHEADS

The loggerhead turtle *(Caretta caretta)* is one of Europe's most beautiful yet most endangered marine species. In Greece the loggerhead turtle nests on two of the Ionian Islands (Zakynthos and Kefallonia), on the Peloponnese coast and in Crete. It prefers large tracts of clean, flat and uninhabited sand – so too do basking tourists from northern Europe, and it's this fateful convergence of interests that has led to the turtle being placed under the threat of extinction.

The female turtle lays about 120 eggs the size of ping-pong balls in the sand in preferred sites. After laying her eggs she returns to the sea and the eggs must lie undisturbed for up to 60 days before the hatchlings emerge. Zakynthos hosts the largest congregation of nests – there's an average of 1300 nests per year along the 5km stretch of the Bay of Laganas on the island's south coast. In recent years this busy resort area has come under repeated fire with conservation lobbies clashing with local authorities and businesses involved in the lucrative tourist trade.

In 1999 the Greek government declared the Bay of Laganas area a National Marine Park (www.nmp-zak.org), and strict regulations are now in force regarding boating, mooring, fishing and watersports in designated zones. At the resort of Laganas itself much of the damage has already been done, but other beaches in the area, such as Gerakas, are now completely off-limits between dusk and dawn during the breeding season (nesting occurs from late May to late August, hatching from late July to late October). There are other regulations in effect (ie cars and bikes are not allowed on nesting beaches, umbrellas are only allowed in designated areas, lights cannot be shone directly onto nesting beaches), but these laws are not particularly well enforced.

The Zakynthos branch of **Archelon** (www.archelon.gr), the Sea Turtle Protection Society of Greece, has an excellent public information centre at Gerakas and regularly hosts informative slide shows at hotels in the area. The organisation accepts volunteers (minimum one-month commitment) for its monitoring and research programmes.

SHIPWRECK BEACH

The famous Shipwreck Beach (Navagio), whose photos grace virtually every tourist brochure about Zakynthos, is at the northwest tip of the island. It truly is a splendid beach, but when some seven large excursion boats on round-the-island cruises pull up here at around noon every day and offload their passengers by the hundreds, the place really loses its appeal. Don't go on one of these cruises unless you fancy nine hours on a crowded boat offering overpriced snack food and generally travelling too far from the coastline to allow you to see much of interest.

You're better off taking a small-boat trip to see Shipwreck Beach or the Blue Caves (in the island's northeast), and these are best done from the lighthouse at Cape Skinari at the far northern tip of the island (3km beyond Agios Nikolaos). From here, the **Potamitis brothers** (☎ 2695 031 132) take small boats at frequent intervals to either venue – a trip to Shipwreck Beach is €10, inside the Blue Caves on a glass-bottom boat is €7, or you can do both trips for €14 (they will also act as a taxi boat to Shipwreck Beach, taking you there and picking you up a pre-arranged time).

You can also visit Shipwreck Beach on a small excursion boat from the little harbour of Porto Vromi on the west coast, which in turn is reached from Anafonitria. Avoid the crowds by visiting in the morning or from mid-afternoon, and take food, drink and a beach umbrella as there are no facilities. And be sure to visit the precariously perched lookout platform over Shipwreck Beach, on the west coast, signposted between Anafonitria and Volimes. Be warned that this is not a place for those afraid of heights, but the picture-perfect view is well worth the adrenaline rush.

well-equipped studios and apartments are above the beachfront Keri Tourist Center (really just a gift shop) at Keri Beach. Their bright, modern decor is enhanced by artwork done by the friendly owner, and all have large balconies with wonderful sea views.

Sea View Village (☎ 2695 035 178; www.seaview village.gr; d €97, 4-person apt €130; ❄ 🏊) One of the most appealing complexes on the island is this smart resort just south of the turn-off to Kaminia, well positioned for exploration of the peninsula's fine beaches. Modern, spacious studios and apartments are a cut above many others on offer, and the central pool and bar area is fabulous.

Gerakas Taverna & Bar (☎ 2695 035 248; mains €5-12) This pleasant family-run restaurant is on the road heading to the Gerakas beach. It offers an extensive menu featuring many Greek favourites – grilled meats, oven-baked dishes, fish etc. There's also a cocktail bar, plus sales of local organic produce (oil, honey, olives, wine and cheese).

If you're looking for a relaxing retreat, there are numerous studios and villas in the Gerakas area, and many can be rented through UK-based **SunIsle** (UK ☎ 01285-750742; www.sunisle.co.uk). Most bookings are on a weekly basis, but if you're in the area and fancy an impromptu stay, drop into the Gerakas Taverna & Bar to see if there are any short-term vacancies (double studios

from around €30 per night). This area is beginning to embrace eco-tourism and there are a few activities available (all approved by marine park authorities), including nature walks, snorkelling, horse riding and sailing. Make enquiries with SunIsle, or at the public information centre next to the restaurant.

At Cape Skinari, 3km beyond Agios Nikolaos, you can enjoy the novelty of staying in a **windmill** (☎ 2695 031 132; d €75) converted into a small studio sleeping two people, or pleasant rooms in a nearby stone cottage. All enjoy spectacular views. Also here are a snack bar-café and steps down to a lovely swimming area; and nearby is the departure point for the Potamitis brothers' boat-trips (see Shipwreck Beach above).

KYTHIRA & ANTIKYTHIRA

KYTHIRA ΚΥΘΗΡΑ

pop 3334

The island of Kythira (*kee*-thih-rah), 12km south of Neapoli, is the perfect destination for people who want to get away from it all and unwind for a few days.

Some 30km long and 18km wide, Kythira dangles off the tip of the Peloponnese's eastern Laconian Peninsula, between the Aegean and Ionian Seas. The landscape is largely barren, dominated by a rocky pla-teau that covers most of the island, and the population is spread among more than 40 villages scattered across the island, taking advantage of small pockets of land where agricultural activity is possible. The villages are linked by narrow, winding lanes flanked by ancient dry-stone walls.

Despite its proximity to the mainland, Kythira is regarded by many Greeks as the Holy Grail of island-hopping, a reputation that owes much to a well-known 1973 song by Dimitris Mitropanos called 'Road to Kythira', which portrayed the island as the end of a line that is never reached.

Kythira's status is something of an enigma. It was part of the British Ionian Protectorate from 1815 to 1864, and is often grouped with the modern Ionian Islands, even though its nearest Ionian neighbour lies more than 100km to the northwest. Administratively it belongs to the prefecture of Piraeus, along with the Saronic Gulf Islands. Historically, and for all practical purposes, its closest ties are with the Peloponnese.

Mythology suggests that Aphrodite was born in Kythira. She is supposed to have risen from the foam where Zeus had thrown Cronos' sex organ after castrating him. The goddess of love then re-emerged near Pa-phos in Cyprus, so both islands haggle over her birthplace.

Tourism remains very low-key for most of the year, but the place goes mad during the months of July and August. Most of the visitors are members of the Kythiran diaspora returning from Australia to visit family and friends. Accommodation is virtually impossible to find at this time, and restaurants are flat-out catering for the crowds. For the remaining 10 months, Kythira is a wonderfully peaceful place with some fine, uncrowded beaches and remarkably clear water. The best times to visit Kythira are in late spring and in September/October.

Getting There & Away
AIR
There are daily flights between Kythira and Athens (€52). The airport is 10km east of Potamos, and **Olympic Airways** (☎ 2736 033 362) is on the central square in Potamos. Book also at **Kythira Travel** (☎ 2736 031 490) in Hora.

FERRY
The island's main connection is between its northern port of Agia Pelagia and Ne-apoli (€5.20, car €17.20, one hour) in the Peloponnese. The frequency of the service ranges from four times daily in July and August down to one a day in winter. Tick-ets are sold at the quay before departure, or from **Sirenes Travel Club** (☎ 2736 034 371) in Potamos. In case of bad weather, the boat arrives and departs from Diakofti, not Agia Pelagia.

ANEN Lines (www.anen.gr) calls at the south-ern port of Diakofti on its weekly schedule between Piraeus, Kythira, Antikythira, Kis-samos (Crete) and Gythio (Peloponnese). From the month of July to September, there are five ferries weekly to Gythio (€8.90, 2½ hours) and five to Kissamos (€14.10, four hours), of which three call at Antikythira (€8.10, two hours). There are also two services weekly to Pireaus (€19.30, 6½ hours). Information and tickets are avail-able from **Porfyra Travel** (☎ /fax 2736 031 888; porfyra@otenet.gr) in Livadi.

HYDROFOIL
Flying Dolphin services to Diakofti had been suspended at the time of research, but were expected to resume. Check www.dolphins.gr for the latest news, or ask at **Kythira Travel** (☎ 2736 031 490) on the main square in Hora.

Getting Around
The only public transport on the island is provided by school buses, which are pressed into service carrying tourists during the July/August school holidays. Not surpris-ingly, there are taxis, but the best way to see the island is with your own transport. Panayotis at **Moto Rent** (☎ 2736 031 600; fax 2736 031 789) on Kapsali's waterfront rents cars and mopeds.

Hora Χώρα
pop 267
Hora (or Kythira), the island's capital, is a pretty village of Cycladic style white, blue-shuttered houses, perched on a long, slender ridge stretching north from an im-pressive 13th-century Venetian kastro. The central square, planted with hibiscus, bou-gainvillea and palms, is Plateia Dimitriou Staï. The main street, Spiridonos Staï, runs south from the square to the kastro.

IONIAN ISLANDS

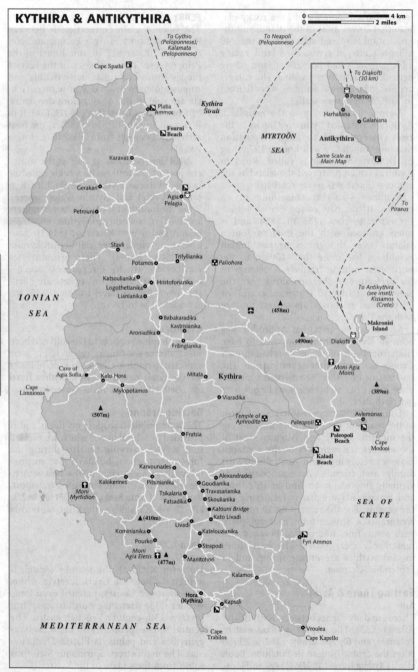

KYTHIRA & ANTIKYTHIRA

0 — 4 km
0 — 2 miles

To Gythio (Peloponnese); Kalamata (Peloponnese)

To Neapoli (Peloponnese)

Cape Spathi

Kythira Strait

Platia Ammos
Fourni Beach

MYRTOÖN SEA

Karavas

Agia Pelagia

Gerakari

Petrouni

To Piraeus

IONIAN SEA

Stavli

Potamos
Trifyllianika
Paliohora

Katsoulianika
Hristoforianika
Logothetianika
Lianianika

(458m)

Babakaradika
Kastrisianika
Aroniadika
Frilingianika

To Antikythira (see inset); Kissamos (Crete)

(490m)

Makronisi Island

Diakofti

Cave of Agia Sofia
Kato Hora
Mylopotamos
Mitata
Kythira

Moni Agia Monis

Cape Limnionas

(507m)

Viaradika

(389m)

Temple of Aphrodite
Paleopoli
Avlemonas

Fratsia

Paleopoli Beach
Cape Modoni

Kaladi Beach

Karvounades
Alexandrades
Goudianika
Kalokerines
Pitsinianika
Travasarianika
Tsikalaria
Skoulianika
Fatsadika
Katouni Bridge
Kato Livadi

SEA OF CRETE

(410m)
Livadi
Katelouzianika
Kominianika
Pourko
Moni Agia Elesis
(477m)
Strapodi
Fyri Ammos
Manitohori

Moni Myrtidion

Kalamos

Hora (Kythira)
Kapsali

MEDITERRANEAN SEA

Cape Trahilos
Vroulea
Cape Kapello

Antikythira (inset)

To Diakofti (30 km)

Potamos
Harhaliana
Galaniana

Same Scale as Main Map

Travellers can check email at **Internet Service** (☎ 2735 039 016; Spiridonos Staï 38; ☺ 9am-2pm & 5.30-9.30pm Mon-Sat). Branches of the National Bank of Greece and **Bank Agoritiki**, both with ATMs, are on the square, as is the **post office** (☺ 7.30am-2pm Mon-Fri). The **police station** (☎ 2736 031 206) is near the kastro.

SIGHTS

Hora's Venetian **kastro**, built in the 13th century, is at the southern end of town. If you walk to its southern extremity, passing the Church of Panagia, you will come to a sheer cliff – from here there's a stunning view of Kapsali and on a good day of Antikythira.

The **archaeological museum** (☎ 2736 031 789; admission free; ☺ 8.45am-3pm Tue-Sat, 9.30am-2.30pm Sun) is north of the central square, near the turn-off to Kapsali. It features gravestones of British soldiers who died on the island in the 19th century. A large marble lion from around 550 BC is also exhibited.

Call in to **Stavros** (☎ 2736 031 857), a store north of the square (opposite the turn-off to Kapsali) and pick up some of the local produce, including Greece's best honey.

SLEEPING & EATING

Castello Rooms (☎ 2736 031 069; jfatseas@otenet.gr; d/tr with bathroom €40/50) These comfortable rooms represent the best deal in town, set back from the main street and surrounded by a well-tended garden full of flowers, vegetables and fruit trees. Most of the rooms also have kitchen facilities. They are signposted at the southern end of Spiridonos Staï.

Hotel Margarita (☎ 2736 031 711; www.hotel-margarita.com; off Spiridonos Staï; s/d/tr/q €70/90/108/132; ☒) This charming hotel offers very pleasant rooms (all with TV and telephone) in a renovated 19th-century mansion featuring beautiful polished timber floors and a fine old spiral staircase. Breakfast is served on a lovely whitewashed terrace.

Zorba's (☎ 2736 031 655; Spiridonos Staï 36; mains €3.50-5.50) Zorba told me to love life and never to fear death, announces the sign in the window. It's a philosophy that the staff appear to endorse wholeheartedly, encouraging customers to enjoy their outing to the max while sampling the grilled meats and salads.

Myrtoon (☎ 2736 031 705; mains €3-6) A good local taverna serving tasty traditional food at realistic prices.

Kapsali Καπσάλι
pop 34

The picturesque village of Kapsali, 2km south of Hora, served as Hora's port in Venetian times. It looks stunning viewed from Hora's castle, with its twin sandy bays and curving waterfront. Restaurants and cafés line the beach, and safe sheltered swimming is Kapsali's trademark. It can also get pretty crowded in high season.

Offshore you can see the stark rock island known as the **Avgo (Egg)** rearing above the water. It is here that Kytherians claim Aphrodite sprang from the sea.

Kapsali goes into hibernation in winter, coming to life only between April and October. **Creperie Vanilia** (☎ 2736 031 881) has a computer for Internet access. There's a small supermarket, while the Kytherian Gallery sells international newspapers as well as souvenirs.

SIGHTS & ACTIVITIES

Panayotis at **Moto Rent** (☎ 2736 031 600), on the waterfront, offers **water-skiing** lessons (€15) and hires canoe and pedal boats as well as cars, mopeds and bicycles.

Spiros Kasimatis (☎ 697 402 2079) offers trips in his glass-bottom boat (€8) every afternoon from May to October. Viewing conditions are ideal in the crystal-clear waters, and Spiros knows all the best spots. He is normally to be found somewhere around the quay where his boat is moored.

SLEEPING & EATING

Camping Kapsali (☎ 2736 031 580; camp sites per adult/tent €4.50/4; ☺ Jun-Sep 15) This small pine-shaded ground (well signposted from the road from Hora) is 400m from Kapsali's quay, behind the village. It's a quiet spot with minimum facilities and is better suited to small tents rather than large campervan set-ups.

Aphrodite Apartments (☎ 2736 031 328; afrodite@aias.gr; d/tr studios €53.70/70.50) This place is ideally situated just 50m behind the main beach. The furnishings are pretty basic, but there are kitchen facilities and all the essentials.

Vassilis Studios (☎ 2736 031 125; www.kythira bungalowsvasili.gr; d €110, tr/q €120) This attractive green-and-white complex of studios has a wonderful setting overlooking Kapsali Beach. Olga, the friendly owner, offers spacious rooms with lovely timber floors and good bay views. It is on the right as you approach Kapsali from Hora.

Raikos Hotel (☎ 2736 031 629; raikoshotel@ techlink.gr; d/tr €100/135; 🖼 💂) Signposted off the Hora–Kapsali road is this very smart, friendly hotel, offering spacious, pleasantly decorated rooms with terraces overlooking Kapsali and Hora's kastro. There's a lovely pool and bar area too, complete with billiards table.

Estiatorio Magos (☎ 2736 031 407; mains €2.80-6, fish priced per kg) The magician (*magos*) in question is owner Antonis, whose assortment of tricks includes pasta (€2.80) and a tasty fish soup (€3).

Hydragogio (☎ 2736 031 065; mains to €14.50, lobster & fish priced per kg) This lively eatery at the far end by the rocks specialises in fresh fish and mezedes. It's a good place to splurge on lobster if your budget stretches that far. The wine list is comprehensive and excellent.

Potamos Ποταμός
pop 680

Potamos, 10km from Agia Pelagia, is the island's commercial hub. Its Sunday morning market seems to attract just about everyone on the island.

Kafe Selena (☎ 2736 033 997), on the square, has Internet access. The National Bank of Greece (with ATM) is also on the central square. The **post office** (⏲ 7.30am-2pm Mon-Fri) is just north of the square.

SLEEPING & EATING

Xenonas Porfyra (☎ 2736 033 329/924; d/tr studios €55/65; 🖼) At Potamos' only hotel, spotless self-contained units surround a pleasant internal courtyard. The sign is in Greek only – look for it almost opposite the post office north of the main square.

Taverna Panaretos (☎ 2736 034 290; mains €4-9) This bustling taverna on the central square serves well-prepared international and Greek dishes, including tempting seafood risotto and pasta.

Ta Katsigouro (☎ 2736 033 880; burgers & snacks €1.50-7) Ta Katsigouro has become something of a tourist attraction thanks to its sign featuring a wonderful new-age mythical beast with a kangaroo's body and a goat's head. Inside, former Sydneysider Maria turns out the best burger with the works (€3.50) west of Perth, as well as Greek fast food like gyros and souvlaki.

Mylopotamos Μυλοπόταμος
pop 680

Mylopotamos is a charming traditional village nestled in a small valley about 12km southwest of Potamos. Its central square is flanked by a much-photographed church and the charming traditional **Kafeneio O Platanos** (☎ 2736 033 397), which becomes a restaurant in summer serving simple meals in a gorgeous setting. It's worth a stroll to the **Neraïda** (water nymph) waterfall, with luxuriant greenery and mature, shady trees. As you reach the church, take the right fork and follow the signs to an unpaved road leading down to the falls.

To reach the abandoned **kastro** of Mylopotamos, take the left fork after the kafeneio and follow the sign for Kato Hora (Lower Village). The road leads to the centre of Kato Hora, from where a portal leads into the spooky kastro, with derelict houses and well-preserved little churches (usually locked).

Further along the same road is the **Cave of Agia Sofia**, reached by a precipitous, unpaved 2km road. The staff at Kafeneio O Platanos can tell you if it's open.

Agia Pelagia Αγία Πελαγία
pop 280

Kythira's northern port of Agia Pelagia is a simple, friendly waterfront village ideal for relaxing and swimming. Mixed sand and pebble beaches are to either side of the quay.

SLEEPING & EATING

Prebooking in high season is almost essential in Agia Pelagia.

Hotel Kytthereia (☎ 2736 033 321; kythereia2001@ yahoo.com; s/d with bathroom €62.50/75; 🖼) This welcoming hotel is right opposite the ferry dock in the middle of the seafront. The rooms are clean and simply furnished, and come with balcony and TV. Helpful owner Angelo from Australia is full of useful information. Prices include breakfast.

Hotel Pelagia Aphrodite (☎ 2736 033 926; pela gia@otenet.gr; s/d/tr 73/87.50/105; 🖼) Has a great location on a small headland on the southern edge of the village. Red Beach, south of the headland, is the best in the area, named for its red pebbles. The hotel is modern with large, airy rooms; most have balconies overlooking the sea. The hotel is open April to October.

Estiatorio Stella (☎ 2736 033 613; mains €4-11) Stella's establishment is the first of half a dozen cafés and eating places spread along the seafront. A hearty plate of spaghetti marinara (€5.50) comes loaded with mussels, calamari and prawns – perfect with a large draught Alpha beer (€1.80).

Moustakias (☎ 2736 033 519; mains to €8.80) This ouzeri, next to the minimarket, is named after the mighty moustache of cheerful owner Panayiotis. He has a selection food ranging from mezedes to grilled meats to seafood, including all the traditional Greek favourites.

Around Kythira

If you have transport, a tour round the island is rewarding. The monasteries of **Agia Moni** and **Agia Elesis** are mountain refuges with superb views. **Moni Myrtidion** is a beautiful monastery surrounded by trees. From Hora, drive northeast to the picturesque village of **Avlemonas** via **Paleopoli** with its wide, pebbled beach. Here, archaeologists spent years searching for evidence of a temple at Aphrodite's birthplace. Be sure to also visit the spectacularly situated ruins of the Byzantine capital of **Paliohora**, in the island's northeast.

Just north of the village of **Kato Livadi** make a detour to see the remarkable, and seemingly out-of-place, British-made **Katouni Bridge**, a legacy of Kythira's time as part of the British Protectorate in the 19th century. In the far north of the island the village of **Karavas** is verdant and very attractive and close to both Agia Pelagia and the reasonable beach at **Platia Ammos**. Beachcombers should seek out **Kaladi Beach**, near Paleopoli. **Fyri Ammos**, closer to Hora, is another good beach – but hard to access.

EATING

Estiatorion Pierros (☎ 2736 031 014; Livadi; mains €3-6) Pierros, on the main road through Livadi, is a long-standing favourite where you'll find no-nonsense Greek staples. There's no menu – visit the kitchen to see what's been freshly cooked.

Rouga (☎ 2736 033 766; Arionadika; mains €5-7) The place to go to sample traditional Kytheran dishes like *kamares* (artichokes and leeks with lemon sauce, €4.50) and baked wild goat (€7). It also sells a range of homemade *gyka* (preserved fruit in syrup), which form a colourful counter display. Arionadika is about 4km south of Potamos.

Sotiris (☎ 2736 033 722; Avlemonas; fish & lobster priced per kg) This popular fish taverna in pretty Avlemonas is famous for its lobster and its fish soup.

Psarotaverna H Manolis (☎ 2736 033 748; fish & lobster priced per kg) This small family-run fish taverna is about the only thing the port of Diakofti has going for it.

ANTIKYTHIRA ΑΝΤΙΚΥΘΗΡΑ

pop 70

The tiny island of Antikythira, 38km southeast of Kythira, is the most remote island in the Ionian group. It has only one settlement (Potamos), one doctor, one police officer, one teacher (with a handful of pupils), one telephone and a monastery. It has no post office or bank. The only accommodation for tourists is 10 basic rooms in two purpose-built blocks, open in summer only. Potamos has a kafeneio and taverna.

Getting There & Away

ANEN Lines (www.anen.gr) calls at Antikythira on its route between Kythira and Kissamos on Crete, offering three services a week in each direction. Both trips cost €8.10 and take two hours. This is not an island for tourists on a tight schedule, and will probably only appeal to those who really like their isolation. For information and tickets, contact **Porfyra Travel** (☎ /fax 2736 031 888; porfyra@otenet.gr) in Livadi on Kythira.

IONIAN ISLANDS

Directory

CONTENTS

ACCOMMODATION

The Greek islands boast accommodation to suit every taste and budget. All places to stay are subject to strict price controls set by the tourist police. By law, a notice must be displayed in every room, which states the category of the room and the maximum price that can be charged. The price includes a 4.5% community tax and 8% VAT.

Accommodation owners may add a 10% surcharge for a stay of less than three nights, but this is not mandatory. A mandatory charge of 20% is levied if an extra bed is put into a room. During July and August, accommodation owners will charge the maximum price, but in spring and autumn, prices will drop by about 20%, and perhaps by even more in winter.

Rip-offs rarely occur, but if you do suspect that you have been exploited by an accommodation owner, make sure you report it to either the tourist police or regular police and they will act swiftly.

Throughout this book we have divided accommodation into budget, mid-range and top-end categories, and within each section the options are listed in order of preference. It's difficult however to generalise accommodation prices in Greece as rates can depend entirely on the season and location. Don't expect to pay the same price for a double on one of the islands as you would for a double in Athens.

Camping

Camping is a good option, especially in summer. There are almost 200 camping grounds dotted around the islands, some of them in great locations. Standard facilities include hot showers, kitchens, restaurants and minimarkets – and often a swimming pool.

Most camping grounds are open only between April and October. The **Panhellenic Camping Association** (☎ /fax 2103 621 560; Solonos 102, Athens 106 80) publishes an annual booklet

---

PRACTICALITIES

- Greece is two hours ahead of GMT/UTC and three hours ahead during daylight-saving time.

- Greece uses the metric system for weights and measures.

- Plug your electrical appliances into a two-pin adaptor before plugging into the electricity supply (220V AC, 50Hz).

- Keep up with Greek current affairs by reading the daily English-language edition of *Kathimerini* that comes with the *Herald Tribune*.

- Channel hop through a choice of nine free-to-air TV channels and an assortment of pay channels.

- Be aware that Greece uses the PAL system if you buy videos to watch back home.

listing all camping grounds, their facilities and months of operation.

Camping fees are highest from 15 June to the end of August. Most camping grounds charge from €4.50 to €6 per adult and €2.50 to €3.50 for children aged four to 12. There's no charge for children four to 12. There's no charge for children aged under four. Tent sites cost from €3.50 per night for small tents, and from €5 per night for large tents.

Between May and mid-September the weather is warm enough to sleep out. Many camping grounds have covered areas where tourists who don't have tents can sleep in summer, so you can get by with a lightweight sleeping bag and foam bedroll. It's a good idea to have a foam pad to lie on and a waterproof cover for your sleeping bag. Pitching a tent in a nondesignated camping area is illegal, but the law is seldom enforced – to the irritation of camping-ground owners.

Domatia

Domatia are the Greek equivalent of the British bed and breakfast, minus the breakfast. Once upon a time domatia comprised little more than spare rooms, in the family home, that could be rented out to travellers in summer; nowadays, many are purpose-built appendages. Some come complete with fully-equipped kitchens. Standards of cleanliness are generally high. The décor runs the gamut from cool marble floors, coordinated pine furniture and pretty lace curtains, to so much kitsch you're afraid to move in case you break an ornament.

Domatia remain a popular option for budget travellers. They are classified A, B or C. Expect to pay from €25 to €35 for a single, and €40 to €50 for a double, depending on the class, whether bathrooms are shared or private, the season and how long you plan to stay. Domatia are found on almost every island that has a permanent population. Many are open only between April and October.

From June to September domatia owners are out in force, touting for customers. They meet buses and boats, shouting 'Room, room!' and often carrying photographs of their rooms. In peak season, it can prove a mistake not to take up an offer – but be wary of owners who are vague about the location of their accommodation. 'Close to town' can turn out to be way out in the sticks. If you are at all dubious, insist they show you the location on a map.

Hostels

The **Athens International Youth Hostel** (Map pp68-9; ☎ 2105 234 170; fax 2105 234 015; Victor Hugo 16, Omonia; members €8.66, nonmembers €8.66 plus daily stamp, joining fee €15, daily stamp €2.50) is the only hostel in Greece affiliated to the International Youth Hostel Federation (IYHF). You don't need a membership card to stay there; temporary membership costs €2.50 per day (ie the daily stamp fee).

Most other youth hostels in Greece are run by the **Greek Youth Hostel Organisation** (☎ 2107 519 530; y-hostels@otenet.gr; Damareos 75, 116 33 Athens) There are affiliated hostels in Athens, Patra and Thessaloniki on the mainland, and on the islands of Crete and Santorini.

Hostel rates vary from €8 to €10 and you don't have to be a member to stay in any of them.

Hotels

Hotels in Greece are divided into six categories: deluxe, A, B, C, D and E. Hotels are categorised according to the size of the room, whether or not they have a bar, and the ratio of bathrooms to beds, rather than standards of cleanliness, comfort of the beds and friendliness of staff – all elements that may be of greater relevance to guests.

As one would expect, deluxe, A- and B-class hotels have many amenities, private bathrooms and constant hot water. C-class hotels have a snack bar, rooms have private bathrooms, but hot water may only be available at certain times of the day. D-class hotels may or may not have snack bars, most rooms will share bathrooms, but there may be some with private bathrooms, and they may have solar-heated water, which means hot water is not guaranteed. E classes do not have a snack bar, bathrooms are shared and you may have to pay extra for hot water – if it exists at all.

Hotel prices are controlled by the tourist police and the maximum rate that can be charged for a room must be displayed on a board behind the door of each room. The classification is not often much of a guide to price. Rates in D- and E-class hotels are generally comparable with domatia. You can pay from €50 to €80 for a single in high season in C class and €70 to €120 for a double. Prices in B class range from €80 to €120 for singles, and from €100 to €150 for doubles. A-class prices are not much higher.

Mountain Refuges

You're unlikely to have much need of Greece's mountain refuges – unless you're going trekking in the mountains of Crete or Evia. See p241 for details of the refuges at Mt Ida and in the Lefka Ori in Crete, and p383 for information about the Dirfys Refuge on Mt Dirfys in Evia. The EOT (Ellinikos Organismos Tourismou; Greek National Tourist Organisation) publication *Greece: Mountain Refuges & Ski Centres* has details on all of the refuges in Greece; copies should be available at all EOT branches. See Tourist Information (p461) for more information about EOT.

Pensions

Pensions in Greece are virtually indistinguishable from hotels. They are classed A, B or C. An A-class pension is equivalent in amenities and price to a B-class hotel, a B-class pension is equivalent to a C-class hotel and a C-class pension is equivalent to a D- or E-class hotel.

Rental Accommodation

There are plenty of places around the islands, offering self-contained family apartments for rent, either long- or short-term. Prices vary considerably according to the season and the amenities offered.

If you're looking for long-term accommodation, it's worth checking out the classified section of the *Athens News* – although most of the places are in Athens. In rural areas and islands, the local *kafeneio* (coffee house) is a good place is start asking about your options.

Traditional Settlements

Traditional settlements are old buildings of architectural merit that have been renovated and converted into tourist accommodation. You'll find them on many of the islands. There are some terrific places among them, but they are expensive – most are equivalent in price to an A- or B-class hotel. Some of the best examples are in Hania (p242) in Crete and in Rhodes Town (p265), Rhodes.

ACTIVITIES

For details on popular activities throughout the Greek islands, see the Greek Islands Outdoors chapter on p50.

BUSINESS HOURS

Banks are open 8am to 2pm Monday to Thursday, and 8am to 1.30pm Friday. Some banks in large towns and cities open between 3.30pm and 6.30pm in the afternoon and on Saturday morning.

Post offices are open 7.30am to 2pm Monday to Friday. In the major cities they stay open until 8pm, and open 7.30am to 2pm Saturday.

In summer, the usual opening hours for shops are 8am to 1.30pm and 5.30pm to 8.30pm on Tuesday, Thursday and Friday, and 8am to 2.30pm on Monday, Wednesday and Saturday. Shops open 30 minutes later in winter. These times are not always strictly adhered to. Many shops in tourist resorts are open seven days a week.

The opening hours of OTE offices (for long-distance and overseas telephone calls) vary according to the size of the town. In smaller towns they are usually open 7.30am to 3pm daily, 6am to 11pm in larger towns, and 24 hours in major cities like Athens and Thessaloniki.

Department stores and supermarkets are open 8am to 8pm Monday to Friday, 8am to at least 3pm on Saturday and are closed Sunday.

Periptera (street kiosks) are open from early morning until late at night. They sell everything from bus tickets and cigarettes to hard-core pornography.

Restaurant hours vary enormously. They are normally open for lunch from 11am to 2pm, and for dinner between 7pm and 1am, while restaurants in tourist areas remain open all day. Cafés normally open at about 10am, and stay open until midnight.

Bars open from about 8pm until late, while nightclubs don't open until at least 10pm; it's rare to find much of a crowd before midnight. They close at about 4am, later on Friday and Saturday.

CHILDREN

The Greek islands are a safe and relatively easy place to travel with children. Greeks are well known for making a fuss of children, who will always be made the centre of attention.

Despite this, it's quite rare for younger children to have much success making friends with local children their own age, partly because Greek children tend to play at home and partly because of the language barrier. The language barrier starts to recede by about the age of 12, by which time many local children are sufficiently advanced in their studies to communicate in English.

Matt Barrett's website (www.greektravel .com) has lots of useful tips for parents, while daughter Amarandi has put together some tips for kids (www.greece4kids.com).

Practicalities

Travelling is especially easy if you're staying at a resort hotel by the beach, where everything is set up for families with children. As well as facilities like paddling pools and playgrounds, they also have cots and high chairs. Best of all, there's a strong possibility of making friends with other kids.

Elsewhere, it's rare to find cots and high chairs, although most hotels and restaurants will do their best to help.

Mobility is an issue for parents with very small children. Strollers (pushchairs) aren't much use. They are hopeless on rough stone paths and up steps, and a curse when getting on/off buses and ferries. Backpacks or front pouches are best.

Fresh milk is available in large towns and tourist areas, but not on the smaller islands. Supermarkets are the best place to look. Formula is available everywhere, as is condensed and heat-treated milk.

Disposable nappies are an environmental curse, but they can be a godsend on the road. They are also available everywhere.

Travel on ferries, buses and trains is free for children under four. They pay half fare up to the age of 10 (ferries) or 12 (buses and trains). Full fares apply otherwise. On domestic flights, you'll pay 10% of the fare to have a child under two sitting on your knee. Kids aged two to 12 pay half fare.

Sights & Activities

If you're travelling around, the shortage of decent playgrounds and other recreational facilities can be a problem, however it's impossible to be far from a beach anywhere on the islands.

Don't be afraid to take children to the ancient sites. Many parents are surprised by how much their children enjoy them. Young imaginations go into overdrive in a place like the 'labyrinth' at Knossos (p215).

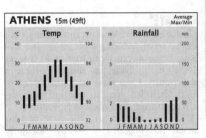

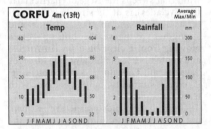

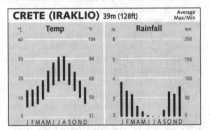

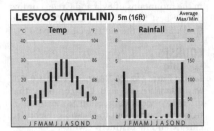

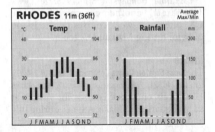

CLIMATE

Greece has a mild Mediterranean climate but can be very hot during summer – in July and August the mercury can soar to 40°C (over 100°F) in the shade, just about anywhere in the country. Crete stays warm the longest of all the islands – you can swim off its southern coast from mid-April to November.

The summer is also the time of year when the *meltemi*, a strong northerly wind that sweeps the Aegean (particularly the Cyclades) is at its strongest. It starts off as a mild wind in May and June, and strengthens as the weather hots up – often blowing from a clear blue sky. In August and September it can blow at gale force for days on end. The wind is a mixed blessing: it reduces humidity, but plays havoc with ferry schedules.

The Ionian Islands escape the *meltemi*, but here the main summer wind is the *maistros*, a light to moderate northwesterly that rises in the afternoon – it usually dies away at sunset.

In the winter, the Ionians are effected by the *gregali*, a northeasterly wind created by depressions moving east in the central Mediterranean. The *gregali* can blow up to Force 8 on the 12-point Beaufort Scale used by Greek meteorologists.

November to February are the wettest months, and it can also get surprisingly cold. Snow is common on the mainland and in the mountains of Evia and Crete. For tips on the best times to visit see When to Go (p13). See also the climate charts (p451).

COURSES
Cooking

Tasting Places (☎ 020-7460 0077; fax 020-7460 0029; www.tastingplaces.com) is a UK company that offers two-week courses on Santorini. Participants learn about the island's celebrated cuisine and its distinctive wines.

Laskarina Holidays (☎ 01629 822203; www .laskarina.co.uk), another company from the UK, offers one-week courses on the island of Symi during May and October.

Dance

The **Dora Stratou Dance Company** (☎ 2103 244 395; fax 2103 246 921; www.grdance.org; Sholiou 8, Plaka, Athens 105 58) runs one-week courses for visitors at its headquarters in Plaka, Athens, during July and August.

Language

If you are serious about learning the language, an intensive course at the start of your stay is a good way to go about it. Most of the courses are in Athens, but there are also special courses on the islands in summer.

The **Hellenic Culture Centre** (☎ 2275 061 140; fax 2275 061 139; www.hcc.gr; Arethoussa, Ikaria 85 302) runs courses on the island of Ikaria from June to October. Two-week intensive courses for beginners cost €470 and involve 40 classroom hours. The centre can also arrange accommodation.

The **Athens Centre** (☎ 2107 012 268; fax 2107 018 603; www.athenscentre.gr; Arhimidous 48) in the suburb of Mets, runs courses on the island of Spetses in June and July. The three-week courses cost €1000, and involve 60 hours of classwork.

Painting

Painting courses are becoming increasingly popular, and British tour operators offer a range of possibilities.

Laskarina Holidays (☎ 01629 822203; www.laskarina.co.uk) offers a selection of two-week courses on the islands of Halki, Samos and Symi.

Simply Travel (☎ 020-8541 2200; fax 020-8541 2280; www.simply-travel.com) runs two-week tours to western Crete.

Travelux (www.travelux.co.uk) offers a week in the wonderful Zagorohoria region of Epiros in northern Greece, followed by a week on the Ionian Island, Lefkada.

The **Hellenic Culture Centre** (☎ 2275 061 140; fax 2275 061 139; www.hcc.gr; Arethoussa, Ikaria 85 302) runs an annual two-week painting course on Ikaria in May.

Photography

Hania-based British photographer **Steve Outram** (☎ 2821 032 201; www.steveoutram.com) runs courses in Crete twice a year.

Photo-Tours Naxos (☎ 2285 022 367; www.naxos photoworkshop.com) runs one-day photo outings for small groups (€35 per person) to great locations with on-the-spot advice (from professional Stuart Thorpe) on taking better pictures.

CUSTOMS

There are no longer duty-free restrictions within the EU. This does not mean, however, that customs checks have been dispensed with; random searches for drugs are still made.

Upon entering the country from outside the EU, customs inspection is usually cursory for foreign tourists. There may be spot checks, but you probably won't have to open your bags. A verbal declaration is usually all that is required.

You may bring the following into Greece duty-free: 200 cigarettes or 50 cigars; 1L of spirits or 2L of wine; 50g of perfume; 250mL of eau de cologne; one camera (still or video) and film; a pair of binoculars; a portable musical instrument; a portable radio or tape recorder; sports equipment; and dogs and cats (with a veterinary certificate).

Importation of works of art and antiquities is free, but they must be declared on entry, so that they can be re-exported. Import regulations for medicines are strict; if you are taking medication, make sure you get a statement from your doctor before you leave home. It is illegal, for instance, to take codeine into Greece without an accompanying doctor's certificate.

An unlimited amount of foreign currency and travellers cheques may be brought into Greece. If you intend to leave the country with foreign banknotes in excess of US$1000, you must declare the sum upon entry.

Restrictions apply to the importation of sailboards into Greece. See the Greek Islands Outdoors chapter (p54) for more details.

It is strictly forbidden to export antiquities (anything over 100 years old) without an export permit. This crime is second only to drug smuggling in the penalties imposed. It is an offence to remove even the smallest article from an archaeological site.

The place to apply for an export permit is the Antique Dealers & Private Collections Section, **Athens Archaeological Service** (Map pp74-5; Polygnotou 13, Athens).

DANGERS & ANNOYANCES
Scams
Bar scams continue to be an unfortunate fact of life in Athens and are particularly prevalent in the Syntagma area. See Dangers & Annoyances on p71 for the full rundown on this scam.

Theft
Crime, especially theft, is low in Greece, but unfortunately it's on the increase. The area worst affected is around Omonia in central Athens – keep track of your valuables here, on the metro and at the Sunday flea market.

The vast majority of thefts from tourists are still committed by other tourists; the biggest danger of theft is probably in dormitory rooms in hostels and at camping grounds – so make sure you do not leave valuables unattended in such places. If you are staying in a hotel room, and the windows and door do not lock securely, ask for your valuables to be locked in the hotel safe – hotel proprietors are happy to do this.

DISABLED TRAVELLERS
If mobility is a problem and you wish to visit Greece, the hard fact is that most hotels, museums and ancient sites in Greece are not wheelchair accessible. This is partly due to the uneven terrain of much of the country, which presents a challenge even for able-bodied people, with its abundance of stones, rocks and marble.

If you are determined, then take heart in the knowledge that disabled people do come to Greece for holidays. But the trip needs careful planning, so get as much information as you can before you go. The British-based **Royal Association for Disability and Rehabilitation** (Radar; ☎ 020-7250 3222; fax 020-7250 0212; radar@radar.org.uk; 12 City Forum, 250 City Road, London EC1V 8AF) publishes a useful guide called *Holidays & Travel Abroad: A Guide for Disabled People*, which gives a good overview of facilities available to disabled travellers in Europe.

DISCOUNT CARDS
Senior Cards
Card-carrying EU pensioners can claim a range of benefits, such as reduced admission at ancient sites and museums, and discounts on bus and train fares.

Student & Youth Cards
The most widely recognised form of student ID is the International Student Identity Card (ISIC).

These cards qualify the holder to some significant discounts including half-price admission to museums and ancient sites and for discounts at some budget hotels and hostels. Aegean Airlines offer student discounts on some domestic flights, but there are none to be had on buses, ferries or trains. Students will find some good deals on international air fares.

Some travel agencies in Athens are licensed to issue cards. You must show documents proving you are a student, provide a passport photo and cough up €10.

Euro<26 (www.euro26.org) youth cards are not valid in Greece. Visit www.istc.org for more information.

EMBASSIES & CONSULATES
Greek Embassies
The following is a selection of Greek diplomatic missions abroad:

Albania (☎ 54-223 959; Ruga Frederik Shiroka, Tirana)
Australia (☎ 02-6273 3011; 9 Turrana St, Yarralumla, Canberra ACT 2600)
Bulgaria (☎ 2-946 1027; San Stefano 33, Sofia 1504)
Canada (☎ 613-238 6271; 76-80 Maclaren St, Ottawa, Ontario K2P OK6)
Cyprus (☎ 02-680 670/671; Byron Boulevard 8-10, Nicosia)
Denmark (☎ 33-114 533; Borgergade 16, 1300 Copenhagen K)
Egypt (☎ 02-795 0443; 18 Aisha el Taymouria, Garden City, Cairo)
France (☎ 01-47 23 72 28; www.amb-grece.fr/presse;17 Rue Auguste Vacquerie, Paris 75116)
Germany (☎ 30-213 7033/4; www.griechische-botschaft.de; Jaegerstrasse 54-55, 10117 Berlin-Mitte)
Ireland (☎ 01-676 7254; 1 Upper Pembroke St, Dublin 2)
Israel (☎ 03-695 3060; Tower Building, Daniel Grise 3, Tel Aviv 64731)
Italy (☎ 06-853 7551; Via S Mercadante 36, Rome 00198)
Japan (☎ 03-3403 0871/0872; www.greekemb.jp; 3-16-30 Nishi Ajabu, Minato-ku, Tokyo 106-0031)
Netherlands (☎ 070-363 87 00; Amaliastraat 1, 2514 JC, The Hague)
New Zealand (☎ 04-473 7775; 5-7 Willeston St, Wellington)
Norway (☎ 2244 2728; Nobels Gate 45, 0244 Oslo 2)
South Africa (☎ 12-430 7351;1003 Church St, Hatfield, Pretoria 0028)
Spain (☎ 01-564 4653; Avenida Doctor Arce 24, Madrid 28002)
Sweden (☎ 08-545 66 019; Riddargatan 60, 11457 Stockholm)
Switzerland (☎ 31-356 1414; Laubeggstrasse, 3006 Bern)
Turkey (☎ 312-436 8860; Ziya-ul-Rahman Caddesi 9-11, Gaziosmanpasa 06700, Ankara)

UK (☎ 020-7229 3850; www.greekembassy.org.uk;1A Holland Park, London W11 3TP)
USA (☎ 202-939 1300; www.greekembassy.org; 2221 Massachusetts Ave NW, Washington DC 20008)

Embassies & Consulates in Greece
All foreign embassies in Greece are in Athens and its suburbs:

Albania (☎ 2107 234 412; Karahristou 1, Athens 115 21)
Australia (☎ 2106 450 404; Dimitrou Soutsou 37, Ambelokipi, Athens 115 21)
Bulgaria (☎ 2106 478 105; Stratigou Kalari 33A, Psyhiko, Athens 154 52)
Canada (☎ 2107 273 400; Genadiou 4, Athens 115 21)
Cyprus (Map pp74-5; ☎ 2107 237 883; Irodotou 16, Athens 106 75)
Egypt (Map pp74-5; ☎ 2103 618 612; Leof Vassilissis Sofias 3, Athens 106 71)
France (Map pp74-5; ☎ 2103 611 663; Leof Vasilissis Sofias 7, Athens 106 71)
Germany (Map pp68-9; ☎ 2107 285 111; Dimitriou 3 & Karaoli, Kolonaki, Athens 106 75)
Hungary (☎ 2106 725 337; Kalvou 16, Athens 154 52)
Ireland (Map pp68-9; ☎ 2107 232 771; Leof Vasileos Konstantinou 7, Athens 106 74)
Israel (☎ 2106 719 530; Marathonodromou 1, Athens 154 52)
Italy (Map pp68-9; ☎ 2103 617 260; Sekeri 2, Athens 106 74)
Japan (☎ 2107 758 101; Athens Tower, Leof Messogion 2-4, Athens 115 27)
Netherlands (Map pp74-5; ☎ 2107 239 701; Vasileos Konstantinou 5-7, Athens 106 74)
New Zealand Consulate (☎ 2106 874 701; Kifissias 268, Halandri)
South Africa (☎ 2106 806 645; Kifissias 60, Maroussi, Athens 151 25)
Turkey (☎ 2107 245 915; Vasilissis Georgiou 8, Athens 106 74)
UK (Map pp68-9; ☎ 2107 236 211; Ploutarhou 1, Athens 106 75)
USA (☎ 2107 212 951; Leof Vasilissis Sofias 91, Athens 115 21)
Yugoslavia (☎ 2107 774 355; Leof Vasilissis Sofias 106 Athens 115 21)

It's important to realise what your own embassy – the embassy of the country of which you are a citizen – can and can't do to help you if you get into trouble. Generally speaking, it won't be much help in emergencies if the trouble you're in is remotely your own fault. Remember that you are bound by the laws of the country you are in. Your embassy will not be sympathetic if you end up in jail after committing a crime locally, even if such actions are legal in your own country.

In genuine emergencies you might get some assistance, but only if other channels have been exhausted. For example, if you need to get home urgently, a free ticket home is exceedingly unlikely – the embassy would expect you to have insurance. If you have all your money and documents stolen, it might assist with getting a new passport, but a loan for onward travel is out of the question.

Some embassies used to keep letters for travellers or have a small reading room with home newspapers, but these days the mail-holding service has usually been stopped and even newspapers tend to be out of date.

FESTIVALS & EVENTS

The Greek year is a succession of festivals and events, some of which are religious, some cultural, others just an excuse for a good party, and some a combination of all three. The following is by no means an exhaustive list, but it covers the most important events, both national and regional. If you're in the right place at the right time, you'll certainly be invited to join the revelry.

More information about festivals and events can be found at www.cultureguide.gr.

January

Feast of Agios Vasilios (St Basil) The year kicks off with this festival on 1 January. A church ceremony is followed by the exchanging of gifts, singing, dancing and feasting; the New Year pie *(vasilopitta)* is cut and the person who gets the slice containing a coin will supposedly have a lucky year.

Epiphany (the Blessing of the Waters) The day Christ's baptism by St John is celebrated throughout Greece on 6 January. Seas, lakes and rivers are blessed and crosses immersed in them. The largest ceremony occurs at Piraeus.

February

Carnival Season The three-week period before the beginning of Lent (the 40-day period before Easter, which is traditionally a period of fasting) is carnival season. The carnivals are ostensibly Christian pre-Lenten celebrations, but many derive from pagan festivals. There are many regional variations, but fancy dress, feasting, traditional dancing and general merry-making prevail. The Patra carnival is the largest and most exuberant, with elaborately decorated chariots parading through

the streets. The most bizarre carnival takes place on the island of Skyros where the men transform themselves into grotesque 'half-man, half-beast' creatures by donning goat-skin masks and hairy jackets.

Shrove Monday (Clean Monday) On the Monday before Ash Wednesday (the first day of Lent), people take to the hills throughout Greece to have picnics and fly kites.

March

Independence Day The anniversary of the hoisting of the Greek flag by Bishop Germanos at Moni Agias Lavras is celebrated on 25 March with parades and dancing. Germanos' act of revolt marked the start of the War of Independence. Independence Day coincides with the **Feast of the Annunciation**, so it is also a religious festival.

April

Easter This is the most important festival in the Greek Orthodox religion. Emphasis is placed on the Resurrection rather than on the Crucifixion, so it is a joyous occasion. The festival begins on the evening of Good Friday with the *perifora epitavios*, when a shrouded bier (representing Christ's funeral bier) is carried through the streets to the local church. This moving candle-lit procession can be seen in towns and villages throughout the country. From a spectator's viewpoint, the most impressive of these processions climbs Lykavittos Hill in Athens to the Chapel of Agios Georgios. The Resurrection Mass starts at 11pm on Saturday night. At midnight, packed churches are plunged into darkness to symbolise Christ's passing through the underworld. The ceremony of the lighting of candles, which follows, is the most significant moment in the Orthodox year, for it symbolises the Resurrection. Its poignancy and beauty are spellbinding. If you are in Greece at Easter you should endeavour to attend this ceremony, which ends with fireworks and candle-lit processions through the streets. The Lenten fast ends on Easter Sunday with the cracking of red-dyed Easter eggs and an outdoor feast of roast lamb followed by Greek dancing. The day's greeting is *Hristos anesti* (Christ is risen), to which the reply is *Alithos anesti* (Truly He is risen). On both Palm Sunday (the Sunday before Easter) and Easter Sunday, St Spyridon (the mummified patron saint of Corfu) is taken out for an airing and joyously paraded through Corfu Town. He is paraded again on 11 August.

Feast of Agios Georgos (St George) The feast day of St George, Greece's patron saint, and patron saint of shepherds, takes place on 23 April or the Tuesday following Easter (whichever comes first).

May

May Day On the first day of May there is a mass exodus from towns to the country. During picnics, wildflowers are gathered and made into wreaths to decorate houses.

June

Navy Week The festival celebrates the long relationship between Greeks and the sea with events in fishing villages and ports throughout the country. Volos and Hydra each have unique versions of these celebrations. Volos re-enacts the departure of the Argo, for legend has it that Iolkos (from where Jason and the Argonauts set off in search of the Golden Fleece) was near the city. Hydra commemorates War of Independence-hero Admiral Andreas Miaoulis, who was born on the island, at its Miaoulia Festival, which includes a re-enactment of one of his naval victories, accompanied by feasting and fireworks.

Feast of St John the Baptist This feast day on 24 June is widely celebrated around Greece. Wreaths made on May Day are kept until this day, when they are burned on bonfires.

Hellenic Festival The Hellenic Festival is the most important of the many festivals staged throughout Greece during summer. It features performances of music, dance and drama at the Theatre of Herodes Atticus in Athens, and performances of ancient Greek drama at the world famous Theatre of Epidavros, near Nafplio in the Peloponnese.

July

Feast of Agia Marina (St Marina) This feast day is celebrated on 17 July in many parts of Greece, and is a particularly important event on the Dodecanese island of Kasos.

Feast of Profitis Ilias This feast day is celebrated on 20 July at the many hilltop churches and monasteries throughout Greece that are dedicated to the prophet Ilias.

Folegandros Festival The Folegandros Festival features a week-long programme of music and feasting at a range of locations around the island's beautiful old Hora.

August

Assumption Greeks celebrate Assumption Day (15 August) with family reunions. The whole population seems to be on the move either side of the big day, so it's a good time to avoid public transport. The island of Tinos gets particularly busy because of its miracle-working icon of Panagia Evangelistria. It becomes a place of pilgrimage for thousands, who come to be blessed, healed or baptised.

Samothraki Dance Festival The Northeastern Aegean Island, Samothraki, plays host to Greece's biggest rave party for a week starting at the end of August.

September

Genesis Tis Panagias The birthday of the Virgin Mary is celebrated on 8 September throughout Greece with religious services and feasting.

Exaltation of the Cross This is celebrated on 14 September throughout Greece with processions and hymns.

October

Feast of Agios Dimitrios This feast day is celebrated in Thessaloniki on 26 October with wine drinking and revelry.

Ohi (No) Day Metaxas' refusal to allow Mussolini's troops free passage through Greece in WWII is commemorated on 28 October with remembrance services, military parades, folk dancing and feasting.

December

Christmas Day Although not as important as Easter, Christmas is still celebrated with religious services and feasting. Nowadays much 'Western' influence is apparent, including Christmas trees, decorations and presents.

FOOD

For large cities and towns, restaurant listings in this book are given in the following order: budget (under €15), mid-range (€15 to €30) and top end (over €30), and within each section the restaurants are listed in order of preference. For information on the staples of Greek food, see the Food & Drink chapter (p56).

GAY & LESBIAN TRAVELLERS

In a country where the church still plays a prominent role in shaping society's views on issues such as sexuality, it should come as no surprise that homosexuality is generally frowned upon – especially outside the major cities. While there is no legislation against homosexual activity, it pays to be discreet and to avoid open displays of togetherness.

This has not prevented Greece from becoming an extremely popular destination for gay travellers. Athens has a busy gay scene – but most gay travellers head for the islands. Mykonos (p134) has long been famous for its bars, beaches and general hedonism, while Paros (and Antiparos), Rhodes, Santorini and Skiathos all have their share of gay hang-outs.

The town of Eresos (p358) on the island of Lesvos (Mytilini), birthplace of the lesbian poet Sappho, has become something of a place of pilgrimage for lesbians.

Information

The *Spartacus International Gay Guide*, published by Bruno Gmünder (Berlin), is widely regarded as the leading authority on the gay travel scene. The Greek section contains a wealth of information on gay venues throughout the country.

There's also stacks of information on the Internet. For example, the website **Roz Mov** (www.geocities.com/WestHollywood/2225/index.html), is a good place to start. It has pages on travel information, gay health, the gay press, organisations, events and legal issues – and links to lots more sites.

Gayscape (www.gayscape.com/gayscape/menugreece .html) also has a useful website with lots of links.

HOLIDAYS
Public Holidays
All banks and shops and most museums and ancient sites close on public holidays. Following are national public holidays in Greece:

New Year's Day 1 January
Epiphany 6 January
First Sunday in Lent February
Greek Independence Day 25 March
Good Friday March/April
(Orthodox) Easter Sunday March/April
Spring Festival/Labour Day 1 May
Feast of the Assumption 15 August
Ohi Day 28 October
Christmas Day 25 December
St Stephen's Day 26 December

School Holidays
The Greek school year is divided into three terms. The main school holidays are in July/August.

INSURANCE
A travel insurance policy to cover theft, loss and medical problems is a good idea. Some policies offer lower and higher medical-expense options; the higher ones are chiefly for countries such as the USA, which have extremely high medical costs. There is a wide variety of policies available, so check the small print.

Some policies specifically exclude 'dangerous activities', eg, scuba diving, motorcycling, even trekking. A locally acquired motorcycle licence is not valid under some policies.

You may prefer a policy that pays doctors or hospitals directly rather than you having to pay on the spot and claim later. If you have to claim later make sure you retain all documentation related to the claim. Some policies ask you to call back (reverse charges) to a centre in your home country

where an immediate assessment of your problem is made.

Check that the policy covers ambulances or an emergency flight home.

Buy travel insurance as early as possible. If you buy it just before you fly, you may find you're not covered for such problems as delays caused by industrial action. Make sure you have a separate record of all your ticket details – preferably a photocopy (for information on what else to copy see Copies on p462).

Paying for your ticket with a credit card sometimes provides limited travel insurance, and you may be able to reclaim the payment if the operator doesn't deliver. In the UK, for instance, credit-card providers are required by law to reimburse consumers if a company goes into liquidation and the amount in contention is more than UK£100.

INTERNET ACCESS
Internet cafés are to be found almost everywhere in Greece, and are listed under the Information section for cities and islands in this book. Some hotels also offer Internet access.

If you need to rely on Internet cafés you'll need to carry three pieces of information with you to enable you to access your Internet mail account: your incoming (POP or IMAP) mail server name, your account name and your password. Armed with this information, you should be able to access your Internet mail account from any Net-connected machine in the world, provided it runs some kind of email software (remember that Netscape and Internet Explorer both have mail modules). It pays to become familiar with the process for doing this before you leave home.

Check out www.netcafeguide.com for an up-to-date list of Internet cafés throughout Greece. You may also find public Net access in post offices, libraries, hostels, hotels, universities and so on.

LEGAL MATTERS
Drugs
Drug laws in Greece are the strictest in Europe. Greek courts make no distinction between the possession of drugs and dealing them. Possession of even a small amount of marijuana is likely to land you in jail.

COMING OF AGE

For the record:

- You can drive when you're 18.
- The legal age for voting in Greece is 18.
- The age of consent for homosexual/heterosexual sex for girls is 15/15 and boys 16/17.
- The legal drinking age is 16.

MAPS

Mapping is an important feature of this guide, and unless you are going to trek or drive, you probably won't need to buy additional maps.

Most tourist offices hand out free maps, but they are often out of date and not particularly accurate. The same applies to the cheap 'tourist maps' sold on every island.

The best maps are published by the Greek company Road Editions. There is a wide range of maps to suit various needs, starting with a 1:500,000 map of Greece.

Crete is well covered by the company's maroon-covered 1:250,000 mainland series. Other islands are covered by its blue-cover island series. At the time of writing, the series featured Alonnisos, Andros, Chios, Corfu, Karpathos and Kasos, Kea (Tzia), Kefallonia and Ithaki, Kos, Lefkada, Lesvos, Milos and Kimolos, Mykonos, Naxos, Paros, Paxi and Antipaxi, Rhodes, Samos, Santorini, Skiathos, Skopelos, Syros, Tinos and Zakynthos. The scale of these maps ranges from 1:100,000 for larger islands like Corfu and Rhodes to 1:25,000 for Skiathos.

Even the smallest roads and villages are clearly marked, and the distance indicators are spot-on – important when negotiating your way around the backblocks. Useful features include symbols to indicate the location of petrol stations and tyre shops.

Freytag & Berndt's 15-map Greece series also has good coverage of the islands.

MONEY

Greece dropped the drachma and adopted the euro at the beginning of 2002.

The only place that will now convert outstanding drachma into euro is the Bank of Greece, and only at its central offices in major cities like Athens, Patra

and Thessaloniki. The Athens branch is at Panepistimiou 15, near Syntagma.

There are eight euro coins, in denominations of two and one euros, then 50, 20, 10, five, two and one cents, and six notes: €5, €10, €20, €50, €100 and €200. Prices in many shops are still displayed in both drachma and euros.

See the Quick Reference (inside front cover) for currency exchange rates, and see p15 for information on costs in Greece.

ATMs

ATMs are to be found in every town large enough to support a bank – and certainly in all of the well-tourist areas. If you've got MasterCard or Visa/Access, there are plenty of places to withdraw money. Cirrus and Maestro users can make withdrawals in all major towns and tourist areas.

AFEMs (automated foreign-exchange machines) are common in major tourist areas. They take all the major European currencies, Australian and US dollars and Japanese yen, and can come in handy in an emergency. It's worth noting that you are charged a hefty commission though.

Cash

Nothing beats cash for convenience – or for risk. If you lose cash, it's gone for good and very few travel insurers will bother to come to your rescue. It's best to carry no more cash than you need for the next few days, which means working out your potential costs whenever you change travellers cheques or withdraw cash from an ATM.

It's also a good idea to set aside a small amount of cash, say €100, as an emergency stash.

Credit Cards

The great advantage of credit cards is that they allow you to pay for major items without carrying around great wads of cash. Credit cards are now an accepted part of the commercial scene just about everywhere in Greece. They can be used to pay for a wide range of goods and services such as meals (in better restaurants), accommodation, car hire and souvenirs.

Be sure to ask whether it's possible to have your card replaced in Greece if it is lost or stolen.

The main credit cards are MasterCard, Visa and Eurocard, all of which are widely accepted in Greece. They can also be used as cash cards to draw cash from the ATMs of affiliated Greek banks in the same way as at home. Daily withdrawal limits are set by the issuing bank. Cash advances are given in local currency only.

The main charge cards are American Express (AmEx) and Diners Club, which are widely accepted in tourist areas but unheard of elsewhere.

Travellers Cheques

The main reason to carry travellers cheques rather than cash is the protection they offer against theft. They are, however, losing popularity as more and more travellers opt to put their money in a bank at home and withdraw it from ATMs as they go along.

AmEx, Visa and Thomas Cook cheques are all widely accepted and have efficient replacement policies. Maintaining a record of the cheque numbers and recording when you use them is vital when it comes to replacing lost cheques – keep this record separate from the cheques themselves.

PHOTOGRAPHY & VIDEO

Major brands of film are widely available, although they can be expensive in smaller towns. In Athens, expect to pay about €4.50 for a 36-exposure roll of Kodak Gold ISO 100; less for other brands. You'll find all the gear you need in the photography shops of Athens and major cities.

It is possible to obtain video cartridges easily in large towns and cities, but make sure you buy the correct format. It is usually worth buying at least a few cartridges duty-free to start off your trip.

As elsewhere in the world, developing film is a competitive business. Most places charge around €8.80 to develop a roll of 36 colour prints.

Lonely Planet's *Travel Photography: A Guide to Taking Better Pictures* by respected photographer Richard I'Anson offers a comprehensive guide to technical and creative travel photography.

Restrictions & Etiquette

Never photograph a military installation or anything else that has a sign forbidding photography. Flash photography is not allowed inside churches, and it's considered taboo to photograph the main altar.

Greeks usually love having their photos taken but always ask permission first. The same goes for video cameras, probably even more annoying and offensive for locals than a still camera.

POST

Post offices *(tahydromia)* are easily identifiable by the yellow signs outside. Regular post boxes are also yellow. The red boxes are for express-mail only.

Postal Rates

The postal rate for postcards and airmail letters to destinations within the EU is €0.60 for up to 20g and €0.85 for up to 50g. To other destinations the rate is €0.65 for up to 20g and €0.90 for up to 150g. Post within Europe takes between five and eight days and to the USA, Australia and New Zealand, nine to 11 days. Some tourist shops also sell stamps, but with a 10% surcharge.

Express mail costs an extra €2 and should ensure delivery in three days within the EU – use the special red post boxes. Valuables should be sent via registered post.

Sending Mail

Do not wrap a parcel until it has been inspected at a post office. In Athens, take your parcel to the **Parcel Post Office** (☎ 2103 228 940; Stadiou 4) located in the arcade, and elsewhere to the parcel counter of a regular post office.

Receiving Mail

You can receive mail poste restante (general delivery) at any main post office. The service is free, but you are required to show your passport. Ask senders to write your family name in capital letters and underline it, and also to mark the envelope 'poste restante'. It is a good idea to ask the post office clerk to check under your first name as well if letters you are expecting cannot be located. After one month, uncollected mail is returned to the sender. If you are about to leave a town and expected mail hasn't arrived, ask at the post office to have it forwarded to your next destination, c/o poste restante. Both Athens' **Central Post Office** (Map pp68-9;

Eolou 100, Omonia; 102 00; ☺ 7.30am-8pm Mon-Fri, 7.30am-2pm Sat) and **Syntagma Post Office** (Map pp74-5; cnr Mitropoleos & Plateia Syntagmatos 103 00; ☺ 7.30am-8pm Mon-Fri, 7.30am-2pm Sat) hold poste-restante mail.

Parcels are not delivered in Greece; they must be collected from the parcel counter of a post office – or, in Athens, from the Parcel Post Office.

SOLO TRAVELLERS

Greece is a great destination for solo travellers, especially in summer when the islands become an international meeting point. Hostels and other backpacker-friendly accommodation are good places to meet up with other solo travellers.

Many women travel alone in Greece. The crime rate remains relatively low and solo travel is probably safer than in most European countries. This does not mean that you should be lulled into complacency; bag snatching and rapes do occur, although violent offences are rare.

The biggest nuisance to foreign women travelling alone are the guys the Greeks have nicknamed *kamaki*. The word means 'fishing trident' and refers to the *kamaki*'s favourite pastime: 'fishing' for women. You'll find them everywhere there are lots of tourists; young (for the most part), smooth-talking guys who aren't in the least bashful about sidling up to foreign women in the street. They can be very persistent, but they are a hassle rather than a threat.

The majority of Greek men treat foreign women with respect, and are genuinely helpful.

TELEPHONE

The Greek telephone service is maintained by the public corporation known as Organismos Tilepikoinonion Ellados, which is always referred to by the acronym OTE (pronounced o-*teh*).

The system is modern and reasonably well maintained. There are public telephones just about everywhere, including some unbelievably isolated spots. The phones are easy to operate and can be used for local, long-distance and international calls. The 'i' at the top left of the push-button dialling panel brings up the operating instructions in English. All public phones use phonecards (known as *telekartes*) not coins. These

cards (€3, €5 and €9) are widely available at *periptera*, corner shops and tourist shops. A local call costs €0.30 for three minutes.

It's also possible to operate these phones using a growing range of discount-card schemes, which involve dialling an access code and then punching in your card number. The cards come with instructions in Greek and English. They are easy to use and buy double the time. The best of these cards is Smile, also widely available.

Mobile Phones

Few countries in the world have embraced the mobile phone with such enthusiasm as Greece. It has become the essential Greek accessory; everyone seems to have one.

If you have a compatible GSM mobile phone from a country with an overseas global roaming arrangement with Greece, you will be able to use your phone in Greece. You must inform your mobile phone service provider before you depart in order to have global roaming activated.

There are three mobile-service providers in Greece – Panafon, CosmOTE and Telestet. Of the three CosmOTE tends to have the best coverage in more remote areas like some of the villages, so you could try re-tuning your phone to CosmOTE if you find mobile coverage is patchy. All three companies offer pay-as-you-talk services by which you can buy a rechargeable SIM card and have your own Greek mobile number:

USEFUL PHONE NUMBERS

Domestic operator	☎ 151 or 152
General telephone information	☎ 134
International access code for Greece	☎ 30
International access code from within Greece	☎ 00
International dialling instructions in English, French and German	☎ 169
International telegrams	☎ 165
International telephone information	☎ 161 or 162
Numbers in Athens	☎ 131
Numbers elsewhere in Greece	☎ 132
Wake-up service	☎ 182
Weather	☎ 149

a good idea if you plan to spend some time in Greece. The Panafon system is called 'á la Carte', the Telestet system 'B-free' and Cosmote's 'Cosmo Karta'.

US and Canadian mobile-phone users won't be able to use their mobile phones in Greece, unless they are dual system equipped.

See Telephone on p70 for information about hiring a mobile phone.

TOILETS
Most places in Greece have Western-style toilets. You'll occasionally come across Asian-style squat toilets in older houses, *kafeneia* and public toilets.

Public toilets are a rarity, except at airports and bus and train stations. Cafés are usually the best option if you happen to get caught short, but you'll most likely be expected to purchase something for the privilege.

One peculiarity of the Greek plumbing system is that it can't handle toilet paper; apparently the pipes are too narrow. Whatever the reason, anything larger than a postage stamp seems to cause a serious problem. Toilet paper etc should be placed in the small bin that is provided near every toilet.

TOURIST INFORMATION
Tourist information is handled by the Greek National Tourist Organisation, known by the initials GNTO abroad and EOT (Ellinikos Organismos Tourismou) in Greece.

Local Tourist Offices
EOT (Map pp68-9; Ellinikos Organismos Tourismou; ☎ 2108 707 000; info@gnto.gr; www.gnto.gr; Tsoha 7, Ambelokipi; ☺ 9am-4pm Mon-Fri) was in turmoil at the time of research, following the relocation of its administrative headquarters from Amerikis 2, near Syntagma, to Ambelokipi. The move has also meant the closure of the ground-floor information office at Amerikis 2, leaving the city temporarily without a city-centre tourist office. Until a new location is found, EOT will be dispensing its usual range of information sheets from Tsoha 7. This information includes a useful timetable of the week's ferry departures from Piraeus, and details about public-transport prices and schedules

from Athens. Its free map of Athens is in need of an update, although most places of interest to travellers are clearly marked. The office is about 500m from Ambelokipi metro station.

Tourist Offices Abroad
GNTO offices abroad:

Australia (☎ 02-9241 1663/5; hto@tpg.com.au; 51-57 Pitt St, Sydney NSW 2000)

Austria (☎ 1-512 5317; grect@vienna.at; Opernring 8, Vienna A-10105)

Belgium (☎ 2-647 5770; 647 5142; 172 Ave Louise Louizalaan, B1050 Brussels)

Canada Toronto (☎ 416-968 2220; gnto.tor@sympatico.ca; 91 Scollard St, Toronto, Ontario M5R 1G4) Montreal (☎ 514-871 1535; 1170 Place Du Frere Andre, Montreal, Quebec H3B 3C6)

Denmark (☎ 33-325 332; Vester Farimagsgade 1, 1606 Copenhagen)

France (☎ 01-42 60 65 75; eot@club-internet.fr; 3 Ave de l'Opéra, Paris 75001)

Germany Berlin (☎ 30-217 6262; Wittenbergplatz 3A, 10789 Berlin 30) Frankfurt (☎ 69-236 561; info@gzf-eot.de; Neue Mainzerstrasse 22, 60311 Frankfurt) Hamburg (☎ 40-454 498; info-hamburg@gzf-eot.de; Neurer Wall 18, 20254 Hamburg) Munich (☎ 89-222 035/036; Pacellistrasse 5, 2W 80333 Munich)

Israel (☎ 3-517 0501; hellenic@netvision.net.il; 5 Shalom Aleichem St, Tel Aviv 61262)

Italy Rome (☎ 06-474 4249; www.enteturismoellenico .com; Via L Bissolati 78-80, 00187 Roma) Milan (☎ 02-860 470; Piazza Diaz 1, 20123 Milano)

Japan (☎ 03-350 55 917; gnto-jpn@t3.rim.or.jp; Fukuda Building West, 5F 2-11-3 Akasaka, Minato-Ku, Tokyo 107)

Netherlands (☎ 20-625 4212; gnto@planet.nl; Kerkstraat 61, Amsterdam GC 1017)

Sweden (☎ 8-679 6480; grekiska.statens.turistbyra@ swipnet.se; Birger Jarlsgatan 30, Box 5298 S, 10246 Stockholm)

Switzerland (☎ 01-221 0105; eot@bluewin.ch; Loewenstrasse 25, 8001 Zürich)

UK (☎ 020-7734 5997; 4 Conduit St, London W1R ODJ)

USA Chicago (☎ 312-782 1084; www.greektourism.com; Suite 600, 168 North Michigan Ave, Chicago, Illinois 60601) Los Angeles (☎ 213-626 6696; Suite 2198, 611 West 6th St, Los Angeles, California 92668) New York (☎ 212-421 5777; Olympic Tower, 645 5th Ave, New York, NY 10022)

Tourist Police
The tourist police work in cooperation with the regular Greek police and EOT. Each tourist-police office has at least one member of staff who speaks English. Hotels, restaurants, travel agencies, tourist

shops, tourist guides, waiters, taxi drivers and bus drivers all come under the jurisdiction of the tourist police. If you think that you have been ripped off by any of these, report it to the tourist police and they will investigate. If you need to report a theft or loss of passport, then go to the tourist police first, and they will act as interpreters between you and the regular police. The tourist police also fulfil the same functions as the EOT and municipal tourist offices, dispensing maps and brochures, and giving information on transport. They can often help to find accommodation.

VISAS

The list of countries whose nationals can stay in Greece for up to three months without a visa includes Australia, Canada, all EU countries, Iceland, Israel, Japan, New Zealand, Norway, Switzerland and the USA. Other countries included are Cyprus, Malta, the European principalities of Monaco and San Marino and most South American countries. The list changes; contact Greek embassies for the full list (up-to-date visa information is also available on www.lonelyplanet.com). Those not included can expect to pay about US$20 for

---

COPIES

All important documents (passport data page and visa page, credit cards, travel insurance policy, air/bus/train tickets, driving licence etc) should be photocopied before you leave home. Leave one copy with someone at home and keep another with you, separate from the originals.

---

a three-month visa.

North Cyprus

Greece will refuse entry to people whose passport indicates that, since November 1983, they have visited Turkish-occupied North Cyprus. This can be overcome if, upon entering North Cyprus, you ask officials to stamp a piece of paper (loose-leaf visa) rather than your passport. If you enter North Cyprus from the Greek Republic of Cyprus (only possible for a day visit), an exit stamp is not put into your passport.

Visa Extensions

If you wish to stay in Greece for longer than

three months, apply at a consulate abroad or at least 20 days in advance to the **Aliens Bureau** (☎ 2107 705 711; Leof Alexandras 173; ◷ 8am-1pm Mon-Fri) in Athens. Take your passport and four passport photographs along. You may be asked for proof that you can support yourself financially, so keep all your bank exchange slips (or the equivalent from a post office). These slips are not always automatically given – you may have to ask for them. Elsewhere in Greece apply to the local police authority. You will be given a permit that will authorise you to stay in the country for a period of up to six months.

Most travellers get around this by visiting neighbouring countries (such as Bulgaria or Turkey) briefly and then re-entering Greece.

WORK
Bar & Hostel Work

The bars of the Greek islands could not survive without foreign workers and there are thousands of summer jobs up for grabs every year. The pay is not fantastic, but you get to spend a summer in the islands. April and May is the time to go looking. Hostels and travellers hotels are other places that regularly employ foreign workers.

English Tutoring

If you're looking for a permanent job, the most widely available option is to teach English. A TEFL (Teaching English as a Foreign Language) certificate or a university degree is an advantage but not essential. In the UK, look through the *Times Educational Supplement* or Tuesday's edition of the *Guardian* newspaper for job opportunities – in other countries, contact the Greek embassy.

Another possibility is to find a job teaching English once you are in Greece. You will see language schools everywhere. Strictly speaking, you need a licence to teach in these schools, but many will employ teachers without one. The best time to look around for such a job is late summer.

The notice board at the **Compendium** (Map pp74-5; ☎ 2103 221 248; Nikis 28, Plaka) bookshop in Athens sometimes has advertisements looking for private English lessons.

Permits

EU nationals don't need a work permit, but

they need a residency permit if they intend to stay longer than three months. Nationals of other countries are supposed to have a work permit.

Street Performers
The islands offer some rich pickings for buskers, particularly Mykonos, Paros and Santorini. Athens can also be rewarding; the best spots are south of Plateia Syntagmatos on Ermou, and the area outside the church on Kydathineon in Plaka.

Volunteer Work
The **Hellenic Society for the Study & Protection of the Monk Seal** (☎ 2105 222 888; fax 2105 222 450; Solomou 53, Athens 104 32) and **Archelon** (Sea Turtle Protection Society of Greece; ☎ /fax 2105 231 342; www.archelon.gr; Solomou 57, Athens 104 32) use volunteers for the monitoring programmes they run on the Ionian Islands.

The **Hellenic Wildlife Rehabilitation Centre** (Elliniko Kentro Perithalifis Agrion Zoon; ☎ 2297 028 367; www.ekpaz.gr in Greek; ☺11am-1pm) in Aegina welcomes volunteers, particularly during the winter months. The new centre has accommodation available for volunteer workers. For more information see p106.

Other Work
Jobs are advertised in the classifieds section of English-language newspapers, or you can place an advertisement yourself. EU nationals can also make use of the OAED (Organismos Apasholiseos Ergatikou Dynamikou), the Greek National Employment Service. The OAED has offices throughout Greece.

Seasonal harvest work is handled by migrant workers from Albania and other Balkan nations, and is no longer a viable option for travellers.

Transport

CONTENTS

GETTING THERE & AWAY

ENTERING THE COUNTRY

As long as you have your documents in order and are willing to answer a few questions about the aim of your visit, your entry into Greece shouldn't be too taxing. All visitors must have a passport and, depending on your nationality, a visa. For more information on visas, see p462.

Passport

Greece will refuse entry to people whose passport indicates that, since November 1983, they have visited Turkish-occupied North Cyprus. This can be overcome if, upon entering North Cyprus, you ask the

---

THINGS CHANGE...

The information in this chapter is particularly vulnerable to change. Check directly with the airline or a travel agent to make sure you understand how a fare (and ticket you may buy) works and be aware of the security requirements for international travel. Shop carefully. The details given in this chapter should be regarded as pointers and are not a substitute for your own careful, up-to-date research.

---

immigration officials to stamp a piece of paper (loose-leaf visa) rather than them stamp your passport. For more information on passports, see p462.

AIR

Most travellers arrive in Greece by air, which is often the cheapest and quickest way to get there.

Airports & Airlines

Greece has 16 international airports, but only those in Athens, Thessaloniki and Iraklio (Crete) take scheduled flights.
Athens Eleftherios Venizelos International Airport (Code ATH; ☎ 2103 530 000; www.aia.gr)
Thessaloniki Macedonia International Airport (Code SKG; ☎ 2310 473 700; users.otenet.gr/~cpnchris/skg.html)
Iraklio Nikos Kazantzakis International Airport (Code HER; ☎ 2810 228 401)

Athens handles the vast majority of the flights, including all intercontinental traffic. Thessaloniki has direct flights to Amsterdam, Belgrade, Berlin, Brussels, Cyprus, Düsseldorf, Frankfurt, Istanbul, London, Milan, Moscow, Munich, Paris, Stuttgart, Tirana, Vienna and Zürich. Most of these flights are with Greece's national airline, Olympic Airways, or whichever flag carrier of the country concerned. Iraklio has direct flights to Cyprus with Olympic, while Aegean Airlines flies direct to Paris, Germany and Italy.

Greece's other international airports are found at Mykonos, Santorini (Thira), Hania (Crete), Kos, Karpathos, Samos, Skiathos, Hrysoupolis (for Kavala), Aktion (for Lefkada), Kefallonia and Zakynthos. These airports are used exclusively for charter flights, mostly from the UK, Germany and Scandinavia. Charter flights also fly to all of Greece's other international airports.

Olympic Airways (OA; ☎ 2013 569 111; www.olympic-airways.gr) is the country's national airline. Olympic has been through dire times in recent years, and the government has been searching in vain for a suitable buyer since 2001. Olympic is no longer Greece's only international airline. **Aegean Airlines** (A3;

☎ 8111 120 000; www.aegeanair.com) flies direct from Athens to Rome and Venice, and via Thessaloniki to Cologne, Dusseldorf, Frankfurt, Munich and Stuttgart.

Contact details for local Olympic and Aegean offices are listed in the appropriate sections throughout this book.

DEPARTURE TAX

The airport tax is €12 for passengers travelling to destinations within the EU, and €22 for other destinations. It applies to travellers aged over five, and is paid when you buy your ticket, not at the airport.

Passengers aged over two departing Athens are liable for a further €8.02 as a contribution to facilities at the new airport, and a security charge of €2.64. These charges also are paid when you buy your ticket.

From Asia

Most Asian countries offer fairly competitive deals, with Bangkok, Singapore and Hong Kong the best places to shop around for discount tickets.

Khao San Rd in Bangkok is the budget travellers' headquarters. Bangkok has a number of excellent travel agents, but there are also some suspect ones; ask the advice of other travellers before handing over your cash. **STA Travel** (☎ 02-236 0262; www.statravel.co.th) is a good place to start.

In Singapore, **STA Travel** (☎ 65-6737 7188; www.statravel.com.sg) offers competitive discount fares for most destinations. Singapore, like Bangkok, has hundreds of travel agents, so it is possible to compare prices on flights. Chinatown Point shopping centre on New Bridge Rd has a good selection of travel agents.

Hong Kong has a number of excellent, reliable travel agencies and some that are not so reliable. A good way to check on a travel agent is to look it up in the phone book: fly-by-night operators don't usually stay around long enough to get listed. In Hong Kong, **Four Seas Tours** (☎ 2200 7760; www.fourseastravel.com) is recommended, as is **Shoestring Travel** (☎ 2723 2306). Hong Kong's travel market can be unpredictable, but if you're lucky some excellent bargains may be available.

From Australia

Two well-known agents for cheap fares are STA Travel and Flight Centre. **STA Travel** (☎ 1300 733 035; www.statravel.com.au) has its main office in Melbourne, but also has offices in all major cities and on many university campuses. Call for the location of your nearest branch. **Flight Centre** (☎ 133 133; www.flightcentre.com.au) has its central office in Sydney, and dozens of offices throughout Australia.

Thai Airways International and Singapore Airlines both have convenient connections to Athens, as well as a reputation for good service. If you're planning on doing a bit of flying around Europe, it's worth checking around for special deals from the major European airlines. Alitalia, KLM and Lufthansa are three likely candidates with good European networks.

From Canada

Canadian discount air ticket sellers are known as consolidators and their air fares tend to be about 10% higher than those sold in the USA. The *Globe and Mail*, the *Toronto Star*, the *Montreal Gazette* and the *Vancouver Sun* carry travel agents' ads and are a good place to look for cheap fares.

Canada's national student travel agency is **Travel CUTS** (☎ 1-866-246-9762; www.travelcuts.com), which has offices in all major cities. For online bookings try www.expedia.ca or www.travelocity.ca.

Olympic Airways has two flights weekly from Toronto to Athens via Montreal. There are no direct flights from Vancouver, but there are connecting flights via Toronto, Amsterdam, Frankfurt and London on Canadian Airlines, KLM, Lufthansa and British Airways. You should be able to get to Athens from Toronto and Montreal for about C$1200/1000 in high/low season or from Vancouver for C$1500/1300.

For courier flights originating in Canada, contact **FB On Board Courier Services** (☎ 514-631-7929) in Montreal.

From Continental Europe

Athens is linked to every major city in Europe by either Olympic Airways or the flag carrier of each country.

Across Europe many travel agencies have ties with STA Travel, where cheap tickets can be purchased and STA-issued tickets

TRANSPORT

can be altered (usually for a US$25 fee). Outlets in major cities include: **Voyages Wasteels** (☎ 08 03 88 70 04) in Paris; **STA Travel** (☎ 03 03 11 09 50) in Berlin; and **Passaggi** (☎ 06 47 409 23) in Rome.

France has a network of travel agencies that can supply discount tickets to travellers of all ages. They include **OTU Voyages** (☎ 01 40 29 12 12; www.otu.fr), which has branches across the country and specialises in tickets for students and young people. Other recommendations include **Voyageurs du Monde** (☎ 01 42 86 16 00; www.vdm.com) and **Nouvelles Frontières** (nationwide ☎ 08 25 00 08 25; Paris ☎ 01 45 68 70 00; www.nouvelles-frontieres.fr).

In Germany, **STA Travel** (☎ 01805 456 422; www.statravel.de) has several offices around the country. For online fares try **Just Travel** (☎ 08 97 47 33 30; www.justtravel.de) and **Expedia** (☎ 018 05 00 60 25; www.expedia.de).

In the Netherlands, **Airfair** (☎ 020-620 5121; www.airfair.nl) and **My Travel** (☎ 0900 10 20 300; www.mytravel.nl) are recommended.

From Cyprus

Olympic Airways and Cyprus Airways share the Cyprus–Greece routes. Both airlines have three flights daily from Larnaka to Athens, and there are five flights weekly to Thessaloniki. Cyprus Airways also flies from Pafos to Athens once a week in winter, and twice a week in summer, while Olympic has two flights weekly between Larnaka and Iraklio.

From Turkey

Olympic Airways and Turkish Airlines share the Istanbul–Athens route, with at least one flight a day each. There are no direct flights from Ankara to Athens; all flights go via Istanbul.

From the UK

Airline ticket discounters are known as bucket shops in the UK. Despite the somewhat disreputable name, there is nothing under the counter about them. Discount air travel is big business in London. Advertisements for many travel agencies appear in the travel pages of the weekend broadsheet newspapers, such as the *Independent* on Saturday and the *Sunday Times*. Look out for the free magazines, such as *TNT*, which are widely available in London – start by looking outside the main train and underground stations.

For students or travellers under 26, a popular travel agency in the UK is **STA Travel** (☎ 087-016 00 599; www.statravel.co.uk). It sells tickets to all travellers but caters especially to young people and students. Charter flights can work out as a cheaper alternative to scheduled flights, especially if you do not qualify for the under-26 and student discounts.

Other recommended bucket shops in London include **Trailfinders** (☎ 020-7938 3939; www.trailfinders.co.uk), **Bridge the World** (☎ 0870-443 2399; www.b-t-w.co.uk) and **Flightbookers** (☎ 087-0010 7000; www.ebookers.com).

British Airways, Olympic Airways and Virgin Atlantic operate daily flights between London and Athens. Pricing is very competitive, with all three offering return tickets for around UK£220 in high season, plus tax. At other times, prices fall as low at UK£104, plus tax. British Airways has flights from Edinburgh, Glasgow and Manchester.

The cheapest scheduled flights are with **easyJet** (☎ 087-1750 0100; www.easyjet.com), the no-frills specialist, which has flights from Luton and Gatwick to Athens. There are numerous charter flights between the UK and Greece. Typical London–Athens charter fares are around UK£99/149 one way/return in the low season and UK£119/209 in the high season. These prices are for advance bookings, but even in high season it's possible to pick up last-minute deals for as little as UK£69/109. There are also charter flights from Birmingham, Cardiff, Glasgow, Luton, Manchester and Newcastle.

If you're flying from Athens to the UK, budget fares start at €75 to London or €90 to Manchester, plus airport tax.

From the USA

Discount travel agents in the USA are known as consolidators (although you won't see a sign on the door saying Consolidator). San Francisco is the ticket consolidator capital of America, although some good deals can be found in Los Angeles, New York and other big cities.

STA Travel (☎ 800-781-4040; www.statravel.com) has offices in Boston, Chicago, Miami, New York, Philadelphia, San Francisco and other major cities. Contact them for office locations. For online bookings try www.cheaptickets.com, www.expedia.com and www.orbitz.com.

New York has the widest range of options to Athens. The route to Europe is very competitive and there are new deals almost every day. Both Olympic Airways and Delta Airlines have direct flights but there are numerous other connecting flights.

There are no direct flights to Athens from the west coast. There are, however, connecting flights to Athens from many US cities, either linking with Olympic Airways in New York or flying with one of the European national airlines to their home country, and then on to Athens. Courier flights to Athens are occasionally advertised in the newspapers, or you could contact air-freight companies listed in the phone book. The **International Association of Air Travel Couriers** (☎ 561-582-8320; www.courier.org) sends members a bimonthly update of air-courier offerings.

LAND
Border Crossings
ALBANIA
There are a few crossing points between Greece and Albania. The main one is at Kakavia, 60km northwest of Ioannina. Two others are at Krystallopigi, 14km west of Kotas on the Florina–Kastoria road, and at Mertziani, 17km west of Konitsa. Kapshtica is the closest town on the Albanian side to Krystallopigi.

BULGARIA
There are two Bulgarian border crossings; one is located at Promahonas, 109km northeast of Thessaloniki and 41km from Serres, and the other at Ormenio, in northeastern Thrace.

FORMER YUGOSLAV REPUBLIC OF MACEDONIA
There are a few border crossings between Greece and FYROM. One is at Evzoni, 68km north of Thessaloniki. This is the main highway to Skopje, which continues to Belgrade. Another border crossing is at Niki, 16km north of Florina. This road leads to Bitola, and continues to Ohrid, once a popular tourist resort on the shores of Lake Ohrid.

TURKEY
Crossing points are at Kipi, 43km northeast of Alexandroupolis, and at Kastanies,

139km northeast of Alexandroupolis. Kipi is probably more convenient if you're heading for Istanbul, but the route through Kastanies goes via the fascinating towns of Soufli and Didymotiho, in Greece, and Edirne (ancient Adrianople) in Turkey.

Albania
BUS
The Hellenic Railways Organisation (OSE) operates a daily bus between Athens and Tirana (€35.20) via Ioannina and Gjirokastra. The bus departs Athens (Peloponnese train station) at 7pm, arriving in Tirana the following day at 5pm. There are also buses from Thessaloniki to Korça (Korytsa, €19, six hours), travelling via Florina.

Bulgaria
BUS
The OSE operates a bus from Athens to Sofia (€45.50, 15 hours) at 7am daily, except Monday. It also operates Thessaloniki–Sofia buses (€19, 7½ hours, four daily). There is a private bus service to Plovdiv (€29.50, six hours) and Sofia (€35.50, seven hours) from Alexandroupolis on Wednesday and Sunday at 8.30am.

TRAIN
There is a daily train to Sofia from Athens (€30.65, 18 hours) via Thessaloniki (€17.90, nine hours). From Sofia, there are connections to Budapest (€67.50) and Bucharest (€37.30).

Former Yugoslav Republic of Macedonia
TRAIN
There are two trains daily from Thessaloniki to Skopje (€14.50, three hours), crossing the border between Idomeni and Gevgelija. They continue from Skopje to the Serbian capital of Belgrade (€31.70, 12 hours).

There are no trains between Florina and FYROM, although there may be trains to Skopje from the FYROM side of the border.

Turkey
BUS
OSE operates a bus from Athens to Istanbul (22 hours) daily except Wednesday, leaving the Peloponnese train station in Athens at 7pm and travelling via Thessaloniki and

Alexandroupolis. One-way fares are €67.50 from Athens, €44 from Thessaloniki and €15 from Alexandroupolis. Students qualify for a 20% discount and children under 12 travel for half-fare. See the Getting There & Away sections for each city for information on where to buy tickets.

Buses from Istanbul to Athens leave the Anadolu Terminal (Anatolia Terminal) at the Topkapı *otogar* (bus station) at 10am daily except Sunday.

TRAIN
There are daily trains between Athens and Istanbul (€63) via Thessaloniki (€42.50) and Alexandroupolis (€20). The service is incredibly slow and the train gets uncomfortably crowded. There are often delays at the border and the journey can take much longer than the advertised 22 hours. You'd be well advised to take the bus instead. Inter-Rail passes are valid in Turkey, but Eurail passes are not.

Western Europe
Overland travel between Western Europe and Greece is almost a thing of the past. Air fares are so cheap that land transport cannot compete. Travelling from the UK to Greece through Europe means crossing various borders, so check whether any visas are required before setting out.

BUS
There are no bus services to Greece from the UK, nor from anywhere else in northern Europe. Bus companies can no longer compete with cheap air fares.

CAR & MOTORCYCLE
Before the troubles in the former Yugoslavia began, most motorists driving from the UK to Greece opted for the direct route: Ostend, Brussels, Salzburg and then down the Yugoslav highway through Zagreb, Belgrade and Skopje, then crossing the border to Evzoni.

These days most people drive to an Italian port and get a ferry to Greece. Coming from the UK, this means driving through France, where petrol costs and road tolls are exorbitant.

TRAIN
Unless you have a **Eurail** (www.eurail.com) pass or are aged under the age of 26 and eligible for a discounted fare, travelling to Greece by train is prohibitively expensive. Indeed, the chances of anyone wanting to travel from London to Athens by train are considered so remote, it's no longer possible to buy a single ticket for this journey. The trip involves travelling from London to Paris on the Eurostar, followed by Paris to Brindisi, then a ferry from Brindisi to Patra – and finally a train from Patra to Athens.

Greece is part of the Eurail network. Eurail passes can only be bought by residents of non-European countries and are supposed to be purchased before arriving in Europe. They can, however, be bought in Europe as long as your passport proves that you've been there for less than six months. In London, head for the **Rail Europe Travel Centre** (☎ 087-0584 8848; 179 Piccadilly). Check the Eurail website for full details of passes and prices.

If you are starting your European travels in Greece, you can buy your Eurail pass from the OSE office in Athens at Karolou 1, and at the stations in Patra and Thessaloniki.

Greece is also part of the **Inter-Rail** (www .interrailnet.com) pass system, available to residents in Europe for six months or more.

SEA
Albania
Corfu-based Petrakis Lines has daily ferries to the Albanian port of Saranda (€15, 25 minutes), plus twice-weekly services to Himara (€25, 1¼ hours) and Vlora (€38, 2½ hours).

Cyprus & Israel
Passenger services from Greece to Cyprus and Israel had been suspended at the time of research. **Salamis Lines** (www.viamare.com/Salamis) was still operating on the route, but carrying only vehicles and freight, while **Poseidon Lines** (www.ferries.gr/poseidon) had stopped all services.

Italy
There are ferries to Greece from the Italian ports of Ancona, Bari, Brindisi, Trieste and Venice. For more information about these services, see the Patra (p93), Igoumenitsa (p94), Corfu (p407) and Kefallonia (p407) sections.

The ferries can get very crowded in summer. If you want to take a vehicle across it's a good idea to make a reservation beforehand.

In the UK, reservations can be made on almost all of these ferries through **Viamare Travel Ltd** (☎ 020-7431 4560; ferries@viamare.com).

You'll find all the latest information about ferry routes, schedules and services on the Internet. For an overview try www.greekferries.gr.

Most of the ferry companies have their own websites. Some of them are included in the following list:
Agoudimos Lines (www.agoudimos-lines.com)
ANEK Lines (www.anek.gr)
Blue Star Ferries (www.bluestarferries.com)
Fragline (www.fragline.gr)
Hellenic Mediterranean Lines (www.hml.gr)
Minoan Lines (www.minoan.gr)
Superfast (www.superfast.com)
Ventouris Ferries (www.ventouris.gr)

The following ferry services are for high season (July and August), and prices are for oneway deck class. Deck class on these services means exactly that. If you want a reclining, aircraft-type seat, you'll be up for another 10% to 15% on top of the listed fares. All companies offer discounts for return travel. Prices are about 30% less in the low season.

FROM ANCONA
The route to Igoumenitsa and Patra has become increasingly popular in recent years. There can be up to three boats daily in summer, and at least one a day year round. All ferry operators in Ancona have booths at the *stazione marittima* (ferry terminal) off Piazza Candy, where you can pick up timetables and price lists and make bookings.

Blue Star Ferries and Superfast Ferries have two boats daily, taking 19 hours direct to Patra, or 21 hours via Igoumenitsa. Both charge €80 and sell tickets through **Morandi & Co** (☎ 071-20 20 33; Via XXIX Settembre 2/0). Superfast accepts Eurail passes. **ANEK Lines** (☎ 071-207 23 46; Via XXIX Settembre 2/0; €68) and **Minoan** (☎ 071-20 17 08; Via Astagno 3; €72) do the trip daily in 19½ hours via Igoumenitsa.

FROM BARI
Minoan (☎ 080-521 02 66; Via Latilla 14; €56) and **Superfast** (☎ 080-52 11 416; Corso de Tullio 6; €57) have daily sailings to Patra via Igoumenitsa. Minoan does the trip to Patra in 14 hours, which is slightly faster than Superfast. Minoan stops at Corfu three times a week, while Superfast accepts Eurail passes.

Ventouris (☎ 080-521 76 09) has daily boats to Corfu (10 hours) and Igoumenitsa (11½ hours) for €45.

FROM BRINDISI
The trip from Brindisi was once the most popular crossing, but it now operates only between April and early October. **Med Link** (Discovery Shipping; ☎ 083-154 81 16/7; Costa Morena) and **Hellenic Mediterranean** (☎ 083-154 80 01; Costa Morena) offer at least one boat a day to Patra between them.

Hellenic Mediterranean calls at Igoumenitsa on the way, and also has services that call at Corfu, Kefallonia, Paxi and Zakynthos, while Med Link calls at Kefallonia during July and August. All these services cost €50. Hellenic Mediterranean accepts Eurail passes, and issues vouchers for travel with Med Link on days when there is no Hellenic Mediterranean service.

Agoudimos Lines (☎ 083-155 01 80; Via Provinciale per Lecce 29) and **Fragline** (☎ 083-154 85 40; Via Spalato 31) sail only to Igoumenitsa.

FROM TRIESTE
ANEK Lines (☎ 040-322 05 61; Via Rossini 2) has boats to Patra (€68, 32 hours) every day except Thursday, calling at Corfu and Igoumenitsa.

FROM VENICE
Minoan Lines (☎ 041-240 71 77; Stazione Marittima 123) sails to Patra (€75, 29 hours) daily except Wednesday, calling at Corfu and Igoumenitsa. **Blue Star Ferries** (☎ 041-277 05 59; Stazione Marittima 123; €64) plys the route four times weekly.

Turkey
There are five regular ferry services between Turkey's Aegean coast and the Greek islands. Tickets for all ferries to Turkey must be bought a day in advance. You'll be asked to turn in your passport the night before the trip but don't worry, you'll get it back the next day before you board the boat. Port tax for departures to Turkey is €9.

In addition to the services listed below, see Kastellorizo (p284) and Symi (p286) for information about excursion boats to Turkey. See the relevant sections under individual island entries for more information.

FROM CHIOS
There are daily Chios–Çeşme boats from July to September, dropping back to two

boats a week in winter. Tickets cost €40/50 one-way/return (plus €9 port tax). See p343 for more details.

FROM KOS

There are daily ferries in summer from Kos to Bodrum (ancient Halicarnassus) in Turkey. Boats leave at 8.30am and return at 4.30pm. The one-hour journey costs €34. See p297 for more details.

FROM LESVOS

There are up to four boats weekly on this route in high season. Tickets cost €39 one way or return, including port taxes. See p351 for more details.

FROM RHODES

There are two daily catamarans from Rhodes to Marmaris at 8am and 4pm respectively from June to September, dropping back to only three or four services a week in winter. Tickets cost €30 one way plus €15 Turkish arrival tax. In addition there is a weekly passenger and car ferry service once a week on Friday at 4pm. The cost of ferrying a car to the Turkish mainland is €180 one way, while passengers pay €55 including taxes. Return rates usually work out cheaper.

FROM SAMOS

There are two boats daily to Kuşadası (for Ephesus) from Samos in summer, dropping to one or two boats weekly in winter. Tickets cost around €45 return (plus €21 port taxes). See p334 for more details.

GETTING AROUND

Greece is an easy place to travel around thanks to a comprehensive public transport system.

Buses are the mainstay of land transport, with a network that reaches out to the smallest villages. Trains are a good alternative, where available. To most visitors, though, travelling in the Greek islands means island-hopping on the multitude of ferries that crisscross the Adriatic and the Aegean. If you're in a hurry, Greece also has an extensive domestic air network.

The information in this chapter was for the 2003 high season. You'll find lots of travel information on the Internet. The website www.ellada.com has lots of useful links, including airline timetables.

AIR

The majority of domestic flights are handled by the country's maligned national carrier, **Olympic Airways** (www.olympic-airways.gr), together with its offshoot, Olympic Aviation.

Olympic has offices wherever there are flights, as well as in other major towns. The **head office** (☎ 2109 269 111) is at Leof Syngrou 96 in Athens. The toll-free number (within Greece) for reservations is ☎ 8011 144 444.

The prices listed in this book are for full-fare economy, and include domestic taxes and charges. Olympic also offers cheaper options between Athens and some of the more popular destinations such as Corfu, Iraklio, Lesvos, Rhodes and Thessaloniki (see p79). There are discounts for return tickets for travel between Monday and Thursday, and bigger discounts for trips that include a Saturday night away.

DOMESTIC DEPARTURE TAX

Airport tax for domestic flights is €12, paid as part of the ticket. It applies to all passengers aged over five. Passengers aged over two departing from Athens must pay an additional €8.02 for using the facilities at the new Eleftherios Venizelos International Airport, plus a security charge of €2.64. These charges are paid as part of the ticket.

All of the prices quoted in this book include these taxes and charges where applicable.

The baggage allowance on domestic flights is 15kg, or 20kg if the domestic flight is part of an international journey. Olympic offers a 25% student discount on domestic flights, but only if the flight is part of an international journey.

Crete-based **Aegean Airlines** (☎ 8011 120 000; www.aegeanair.com) is the sole survivor of the many new airlines that emerged to challenge Olympic following the 1993 decision to end Olympic's monopoly on domestic flights.

It offers flights from Athens (p79) to Alexandroupolis, Corfu, Hania, Iraklio, Kavala, Lesvos, Mykonos, Rhodes, Santorini and Thessaloniki; from Thessaloniki (p87) to Iraklio, Lesvos, Mykonos, Rhodes and Santorini; and from Iraklio (p214) to Rhodes.

Full-fare economy seats cost the same as Olympic, but Aegean often has special deals. It offers a 20% youth discount for travellers under 26, and a similar discount for the over-60s.

BICYCLE

Cycling is a cheap, healthy, environmentally sound and, above all, fun way of travelling.

Crete has become a popular destination for cycling fans, but you'll find cyclists wherever the roads are good enough to get around. Most of them are foreigners; few locals show much enthusiasm for peddling.

The time of year is an important consideration. It's too hot to cycle around in summer and it can get very cold in winter, but for the rest of the year conditions are ideal.

If you want a decent touring bike, you should bring your own. Bicycles pose few problems for airlines. You can take it to pieces and put it in a bike bag or box, but it's much easier simply to wheel your bike to the check-in desk, where it should be treated as a piece of baggage. You may have to remove the pedals and turn the handlebars sideways so that it takes up less space in the aircraft's hold; check all this with the airline well in advance. Bikes are carried free of charge on ferries.

One note of caution: before you leave home, go over your bike with a fine-toothed comb and fill your repair kit with every imaginable spare. As with cars and motorbikes, you won't necessarily be able to buy spares for your machine if it breaks down in the middle of nowhere.

You can hire bicycles in some tourist places, but they are not as widely available as cars and motorbikes. Prices range from €5 to €12 per day, depending on the type and age of the bike.

BOAT
Catamaran

High-speed catamarans have become an important part of the island travel scene. They are just as fast as the hydrofoils – if not faster – and much more comfortable. They are also much less prone to cancellation in rough weather. Fares are the same as for hydrofoils.

Hellas Flying Dolphins (www.dolphins.gr) is the major player in the field. It operates huge, vehicle-carrying Highspeed Cats from Piraeus and Rafina to the Cyclades, and smaller Flying Cats from Rafina to the central and northern Cyclades and on many of the routes around the Saronic Gulf.

Blue Star Ferries (www.bluestarferries.com) operates its Seajet catamarans on the run from Rafina to Tinos, Mykonos and Paros.

These services are very popular; book as far in advance as possible, especially if you want to travel on weekends.

Ferry

Every island has a ferry service of some sort, although in winter, services to some of the smaller islands are fairly skeletal. Services start to pick up again from April onwards, and by July and August there are countless services crisscrossing the Aegean. Ferries come in all shapes and sizes, from the giant 'superferries' that work the major routes to the small, ageing open ferries that chug around the backwaters.

CLASSES

The large ferries usually have four classes: 1st class has air-con cabins and a posh lounge and restaurant; 2nd class has smaller cabins and sometimes a separate lounge; tourist class gives you a berth in a shared four-berth cabin; and 3rd (deck) class gives you access to a room with 'airline' seats, a restaurant, a lounge/bar and, of course, the deck.

Deck class remains an economical way to travel, while a 1st-class ticket can cost almost as much as flying on some routes. Children under four travel free, while children between four and 10 pay half fare. Full fares apply for children over 10. Unless you state otherwise, when purchasing a ticket you will automatically be given deck class. Prices quoted in this book are for deck class as this is the most popular with tourists.

COSTS

Prices are fixed by the government, and are determined by the distance of the destination from the port of origin. The small differences in price you may find at ticket agencies are the results of some agents sacrificing part of their designated commission to qualify as a 'discount service'. The discount is seldom more than €0.30. Ticket prices include embarkation tax, a contribution to NAT (the seamen's union) and 8% VAT.

TRANSPORT

ROUTES

Greece's major ferry port is Piraeus, Athens (p84). Ferries leave here for the Cyclades, the Dodecanese, the Northeastern Aegean Islands, the Saronic Gulf Islands and Crete. Athens' second port is Rafina (p85), 70km east of the city and served by an hourly bus service. It has ferries to the northern Cyclades, Evia, Lesvos and Limnos. The port of Lavrio (p91), in southern Attica, is the port for ferries to the Cycladic island of Kea.

Ferries for the Ionian Islands leave from the Peloponnese ports of Patra (p93), for Kefallonia, Ithaki, Paxi and Corfu, and Kyllini (p94) for Kefallonia and Zakynthos; and from Igoumenitsa (p94) in Epiros for Corfu and Paxi.

Ferries for the Sporades leave from Volos (p96), Thessaloniki (p89), Agios Konstantinos (p95) and Kymi on Evia. The last two ports are easily reached by bus from Athens.

Some of the Northeastern Aegean Islands have connections with Thessaloniki as well as Piraeus. The odd ones out are Thasos, which is reached from Kavala (p98), and Samothraki, which can be reached from Alexandroupolis (p100) year-round and also from Kavala in summer.

SCHEDULES

Ferry timetables change from year to year and season to season, and ferries can be subject to delays and cancellations at short

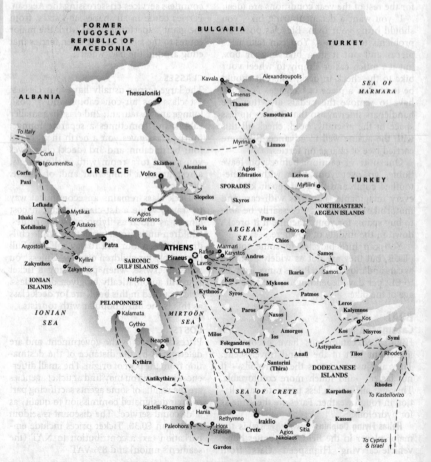

notice due to bad weather, strikes or the boats simply conking out. No timetable is infallible, but the comprehensive weekly list of departures from Piraeus put out by the EOT (Ellinikos Organismos Tourismou) in Athens is as accurate as is humanly possible. The people to go to for the most up-to-date ferry information are the local port police *(limenarheio)*, whose offices are usually located on or near the quay side.

There's lots of information about ferry services available on the Internet. Try www.greekferries.gr. Many of the larger ferry companies have their own sites, including the following:

ANEK Lines (www.anek.gr)
Blue Star Ferries (www.bluestarferries.com)
GA Ferries (www.gaferries.com)
Hellas Flying Dolphins (www.dolphins.gr)
Italian Ferries (www.italianferries.it)
LANE Lines (www.lane.gr)
Minoan Lines (www.minoan.gr)
NEL Lines (www.nel.gr)

Throughout the year there is at least one ferry a day from a mainland port to the major island in each group, and during the high season (from June to mid-September) there are considerably more. Ferries sailing from one island group to another are not so frequent, and if you're going to travel in this way you'll need to plan carefully, otherwise you may end up having to backtrack to Piraeus.

Travelling time can vary from one ferry to another, depending on how many islands are visited on the way to your destination. For example, the Piraeus–Rhodes trip can take between 15 and 18 hours depending on the route. Before buying your ticket, check how many stops the boat makes, and its estimated arrival time. It can make a big difference.

TICKET PURCHASE

Given that ferries are prone to delays and cancellations, it's best not to purchase a ticket until it has been confirmed that the ferry is leaving. If you need to reserve a car space, however, you may need to pay in advance. If the service is then cancelled you can transfer your ticket to the next available service with that company.

Agencies selling tickets line the waterfront of most ports, but rarely is there one that sells tickets for every boat, and often an agency is reluctant to give you information about a boat they do not sell tickets for. This means you have to check the timetables displayed outside each agency to find out which ferry is next to depart – or ask the port police.

High-Speed Ferries

These are the latest addition to the ferry network, slashing travel times on some of the longer routes. **Nel Lines** (☎ 2251 026 299; www.nel.gr) leads the way with its futuristic-looking *Aeolis Express*, which operates from Piraeus to the Northeast Aegean islands of Chios (4½ hours), Ikaria (5½ hours), Lesvos (six hours) and Samos (seven hours). These services cost roughly twice as much as standard ferries.

Blue Star Ferries (www.bluestarferries.com) aren't in quite the same league, but its *Blue Star 1* sails from Piraeus to Kos in eight hours and to Rhodes in 11 hours. It charges about 20% more than the regular ferries.

Hydrofoil

Hydrofoils offer a faster alternative to ferries on some routes, particularly to islands close to the mainland. They take half the time, but cost twice as much. They don't take cars or motorbikes. Most routes operate only during high season, and according to demand, and all are prone to cancellations if the sea is rough.

Hellas Flying Dolphins (www.dolphins.gr) runs the busy Argosaronic network linking Piraeus with the Saronic Gulf Islands and the ports of the eastern Peloponnese, as well as services to the Sporades from Agios Konstantinos and Volos.

Kyriacoulis Hydrofoils (☎ 2241 024 000), based in Rhodes, serves the Dodecanese and provides connections to the Northeastern Aegean islands of Ikaria and Samos. Other routes are between Kavala and Thasos in the Northeastern Aegean, and from Alexandroupolis to Samothraki and Limnos.

Tickets can't be bought on board hydrofoils – buy them in advance from an agent. You will be allocated a seat number.

Interisland Boat

In addition to the large ferries that ply between the large mainland ports and island groups, there are smaller boats that link islands within a group, and occasionally, an island in one group with an island in another.

TRANSPORT

In the past these boats were invariably caïques – sturdy old fishing boats – but gradually these are being replaced by new purpose-built boats, which are called express or excursion boats. Tickets tend to cost more than tickets for the large ferries, but the boats are useful if you're island-hopping.

Taxi Boat

Most islands have taxi boats – small speed-boats that operate like taxis, transporting people to difficult to get to places. Some owners charge a set price for each person, others charge a flat rate for the boat, and this cost is divided by the number of passengers. Either way, prices are usually quite reasonable.

BUS

All long-distance buses, on the mainland and the islands, are operated by regional collectives known as **KTEL** (Koino Tamio Eispraxeon Leoforion; www.ktel.org). Every prefecture on the mainland has a KTEL, which operates local services within the prefecture and services to the main towns of other prefectures. Fares are fixed by the government.

Island Buses

Island services are less simple to summarise! There's an enormous difference in the level of services. Crete (which is split into three prefectures) is organised in the same way as the mainland – each prefecture has its own KTEL providing local services and services to the main towns of other prefectures. Most islands have just one bus company, some have just one bus.

On islands where the capital is inland, buses normally meet the boats. Some of the more remote islands have not yet acquired a bus, but most have some sort of motorised transport – even if it is only a bone-shaking, three-wheeled truck.

Mainland Buses

The network is comprehensive. All major ports on the mainland have daily connections to Athens. The islands of Corfu, Kefallonia and Zakynthos can also be reached directly from Athens by bus – the fares include the price of the ferry ticket. For details, see p79.

When you buy a ticket you will be allotted a seat number, which is noted on the ticket. The seat number is indicated on the back of

each seat of the bus, not on the back of the seat in front; this can cause confusion among Greeks and tourists alike. You can board a bus without a ticket and pay on board, but this may mean that you have to stand. Keep your ticket for the duration of the journey; it will be checked several times en route.

Buses do not have toilets or refreshments on board, so make sure you are prepared on both counts. Buses stop about every three hours on long journeys. Smoking is prohibited on all buses in Greece; only the drivers dare to ignore the no-smoking signs.

Bus travel is very reasonably priced, with a journey costing approximately €5 per 100km. Following are fares and journey times on some of the major routes.

Route	Duration	Cost
Athens–Thessaloniki	7½hr	€29.40
Athens–Patra	3hr	€12.90
Athens–Volos	5hr	€18.60
Athens–Corfu*	5hr	€29.50
* including ferry		

CAR & MOTORCYCLE

Many of the islands are plenty big enough to warrant having your own vehicle. Roads have improved enormously in recent years, particularly on the larger, more visited islands, such as Crete. Few people bother to bring their own vehicle from Europe; there are plenty of places to hire cars.

Almost all islands are served by car ferries. Sample prices for small vehicles include Piraeus–Mykonos (€66.60); Piraeus–Crete (Hania and Iraklio; €70); and Piraeus–Samos (€79.80). The charge for a large motorbike is about the same as the price of a 3rd-class passenger ticket.

Petrol is expensive, the further you get from major cities the more it costs. Prices vary from station to station. Super can be as cheap as €0.70 per litre at city discount places, but €0.75 to €0.85 is the norm. You'll pay closer to €0.90 per litre in remote areas. The price range for unleaded – available everywhere – is from €0.75 to €0.85 per litre. Diesel costs about €0.60 per litre.

Bringing Your Own Vehicle

Cars can be brought into Greece for four months without a carnet; a green card (international third-party insurance) is the only requirement. Your vehicle will be registered in your passport when you enter Greece to prevent you leaving the country without it.

Driving Licence

Greece recognises all national driving licences, provided the licence has been held for at least one year. It also recognises an International Driving Permit, which should be obtained before you leave home.

Greece has introduced new regulations for hiring mopeds and motorcycles – to rent one you must produce a licence that shows proficiency in riding the category of bike you wish to rent; this applies to everything from 50cc up. Standard British driving licences are not sufficient – British citizens must obtain a Category A licence from the DVLA. In most other EU countries separate licences are automatically issued

Rental

CAR

Rental cars are available almost everywhere, but it's best to hire from major cities where competition lowers the prices. All the multinational car-hire companies are represented in Athens, and most have branches in other major towns and tourist destinations. Smaller islands often have only one outlet.

High-season weekly rates with unlimited mileage start at about €280 for the smallest models, dropping to about €200 per week in winter. To these prices must be added VAT of 18%, or 13% on the islands of the Dodecanese, the Northeastern Aegean and the Sporades, and optional extras such as a collision damage waiver of €12 per day (more for larger models), without which you'll find yourself liable for the first €295 of the repairs (more for larger models). Other costs include a theft waiver (at least €6 per day) and personal accident insurance.

You can find better deals at local companies. Their advertised rates can be up to 50% cheaper, and they are normally more open to negotiation, especially if business is slow.

If you want to take a hire car to another country or onto a ferry, you will need advance written authorisation from the hire company. Unless you pay with a credit card, most hire companies will require a minimum deposit of €120 per day. See the Getting Around sections of cities and islands for details of places to rent cars.

The minimum driving age in Greece is 18 years, but most car-hire firms require you to be at least 21 – or 23 for larger vehicles.

MOTORCYCLE

Mopeds and motorcycles are available for hire wherever there are tourists to rent them. In many cases their maintenance has been minimal, so check the machine thoroughly before you hire it – especially the brakes: you'll need them!

Motorbikes are a cheap way to travel around. Rates range from €10 to €15 per day for a moped or 50cc motorbike to €25 per day for a 250cc motorbike. Out of season these prices drop considerably, so use your bargaining skills. By October it is sometimes possible to hire a moped for as little as €5 per day. Most motorcycle hirers include third-party insurance in the price, but it's wise to check this. This insurance will not include medical expenses.

Road Rules

In Greece, as in Continental Europe, you drive on the right and overtake on the left. Outside built-up areas, main road traffic has right of way at intersections. In towns, vehicles coming from the right have right of way. Seat belts must be worn in front seats, and in back seats if the car is fitted with them. Children under 12 years of age are not allowed in the front seat. It's compulsory to carry a first-aid kit, fire extinguisher and warning triangle, and it's forbidden to carry cans of petrol. Helmets are compulsory for motorcyclists if the motorbike is 50cc or more.

Outside residential areas the speed limit is 120km/h on highways, 90km/h on other roads and 50km/h in built-up areas. The speed limit for motorbikes up to 100cc is 70km/h and for larger motorbikes, 90km/h.

WARNING

The islands are not the best place to initiate yourself into the art of motorcycling. There are still a lot of gravel roads, and dozens of tourists have accidents every year. If you are planning to use a motorcycle or moped, check that your travel insurance covers you for injury resulting from a motorbike accident. Many insurance companies don't offer this cover, so check the fine print!

TRANSPORT

Drivers exceeding the speed limit by 20% are liable to receive a fine of €60; and by 40%, €150.

The police have also cracked down on drink-driving laws – at last. A blood-alcohol content of 0.05% is liable to incur a fine of €147.75, and over 0.08% is a criminal offence.

If you are involved in an accident and no-one is hurt, the police will not be required to write a report, but it is advisable to go to a nearby police station and explain what happened. A police report may be required for insurance purposes. If an accident involves injury, a driver who does not stop and does not inform the police may face a prison sentence.

HITCHING

Hitching is never entirely safe in any country in the world, and we don't recommend it. Travellers who decide to hitch should understand that they are taking a small but potentially serious risk. People who do choose to hitch will be safer if they travel in pairs and should let someone know where they are planning to go. Greece has a reputation for being a relatively safe place for women to hitch, but it is still unwise to do it alone. It's better for a woman to hitch with a companion, preferably a male one.

Some parts of Greece are much better for hitching than others. Getting out of major cities tends to be hard work, and Athens is notoriously difficult. Hitching is much easier in remote areas and on islands with poor public transport. On country roads, it is not unknown for someone to stop and ask if you want a lift even if you haven't stuck a thumb out.

LOCAL TRANSPORT
Bus

Most Greek island towns are small enough to get around on foot. The only island towns where tourists are likely to use buses are Iraklio and Rhodes. The procedure for buying tickets for local buses is covered in the Getting Around section for each city.

Metro

Athens is the only city in Greece large enough to warrant the building of an underground system. See p81 for details.

Taxi

Taxis are widely available except on the very smallest islands. They are reasonably priced by European standards, especially if three or four people share costs.

Yellow city cabs are metered. Flag fall is €0.75, followed by €0.24 per kilometre (€0.44 per kilometre outside town). These rates double between midnight and 5am. Costs additional to the per-kilometre rate are €1.18 from an airport, €0.59 from a bus, port or train station and €0.30 for each piece of luggage over 10kg. Grey rural taxis do not have meters, so you should always settle on a price before you get in.

TRAIN

None of the islands have trains. On the mainland, however, trains are operated by the **Greek Railways Organisation** (Organismos Sidirodromon Ellados; www.ose.gr), referred to as the OSE.

The biggest problem with the Greek railway network is that it's so limited. There are essentially only two main lines: the standard gauge service from Athens to Alexandroupolis via Thessaloniki, and the Peloponnese network, a narrow-gauge track.

The services that do exist are of a good standard, and improving. In fact, the network was in the middle of a major pre-Olympic overhaul at the time of research.

There are two types of service: regular (slow) trains that stop at all stations, and faster intercity trains that link major cities.

Slow trains are the country's cheapest public transport: 2nd-class fares are absurdly cheap, and even 1st class is cheaper than bus travel. Sample journey times and 1st- and 2nd-class fares include Athens–Thessaloniki (€21/14, 7½ hours) and Thessaloniki–Alexandroupolis (€14.60/9.70, seven hours).

Intercity trains linking the major cities are an excellent way to travel. Services aren't always express – Greece is too mountainous for that – but the trains are modern and comfortable. Sample journey times and 1st- and 2nd-class fares include Athens–Thessaloniki (€37.30/27.60, six hours) and Thessaloniki–Alexandroupolis (€21.90/16.20, 5½ hours).

Eurail and Inter-Rail passes are valid in Greece, but it's not worth buying one if Greece is the only place you plan to use it. The passes can be used for 2nd-class travel on intercity services.

Health

CONTENTS

BEFORE YOU GO

Prevention is the key to staying healthy while abroad. A little planning before departure, particularly for pre-existing illnesses, will save trouble later. Bring medications in their original, clearly labelled, containers. A signed and dated letter from your physician describing your medical conditions and medications, including generic names, is also a good idea. If carrying syringes or needles, be sure to have a physician's letter documenting their medical necessity. If you are embarking on a long trip, make sure your teeth are OK and take your optical prescription with you.

INSURANCE

If you're an EU citizen, an E111 form, available from health centres (and post offices in the UK), covers you for most medical care but not emergency repatriation home or nonemergencies. Citizens from other countries should find out if there is a reciprocal arrangement for free medical care between their country and Greece. If you do need health insurance, make sure you get a policy that covers you for the worst possible scenario, such as an accident requiring an emergency flight home. Find out in advance if your insurance plan will make payments directly to providers or reimburse you later for overseas health expenditures.

RECOMMENDED VACCINATIONS

No jabs are required to travel to Greece, but a yellow-fever vaccination certificate is required if you are coming from an infected area. The WHO recommends that all travellers should be covered for diphtheria, tetanus, measles, mumps, rubella and polio.

ONLINE RESOURCES

The WHO's publication *International Travel and Health* is revised annually and is available online at www.who.int/ith/. Other useful websites include www.mdtravelhealth.com (travel health recommendations for every country; updated daily), www.fitfortravel .scot.nhs.uk (general travel advice for the layperson), www.ageconcern.org.uk (advice on travel for the elderly) and www.marie stopes.org.uk (information on women's health and contraception).

IN TRANSIT

DEEP VEIN THROMBOSIS (DVT)

Blood clots may form in the legs during plane flights, chiefly because of prolonged immobility (the longer the flight, the greater the risk). The chief symptom of DVT is swelling or pain of the foot, ankle, or calf, usually but not always on just one side. When a blood clot travels to the lungs, it may cause chest pain and breathing difficulties. Travellers with any of these symptoms should immediately seek medical attention. To prevent the development of DVT on long flights you should walk about the cabin, contract

---

WARNING

Codeine, which is commonly found in headache preparations, is banned in Greece; check labels carefully, or risk prosecution. There are strict regulations applying to the importation of medicines into Greece, so obtain a certificate from your doctor that outlines any medication you may have to carry into the country with you.

HEALTH

the leg muscles while sitting, drink plenty of fluids and avoid alcohol and tobacco.

JET LAG

To avoid jet lag drink plenty of nonalcoholic fluids and eat light meals. Upon arrival, get exposure to natural sunlight and readjust your schedule (for meals, sleep etc) as soon as possible.

IN GREECE

AVAILABILITY & COST OF HEALTH CARE

If you need an ambulance in Greece call ☎ 166. There is at least one doctor on every island and larger islands have hospitals. Pharmacies can dispense medicines that are available only on prescription in most European countries, so you can consult a pharmacist for minor ailments.

All this sounds fine but, although medical training is of a high standard in Greece, the health service is badly underfunded. Hospitals can be overcrowded, hygiene is not always what it should be and relatives are expected to bring in food for the patient – which could be a problem for a tourist. Conditions and treatment are better in private hospitals, which are expensive. All this means that a good health-insurance policy is essential.

TRAVELLER'S DIARRHOEA

If you develop diarrhoea, be sure to drink plenty of fluids, preferably in the form of an oral rehydration solution such as dioralyte. If diarrhoea is bloody, persists for more than 72 hours or is accompanied by fever, shaking, chills or severe abdominal pain you should seek medical attention.

ENVIRONMENTAL HAZARDS
Bites, Stings & Insect-Borne Diseases

Watch out for sea urchins around rocky beaches; if you get some of their needles embedded in your skin, olive oil will help to loosen them. If they are not removed they will become infected. Be wary also of jellyfish, particularly during the months of September and October. Although they are not lethal in Greece, their stings can be painful. Dousing in vinegar will deactivate any stingers that have not 'fired'. Calamine lotion, antihistamines and analgesics may reduce the reaction and relieve the pain. Much more painful than either of these, but thankfully much rarer, is an encounter with the weever fish. It buries itself in the sand of the tidal zone with only its spines protruding, and injects a painful and powerful toxin if trodden on. Soaking your foot in very hot water (which breaks down the poison) should solve the problem. It can cause permanent local paralysis in the worst case.

Greece's only dangerous snake is the adder. To minimise the possibilities of being bitten, always wear boots, socks and long trousers when walking through undergrowth where snakes may be present. Don't put your hands into holes and crevices, and be careful when collecting firewood. Snake bites do not cause instantaneous death and an antivenin is widely available. Keep the victim calm and still, wrap the bitten limb tightly, as you would for a sprained ankle, and attach a splint to immobilise it. Seek medical help, if possible with the dead snake for identification. Don't attempt to catch the snake if there is a possibility of being bitten again. Tourniquets and sucking out the poison are now comprehensively discredited.

Always check all over your body if you have been walking through a potentially tick-infested area as ticks can cause skin infections and other more serious diseases such as lyme disease and typhus. If a tick is found attached, press down around the tick's head with tweezers, grab the head and gently pull upwards. Avoid pulling the rear of the body as this may squeeze the tick's gut contents through the attached mouth parts into the skin, increasing the risk of infection and disease. Lyme disease begins with the spreading of a rash at the site of the bite, accompanied by fever, headache, extreme fatigue, aching joints and muscles and severe neck stiffness. If left untreated symptoms usually disappear but disorders of the nervous system, heart and joints can develop later. Treatment works best early in the illness – medical help should be sought. Typhus begins with a fever, chills, headache and muscle pains, followed a few days later by a body rash. There is often a large painful sore at the site of the bite and nearby lymph nodes are swollen and painful. There is no vaccine available.

Rabies is still found in Greece but only in isolated areas. Any bite, scratch or even lick from a warm-blooded, furry animal should scrubbed with soap and running water immediately and then cleaned with an alcohol solution. If there is any possibility that the animal is infected medical help should be sought immediately. Even if the animal is not rabid, all bites should be treated seriously as they can become infected or can result in tetanus.

Heatstroke
Heatstroke occurs following excessive fluid loss with inadequate replacement of fluids and salt. Symptoms include headache, dizziness and tiredness. Dehydration is already happening by the time you feel thirsty – aim to drink sufficient water to produce pale, diluted urine. To treat heatstroke drink water and/or fruit juice, and cool the body with cold water and fans.

Hypothermia
Hypothermia occurs when the body loses heat faster than it can produce it. As ever, proper preparation will reduce the risks of getting it. Even on a hot day in the mountains, the weather can change rapidly so carry waterproof garments, warm layers and a hat, and inform others of your route. Hypothermia starts with shivering, loss of judgment and clumsiness. Unless re-warming occurs, the sufferer deteriorates into apathy, confusion and coma. Prevent further heat loss by seeking shelter, warm dry clothing, hot sweet drinks and shared bodily warmth.

TRAVELLING WITH CHILDREN
Make sure children are up to date with routine vaccinations and discuss possible travel vaccines well before departure as some vaccines are not suitable for children under a year. Lonely Planet's *Travel with Children* includes travel health advice for younger children.

WOMEN'S HEALTH
Emotional stress, exhaustion and travelling through different time zones can all contribute to an upset in the menstrual pattern.

If using oral contraceptives, remember some antibiotics, diarrhoea and vomiting can stop the pill from working. Time zones, gastrointestinal upsets and antibiotics do not affect injectable contraception.

Travelling during pregnancy is usually possible but always consult your doctor before planning your trip. The most risky times for travel are during the first 12 weeks of pregnancy and after 30 weeks.

SEXUAL HEALTH
Condoms are readily available but emergency contraception may not be, so take the necessary precautions.

HEALTH

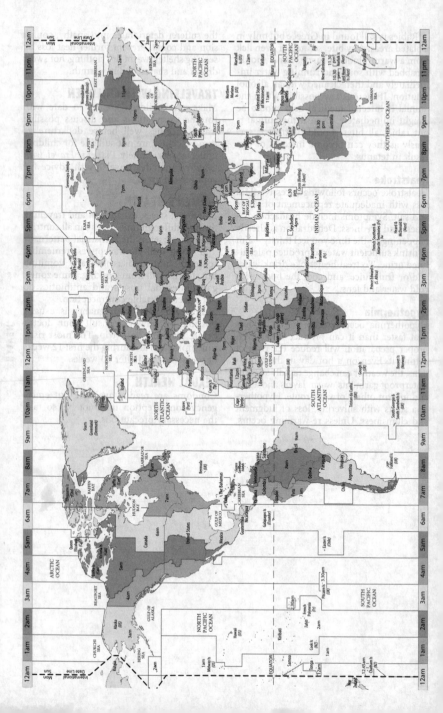

Language

CONTENTS

The Greek language is probably the oldest European language, with an oral tradition of 4000 years and a written tradition of approximately 3000 years. Its evolution over the four millennia was characterised by its strength during the golden age of Athens and the Democracy (mid-5th century BC); its use as a lingua franca throughout the Middle Eastern world, spread by Alexander the Great and his successors as far as India during the Hellenistic period (330 BC to AD 100); its adaptation as the language of the new religion, Christianity; its use as the official language of the Eastern Roman Empire; and its eventual proclamation as the language of the Byzantine Empire (380–1453).

Greek maintained its status and prestige during the rise of the European Renaissance and was employed as the linguistic perspective for all contemporary sciences and terminologies during the period of Enlightenment. Today, Greek constitutes a large part of the vocabulary of any Indo-European language, and much of the lexicon of any scientific repertoire.

The modern Greek language is a southern Greek dialect which is now used by most Greek speakers both in Greece and abroad. It is the result of an intralinguistic influence and synthesis of the ancient vocabulary combined with words from Greek

regional dialects, namely Cretan, Cypriot and Macedonian.

Greek is spoken throughout Greece by a population of around 10 million, and by some five million Greeks who live abroad.

PRONUNCIATION

All Greek words of two or more syllables have an acute accent which indicates where the stress falls. For instance, άγαλμα (statue) is pronounced *aghalma*, and αγάπη (love) is pronounced *aghapi*. In the following transliterations, italic lettering indicates where stress falls. Note also that **dh** is pronounced as 'th' in 'then' and **gh** is a softer, slightly guttural version of 'g'.

ACCOMMODATION

I'm looking for ...

*psa·*hno yi·a ...	Ψάχνω για ...
a room	
e·na dho·*ma*·ti·o	ένα δωμάτιο
a hotel	
e·na kse·no·dho·*chi*·o	ένα ξενοδοχείο
a youth hostel	
e·nan kse·*no*·na ne·*o*·ti·tas	έναν ξενώνα νεότητας

Where is a cheap hotel?
pou *i·*ne e·na fti·*no* xe·no·do·*hi·*o?
Πού είναι ένα φτηνό ξενοδοχείο?

What is the address?
pya *i·*ne i dhi·*ef·*thin·si
Ποια είναι η διεύθυνση

Could you write the address, please?
pa·ra·ka·*lo,* bo·*ri·*te na *ghra·*pse·te ti· dhi·*ef·*thin·si
Παρακαλώ, μπορείτε να γράψετε τη διεύθυνση;

Are there any rooms available?
i·*par·*chun e·*lef·*the·ra dho·*ma·*ti·a?
Υπάρχουν ελεύθερα δωμάτια;

I'd like to book ...

tha *i·*the·la na *kli·*so	Θα ήθελα να κλείσω ...
a bed	
e·na kre·*va·*ti	ένα κρεββάτι
a single room	
e·na mo·*no*·kli·o·no dho·*ma·*ti·o	ένα μονόκλινο δωμάτιο
a double room	
e·na *dhi·*kli·no dho·*ma·*ti·o	ένα δίκλινο δωμάτιο

THE GREEK ALPHABET & PRONUNCIATION

Greek	Pronunciation Guide		Example		
Α α	a	as in 'father'	αγάπη	a·gha·pi	love
Β β	v	as in 'vine'	βήμα	vi·ma	step
Γ γ	gh	like a rough 'g'	γάτα	gha·ta	cat
	y	as in 'yes'	για	ya	for
Δ δ	dh	as in 'there'	δέμα	dhe·ma	parcel
Ε ε	e	as in 'egg'	ένας	e·nas	one (m)
Ζ ζ	z	as in 'zoo'	ζώο	zo·o	animal
Η η	i	as in 'feet'	ήταν	i·tan	was
Θ θ	th	as in 'throw'	θέμα	the·ma	theme
Ι ι	i	as in 'feet'	ίδιος	i·dhyos	same
Κ κ	k	as in 'kite'	καλά	ka·la	well
Λ λ	l	as in 'leg'	λάθος	la·thos	mistake
Μ μ	m	as in 'man'	μαμά	ma·ma	mother
Ν ν	n	as in 'net'	νερό	ne·ro	water
Ξ ξ	x	as in 'ox'	ξύδι	ksi·dhi	vinegar
Ο ο	o	as in 'hot'	όλα	o·la	all
Π π	p	as in 'pup'	πάω	pa·o	I go
Ρ ρ	r	as in 'road'	ρέμα	re·ma	stream
		a slightly trilled r	ρόδα	ro·dha	tyre
Σ σ, ς	s	as in 'sand'	σημάδι	si·ma·dhi	mark
Τ τ	t	as in 'tap'	τόπι	to·pi	ball
Υ υ	i	as in 'feet'	ύστερα	is·tera	after
Φ φ	f	as in 'find'	φύλλο	fi·lo	leaf
Χ χ	h	as the ch in Scottish loch, or	χάνω	ha·no	I lose
		like a rough h	χέρι	he·ri	hand
Ψ ψ	ps	as in 'lapse'	ψωμί	pso·mi	bread
Ω ω	o	as in 'hot'	ώρα	o·ra	time

Combinations of Letters
The combinations of letters shown here are pronounced as follows:

Greek	Pronunciation Guide		Example		
ει	i	as in 'feet'	είδα	i·dha	I saw
οι	i	as in 'feet'	οικόπεδο	i·ko·pe·dho	land
αι	e	as in 'bet'	αίμα	e·ma	blood
ου	u	as in 'mood'	πού	pou	who/what
μπ	b	as in 'beer'	μπάλα	ba·la	ball
	mb	as in 'amber'	κάμπος	kam·bos	forest
ντ	d	as in 'dot'	ντουλάπα	dou·la·pa	wardrobe
	nd	as in 'bend'	πέντε	pen·de	five
γκ	g	as in 'God'	γκάζι	ga·zi	gas
γγ	ng	as in 'angle'	αγγελία	an·ge·lia	announcement
γξ	ks	as in 'minks'	σφιγξ	sfinks	sphynx
τζ	dz	as in 'hands'	τζάκι	dza·ki	fireplace

The pairs of vowels shown above are pronounced separately if the first has an acute accent, or the second a dieresis, as in the examples below:

γαϊδουράκι	gai·dhou·ra·ki	little donkey
Κάιρο	kai·ro	Cairo

Some Greek consonant sounds have no English equivalent. The υ of the groups αυ, ευ and ηυ is generally pronounced 'v'. The Greek question mark is represented with the English equivalent of a semicolon ';'.

a room with a double bed
e·na dho·*ma*·ti·o me   ένα δωμάτιο με δυό
dhy·o kre·*va*·ti·a   κρεββάτια

a room with a bathroom
e·na dho·*ma*·ti·o me   ένα δωμάτιο με
ba·ni·o   μπάνιο

I'd like to share a dorm.
tha i·the·la na mi·*ra*·so e·na ki·*no* dho·*ma*·ti·o
me *al*·la *a*·to·ma
Θα ήθελα να μοιράσω ένα κοινό δωμάτιο
με άλλα άτομα

How much is it ...? *po*·so ka·ni ...?   Πόσο κάνει ...;
per night   ti ·vra·*dhya*   τη βραδυά
per person   to *a*·to·mo   το άτομο

May I see it?
bo·*ro* na to dho?   Μπορώ να το δω;

Where is the bathroom?
pou i·ne to·*ba*·ni·o?   Πού είναι το μπάνιο;

I'm/We're leaving today.
fev·gho/*fev*·ghou·me   Φεύγω/φεύγουμε
si·me·ra   σήμερα

CONVERSATION & ESSENTIALS

Hello.
ya·sas (polite)   Γειά σας.
ya·su (informal)   Γειά σου.

Goodbye.
an·*di*·o   Αντίο.

Yes.
ne   Ναι.

No.
o·hi   Όχι.

Please.
pa·ra·ka·*lo*   Παρακαλώ.

Thank you.
ef·ha·ri·*sto*   Ευχαριστώ.

That's fine/You're welcome
pa·ra·ka·*lo*   Παρακαλώ.

Sorry. (excuse me, forgive me)
sigh·*no*·mi   Συγγνώμη.

What's your name?
pos sas *le*·ne?   Πώς σας λένε;

My name is ...
me *le*·ne ...   Με λένε ...

Where are you from?
a·*po* pou i·ste?   Από πού είστε;

I'm from ...
i·me a·*po* ...   Είμαι από ...

I (don't) like ...
(dhen) ma·*re*·si ...   (Δεν) μ' αρέσει ...

Just a minute.
mi·*so* lep·*to*   Μισό λεπτό.

DIRECTIONS

Where is ...?
pou i·ne ...?   Πού είναι...;

Straight ahead.
o·lo ef·*thi*·a   Όλο ευθεία.

Turn left.
strips·te a·ri·ste·*ra*   Στρίψτε αριστερά

Turn right.
strips·te dhe·ksi·*a*   Στρίψτε δεξιά

at the next corner
stin epo·me·ni gho·*ni*·a   στην επόμενη γωνία

at the traffic lights
sta *fo*·ta   στα φώτα

SIGNS

ΕΙΣΟΔΟΣ	Entry
ΕΞΟΔΟΣ	Exit
ΠΛΗΡΟΦΟΡΙΕΣ	Information
ΑΝΟΙΧΤΟ	Open
ΚΛΕΙΣΤΟ	Closed
ΑΠΑΓΟΡΕΥΕΤΑΙ	Prohibited
ΥΠΑΡΧΟΥΝ ΔΩΜΑΤΙΑ	Rooms Available
ΠΛΗΡΕΣ	Full/No Vacancies
ΑΣΤΥΝΟΜΙΑ	Police
ΑΣΤΥΝΟΜΙΚΟΣ ΣΤΑΘΜΟΣ	Police Station
ΓΥΝΑΙΚΩΝ	Toilets (women)
ΑΝΔΡΩΝ	Toilets (men)

---

behind   pi·so   πίσω
in front of bro·*sta*   μπροστά
far   ma·kri·*a*   μακριά
near (to)   kon·*da*   κοντά
opposite   a·*pe*·nan·di απέναντι

acropolis   a·*kro*·po·li ακρόπολη
beach   pa·ra·*li*·a   παραλία
bridge   yefira   γέφυρα
castle   *ka*·stro   κάστρο
island   ni·*si*   νησί
main square ken·dri·*ki*· pla·*ti*·a κεντρική πλατεία
market   a·gho·*ra*   αγορά
museum   mu·*si*·o   μουσείο
old quarter pa·li·a po·li παλιά πόλη
ruins   ar·he·a   αρχαία
sea   tha·las·sa   θάλασσα
square   pla·*ti*·a   πλατεία
temple   na·os   ναός

HEALTH

I'm ill.   i·me a·ro·stos   Είμαι άρρωστος.
It hurts here.   po·*nai*· e·*dho* πονάει εδώ

TRANSLITERATION & VARIANT SPELLINGS: AN EXPLANATION

The issue of correctly transliterating Greek into the Latin alphabet is a vexed one, fraught with inconsistencies and pitfalls. The Greeks themselves are not very consistent in this respect, though things are gradually improving. The word 'Piraeus', for example, has been variously represented by the following transliterations: *Pireas, Piraievs* and *Pireefs*; and when appearing as a street name (eg Piraeus Street) you will also find *Pireos*!

This has been compounded by the linguistic minefield of diglossy, or the two forms of the Greek language. The purist form is called *Katharevousa* and the popular form is *Dimotiki* (Demotic). The Katharevousa form was never more than an artificiality and Dimotiki has always been spoken as the mainstream language, but this linguistic schizophrenia means there are often two Greek words for each English word. Thus, the word for 'baker' in everyday language is *fournos*, but the shop sign will more often than not say *artopoieion*. The baker's product will be known in the street as *psomi*, but in church as *artos*.

A further complication is the issue of anglicised vs hellenised forms of place names: Athina vs Athens, Patra vs Patras, Thiva vs Thebes, Evia vs Euboia – the list goes on and on! Toponymic diglossy (the existence of both an official and everyday name for a place) is responsible for Kerkyra/ Corfu, Zante/Zakynthos, and Santorini/Thira. In this guide we usually provide modern Greek equivalents for town names, with one or two well known exceptions, eg Athens and Patras. For ancient sites, settlements or people from antiquity, we have tried to stick to the more familiar classical names; so we have Thucydides instead of Thoukididis, Mycenae instead of Mykines.

Problems in transliteration have particular implications for vowels, especially given that Greek has six ways of rendering the vowel sound 'ee', two ways of rendering the 'o' sound and two ways of rendering the 'e' sound. In most instances in this book, **y** has been used for the 'ee' sound when a Greek *upsilon* (υ, Υ) has been used, and **i** for Greek *ita* (η, Η) and *iota* (ι, Ι). In the case of the Greek vowel combinations that make the 'ee' sound, that is οι, ει and υι, an **i** has been used. For the two Greek 'e' sounds αι and ε, an **e** has been employed.

As far as consonants are concerned, the Greek letter *gamma* (γ, Γ) appears as **g** rather than **y** throughout this book. This means that *agios* (Greek for male saint) is used rather than *ayios*, and *agia* (female saint) rather than *ayia*. The letter *fi* (φ, Φ) can be transliterated as either **f** or **ph**. Here, a general rule of thumb is that classical names are spelt with a **ph** and modern names with an **f**. So Phaistos is used rather than Festos, and Folegandros is used rather than Pholegandros. The Greek *chi* (ξ, Ξ) has usually been represented as **h** in order to approximate the Greek pronunciation as closely as possible. Thus, we have Haralambos instead of Charalambos and Polytehniou instead of Polytechniou. Bear in mind that the **h** is to be pronounced as an aspirated 'h', much like the 'ch' in *loch*. The letter *kapa* (κ, Κ) has been used to represent that sound, except where well known names from antiquity have adopted by convention the letter **c**, eg Polycrates, Acropolis.

Wherever reference to a street name is made, we have omitted the Greek word *odos*, but words for avenue (*leoforos*) and square (*plateia*) have been included.

I have ...		penicillin	
*e·*ho ...	Εχω ...	stin pe·ni·ki·*li·*ni	στην πενικιλλίνη
asthma		**bees**	
*asth·*ma	άσθμα	stis *me·*li·ses	στις μέλισσες
diabetes		**nuts**	
za·ha·ro·dhi·a·*vi·*ti	ζαχαροδιαβήτη	sta fi·*sti·*ki·a	στα φυστίκια
epilepsy			
e·pi·lip·*si·*a	επιληψία	**condoms**	pro·fi·la·kti·*ka*	προφυλακτικά
			(ka·*po·*tez)	(καπότες)
I'm allergic to ...		**contraceptive**	pro·fi·lak·ti·*ko*	προφυλακτικό
*i·*me a·ler·yi·*kos*/	Είμαι αλλεργικός/	**diarrhoea**	dhi·*a·*ri·a	διάρροια
a·ler·yi·ki ... (m/f)	αλλεργική ...	**medicine**	*farm·*a·ko	φάρμακο
antibiotics		**sunblock cream**	*kre·*ma i·*li·*u	κρέμα ηλίου
sta an·di·vi·o·ti·*ka*	στα αντιβιωτικά	**tampons**	tam·*bon*	ταμπόν
aspirin				
stin a·spi·*ri·*ni	στην ασπιρίνη			

LANGUAGE DIFFICULTIES

Do you speak English?
mi·la·te an·gli·ka?   Μιλάτε Αγγλικά;
Does anyone speak English?
mi·lai ka·nis an·gli·ka?   Μιλάει κανείς αγγλικά;
How do you say ... in Greek?
ps le·ghe·te ... sta   Πώς λέγεται ... στα
el·li·ni·ka   ελληνικά;
I understand.
ka·ta·la·ve·no   Καταλαβαίνω.
I don't understand.
dhen ka·ta·la·ve·no   Δεν καταλαβαίνω.
Please write it down.
ghrap·ste to, pa·ra·ka·lo   Γράψτε το, παρακαλώ.
Can you show me on the map?
bo·ri·te na mo·u to   Μπορείτε να μου το
dhi·xe·te sto har·ti?   δείξετε στο χάρτη;

NUMBERS

0	mi·dhen	μηδέν
1	e·nas	ένας (m)
	mi·a	μία (f)
	e·na	ένα (n)
2	dhi·o	δύο
3	tris	τρεις (m&f)
	tri·a	τρία (n)
4	te·se·ris	τέσσερεις (m&f)
	te·se·ra	τέσσερα (n)
5	pen·de	πέντε
6	e·xi	έξη
7	ep·ta	επτά
8	oh·to	οχτώ
9	e·ne·a	εννέα
10	dhe·ka	δέκα
20	ik·o·si	είκοσι
30	tri·an·da	τριάντα
40	sa·ran·da	σαράντα
50	pe·nin·da	πενήντα
60	exin·da	εξήντα
70	ev·dho·min·da	εβδομήντα
80	oh·dhon·da	ογδόντα
90	eneninda	ενενήντα
100	e·ka·to	εκατό
1000	hi·li·i	χίλιοι (m)
	hi·li·ez	χίλιες (f)
	hi·li·a	χίλια (n)
2000	dhi·o chi·li·a·dhez	δυό χιλιάδες

PAPERWORK

name
o·no·ma·te·po·ni·mo   ονοματεπώνυμο
nationality
i·pi·ko·o·ti·ta   υπηκοότητα
date of birth
i·me·ro·mi·ni·a yen·ni·se·os   ημερομηνία γεννήσεως

place of birth
to·pos yen·ni·se·os   τόπος γεννήσεως
sex (gender)
fil·lon   φύλλον
passport
dhia·va·ti·ri·o   διαβατήριο
visa
vi·za   βίζα

QUESTION WORDS

Who/Which?
pi·os/pi·a/pi·o? (sg m/f/n)   Ποιος/Ποια/Ποιο;
pi·i/pi·es/pi·a? (pl m/f/n)   Ποιοι/Ποιες/Ποια;
Who's there?
pi·os i·ne e·ki?   Ποιος είναι εκεί;
Which street is this?
pi·a o·dhos i·ne af·ti?   Ποια οδός είναι αυτή;
What?
ti?   Τι;
What's this?
ti i·ne af·to?   Τι είναι αυτό;
Where?
pu?   Πού;
When?
po·te?   Πότε;
Why?
yi·a·ti?   Γιατί;
How?
pos?   Πώς;
How much?
po·so?   Πόσο;
How much does it cost?
po·so ka·ni?   Πόσο κάνει;

SHOPPING & SERVICES

I'd like to buy ...
the·lo n'a·gho·ra·so ...   Θέλω ν' αγοράσω ...
How much is it?
po·so ka·ni?   Πόσο κάνει;
I don't like it
dhen mu a·re·si   Δεν μου αρέσει.

May I see it?
bo·*ro* na to dho?   Μπορώ να το δω;
I'm just looking.
ap·*los* ki·*ta*·zo   Απλώς κοιτάζω.
It's cheap.
i·ne fti·*no*   Είναι φτηνό
It's too expensive.
i·ne po·*li* a·kri·*vo*   Είναι πολύ ακριβό.
I'll take it.
tha to *pa*·ro   Θα το πάρω

Do you accept ...   dhe·che·ste ...   Δέχεστε ...;
 credit cards   pi·sto·ti·*ki kar*·ta   πιστωτική κάρτα
 travellers   tak·si·dhi·o·ti·*kes*   ταξιδιωτικές
  cheques   e·pi·ta·*ghes*   επιταγές

more   pe·ri·*so*·te·ro   περισσότερο
less   li·*gho*·te·ro   λιγότερο
smaller   mi·*kro*·te·ro   μικρότερο
bigger   me·gha·*li*·te·ro   μεγαλύτερο

I'm looking for ...   *psach*·no ya ...   Ψάχνω για ...
 a bank   mya *tra*·pe·za   μια τράπεζα
 the church   tin ek·kli·*si*·a   την εκκλησία
 the city centre   to *ken*·dro tis   το κέντρο της
   po·lis   πόλης
 the ... embassy   tin ... pres·*vi*·a   την ... πρεσβεία
 the market   ti· lai·*ki*· a·gho·*ra*   τη λαϊκή αγορά
 the museum   to mu·*si*·o   το μουσείο
 the post office   to ta·chi·dhro·*mi*·o   το ταχυδρομείο
 a public toilet   mya dhi·*mo*·sia   μια δημόσια
   tu·a·*let*·ta   τουαλέττα
 the telephone   to ti·le·fo·ni·*ko*   το τηλεφωνικό
  centre   *ken*·dro   κέντρο
 the tourist office   to tu·ri·st·*iko*   το τουριστικό
   ghra·*fi*·o   γραφείο

TIME & DATES

What time is it?   ti o·*ra i*·ne?   Τι ώρα είναι;
It's (2 o'clock).   *i*·ne (dhi·o i· o·ra)   είναι (δύο η ώρα).
in the morning   to pro·*i*   το πρωί
in the afternoon   to a·*po*·yev·ma   το απόγευμα
in the evening   to *vra*·dhi   το βράδυ
When?   *po*·te   Πότε;
today   *si*·me·ra   σήμερα
tomorrow   *av*·ri·o   αύριο
yesterday   hthes   χθες

Monday   dhef·*te*·ra   Δευτέρα
Tuesday   *tri*·ti   Τρίτη
Wednesday   te·*tar*·ti   Τετάρτη
Thursday   *pemp*·ti   Πέμπτη
Friday   pa·ras·ke·*vi*   Παρασκευή
Saturday   *sa*·va·to   Σάββατο
Sunday   kyri·a·*ki*   Κυριακή

January   ia·nou·*ar*·i·os   Ιανουάριος
February   fev·rou·*ar*·i·os   Φεβρουάριος
March   *mar*·ti·os   Μάρτιος
April   a·*pri*·li·os   Απρίλιος
May   *mai*·os   Μάιος
June   i·*ou*·ni·os   Ιούνιος
July   i·*ou*·li·os   Ιούλιος
August   *av*·ghous·tos   Αύγουστος
September   sep·*tem*·vri·os   Σεπτέμβριος
October   ok·*to*·vri·os   Οκτώβριος
November   no·*em*·vri·os   Νοέμβριος
December   dhe·*kem*·vri·os   Δεκέμβριος

TRANSPORT
Public Transport

What time does   ti o·ra fev·yi/   Τι ώρα φεύγει/
the ... leave/   *fta*·ni to ...?   φτάνει το ...;
arrive?
 boat   *pli*·o   πλοίο
 (city) bus   a·sti·*ko*   αστικό
 (intercity) bus   le·o·fo·*ri*·o   λεωφορείο
 plane   ae·ro·*pla*·no   αεροπλάνο
 train   *tre*·no   τραίνο

I'd like   tha *i*·the·la   θα ήθελα
(a) ...   (e·na) ...   (ένα) ...
 one way ticket   a·*plo* isi·*ti*·ri·o   απλό εισιτήριο
 return ticket   i·si·*ti*·ri·o me   εισιτήριο με
   e·pi·stro·*fi*   επιστροφή
 1st class   *pro*·ti· *the*·si   πρώτη θέση
 2nd class   *def*·te·ri *the*·si   δεύτερη θέση

I want to go to ...
the·lo na *pao* sto/sti...
θέλω να πάω στο/στη ...
The train has been cancelled/delayed.
to *tre*·no a·ki·rothi·ke/ka·thi·*ste*·ri·se
Το τραίνο ακυρώθηκε/καθυστέρησε

the first
to *pro*·to   το πρώτο
the last
to te·lef·*te*·o   το τελευταίο
platform number
a·*rithmos* a·po·*va*·thras   αριθμός αποβάθρας
ticket office
ek·dho·*ti*·ri·o i·si·ti·*ri*·on   εκδοτήριο εισιτηρίων
timetable
dhro·mo·*lo*·gio   δρομολόγιο
train station
si·dhi·ro·dhro-   σιδηροδρομικός
  mi·*kos* stath·*mos*   σταθμός

Private Transport

I'd like to hire   tha *i*·the·la na   θα ήθελα να
a ...   ni·ki·a·so ...   νοικιάσω ...

car	e·na af·ti·ki·ni·to	ένα αυτοκίνητο
4WD	e·na tes·se·ra	ένα τέσσερα
	e·pi tes·se·ra	επί τέσσερα
(a jeep)	(e·na tzip)	(ένα τζιπ)
motorbike	mya mo·to·si·klet·ta	μια μοτοσυ-κλέττα
bicycle	e·na po·dhi·la·to	ένα ποδήλατο

Is this the road to ...?
af·tos i·ne o dhro·mos ya ...
Αυτός είναι ο δρόμος για ...
Where's the next service station?
pu i·ne to e·po·me·no ven·zi·na·dhi·ko
Πού είναι το επόμενο βενζινάδικο;
Please fill it up.
ye·mi·ste to pa·ra·ka·lo
Γεμίστε το, παρακαλώ.
I'd like (30) euros worth.
tha i·the·la (30) ev·ro
Θα ήθελα (30) ευρώ.

ROAD SIGNS

ΠΑΡΑΚΑΜΨΗ	Detour
ΑΠΑΓΟΡΕΥΕΤΑΙ Η ΕΙΣΟΔΟΣ	No Entry
ΑΠΑΓΟΡΕΥΕΤΑΙ Η ΠΡΟΣΠΕΡΑΣΗ	No Overtaking
ΑΠΑΓΟΡΕΥΕΤΑΙ Η ΣΤΑΘΜΕΥΣΗ	No Parking
ΕΙΣΟΔΟΣ	Entrance
ΜΗΝ ΠΑΡΚΑΡΕΤΕ ΕΔΩ	Keep Clear
(lit: don't park here)	
ΔΙΟΔΙΑ	Toll
ΚΙΝΔΥΝΟΣ	Danger
ΑΡΓΑ	Slow Down
ΕΞΟΔΟΣ	Exit

---

diesel	pet·re·le·o	πετρέλαιο
leaded petrol	su·per	σούπερ
unleaded petrol	a·mo·liv·dhi	αμόλυβδη

Can I park here?
bo·ro na par·ka·ro e·dho
Μπορώ να παρκάρω εδώ;
Where do I pay?
pu pli·ro·no
Πού πληρώνω;
The car/motorbike has broken down (at ...)
to af·to·ki·ni·to/mo·to·si·klet·ta cha·la·se sto ...
Το αυτοκίνητο/η μοτοσυκλέττα χάλασε στο ...
The car/motorbike won't start.
to af·to·ki·ni·to/mo·to·si·klet·ta dhen per·ni· bros
Το αυτοκίνητο/η μοτοσυκλέττα δεν παίρνει μπρος.
I have a flat tyre.
e·pa·tha la·sti·cho
Έπαθα λάστιχο.

I've run out of petrol.
e·mi·na a·po ven·zi·ni
Έμεινα από βενζίνη.
I've had an accident.
e·pa·tha a·ti·chi·ma
Έπαθα ατύχημα.

TRAVEL WITH CHILDREN

Is there a/an ...	i·par·chi ...	Υπάρχει ...
I need a/an ...	chri·a·zo·me ...	Χρειάζομαι ...
a baby change room	me·ros nal·lak·so to mo·ro	μέρος ν'αλλάξω το μωρό
car baby seat	ka·this·ma ya mo·ro	κάθισμα για μωρό.
child-minding service	ba·bi sit·ter	μπέιμπι σίττερ
children's menu	me·nu ya pe·dhya	μενού για παιδία
(disposable) nappies/diapers	pan·nez Pam·pers	πάννες Pampers
(English-speaking) babysitter	ba·bi sit·ter pu mi·la an·ghl·ika	μπέιμπι σίττερ που μιλά αγγλικά
highchair	pe·dhi·ki ka·rek·la	παιδική καρέκλα
potty	yo·yo	γιογιό
stroller	ka·rot·sa·ki	καροτσάκι

Do you mind if I breastfeed here?
bo·ro na thi·la·so e·dho
Μπορώ να θηλάσω εδώ
Are children allowed?
e·pi·tre·pon·de ta pe·dhya
Επιρέπονται τα παιδιά

Also available from Lonely Planet:
Greek phrasebook

Glossary

A

Achaean civilisation – see *Mycenaean civilisation*

acropolis – citadel; highest point of an ancient city

agia (f), agios (m) – saint

agora – commercial area of an ancient city; shopping precinct in modern Greece

Archaic period (800–480 BC) – also known as the Middle Age; period in which the city-states emerged from the 'dark age' and traded their way to wealth and power; the city-states were unified by a Greek alphabet and common cultural pursuits, engendering a sense of national identity

arhontika – 17th- and 18th-century AD mansions which belonged to arhons, the leading citizens of a town

askitiria – mini-chapels; places of solitary worship

B

basilica – early Christian church

bouleuterion – council house

bouzouki – stringed lute-like instrument associated with *rembetika* music

bouzoukia – any nightclub where the *bouzouki* is played and low-grade blues songs are sung

Byzantine Empire (324 BC–AD 1453) – characterised by the merging of *Hellenistic* culture and Christianity and named after Byzantium, the city on the Bosphorus that became the capital of the Roman Empire; when the Roman Empire was formally divided in AD 395, Rome went into decline and the eastern capital, renamed Constantinople, flourished; the Byzantine Empire dissolved after the fall of Constantinople to the Turks in 1453

C

caïque – small, sturdy fishing boat often used to carry passengers

Classical period (480–323 BC) – era in which the city-states reached the height of their wealth and power after the defeat of the Persians in the 5th century BC; ended with the decline of the city-states as a result of the Peloponnesian Wars, and the expansionist aspirations of Philip II, King of Macedon (ruled 359–336 BC), and his son, Alexander the Great (ruled 336–323 BC)

Corinthian – order of Greek architecture recognisable by columns with bell-shaped capitals with sculpted elaborate ornaments based on acanthus leaves

Cycladic civilisation (3000–1100 BC) – civilisation which emerged following the settlement of Phoenician colonists on the Cycladic islands

cyclopes – mythical one-eyed giants

D

dark age (1200–800 BC) – period in which Greece was under *Dorian* rule

delfini – dolphin; common name for a hydrofoil

domatio (s), domatia (pl) – room, usually in a private home; cheap accommodation option

Dorians – Hellenic warriors who invaded Greece around 1200 BC, demolishing the city-states and destroying the *Mycenaean civilisation*; heralded Greece's 'dark age', when the artistic and cultural advancements of the Mycenaean's and Minoan's were abandoned; the Dorians later developed into land-holding aristocrats which encouraged the resurgence of independent city-states led by wealthy aristocrats

Doric – order of Greek architecture characterised by a column which has no base, a fluted shaft and a relatively plain capital, when compared with the flourishes evident on *Ionic* and *Corinthian* capitals

E

Ellada or Ellas – the Greek name for Greece

EOT – Ellinikos Organismos Tourismou; national tourism organisation which has offices providing tourist information and services in most major towns

F

Filiki Eteria – friendly society; a group of Greeks in exile; formed during Ottoman rule to organise an uprising against the Turks

flokati – shaggy woollen rug produced in central and northern Greece

G

Geometric period (1200–800 BC) – period characterised by pottery decorated with geometric designs; sometimes referred to as Greece's 'dark age'

H

Hellas – the Greek name for Greece

Hellenistic period (323–146 BC) – prosperous, influential period of Greek civilisation ushered in by Alexander the Great's empire building and lasting until the Roman sacking of Corinth in 146 BC

hora – main town (usually on an island)

horio – village

I

Ionic – order of Greek architecture characterised by a column with truncated flutes and capitals with ornaments resembling scrolls

K
kafeneio (s), kafeneia (pl) – traditionally a male-only coffee house where cards and backgammon are played

kastro – walled-in town; also used for a fort and castle

katholikon – principal church of a monastic complex

kore – female statue of the *Archaic period;* see also *kouros*

kouros – male statue of the *Archaic period,* characterised by a stiff body posture and enigmatic smile; see also *kore*

KTEL – Kino Tamio Ispraxeon Leoforion; national bus cooperative; runs all long-distance bus services

L
leoforos – avenue

M
mayiria – cook houses

meltemi – northeasterly wind which blows throughout much of Greece during the summer

meze (s), mezedes (pl) – appetiser

Middle Age – see *Archaic period*

Minoan civilisation (3000–1100 BC) – Bronze Age culture of Crete named after the mythical king Minos, and characterised by pottery and metalwork of great beauty and artisanship

moni – monastery or convent

Mycenaean civilisation (1900–1100 BC) – first great civilisation of the Greek mainland, characterised by powerful independent city-states ruled by kings; also known as the *Achaean civilisation*

O
odos – street

OSE – Organismos Sidirodromon Ellados; Greek railways organisation

OTE – Organismos Tilepikinonion Ellados; Greece's major telecommunications carrier

ouzeri (s), ouzeria (pl) – place that serves ouzo and light snacks

P
Panagia – Mother of God; name frequently used for churches

Pantokrator – painting or mosaic of Christ in the centre of the dome of a Byzantine church

periptero (s), periptera (pl) – street kiosk

plateia – square

R
rembetika – blues songs commonly associated with the underworld of the 1920s

S
Sarakatsani – Greek-speaking nomadic shepherd community from northern Greece

spilia – cave

stele (s), stelae (pl) – upright stone decorated with inscriptions or figures

stoa – long colonnaded building, usually in an *agora*; used as a meeting place and shelter in ancient Greece

T
taverna – traditional restaurant that serves food and wine

tholos – Mycenaean tomb shaped like a beehive

V
Vlach – traditional, seminomadic shepherds from northern Greece who speak a Latin-based dialect

Behind the Scenes

THIS BOOK

The 1st edition of *Greek Islands* was coordinated by David Willett, and updated by Brigitte Barta, Rosemary Hall, Paul Hellander and Jeanne Oliver. These same authors, along with Carolyn Bain and Kate Daly, also put together the 2nd edition. The 3rd edition saw the return of David (coordinating author for a third time), Carolyn, Paul and Jeanne, this time with Michael Clark and Des Hannigan also on board. The Food & Drink chapter was based on Lonely Planet's *World Food Greece*, written by Richard Sterling, Georgia Dacakis and Kate Reeves, and the health chapter was written by Dr Caroline Evans.

THANKS FROM THE AUTHORS

David Willett I'd like to thank all the friends who have contributed so much to my understanding of Greece over the years, especially Maria Economou from the Greek National Tourism Office; the Kanakis family; Ana Kamais; Tolis Houtzoumis; Vassilis Dimitreakis; George Constantinides; Elisavet Nazli; Petros and Dimitris in Nafplio; Yiannis is Sparti; the irrepressible Voula in Gythio; Karen and Andreas the magician from Patra.

Many thanks also to family and friends who have helped to road-test the book: Rowan Lunney and Tom Willett; Dan and Suzi Maher; Mark Jarvinen and Jenny Nolan; and Colin Clement.

Carolyn Bain Many thanks to LP's Michala Green for giving me the chance to return to one of my favourite parts of the world, and kudos to the talented LP production team who put this book together. It was wonderful to return to the Ionians

for this project and to be warmly welcomed back by so many familiar faces. *Efharisto poli* once again to Noula and her trusty gang – Marta, Yiannis and Sue – in Agios Stefanos; Fiona, Bart and the people of Paxi, who made me fall in love with their island all over again; Dora in Nydri; Thomas in Athani; Nick and Vivian in Argostoli; Katrina in Zakynthos Town; Pia in Keri, and everyone else who made this trip so enjoyable. Cheers to JJJ and Sandro for a great day in and around Paleokastritsa despite the rain, and huge thanks to Kelvin Adams for his fabulous company on much of this trip – thanks doll for gin, giggles, bad accents and dodgy CD selections, and for making sure the beaches were thoroughly researched.

Michael Clark My contribution to this book was made possible by the kindness of strangers throughout Greece, and the help of friends, relatives and acquaintances there and at home, among them: my Athenian hosts Tolis, Takis and George; in Delphi, Yannis Christopoulos, and archaeologist Efi Marcellou; Kostas Gekas and Arthur in Kalambaka for support when it mattered most; in the Pelion, Mariana and Eleni; in Skiathos, Keyrillos Sinioris; in Skopelos, Makis at Thalpos Travel, Nana Kobro; in Alonnisos, Chris Browne.

Closer to home, Kostas and Nana Vatsis, Maria Kotzamanidou, Sofia Vamvaka, Angelo and Vangie Kallipolitis, and Dessine Fricioni provided advice, spiritual sustenance and humour; Doris Kyburz and Lynne Cummings made last-minute computer rescues. Special thanks to my editor Michala Green

---

THE LONELY PLANET STORY

The story begins with a classic travel adventure: Tony and Maureen Wheeler's 1972 journey across Europe and Asia to Australia. There was no useful information about the overland trail then, so Tony and Maureen published the first Lonely Planet guidebook to meet a growing need.

From a kitchen table, Lonely Planet has grown to become the largest independent travel publisher in the world, with offices in Melbourne (Australia), Oakland (USA), London (UK) and Paris (France).

Today Lonely Planet guidebooks cover the globe. There is an ever-growing list of books and information in a variety of media. Some things haven't changed. The main aim is still to make it possible for adventurous travellers to get out there – to explore and better understand the world.

At Lonely Planet we believe travellers can make a positive contribution to the countries they visit – if they respect their host communities and spend their money wisely.

at LP, and fellow authors David Willett and Paul Hellander, along with my oft-remembered predecessor in Central Greece, Rosemary Hall. And to my splendiferous and loving family – wife Janet White and kids Melina and Alexander – the next trip is all together!

Finally, I wish to dedicate this work to the memory of my mother, Mary Efimedia Raptis Kent, who taught me to appreciate all things Greek, most of all the voyage.

Des Hannigan Des sends his thanks and affection to the many friends who helped and advised him in his hugely rewarding odyssey through the Cyclades. Special thanks go to Kostas Karabetsos and Zelena Mihalopoyloy on Mykonos for great company, and especially for navigating the night life in style; to John van Lerberghe on Mykonos for problem solving; Margarita Gavalas and Dee Skaramagas on Paros for great advice; Alex Reichardt on Naxos for his inspiring company, and Tassos for his thoughtful words. Lisos Zilelides on Santorini for knowledge, wit, and a great big Greek wedding; Sara Donnelly on Folegandros for her kindness and time. Thanks also to Helena Prodroumou, Achilles Gazis, Jutta Kalogeropoulou, Aaron McIntyre, Maria Quemada, Gregorios Mavrides, Despina Kitini, Antonio Gotsis and Stelios Platonos for their insights and great conversation. Finally, my gratitude to Michala Green at Lonely Planet's London Office and to coordinating author David Willett, for their patience and professionalism.

Paul Hellander Putting a guide like this together is more often than not the result of collaborative team work. For their unstinting and invaluable assistance in collating my *Greek Islands* data I thank the following unsung heroes of my own team: Angeliki Kanelli (Athens); Vasilis and Giannis Kambouris (Ikaria); Giakoumina Matheou (Patmos); Nick Hristodoulou (Lipsi); Kostas Kourounis (Kos); Alexis Zikas (Kos); Kim Sjogren (Rhodes); Constance Rivemal (Rhodes); Alex and Christine Sakellaridis (Halki); Minas Gializis (Karpathos); Nikos Perakis (Kato Zakros); Manolis Tsangarakis (Iraklio); Evangelos and Stella Skoulakis (Kissamos). Special thanks also to Hotel Lato (Iraklio), Elotia Travel (Rethymno), Casa Delfino (Hania), Hotel Amphora (Hania), Blue Star Ferries (Patra), Dodecanese Express (Rhodes), Peugeot Sodexa (Paris) and DriveAway Holidays (Sydney) for their extremely valuable logistical help in making it all happen. Byron, Marcus, Stella – my work in this guide is dedicated, as ever, to the three of you. Bubble (Eleni), your turn next!

Jeanne Oliver First, I'd like to deliver a warm thanks to my colleague Paul Hellander and his wife Stella for providing an unforgettable Orthodox Easter celebration in Ikaria. Same time next year, Paul? Also on Ikaria, Vasilis Dionysos was a wonderfully informative host and demonstrated the true meaning of *kefi*. On Samos, Dimitris Eleni and his wife Helena couldn't have been more helpful and welcoming. Theodore and Gûher Spordilis on Chios went above and beyond the call of hospitality in showing me their island. Finally, big *bisoux* to John Enée whose patience and good humour made the trip a joy.

CREDITS

Coordinating the production of *Greek Islands* were Gina Tsarouhas (editorial), Chris Tsismetzis (cartography) and Dianne Zammit (layout). Overseeing production were Huw Fowles (project manager), Jane Thompson (managing editor) and Mark Griffiths (managing cartographer). Quentin Frayne compiled the language chapter. This title was commissioned and developed in Lonely Planet's London office by Michala Green. Cartography for this guide was developed by Ed Pickard and Corinne Waddell. Cover Designers were Pepi Bluck and Annika Roojun.

A bevy of talented editors, proofers and indexers helped behind the scenes: Imogen Bannister, Miriam Cannell, Monique Choy, Emily Coles, Adrienne Costanzo, Melanie Dankel, Justin Flynn, Jennifer Garrett, Victoria Harrison, Evan Jones, Thalia Kalkipsakis, Anne Mulvaney, Danielle North, Kristen Odijk, Kalya Ryan, Anastasia Safioleas, Katrina Webb and Helen Yeates. To each and everyone of you: *efharisto!*

Assisting with cartography were Christopher Crook, Louise Klep and Valentina Kremenchutskaya.

Series Publishing Manager Virginia Maxwell oversaw the redevelopment of the regional guides series with help from Maria Donohoe. Regional Publishing Manager Katrina Browning steered the development of this title. The series was designed by James Hardy, with mapping development by Paul Piaia. The series development team included Shahara Ahmed, Susie Ashworth, Gerilyn Attebery, Jenny Blake, Anna Bolger, Verity Campbell, Erin Corrigan, Nadine Fogale, Dave McClymont, Leonie Mugavin, Rachel Peart, Lynne Preston and Howard Ralley.

THANKS FROM LONELY PLANET

Many thanks to the travellers who used the last edition and wrote to us with helpful hints, useful advice and interesting anecdotes:

A Steve Akeroyd, Tanya Allen, Mike Alton, Jonathan Amies, Ellen Andersen, Anthony Angelucci, Panagiotis Antonopoulos,

Mary Ara, Nathalène Armand-Gouzi, Shlomit Aviram **B** Morten Bagger, John Baker, SD Baker, Rebecca Balsamo, Chris Barber, Gabi Barkay, Irene Barrett, Mark, Beth, Nick and Maggie Bauer, Liz and Diego Becker, Helen Bell, Iris Bertz, Ellis Bijlmakers, Dionne Black, Marcel Boer, Danielle Brand, Ineke and Hans Breeman, David Brett, Jeroen Bruijns, Bruce Budd, Irena Bushandrova **C** Lisa Calabro, J H Callen, Brooke Cameron, Jack Ceaser, K Chau, Nikitas Chondroyannos, Edward and Connie Chung Ramos, Sarah Citrin, Odile Ayral Claure, Daniele Clavenzani, Marie Coffey, Caroline Cohen, Joshu Cohen, Gael Connell, Bill Crook, Marilyn and Eric Crump, Jennifer Currie **D** George Dalidakis, Maureen P Davies, Rosemarie Dawson, Karsten Dax, Nikias De Feyter, Riemke de Groot, Frank and Rita De Rijck, Valentijn Delie, Regine Denaegel, Ina Deschouwer, Constantine Dimaras, Marianna Dioxini, Jennifer Ditchburn, Beverley Dobbie, Paul Dobbie, Julie Doring, Noah Duguid **E** Ken E Edwards, Demetre Eliopoulos, John Engel, Dimos Ermoupolis **F** Rhonda Falk, Maureen Farrer, Franklin M Fernandez, Wendy Finch-Turner, Harvey Florman, Glenn Fowler, John Francis, Sarah French **G** Marco Garrone, Christina Gellura, Jean-Philippe Genieys, Jill and Ian Gibson, Wayne Gin, Raih Glick, Kerry Gonzales, Jules and Laura Gorgone, Chrissie Graboski, Nagy Atilla Gyorgy **H** Dr June Hagen (Hofmeyr), Chee Juan Han, Michael Hardcastle, Paul Harris, Rosemary Hay, Marie Hazelwood, Allan Healy, Dr Franz Hebestreit, Dale Henderson, Joke Hermans, Jan Hogenbirk, David Horan, Andrew Hoshkiw, Gail and John Houston, Alan Hoyle, Yasuko Hudson, Jennifer Hughes, Tony Hughes **I** Cynthia Iles **J** Richard Jackson, Rommary Jenkins **K** Martin and Esther Kafer, Lili Kalp, Nancy Kartsonas, Kanella Kastanias, Gordon Kelly, Melanie Kelly, Reza Khosroshahy, Don Kidd, Kalervo Kiianmaa, Elizabeth Klawiter, Josef Koberl, Olka Kolker, Steve Kotlarchuk, Penny Koutsouradis, Marcia Kran, Peter Kromp, Richard C Kruse, Danuta and Bogmil Kusiba **L** Peter Lamont, Birgith Lange Neilsen, Vivian Lee, Marie-France Legault, Jonas Leurman, Leif Lie, Ville Liukka, Andrew Logan, Georgios Lokas, Bud Long, Penelope Lumley **M** John Macadam, Veronique Manapeau, Patrick Martin, Eleni Martini, Dubravka Martinovic, Eleni Martonis, Doug Matheson, Jane and David Maw Cornish, Stuart McBeath, Eva Meer, Mark Melville, JP Michaels, David and Susan Miller, Ron Miller, Phillip and Janine Mills, Steven R Mills, Lucy Mitchell, Luis Molina, Dominique Moollan, Jo Mooney, Christian Mooser, Geoffrey Morant, Brian and Ruth Morris, Mollie Murray **N** Helene Naidis, Owen Napier, Mark Newman, Sarah Newton, Tracy Newton, Stelios Nikolaou **O** Maureen O Keefe, Sarah O'Connor, Mike O'Flaherty, Jorg Ostermann **P** Giorgio Pagnotta, Darja Pahic, Catherine Paine, Katerina Panagiotakis, Athanasios Panagiotopoulos, Sotirios Papastathopoulos, Matt Paradise, Dan Parsons, Panayiotis Patrikios, Gordon Stanley Payne, Laura Pearce, William Peden, Marco Perezzani, Rossen Petrov, Jonathan Piesse, Niki Pilidou, David John Pitts, Jacek Pliszka, Orpheus Polioudakis, Doreen Pon, Karen Poole, Patrice Powers, Emiko Priest, Pierre Prince, Brit Ragnhild Manengen **R** Matine Rahmani, Bernt Rane, Chris Rees, Tony Richmond, Dan Robinson, Sharon Rollisson, Georgina Ross, Nagiller Rudolf, Tony Rymer **S** Milan Sahanek, Ashley Salisbury, Stritof Samo, Alejandro Sanfeliu, Kypp Saunders, Ed Schlenk, Dara Schlissel, Jeremias Schmidt, Nicolas Schmidt, Claudia Schmitz,

Marije Scholma, Michiel Schreve, Rebecca Schroeder, Elan Schultz, Hannah Schumann, Marilyn Schwam, Michel Semienchuk, Eyal Shaham, Justin Sinodinos, Mikkel Skovbo, Nicola Slade, Owen Smith, Ioannis Sofilos, Michael and Teresa Spezio, Laura Stanning, Alexandra Sternin, Arzelie Stewart, Kim Stewart, Jasmine St-Laurent, Sarah Straus, Regine Striegel, Samo Stritof, Wendy Stronge, Roxane Suchier, Jord Swart, Peter Symonds **T** Terence Tam, Martin Tatuch, David Tisdale, Tony Titchener, Steve and Kathleen Turner **V** Jeremy Vann, B Verlaan, Jessica Vincent, S Vitakis, Maria Vlachou **W** Andrea Wachenfeld, David Wade-Smith, Glen G Walker, James Walker, Kevin Walters, Charles and Samantha Warren, Rebecca Wassell, Nick Weber, Kenny Wheeler, Kym Wheeler, Thelma White, Winston White, Kathleen Whittle, Veryan Wilkie-Jones, Raymond Wu **Z** Jean Zachos

ACKNOWLEDGMENTS

Many thanks to the following for the use of their content;

Mountain High Maps® Copyright ©1993 Digital Wisdom, Inc.

Portions of this document include intellectual property of EPSILON and are used herein by permission. Copyright ©2001 Epsilon International SA. All rights reserved.

Index

000 Map pages
000 Location of colour photographs

INDEX

INDEX

INDEX

500

MAP LEGEND

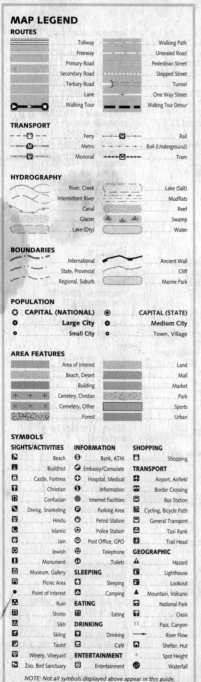

ROUTES

Tollway	Walking Path
Freeway	Unsealed Road
Primary Road	Pedestrian Street
Secondary Road	Stepped Street
Tertiary Road	Tunnel
Lane	One Way Street
Walking Tour	Walking Tour Detour

TRANSPORT

Ferry	Rail
Metro	Rail (Underground)
Monorail	Tram

HYDROGRAPHY

River, Creek	Lake (Salt)
Intermittent River	Mudflats
Canal	Reef
Glacier	Swamp
Lake (Dry)	Water

BOUNDARIES

International	Ancient Wall
State, Provincial	Cliff
Regional, Suburb	Marine Park

POPULATION

◎ CAPITAL (NATIONAL)	◉ CAPITAL (STATE)
● Large City	● Medium City
○ Small City	● Town, Village

AREA FEATURES

Area of Interest	Land
Beach, Desert	Mall
Building	Market
Cemetery, Christian	Park
Cemetery, Other	Sports
Forest	Urban

SYMBOLS

SIGHTS/ACTIVITIES
- Beach
- Buddhist
- Castle, Fortress
- Christian
- Confucian
- Diving, Snorkeling
- Hindu
- Islamic
- Jain
- Jewish
- Monument
- Museum, Gallery
- Picnic Area
- Point of Interest
- Ruin
- Shinto
- Sikh
- Skiing
- Taoist
- Winery, Vineyard
- Zoo, Bird Sanctuary

INFORMATION
- Bank, ATM
- Embassy/Consulate
- Hospital, Medical
- Information
- Internet Facilities
- Parking Area
- Petrol Station
- Police Station
- Post Office, GPO
- Telephone
- Toilets

SLEEPING
- Sleeping
- Camping

EATING
- Eating

DRINKING
- Drinking
- Café

ENTERTAINMENT
- Entertainment

SHOPPING
- Shopping

TRANSPORT
- Airport, Airfield
- Border Crossing
- Bus Station
- Cycling, Bicycle Path
- General Transport
- Taxi Rank
- Trail Head

GEOGRAPHIC
- Hazard
- Lighthouse
- Lookout
- Mountain, Volcano
- National Park
- Oasis
- Pass, Canyon
- River Flow
- Shelter, Hut
- Spot Height
- Waterfall

NOTE: Not all symbols displayed above appear in this guide.

LONELY PLANET OFFICES

Australia
Head Office
Locked Bag 1, Footscray, Victoria 3011
☎ 03 8379 8000, fax 03 8379 8111
talk2us@lonelyplanet.com.au

USA
150 Linden St, Oakland, CA 94607
☎ 510 893 8555, toll free 800 275 8555
fax 510 893 8572, info@lonelyplanet.com

UK
72–82 Rosebery Ave,
Clerkenwell, London EC1R 4RW
☎ 020 7841 9000, fax 020 7841 9001
go@lonelyplanet.co.uk

France
1 rue du Dahomey, 75011 Paris
☎ 01 55 25 33 00, fax 01 55 25 33 01
bip@lonelyplanet.fr, www.lonelyplanet.fr

Published by Lonely Planet Publications Pty Ltd
ABN 36 005 607 983

© Lonely Planet 2004

© photographers as indicated 2004

Cover photographs by Lonely Planet Images: Blue-domed church at sunset, Glenn Beanland/Lonely Planet Images (front); Dining alfresco: Outdoor cafe, Aegina, Kim Wildman/Lonely Planet Images (back).

Many of the images in this guide are available for licensing from Lonely Planet Images: www.lonelyplanetimages.com.

Although the authors and Lonely Planet have taken all reasonable care in preparing this book, we make no warranty about the accuracy or completeness of its content and, to the maximum extent permitted, disclaim all liability arising from its use.